First Philosophy

VOLUME I: VALUES AND SOCIETY

First Philosophy
Fundamental Problems and Readings in Philosophy

SECOND EDITION

VOLUME I
Values and Society

General Editor
ANDREW BAILEY

Contributing Editor
ROBERT M. MARTIN

broadview press

Library and Archives Canada Cataloguing in Publication

   First philosophy : fundamental problems and readings in philosophy / general editor Andrew Bailey ; contributing editor Robert M. Martin. — 2nd ed.

Includes bibliographical references.
Contents: v. 1. Values and society — v. 2. Knowledge and reality — v. 3. God, mind, and freedom.
ISBN 978-1-55111-972-4 (v. 1).—ISBN 978-1-55111-973-1 (v. 2).— ISBN 978-1-55111-974-8 (v. 3)

   1. Philosophy—Textbooks. I. Bailey, Andrew, 1969- II. Martin, Robert M.

B29.F57 2011a   100   C2011-901810-1

Broadview Press is an independent, international publishing house, incorporated in 1985.

We welcome comments and suggestions regarding any aspect of our publications—please feel free to contact us at the addresses below or at broadview@broadviewpress.com.

North America   PO Box 1243, Peterborough, Ontario, Canada K9J 7H5
                         2215 Kenmore Ave., Buffalo, New York, USA 14207
                         Tel: (705) 743-8990; Fax: (705) 743-8353
                         email: customerservice@broadviewpress.com

UK, Europe, Central Asia,   Eurospan Group, 3 Henrietta St., London WC2E 8LU, UK
Middle East, Africa, India,   Tel: 44 (0) 1767 604972; Fax: 44 (0) 1767 601640
and Southeast Asia   email: eurospan@turpin-distribution.com

Australia and New Zealand   NewSouth Books, c/o TL Distribution
                         15-23 Helles Ave., Moorebank, NSW, Australia 2170
                         Tel: (02) 8778 9999; Fax: (02) 8778 9944
                         email: orders@tldistribution.com.au

www.broadviewpress.com

Broadview Press acknowledges the financial support of the Government of Canada through the Canada Book Fund for our publishing activities.

This book is printed on paper containing 100% postconsumer fibre.

PRINTED IN CANADA

For Jack and Max

CONTENTS

How to Use This Book ix

Suggestions for Abridgement xi

Chapter 1: Philosophy

What Is Philosophy? 1

A Brief Introduction to Arguments 5

Introductory Tips on Reading and Writing Philosophy 12

Chapter 2: Ethics—How Ought We to Live Our Lives?

Introduction to the Question 15

Plato 17

    Republic, Book II (357a–367e) 24

Aristotle 31

    from *The Nicomachean Ethics*, Books I, II, and X 38

Immanuel Kant 50

    Foundations of the Metaphysics of Morals, First and Second Sections 61

John Stuart Mill 85

    Utilitarianism, Chapters 1–4 94

Friedrich Nietzsche 118

    Beyond Good and Evil, §§259–261 125

Virginia Held 129

    "Feminist Transformations of Moral Theory" 131

Mary Midgley 148

    "Is a Dolphin a Person?" 149

Chapter 3: Social/Political Philosophy—What Is Justice?

Introduction to the Question 157

Aristotle 159

    The Nicomachean Ethics, Book V, Sections 1-5 162

Thomas Hobbes 169

    from *Leviathan*, Parts I and II 179

John Stuart Mill 197

    from *On Liberty* 200

Karl Marx and Friedrich Engels 241

    from *The Communist Manifesto* 249

Simone de Beauvoir 262

    The Second Sex, Introduction 267

John Rawls..278

    Justice as Fairness: A Restatement, Part II: "Principles of Justice," §§12-13 282

Robert Nozick..290

    from *Anarchy, State, and Utopia*...292

Susan Moller Okin...307

    "Justice and Gender"...309

Appendix 1: Philosophical Puzzles and Paradoxes 329

Appendix 2: Philosophical Lexicon 345

Image Credits 375

Acknowledgments..377

Sources for Quotations 379

HOW TO USE THIS BOOK

This book is an introduction to ethics and social/political philosophy. Within this field, it is intended to be a reasonably representative—though very far from exhaustive—sampling of important philosophical questions, major philosophers and their most important works, periods of philosophical history, and styles of philosophical thought.[1] A third of the included readings, however, were published since 1950, and another important aim of the book is to provide some background for *current* philosophical debates, to give the interested reader a springboard for the plunge into the exciting world of contemporary philosophy.

The aim of this book is to introduce philosophy through philosophy itself: it is not a book *about* philosophy but a book *of* philosophy, in which more than a dozen great philosophers speak for themselves. Each of the readings is prefaced by a set of notes, but these notes make no attempt to explain or summarize the reading. Instead, the goal of the notes is to provide *background information* helpful for understanding the reading—to remove as many of the unnecessary barriers to comprehension as possible, and to encourage a deeper and more sophisticated encounter with great pieces of philosophy. The notes to selections, therefore, do not stand alone and *certainly* are not a substitute for the reading itself: they are meant to be consulted in combination with the reading. (The philosophical selections are also quite heavily annotated throughout by the editor, again in an effort to get merely contingent difficulties for comprehension out of the way and allow the reader to devote all his or her effort to understanding the philosophy itself.)

The reader can of course take or leave these notes as they choose, and read them (or not) in any order. One good way of proceeding, however, would be the following. First, read the selection (so that nothing said in the notes inadvertently taints your first impression of the piece). Then, go back and read some of the notes—the biographical sketch, information on the author's philosophical project, structural and background information—and with these things in mind read the selection again. Spend some time *thinking* about the reading: ask yourself if you really feel you have a good grasp on what the author is trying to say, and then—no less importantly—ask yourself whether the author gives good reasons to believe that their position is *true*. (Chapter 1 tries to give some helpful suggestions for this process of critical reflection.) After this, it should be worthwhile going back to the notes, checking your impressions against any 'common misconceptions,' and then running through at least some of the suggestions for critical reflection. Finally, you might want to go on and read more material by the philosopher in question, or examine what other philosophers have said about his or her ideas: the suggestions for further reading will point you in the right direction.

A word of explanation about the 'Suggestions for Critical Reflection' section: although the notes to the readings contain no philosophical critique of the selection, the questions in this section are largely intended to help the reader generate his or her own critique. As such, they are supposed to be thought-provoking, rather than straightforwardly easy to answer. They try to suggest fruitful avenues for critical thought (though they do not cover every possible angle of questioning, or even all the important ones), and only very rarely is there some particular 'right answer' to the question. Thus, these questions should not be considered a kind of 'self-test' to see if you understand the material: even people with a very good grasp of the material will typically be puzzled by the questions—because they are *supposed* to be puzzling questions.

---

1   There are two major exceptions to this. First, this book focuses exclusively on 'Western' philosophy—that is, roughly, on the philosophical traditions of Europe and of the descendents of European settlers in North America and Australasia. In particular, it does not attempt to encompass the rich philosophical heritage of Asia or Africa. Second, this collection generally ignores an important strain of twentieth-century philosophy, so-called 'Continental' philosophy, which includes thinkers such as Husserl, Heidegger, Sartre, Foucault, Derrida, and Habermas, and is characterized by such movements as existentialism, hermeneutics, structuralism, and deconstructionism.

The readings and their accompanying notes are designed to be 'modular'; that is, in general, one reading can be understood without the benefit of having read any of the other selections. This means that the selections can be read in any order. One natural way of doing the readings is chronologically; here is a list of the contents of the book arranged according to the date of the first 'publication' of the work in its original language:

Plato, *Republic*	c. 380 BCE
Aristotle, *The Nicomachean Ethics*	c. 330 BCE
Hobbes, *Leviathan*	1651
Kant, *Foundations of the Metaphysics of Morals*	1785
Marx and Engels, *The Communist Manifesto*	1848
Mill, *On Liberty*	1859
Mill, *Utilitarianism*	1861
Nietzsche, *Beyond Good and Evil*	1886
de Beauvoir, *The Second Sex*	1952
Nozick, *Anarchy, State, and Utopia*	1974
Midgley, "Is a Dolphin a Person?"	1985
Okin, "Justice and Gender"	1987
Held, "Feminist Transformations of Moral Theory"	1990
Rawls, *Justice as Fairness: A Restatement*	2001

The readings in this anthology are, so far as is practicable, 'complete': that is, they are entire articles, chapters, or sections of books. The editors feel it is important for students to be able to see an argument in the context in which it was originally presented; also, the fact that the readings are not edited to include only what is relevant to one particular philosophical concern means that they can be used in a variety of different ways following a variety of different lines of thought across the ages. Some instructors will wish to assign for their students shorter excerpts of some of these readings, rather than having them read all of the work included: the fact that complete, or almost complete, pieces of philosophy are included in this anthology gives the instructor the freedom to pick the excerpts that best fit their pedagogical aims. We have also included an alternative table of contents giving suggestions for abridgement corresponding to the shortened pieces most commonly found in other introductory philosophy anthologies.

The notes to the readings in this anthology are almost entirely a work of synthesis, and a large number of books and articles were consulted in their preparation; it is impossible—without adding an immense apparatus of notes and references—to acknowledge them in detail, but all my main sources have been included as suggestions for further reading. This is, I believe, appropriate for a textbook, but it is not intended to model good referencing practices for student essays. All the material and annotations accompanying the readings were written by the editors, and none of it (unless otherwise noted) was copied from other sources. Typically, the notes for each reading amalgamate information from a dozen or so sources; in a few instances, especially for biographical information on still-living philosophers, the notes rely heavily on a smaller number of sources (and I tried to indicate this in the text when it occurred). These sources are not footnoted in the body of the text, as they should be in a student (or professional) essay. However, citations are provided at the back of the book for all direct quotations. All of the books, articles and websites that I referred to and found useful are also listed in bibliographies: Chapter 1 lists general works of reference, and the introductory material for each selection includes suggestions for further reading which include the works I looked at (when I found them helpful).

Students should make sure they are aware of the citation system that their instructor prefers them to use in their class work.

Thanks to Alan Belk, Lance Hickey, Peter Loptson, and Mark Migotti for pointing out errors and omissions in the first edition. In case of a third edition but also, more importantly, for the general good of his soul, the editor would warmly welcome further corrections or suggestions for improvement:

Andrew Bailey
Department of Philosophy
The University of Guelph
Guelph, Ontario N1G 2W1
Canada
abailey@uoguelph.ca

SUGGESTIONS FOR ABRIDGEMENT

The following version of the table of contents identifies shorter excerpts of the readings—often those selections most frequently reprinted in other introductory philosophy anthologies—as suggestions for instructors who wish to assign briefer readings for their students.

Chapter 2: Ethics—How Ought We to Live Our Lives?

Plato, *Republic*, Book II (357a-367e) 24-31

Aristotle, from *The Nicomachean Ethics*, Book I, Section 7; Book II, Sections 5–9 . . . . 39-41, 41-46

Immanuel Kant, *Foundations of the Metaphysics of Morals*,
     First and Second Sections 61-84

John Stuart Mill, *Utilitarianism*, Chapters 1 and 2 94-109

Friedrich Nietzsche, *Beyond Good and Evil*, §§ 259-261 125-129

Virginia Held, "Feminist Transformations of Moral Theory" 131-147

Mary Midgley, "Is a Dolphin a Person?" 149-156

Chapter 3: Social/Political Philosophy—What Is Justice?

Aristotle, *The Nicomachean Ethics*, Book V, Sections 1-5 162-169

Thomas Hobbes, from *Leviathan*, Part I, Chapters XIII–XV 179-190

John Stuart Mill, from *On Liberty*, Chapter IV 230-240

Karl Marx and Friedrich Engels, from *The Communist Manifesto*, Sections I and II 249-261

Simone de Beauvoir, *The Second Sex*, Introduction 267-278

John Rawls, *Justice as Fairness: A Restatement*, Part II: "Principles of Justice," §§ 12-13 282-289

Robert Nozick, from *Anarchy, State, and Utopia* 292-307

Susan Moller Okin, "Justice and Gender," Section 1, "Justice as Fairness";
     Section 3, "Women and Justice in Theory and Practice" 311-316, 323-328

CHAPTER 1

Philosophy

WHAT IS PHILOSOPHY?

Philosophy, at least according to the origin of the word in classical Greek, is the "love of wisdom"—philosophers are lovers of wisdom. The first philosophers of the Western tradition lived on the shores of the Mediterranean in the sixth century BCE (that is, more than 2,500 years ago);[1] thinkers such as Thales, Xenophanes, Pythagoras, Heraclitus, and Protagoras tried systematically to answer questions about the ultimate nature of the universe, the standards of knowledge, the objectivity of moral claims, and the existence and nature of God. Questions like these are still at the core of the discipline today.

So what is philosophy? It can be characterized either as a particular sort of *method*, or in terms of its *subject matter*, or as a kind of intellectual *attitude*.

Philosophy as a Method

One view is that philosophy studies the same things—the same world—as, for example, scientists do, but that they do so in a different, and complementary, way. In particular, it is often claimed that while scientists draw conclusions from empirical *observations* of the world, philosophers use *rational arguments* to justify claims about the world. For instance, both scientists and philosophers are involved in contemporary studies of the human mind. Neuroscientists and psychologists are busily mapping out correlations between brain states and mental states—finding which parts of the visual

cortex play a role in dreaming, for example—and building computer models of intelligent information processing (such as chess-playing programs). Philosophers are also involved in cognitive science, trying to discover just what would *count* as discovering that dreaming is really nothing more than certain electro-chemical events in the brain, or would count as building a computer which feels pain or genuinely has beliefs. These second kinds of questions are crucial to the whole project of cognitive science, but they are not empirical, scientific questions: there simply is no fact about the brain that a scientist could observe to answer them. And so these questions—which are part of cognitive science—are dealt with by philosophers.

Here are two more examples. Economists study the distribution of wealth in society, and develop theories about how wealth and other goods can come to be distributed one way rather than another (e.g., concentrated in a small proportion of the population, as in Brazil, or spread more evenly across society, as in Sweden). However, questions about which kind of distribution is more *just*, which kind of society is best to live in, are not answered within economic theory—these are philosophical questions. Medical professionals are concerned with facts about sickness and death, and often have to make decisions about the severity of an illness or weigh the risk of death from a certain procedure. Philosophers also examine the phenomenon of death, but ask different questions: for example, they ask whether people can survive their own deaths (i.e., if there is a soul), whether death is really a harm for the person who dies, under what conditions—if any—we should assist people in committing suicide, and so on.

---

1   In the East, Lao-Tzu, the founder of Taoism, probably lived at about the same time in China. Buddha and Confucius were born a few decades later. In India, an oral literature called the *Veda* had been asking philosophical questions since at least 1500 BCE.

One reason why philosophers deal differently with phenomena than scientists do is that philosophers are using different techniques of investigation. The core of the philosophical method is the application of *rational thought* to problems. There are (arguably) two main aspects to this: the use of conceptual or linguistic *analysis* to clarify ideas and questions; and the use of formal or informal *logic* to argue for certain answers to those questions.

For example, questions about the morality of abortion often pivot on the following question: is a foetus a *person* or not? A person is, roughly, someone who has similar moral status to a normal adult human being. Being a person is not simply *the same thing* as being a member of the human species, however, since it is at least possible that some human beings are not persons (brain-dead individuals in permanent comas, for example?) and some persons might not be human beings (intelligent life from other planets, or gorillas, perhaps?). If it turns out that a foetus *is* a person, abortion will be morally problematic—it may even be a kind of murder. On the other hand, if a foetus is no more a person than, say, one of my kidneys, abortion may be as morally permissible as a transplant. So *is* a foetus a person? How would one even go about discovering the answer to this question? Philosophers proceed by using *conceptual analysis*. What we need to find out, first of all, is what makes something a person—what the essential difference is between persons and non-persons—and then we can apply this general account to human foetuses to see if they satisfy the definition. Put another way, we need to discover precisely what the word "person" means.

Since different conceptual analyses will provide importantly different answers to questions about the morality of abortion, we need to *justify* our definition: we need to give reasons to believe that one particular analysis of personhood is correct. This is where logic comes in: logic is the study of arguments, and its techniques are designed to distinguish between good arguments—by which we should be persuaded—and bad arguments, which we should not find persuasive. (The next main section of this chapter will tell you a little more about logic.)

Philosophy as a Subject Matter

Another way of understanding philosophy is to say that philosophers study a special set of issues, and that it is this subject matter which defines the subject. Philosophical questions fit three major characteristics:

1. They are of deep and lasting interest to human beings;
2. They have answers, but the answers have not yet been settled on;
3. The answers cannot be decided by science, faith or common sense.

Philosophers try to give the best possible answers to such questions. That is, they seek the one answer which is more justified than any other possible answer. There are lots of questions which count as philosophical, according to these criteria. All can be classified as versions of one of three basic philosophical questions.

The first foundational philosophical question is *What exists?* For example: Does God exist? Are quarks really real, or are they just fictional postulates of a particular scientific theory? Are numbers real? Do persons exist, and what is the difference between a person and her physical body, or between a person and a 'mere animal'? The various questions of existence are studied by the branch of philosophy called Metaphysics, and by its various sub-fields such as Philosophy of Mind and Philosophy of Religion.

The second fundamental philosophical question is *What do we know?* For example, can we be sure that a scientific theory is actually true, or is it merely the currently dominant simplification of reality? The world appears to us to be full of colors and smells, but can we ever find out whether it really is colored or smelly (i.e., even if no one is perceiving it)? Everyone believes that 5+6=11, but what makes us so sure of this—could we be wrong, and if not, why not? The branch of philosophy which deals with these kinds of questions is called Epistemology. Philosophy of Science examines the special claims to knowledge made by the natural sciences, and Logic is the study of the nature of rational justification.

The third major philosophical question is *What should we do?* If I make a million dollars selling widgets or playing basketball, is it okay for me to keep all of that money and do what I want with it, or do I have some kind of moral obligation to give a portion of my income to the less well off? If I could get out of trouble by telling a lie, and no one else will really be harmed by my lie, is it alright to do so? Is Mozart's *Requiem* more or less artistically valuable than The Beatles' *Sergeant Pepper's Lonely Hearts Club Band*? Questions like these are addressed by Value Theory, which includes such philosophical areas as Ethics, Aesthetics, Political Philosophy, and Philosophy of Law.

Philosophy as an Attitude

A third view is that philosophy is a state of being—a kind of intellectual independence. Philosophy is a reflective activity, an attitude of critical and systematic thoughtfulness. To be philosophical is to continue to question the assumptions behind every claim until we come to our most basic beliefs about reality, and then to critically examine those beliefs. For example, most of us assume that criminals are responsible for their actions, and that this is at least partly why we punish them. But *are* they responsible for what they do? We know that social pressures are very powerful in affecting our behavior. Is it unfair to make individuals entirely responsible for society's effects on them when those effects are negative? How much of our personal identity is bound up with the kind of community we belong to, and how far are we free to choose our own personalities and values? Furthermore, it is common to believe that the brain is the physical cause of all our behavior, that the brain is an entirely physical organ, and that all physical objects are subject to deterministic causal laws. If all of this is right, then presumably all human behavior is just the result of complex causal laws affecting our brain and body, and we could no more choose our actions than a falling rock could choose to take a different route down the mountainside. If this is true, then can we even make sense of the notion of moral responsibility? If it is not true, then where does free will come from and how (if at all) does it allow us to escape the laws of physics? Here, a questioning attitude towards our assumptions about criminals has shown that we might not have properly considered the bases of our assumptions. This ultimately leads us to fundamental questions about the place of human beings in the world.

Here are three quotes from famous philosophers which give the flavor of this view of philosophy as a critical attitude:

Socrates, one of the earliest Western philosophers, who lived in Greece around 400 BCE, is said to have declared that "it is the greatest good for a man to discuss virtue every day and those other things about which you hear me conversing and testing myself and others, for the unexamined life is not worth living."

Immanuel Kant—the most important thinker of the late eighteenth century—called this philosophical state of being "Enlightenment."

> Enlightenment is the emergence of man from the immaturity for which he is himself responsible. Immaturity is the inability to use one's understanding without the guidance of another. Man is responsible for his own immaturity, when it is caused, by lack not of understanding, but of the resolution and the courage to use it without the guidance of another. *Sapere aude!* Have the courage to use your own reason! is the slogan of Enlightenment.

Finally, in the twentieth century, Bertrand Russell wrote the following assessment of the value of philosophy:

> Philosophy is to be studied, not for the sake of any definite answers to its questions, since no definite answers can, as a rule, be known to be true, but rather for the sake of the questions themselves; because these questions enlarge our conception of what is possible, enrich our intellectual imagination and diminish the dogmatic assurance which closes the mind against speculation; but above all because, through the greatness of the universe which philosophy contemplates, the mind also is rendered great, and becomes capable of that union with the universe which constitutes its highest good.

Questions for Further Thought:

1. Here are some more examples of phenomena which are studied by both scientists and philosophers: color, sense perception, medical practices like abortion and euthanasia, human languages, mathematics, quantum mechanics,

the evolution of species, democracy, taxation. What contribution (if any) might philosophers make to the study of these topics?

2. How well does *mathematics* fit into the division between science and philosophy described above? How does *religion* fit into this classification?

3. Here are a few simple candidate definitions of "person": a person is anything which is capable of making rational decisions; a person is any creature who can feel pain; a person is any creature with a soul; a person is any creature which has the appropriate place in a human community. Which of these, if any, do you think are plausible? What are the consequences of these definitions for moral issues like abortion or vegetarianism? Try to come up with a more sophisticated conceptual analysis of personhood.

4. Do you think criminals are responsible for their actions?

5. Should society support philosophy, and to what degree (e.g., should tax dollars be spent paying philosophers to teach at public universities? Why (not)?)?

Suggestions for Further Reading

As a general rule, it is far better to read philosophy than to read *about* philosophy. A brief but moving work often anthologized in the "what is philosophy" section of introductory textbooks is Plato's *Apology*, which features a speech by Socrates defending the practice of philosophy in the face of his fourth-century BCE Athenian contemporaries, who are about to condemn him to death for it. Two more modern works, which are introductions to philosophy but also significant pieces of philosophy in their own right, are Bertrand Russell's *The Problems of Philosophy* (Oxford University Press, 1912) and *The Central Questions of Philosophy* by A.J. Ayer (Penguin, 1973).

Two aging, slightly idiosyncratic, but nevertheless well-respected histories of western philosophy are Bertrand Russell's *A History of Western Philosophy* (George Allen & Unwin, 1961) and the massive *History of Philosophy* by Frederick Copleston, originally published between 1946 and 1968 and recently re-issued in nine garish volumes by Image Books. Two shorter and more recent histories are *A Brief History of Western Philosophy* by Anthony Kenny (Blackwell, 1998) and *The Oxford Illustrated History of Western Philosophy*, edited by Anthony Kenny (Oxford University Press, 1994).

Finally, there are a number of useful philosophical reference works. The major encyclopedia of philosophy is now the ten-volume *Routledge Encyclopedia of Philosophy*, published in 1998. This replaced the old standby—which is still a useful work, consisting of eight volumes—*The Encyclopedia of Philosophy* edited by Paul Edwards (Macmillan, 1967). Shorter philosophy reference works include *The Concise Routledge Encyclopedia of Philosophy* (Routledge, 2000); *The Cambridge Dictionary of Philosophy*, edited by Robert Audi (Cambridge University Press, 1999); the *Oxford Dictionary of Philosophy*, by Simon Blackburn (Oxford University Press, 1996); *The Blackwell Companion to Philosophy*, edited by Nicholas Bunnin and E.P. Tsui-James (Blackwell, 1996); *The Oxford Companion to Philosophy*, edited by Ted Honderich (Oxford University Press, 1995); *The Philosopher's Dictionary*, by Robert Martin (Broadview, 1994); and the *Penguin Dictionary of Philosophy*, edited by Thomas Mautner (Penguin, 1997). Online philosophy is not always very reliable and should be treated with caution, but two websites which are dependable and likely to be around for a while are the *Stanford Encyclopedia of Philosophy* (http://plato.stanford.edu/) and *The Internet Encyclopedia of Philosophy* (http://www.utm.edu/research/iep/).

A BRIEF INTRODUCTION TO ARGUMENTS

Evaluating Arguments

The main tool of philosophy is the *argument*. An argument is any sequence of statements intended to establish—or at least to make plausible—some particular claim. For example, if I say that Vancouver is a better place to live than Toronto because it has a beautiful setting between the mountains and the ocean, is less congested, and has a lower cost of living, then I am making an argument. The claim which is being defended is called the *conclusion*, and the statements which together are supposed to show that the conclusion is (likely to be) true are called the *premises*. Often arguments will be strung together in a sequence, with the conclusions of earlier arguments featuring as premises of the later ones. For example, I might go on to argue that since Vancouver is a better place to live than Toronto, and since one's living conditions are a big part of what determines one's happiness, then the people who live in Vancouver must, in general, be happier than those living in Toronto. Usually, a piece of philosophy is primarily made up of chains of argumentation: good philosophy consists of good arguments; bad philosophy contains bad arguments.

What makes the difference between a good and a bad argument? It's important to notice, first of all, that the difference is *not* that good arguments have true conclusions and bad arguments have false ones. A perfectly good argument might, unluckily, happen to have a conclusion that is false. For example, you might argue that you know this rope will bear my weight because you know that the rope's rating is greater than my weight, you know that the rope's manufacturer is a reliable one, you have a good understanding of the safety standards which are imposed on rope makers and vendors, and you have carefully inspected this rope for flaws. Nevertheless, it still might be the case that this rope is the one in 50 million which has a hidden defect causing it to snap. If so, that makes me unlucky, but it doesn't suddenly make your argument a bad one—we were still being quite reasonable when we trusted the rope. On the other hand, it is very easy to give appallingly bad arguments for true conclusions: Every sentence beginning with the letter "c" is true; "Chickens lay eggs" begins with the letter "c"; Therefore, chickens lay eggs.

But there is a deeper reason why the evaluation of arguments doesn't begin by assessing the truth of the conclusion. The whole point of making arguments is to establish *whether or not* some particular claim is true or false. An argument works by starting from some claims which, ideally, everyone is willing to accept as true—the premises—and then showing that something interesting—something *new*—follows from them: i.e., an argument tells you that *if* you believe these premises, *then* you should also believe this conclusion. In general, it would be unfair, therefore, to simply reject the conclusion and suppose that the argument must be a bad one—in fact, it would often be intellectually dishonest. If the argument *were* a good one, then it would show you that you might be *wrong* in supposing its conclusion to be false; and to refuse to accept this is not to respond to the argument but simply to ignore it.[2]

It follows that there are exactly two reasonable ways to criticize an argument: the first is to question the truth of the *premises*; and the second is to question the claim that if the premises are true then the conclusion is true as well—that is, one can critique the *strength* of the argument. Querying the truth of

---

2   Of course, occasionally, you might legitimately know *for sure* that the conclusion is false, and then you could safely ignore arguments which try to show it is true: for example, *after* the rope breaks, I could dismiss your argument that it is safe (again, though, this would not show that your argument was *bad*, just that I need not be persuaded that the conclusion is true). However, this will not do for philosophical arguments: all interesting philosophy deals with issues where, though we may have firm opinions, we cannot just insist that we know all the answers and can therefore afford to ignore relevant arguments.

the premises (i.e., asking whether it's really true that Vancouver is less congested or cheaper than Toronto) is fairly straightforward. The thing to bear in mind is that you will usually be working backwards down a chain of argumentation: that is, each premise of a philosopher's main argument will often be supported by sub-arguments, and the controversial premises in these sub-arguments might be defended by further arguments, and so on. Normally it is not enough to merely demand to know whether some particular premise is true: one must look for *why* the arguer thinks it is true, and then engage with *that* argument.

Understanding and critiquing the strength of an argument (either your own or someone else's) is somewhat more complex. In fact, this is the main subject of most books and courses in introductory logic. When dealing with the strength of an argument, it is usual to divide arguments into two classes: *deductive* arguments and *inductive* arguments. Good deductive arguments are the strongest possible kind of argument: if their premises are true, then their conclusion *must necessarily* be true. For example, if all bandicoots are rat-like marsupials, and if Billy is a bandicoot, then it cannot possibly be false that Billy is a rat-like marsupial. On the other hand, good inductive arguments establish that, if the premises are true, then the conclusion is *highly likely* (but not absolutely certain) to be true as well. For example, I may notice that the first bandicoot I see is rat-like, and the second one is, and the third, and so on; eventually, I might reasonably conclude that all bandicoots are rat-like. This is a good argument for a probable conclusion, but nevertheless the conclusion can never be shown to be *necessarily* true. Perhaps a non-rat-like bandicoot once existed before I was born, or perhaps there is one living now in an obscure corner of New Guinea, or perhaps no bandicoot so far has ever been non-rat-like but at some point, in the future, a mutant bandicoot will be born that in no way resembles a rat, and so on.

Deductive Arguments and Validity

The strength of deductive arguments is an on/off affair, rather than a matter of degree. Either these arguments are such that if the premises are true then the conclusion necessarily must be, or they are not. Strong deductive arguments are called *valid*; otherwise, they are called *invalid*. The main thing to notice about validity is that its definition is an *if… then…* statement: *if* the premises *were* true, then the conclusion *would* be. For example, an argument can be valid even if its premises and its conclusion are not true: all that matters is that if the premises *had* been true, the conclusion necessarily would have been as well. This is an example of a valid argument:

1. Either bees are rodents or they are birds.
2. Bees are not birds.
3. Therefore bees are rodents.

If the first premise were true, then (since the second premise is already true), the conclusion would *have* to be true—that's what makes this argument valid. This example makes it clear that validity, though a highly desirable property in an argument, is not enough all by itself to make a good argument: good deductive arguments are both valid *and* have true premises. When arguments are good in this way they are called *sound*: sound arguments have the attractive feature that they necessarily have true conclusions. To show that an argument is unsound, it is enough to show that it is either invalid or has a false premise.

It bears emphasizing that even arguments which have true premises and a true conclusion can be unsound. For example:

1. Only US citizens can become the President of America.
2. George W. Bush is a US citizen.
3. Therefore, George W. Bush was elected President of America.

This argument is not valid, and therefore it should not convince anyone who does not already believe the conclusion to start believing it. It is not valid because the conclusion could have been false even though the premises were true: Bush could have lost to Gore in 2000, for example. The question to ask, in thinking about the validity of arguments is this: Is there a coherent possible world, which I can even *imagine*, in which the premises are true and the conclusion false? If there is, then the argument is invalid.

When assessing the deductive arguments that you encounter in philosophical work, it is often useful to try to lay out, as clearly as possible, their *structure*. A standard and fairly simple way to do this is simply to pull out the logical connecting phrases and to replace, with letters, the sentences they connect. Five of the most common and important 'logical operators' are *and, or, it is not the case that, if … then …,* and *if and only if…*. For example, consider the following argument: "If God is perfectly powerful (omnipotent) and perfectly good, then no evil would exist. But evil does exist. Therefore, God cannot be both omnipotent and perfectly good, so either God is not all-powerful or he is not perfectly good." The structure of this argument could be laid bare as follows:

1. If (O and G) then not-E.
2. E.
3. Therefore not-(O and G).
4. Therefore either not-O or not-G.

Revealing the structure in this way can make it easier to see whether or not the argument is valid. And in this case, it is valid. In fact, no matter what O, G, and E stand for—no matter how we fill in the blanks— *any* argument of this form must be valid. You could try it yourself—invent random sentences to fill in for O, G, and E, and no matter how hard you try, you will never produce an argument with all true premises and a false conclusion.[3] What this shows is that validity is often a property of the *form* or structure of an argument. (This is why deductive logic is known as "formal logic." It is not formal in the sense that it is stiff and ceremonious, but because it has to do with argument forms.)

Using this kind of shorthand, therefore, it is possible to describe certain general argument forms which are *invariably* valid and which—since they are often used in philosophical writing—it can be handy to look out for. For example, a very common and valuable form of argument looks like this: if P then Q; P; therefore Q. This form is often called *modus ponens*. Another—

which appears in the previous argument about God and evil—is *modus tollens*: if P then Q; not-Q; therefore not-P. A *disjunctive syllogism* works as follows: either P or Q; not-P; therefore Q. A *hypothetical syllogism* has the structure: if P then Q; if Q then R; therefore if P then R. Finally, a slightly more complicated but still common argument structure is sometimes called a *constructive dilemma*: either P or Q; if P then R; if Q then R; therefore R.

Inductive Arguments and Inductive Strength

I noted above that the validity of deductive arguments is a yes/no affair—that a deductive argument is either extremely strong or it is hopelessly weak. This is not true for inductive arguments. The strength of an inductive argument—the amount of support the premises give to the conclusion—is a matter of degree, and there is no clear dividing line between the 'strong' inductive arguments and the 'weak' ones. Nevertheless, some inductive arguments are obviously much stronger than others, and it is useful to think a little bit about what factors make a difference.

There are lots of different types and structures of inductive arguments; here I will briefly describe four which are fairly representative and commonly encountered in philosophy. The first is *inductive generalization*. This type of argument is the prototype inductive argument—indeed, it is often what people mean when they use the term "induction"—and it has the following form:

1. *x* per cent of observed Fs are G.
2. Therefore *x* per cent of all Fs are G.

That is, inductive generalizations work by inferring a claim about an entire *population* of objects from data about a *sample* of those objects. For example:

(a) Every swan I have ever seen is white, so all swans (in the past and future, and on every part of the planet) are white.

(b) Every swan I have ever seen is white, so probably all the swans around here are white.

(c) 800 of the 1,000 rocks we have taken from the Moon contain silicon, so probably around 80% of the Moon's surface contains silicon.

---

3   Since the argument about God and evil is valid, then we are left with only two possibilities. Either all its premises are true, and then it is sound and its conclusion *must* inescapably be true. Or one of its premises is false, in which case the conclusion *might* be false (though we would still not have shown that it *is* false). The only way to effectively critique this argument, therefore, is to argue against one of the claims 1 and 2.

(d) We have tested two very pure samples of copper in the lab and found that each sample has a boiling point of 2,567°C; we conclude that 2,567°C is the boiling point for copper.

(e) Every intricate system I have seen created (such as houses and watches) has been the product of intelligent design, so therefore all intricate systems (including, for example, frogs and volcanoes) must be the product of intelligent design.

The two main considerations when assessing the strength of inductive generalizations are the following. First, ask how *representative* is the sample? How likely is it that whatever is true of the sample will also be true of the population as a whole? For instance, although the sample size in argument (c) is much larger than that in argument (d), it is much more likely to be biased: we know that pure copper is very uniform, so a small sample will do; but the surface of the Moon might well be highly variable, and so data about the areas around moon landings may not be representative of the surface as a whole. Second, it is important to gauge how cautious and *accurate* the conclusion is, given the data—how far beyond the evidence does it go? The conclusion to argument (a) is a much more radical inference from the data than that in argument (b); consequently, though less exciting, the conclusion of argument (b) is much better supported by the premise.

A second type of inductive argument is an *argument from analogy*. It most commonly has the following form:

1. Object (or objects) A and object (or objects) B are alike in having features F, G, H, …
2. B has feature X.
3. Therefore A has feature X as well.

These examples illustrate arguments from analogy:

(a) Human brains and dolphin brains are large, compared to body size. Humans are capable of planning for the future. So, dolphins must also be capable of planning for the future.

(b) Humans and dolphins are both mammals and often grow to more than five feet long. Humans are capable of planning for the future. So, dolphins must also be capable of planning for the future.

(c) Eagles and robins are alike in having wings, feathers, claws, and beaks. Eagles kill and eat sheep. Therefore, robins kill and eat sheep.

(d) Anselm's ontological argument has the same argumentative form as Gaunilo's "perfect island" argument. But Gaunilo's argument is a patently bad argument. So there must be something wrong with the ontological argument.

(e) An eye and a watch are both complex systems in which all of the parts are inter-dependent and where any small mis-adjustment could lead to a complete failure of the whole. A watch is the product of intelligent design. Therefore, the eye must also be the product of intelligent design (i.e., God exists).

The strength of an argument from analogy depends mostly on two things: first, the degree of *positive relevance* that the noted similarities (F, G, H …) have to the target property X; and second, the absence of *relevant dissimilarities*—properties which A has but B does not, which make it *less* likely that A is X. For example, the similarity (brain size) between humans and dolphins cited in argument (a) is much more relevant to the target property (planning) than are the similarities cited in argument (b). This, of course, makes (a) a much stronger argument than (b). The primary problem with argument (c), on the other hand, is that we know that robins are much smaller and weaker than eagles and this dissimilarity makes it far less likely that they kill sheep.

A third form of inductive argument is often called *inference to the best explanation* or sometimes *abduction*. This kind of argument works in the following way. Suppose we have a certain quantity of data to explain (such as the behavior of light in various media, or facts about the complexity of biological organisms, or a set of ethical claims). Suppose also that we have a number of theories which account for this data in different ways (e.g., the theory that light is a particle, or the theory that light is a wave, or the theory that it is somehow both). One way of arguing for the truth of one of these theories, over the others, is to show that one theory provides a much *better explanation* of the data than the others. What counts as making a theory a better explanation can be a bit tricky, but some basic criteria would be:

1. The theory predicts all the data we know to be true.
2. The theory explains all this data in the most economical and theoretically satisfying way (scientists and mathematicians often call this the most *beautiful* theory).
3. The theory predicts some *new* phenomena which turn out to exist and which would be a big surprise if one of the competing theories were true. (For example, one of the clinchers for Einstein's theory of relativity was the observation that starlight is bent by the sun's gravity. This would have been a big surprise under the older Newtonian theory, but was predicted by Einstein's theory.)

Here are some examples of inferences to the best explanation:

(a) When I inter-breed my pea plants, I observe certain patterns in the properties of the plants produced (e.g., in the proportion of tall plants, or of plants which produce wrinkled peas). If the properties of pea plants were generated randomly, these patterns would be highly surprising. However, if plants pass on packets of information (genes) to their offspring, the patterns I have observed would be neatly explained. Therefore, genes exist.

(b) The biological world is a highly complex and inter-dependent system. It is highly unlikely that such a system would have come about (and would continue to hang together) from the purely random motions of particles. It would be much less surprising if it were the result of conscious design from a super-intelligent creator. Therefore, the biological world was deliberately created (and therefore, God exists).

(c) The biological world is a highly complex and inter-dependent system. It is highly unlikely that such a system would have come about (and would continue to hang together) from the purely random motions of particles. It would be much less surprising if it were the result of an evolutionary process of natural selection which mechanically preserves order and eliminates randomness, and which (if it existed) would produce a world much like the one we see

around us. Therefore, the theory of evolution is true.

The final type of inductive argument that I want to mention here is usually called *reductio ad absurdum*, which means "reduction to absurdity." It is always a negative argument, and has this structure:

1. Suppose (for the sake of argument) that position p were true.
2. If p were true then something else, q, would also have to be true.
3. However q is absurd—it can't possibly be true.
4. Therefore p can't be true either.

In fact, this argument style can be either inductive or deductive, depending on how rigorous the premises 2 and 3 are. If p logically implies q, and if q is a logical contradiction, then it is deductively certain that p can't be true (at least, assuming the classical laws of logic). On the other hand, if q is merely absurd but not literally *impossible,* then the argument is inductive: it makes it highly likely that p is false, but does not prove it beyond all doubt.

Here are a few examples of *reductio* arguments:

(a) Suppose that gun control were a good idea. That would mean it's a good idea for the government to gather information on anything we own which, in the wrong hands could be a lethal weapon, such as kitchen knives and baseball bats. But that would be ridiculous. This shows gun control cannot be a good idea.

(b) If you think that foetuses have a right to life because they have hearts and fingers and toes, then you must believe that *anything* with a heart, fingers, and toes has a right to life. But that would be absurd. Therefore, a claim like this about foetuses cannot be a good argument against abortion.

(c) Suppose, for the sake of argument, that this is not the best possible world. But that would mean God had either deliberately chosen to create a sub-standard world or had failed to notice that this was not the best of all possible worlds, and either of these options is absurd. Therefore, it must be true that this is the best of all possible worlds.

(d) "The anti-vitalist says that there is no such thing as vital spirit. But this claim is self-refuting. The speaker can be taken seriously only if his claim cannot. For if the claim is true, then the speaker does not have vital spirit and must be *dead*. But if he is dead, then his statement is a meaningless string of noises, devoid of reason and truth." (If you want more information, see Paul Churchland's "Eliminative Materialism and the Propositional Attitudes," *Journal of Philosophy* 78 [1981].)

The critical questions to ask about *reductio* arguments are simply: *Does* the supposedly absurd consequence follow from the position being attacked? and Is it *really* absurd?

A Few Common Fallacies

Just as it can be useful to look for common patterns of reasoning in philosophical writing, it can also be helpful to be on guard for a few recurring fallacies—and, equally importantly, to take care not to commit them in your own philosophical writing. Here are four common ones:

Begging the question does not mean, as the media would have us believe, stimulating one to ask a further question; instead, it means to assume as true (as one of your premises) the very same thing which you are supposedly attempting to prove. This fallacy is sometimes called *circular reasoning* or even (the old Latin name) *petitio principii*. To argue, for example, that God exists because (a) it says in the Bible that God exists, (b) God wrote the Bible, and (c) God would not lie, is to commit a blatant case of begging the question. In this case, of course, one would have no reason to accept the premises as true unless one *already* believed the conclusion. Usually, however, arguments that beg the question are a little more disguised. For example, "Adultery is immoral, since sexual relations outside marriage violate ethical principles," or "Terrorism is bad, because it encourages further acts of terrorism," are both instances of circular reasoning.

Arguing *ad hominem* means attacking or rejecting a position not because the arguments for it are poor, but because the person presenting those arguments is unattractive in some way: i.e., an attack is directed at the person (*ad hominem*) rather than at their argu-

ment. The following are implicit *ad hominem* arguments: "You say you want to close down the church? Well, Hitler and Stalin would agree with you!" and "We shouldn't trust the claim, by philosophers such as Anselm, Aquinas, and Leibniz, that God exists, since they were all Christian philosophers and so of course they were biased." Such attacks are fallacious because they have nothing at all to do with how reasonable a claim is: even if the claim is false, *ad hominem* attacks do nothing to show this.

Straw man arguments are particularly devious, and this fallacy can be hard to spot (or to avoid committing) unless great care is taken. The *straw man* fallacy consists in misrepresenting someone else's position so that it can be more easily criticized. It is like attacking a dummy stuffed with straw instead of a real opponent. For example, it's not uncommon to see attacks on "pro-choice" activists for thinking that abortion is a good thing. However, whatever the merits of either position, this objection is clearly unfair— no serious abortion advocates think it is a positively *good thing* to have an abortion; at most they claim that (at least in some circumstances) it is a lesser evil than the alternative. Here's an even more familiar example, containing two straw men, one after the other: "We should clean out the closets. They're getting a bit messy." "Why, we just went through those closets last year. Do we have to clean them out every day?" "I never said anything about cleaning them out every day. You just want to keep all your junk forever, which is simply ridiculous."

Arguments from ignorance, finally, are based on the assumption that lack of evidence *for* something is evidence that it is false, or that lack of evidence *against* something is evidence for its truth. Generally, neither of these assumptions are reliable. For example, even if we could find no good proof to show that God exists, this would not, all by itself, suffice to show that God does *not* exist: it would still be possible, for example, that God exists but transcends our limited human reason. Consider the following 'argument' by Senator Joseph McCarthy, about some poor official in the State Department: "I do not have much information on this except the general statement of the agency that there is nothing in the files to disprove his Communist connections."

Suggestions for Critical Reflection

1. Suppose some deductive argument has a premise which is necessarily false. Is it a valid argument?

2. Suppose some deductive argument has a conclusion which is necessarily true. Is it a valid argument? From this information alone, can you tell whether it is sound?

3. Is the following argument form valid: if P then Q; Q; therefore P? How about: if P then Q; not-P; so not-Q?

4. No inductive argument is strong enough to *prove* that its conclusion is true: the best it can do is to show that the conclusion is highly probable. Does this make inductive arguments bad or less useful? Why don't we restrict ourselves to using only deductive arguments?

5. Formal logic provides mechanical and reliable methods for assessing the validity of deductive arguments. Do you think there might be some similar system for evaluating the strength of inductive arguments?

6. I have listed four important fallacies; can you identify any other common patterns of poor reasoning?

Suggestions for Further Reading

An entertaining, thought-provoking and brief introduction to logic can be found in Graham Priest's *Logic: A Very Short Introduction* (Oxford University Press, 2000); an equally brief but highly practical primer on arguing is Anthony Weston's *A Rulebook for Arguments* (Hackett, 2001). There are many books which competently lay out the nuts and bolts of formal logic: Richard Jeffrey's *Formal Logic: Its Scope and Limits* (McGraw-Hill, 1991) is short but rigorous and clear; *The Logic Book* by Bergmann, Moor, and Nelson (McGraw-Hill, 1998), on the other hand, is rather painstaking but is one of the most complete texts. An interesting book which explains not only classical formal logic but also makes accessible some more recently developed logical languages, such as modal logic and intuitionistic logic, is Bell, DeVidi, and Solomon's *Logical Options* (Broadview Press, 2001). Two somewhat older texts, which were used to teach many of the current generation of professional philosophers and are still much used today, are Wilfrid Hodges's *Logic* (Penguin, 1977) and E.J. Lemmon's *Beginning Logic* (Hackett, 1978).

One of the best introductory texts on inductive logic is Brian Skyrms's *Choice & Chance* (Wadsworth, 2000). Other good texts include Copi and Burgess-Jackson's *Informal Logic* (Prentice Hall, 1995), Fogelin and Sinnott-Armstrong's *Understanding Arguments* (Harcourt, 2001), and Douglas Walton's *Informal Logic: A Handbook for Critical Argumentation* (Cambridge University Press, 1989). Quite a good book on fallacies is *Attacking Faulty Reasoning* by T. Edward Damer (Wadsworth, 2000), while Darrell Huff's *How to Lie with Statistics* (W.W. Norton, 1954) is an entertaining guide to the tricks that can be played with bad inductive arguments in, for example, advertising.

INTRODUCTORY TIPS ON READING AND WRITING PHILOSOPHY

Reading Philosophy

As you will soon find out, if you haven't already, it is not easy to read philosophy. It can be exhilarating, stimulating, life-changing, or even annoying, but it isn't easy. There are no real shortcuts for engaging with philosophy (though the notes accompanying the readings in this book are intended to remove a few of the more unnecessary barriers); however, there are two things to remember which will help you get the most out of reading philosophy—*read it several times*, and *read it actively*.

Philosophical writing is not like a novel, a historical narrative, or even a textbook: it is typically dense, compressed, and written to contribute to an ongoing debate with which you may not yet be fully familiar. This means, no matter how smart you are, it is highly unlikely that you will get an adequate understanding of any halfway interesting piece of philosophy the first time through, and it may even take two or three more readings before it really becomes clear. Furthermore, even after that point, repeated readings of good philosophy will usually reveal new and interesting nuances to the writer's position, and occasionally you will notice some small point that seems to open a mental door and show you what the author is trying to say in a whole new way. As they say, if a piece of philosophy isn't worth reading at least twice, it isn't worth reading once. Every selection in this book, I guarantee, is well worth reading once.

As you go through a piece of philosophy, it is very important to engage with it: instead of just letting the words wash over you, you should make a positive effort, first, to understand and then, to critically assess the ideas you encounter. On your first read-through it is a good idea to try to formulate a high-level understanding of what the philosopher is attempting: What are the main claims? What is the overall structure of the arguments behind them? At this stage, it can be useful to pay explicit attention to section headings and introductory paragraphs.

Ideally during a second reading, you should try to reconstruct the author's arguments and sub-arguments in more detail. To help yourself understand them, consider jotting down their outlines on a sheet of paper. At this point, it can be extremely fruitful to pay attention to special definitions or distinctions used by the author in the arguments. It is also helpful to consider the historical context in which the philosopher wrote, and to look for connections to ideas found in other philosophical works.

Finally, on third and subsequent readings, it is valuable to expressly look for *objections* to the writer's argument (Are the premises true? Is the argument strong?), *unclarities* in position statements, or *assumptions* they depend upon, but do not argue for. I make these suggestions partly because the process of critical assessment is helpful in coming to understand a philosopher's work; but more importantly for the reason that—perhaps contrary to popular opinion—philosophers are typically playing for very high stakes. When philosophers write about whether God exists, whether science is a rational enterprise, or whether unfettered capitalism creates a just society, they are seriously interested in discovering the *answers* to these questions. The arguments they make, if they are good enough, will be strong reasons to believe one thing rather than another. If you are reading philosophy properly, you must sincerely join the debate and be honestly prepared to be persuaded—but it is also important not to let yourself be persuaded too easily.

Writing Philosophy

Writing philosophy consists, in roughly equal measures, of *thinking* about philosophy and then of trying to express your ideas *clearly and precisely*. This makes it somewhat unlike other writing: the point of writing philosophy is not, alas, to entertain, nor to explain some chunk of knowledge, nor to trick or cajole the reader into accepting a certain thesis. The point of philosophical writing is, really, to *do* philosophy.

This means that, since philosophy is based on arguments, most philosophical essays will have the underlying structure of an argument. They will seek to defend some particular philosophical claim by developing one or more good arguments for that claim.[4]

There is no particular template to follow for philosophical writing (there are lots of different kinds of good philosophical writing—lots of different ways of arguing well), but here are seven suggestions you might find useful:

1. Take your time. Spend time thinking, and then leave yourself enough time to get the writing right.

2. After you've thought for a while, begin by making an outline of the points you want to make (rather than immediately launching into prose). Then write several drafts, preferably allowing some cooling-off time between drafts so you can come back refreshed and with a more objective eye. Be prepared for the fact that writing a second draft doesn't mean merely tinkering with what you've already got, but starting at the beginning and writing it again.

3. Strive to be clear. Avoid unnecessary jargon, and use plain, simple words whenever possible; concrete examples can be extremely useful in explaining what you mean. It's also worth remembering that the clarity of a piece of writing has a lot to do with its structure. Ideally, the argumentative structure of your essay should be obvious to the reader, and it is a good idea to use your introduction to give the reader a 'road map' of the argument to follow.

4. Aim for precision. Make sure the *thesis* of your essay is spelled out in sufficient detail that the reader is left in no doubt about what you are arguing for (and therefore, what the implications will be, if your arguments are strong ones). Also, take care to define important terms so the reader knows exactly what you mean by them. Terms should normally be defined under any of the following three conditions: (a) the word is a technical term which a layperson probably won't know the meaning of (e.g., "intrinsic value"); (b) it is an ordinary word whose meaning is not sufficiently clear or precise for philosophical purposes (e.g., "abortion"); or (c) it is an ordinary word that you are going to use to mean something other than what it normally means (e.g., "person").

5. Focus. Everything you write should directly contribute to establishing your thesis. Anything which is unnecessary for your arguments should be eliminated. Make every word count. Also, don't be over-ambitious; properly done, philosophy moves at a fairly slow pace—it is unlikely that anyone could show adequately that, for example, there is no such thing as matter in three or fewer pages.

6. Argue as well and as carefully as you can. Defend your position using reason and not rhetoric; critically assess the strength of your arguments, and consider the plausibility of your premises. It's important to consider alternatives to your own position and possible counter-arguments; don't be afraid to raise and attempt to reply to objections to your position. (If you make a serious objection, one which you cannot answer, perhaps you should change your position.)

7. When you think you are finished, read the essay out loud and/or give it to someone else to read—at a minimum, this is a good way of checking for ease of reading, and it may reveal problems with your essay or argument that hadn't previously occurred to you.

---

4   The conclusion of a philosophical essay, however, need not always be something like: "God exists," or "Physical objects are not colored." It could just as legitimately be something like: "Philosopher A's third argument is flawed," or "When the arguments of philosopher A and those of philosopher B are compared, B wins," or "No one has yet given a good argument to show either P or not-P," or even "Philosopher A's argument is not, as is widely thought, X but instead it is Y." Though these kinds of claims are, perhaps, less immediately exciting than the first two examples, they are still philosophical claims, they still need to be argued for, and they can be extremely important in an overall debate about, say, the existence of God.

Suggestions for Further Reading

There are several short books devoted to helping students do well in philosophy courses. Perhaps the best of the bunch is Jay Rosenberg's *The Practice of Philosophy: A Handbook for Beginners* (Prentice Hall, 1995); A.P. Martinich's *Philosophical Writing* (Blackwell, 1996) is also very good. Also useful are: Anne M. Edwards, *Writing to Learn: An Introduction to Writing Philosophical Essays* (McGraw-Hill, 1999); Graybosch, Scott, and Garrison, *The Philosophy Student Writer's Manual* (Prentice Hall, 1998); and Zachery Seech, *Writing Philosophy Papers* (third edition, Wadsworth, 2000).

CHAPTER 2

Ethics—How Ought We to Live Our Lives?

INTRODUCTION TO THE QUESTION

Ethics, of course, is the philosophical sub-discipline which examines morality;[1] along with metaphysics and epistemology, it is one of the largest and most important areas of philosophy. It can usefully be thought of as divided into three main parts: *normative ethics, applied ethics* and *meta-ethics.*

i) Normative ethics is the philosophical study of the standards of right and wrong, or of good and bad. Normative ethical theories do not attempt to merely *describe* how people actually do behave, or report what people *think* is right: they lay out prescriptions (rooted in rationally supported philosophical theory) for how people *really ought* to think and behave. It is common—though by no means universal—to assume that the proper aim of normative ethics should be to develop a systematic and comprehensive moral theory which has as many of the virtues of a scientific theory as possible: it should capture all the phenomena of moral life, place them within a simple and unified theoretical structure, and provide the resources for answering any ethical question whatsoever—i.e.,

an adequate moral theory should always be able to tell you what to do, and it should always give you the correct answer.

One way of classifying different normative moral theories is in terms of their emphasis on 'the Right' or 'the Good.' Some moral theories—such as that of Kant—are primarily theories of *right action*: they are moral codes (usually derived from, and justified by, some fundamental principle or set of principles, such as Kant's Categorical Imperative) that define the duties human beings have to themselves and others. A (morally) good life is then defined simply as a life of duty—a life spent doing the right thing. By contrast, other moral theories—such as Mill's utilitarianism— *begin* by developing a theory of the good: they are accounts of those things that are *good in themselves* (or at least which are essential components of human flourishing). For example, for Mill, what is good is the happiness of sentient creatures. Right actions are then defined derivatively as those (whichever they are) that best contribute to the good.

ii) Applied ethics is the study of how ethical norms or rules ought to be applied in particular cases of unusual difficulty, such as abortion, mercy-killing, the treatment of animals, genetic research, corporate responsibility to the community, 'just' wars, and so on. It encompasses several sub-fields, such as bioethics, business ethics, environmental ethics, legal ethics, and so forth.

iii) Metaethics deals with the philosophical underpinnings of normative ethics: that is, it applies philosophical scrutiny to a part of philosophy itself. The main kinds of metaethical inquiry are the study of

---

1   There are various important philosophical usages which treat 'ethical' and 'moral' as meaning slightly different things. For example, some philosophers (such as Bernard Williams) use the word 'ethics' to denote systems of *rules* for conduct, whilst 'morality' has a more open-ended, less institutionalized content ... while others (such as Jürgen Habermas), interestingly, use the terms in almost exactly the opposite way! I am ignoring such niceties here, however, and simply treat the two words as being interchangeable.

the ethical *concepts* used in normative ethics (such as 'duty,' 'right,' 'good,' 'responsibility'), moral *epistemology* (questions about whether and how moral truths can be known), and moral *ontology* (which is concerned with the nature of 'moral reality'— e.g., whether it is objective or subjective, relative or absolute).

The sequence of readings in this chapter begins in the realm of metaethics, then moves into normative ethics, and finally returns to metaethics; the question which is being pursued throughout is simple, but profound: it is "How should I live my life?" That is, what kind of *person* should I be? What *values* should guide my plans and choices? Which kinds of *behavior* are morally acceptable, and which unacceptable?

The first selection, from Plato, is a metaethical consideration of the notion of moral value itself: what exactly is the connection between moral virtue and 'the good life'? Are moral goodness and well-being *simply the same thing* (perhaps because only the virtuous are really happy, as Plato goes on to argue, or because what is morally good just is happiness, which is Mill's view)? Or do happiness and virtue come apart (as Kant believes): could one be moral but miserable, vicious yet fulfilled?

The next readings introduce three of the historically most important and influential theories of normative ethics. Aristotle lays the foundations for a theory called 'virtue ethics,' which holds that morality cannot be captured by any set of moral rules or principles— instead that what is right or wrong will vary from situation to situation and the trick is to educate people to be wise in their ethical judgments. Kant defends the view that moral actions have to be understood independently of their merely contingent motivations, and thus that certain actions are simply right or wrong *in themselves*. Mill lays out a moral theory, called utilitarianism, which is based on the principle that the moral value of actions must be understood in terms of their effect on human happiness or well-being.

The final three readings can be thought of as critiques of traditional approaches to ethics. Nietzsche, who called himself an 'immoralist,' argues that our modern moral views are merely historically contingent opinion (rather than any kind of insight into 'the truth'), and furthermore that they are heavily infected with what he labels "slave morality." He urges a 'revaluation' of our moral values which will take us "beyond good and evil." Virginia Held presents a feminist critique of traditional moral theory, arguing that the history of ethical thought has been dominated by sexist attitudes towards women and that only a *radical transformation* of moral philosophy will allow us to escape from these distorting preconceptions. Mary Midgley argues that we need to develop a more flexible notion of moral personhood that will allow us to treat non-human animals as morally important in their own right.

Many good introductory books on moral philosophy are available, including: Piers Benn, *Ethics* (McGill-Queen's University Press, 1998); Simon Blackburn, *Being Good: A Short Introduction to Ethics* (Oxford University Press, 2003); Julia Driver, *Ethics: The Fundamentals* (Blackwell, 2006); Fred Feldman, *Introductory Ethics* (Prentice Hall, 1978); William Frankena, *Ethics* (Prentice Hall, 1988); Gilbert Harman, *The Nature of Morality* (Oxford University Press, 1977); Colin McGinn, *Moral Literacy, or How to Do The Right Thing* (Hackett, 1992); Louis Pojman, *Ethics: Discovering Right and Wrong* (Wadsworth, 2005); James Rachels, *The Elements of Moral Philosophy* (McGraw Hill, 2006); Peter Singer, *Practical Ethics* (Cambridge University Press, 1999); and Bernard Williams, *Morality: An Introduction to Ethics* (Cambridge University Press, 1993). Good reference works are Hugh LaFollette (ed.), *The Blackwell Guide to Ethical Theory* (Blackwell, 2000) and Peter Singer (ed.), *A Companion to Ethics* (Blackwell, 1991).

PLATO
Republic

Who Was Plato?

The historical details of Plato's life are shrouded in uncertainty. He is traditionally thought to have been born in about 427 BCE and to have died in 347 BCE. His family, who lived in the Greek city-state of Athens, was aristocratic and wealthy. Legend has it that Plato's father, Ariston, was descended from Codrus, the last king of Athens, and his mother, Perictione, was related to the great Solon, who wrote the first Athenian constitution. While Plato was still a boy, his father died and his mother married Pyrilampes, a friend of the revered Athenian statesman, Pericles, who in the 450s had transformed Athens into one of the greatest cities in the Greek world.

As a young man, Plato probably fought with the Athenian army against Sparta during the Peloponnesian war (431–404 BCE)—which Athens lost—and he may have served again when Athens was involved in the Corinthian war (395–386 BCE).

Given his family connections, Plato looked set for a prominent role in Athenian political life and, as it happens, when he was about 23, a political revolution occurred in Athens which could have catapulted Plato into public affairs. The coup swept the previous democratic rulers—who had just lost the war against Sparta—out of power and into exile, and replaced them with the so-called Thirty Tyrants, several of whom were Plato's friends and relatives. Plato, an idealistic young man, expected this would usher in a new era of justice and good government, but he was soon disillusioned when the new regime was even more violent and corrupt than the old. He withdrew from public life in disgust. The rule of the Thirty lasted only about 90 days before the exiled democrats were restored to power, and Plato—impressed by their relative lenience towards the coup leaders—apparently thought again about entering politics. But then, in 399 BCE, the city rulers arrested Plato's old friend and mentor, Socrates, and accused him of the trumped-up charge of impiety towards the city's gods and of corrupting the youth of Athens. Socrates was convicted by a jury of the townspeople, and—since he declared that he would rather die than give up philosophy, even though he was given a chance to escape—he was executed by being forced to drink poison.

The result was that I, who had at first been full of eagerness for public affairs, when I considered all this and saw how things were shifting about every which way, at last became dizzy. I didn't cease to consider ways of improving this particular situation, however, and, indeed, of reforming the whole constitution. But as far as action was concerned, I kept waiting for favorable moments and finally saw clearly that the constitutions of all actual cities are bad and that their laws are almost beyond redemption without extraordinary resources and luck as well. Hence I was compelled to say in praise of the true philosophy that it enables us to discern what is just for a city or an individual in every case and that the human race will have no respite from evils until those who are really and truly philosophers acquire political power or until, through some divine dispensation, those who rule and have political authority in cities become real philosophers.[1]

After the death of Socrates, it appears that Plato, along with some other philosophical followers of Socrates, fled Athens and went to the city of Megara in east-central Greece to stay with the philosopher Eucleides (a follower of the great Greek philosopher Parmenides of Elea). He may also have visited Egypt, though his travels at this time are shrouded in myth. It appears that Plato started doing philosophy in earnest at about this time, and his earliest writings date from this point. Almost all of Plato's writings are in the form of dialogues between two or more characters and, in most of them, the character leading the discussion is Socrates. Since Plato never wrote himself into any of his dialogues, it is usually—though not uncontroversially—assumed that the views expressed by the character of Socrates more or less correspond with those that Plato is trying to put forward in his dialogues.

Later, when Plato was about 40, he made another trip away from Athens, visiting Italy to talk with the Pythagorean philosophers. Plato was deeply impressed by Pythagorean philosophy—especially their emphasis on mathematics—but he was horrified by the luxury and sensuality of life in Italy, "with men gorging themselves twice a day and never sleeping alone at night."

After Italy, Plato visited Syracuse on the island of Sicily where, during a long stay, he became close friends with Dion, the brother-in-law of the ruling tyrant Dionysius I.[2] Dion became Plato's pupil, and (according to legend) came to prefer the philosophical life of moral goodness to the pleasure, luxury, and power of his surroundings. Exactly what happened next is historically unclear, but there is some reason to believe Plato was captured by a displeased Dionysius, sold into slavery, and subsequently rescued from the slave market when his freedom was purchased by an unidentified benevolent stranger.

On Plato's return to Athens, he bought land in a precinct named for an Athenian hero called Academus, and there, in about 385, he founded the first European university (or at least, the first of which there is any real historical knowledge). Because of its location, this school was called the Academy, and it was to remain in existence for over 900 years, until 529 CE. For most of the rest of his life, Plato stayed at the Academy, directing its studies, and he probably wrote the Republic there (in about 380 BCE). Very quickly, the school became a vital center for research in all kinds of subjects, both theoretical and practical. It was probably one of the first cradles for the subjects of metaphysics, epistemology, psychology, ethics, politics, aesthetics, and mathematical science, and members were invited, by various Greek city-states, to help draft new political constitutions.

In 368 Dionysius I of Sicily died and Dion persuaded his successor, Dionysius II, to send for Plato to advise him on how the state should be run. Plato, by now about 60, agreed with some misgivings, possibly hoping to make the younger Dionysius an example of a philosopher-king and to put the doctrines of the Republic into practice. However, the experiment was a disastrous failure. Dionysius II—though he gave himself airs as a philosopher—had no inclination to learn philosophy and mathematics in order to become a better ruler. Within four months Dion was banished, and Plato returned to Greece shortly afterwards. However, four years later Dionysius II persuaded Plato to return, pressuring him with testimonials from eminent philosophers describing Dionysius's love for philosophy, and bribing him by offering to reinstate Dion at Syracuse within a year. Once again, the king proved false: he not only kept Dion in exile but confiscated and sold his lands and property. Plato was imprisoned on Sicily for nearly two years until, in 360, he finally

---

1   This is a quotation from the so-called *Seventh Letter*, supposed to have been written by Plato when he was 70 years old. It is not certain that Plato actually wrote this document, but if it was not his, it was probably written by one of his disciples shortly after his death. (This translation is by C.D.C. Reeve.)

2   Indeed, Plato later wrote a poem about Dion and spoke of being driven out of his mind with love for him.

escaped and returned to Athens for good. He died thirteen years later, at the ripe age of 80.[3]

What Was Plato's Overall Philosophical Project?

Plato is probably the single person with the best claim to being the inventor of western philosophy. His thought encompassed nearly all the areas central to philosophy today—metaphysics, epistemology, ethics, political theory, aesthetics, and the philosophy of science and mathematics—and, for the first time in European history, dealt with them in a unified way.[4] Plato thought of philosophy as a special discipline with its own intellectual method, and he was convinced it had foundational importance in human life. Only philosophy, Plato thought, could provide genuine understanding, since only philosophy scrutinized the assumptions that other disciplines left unquestioned. Furthermore, according to Plato, philosophy reveals a realm of comprehensive and unitary hidden truths—indeed, a whole level of reality that the senses cannot detect—which goes far beyond everyday common sense and which, when properly understood, has the power to revolutionize the way we live our lives and organize our societies. Philosophy, and only philosophy, holds the key to genuine human happiness and well-being.

This realm of objects which Plato claimed to have discovered is generally known as that of the Platonic Forms. The Forms—according to Plato—are changeless, eternal objects, which lie outside of both the physical world and the minds of individuals, and which can only be encountered through pure thought rather than through sensation. One of Pla-

to's favorite examples of a Form is the mathematical property of Equality. In a dialogue called the *Phaedo* he argues that Equality itself cannot be identical with two equal sticks, or with any other group of physical objects of equal length, since we could always be mistaken about whether any two observed objects are really equal with one another, but we could not possibly be mistaken about Equality itself and somehow take *it* to be unequal. When two sticks are equal in length, therefore, they "participate in" Equality—it is their relation to Equality which makes them equal rather than unequal—but Equality itself is an abstract object which exists over and above all the instances of equal things. The form of Equality is what one succeeds in understanding when one has a proper conception of what Equality really is in itself: real knowledge, therefore, comes not from observation but from acquaintance with the Forms. Other central examples of Platonic Forms, are Sameness, Number, Motion, Beauty, Justice, Piety, and (the most important Form of all) Goodness.

Plato describes the relation of the ordinary world of perceivable, concrete objects to the realm of the Forms in Book VII of the *Republic,* using the allegory of a cave. Ordinary people, lacking the benefit of a philosophical education, are like prisoners trapped underground in a cave since birth and forced to look only at shadows cast on the wall in front of them by puppets behind their backs, dancing in front of a fire. With the proper philosophical encouragement, they can—if they have the courage to do so—break their bonds and turn around to see that what they believed was reality was really only an illusory puppet show. The philosophers among them can even leave the cave to encounter the true reality—of which even the puppets are only copies—illuminated by the light of the sun which, for Plato, represents the form of the Good. The perceptible world is thus merely an imperfect image of—and sustained by—the quasi-divine, eternal realm of the unchanging and unobservable Forms.

What Is the Structure of This Reading?

The *Republic* is written in the form of a dramatic dialogue. The narrator, Socrates, speaking directly to the reader, describes a conversation in which he took part

---

3   Dion, meanwhile, attempted to recover his position at Syracuse by force—an endeavor Plato, wisely, refused to support—and was later assassinated by a supposed friend, and fellow member of the Academy, called Callippus.

4   In fact the mathematician and philosopher Alfred North Whitehead (1861–1947) famously was moved to say that: "The safest general characterization of the European philosophical tradition is that it consists of a series of footnotes to Plato."

and which is supposed to have happened yesterday at the Athenian port city of Piraeus. The dialogue is traditionally divided into ten parts or "Books," and the first half of Book II is reprinted here. In the first book, Thrasymachus, a boorish character, has asserted that justice, or morality, is simply the rule of the strong over the weak, and that it is, in fact, not in everybody's self-interest to be just—it is only in the best interests of the ruling powers for everyone else to follow the social rules they lay down. Socrates has, characteristically, attempted to show that Thrasymachus' reasons for this claim are muddled and confused, but although Thrasymachus is unable to defend himself against Socrates' attacks he remains convinced of the truth of his position. As Book II opens, two brothers, Glaucon and Adeimantus, take up Thrasymachus's cause ... not because they think he is right, but because they want to challenge Socrates to defeat it properly and to conclusively show that being a just and moral person is valuable *in itself*.

Glaucon begins by introducing a classification of "goods" into three types and asks Socrates to which class justice belongs. Socrates replies it belongs to the highest type of good, but Glaucon points out this conflicts with the popularly held assumption that justice belongs in the lowest class of good. Glaucon then presents three arguments in favor of this common view. First, he describes an account of the "origin and essence of justice" which treats it as only a 'second best' solution to a social problem. Second, he uses the myth of the Ring of Gyges to argue that people are unwillingly just and that, given the chance, anyone would behave immorally. Finally, he describes 'ideal cases' of just and unjust people to show that, if one had the option of living a perfectly just or a totally unjust life, the only rational choice would be the latter. When Glaucon has finished, Adeimantus argues at length that even those who defend justice—parents, poets, and politicians—only defend it on the basis of its beneficial *effects*, and never go so far as to claim it is intrinsically worthwhile to be a morally just person. Glaucon and Adeimantus challenge Socrates to refute all of these arguments.

The reading breaks off just as Socrates is about to respond to this challenge (a response not completed until at least the end of Book IX of the *Republic*). Socra-

tes argues, in effect, that the virtue of justice is such a good thing that it is better to be a just person, even if severe misfortune and loss of reputation occur, than it is to be unjust and to enjoy all possible social rewards; that being a just person always makes you *happier* than being an unjust one, no matter what other circumstances may hold.

In crude outline, Plato's response goes like this. There are three fundamentally different kinds of psychological impulses in human beings: *appetitive desires* (e.g., food, sex, money), *spirited desires* (e.g., fame, power, honor), and *rational desires* (knowledge and truth). Because of this three-fold division of desire, the human soul must also be divided into three parts, and people can be classified according to the dominant part of their soul: that is, people are either money-lovers, honor-lovers, or wisdom-lovers (philosophers). Since these three types of people have very different sorts of desires, they must also have quite different views of what it is to lead a good and morally virtuous life. For one it is a life of hedonistic pleasure, for the second, a life of political power and influence, and for the philosopher, a life spent in the pursuit of knowledge.

However, according to Plato, only one of these views of the good life is *correct*. Only the philosopher, he argues, has access to the genuinely good life. This is so because the true nature of reality—including moral reality—is the realm of the Forms, and only the philosopher has knowledge of this fundamental reality. Since philosophers are the only ones to understand the true nature of virtue, it seems, to Plato, to follow that they are the only ones with the specialized knowledge necessary to live a truly good life.[5] Since capacity for the good life is thus connected with the *kind of person* one is (i.e., a money-lover, an honor-lover, or a philosopher), the Platonic conception of

---

5   There is also a quasi-religious interpretation of Plato which sees him holding that the Forms—rather than anything in the shifting, illusory spatio-temporal world—are the supreme objects of value. Instead of wealth, power, or pleasure, the most perfect object of devotion is the realm of the Forms, and in particular the Form of the Good (which Plato seems to think of as almost a kind of divinity).

virtue can thus be understood as a particular kind of balance in the soul. According to Plato, to be virtuous is to have a soul ruled by its rational part. Morality, properly understood, fulfils one's highest nature—it is a kind of psychic harmony or mental health—and so leads to the deepest and most genuine form of happiness.[6]

Some Useful Background Information

1. All the characters who take part in discussions in the *Republic* were historical figures. Of those mentioned here, Glaucon and Adeimantus were actually Plato's brothers and Thrasymachus was a well-known contemporary teacher of rhetoric, oratory, and "sophist" philosophy (roughly, what we might think of today as a "self-help" guru). The main character of the *Republic,* however, is its narrator Socrates, Plato's primary intellectual influence. Though he left no writings, Socrates' personality and ideas were so powerful that he appears to have had a tremendous impact upon everyone he encountered, inspiring either fervent devotion or intense irritation. Socrates' main philosophical concern was the ethical question of how one's life should best be lived, and his method was to engage in systematic cross-examination (*elenchus*) of those he encountered, challenging them to state and then justify their beliefs about justice and virtue. The effect of this was to demonstrate to them that their uncritically

held beliefs about moral virtue are self-contradictory and hence *have* no justification. The state of bewildered awareness of their own ignorance in which Socrates left his unfortunate victims is called *aporia*, and Socrates' technique of remorseless questioning is sometimes known as the "aporetic method."

Though famous for insisting he was wiser than his fellow Athenians only because he alone realized that he knew nothing, Socrates did subscribe to a handful of substantive philosophical positions, two of which he passed on to Plato. First, for Socrates, virtue (*aretē*) is a kind of knowledge. To be a virtuous person is, fundamentally, to *understand* what virtue is, in much the same way as being an expert shoemaker consists in knowing everything there is to know about shoes. Socrates (and Plato after him) held that it was vitally important to find correct definitions—to understand the essence (*eidos*)—of ethical concepts, otherwise we will not know how to live. The second crucial Socratic doctrine is that the real essence of a person is not their body but their soul, and that this soul is immortal. The health of one's own soul is thus of paramount importance, far more significant than the mere slings and arrows of physical life. Indeed, Socrates was convinced that, even while we are living in the physical world, the quality of our souls is a far more important determinant of our happiness than external circumstances like health, wealth, popularity, or power.

2. The topic of the *Republic* is *dikaiosunē*, a Greek word usually translated into English as "justice." Strangely enough, it is a matter of some controversy just what Plato means by *dikaiosunē* (and thus just what, exactly, the *Republic* is about!); clearly, though, the notion covers more than we might normally understand by the word "justice," though probably somewhat less than we would, today, understand by "morality." Plato is not merely interested in the virtue of treating other people fairly and impartially (and, in the *Republic*, he is hardly interested at all in the formulation and administration of civil and criminal law). Rather, Plato is discussing some-

---

6   Plato introduces and explains this account of justice in the human soul by drawing an analogy with the structure of an ideal city-state (which is why the dialogue is called the *Republic*). Briefly, a properly run state would contain three specialized types of citizens: craftspeople, warrior-guardians, and rulers. The rulers would have to have a proper philosophical education, in order to truly know what is best for the state and its citizens, and for this reason they are often called "philosopher kings." The state only functions properly and justly, according to Plato, when these three classes work together in harmony—for example, the craftspeople must be appropriately skilled and must also be properly subservient to the other two classes.

thing like *the right way to live*, where it is understood (as was generally assumed by the ancient Greeks) that human beings are *social* animals, for whom the good life can only exist in a particular sort of political context and all the virtues—such as courage, moderation, generosity, and even piety—have to do, in one way or another, with our relationships with other people. Therefore, by "justice," Plato probably means all the areas of morality that regulate our relationships with other people.

On the other hand, it is important to notice that Plato does *not* think of justice as primarily a way of behaving, as a set of rules for correct action, or as a kind of relationship between people. Justice, for Plato, is an *internal property of individual souls*, and only secondarily of their actions. You have the virtue of justice if your soul has a certain configuration, and then it is this virtue of yours which regulates your treatment of other people; but your treatment of other people is not *itself* justice, it is just the manifestation of your justice. To put it another way, you are not a just person because your actions are just—on the contrary, your actions are just because you are.

3. The description of the "popular view" of justice by Glaucon and Adeimantus is philosophically more complicated than it might at first seem, and the following distinction is a useful one to bear in mind when you are trying to get it straight. This distinction is one between what are often called the "artificial" and the "natural" consequences of justice. The artificial consequences of justice are those "rewards and reputations" which society provides for those who give the appearance of being just. They are artificial rewards because they would not exist if it were not for human social conventions and practices and, more importantly, because they are connected only to the *appearance* of justice rather than justice itself. Thus, someone who appeared just, but was not, would still get all of the artificial rewards of justice. On the other hand, the natural rewards of being just are supposed to follow simply from justice itself, in the

way that health, sight, and knowledge have, in themselves, beneficial consequences for their possessors.

Some Common Misconceptions

1. All the protagonists in this section—Glaucon, Adeimantus, and Socrates—*agree* that justice is good in itself. Glaucon and Adeimantus present certain arguments as strongly as they can in order to force Socrates to properly respond to them, but they do not, themselves, endorse the conclusion of those arguments (and they hope Socrates will give them a way to legitimately evade that conclusion).

2. The discussion is about the benefits of justice *for just people themselves*, not for those with whom they interact or for society generally. The topic asks whether *acting justly* is intrinsically worthwhile (rather than whether it is nice to be *treated* justly).

How Important and Influential Is This Passage?

The *Republic* is generally acknowledged to be Plato's greatest work (indeed, one of the very greatest works in all philosophy), and is often thought of as the centerpiece of Plato's philosophy. Though it presents only a partial picture of his developing philosophical views, it is the dialogue where most of Plato's central ideas about ethics, metaphysics, epistemology, politics, psychology, aesthetics, and so on, come together into a single unified theory. This excerpt from the *Republic* is by no means the best-known part of the work, but it is where Plato sets up the philosophical question his book is intended to answer. As with much of Plato's writing, it is the questions he asked which have proved to be of enduring philosophical importance as much as the answers he gave to them. The questions developed here about the relationship between morality and self-interest lie at the very foundation of ethical study, and the myth of the Ring of Gyges, in particular, has been a particularly evocative image through the centuries for exploring these issues.

Suggestions for Critical Reflection

1. How does Glaucon distinguish between the three different kinds of good? Do his examples make sense, and can you think of any examples of goods that do not fit easily into his classification? Into which of the three classes would *you* place justice?

2. Most modern debates about justice or morality tend to assume that there are only two fundamental, mutually exclusive positions one might take. Either something is morally right in itself, *regardless* of its consequences—often called a "deontological" view—or things are morally right or wrong *because* of their consequences (a view called "consequentialism"). For example, one might hold that taking human life is intrinsically morally wrong, no matter what the justification (e.g., because human life is 'sacred'); alternately, one might believe killing is wrong because of its harmful consequences (suffering, death, etc.), or perhaps even that sometimes it can be morally justified to kill human beings if the net consequences of doing so are sufficiently desirable (e.g., if a killing prevents more deaths than it brings about). How does the view of justice Socrates is being asked to defend fit here? Is his position *either* deontological or consequentialist? If not, what is it? How tenable a view is it?

3. How plausible is Glaucon's story of the origin of justice? If he were historically right about it, what would this show us (if anything) about the *moral* value of behaving justly?

4. If you had the Ring of Gyges, how would you behave? Do you agree with the claim that nearly everybody who possessed such a ring would behave immorally? What, if anything, would the answer to this question show about how people *ought* to behave?

5. Do unjust people generally lead more pleasant lives than just people? If so, what, if anything, would this show about the nature of morality?

6. Some commentators have claimed that the speeches of Glaucon and Adeimantus are not, as they purport to be, making the same point, but, in fact, are arguing for two quite *different* conclusions. Glaucon, it is said, emphasizes the need to defend justice *in itself*, without concern for the consequences, while Adeimantus urges that the virtue of justice must be shown to have beneficial *consequences* for those who have it. What do you think about this? Is this characterization of the speeches correct and, if so, does it mean they must be arguing for different conclusions?

7. Socrates agrees with Glaucon and Adeimantus that if justice is to be properly defended, it must be defended in isolation from its artificial or conventional consequences (such as reputation, wealth, and political influence). He also agrees that a good theory of justice must be capable of accommodating such extreme and unrealistic examples as the Ring of Gyges. But is this the right methodology to adopt? Couldn't we say that an essential part of what makes justice valuable is its pragmatic role in regulating social interactions in the kind of political societies in which we find ourselves? For example, perhaps part of the *point* of being just *is* that it entitles us to certain social rewards, or allows us to escape social penalties, and so justice does lose at least some of its value if this connection to social reality breaks down. What do you think?

8. If being just would make a person unhappy, would it then be irrational to be moral? Does Plato think so? Why does Socrates accept the challenge of showing that being just is in one's self-interest? Why not agree that justice is onerous, but is, nevertheless, our moral duty?

Suggestions for Further Reading

Various translations of the *Republic* are available. The one used here is by G.M.A. Grube and C.D.C. Reeve and was published by Hackett in 1992. Another much-used translation is F.M. Cornford's *The Republic of Plato* (Oxford University Press, 1941), and an interesting newer one is *Republic*, translated by Robin Waterfield (Oxford University Press, 1993). The rest of Plato's writings can be found in either *The Collected Dialogues of Plato*, edited by Hamilton and Cairns (Princeton University Press, 1971) or *Plato: Complete Works*, edited by

John Cooper (Hackett, 1997). If you like the fragments of poetry quoted by Plato, you can find more of it in Richard Lattimore's *Greek Lyrics* (University of Chicago Press, 1960). There isn't enough historical detail available about Plato's life for extensive biographies to be possible, but an entertaining historical novel, which includes a fictionalized account of Plato's adventures in Syracuse, is *The Mask of Apollo* by Mary Renault (Pantheon Books, 1966).

Probably the best short introduction to the philosophical context in which Plato was writing is Terence Irwin's superb *Classical Thought* (Oxford University Press, 1989). A fine, brief account of the theories of Plato's predecessors is Edward Hussey's, *The Presocratics* (Hackett, 1972). The British Joint Association of Classical Teachers has produced a reliable, readable (illustrated) book called *The World of Athens: An Introduction to Classical Athenian Culture* (Cambridge University Press, 1984). Finally, K.J. Dover's *Greek Popular Morality in the Time of Plato and Aristotle* (Basil Blackwell, 1974, reprinted by Hackett in 1994) is immensely interesting.

Plato's mentor Socrates wrote nothing, and the best access to his views is in Plato's early dialogues, the *Apology, Crito, Euthyphro, Protagoras,* and *Gorgias.* In fact, Socrates' trial and conviction are the setting for a sequence of Platonic dialogues: in the *Euthyphro* Socrates is on his way to court to be indicted; the *Apology* depicts his trial; in the *Crito* Socrates refuses his friends' pleas to escape from prison; and the *Phaedo* describes Socrates' last conversation and his death. Modern accounts of the trial of Socrates include Brickhouse and Smith, *Socrates on Trial* (Princeton University Press, 1989) and C.D.C. Reeve, *Socrates in the Apology* (Hackett, 1989). A general account of the philosophy of Socrates is Gregory Vlastos, *Socrates: Ironist and Moral Philosopher* (Cambridge University Press, 1991).

The history of modern Plato scholarship dates back to the nineteenth century and, as you might expect, there is a wealth of published description and analysis of his philosophical views. Some of the best (accessible, relatively recent) work is: I.M. Crosbie, *An Examination of Plato's Doctrines* (2 vols., Routledge & Kegan Paul, 1962/1963); J.C.B. Gosling, *Plato* (Routledge & Kegan Paul, 1973); G.M.A. Grube, *Plato's*

Thought (Hackett, 1980); W.K.C. Guthrie, *A History of Greek Philosophy*, Vols. 4 and 5 (Cambridge University Press, 1986); Terence Irwin, *Plato's Moral Theory* (Oxford University Press, 1977); Richard Kraut (ed.), *The Cambridge Companion to Plato* (Cambridge University Press, 1992); W.D. Ross, *Plato's Theory of Ideas* (Oxford University Press, 1951); Gregory Vlastos (ed.), *Plato: A Collection of Critical Essays* (2 vols., Doubleday, 1971); Gregory Vlastos, *Platonic Studies* (Princeton University Press, 1981); and Nicholas White, *Plato on Knowledge and Reality* (Hackett, 1976).

There are also a number of works specifically about Plato's *Republic.* The best is by Julia Annas, *An Introduction to Plato's Republic* (Oxford University Press, 1981). Nicholas White, *A Companion to Plato's Republic* (Hackett, 1979), Cross and Woozley, *Plato's Republic: A Philosophical Commentary* (Macmillan, 1964), and C.D.C. Reeve, *Philosopher-Kings* (Princeton University Press, 1988) are also good. The following articles deal with material found in the first half of Book II of the *Republic* and are well worth looking at: C.A. Kirwan, "Glaucon's Challenge," *Phronesis* 10 (1965); J.D. Mabbott, "Is Plato's *Republic* Utilitarian?" *Mind* 46 (1937); H.A. Prichard, "Duty and Interest" in *Moral Obligation and Duty and Interest* (Oxford University Press, 1968); David Sachs, "A Fallacy in Plato's *Republic,*" *Philosophical Review* 72 (1963); and Nicholas White, "The Classification of Goods in Plato's *Republic,*" *Journal of the History of Philosophy* 22 (1984).

Republic
Book II
(357a–367e)[7]

When I said this, I thought I had done with the discussion, but it turned out to have been only a prelude. Glaucon showed his characteristic courage on this occasion too and refused to accept Thrasymachus'

---

7   The *Republic* was probably written in about 380 BCE. This translation is by G.M.A. Grube, revised by C.D.C. Reeve, and published in 1992 by the Hackett Publishing Company. Reprinted by permission of Hackett Publishing Company, Inc. All rights reserved.

abandonment of the argument. Socrates, he said, do you want to seem to have persuaded us that it is better in every way to be just than unjust, or do you want truly to convince us of this?

I want truly to convince you, I said, if I can.

Well, then, you certainly aren't doing what you want. Tell me, do you think there is a kind of good we welcome, not because we desire what comes from it, but because we welcome it for its own sake—joy, for example, and all the harmless pleasures that have no results beyond the joy of having them?

Certainly, I think there are such things.

And is there a kind of good we like for its own sake and also for the sake of what comes from it—knowing, for example, and seeing and being healthy? We welcome such things, I suppose, on both counts.

Yes.

And do you also see a third kind of good, such as physical training, medical treatment when sick, medicine itself, and the other ways of making money? We'd say that these are onerous[8] but beneficial to us, and we wouldn't choose them for their own sakes, but for the sake of the rewards and other things that come from them.

There is also this third kind. But what of it?

Where do you put justice?

I myself put it among the finest goods, as something to be valued by anyone who is going to be blessed with happiness, both because of itself and because of what comes from it.

That isn't most people's opinion. They'd say that justice belongs to the onerous kind, and is to be practiced for the sake of the rewards and popularity that come from a reputation for justice, but is to be avoided because of itself as something burdensome.

I know that's the general opinion. Thrasymachus faulted justice on these grounds a moment ago and praised injustice, but it seems that I'm a slow learner.

Come, then, and listen to me as well, and see whether you still have that problem, for I think that Thrasymachus gave up before he had to, charmed by you as if he were a snake.[9] But I'm not yet satisfied by the argument on either side. I want to know what justice and injustice are and what power each itself has when it's by itself in the soul. I want to leave out of account their rewards and what comes from each of them. So, if you agree, I'll renew the argument of Thrasymachus. First, I'll state what kind of thing people consider justice to be and what its origins are. Second, I'll argue that all who practice it do so unwillingly, as something necessary, not as something good. Third, I'll argue that they have good reason to act as they do, for the life of an unjust person is, they say, much better than that of a just one.

It isn't, Socrates, that I believe any of that myself. I'm perplexed, indeed, and my ears are deafened listening to Thrasymachus and countless others. But I've yet to hear anyone defend justice in the way I want, proving that it is better than injustice. I want to hear it praised *by itself*, and I think that I'm most likely to hear this from you. Therefore, I'm going to speak at length in praise of the unjust life, and in doing so I'll show you the way I want to hear you praising justice and denouncing injustice. But see whether you want me to do that or not.

I want that most of all. Indeed, what subject could someone with any understanding enjoy discussing more often?

Excellent. Then let's discuss the first subject I mentioned—what justice is and what its origins are.

They say that to do injustice is naturally good and to suffer injustice bad, but that the badness of suffering it so far exceeds the goodness of doing it that those who have done and suffered injustice and tasted both, but who lack the power to do it and avoid suffering it, decide that it is profitable to come to an agreement with each other neither to do injustice nor to suffer it. As a result, they begin to make laws and covenants, and what the law commands they call lawful and just. This, they say, is the origin and essence of justice. It is intermediate between the best and the worst. The best is to do injustice without paying the penalty; the worst is to suffer it without being able to take revenge. Justice is a mean between these two extremes. People value it not as a good but because they are too weak to do injustice with impunity. Someone who has the power to do this, however, and is a true man wouldn't make an agreement with anyone not to do injustice in

---

8   Burdensome, troublesome.

9   As if he were calmed by the music of a snake-charmer.

order not to suffer it. For him that would be madness. This is the nature of justice, according to the argument, Socrates, and these are its natural origins.

We can see most clearly that those who practice justice do it unwillingly and because they lack the power to do injustice, if in our thoughts we grant to a just and an unjust person the freedom to do whatever they like. We can then follow both of them and see where their desires would lead. And we'll catch the just person red-handed travelling the same road as the unjust. The reason for this is the desire to outdo others and get more and more.[10] This is what anyone's nature naturally pursues as good, but nature is forced by law into the perversion of treating fairness with respect.

The freedom I mentioned would be most easily realized if both people had the power they say the ancestor of Gyges of Lydia[11] possessed. The story goes that he was a shepherd in the service of the ruler of Lydia. There was a violent thunderstorm, and an earthquake broke open the ground and created a chasm at the place where he was tending his sheep. Seeing this, he was filled with amazement and went down into it. And there, in addition to many other wonders of which we're told, he saw a hollow bronze horse. There were windowlike openings in it, and, peeping in, he saw a corpse, which seemed to be of more than human size, wearing nothing but a gold ring on its finger. He took the ring and came out of the chasm. He wore the ring at the usual monthly meeting that reported to the king on the state of the flocks. And as he was sitting among the others, he happened to turn the setting[12] of the ring towards himself to the inside of his hand. When he did this, he became invisible to those sitting near him, and they went on talking as if he had gone. He wondered at this, and, fingering the ring, he turned the setting outwards again and became visible. So he experimented with the ring to test whether it indeed had this power—and it did. If he turned the setting inward, he became invisible; if he turned it outward, he became visible again. When he realized this, he at once arranged to become one of the messengers sent to report to the king. And when he arrived there, he seduced the king's wife, attacked the king with her help, killed him, and took over the kingdom.

Let's suppose, then, that there were two such rings, one worn by a just and the other by an unjust person. Now, no one, it seems, would be so incorruptible that he would stay on the path of justice or stay away from other people's property, when he could take whatever he wanted from the marketplace with impunity, go into people's houses and have sex with anyone he wished, kill or release from prison anyone he wished, and do all the other things that would make him like a god among humans. Rather his actions would be in no way different from those of an unjust person and both would follow the same path. This, some would say, is a great proof that one is never just willingly but only when compelled to be. No one believes justice to be a good when it is kept private, since, wherever either person thinks he can do injustice with impunity, he does it. Indeed, every man believes that injustice is far more profitable to himself than justice. And any exponent of this argument will say he's right, for someone who didn't want to do injustice, given this sort of opportunity, and who didn't touch other people's property would be thought wretched and stupid by everyone aware of the situation, though, of course, they'd praise him in public, deceiving each other for fear of suffering injustice. So much for my second topic.

As for the choice between the lives we're discussing, we'll be able to make a correct judgment about that only if we separate the most just and the most unjust. Otherwise we won't be able to do it. Here's the

---

10   This is the vice of *pleonexia*, the desire to out-compete everybody else and get more than you are entitled to. According to Plato, *pleonexia* is the root cause of injustice, and proper virtue consists in keeping *pleonexia* in check; Thrasymachus, however, has argued that *pleonexia* is not a vice at all, but a reasonable impulse which is only stifled by artificial social conventions.

11   Lydia was an ancient kingdom located in western Asia Minor, where northwestern Turkey lies today. Gyges was king of Lydia from 670 to 652 BCE. Probably the first realm to use coins as money, Lydia was renowned for its immense wealth and reached the height of its power in the seventh century BCE. In 546 BCE its final king, Croesus, was defeated by the Persians and Lydia was absorbed into the Persian Empire.

12   The setting for a jewel.

separation I have in mind. We'll subtract nothing from the injustice of an unjust person and nothing from the justice of a just one, but we'll take each to be complete in his own way of life. First, therefore, we must suppose that an unjust person will act as clever craftsmen do: A first-rate captain or doctor, for example, knows the difference between what his craft can and can't do. He attempts the first but lets the second go by, and if he happens to slip, he can put things right. In the same way, an unjust person's successful attempts at injustice must remain undetected, if he is to be fully unjust. Anyone who is caught should be thought inept, for the extreme of injustice is to be believed to be just without being just. And our completely unjust person must be given complete injustice; nothing may be subtracted from it. We must allow that, while doing the greatest injustice, he has nonetheless provided himself with the greatest reputation for justice. If he happens to make a slip, he must be able to put it right. If any of his unjust activities should be discovered, he must be able to speak persuasively or to use force. And if force is needed, he must have the help of courage and strength and of the substantial wealth and friends with which he has provided himself.

Having hypothesized such a person, let's now in our argument put beside him a just man, who is simple and noble and who, as Aeschylus[13] says, doesn't want to be believed to be good but to be so.[14] We must take away his reputation, for a reputation for justice would bring him honour and rewards, so that it wouldn't be clear whether he is just for the sake of justice itself or for the sake of those honours and rewards. We must strip him of everything except justice and make his situation the opposite of an unjust person's. Though he does no injustice, he must have the greatest reputation

for it, so that his justice may be tested full-strength and not diluted by wrong-doing and what comes from it. Let him stay like that unchanged until he dies—just, but all his life believed to be unjust. In this way, both will reach the extremes, the one of justice and the other of injustice, and we'll be able to judge which of them is happier.

Whew! Glaucon, I said, how vigorously you've scoured each of the men for our competition, just as you would a pair of statues for an art competition.

I do the best I can, he replied. Since the two are as I've described, in any case, it shouldn't be difficult to complete the account of the kind of life that awaits each of them, but it must be done. And if what I say sounds crude, Socrates, remember that it isn't I who speak but those who praise injustice at the expense of justice. They'll say that a just person in such circumstances will be whipped, stretched on a rack, chained, blinded with fire, and, at the end, when he has suffered every kind of evil, he'll be impaled, and will realize then that one shouldn't want to be just but to be believed to be just. Indeed, Aeschylus' words are far more correctly applied to unjust people than to just ones, for the supporters of injustice will say that a really unjust person, having a way of life based on the truth about things and not living in accordance with opinion, doesn't want simply to be believed to be unjust but actually to be so —

Harvesting a deep furrow in his mind,
Where wise counsels propagate.

He rules his city because of his reputation for justice; he marries into any family he wishes; he gives his children in marriage to anyone he wishes; he has contracts and partnerships with anyone he wants; and besides benefiting himself in all these ways, he profits because he has no scruples about doing injustice. In any contest, public or private, he's the winner and outdoes his enemies. And by outdoing them, he becomes wealthy, benefiting his friends and harming his enemies. He makes adequate sacrifices to the gods and sets up magnificent offerings to them. He takes better care of the gods, therefore, (and, indeed, of the human beings he's fond of) than a just person does. Hence it's likely that the gods, in turn, will take better care of him than of a just person. That's what they say,

---

13　Aeschylus (525–456 BCE) was a great and influential Greek tragic dramatist. He is sometimes said to have created drama itself, through his innovative introduction of multiple actors speaking different parts. His most famous plays are the *Oresteia* trilogy—*Agamemnon, The Libation Bearers,* and *The Eumenides.*

14　This refers to Aeschylus's play *Seven Against Thebes.* It is said of a character that "he did not wish to be believed to be the best but to be it." The next two lines of the passage are quoted by Glaucon below.

Socrates, that gods and humans provide a better life for unjust people than for just ones.

When Glaucon had said this, I had it in mind to respond, but his brother Adeimantus intervened: You surely don't think that the position has been adequately stated?

Why not? I said.

The most important thing to say hasn't been said yet.

Well, then, I replied, a man's brother must stand by him, as the saying goes.[15] If Glaucon has omitted something, you must help him. Yet what he has said is enough to throw me to the canvas[16] and make me unable to come to the aid of justice.

Nonsense, he said. Hear what more I have to say, for we should also fully explore the arguments that are opposed to the ones Glaucon gave, the ones that praise justice and find fault with injustice, so that what I take to be his intention may be clearer.

When fathers speak to their sons, they say that one must be just, as do all the others who have charge of anyone. But they don't praise justice itself, only the high reputations it leads to and the consequences of being thought to be just, such as the public offices, marriages, and other things Glaucon listed. But they elaborate even further on the consequences of reputation. By bringing in the esteem of the gods, they are able to talk about the abundant good things that they themselves and the noble Hesiod and Homer say that the gods give to the pious, for Hesiod says that the gods make the oak trees

> *Bear acorns at the top and bees in the middle*
> *And make fleecy sheep heavy laden with wool*[17]

for the just, and tells of many other good things akin to these. And Homer is similar:

> *When a good king, in his piety,*
> *Upholds justice, the black earth bears*
> *Wheat and barley for him, and his trees are*
> *heavy with fruit.*
> *His sheep bear lambs unfailingly, and the sea*
> *yields up its fish.*[18]

Musaeus[19] and his son make the gods give the just more headstrong goods than these. In their stories, they lead the just to Hades,[20] seat them on couches, provide them with a symposium[21] of pious people, crown them with wreaths, and make them spend all their time drinking—as if they thought drunkenness was the finest wage of virtue. Others stretch even further the wages that virtue receives from the gods, for they say that someone who is pious and keeps his promises leaves his children's children and a whole race behind him. In these and other similar ways, they praise justice. They bury the impious and unjust in mud in Hades; force them to carry water in a sieve; bring them into bad repute while they're still alive, and all those penalties that Glaucon gave to the just person they give to the unjust. But they have nothing else to say. This, then, is the way people praise justice and find fault with injustice.

Besides this, Socrates, consider another form of argument about justice and injustice employed both by private individuals and by poets. All go on repeating with one voice that justice and moderation are

---

15 In Homer's *Odyssey* (part 16, lines 97–98).

16 To throw me to the floor of a wrestling ring.

17 Hesiod, *Works and Days*, lines 232–234. Hesiod was an early Greek poet—considered the second greatest Greek epic poet after Homer—who lived around 700 BCE. His poem *Works and Days* reflects his experiences as a farmer, giving practical advice on how to live, and also shows Hesiod lamenting the loss of a historic Golden Age which has been replaced, he complains, with a modern era of immorality and suffering.

18 Homer, *Odyssey*, part 19, lines 109 and 111–113.

19 This Musaeus (as opposed to a Greek poet of the same name, who lived some 1000 years later) was a mythical poet and singer connected with the cult of Orphism, a Greek mystery religion of the sixth century BCE. His son, Eumolpus, is said to have founded the Eleusinian mysteries, an annual celebration to honor Demeter, goddess of agriculture and fertility.

20 The site of the Greek afterlife, where the good were rewarded and the wicked punished.

21 A gathering for drinking, music, and intellectual conversation. (Greek—*sumposion*, literally, drinking party.)

fine things, but hard and onerous, while licentiousness and injustice are sweet and easy to acquire and are shameful only in opinion and law. They add that unjust deeds are for the most part more profitable than just ones, and, whether in public or private, they willingly honour vicious people[22] who have wealth and other types of power and declare them to be happy. But they dishonour and disregard the weak and the poor, even though they agree that they are better than the others.

But the most wonderful of all these arguments concerns what they have to say about the gods and virtue. They say that the gods, too, assign misfortune and a bad life to many good people, and the opposite fate to their opposites. Begging priests and prophets frequent the doors of the rich and persuade them that they possess a god-given power founded on sacrifices and incantations. If the rich person or any of his ancestors has committed an injustice, they can fix it with pleasant rituals. Moreover, if he wishes to injure some enemy, then, at little expense, he'll be able to harm just and unjust alike, for by means of spells and enchantments they can persuade the gods to serve them. And the poets are brought forward as witnesses to all these accounts. Some harp on the ease of vice, as follows:

> Vice in abundance is easy to get;
> The road is smooth and begins beside you,
> But the gods have put sweat between us and
>   virtue,[23]

and a road that is long, rough, and steep. Others quote Homer to witness that the gods can be influenced by humans, since he said:

> The gods themselves can be swayed by prayer,
> And with sacrifices and soothing promises,
> Incense and libations, human beings turn
>   them from their purpose
> When someone has transgressed and sinned.[24]

And they present a noisy throng of books by Musaeus and Orpheus,[25] offspring as they say of Selene and the Muses,[26] in accordance with which they perform their rituals. And they persuade not only individuals but whole cities that the unjust deeds of the living or the dead can be absolved or purified through sacrifices and pleasant games, whether those who have committed them are still alive, or have died. These initiations, as they call them, free people from punishment hereafter, while a terrible fate awaits those who have not performed rituals.

When all such sayings about the attitudes of gods and humans to virtue and vice are so often repeated, Socrates, what effect do you suppose they have on the souls of young people? I mean those who are clever and are able to flit from one of these sayings to another, so to speak, and gather from them an impression of what sort of person he should be and of how best to travel the road of life. He would surely ask himself Pindar's[27] question, "Should I by justice or by crooked deceit scale this high wall and live my life guarded and secure?" And he'll answer: "The various sayings suggest that there is no advantage in my being just if I'm not also thought just, while the troubles and penalties of being just are apparent. But they tell me that an unjust person, who has secured for himself a reputation for justice, lives the life of a god. Since, then, 'opinion forcibly overcomes truth'

---

22   Those having many vices, wicked people.

23   *Works and Days*, lines 287–289.

24   *Iliad*, part 9, lines 497 and 499–501.

25   Orpheus was a legendary poet who lived (if he is a real figure at all) in the sixth or seventh century BCE. According to Greek myth, he was the first living mortal to travel to the underworld, on a quest to retrieve his dead wife Eurydice. Hades, ruler of the underworld, was so moved by the poet's music that he gave back Eurydice, on the condition that Orpheus not look back at her until they reached the world of the living. Orpheus glanced back a moment too soon, and Eurydice vanished. Heart-broken, he wandered alone in the wilds until a band of Thracian women killed him and threw his severed head in the river, where it continued to call for his lost love, Eurydice.

26   Selene is the Greek goddess of the Moon. The Muses were nine goddesses, daughters of Zeus, who presided over the arts and sciences.

27   Pindar (520–440 BCE) was a Greek lyric poet.

and 'controls happiness,' as the wise men[28] say, I must surely turn entirely to it. I should create a façade of illusory virtue around me to deceive those who come near, but keep behind it the greedy and crafty fox of the wise Archilochus."[29]

"But surely," someone will object, "it isn't easy for vice to remain always hidden." We'll reply that nothing great is easy. And, in any case, if we're to be happy, we must follow the path indicated in these accounts. To remain undiscovered we'll form secret societies and political clubs. And there are teachers of persuasion to make us clever in dealing with assemblies and law courts. Therefore, using persuasion in one place and force in another, we'll outdo others without paying a penalty.

"What about the gods? Surely, we can't hide from them or use violent force against them!" Well, if the gods don't exist or don't concern themselves with human affairs, why should we worry at all about hiding from them? If they do exist and do concern themselves with us, we've learned all we know about them from the laws and the poets who give their genealogies—nowhere else. But these are the very people who tell us that the gods can be persuaded and influenced by sacrifices, gentle prayers, and offerings. Hence, we should believe them on both matters or neither. If we believe them, we should be unjust and offer sacrifices from the fruits of our injustice. If we are just, our only gain is not to be punished by the gods, since we lose the profits of injustice. But if we are unjust, we get the profits of our crimes and transgressions and afterwards persuade the gods by prayer and escape without punishment.

"But in Hades won't we pay the penalty for crimes committed here, either ourselves or our children's children?" "My friend," the young man will say as he does his calculation, "mystery rites have great power and the gods have great power of absolution. The greatest cities tell us this, as do those children of the gods who have become poets and prophets."

---

28   Simonides of Ceos (c. 556–468 BCE), a Greek poet.
29   Archilochus of Paros (who lived around 650 BCE), yet another Greek poet, and author of the famous fable about a fox and a hedgehog.

Why, then, should we still choose justice over the greatest injustice? Many eminent authorities agree that, if we practice such injustice with a false façade, we'll do well at the hands of gods and humans, living and dying as we've a mind to. So, given all that has been said, Socrates, how is it possible for anyone of any power—whether of mind, wealth, body, or birth—to be willing to honor justice and not laugh aloud when he hears it praised? Indeed, if anyone can show that what we've said is false and has adequate knowledge that justice is best, he'll surely be full not of anger but of forgiveness for the unjust. He knows that, apart from someone of godlike character who is disgusted by injustice or one who has gained knowledge and avoids injustice for that reason, no one is just willingly. Through cowardice or old age or some other weakness, people do indeed object to injustice. But it's obvious that they do so only because they lack the power to do injustice, for the first of them to acquire it is the first to do as much injustice as he can.

And all of this has no other cause than the one that led Glaucon and me to say to you: "Socrates, of all of you who claim to praise justice, from the original heroes of old whose words survive, to the men of the present day, not one has ever blamed injustice or praised justice except by mentioning the reputations, honours, and rewards that are their consequences. No one has ever adequately described what each itself does of its own power by its presence in the soul of the person who possesses it, even if it remains hidden from gods and humans. No one, whether in poetry or in private conversations, has adequately argued that injustice is the worst thing a soul can have in it and that justice is the greatest good. If you had treated the subject in this way and persuaded us from youth, we wouldn't now be guarding against one another's injustices, but each would be his own best guardian, afraid that by doing injustice he'd be living with the worst thing possible."

Thrasymachus or anyone else might say what we've said, Socrates, or maybe even more, in discussing justice and injustice—crudely inverting their powers, in my opinion. And, frankly, it's because I want to hear the opposite from you that I speak with all the force I can muster. So don't merely give us a theoretical argument that justice is stronger than injustice, but tell us what each itself does, because of its own powers, to someone who possesses it, that makes injustice bad and justice good. Follow Glaucon's advice, and don't take reputations into account, for if you don't deprive justice and injustice of their true reputations and attach false ones to them, we'll say that you are not praising them but their reputations and that you're encouraging us to be unjust in secret. In that case, we'll say that you agree with Thrasymachus that justice is the good of another, the advantage of the stronger, while injustice is one's own advantage and profit, though not the advantage of the weaker.

You agree that justice is one of the greatest goods, the ones that are worth getting for the sake of what comes from them, but much more so for their own sake, such as seeing, hearing, knowing, being healthy, and all other goods that are fruitful by their own nature and not simply because of reputation. Therefore, praise justice as a good of that kind, explaining how—because of its very self—it benefits its possessors and how injustice harms them. Leave wages and reputations for others to praise.

Others would satisfy me if they praised justice and blamed injustice in that way, extolling the wages of one and denigrating those of the other. But you, unless you order me to be satisfied, wouldn't, for you've spent your whole life investigating this and nothing else. Don't, then, give us only a theoretical argument that justice is stronger than injustice, but show what effect each has because of itself on the person who has it—the one for good and the other for bad—whether it remains hidden from gods and human beings or not....

ARISTOTLE

The Nicomachean Ethics

Who Was Aristotle?

Aristotle was born in 384 BCE in Stageira, a small town in the northeast corner of the Chalcidice peninsula in the kingdom of Macedon, many days journey north of the intellectual centers of Greece. His father—Nicomachus, a physician at the Macedonian court—died when Aristotle was young, and he was brought up by his mother's wealthy family. At 17 Aristotle traveled to Athens to study at Europe's most important center of learning, the Academy, set up and presided over by Plato. As a young philosopher, Aristotle showed exceptional promise and made a name for himself as being industrious and clever, a good speaker, argumentative (if rather sarcastic), original, and independent of thought. He was apparently a bit of a dandy—cutting his hair in a fashionably short style, and wearing jeweled rings—and is said to have suffered from poor digestion, to have lisped, and to have had spindly legs.

After Plato's death in about 347 BCE, Aristotle left Athens (possibly pushed out by a surge of anti-Macedonian feeling in the city—though one story suggests he left in a fit of pique after failing to be granted leadership of the Academy, and yet another account has it that Aristotle was unhappy with the Academy's turn towards pure mathematics under Plato's successor Speusippus). He traveled to Atarneus on the coast of Asia Minor (present-day Turkey) where his mother's family had connections and where the pro-Macedonian tyrant, Hermias, was a patron of philosophical studies. There, with three colleagues from the Academy, Aristotle started his own school at the town of Assos. Aristotle married Hermias's niece and adopted daughter, Pythias, and they had a daughter, also called Pythias.

This happy familial situation did not last long, however. In about 345 BCE Hermias was betrayed and executed (in a particularly grisly fashion) by the Persians. Aristotle and his family fled to the nearby island of Lesbos, in the eastern Aegean Sea, where Aristotle founded another school at a town called Mytilene. There, with his student Theophrastus, he engaged in a hugely impressive series of studies in botany, zoology, and marine biology, collecting observations which were still of unrivaled scientific interest some 2000 years later. (Indeed, as late as the nineteenth century, Charles Darwin was able to praise Aristotle's biological researches as a work of genius which every professional biologist should read.)

Aristotle's stay on Lesbos was of short duration. In 343 BCE, invited by Philip II, the ruler of Macedonia, he returned home to tutor the 13-year-old prince Alexander. Little is reliably known about Aristotle's life during this period, though many fanciful stories have been written, enshrouding it in myth. Three years later, on Philip's death, Alexander became king and launched the military career which, in fairly short order, made him conqueror of much of the known world and earned him the epithet Alexander the Great. (One history claims that when Alexander embarked on his conquest of the East—his armies advanced as far as the Indian sub-continent—he took along scientists whose sole job it was to report their discoveries back to Aristotle.)

In 335 BCE, after Alexander's troops had completed their conquest of the Greek city-states, Aristotle moved back to Athens where, once again, he started his own research institute. This university became known as the Lyceum (after the grove, dedicated to Apollo Lyceus, where it was located), and it continued to flourish for 500 years after Aristotle's death.[1] There he spent the next twelve years teaching, writing, and building up the first great library of the ancient world. Most of his known philosophical writings probably date from this time. After his wife Pythias died, Aristotle became the lover of a woman called Herpyllis. Their son Nicomachus, was named, following the Greek custom, after his grandfather.

This peaceful existence was shattered in 323 BCE by news of Alexander's death in Babylon at the age of 33. Almost instantly, open revolt against the Macedonian conquerors broke out, and Aristotle—because of his connection with Alexander—was suddenly no longer welcome in Athens. One of the citizens brought an indictment of impiety towards him—the same 'crime' for which the Athenians had executed Socrates three-quarters of a century earlier. In order, as one tradition has it, to prevent the Athenians from sinning against philosophy a second time, Aristotle and his family beat a hasty retreat to Chalcis, on the island of Euboea, where his mother's family had estates. There Aristotle soon died, in November 322 BCE, at age 62. In his humane and sensible will, which has been preserved for posterity, Aristotle directed that Pythias's bones should be placed in his grave, in accordance with her wishes. He also freed several of his slaves and made generous and flexible financial provisions for Herpyllis and Nicomachus.

What Was Aristotle's Overall Philosophical Project?

Aristotle's life-work was nothing less than the attempt to collect together and systematically arrange all human knowledge. His consuming ambition was to get

---

1   Because philosophical discussions at the Lyceum were often conducted whilst strolling around a colonnaded walk called a *peripatos*, Aristotle's group became known as "the Peripatetics" (the walkers).

as close as possible to *knowing everything*—about the natural world, the human social world, and even the unchanging and eternal world of the heavens and the gods. However, unlike many other philosophers with similar ambitions before and since, Aristotle probably did not believe that there is some single, unified set of truths—some single *theory*—which provides the key to unlocking all of reality. He was not looking for a deeper, more authentic realm lying behind and explaining the world we live in, but instead was simply trying to find out as much as he could about *our* world, as we experience it. Thus, it is sometimes said, Aristotle's basic theoretical commitment was to *common sense*: he wanted to develop a system that provided a place for both scientific and moral-political truths, but did not depend on mysteriously invisible and inaccessible objects such as Plato's Forms (see the notes to the previous reading).[2] For Aristotle, the ultimate reality is the concrete world with which we are already acquainted—people, animals, plants, minerals—which Aristotle thought of as *substances* and their properties.

Often, Aristotle worked in the following way: after choosing a domain of study (such as rhetoric or metaphysics), he would begin by summarizing and laying out all the serious claims made about it—"what seems to be the case," including all the "reputable opinions." He would also pay attention to the way in which the matters in question were ordinarily spoken of—the assumptions about them built into everyday language. Then, Aristotle would survey the puzzles or problems generated by this material, and would set out to solve those puzzles, preferably without disturbing too many of the received opinions. Typically he would not stop there: new puzzles or objections

would be raised by the solutions, and he would try to clear up those matters, and then the new puzzles generated, and so on, each time, he hoped, getting closer to the final truth.

Since Aristotle did not believe in a single "theory of everything," he divided the branches of knowledge, or "sciences," into three main groups: theoretical sciences (whose aim is to discover truths), practical sciences (governing the performance of actions), and productive sciences (whose goal is the making of objects). The major theoretical sciences, according to Aristotle, are theology (which he thought of as the study of "changeless items"), mathematics, and the natural sciences. The chief practical sciences are ethics and politics. Examples of productive sciences are poetics, rhetoric, medicine, and agriculture. According to Aristotle, these various sciences are quite different: although they add up to a composite picture of reality, they share no single set of theoretical concepts or assumptions, no single methodology, and no single set of standards for scientific rigor. The proper methods of mathematics differ from those of zoology, which differ again from those of ethics.

On the other hand, Aristotle hoped each science, or at least all theoretical sciences, would share the same *structure*: Aristotle was the first philosopher to conceive of science as a body of knowledge arranged according to a particular logical structure, which he modeled on that of geometry. As in geometry, there are two kinds of scientific truth, according to Aristotle: truths which are simply "evident" and need no explanation, and a much larger body of further truths which are justified or explained by being logically derived from the self-evident truths. (Aristotle, more or less single-handedly, *invented* the study of logic—which he called the science of "syllogisms"—partly to be able to describe the proper structure of scientific knowledge.) Unlike the case with geometry, however, Aristotle insisted that the "axioms" of any theoretical science—the self-evident truths upon which it is based—should ideally capture the *essences* of the things being described by that science. In this way, according to Aristotle, the logical structure of science would exactly reflect the structure of the world itself. Just as the properties of things (say, plants) are caused by their essential natures, so will the claims of

---

2   Another, then contemporary, theory which Aristotle opposed, also on the grounds of mystery-mongering, was a theory called "atomism," put forward by philosophers like Leucippus (who flourished between 450 and 420 BCE) and Democritus (c. 460–371 BCE). This theory postulated the existence of huge numbers of invisibly tiny, eternal, unchangeable particles—*atoma*, Greek for "uncuttables"—whose hidden behaviors and interactions were supposed to explain all the observable properties of the visible spatio-temporal world.

the relevant science (e.g., botany) be logically derived from its basic assumptions about the essences of the things in its domain.

So *where*, according to Aristotle, do we get these first principles of the different sciences? The answer, Aristotle believed, was not from the exercise of pure reason but from careful *observation* of the world around us. By looking very hard and carefully at a particular domain (such as botany or ethics) we discern some fundamental truths about the things in that domain, from which everything else about it will follow. Because of this practical emphasis on observation rather than mere thought, Aristotle is described as "the father of modern empiricism." On the other hand, Aristotle never developed anything like an experimental method: his method for testing theories—verifying and falsifying them—consisted more in reasoned analysis than in empirical testing.

What Is the Structure of This Reading?

Judging by Alexandrian-age library catalogues, Aristotle wrote some 150 works in his lifetime—ranging in length from essays to books—covering a huge variety of topics: logic, physics, biology, meteorology, philosophy of science, history of science, metaphysics, psychology (including works on love, friendship, and the emotions), ethics and political theory, political science, rhetoric, poetics (and some original poetry), and political and legal history. Only a fraction of these writings—perhaps less than a fifth—survive: many of Aristotle's works, including all the dialogues he wrote for popular consumption, are now lost.[3] Most of what remains are summaries of lectures delivered at various times during his career, which were deposited in Aristotle's own library at the Lyceum to be consulted by teachers and students. Most of these

notes were probably edited and re-edited, both by Aristotle and his successors; the *Nicomachean Ethics*, for example, is so-called because it is thought to have been edited by Aristotle's son Nicomachus after his father's death.[4]

The *Nicomachean Ethics* is traditionally divided into ten books (though the divisions were probably not Aristotle's own). Book I examines the nature of the good for human beings—happiness—and divides it into two categories: intellectual excellence and moral excellence. Books II to IV deal with moral excellence, beginning with a general account of it and going on to discuss several of the moral virtues in detail. Book V looks at the virtue of justice, while Book VI describes some of the forms of intellectual excellence. Book VII deals with moral self-control and the nature of pleasure, and Books VIII and IX are about friendship. Finally, Book X concludes with a discussion of *eudaimonia* or well-being, and of the role that education and society play in bringing about individual happiness.

Excerpted here are the first few pages of Book I, which introduce Aristotle's view of the study of ethics, and then section 7 of Book I, where Aristotle lays out his so-called "function argument" for the view that human happiness consists in a life of excellent activity in accordance with reason. There follows the second half of Book II, where Aristotle defines moral virtue as a disposition to choose the mean—illustrating this with examples of particular moral virtues—and then discusses the practical corollaries of this account of virtue. Finally, part of Book X is included: here, Aristotle discusses further the nature of happiness and argues that the highest form of happiness is to be found in a life of philosophical "contemplation."

Much of Book V of the *Nicomachean Ethics* is also reprinted in Chapter 3.

---

3   This lost *oeuvre* is a particular tragedy because Aristotle's prose style was greatly admired by the ancients—more so than Plato's, for example—and yet (not unnaturally, considering their purpose) the lecture notes, which are the only things of Aristotle's we have left to us, are generally agreed to be rather dryly written: terse and elliptical, full of abrupt transitions, inadequate explanations, and technical jargon.

---

4   Aristotle's other main ethical work—an earlier set of lecture notes, generally thought to be superseded by the more mature *Nicomachean Ethics*—is similarly called the *Eudemian Ethics*, possibly after its ancient editor Eudemus of Rhodes.

Some Useful Background Information

1. Aristotle categorized ethics as a practical, rather than a theoretical, science. The *Nicomachean Ethics* is written "not in order to know what virtue is, but in order to become good." In other words, for Aristotle, the point of ethics is not merely to know what good people are like, but to learn to act as good people do: the *Nicomachean Ethics* is intended to foster what he calls "practical wisdom" (*phronesis*) in those who study it. The science of ethics is continuous, for Aristotle, with two others—biology and politics. It is continuous with biology because ethics is the study of the good life for humankind *as a biological species*. A good life for the member of *any* species (whether a horse or a rubber plant) is a life of continuous flourishing, but what *counts* as flourishing will depend upon the biological nature of that species. Ethics is continuous with politics—the study of human society—because the arena in which human beings live their lives, in which they develop as moral agents and exercise their moral capacities, is necessarily a social one.

2. According to Aristotle, the goal of human life is to achieve *eudaimonia*. *Eudaimonia* is usually—as it is in our selection—translated as "happiness," but this can be misleading. The Greek word does not refer to a psychological state or feeling, such as pleasure, but instead means a certain kind of desirable *activity* or *way of life*— it is the activity of living well. The happy person is, for Aristotle, someone who has lived a genuinely *successful* or fulfilling life.

3. Aristotle's understanding of nature, and in particular of biology, is what is called *teleological*: a thing's *telos* is its goal or purpose and, for Aristotle, all of nature is goal-directed. For example, the nature of some processes (such as digestion) or biological organs (such as the eye) is plausibly determined by their *function*—their goal or *telos*—and not by their physical composition at some particular time. Eyes are things— any things—that have the function of seeing. Aristotle extended this model to the entire natural world, so that, in his view, the essence of fire consists in its goal (of, roughly, rising upwards), the essence of an acorn is its purpose to grow into an oak tree, and the essence of the species *horse* is to flourish and procreate as horses are supposed to do. Since human beings are as much a part of the biological world as anything else, it follows that a proper understanding of human nature—and thus of the good life for human beings—must involve an investigation into the function of the human species.

Some Common Misconceptions

1. When Aristotle refers to the *telos*—the function or goal—of living creatures like plants, animals, and human beings, he is not thinking of these creatures as having a purpose for *something else*. He is not, for example, assuming that there is some great universal plan (perhaps God's plan) and that living creatures have a role to play in fulfilling this plan. Instead, the *telos* of living creatures is *internal* to them: it is, so to speak, built into their biological natures.

2. It is sometimes easy to forget that Aristotle's Doctrine of the Mean urges us to avoid *both* excess and deficiency. Aristotle's account not only instructs us to moderate our anger or curb our drinking, it also warns us against feeling too *little* anger or not drinking *enough* wine.

3. When Aristotle refers to "the mean" of a spectrum of behavior, he does not intend to speak of something like an arithmetical average, and thus does not suggest we should, literally, choose the *mid-point* of that range of behavior. The mean or mid-point of two numbers (as 6 is the mean of 2 and 10) is an example of what Aristotle calls a mean "in terms of the object." Aristotle contrasts this mathematical use with his own usage of "mean," which is a mean "relatively to us." For example, we should eat neither too many, nor too few, cookies; but exactly how many cookies we should eat depends on our personal circumstances (our weight, our lifestyle, how many other people also want cookies, whether we are allergic to ingredients in the

cookies, and so on). Certainly, Aristotle does not want to say that we should eat *exactly half* of all the available cookies. As Jonathan Barnes put it, "it is as though I were to hand a man a pack of cards and urge him to pick the middle one—adding that by 'middle' I meant 'middle relative to the chooser,' and that any card in the pack may be middle in this sense."

4. Aristotle does not think of his ethical theory as a sort of moral rulebook. Unlike most modern moral philosophers, such as Immanuel Kant and J.S. Mill, Aristotle is not trying to find a theory that will, by itself, generate moral principles to tell us how to act. Instead, he is trying to develop an account of moral *character*—a theory of the good person. It is salutary to recall that, although the topic of Aristotle's book is indeed *ēthika*, which is usually translated as "ethics," the Greek word means "matters to do with character." Similarly, when Aristotle writes of *ēthikē aretē*—which is almost invariably translated as "moral virtue"—the literal meaning is "excellence of character," and by "excellence" is meant simply what we would mean if we spoke of an excellent horse or an excellent ax. The modern sense of ethics, as involving *obedience to some sort of moral law,* is substantially more recent than Aristotle, and arose (more or less) with the monotheistic religions of Judaism, Christianity, and Islam.

5. The Doctrine of the Mean does not apply to particular *actions*, but to *virtues*—to states of character. Thus, the idea is not that one always *acts* in a way which is intermediate between two extremes, but that one's actions are guided by a *character trait* which is neither excessive nor insufficient. For example, in certain situations, someone possessing the virtue of generosity might nevertheless refuse to give anything at all to a particular person in a particular circumstance (or, conversely, might give away everything they own); or a person with the virtue of being even-tempered might nevertheless find it appropriate, sometimes, to become very angry (or, in another situation, to meekly suppress any angry feelings whatsoever).

How Important and Influential Is This Passage?

Many professional philosophers consider Aristotle to be the greatest philosopher who ever lived (for example, Oxford philosopher J.L. Ackrill calls him "a philosophical super-genius"); throughout the Middle Ages he was simply "the Philosopher." The system of ethics developed in the *Nicomachean Ethics* has had a profound effect on all subsequent moral philosophy. In every age of philosophy it has been either fervently embraced or fiercely rejected, but never ignored. Several of its central tenets—that morality consists in finding a "golden mean," or that the rational aim of human life is happiness (though not necessarily pleasure)—have become part of our everyday moral consciousness. On the other hand, for much of the post-medieval period, Aristotle's emphasis on the *virtues*, rather than on *types of action*, as the basis of morality was paid relatively little attention. More recently, there has been a surge of interest in so-called "virtue ethics," and Aristotle is generally considered the original source for this 'new' theory. (Modern virtue theories, however, diverge from Aristotle's ethical philosophy in important ways. In particular, they tend to reject or ignore his emphasis on *eudaimonia* as the ultimate moral good.)

Suggestions for Critical Reflection

1. When Aristotle talks of the "precision" of a subject matter, what exactly does he mean? What kind of precision can mathematics have which ethics must always lack? Does this mean there can be no universally true moral principles (but, perhaps, just 'rules of thumb')?

2. Does Aristotle assume there is just one thing which is the goal of every human life? Is he right?

3. Aristotle seems to define the (biological) function of human beings as the thing "which is peculiar to man"—i.e., as something only human beings can do. Is this a plausible way of identifying the human function? Is reason the *only* capacity which human beings have uniquely? Does Aristotle believe that only human beings are rational, or does he say things elsewhere which are inconsistent with this?

4. What if human beings do not *have* a function? How much damage would this do to Aristotle's moral theory?

5. Aristotle concedes that not every *vice* is a matter of degree, but he does seem to hold that every *virtue is* in the middle between two vices. Does this claim seem plausible? What about, for example, the virtue of kindness?

6. Does Aristotle's Doctrine of the Mean actually help us at all in making moral decisions? If not, how much of a problem is this for Aristotle's ethics? Do you think Aristotle *expects* his Doctrine of the Mean to guide our moral behavior? If the Doctrine of the Mean *cannot* tell us what to do, then what (if anything) is its point?

7. Many commentators on Aristotle's ethics have worried about what is sometimes called the "Aristotelian circle." Aristotle can be seen as making the following claims: virtuous action is what the practically wise person would choose; the practically wise are those who can successfully act in such a way as to achieve *eudaimonia*; but *eudaimonia*, for Aristotle, simply consists in wise action (it is "activity of soul exhibiting excellence"). If this is an accurate description of Aristotle's claims, how are we to *recognize* wise or virtuous action without an independent standard by which to judge it, and when Aristotle's inter-connected definitions go around in an endless circle? Do you agree that Aristotle's theory is circular? If so, do you think that makes it simply vacuous?

8. How plausible do you find Aristotle's arguments that the life of a philosopher is the best and happiest possible kind of life for human beings? How consistent is the emphasis in Book X on the activity of *theoria*—on *theoretical* reason—with Aristotle's earlier focus on *practical* wisdom?

9. Is Aristotle too egoistic? Does he pay too much attention to the question of how *individuals* can lead a good life, and not enough on moral issues to do with helping other people? For example, is generosity a virtue just because of its good effects on others, or simply because being generous makes one happy?

Suggestions for Further Reading

The standard English edition of Aristotle's works is *The Complete Works of Aristotle*, edited by Jonathan Barnes (2 vols., Princeton University Press, 1984). The translation of the *Nicomachean Ethics* reprinted here—that by W.D. Ross, revised by J.L. Ackrill and J.O. Urmson (Oxford University Press, 1998)—is the classic English version, but there are several other good ones, including the translations by J.A.K. Thomson, revised by Hugh Tredennick (Penguin, 1976), and Terence Irwin, which includes very extensive notes (Hackett, 1999).

By common consensus, the best short introduction to Aristotle's philosophy is J.L. Ackrill's *Aristotle the Philosopher* (Oxford University Press, 1981). Another good short book (which gives a strong impression of the breadth of Aristotle's interests, though it places very little emphasis on his ethics) is *Aristotle* by Jonathan Barnes (Oxford University Press, 1982). Somewhat longer but very valuable books are: W.D. Ross, *Aristotle* (Routledge, 1995); Jonathan Lear, *Aristotle: The Desire to Understand* (Cambridge University Press, 1988); G.E.R. Lloyd, *Aristotle: The Growth and Structure of his Thought* (Cambridge University Press, 1968); and Terence Irwin, *Aristotle's First Principles* (Oxford University Press, 1990). *The Cambridge Companion to Aristotle*, edited by Jonathan Barnes (Cambridge University Press, 1995), is also very good.

Perhaps the best guide to Aristotle's ethical philosophy is W.F.R. Hardie's *Aristotle's Ethical Theory* (Oxford University Press, 1980). Sarah Broadie's *Ethics with Aristotle* (Oxford University Press, 1995), John M. Cooper's *Reason and Human Good in Aristotle* (Hackett, 1986), Gerard Hughes's *Aristotle's Ethics* (Routledge, 2001), D.S. Hutchinson's *The Virtues of Aristotle* (Routledge & Kegan Paul, 1986), Harold H. Joachim's *Aristotle: The Nicomachean Ethics* (Oxford University Press, 1955), Richard Kraut's *Aristotle on the Human Good* (Princeton University Press, 1990), C.D.C. Reeve's *Practices of Reason: Aristotle's Nicomachean Ethics* (Oxford University Press, 1995), and J.O. Urmson's *Aristotle's Ethics* (Blackwell, 1988) are also good.

There are two particularly useful collections of articles on the *Nicomachean Ethics*: Nancy Sherman (ed.), *Aristotle's Ethics: Critical Essays* (Rowman and Littlefield, 1999), and Amélie O. Rorty (ed.), *Essays on Aristo-*

tle's Ethics (University of California Press, 1981). Three additional interesting articles, not included in these collections, are: J.E. Whiting, "Aristotle's Function Argument: A Defence," *Ancient Philosophy* 8 (1988); Richard Kraut, "Two Conceptions of Happiness," *Philosophical Review* 88 (1979); and Gavin Lawrence, "Aristotle on the Ideal Life," *Philosophical Review* 102 (1993).

Finally, descendents of Aristotle's ethical ideas are discussed in Georg Henrik Von Wright, *The Varieties of Goodness* (Routledge & Kegan Paul, 1963); Peter Geach, *The Virtues* (Cambridge University Press, 1977); Stuart Hampshire, *Two Theories of Morality* (Oxford University Press, 1977); Philippa Foot, *Virtues and Vices* (University of California Press, 1978); James D. Wallace, *Virtues and Vices* (Cornell University Press, 1978); Bernard Williams, *Ethics and the Limits of Philosophy* (Harvard University Press, 1986); Michael Slote, *From Morality to Virtue* (Oxford University Press, 1995); Crisp and Slote (eds.), *Virtue Ethics* (Oxford University Press, 1997); Roger Crisp (ed.), *How Should One Live?* (Oxford University Press, 1998); Christine MacKinnon, *Character, Virtue Theories, and the Vices* (Broadview Press, 1999); and Thomas Hurka, *Virtue, Vice, and Value* (Oxford University Press, 2000).

from *The Nicomachean Ethics*[5]
Book I

1: All human activities aim at some good: some goods subordinate to others.

Every art and every inquiry, and similarly every action and pursuit, is thought to aim at some good; and for this reason the good has rightly been declared to be that at which all things aim.[6] But a certain difference is found among ends;[7] some are activities, others are products apart from the activities that produce them. Where there are ends apart from the actions, it is the nature of the products to be better than the activities. Now, as there are many actions, arts, and sciences, their ends also are many; the end of the medical art is health, that of shipbuilding a vessel, that of strategy victory, that of economics wealth. But where such arts fall under a single capacity—as bridle-making and the other arts concerned with the equipment of horses fall under the art of riding, and this and every military action under strategy, in the same way other arts fall under yet others—in all of these the ends of the master arts are to be preferred to all the subordinate ends; for it is for the sake of the former that the latter are pursued. It makes no difference whether the activities themselves are the ends of the actions, or something else apart from the activities, as in the case of the sciences just mentioned.

2: The science of the good for man is politics.

If, then, there is some end of the things we do, which we desire for its own sake (everything else being desired for the sake of this), and if we do not choose everything for the sake of something else (for at that rate the process would go on to infinity, so that our desire would be empty and vain), clearly this must be the good and the chief good. Will not the knowledge of it, then, have a great influence on life? Shall we not, like archers who have a mark to aim at, be more likely to hit upon what is right? If so, we must try, in outline at least, to determine what it is, and of which of the sciences or capacities it is the object. It would seem to belong to the most authoritative art and that which

5   The *Nicomachean Ethics* was probably written, as a series of lecture notes which would have undergone frequent revision, sometime between 334 and 322 BCE. This selection is reprinted from *Aristotle: The Nicomachean Ethics*, translated with an Introduction by David Ross [aka W.D. Ross], revised by J.O. Urmson and J.L. Ackrill (Oxford World's Classics, 1998), by permission of Oxford University Press. The section headings are not Aristotle's own, but are supplied by the translators.

6   This definition is consistent with the views of Plato, but Aristotle is probably thinking mostly of the work of a philosopher, mathematician, and astronomer called Eudoxus of Cnidus. Eudoxus taught at Plato's Academy in Athens from 368 until his death in 355 BCE, and was in charge of the school (during one of Plato's absences in Sicily) when Aristotle arrived there to study at the age of 17.

7   Here, and throughout this reading, "end" means "goal" or "purpose," rather than merely "stopping place."

is most truly the master art. And politics[8] appears to be of this nature; for it is this that ordains which of the sciences should be studied in a state, and which each class of citizens should learn and up to what point they should learn them; and we see even the most highly esteemed of capacities to fall under this, e.g., strategy, economics, rhetoric; now, since politics uses the rest of the sciences, and since, again, it legislates as to what we are to do and what we are to abstain from, the end of this science must include those of the others, so that this end must be the good for man. For even if the end is the same for a single man and for a state, that of the state seems at all events something greater and more complete whether to attain or to preserve; though it is worth while to attain the end merely for one man, it is finer and more godlike to attain it for a nation or for city-states. These, then, are the ends at which our inquiry aims, since it is political science, in one sense of that term.

3: We must not expect more precision than the subject-matter admits of.

Our discussion will be adequate if it has as much clearness as the subject-matter admits of, for precision is not to be sought for alike in all discussions, any more than in all the products of the crafts. Now fine and just actions, which political science investigates, admit of much variety and fluctuation of opinion, so that they may be thought to exist only by convention, and not by nature. And goods also give rise to a similar fluctuation because they bring harm to many people; for before now men have been undone by reason of their wealth, and others by reason of their courage. We must be content, then, in speaking of such subjects and with such premises to indicate the truth roughly and in outline, and in speaking about things which are only for the most part true and with premises of the

same kind to reach conclusions that are no better. In the same spirit, therefore, should each type of statement be received; for it is the mark of an educated man to look for precision in each class of things just so far as the nature of the subject admits; it is evidently equally foolish to accept probable reasoning from a mathematician and to demand from a rhetorician scientific proofs....

7: The good must be something final and self-sufficient. Definition of happiness reached by considering the characteristic function of man.

Let us again return to the good we are seeking, and ask what it can be. It seems different in different actions and arts; it is different in medicine, in strategy, and in the other arts likewise. What then is the good of each? Surely that for whose sake everything else is done. In medicine this is health, in strategy victory, in architecture a house, in any other sphere something else, and in every action and pursuit the end; for it is for the sake of this that all men do whatever else they do. Therefore, if there is an end for all that we do, this will be the good achievable by action, and if there are more than one, these will be the goods achievable by action.

So the argument has by a different course reached the same point; but we must try to state this even more clearly. Since there are evidently more than one end, and we choose some of these (e.g., wealth, flutes,[9] and in general instruments) for the sake of something else, clearly not all ends are final ends; but the chief good is evidently something final. Therefore, if there is only one final end, this will be what we are seeking, and if there are more than one, the most final of these will be what we are seeking. Now we call that which is in itself worthy of pursuit more final than that which is worthy of pursuit for the sake of something else, and that which is never desirable for the sake of something else more final than the things that are desirable both in themselves and for the sake of that other thing, and therefore we call final without qualification that which is always desirable in itself and never for the sake of something else.

---

8   For Aristotle the study of politics (*politikē*) would be broader than our modern political science, and would include all aspects of the study of society. The goal of political science, according to Aristotle, ought to be to achieve happiness (*eudaimonia*) for all the citizens of the state, and this is why he thinks that the investigation into human happiness (ethics) is continuous with politics.

---

9   Strictly speaking, Aristotle means an *aulos*, an ancient Greek double-reed instrument.

Now such a thing happiness,[10] above all else, is held to be; for this we choose always for itself and never for the sake of something else, but honour, pleasure, reason, and every virtue we choose indeed for themselves (for if nothing resulted from them we should still choose each of them), but we choose them also for the sake of happiness, judging that by means of them we shall be happy. Happiness, on the other hand, no one chooses for the sake of these, nor, in general, for anything other than itself.

From the point of view of self-sufficiency the same result seems to follow; for the final good is thought to be self-sufficient. Now by self-sufficient we do not mean that which is sufficient for a man by himself, for one who lives a solitary life, but also for parents, children, wife, and in general for his friends and fellow citizens, since man is born for citizenship. But some limit must be set to this; for if we extend our requirement to ancestors and descendants and friends' friends we are in for an infinite series. Let us examine this question, however, on another occasion; the self-sufficient we now define as that which when isolated makes life desirable and lacking in nothing; and such we think happiness to be; and further we think it most desirable of all things, without being counted as one good thing among others—if it were so counted it would clearly be made more desirable by the addition of even the least of goods; for that which is added becomes an excess of goods, and of goods the greater is always more desirable. Happiness, then, is something final and self-sufficient, and is the end of action.

Presumably, however, to say that happiness is the chief good seems a platitude, and a clearer account of what it is is still desired. This might perhaps be given, if we could first ascertain the function of man. For just as for a flute-player, a sculptor, or any artist, and, in general, for all things that have a function or activity, the good and the 'well' is thought to reside in the function, so would it seem to be for man, if he has a function. Have the carpenter, then, and the tanner certain functions or activities, and has man none? Is he born without a function?[11] Or as eye, hand,

foot, and in general each of the parts evidently has a function, may one lay it down that man similarly has a function apart from all these? What then can this be? Life seems to belong even to plants, but we are seeking what is peculiar to man. Let us exclude, therefore, the life of nutrition and growth. Next there would be a life of perception, but *it* also seems to be shared even by the horse, the ox, and every animal. There remains, then, an active life of the element that has a rational principle; of this, one part has such a principle in the sense of being obedient to one, the other in the sense of possessing one and exercising thought. And, as 'life of the rational element' also has two meanings, we must state that life in the sense of activity is what we mean; for this seems to be the more proper sense of the term. Now if the function of man is an activity of soul[12] which follows or implies a rational principle, and if we say 'a so-and-so' and 'a good so-and-so' have a function which is the same in kind, e.g., a lyre-player and a good lyre-player, and so without qualification in all cases, eminence in respect of goodness being added to the name of the function (for the function of a lyre-player is to play the lyre, and that of a good lyre-player is to do so well): if this is the case [and we state the function of man to be a certain kind of life, and this to be an activity or actions of the soul implying a rational principle, and the function of a good man to be the good and noble performance of these, and if any action is well performed when it is performed in accordance with the appropriate excellence: if this is the case], human good turns out to be activity of soul exhibiting excellence, and if there are more than one excellence, in accordance with the best and most complete.

But we must add 'in a complete life'. For one swallow does not make a summer, nor does one day; and

---

10 *Eudaimonia* (see the introductory notes to this reading).

11 In the original Greek, this would have been a pun: the word for being "without function" (*argon*) was also

used colloquially to mean a "good for nothing" or a "dropout."

12 By "soul"—*psuchē*—Aristotle means, very roughly, that which makes us alive or animates us. The religious or Cartesian connotations of the word—the notion of the soul as a sort of substantial spiritual self, housed in a temporary material vessel (the body)—only came about much later in history.

so too one day, or a short time, does not make a man blessed and happy.

Let this serve as an outline of the good; for we must presumably first sketch it roughly, and then later fill in the details. But it would seem that any one is capable of carrying on and articulating what has once been well outlined, and that time is a good discoverer or partner in such a work; to which facts the advances of the arts are due; for any one can add what is lacking. And we must also remember what has been said before, and not look for precision in all things alike, but in each class of things such precision as accords with the subject-matter, and so much as is appropriate to the inquiry. For a carpenter and a geometer investigate the right angle in different ways; the former does so in so far as the right angle is useful for his work, while the latter inquires what it is or what sort of thing it is; for he is a spectator of the truth. We must act in the same way, then, in all other matters as well, that our main task may not be subordinated to minor questions. Nor must we demand the cause in all matters alike; it is enough in some cases that the *fact* be well established, as in the case of the first principles; the fact is a primary thing or first principle. Now of first principles we see some by induction,[13] some by perception,[14] some by a certain habituation,[15] and others too in other ways. But each set of principles we must try to investigate in the natural way, and we must take pains to determine them correctly, since they have a great influence on what follows. For the beginning

is thought to be more than half of the whole,[16] and many of the questions we ask are cleared up by it....

Book II

5: The genus of moral virtue: it is a state of character, not a passion, nor a faculty.

Next we must consider what virtue is. Since things that are found in the soul are of three kinds—passions, faculties, states of character—virtue must be one of these. By passions I mean appetite, anger, fear, confidence, envy, joy, friendly feeling, hatred, longing, emulation, pity, and in general the feelings that are accompanied by pleasure or pain; by faculties the things in virtue of which we are said to be capable of feeling these, e.g., of becoming angry or being pained or feeling pity; by states of character the things in virtue of which we stand well or badly with reference to the passions, e.g., with reference to anger we stand badly if we feel it violently or too weakly, and well if we feel it moderately; and similarly with reference to the other passions.

Now neither the virtues nor the vices are *passions*, because we are not called good or bad on the ground of our passions, but are so called on the ground of our virtues and our vices, and because we are neither praised nor blamed for our passions (for the man who feels fear or anger is not praised, nor is the man who simply feels anger blamed, but the man who feels it in a certain way), but for our virtues and our vices we *are* praised or blamed.

Again, we feel anger and fear without choice, but the virtues are modes of choice or involve choice. Further, in respect of the passions we are said to be moved, but in respect of the virtues and the vices we are said not to be moved but to be disposed in a particular way.

For these reasons also they are not *faculties*; for we are neither called good nor bad, nor praised nor blamed, for the simple capacity of feeling the passions; again, we have the faculties by nature, but we are not made good or bad by nature; we have spoken of this before.

---

13 This, for Aristotle, is the process of moving from particular facts, observations, or examples to a general or universal claim (for example, from particular examples of courage and cowardice to a general understanding of the relation between them). The Greek word is *epagōgē*, which literally means "leading on."

14 The word Aristotle uses, *aisthēsis*, can be used to mean sense-perception, but Aristotle probably means something more like "direct intuition" of (moral) facts—just *seeing* that something is right or wrong.

15 This, in Aristotle's view, is how the moral virtues are inculcated: by repeatedly and self-consciously acting in a particular way (e.g., bravely) until that manner of behaving (e.g., bravery) becomes a habit or a character trait.

---

16 This was apparently a Greek proverb.

If, then, the virtues are neither passions nor faculties, all that remains is that they should be *states of character*.

Thus we have stated what virtue is in respect of its genus.

6: The differentia of moral virtue: it is a disposition to choose the mean.

We must, however, not only describe virtue as a state of character, but also say what sort of state it is. We may remark, then, that every virtue or excellence both brings into good condition the thing of which it is the excellence and makes the work of that thing be done well; e.g., the excellence of the eye makes both the eye and its work good; for it is by the excellence of the eye that we see well. Similarly the excellence of the horse makes a horse both good in itself and good at running and at carrying its rider and at awaiting the attack of the enemy. Therefore, if this is true in every case, the virtue of man also will be the state of character which makes a man good and which makes him do his own work well.

How this is to happen we have stated already, but it will be made plain also by the following consideration of the specific nature of virtue. In everything that is continuous and divisible it is possible to take more, less, or an equal amount, and that either in terms of the thing itself or relatively to us; and the equal is an intermediate between excess and defect. By the intermediate in the object I mean that which is equidistant from each of the extremes, which is one and the same for all men; by the intermediate relatively to us that which is neither too much nor too little—and this is not one, nor the same for all. For instance, if ten is many and two is few, six is the intermediate, taken in terms of the object; for it exceeds and is exceeded by an equal amount; this is intermediate according to arithmetical proportion. But the intermediate relatively to us is not to be taken so; if ten pounds are too much for a particular person to eat and two too little, it does not follow that the trainer will order six pounds; for this also is perhaps too much for the person who is to take it, or too little—too little for Milo,[17] too much

for the beginner in athletic exercises. The same is true of running and wrestling. Thus a master of any art avoids excess and defect, but seeks the intermediate and chooses this—the intermediate not in the object but relatively to us.

If it is thus, then, that every art does its work well—by looking to the intermediate and judging its works by this standard (so that we often say of good works of art that it is not possible either to take away or to add anything, implying that excess and defect destroy the goodness of works of art, while the mean preserves it; and good artists, as we say, look to this in their work), and if, further, virtue is more exact and better than any art, as nature also is, then virtue must have the quality of aiming at the intermediate. I mean moral virtue; for it is this that is concerned with passions and actions, and in these there is excess, defect, and the intermediate. For instance, both fear and confidence and appetite and anger and pity and in general pleasure and pain may be felt both too much and too little, and in both cases not well; but to feel them at the right times, with reference to the right objects, towards the right people, with the right motive, and in the right way, is what is both intermediate and best, and this is characteristic of virtue. Similarly with regard to actions also there is excess, defect, and the intermediate. Now virtue is concerned with passions and actions, in which excess is a form of failure, and so is defect, while the intermediate is praised and is a form of success; and being praised and being successful are both characteristics of virtue. Therefore virtue is a kind of mean, since, as we have seen, it aims at what is intermediate.

Again, it is possible to fail in many ways (for evil belongs to the class of the unlimited, as the Pythagoreans[18] conjectured, and good to that of the limited), while to succeed is possible only in one way (for

---

17   Milo of Croton, supposed to have lived in the second half of the sixth century BCE in southern Italy, was a

legendary wrestler and athlete, famous for his immense strength.

18   The followers of philosopher and mystic Pythagoras of Samos (c. 570–495 BCE). One of their most influential beliefs was that everything in the universe can be understood in terms of *harmonia* or number, and the notion of a "limit" which Aristotle refers to here is a quasi-mathematical notion.

which reason also one is easy and the other difficult—to miss the mark easy, to hit it difficult); for these reasons also, then, excess and defect are characteristic of vice, and the mean of virtue;

> *For men are good in but one way, but bad in many.*[19]

Virtue, then, is a state of character concerned with choice, lying in a mean, i.e., the mean relative to us, this being determined by a rational principle, and by that principle by which the man of practical wisdom would determine it. Now it is a mean between two vices, that which depends on excess and that which depends on defect; and again it is a mean because the vices respectively fall short of or exceed what is right in both passions and actions, while virtue both finds and chooses that which is intermediate. Hence in respect of what it is, i.e., the definition which states its essence, virtue is a mean, with regard to what is best and right an extreme.

But not every action nor every passion admits of a mean; for some have names that already imply badness, e.g., spite, shamelessness, envy, and in the case of actions adultery, theft, murder; for all of these and suchlike things imply by their names that they are themselves bad, and not the excesses or deficiencies of them. It is not possible, then, ever to be right with regard to them; one must always be wrong. Nor does goodness or badness with regard to such things depend on committing adultery with the right woman, at the right time, and in the right way, but simply to do any of them is to go wrong. It would be equally absurd, then, to expect that in unjust, cowardly, and voluptuous action there should be a mean, an excess, and a deficiency; for at that rate there would be a mean of excess and of deficiency, an excess of excess, and a deficiency of deficiency. But as there is no excess and deficiency of temperance and courage because what is intermediate is in a sense an extreme, so too of the actions we have mentioned there is no mean nor any excess and deficiency, but however they are done they are wrong; for in general there is neither a mean of excess and deficiency, nor excess and deficiency of a mean.

---

19 The source of this quotation is unknown.

7: The above proposition illustrated by reference to particular virtues.

We must, however, not only make this general statement, but also apply it to the individual facts. For among statements about conduct those which are general apply more widely, but those which are particular are more true, since conduct has to do with individual cases, and our statements must harmonize with the facts in these cases. We may take these cases from our table.[20] With regard to feelings of fear and confidence courage is the mean; of the people who exceed, he who exceeds in fearlessness has no name (many of the states have no name), while the man who exceeds in confidence is rash, and he who exceeds in fear and falls short in confidence is a coward. With regard to pleasures and pains—not all of them, and not so much with regard to the pains—the mean is temperance, the excess self-indulgence. Persons deficient with regard to the pleasures are not often found; hence such persons also have received no name. But let us call them 'insensible'.

With regard to giving and taking of money the mean is liberality, the excess and the defect prodigality and meanness. In these actions people exceed and fall short in contrary ways; the prodigal exceeds in spending and falls short in taking, while the mean man exceeds in taking and falls short in spending. (At present we are giving a mere outline or summary, and are satisfied with this; later these states will be more exactly determined.) With regard to money there are also other dispositions—a mean, magnificence (for the magnificent man differs from the liberal man; the former deals with large sums, the latter with small ones), an excess, tastelessness and vulgarity, and a deficiency, niggardliness; these differ from the states opposed to liberality, and the mode of their difference will be stated later.

With regard to honour and dishonour the mean is proper pride, the excess is known as a sort of 'empty vanity', and the deficiency is undue humility; and as we said liberality was related to magnificence, differing from it by dealing with small sums, so there is a state similarly related to proper pride, being concerned

---

20 Aristotle must have used a diagram at this point during his lectures, to illustrate graphically the various virtues and their extremes.

with small honours while that is concerned with great. For it is possible to desire honour as one ought, and more than one ought, and less, and the man who exceeds in his desires is called ambitious, the man who falls short unambitious, while the intermediate person has no name. The dispositions also are nameless, except that that of the ambitious man is called ambition. Hence the people who are at the extremes lay claim to the middle place; and we ourselves sometimes call the intermediate person ambitious and sometimes unambitious, and sometimes praise the ambitious man and sometimes the unambitious. The reason of our doing this will be stated in what follows; but now let us speak of the remaining states according to the method which has been indicated.

With regard to anger also there is an excess, a deficiency, and a mean. Although they can scarcely be said to have names, yet since we call the intermediate person good-tempered let us call the mean good temper; of the persons at the extremes let the one who exceeds be called irascible, and his vice irascibility, and the man who falls short an unirascible sort of person, and the deficiency unirascibility.

There are also three other means, which have a certain likeness to one another, but differ from one another: for they are all concerned with intercourse in words and actions, but differ in that one is concerned with truth in this sphere, the other two with pleasantness; and of this one kind is exhibited in giving amusement, the other in all the circumstances of life. We must therefore speak of these too, that we may the better see that in all things the mean is praise-worthy, and the extremes neither praiseworthy nor right, but worthy of blame. Now most of these states also have no names, but we must try, as in the other cases, to invent names ourselves so that we may be clear and easy to follow. With regard to truth, then, the intermediate is a truthful sort of person and the mean may be called truthfulness, while the pretence which exaggerates is boastfulness and the person characterized by it a boaster, and that which understates is mock modesty and the person characterized by it mock-modest. With regard to pleasantness in the giving of amusement the intermediate person is ready-witted and the disposition ready wit, the excess is buffoonery and the person characterized by it a buffoon, while the man who falls

short is a sort of boor and his state is boorishness. With regard to the remaining kind of pleasantness, that which is exhibited in life in general, the man who is pleasant in the right way is friendly and the mean is friendliness, while the man who exceeds is an obsequious person if he has no end in view, a flatterer if he is aiming at his own advantage, and the man who falls short and is unpleasant in all circumstances is a quarrelsome and surly sort of person.

There are also means in the passions and concerned with the passions; since shame is not a virtue, and yet praise is extended to the modest man. For even in these matters one man is said to be intermediate, and another to exceed, as for instance the bashful man who is ashamed of everything; while he who falls short or is not ashamed of anything at all is shameless, and the intermediate person is modest. Righteous indignation is a mean between envy and spite, and these states are concerned with the pain and pleasure that are felt at the fortunes of our neighbours; the man who is characterized by righteous indignation is pained at undeserved good fortune, the envious man, going beyond him, is pained at all good fortune, and the spiteful man falls so far short of being pained that he even rejoices.[21] But these states there will be an opportunity of describing elsewhere; with regard to justice, since it has not one simple meaning, we shall, after describing the other states, distinguish its two kinds and say how each of them is a mean; and similarly we shall treat also of the rational virtues.

8: The extremes are opposed to each other and to the mean.

There are three kinds of disposition, then, two of them vices, involving excess and deficiency respectively, and one a virtue, viz.[22] the mean, and all are in a sense opposed to all; for the extreme states are contrary both to the intermediate state and to each other, and the intermediate to the extremes; as the equal is greater relatively to the less, less relatively to the greater, so the middle states are excessive relatively to the deficiencies, deficient relatively to the excesses, both in passions and in actions. For the brave man appears

---

21   At the misfortune of others.
22   "In other words."

rash relatively to the coward, and cowardly relatively to the rash man; and similarly the temperate man appears self-indulgent relatively to the insensible man, insensible relatively to the self-indulgent, and the liberal man prodigal relatively to the mean man, mean relatively to the prodigal. Hence also the people at the extremes push the intermediate man each over to the other, and the brave man is called rash by the coward, cowardly by the rash man, and correspondingly in the other cases.

These states being thus opposed to one another, the greatest contrariety is that of the extremes to each other, rather than to the intermediate; for these are further from each other than from the intermediate, as the great is further from the small and the small from the great than both are from the equal. Again, to the intermediate some extremes show a certain likeness, as that of rashness to courage and that of prodigality to liberality; but the extremes show the greatest unlikeness to each other; now contraries are defined as the things that are furthest from each other, so that things that are further apart are more contrary.

To the mean in some cases the deficiency, in some the excess, is more opposed; e.g., it is not rashness, which is an excess, but cowardice, which is a deficiency, that is more opposed to courage, and not insensibility, which is a deficiency, but self-indulgence, which is an excess, that is more opposed to temperance. This happens from two reasons, one being drawn from the thing itself; for because one extreme is nearer and liker to the intermediate, we oppose not this but rather its contrary to the intermediate. E.g., since rashness is thought liker and nearer to courage, and cowardice more unlike, we oppose rather the latter to courage; for things that are further from the intermediate are thought more contrary to it. This, then, is one cause, drawn from the thing itself; another is drawn from ourselves; for the things to which we ourselves more naturally tend seem more contrary to the intermediate. For instance, we ourselves tend more naturally to pleasures, and hence are more easily carried away towards self-indulgence than towards propriety. We describe as contrary to the mean, then, rather the directions in which we more often go to great lengths; and therefore self-indulgence, which is an excess, is the more contrary to temperance.

9: The mean is hard to attain, and is grasped by perception, not by reasoning.

That moral virtue is a mean, then, and in what sense it is so, and that it is a mean between two vices, the one involving excess, the other deficiency, and that it is such because its character is to aim at what is intermediate in passions and in actions, has been sufficiently stated. Hence also it is no easy task to be good. For in everything it is no easy task to find the middle, e.g., to find the middle of a circle is not for every one but for him who knows; so, too, any one can get angry—that is easy—or give or spend money; but to do this to the right person, to the right extent, at the right time, with the right motive, and in the right way, *that* is not for every one, nor is it easy; wherefore goodness is both rare and laudable and noble.

Hence he who aims at the intermediate must first depart from what is the more contrary to it, as Calypso advises—

Hold the ship out beyond that surf and spray.[23]
For of the extremes one is more erroneous, one less so; therefore, since to hit the mean is hard in the extreme, we must as a second best, as people say, take the least of the evils; and this will be done best in the way we describe.

But we must consider the things towards which we ourselves also are easily carried away; for some of us tend to one thing, some to another; and this will be recognizable from the pleasure and the pain we feel. We must drag ourselves away to the contrary extreme; for we shall get into the intermediate state by drawing well away from error, as people do in straightening sticks that are bent.

Now in everything the pleasant or pleasure is most to be guarded against; for we do not judge it impar-

---

23   A line from Homer's *Odyssey* (part 12, lines 219–220). However, it is actually Circe (an enchantress), not Calypso (the nymph who detained Odysseus and his crew on her island), who gave the advice. The actual quotation is from Odysseus' orders to his steersman when he acts on Circe's suggestion that he take the ship closer to Scylla (a sea monster) than to Charybdis (a great whirlpool). Aristotle's quotations from Homer were apparently made from memory, and are rarely exact.

tially. We ought, then, to feel towards pleasure as the elders of the people felt towards Helen, and in all circumstances repeat their saying;[24] for if we dismiss pleasure thus we are less likely to go astray. It is by doing this, then, (to sum the matter up) that we shall best be able to hit the mean.

But this is no doubt difficult, and especially in individual cases; for it is not easy to determine both how and with whom and on what provocation and how long one should be angry; for we too sometimes praise those who fall short and call them good-tempered, but sometimes we praise those who get angry and call them manly. The man, however, who deviates little from goodness is not blamed, whether he do so in the direction of the more or of the less, but only the man who deviates more widely; for *he* does not fail to be noticed. But up to what point and to what extent a man must deviate before he becomes blameworthy it is not easy to determine by reasoning, any more than anything else that is perceived by the senses; such things depend on particular facts, and the decision rests with perception. So much, then, is plain, that the intermediate state is in all things to be praised, but that we must incline sometimes towards the excess, sometimes towards the deficiency; for so shall we most easily hit the mean and what is right....

Book X

6: Happiness is good activity, not amusement.

Now that we have spoken of the virtues, the forms of friendship, and the varieties of pleasure, what remains is to discuss in outline the nature of happiness, since

---

24   See Homer's *Iliad*, part 3, lines 156–160 (here translated by Richmond Lattimore):

   Surely there is no blame on Trojans and strong-
      greaved Achaians
   if for long time they suffer hardship for a woman like
      this one.
   Terrible is the likeness of her face to immortal god-
      desses.
   Still, though she be such, let her go away in the
      ships, lest
   she be left behind, a grief for us and our children.

this is what we state the end of human affairs to be. Our discussion will be the more concise if we first sum up what we have said already. We said, then, that it is not a state; for if it were it might belong to someone who was asleep throughout his life, living the life of a plant, or, again, to someone who was suffering the greatest misfortunes. If these implications are unacceptable, and we must rather class happiness as an activity, as we have said before, and if some activities are necessary, and desirable for the sake of something else, while others are so in themselves, evidently happiness must be placed among those desirable in themselves, not among those desirable for the sake of something else; for happiness does not lack anything, but is self-sufficient. Now those activities are desirable in themselves from which nothing is sought beyond the activity. And of this nature virtuous actions are thought to be; for to do noble and good deeds is a thing desirable for its own sake.

Pleasant amusements also are thought to be of this nature: we choose them not for the sake of other things; for we are injured rather than benefited by them, since we are led to neglect our bodies and our property. But most of the people who are deemed happy take refuge in such pastimes, which is the reason why those who are ready-witted at them are highly esteemed at the courts of tyrants; they make themselves pleasant companions in the tyrants' favourite pursuits, and that is the sort of man they want. Now these things are thought to be of the nature of happiness because people in despotic positions spend their leisure in them, but perhaps such people prove nothing; for virtue and reason, from which good activities flow, do not depend on despotic position; nor, if these people, who have never tasted pure and generous pleasure, take refuge in the bodily pleasures, should these for that reason be thought more desirable; for boys, too, think the things that are valued among themselves are the best. It is to be expected, then, that, as different things seem valuable to boys and to men, so they should to bad men and to good. Now, as we have often maintained, those things are both valuable and pleasant which are such to the good man; and to each man the activity in accordance with his own disposition is most desirable, and, therefore, to the good man that which is in accordance with virtue. Happiness, therefore, does not lie in amusement; it would, indeed, be strange if the end were amusement, and one were to take trouble and suffer hardship all one's life in order to amuse oneself. For, in a word, everything that we choose we choose for the sake of something else—except happiness, which is an end. Now to exert oneself and work for the sake of amusement seems silly and utterly childish. But to amuse oneself in order that one may exert oneself, as Anacharsis[25] puts it, seems right; for amusement is a sort of relaxation, and we need relaxation because we cannot work continuously. Relaxation, then, is not an end; for it is taken for the sake of activity.

The happy life is thought to be virtuous; now a virtuous life requires exertion, and does not consist in amusement. And we say that serious things are better than laughable things and those connected with amusement, and that the activity of the better of any two things—whether it be two elements of our being or two men—is the more serious; but the activity of the better is *ipso facto*[26] superior and more of the nature of happiness. And any chance person—even a slave—can enjoy the bodily pleasures no less than the best man; but no one assigns to a slave a share in happiness—unless he assigns to him also a share in human life. For happiness does not lie in such occupations, but, as we have said before, in virtuous activities.

7: Happiness in the highest sense is the contemplative life.

If happiness is activity in accordance with virtue, it is reasonable that it should be in accordance with the highest virtue; and this will be that of the best thing in us. Whether it be reason or something else that is this element which is thought to be our natural ruler and guide and to take thought of things noble and divine, whether it be itself also divine or only the most divine element in us, the activity of this in accordance with its proper virtue will be perfect happiness. That this activity is contemplative[27] we have already said.

Now this would seem to be in agreement both with what we said before and with the truth. For, firstly, this activity is the best (since not only is reason the best thing in us, but the objects of reason are the best of knowable objects); and secondly, it is the most continuous, since we can contemplate truth more continuously than we can *do* anything. And we think happiness ought to have pleasure mingled with it, but the activity of philosophic wisdom is admittedly the pleasantest of virtuous activities; at all events the pursuit of it is thought to offer pleasures marvellous for their purity and their enduringness, and it is to be expected that those who know will pass their time more pleasantly than those who inquire. And the self-sufficiency that is spoken of must belong most to the contemplative activity. For while a philosopher, as well as a just man or one possessing any other virtue, needs the necessaries of life, when they are sufficiently equipped with things of that sort the just man needs people towards whom and with whom he shall act justly, and the temperate man, the brave man, and each of the others is in the same case, but the philosopher, even when by himself, can contemplate truth, and the better the wiser he is; he can perhaps do so better if he has fellow-workers, but still he is the most self-sufficient. And this activity alone would seem to be loved for its own sake; for nothing arises from it apart from the contemplating, while from practical activities we gain more or less apart from the action. And happiness is thought to depend on leisure; for we are busy that we may have leisure, and make war that

---

25 Anacharsis was a prince of Scythia (today the southern Ukraine), said to have lived early in the sixth century BCE, whose travels throughout the Greek world gave him a reputation for wisdom. He was known for his aphorisms, which were believed to be particularly profound.

26 "By that very fact."

27 The Greek word *theōria*, translated here as "contemplation," denotes something like the theoretical study of reality for the sake of knowledge alone, and would include, for example, astronomy, biology, mathematics, and anthropology as well as what we call philosophy. Furthermore, it is not so much the *search* for this knowledge that Aristotle is thinking of, but the quasi-aesthetic *appreciation* of it—a tranquil surveying of it in one's mind—once it has been acquired. (*Theōrein* is a Greek verb which originally meant to look at something, to gaze at it steadily.)

we may live in peace. Now the activity of the practical virtues is exhibited in political or military affairs, but the actions concerned with these seem to be unleisurely. Warlike actions are completely so (for no one chooses to be at war, or provokes war, for the sake of being at war; anyone would seem absolutely murderous if he were to make enemies of his friends in order to bring about battle and slaughter); but the action of the statesman is also unleisurely, and aims—beyond the political action itself—at despotic power and honours, or at all events happiness, for him and his fellow citizens—a happiness different from political action, and evidently sought as being different. So if among virtuous actions political and military actions are distinguished by nobility and greatness, and these are unleisurely and aim at an end and are not desirable for their own sake, but the activity of reason, which is contemplative, seems both to be superior in serious worth and to aim at no end beyond itself, and to have its pleasure proper to itself (and this augments the activity), and the self-sufficiency, leisureliness, unweariedness (so far as this is possible for man), and all the other attributes ascribed to the supremely happy man are evidently those connected with this activity, it follows that this will be the complete happiness of man, if it be allowed a complete term of life (for none of the attributes of happiness is *in*complete).

But such a life would be too high for man; for it is not in so far as he is man that he will live so, but in so far as something divine is present in him; and by so much as this is superior to our composite nature[28] is its activity superior to that which is the exercise of the other kind of virtue. If reason is divine, then, in comparison with man, the life according to it is divine in comparison with human life. But we must not follow those who advise us, being men, to think of human things, and, being mortal, of mortal things, but must, so far as we can, make ourselves immortal, and strain every nerve to live in accordance with the best thing in us; for even if it be small in bulk, much more does it in power and worth surpass everything. This would seem, too, to *be* each man himself, since it is the authoritative and better part of him. It would

28   The view that human beings are made up of both soul and body, while the divine is pure intellect.

be strange, then, if he were to choose not the life of his self but that of something else. And what we said before will apply now; that which is proper to each thing is by nature best and most pleasant for each thing; for man, therefore, the life according to reason is best and pleasantest, since reason more than anything else *is* man. This life therefore is also the happiest.

8: Superiority of the contemplative life further considered.

But in a secondary degree the life in accordance with the other kind of virtue is happy; for the activities in accordance with this befit our human estate. Just and brave acts, and other virtuous acts, we do in relation to each other, observing our respective duties with regard to contracts and services and all manner of actions and with regard to passions; and all of these seem to be typically human. Some of them seem even to arise from the body, and virtue of character to be in many ways bound up with the passions. Practical wisdom, too, is linked to virtue of character, and this to practical wisdom, since the principles of practical wisdom are in accordance with the moral virtues and rightness in morals is in accordance with practical wisdom. Being connected with the passions also, the moral virtues must belong to our composite nature; and the virtues of our composite nature are human; so, therefore, are the life and the happiness which correspond to these. The excellence of the reason is a thing apart; we must be content to say this much about it, for to describe it precisely is a task greater than our purpose requires. It would seem, however, also to need external equipment but little, or less than moral virtue does. Grant that both need the necessaries, and do so equally, even if the statesman's work is the more concerned with the body and things of that sort; for there will be little difference there; but in what they need for the exercise of their activities there will be much difference. The liberal man will need money for the doing of his liberal deeds, and the just man too will need it for the returning of services (for wishes are hard to discern, and even people who are not just *pretend* to wish to act justly); and the brave man will need power if he is to accomplish any of the acts that correspond to his virtue, and the temperate man will need opportunity; for how else is either he or any of the others to be recognized? It is debated, too, whether the will or the deed is more essential to virtue, which is assumed to involve both; it is surely clear that its perfection involves both; but for deeds many things are needed, and more, the greater and nobler the deeds are. But the man who is contemplating the truth needs no such thing, at least with a view to the exercise of his activity; indeed they are, one may say, even hindrances, at all events to his contemplation; but in so far as he is a man and lives with a number of people, he chooses to do virtuous acts; he will therefore need such aids to living a human life.

But that perfect happiness is a contemplative activity will appear from the following consideration as well. We assume the gods to be above all other beings blessed and happy; but what sort of actions must we assign to them? Acts of justice? Will not the gods seem absurd if they make contracts and return deposits, and so on? Acts of a brave man, then, confronting dangers and running risks because it is noble to do so? Or liberal acts? To whom will they give? It will be strange if they are really to have money or anything of the kind. And what would their temperate acts be? Is not such praise tasteless, since they have no bad appetites? If we were to run through them all, the circumstances of action would be found trivial and unworthy of gods. Still, every one supposes that they *live* and therefore that they are active; we cannot suppose them to sleep like Endymion.[29] Now if you take away from a living being action, and still more production, what is left but contemplation? Therefore the activity of God, which surpasses all others in blessedness, must be contemplative; and of human activities, therefore, that which is most akin to this must be most of the nature of happiness.

This is indicated, too, by the fact that the other animals have no share in happiness, being completely deprived of such activity. For while the whole life of the gods is blessed, and that of men too in so far as some likeness of such activity belongs to them, none of the other animals is happy, since they in no way

share in contemplation. Happiness extends, then, just so far as contemplation does, and those to whom contemplation more fully belongs are more truly happy, not as a mere concomitant but in virtue of the contemplation; for this is in itself precious. Happiness, therefore, must be some form of contemplation.

But, being a man, one will also need external prosperity; for our nature is not self-sufficient for the purpose of contemplation, but our body also must be healthy and must have food and other attention. Still, we must not think that the man who is to be happy will need many things or great things, merely because he cannot be supremely happy without external goods; for self-sufficiency and action do not involve excess, and we can do noble acts without ruling earth and sea; for even with moderate advantages one can act virtuously (this is manifest enough; for private persons are thought to do worthy acts no less than despots—indeed even more); and it is enough that we should have so much as that; for the life of the man who is active in accordance with virtue will be happy. Solon,[30] too, was perhaps sketching well the happy man when he described him[31] as moderately furnished with externals but as having done (as Solon thought) the noblest acts, and lived temperately; for one can with but moderate possessions do what one ought. Anaxagoras[32] also seems to have supposed the happy man not to be rich nor a despot, when he said that he would not be surprised if the happy man were to seem to most people a strange person; for they judge by externals, since these are all they perceive. The opinions of the wise seem, then, to harmonize with our arguments. But while even such things carry some conviction, the truth in practical matters is discerned from the facts of life; for these are the

29 According to Greek myth, Endymion was such a beautiful man that the Moon fell in love with him. She made him immortal, but cast him into an eternal sleep so that she could descend and embrace him every night.

30 Solon (c. 640–558 BCE) was an Athenian lawmaker and poet, considered the founder of Athenian democracy, whose name was a byword for wisdom.

31 As quoted in Book I of Herodotus's *History*.

32 Anaxagoras of Clazomenae (c. 500–428 BCE) was the first philosopher to teach in Athens—though he, like Socrates and Plato, was prosecuted for impiety by the Athenians (in part for believing that the sun is a fiery body larger than Greece and that the light of the moon is reflected light from the sun).

decisive factor. We must therefore survey what we have already said, bringing it to the test of the facts of life, and if it harmonizes with the facts we must accept it, but if it clashes with them we must suppose it to be mere theory. Now he who exercises his reason and cultivates it seems to be both in the best state of mind and most dear to the gods. For if the gods have any care for human affairs, as they are thought to have, it would be reasonable both that they should delight in that which was best and most akin to them (i.e., reason) and that they should reward those who love and honour this most, as caring for the things that are dear to them and acting both rightly and nobly. And that all these attributes belong most of all to the philosopher is manifest. He, therefore, is the dearest to the gods. And he who is that will presumably be also the happiest; so that in this way too the philosopher will more than any other be happy.

IMMANUEL KANT

Foundations of the Metaphysics of Morals

Who Was Immanuel Kant?

Immanuel Kant—by common consent the most important philosopher of the past 300 years, and arguably the most important of the past 2,300—was born in 1724 on the coast of the Baltic Sea, in Königsberg, a regionally important harbor city in East Prussia.[1] Kant spent his whole life living in this town, and never ventured outside its region. His family were devout members of an evangelical Protestant sect (rather like the Quakers or early Methodists) called the Pietists, and Pietism's strong emphasis on moral responsibility, hard work, and distrust of religious dogma had a deep effect on Kant's character. Kant's father was a craftsman (making harnesses and saddles for horses) and his family was fairly poor; Kant's mother, whom he loved deeply, died when he was 13.

Kant's life is notorious for its outward uneventfulness. He was educated at a strict Lutheran school in Königsberg, and after graduating from the University of Königsberg in 1746 (where he supported himself by some tutoring but also by his skill at billiards and card games) he served as a private tutor to various local families until he became a lecturer at the university in 1755. However his position—that of *Privatdozent*—carried no salary, and Kant was expected to support himself by the income from his lecturing; financial need caused Kant to lecture for thirty or more hours a week on a huge range of subjects (including mathematics, physics, geography, anthropology, ethics, and law). During this period Kant published several scientific works and his reputation as a scholar grew; he turned down opportunities for professorships in other towns (Erlangen and Jena), having his heart set on a professorship in Königsberg. Finally, at the age of 46, Kant became professor of logic and metaphysics at the University of Königsberg, a position he held until his retirement twenty-six years later in 1796. After a tragic period of senility he died in

---

1 Prussia is a historical region which included what is today northern Germany, Poland, and the western fringes of Russia. It became a kingdom in 1701, and then a dominant part of the newly unified Germany in 1871. Greatly reduced after World War I, the state of Prussia was formally abolished after World War II, and Königsberg—renamed Kaliningrad during the Soviet era, after one of Stalin's henchmen—now sits on the western rump of Russia (between Poland and Lithuania).

1804, and was buried with pomp and circumstance in the "professors' vault" at the Königsberg cathedral.[2]

Kant's days were structured by a rigorous and unvarying routine—indeed, it is often said that the housewives of Königsberg were able to set their clocks by the regularity of his afternoon walk. He never married (though twice he nearly did), had very few close friends, and lived by all accounts an austere and outwardly unemotional life. He was something of a hypochondriac, hated noise, and disliked all music except for military marches. Nevertheless, anecdotes by those who knew him give the impression of a warm, impressive, rather noble human being, capable of great kindness and dignity and sparkling conversation. He did not shun society, and in fact his regular daily routine included an extended lunchtime gathering at which he and his guests—drawn from the cosmopolitan stratum of Königsberg society—would discuss politics, science, philosophy, and poetry.

Kant's philosophical life is often divided into three phases: his "pre-Critical" period, his "silent" period, and his "Critical" period. His pre-Critical period began in 1747 when he published his first work (*Thoughts on the True Estimation of Living Forces*) and ended in 1770 when he wrote his Inaugural Dissertation—*Concerning the Form and Principles of the Sensible and Intelligible World*—and became a professor. Between 1770 and 1780, Kant published almost nothing. In 1781, however, at the age of 57, Kant made his first major contribution to philosophy with his monumental *Critique of Pure Reason* (written, Kant said, over the course of a few months "as if in flight"). He spent the next

twenty years in unrelenting intellectual labor, trying to develop and answer the new problems laid out in this masterwork. First, in order to clarify and simplify the system of the *Critique* for the educated public, Kant published the much shorter *Prolegomena to Any Future Metaphysics* in 1783. In 1785 came Kant's *Foundations of the Metaphysics of Morals*, and in 1788 he published what is now known as his "second Critique": the *Critique of Practical Reason*. His third and final Critique, the *Critique of Judgement*, was published in 1790—an amazing body of work produced in less than ten years.

By the time he died, Kant had already become known as a great philosopher, with a permanent place in history. Over his grave was inscribed a quote from the *Critique of Practical Reason*, which sums up the impulse for his philosophy: "Two things fill the mind with ever new and increasing admiration and reverence, the more often and more steadily one reflects on them: the starry heavens above me and the moral law within me."

What Was Kant's Overall Philosophical Project?

Kant began his philosophical career as a follower of rationalism. Rationalism was an important seventeenth- and eighteenth-century intellectual movement begun by Descartes and developed by Leibniz and his follower Christian Wolff, which held that all knowledge was capable of being part of a single, complete "science": that is, all knowledge can be slotted into a total, unified system of *a priori*, and certainly true, claims capable of encompassing everything that exists in the world, whether we have experience of it or not. In other words, for the German rationalists of Kant's day, metaphysical philosophy—which then

---

2   His body no longer remains there: in 1950 his sarcophagus was broken open by unknown vandals and his corpse was stolen and never recovered.

included theoretical science—was thought of as being very similar to pure mathematics. Rationalism was also, in Kantian terminology, "dogmatic" as opposed to "critical": that is, it sought to construct systems of knowledge without first attempting a careful examination of the scope and limits of possible knowledge. (This is why Kant's rationalist period is usually called his pre-Critical phase.)

In 1781, after ten years of hard thought, Kant rejected this rationalistic view of philosophy: he came to the view that metaphysics, as traditionally understood, is so far from being a rational science that it is not even a body of knowledge at all. Three major stimuli provoked Kant into being "awakened from his dogmatic slumber," as he put it. First, in about 1769, Kant came to the conclusion that he had discovered several "antinomies"—sets of contradictory propositions *each* of which can apparently be *rationally proven* to be true of reality (if we assume that our intellectual concepts apply to reality at all) and yet which can't both be true. For example, Kant argued that rational arguments are available to prove both that reality is finite but also that it is infinite, and that it is composed of indivisible atoms yet also infinitely divisible. Since both halves of these two pairs can't possibly be true at the same time, Kant argued that this casts serious doubt on the power of pure reason to draw metaphysical conclusions.

Second, Kant was worried about the conflict between free will and natural causality (this is a theme that appears throughout Kant's Critical works). He was convinced that genuine morality must be based on *freely* choosing—or "willing"— to do what is right. To be worthy of moral praise, in Kant's view, one must choose to do X rather than Y, not because some law of nature causes you to do so, but because your rational self is convinced that it is the right thing to do. Yet he also thought that the rational understanding of reality sought by the metaphysicians could only be founded on universally extending the laws we find in the scientific study of nature—and this includes universal causal determination, the principle that nothing (including choosing X over Y) happens without a cause. This, for Kant, produces an antinomy: some actions are free (i.e., *not* bound by the laws of nature) and yet everything that happens *is* determined by a law of nature.

Kant resolved this paradox by arguing that the scientific view of reality (including that pursued by the rationalists) must in principle be *incomplete*. Roughly, he held that although we can only rationally understand reality by thinking of it as causally deterministic and governed by scientific laws, our intellectual reason can never encompass *all* of reality. According to Kant, there must be a level of ultimate reality which is beyond the scope of pure reason, and which allows for the free activity of what Kant calls "practical reason" (which therefore holds open the possibility of genuine morality).

The third alarm bell to rouse Kant from his pre-Critical dogmatism was his reading of the Scottish philosopher David Hume. Hume was not a rationalist but instead represented the culmination of the other main seventeenth- and eighteenth-century stream of philosophical thought, usually called empiricism. Instead of thinking of knowledge as a unified, systematic, *a priori* whole, as the rationalists did, empiricists like Locke and Hume saw knowledge as being a piecemeal accumulation of claims derived primarily, not from pure logic, but from *sensation*— from our experience of the world. Science, for Hume, is thus not *a priori* but *a posteriori*: for example, we cannot just *deduce* from first principles that heavy objects tend to fall to the ground, as the rationalists supposed we could; we can only learn this by observing it to happen in our experience. The trouble was that Hume appeared to Kant (and to many others) to have shown that experience is simply *inadequate* for establishing the kind of metaphysical principles that philosophers have traditionally defended: no amount of sense-experience could ever either prove or disprove that God exists, that substance is imperishable, that we have an immortal soul, or even that there exist mind-independent "physical" objects which interact with each other according to causal laws of nature. Not just what we now think of as "philosophy" but theoretical science itself seemed to be called into question by Hume's "skeptical" philosophy. Since Kant was quite sure that mathematics and the natural sciences were genuine bodies of knowledge, he needed to show how such knowledge was possible despite Hume's skepticism: that is, as well as combatting the excessive claims of rationalism, he needed to show how empiricism went wrong in the other direction.

Prior to Kant, seventeenth- and eighteenth-century philosophers divided knowledge into exactly two camps: "truths of reason" (or "relations of ideas") on the one hand, and "truths of fact" (or "matters of fact") on the other. Rationalism was characterized by the doctrine that all final, complete knowledge was a truth of reason: that is, it was made up entirely of claims that could be proven *a priori* as being necessarily true, as a matter of logic, since it would be self-contradictory for them to be false. Empiricists, on the other hand, believed that all genuinely *informative* claims were truths of fact: if we wanted to find out about the world itself, rather than merely the logical relations between our own concepts, we had to rely upon the (*a posteriori*) data of sensory experience.

Kant, however, reshaped this distinction in a new framework which, he argued, cast a vital new light upon the nature of metaphysics. Instead of merely drawing a distinction between truths of reason and truths of fact, Kant replaced this with *two* separate distinctions: that between "*a priori*" and "*a posteriori*" propositions, and that between "analytic" and "synthetic" judgments. On this more complex scheme, the rationalists' truths of reason turn out to be "analytic *a priori*" knowledge, while empirical truths of fact are "synthetic *a posteriori*" propositions. But, Kant pointed out, this leaves open the possibility that there is at least a *third* type of knowledge: *synthetic a priori* judgments. These are judgments which we know *a priori* and thus do not need to learn from experience, but which nevertheless go beyond merely "analytic" claims about our own concepts. Kant's central claim in the *Critique of Pure Reason* is that he is the first philosopher in history to understand that the traditional claims of metaphysics—questions about God, the soul, free will, the underlying nature of space, time and matter—consist entirely of synthetic *a priori* propositions. (He also argues that pure mathematics is synthetic *a priori* as well.)

Kant's question therefore becomes: *How* is synthetic *a priori* knowledge possible? After all, the source of this knowledge can be neither experience (since it is *a priori*) nor the logical relations of ideas (since it is synthetic), so where could this kind of knowledge possibly come from? Once we have discovered the conditions of synthetic *a priori* knowledge, we can ask what its limits are: in particular, we can ask whether the traditional claims of speculative metaphysics meet those conditions, and thus whether they can be known to be true.

In bald (and massively simplified) summary, Kant's answer to these questions in the *Critique of Pure Reason* is the following: Synthetic *a priori* knowledge is possible insofar as it is knowledge of the *conditions of our experience of the world* (or indeed, of any *possible* experience). For example, for Kant, our judgments about the fundamental nature of space and time are not claims about our experiences themselves, nor are they the results of logic: instead, the forms of space and time are the conditions under which we are capable of having experience *at all*—we *can* only undergo sensations (either perceived or imaginary) that are arranged in space, and spread out in time; anything else is just impossible for us. So we can know *a priori*, but not analytically, that space and time must have a certain nature, since they are the forms of (the very possibility of) our experience.

Kant, famously, described this insight as constituting a kind of "Copernican revolution" in philosophy: just as Copernicus set cosmology on a totally new path by suggesting (in 1543) that the Earth orbits the Sun and not the other way around, so Kant wanted to breathe new life into philosophy by suggesting that, rather than assuming that "all our knowledge must conform to objects," we might instead "suppose that objects must conform to our knowledge." That is, rather than merely passively representing mind-independent objects in a "real" world, Kant held that the mind actively *constitutes* its objects—by *imposing* the categories of time, space, and causation onto our sensory experience, the subject actually *creates* the only kind of reality to which it has access. (This is why Kant's philosophy is often called "transcendental idealism." However, Kant is not a full-out idealist in the way that, say, George Berkeley is. He does not claim that the *existence* of objects is mind-dependent—only God's mind is capable of this kind of creation, according to Kant. Instead, the *a priori properties* of objects are what we constitute, by the structures of our cognition.)

When we turn to speculative metaphysics, however, we try to go beyond experience and its conditions—we attempt to move beyond what Kant called the "phenomena" of experience, and to make judgments about the nature of a reality that lies behind our sensory experience, what Kant called the "noumenal" realm. And here pure reason reaches its limits. If we ask about the nature of "things in themselves," independently of our experience of them, or if we try to show whether a supra-sensible God really exists, then our faculty of reason is powerless to demonstrate that these synthetic *a priori* judgments are either true or false—these metaphysical questions are neither empirical, nor logical, nor about the basic categories of our experience, so there is simply no way to answer them. The questions are meaningful ones (human beings crave answers to them) but they are beyond the scope of our faculty of reason. In short, we can have knowledge only of things that can be objects of possible experience, and cannot know anything that transcends the phenomenal realm.

This result, according to Kant, finally lets philosophy cease its constant oscillation between dogmatism and skepticism. It sets out the area in which human cognition is capable of attaining lasting truth (theoretical science—the metaphysics of experience—and mathematics), and that in which reason leads to self-contradiction and illusion (speculative metaphysics). Importantly, for Kant, this Copernican revolution provides *morality* with all the metaphysical support it needs, by clearing an area for free will.

What Is the Structure of This Reading?

Kant's *Foundations of the Metaphysics of Morals* was written, not just for professional philosophers, but for the general educated reader. Nevertheless, it can be pretty hard going, especially for those coming to Kant for the first time; the effort, however, is richly rewarded.

The *Foundations* forms a single, continuous argument running the whole length of the book, and each step of that overall argument is supported by sub-arguments. Its aim is to lay the preliminary groundwork for the study of morality. It is not intended to be, all by itself, a *moral theory* (though that is often the way it

has been treated in the past). Kant's goals for the work are ambitious enough: first, to establish that there is such a thing as morality—that there really are laws that should govern our conduct—and, second, to discover and justify "the supreme principle of morality." This "supreme principle," which Kant announces he has uncovered, is now famous as the Categorical Imperative.

Each section of the *Foundations* plays a role in Kant's overall argument. He begins, in the First Section, by simply trying to discover *what we already think morality is*. He is not, at this stage, trying to *justify* these beliefs: he merely wants to analyze our moral "common sense" to bring to light the principle behind it. He argues that the only thing which is "unconditionally" morally good is a good will, and that this insight is embedded in our ordinary moral judgments. (He then backs this argument with another, longer but less plausible, which appeals to "the purpose of nature.") The key to understanding morality, therefore, must be a proper understanding of the good will; if we can understand the principles that people of good will try to act on, Kant thinks, then we can see what the moral law tells us to do. In order to carry out this investigation, Kant announces he will focus on examples that make the moral will especially clear: i.e., on cases where the person performing an action has other motives that would normally lead to *not* doing that thing, but where she does it anyway because she recognizes it as her moral duty. He illustrates this contrast between people doing things "from duty" and doing them for some other reason by giving examples (each of which can be done for the sake of duty or not): a merchant who does not overcharge customers, a person who refrains from committing suicide, a man who performs kind actions to help others, and someone taking care to preserve their own happiness.

Consideration of examples like these shows us, Kant argues, that what gives a particular action moral worth is not the kind of action it is, nor the consequences of that action, nor even the purpose for which the action is performed, but the psychological *maxim* motivating that action. This in turn, Kant claims, shows moral worth is a kind of *respect for moral law* and that, in order to have the form of a law, moral principles must be *universalizable*. This important result is then illustrated and further explained using the example of truth-telling.

Kant concludes the First Section by explaining the need for philosophy to bolster these insights of common sense. The Second Section, therefore, is devoted to developing the fundamental elements of a proper "metaphysics of morals," which, in turn, Kant argues, must ultimately be embedded within a general theory of *practical reason*. Since the theory of practical reason is a theory of what reason tells us we ought to do (whether or not we actually do it), it must be a theory of what Kant calls *imperatives*. Kant therefore embarks on a discussion of the different types of imperative, distinguishing between *hypothetical* imperatives and *categorical* imperatives. Moral imperatives, he argues, must be categorical and not hypothetical.

He then asks: What makes these imperatives "possible," that is, what makes them legitimate requirements of rationality? Why are they *laws* that are binding on rational beings? The answer for hypothetical imperatives, Kant argues, is easy: that hypothetical imperatives are laws of reason is an *analytic* truth. However, in the case of categorical imperatives, the issue is more difficult. That these imperatives are rationally binding can only be, in Kant's terms, a *synthetic a priori* practical principle—something which we can know, independently of experience, to be true, but which is not merely true 'logically' or by virtue of the meanings of the words involved. Thus, showing there really *are* moral laws that are binding on all rational creatures is a difficult problem for Kant—and he postpones it until the Third Section of his book.

First, he turns to a more detailed analysis of the concept of a categorical imperative and, by emphasizing the *unconditional* character of categorical imperatives, arrives at his first major formulation of the moral law: the so-called Formula of Universal Law. Kant then illustrates how this law constrains our duties by ruling out certain maxims as being immoral. He gives four (carefully chosen) examples: someone contemplating suicide, someone considering borrowing money by making a false promise to repay it, someone wasting their talents in a life of self-indulgence and idleness, and someone refusing to help others.

If this helps us see *what* the categorical imperative requires us to do, the next issue is to discover *why* our wills should be consistent with the categorical imperative: what could motivate us to adopt universalizable maxims? The imperative is categorical and not hypothetical, so we cannot appeal to any contingent or variable motivations: the goal of morality—the *value of* being moral—must be something shared by every possible rational creature, no matter how they are situated. This, Kant argues, means all rational creatures must be ends-in-themselves and the ultimate source of all objective value. The categorical imperative can thus be expressed according to the Formula of Humanity as End in Itself. The reason non-universalizable maxims are immoral is, according to Kant, because they fail to properly respect rational creatures as ends in themselves; Kant illustrates this by re-considering his four examples in light of this latest formulation.

This notion of rational beings as having (and indeed being the source of) objective, intrinsic worth leads Kant to the idea of the *kingdom of ends*: an ideal human community in which people treat each other as ends in themselves. Acting morally, Kant claims, can be thought of as *legislating* moral laws for this ideal community: we guide our own behavior by principles which we realize should be followed by all the free and equal members of the kingdom of ends. This formulation of the categorical imperative is often called the Formula of Autonomy (autonomy comes from the Greek words for self—*autos*—and law—*nomos*—and hence means something like "following one's own laws"). Again, this shows us something new about the categorical imperative: the reason we ought to follow the moral law is not because we are forced to conform to it by something outside ourselves (such as society or God), but because these are laws that rational people lay down *for themselves*.[3] Morality, thus, does

---

3 Moreover, we do not need to be told, by some external authority, what the moral law is. We can each reliably discover *for ourselves* what we ought to do. In fact, for Kant, acting in accordance with a moral law merely because some moral authority has told you to does not make you a good person. That would be to obey a merely hypothetical, and not a categorical, imperative.

not infringe on freedom—on the contrary, it is the fullest expression of freedom, and also of respect for the freedom of others. Furthermore, it is the capacity of rational creatures to be legislators in the kingdom of ends which is the source of what Kant calls their *dignity*.

This brings us to the final stage of Kant's argument: the last problem he faces is that of showing moral law really does exist—that we really are rationally bound by it. He has shown that we *would* be bound by it if we were autonomous, rational beings capable of being legislative citizens in the kingdom of ends; now Kant has to show that human beings really do have an autonomous will, and this is the project of the Third Section (which is not reprinted here). To do this, Kant needs to show that the human will is not subject to the laws of nature, for otherwise we would not be free to legislate the moral law for ourselves. On the other hand, if we are free, then—since our wills must be governed by *some* law or other or they would not be causal—we must be governed by the moral law. Morality and freedom are thus intimately connected, for Kant, and we cannot have one without the other. He then argues that if we are to think of ourselves as *rational,* we must necessarily think of ourselves as free. Thus, to be rational just is to be governed by the moral law.

But how is this freedom possible—how *can* human beings be rational, given that we are surely part of the natural world and hence entangled in the web of the laws of nature? Here Kant appeals to and summarizes parts of his *Critique of Pure Reason*, where he argued that the empirical world of appearance—the world of nature—is not the way things are in themselves, but merely how they appear to us: 'behind' this world of appearance is the deeper reality of things as they are in themselves. Human beings, too, are subject to this duality: as members of the natural world, we are subject to the laws of causality, but our real selves—our *egos*—are "above nature" and so, at least potentially, are autonomous. Kant's overall conclusion in the *Foundations of the Metaphysics of Morals*, then, is not that we can actually know there *is* a moral law, but that a) if there were a moral law it would have to be the way he has described, b) it is at least possible the moral law really does exist, and c) in any case we are forced to *believe* the moral law exists, simply in virtue of thinking of ourselves as rational beings.

Some Useful Background Information

1. The goal of Kant's *Foundations* is not to tell people how to act or to introduce a new theory of morality. Kant thought that, on the whole, people know perfectly well what they are and are not supposed to do and, indeed, that any moral theory having prescriptions that substantially diverged from "common sense" beliefs about morality was likely to be erroneous. When criticized by his contemporaries for merely providing a new formula for old beliefs, Kant replied, "… who would even want to introduce a new principle of all morality and, as it were, first invent it? Just as if, before him, the world had been ignorant of what duty is, or in thoroughgoing error about it." Instead, Kant aimed to provide a new philosophical *underpinning* for morality: he thought people had misunderstood *why* the prescriptions of morality are the way they are, and that they lacked a reliable *method* for making sure they always did the right thing.

2. In the Preface to the *Foundations of the Metaphysics of Morals* Kant divides philosophy into three parts: logic (the study of thought), physics (the study of the way the world is), and ethics (the study of what we ought to do). Kant thinks of each of these as a domain of *laws*: logic deals with the laws of thought, physics deals with the laws of nature, and ethics deals with what Kant calls the *laws of freedom*—that is, with laws governing the conduct of those beings not subject to the laws of nature. In this way, Kant sets up the study of morality as the study of a particular kind of law (as opposed to, say, of character traits, states of affairs, or types of actions), and he thinks of these laws as being analogous to, but different from, laws of nature.

3. According to Kant, there are in general two routes to knowledge: experience and reason. The study of logic is within the domain of pure reason, but for Kant physics and ethics each have both a "pure" and an empirical part. Par-

ticular physical laws—for example that infection is transmitted by micro-organisms—are empirical, but the general *framework* for these laws—the idea that all events must have a lawlike cause—is not itself empirical (after all, we have not *seen* every event and its cause). That ethics must be built upon a non-empirical foundation is even more obvious, according to Kant. Ethics is the study, not of how things actually are, but of how things *ought* to be. Scrutinizing the way human beings actually behave, and describing the things they actually believe, will never be sufficient to tell you what we *ought* to do and think. Moral laws and concepts, therefore, must be established by pure reason alone (though experience will certainly play a role in determining the *concrete content* of moral principles in actual circumstances). This body of non-empirical knowledge, which sets out what Kant calls the "synthetic *a priori*" framework for physics and ethics, is called *metaphysics*; that is why Kant labels the subject of this work the "metaphysics of morals."

4. While all things in nature are bound by laws, rational beings instead govern their behavior by their *conception* of laws. For example, while objects fall because of the law of gravity, rational entities refrain from stepping off high places, not because of this law itself, but because of their *understanding* or conception of the law. A *maxim*, for Kant, is the subjective psychological principle that lies behind volition. It is, roughly, a stable motive that makes people do things in one way rather than another, a tacit 'rule' that guides their behavior. Examples of maxims might be "never kill innocent people," "don't tell lies unless it is clearly to your advantage to do so," "don't eat meat (except on special occasions)," "always give people the correct change," "never sleep with someone before the third date," and "never shoplift, but it's okay to take office supplies from your workplace."

5. Kant makes frequent mention of the *formal* nature of moral law. Something is *formal* if it concerns the form of something and *material* if it concerns what it is made of. The "matter" of

a maxim is typically the action intended (such as keeping someone's car keys) plus the goal of that action (such as wanting to keep someone safe or wanting their car). The form of the maxim consists in the way those parts are put together. Consider, for example, the way the moral worth of the following maxims changes as their matter is rearranged: (1) "I will keep your car keys because you have had too much to drink and might hurt yourself or others," (2) "I will keep your car keys because I want the car for myself," (3) "I will keep my car keys because I want the car for myself." Maxims 1 and 2 involve the same action and maxims 2 and 3 have the same goal, yet—because of their different forms—1 and 3 are moral maxims while 2 is not.

Some Common Misconceptions

1. Kant is not an ethical grinch or an unfeeling puritan. He does not claim that we cannot be glad to perform a moral action, that we only act morally when we do something we don't want to do, or that happiness is incompatible with goodness. Kant's examples in the *Foundations* are only supposed to be thought experiments which pull apart, as clearly as possible, actions we *want* to do from actions we *ought* to do, in order to show what makes actions distinctively moral. He does not claim that the mere presence of an inclination to do something detracts from its moral worth: the key idea is just that one's *motive* must be duty and not inclination. (In fact, Kant argues that we have a kind of indirect moral duty to seek our own happiness, and that since generous inclinations are helpful in doing good actions, we should cultivate these feelings in ourselves.)

2. Similarly, Kant does not—as is sometimes claimed—assert that the good will is the *only thing* which is good, that everything else which is good is merely a *means* to the achievement of a good will, or even that a good will is *all* we require for a completely good life. It is perfectly consistent with Kant's views to point out that, say, health or pleasure are valuable for their

own sake. Kant's claim is that the good will is the *highest* good, and that it is the *precondition* of all the other goods (i.e., nothing else is good unless it is combined with a good will). When Kant says health is not "unconditionally" good, what he means is that it is not good at all unless it is combined with a good will—though when it *is* so combined, it really does have value in itself. By contrast, a good will is unconditionally good: it has its goodness in all possible circumstances, independently of its relation to anything else, and this is what makes it the "highest" good.

3. The categorical imperative is (arguably) not intended by Kant to be *itself* a recipe for moral action. It does not, and is not supposed to, tell you what you ought to do. Instead, the categorical imperative acts as a *test* for particular maxims—ruling some in and others out—and it is these *maxims* which provide the content of morality. To put it another way, Kant does not expect us to *deduce* particular moral maxims from the categorical imperative alone; rather, we take the maxims upon which we are *already* disposed to act and scrutinize them to see if they are formally consistent with the moral law.

4. The categorical imperative—say, the Formula of Universal Law—applies to maxims, not to actions or even intentions. Thus, for example, there is no requirement that our *actions* be universalizable: it need not be immoral for me to use my toothbrush or live in my house, even though not *everyone* could do those things. Instead, the *maxims* which guide my actions must be universalizable, and one and the same maxim (e.g., the principle of taking care of one's teeth) can give rise to different actions by different people in different circumstances. Conversely, two actions of exactly the same type (e.g., refusing to give someone a loan) could be of vastly different moral significance since the maxims that lie behind them might be of vastly different moral worth. It is also important to notice that maxims are not the same thing as *intentions*: one can intend to do something (such as make someone happy) for any of several quite different maxims (e.g., because you realize that being nice to people is part of moral duty, or because you want to be remembered in their will), and thus sometimes this intention is moral and sometimes it is not.[4]

5. When Kant claims certain maxims cannot be universalized, he cannot mean by this merely that it would be *immoral* or *bad* if these maxims were universal laws. (This would make his reasoning circular; if he is trying to define immorality in terms of non-universalizable maxims, he can't turn around and define universalizability in terms of immorality. Also, Kant has disavowed the relevance of the *consequences* of an action as part of what makes it moral or immoral, so he cannot now appeal to the consequences of making a maxim universal.) Instead, Kant means it is *literally impossible* to will that certain maxims be universal laws—that it would go against rationality itself to do so, rather like willing that 2+2=5 or wanting my will to be always and everywhere frustrated.

6. Kant did not hold that *all* universalizable maxims are moral; it would be a problem for his account if he had done so, since some obviously trivial and non-moral maxims appear to be consistent with the categorical imperative (e.g., a policy of always wearing socks on Tuesdays). Kant is able to exclude such examples from the sphere of the moral by distinguishing between actions that merely *conform* to a law, and actions performed *because* of a law. It is these latter kind of actions that are genuinely moral, since in these cases I decide what to do *by* working out what I would will that every rational being should do (rather than doing

---

4   One significant consequence of this is that Kant is not coldly saying that all of our actions should be done *because* it is our duty, in the sense that the purpose of our acting is to be dutiful. On the contrary, good people will typically do the things they do because they want to help others, or to cultivate their own talents, or to be good parents, and so on: it is just that the maxims they are following in acting on these intentions are maxims which are consistent with the moral law.

something for *other* reasons—e.g., to keep my feet warm—that also happens to be something that every rational being could do).

7. Kant's philosophy is not, as is often assumed, authoritarian or dictatorial. Although he places great emphasis on a rigid adherence to duty, it is important to realize that, for Kant, this duty is not imposed from the outside: it is not a matter of the laying down of moral laws by the state, society, or even by God. Quite the opposite: for Kant, constraining one's own behavior by the moral law actually *constitutes* genuine freedom or autonomy, which is being guided by rationality and not by mere inclination. Moral duty, for Kant, is *self*-legislated.

How Important and Influential Is This Passage?

Kant's *Foundations of the Metaphysics of Morals* is one of the most important ethical works ever written. Philosopher H.J. Patton called it "one of the small books which are truly great: it has exercised on human thought an influence almost ludicrously disproportionate to its size.... Its main topic—the supreme principle of morality—is of the utmost importance to all who are not indifferent to the struggle of good against evil." Since their introduction in this work, some of Kant's themes—the idea that human beings are ends-in-themselves and so not to be treated as mere means by others; that our own humanity finds its greatest expression through the respect we have for others; that morality is freedom and vice a form of enslavement—have become central parts of contemporary moral culture. Many modern moral philosophers have been heavily influenced by his work, and descendents of his moral theory form one of the main strands in contemporary ethical theory. Kant's ethical theory is very much a 'live' philosophical position today.

Suggestions for Critical Reflection

1. Kant gives four examples in which it is supposed to be impossible to will that your maxim become universal law. Just exactly *how* does Kant think this is impossible? Is there more than one kind of 'impossibility' here? Is Kant *correct* that it is, in some way, impossible to universalize these four maxims? (If you don't think he is, what does this show about his moral theory?)

2. Could Kant's moral theory lead to a potential conflict of duties? For example, the duty to tell the truth seems to conflict, potentially, with the duty to save the lives of innocent people: what, for example, if you are faced with a mad axeman demanding to know where his victim—whom you happen to know is cowering under your kitchen table—is hiding? (Here the key idea is that, in some situations, two universalizable *maxims* must tend toward different and incompatible actions. Mere conflicts of rules for action—e.g., "always return what you have borrowed"—will tend to miss the mark as criticisms of Kant, as the maxims which lie behind them may well allow for exceptions in particular cases.) If duties mandated by the categorical imperative *can* conflict with each other, how much destruction does this wreak on Kant's moral theory?

3. On the other hand, does Kant's moral theory produce any concrete ethical prescriptions at all? The German philosopher G.W.F. Hegel called Kant's Formula of Universal Law an "empty formalism" and said it reduced "the science of morals to the preaching of duty for duty's sake.... No transition is possible to the specification of particular duties nor, if some such particular content for acting comes under consideration, is there any criterion in that principle for deciding whether it is or is not a duty. On the contrary, by this means any wrong or immoral line of conduct may be justified." What do you make of this objection?

4. Kant provides several—up to five—different formulations of the categorical imperative. What is the relationship between them? For example, do some of the formulations yield different sets of duties than the others?

5. Kant denies that "the principles of morality are ... to be sought anywhere in knowledge of human nature." Does this seem like a reasonable

position to take? What reasons does he have for this striking claim, and how persuasive are they?

6. At one point Kant argues that the function of reason cannot, primarily, be to produce happiness, since then it would not have been well adapted by nature to its purpose, and it must therefore have some other purpose (to produce a will which is good in itself). What do you think of this argument? How much does it rely upon the assumption that nature has purposes?

7. Kant suggests our ordinary, everyday moral beliefs and practices contain within them the "ultimate principle" of morality (the categorical imperative). Is he successful in showing we *already* tacitly believe the categorical imperative? If not, how much of a problem is this for his later arguments?

8. Do all of our actions rest on maxims? Do you think that Kant thinks they do (and if so, how does that affect your understanding of what he means by "maxim")? If they do not, does this cause serious problems for Kant's moral theory?

9. "There are … many persons so sympathetically constituted that without any motive of vanity or selfishness they find an inner satisfaction in spreading joy and rejoice in the contentment of others which they have made possible. But I say that, however dutiful and however amiable it may be, that kind of action has no true moral worth." What do you think of this claim of Kant's? When properly understood, do you think it is plausible?

10. Does Kant's moral theory require us to be perfectly rational in order to be perfectly moral? If so, is this a reasonable expectation? What place can the irrational elements of human psychology—such as emotions—have in Kant's moral philosophy?

11. How well can Kant's moral theory handle the following question: Now you've shown me what morality is, *why* should I be moral? Why is morality binding on me? For example, when Kant rules out all hypothetical imperatives as grounds for moral behavior, does he thereby rule out all possible *reasons* to be moral?

12. How accurately can we make moral judgments about *other people*, if Kant's theory is correct? How easily could we tell what maxim is guiding their behavior? For that matter, how accurately can we make moral judgments about our *own* behavior? Do we always know our own motives for action? How much, if at all, is any of this a problem for Kant's theory?

13. Even if you disagree with the details in Kant's moral theory, do you think his fundamental claim is sound? Is there a sharp distinction between moral actions and those performed for the sake of self-interest or emotional inclination? Must genuinely moral actions be motivated by a categorical or universally rational duty?

Suggestions for Further Reading

It is important to realize that the *Foundations for the Metaphysics of Morals* is only *part* of Kant's ethical system, and some things which are puzzling or incomplete in the *Foundations* are fleshed out elsewhere. There are three main places to look for the rest of Kant's ethics. In the *Critique of Practical Reason* Kant re-examines the question of whether a categorical imperative is really possible—that is, whether a "purely rational" consideration can provide any kind of incentive for action. In the *Metaphysics of Morals* Kant discusses, in detail, the problems of moral choice in concrete situations, and tries to show how the categorical imperative yields precise and plausible moral prescriptions in everyday life. And in *Religion Within the Limits of Reason Alone* Kant explores important questions about moral choice and responsibility. *The Cambridge Edition of the Works of Immanuel Kant: Practical Philosophy*, translated and edited by Mary J. Gregor (Cambridge University Press, 1996), contains most of his writings on ethics. The Cambridge Edition volume on *Religion and Rational Theology*, translated and edited by Allen Wood and George diGiovanni (Cambridge University Press, 1996), contains *Religion Within the Limits of Reason Alone*.

Mary Gregor's translation of the *Foundations* is also published separately, with an extremely helpful introduction by Christine Korsgaard, as *Kant: Groundwork of the Metaphysics of Morals* (Cambridge University Press, 1997). *Immanuel Kant: Ethical Philosophy* (Hackett, 1994), contains translations by James Ellington of (what is there called) the *Grounding for the Metaphysics of Morals* and the second part of the *Metaphysics of Morals*, along with a clear and useful introductory essay by Warner Wick. Another well-known translation of the *Foundations* is H.J. Paton's *The Moral Law: Kant's Groundwork of the Metaphysic of Morals* (Hutchinson, 1948).

There are many books and articles on Kant's ethical theory, and the *Foundations* in particular. Here are some of the best of recent years: H.B. Acton, *Kant's Moral Philosophy* (Macmillan, 1970); Henry Allison, *Idealism and Freedom: Essays on Kant's Theoretical and Practical Philosophy* (Cambridge University Press, 1996); Bruce Aune, *Kant's Theory of Morals* (Princeton University Press, 1979); Lewis White Beck, *Studies in the Philosophy of Kant* (Bobbs-Merrill, 1965); A.R.C. Duncan, *Practical Reason and Morality: A Study of Immanuel Kant's Foundations for the Metaphysics of Morals* (Thomas Nelson, 1957); Mary J. Gregor, *Laws of Freedom* (Basil Blackwell, 1963); Paul Guyer (ed.), *The Cambridge Companion to Kant* (Cambridge University Press, 1992) and *Kant's Groundwork of the Metaphysics of Morals: Critical Essays* (Rowman & Littlefield, 1998); Barbara Herman, *The Practice of Moral Judgment* (Harvard University Press, 1993); Thomas E. Hill, Jr., *Dignity and Practical Reason in Kant's Moral Theory* (Cornell University Press, 1992); Christine Korsgaard, *Creating the Kingdom of Ends* (Cambridge University Press, 1996); Onora Nell (O'Neill), *Acting on Principle: An Essay on Kantian Ethics* (Columbia University Press, 1975); Onora O'Neill, *Constructions of Reason: Explorations of Kant's Moral Philosophy* (Cambridge University Press, 1989); H.J. Paton, *The Categorical Imperative: A Study in Kant's Moral Philosophy* (University of Chicago Press, 1948); Roger J. Sullivan, *Immanuel Kant's Moral Theory* (Cambridge University Press, 1989) and the shorter *An Introduction to Kant's Ethics* (Cambridge University Press, 1994); Robert Paul Wolff, *The Autonomy of Reason: A Commentary on Kant's Groundwork of the Metaphysics of Morals* (Harper & Row, 1973); Robert Paul Wolff (ed.), *Foundations of the Metaphysics of Morals with Critical Essays* (Bobbs-Merrill, 1969); and Allen Wood, *Kant's Ethical Thought* (Cambridge University Press, 1999).

Kantian ideas have played an important role in recently-published original moral and political philosophy, including Stephen Darwall's *Impartial Reason* (Cornell University Press, 1983), Alan Donagan's *The Theory of Morality* (University of Chicago Press, 1977), Alan Gewirth's *Reason and Morality* (University of Chicago Press, 1978), Thomas Hill, Jr.'s *Autonomy and Self-Respect* (Cambridge University Press, 1991), Christine Korsgaard's *The Sources of Normativity* (Cambridge University Press, 1996), Thomas Nagel's *The Possibility of Altruism* (Princeton University Press, 1978), Onora O'Neill's *Towards Justice and Virtue* (Cambridge University Press, 1996), and, especially, John Rawls's *A Theory of Justice* (Harvard University Press, 1971).

Foundations of the Metaphysics of Morals[5]

First Section

Transition from the Common Rational Moral Cognition to the Philosophical Moral Cognition

Nothing can possibly be conceived in the world, or even out of it, which can be called good without qualification, except a *good will*. Intelligence, wit, judgment, and the other *talents* of the mind, however they may be named, or courage, resolution, perseverance, as qualities of *temperament*, are undoubtedly good and desirable in many respects; but these gifts of nature may also become extremely bad and mischievous if the will which is to make use of them, and which, therefore, constitutes what is called *character*, is not good. It is the same with the *gifts of fortune*. Power, riches, honor, even health, and the general well-being

---

5   Kant's *Grundlegung zur Metaphysik der Sitten* was first published in Riga in 1785. This translation is by Thomas K. Abbott with revisions by Lara Denis, *Groundwork for the Metaphysics of Morals* (Peterborough, ON: Broadview Press, 2005).

and contentment with one's condition which is called *happiness*, inspire pride, and often presumption, if there is not a good will to correct the influence of these on the mind, and with this also to rectify the whole principle of acting, and adapt it to its end. The sight of a being who is not adorned with a single feature of a pure and good will, enjoying unbroken prosperity, can never give pleasure to an impartial spectator. Thus a good will appears to constitute the indispensable condition even of being worthy of happiness.

There are even some qualities which are of service to this good will itself, and may facilitate its action, yet which have no inner unconditional value, but always presuppose a good will, and this qualifies the esteem that we justly have for them, and does not permit us to regard them as absolutely good. Moderation in the affections and passions, self-control, and calm deliberation are not only good in many respects, but even seem to constitute part of the *inner* worth of the person; but they are far from deserving to be called good without qualification, although they have been so unconditionally praised by the ancients. For without the principles of a good will, they may become extremely evil; and the coldness of a villain not only makes him far more dangerous, but also directly makes him more abominable in our eyes than he would have been without it.

A good will is good not because of what it accomplishes or effects, not by its aptness for the attainment of some proposed end, but simply by virtue of the volition—that is, it is good in itself, and considered by itself is to be esteemed much higher than all that can be brought about by it in favor of any inclination, or even the sum total of all inclinations.[6] Even if it should happen that, owing to a step-motherly nature, this will should wholly lack power to accomplish its purpose, if with its greatest efforts it should yet achieve nothing, and there should remain only the good will (not, to be sure, a mere wish, but the summoning of all means in our power), then, like a jewel, it would still shine by its own light, as a thing which has its whole value in itself. Its usefulness or fruitlessness can neither add to nor take away anything from this value. It would be, as it were, only the setting to

enable us to handle it more conveniently in common commerce, or to attract to it the attention of those who are not yet connoisseurs, but not to recommend it to true connoisseurs, or to determine its value.

There is, however, something so strange in this idea of the absolute value of a mere will, in which no account is taken of its utility, that notwithstanding the thorough assent of even common reason to the idea, yet a suspicion must arise that it may perhaps really be the product of mere high-flown fancy, and that we may have misunderstood the purpose of nature in assigning reason as the governor of our will. Therefore we will examine this idea from this point of view.

In the natural constitution of an organized being, that is, a being adapted suitably to the purposes of life, we assume it as a fundamental principle that no organ for any purpose will be found but what is also the fittest and best adapted for that purpose. Now in a being which has reason and a will, if the proper object of nature were its *preservation*, its *welfare*, in a word, its *happiness*, then nature would have hit upon a very bad arrangement in selecting the reason of the creature to carry out this purpose. For all the actions which the creature has to perform with a view to this purpose, and the whole rule of its conduct, would be far more surely prescribed to it by instinct, and that end would have been attained thereby much more certainly than it ever can be by reason. Should reason have been imparted to this favored creature over and above, it must only have served it to contemplate the happy constitution of its nature, to admire it, to congratulate itself on it, and to feel thankful for it to the beneficent cause, but not that it should subject its desires to that weak and delusive guidance, and meddle incompetently with the purpose of nature. In a word, nature would have taken care that reason should not break forth into *practical use*, nor have the presumption, with its weak insight, to think out for itself the plan of happiness and of the means of attaining it. Nature would not only have taken on herself the choice of the ends but also of the means, and with wise foresight would have entrusted both to instinct.

And, in fact, we find that the more a cultivated reason applies itself with deliberate purpose to the enjoyment of life and happiness, so much more does one fall short of true satisfaction. And from this cir-

---

6   One's inclinations are things one wants or likes to do.

cumstance there arises in many, if they are candid enough to confess it, a certain degree of *misology*, that is, hatred of reason, especially in the case of those who are most experienced in the use of it, because after calculating all the advantages they derive—I do not say from the invention of all the arts of common luxury, but even from the sciences (which seem to them to be after all only a luxury of the understanding)—they find that they have, in fact, only brought more trouble on their shoulders rather than gained in happiness; and they end by envying rather than despising the more common run of human beings who keep closer to the guidance of mere instinct, and do not allow their reason much influence on their conduct. And this we must admit, that the judgment of those who would very much lower the lofty eulogies of the advantages which reason gives us in regard to the happiness and satisfaction of life, or who would even reduce them below zero, is by no means morose or ungrateful to the goodness with which the world is governed, but that there lies at the root of these judgments the idea that our existence has a different and far worthier end, to which, and not to happiness, is reason's proper vocation, and which must, therefore, be regarded as the supreme condition to which private ends of human beings must, for the most part, defer.

For as reason is not competent to guide the will with certainty in regard to its objects and the satisfaction of all our needs (which it to some extent even multiplies), this being an end to which an implanted instinct would have led with much greater certainty; and since, nevertheless, reason is imparted to us as a practical faculty, that is, as one which is to have influence on the *will*, therefore admitting that nature generally in the distribution of her capacities has adapted the means to the end, its true vocation must be to produce a *will*, not merely good as a *means* to something else, but *good in itself*, for which reason was absolutely necessary. This will then, though not indeed the sole and complete good, must be the supreme good and the condition of every other, even of the desire of happiness. Under these circumstances, there is nothing inconsistent with the wisdom of nature in the fact that the cultivation of reason, which is requisite for the first and unconditioned purpose, does in many ways interfere, at least in this life,

with the attainment of the second, which is always conditional—namely, happiness. Indeed, it may even reduce it to nothing, without nature thereby failing of her purpose. For reason recognizes the establishment of a good will as its highest practical vocation, and in attaining this purpose is capable only of a satisfaction of its own proper kind, namely, that from the attainment of an end, which in turn is determined by reason only, notwithstanding that this may involve many a disappointment to the ends of inclination.

We have then to develop the concept of a will which deserves to be highly esteemed for itself, and is good without a view to anything further, a concept which exists already in the sound natural understanding, requiring rather to be clarified than to be taught, and which in estimating the value of our actions always takes the first place and constitutes the condition of all the rest. In order to do this, we will take concept of duty, which includes that of a good will, although implying certain subjective limitations and hindrances. These, however, far from concealing it or rendering it unrecognizable, rather bring it out by contrast and make it shine forth so much the brighter.

I omit here all actions which are already recognized as contrary to duty, although they may be useful for this or that purpose, for with these the question whether they are done *from duty* cannot arise at all, since they even conflict with it. I also set aside those actions which really conform to duty, but to which men have *no* immediate *inclination*, performing them because they are impelled thereto by some other inclination. For in this case we can readily distinguish whether the action which agrees with duty is done *from duty* or from a selfish purpose. It is much harder to make this distinction when the action accords with duty, and the subject has besides an *immediate* inclination to it. For example, it is always a matter of duty that a dealer should not overcharge an inexperienced purchaser; and wherever there is much commerce the prudent tradesman does not overcharge, but keeps a fixed price for everyone, so that a child buys from him as well as any other. People are thus *honestly* served; but this is not enough to make us believe that the tradesman has so acted from duty and from principles of honesty; his own advantage required it; it is unwarranted in this case to suppose that he might besides have an immediate inclination in favor of the buyers, so that, as it were, from love he should give no advantage to one over another. Accordingly the action was done neither from duty nor from immediate inclination, but merely with a selfish purpose.

On the other hand, it is a duty to preserve one's life; and, in addition, everyone has also an immediate inclination to do so. But on this account the often anxious care which most people take for it has no intrinsic worth, and their maxim has no moral content. They preserve their life *in conformity with duty*, no doubt, but not *from duty*. On the other hand, if adversity and hopeless sorrow have completely taken away the relish for life, if the unfortunate one, strong in mind, indignant to his fate rather than desponding or dejected, wishes for death, and yet preserves his life without loving it—not from inclination or fear, but from duty—then his maxim has moral content.

To be beneficent when one can is a duty; and besides this, there are many minds so sympathetically constituted that, without any other motive of vanity or self-interest, they find a pleasure in spreading joy around them, and can take delight in the satisfaction of others so far as it is their own work. But I maintain that in such a case an action of this kind, however proper, however amiable it may be, has nevertheless no true moral worth, but is on a level with other inclinations, for example, the inclination to honor, which if it is happily directed to that which is in fact of public utility and accordant with duty, and consequently honorable, deserves praise and encouragement, but not esteem. For the maxim lacks the moral content, namely, that such actions be done *from duty*, not from inclination. Put the case that the mind of that philanthropist was clouded by sorrow of his own, extinguishing all sympathy with the lot of others, and that while he still has the power to benefit others in distress, he is not touched by their trouble because he is absorbed with his own; and now suppose that he tears himself out of this dead insensibility and performs the action without any inclination to it, but simply from duty, then for the first time his action has its genuine moral worth. Further still, if nature has put little sympathy in the heart of this or that man, if he, supposed to be an upright man, is by temperament cold and indifferent to the sufferings of others, perhaps because in respect of his own he is provided with the special gifts of patience and fortitude, and supposes, or even requires, that others should have the same—and such a man would certainly not be the meanest product of nature—but if nature had not specially framed him for a philanthropist, would he not still find in himself a source from which to give himself a far higher worth than that of a good-natured temperament could be? Unquestionably. It is just in this that the moral worth of the character is brought out which is incomparably the highest of all, namely, that he is beneficent, not from inclination, but from duty.

To secure one's own happiness is a duty, at least indirectly; for discontent with one's condition, under a pressure of many anxieties and amidst unsatisfied needs, might easily become a great *temptation to transgression of duty*. But here again, without looking to duty, all men have already the strongest and most intimate inclination to happiness, because it is just in this idea[7] that all inclinations are combined in one total. But the precept of happiness is often of such a sort that it greatly interferes with some inclinations, and yet a human being cannot form any definite and certain conception of the sum of satisfaction of all of them which is called happiness. It is not then to be wondered at that a single inclination, definite both as to what it promises and as to the time within which it can be gratified, is often able to overcome such a fluctuating idea, and that a gouty[8] patient, for instance, can choose to enjoy what he likes, and to suffer what he may, since, according to his calculation, on this occasion at least, he has not sacrificed the enjoyment of the present mo-

---

7   Kant used the word *Idee,* which means a pure concept of reason corresponding to no sensory "intuition"— roughly, concepts that (though they may be derived from the empirical world) correspond to nothing within the empirical world but only to 'something' outside it. Kant thought that ideas, although they do not 'picture reality' in any way we can understand, can act as *precepts* that guide our thoughts and actions in particular directions.

8   Gout is a chronic illness (caused by elevated levels of uric acid in the blood) traditionally thought to be brought on by eating too much rich food and drinking too much alcohol.

ment to a possibly mistaken expectation of a happiness which is supposed to be found in health. But even in this case, if the general inclination to happiness did not influence his will, and supposing that in his particular case health was not a necessary element in this calculation, there yet remains in this, as in all other cases, this law—namely, that he should promote his happiness not from inclination but from duty, and by this would his conduct first acquire true moral worth.

It is in this manner, undoubtedly, that we are to understand those passages of Scripture also in which we are commanded to love our neighbor, even our enemy. For love, as an inclination, cannot be commanded, but beneficence for duty's sake may, even though we are not impelled to it by any inclination—indeed, are even repelled by a natural and unconquerable aversion. This is *practical*[9] love, and not *pathological*[10]—a love which is seated in the will, and not in the propensities of feeling—in principles of action and not of tender sympathy; and it is this love alone which can be commanded.

The second proposition is: That an action done from duty derives its moral worth, *not from the purpose* which is to be attained by it, but from the maxim by which it is determined, and therefore does not depend on the realization of the object of the action, but merely on the *principle of volition* by which the action has taken place, without regard to any object of desire. It is clear from what precedes that the purposes which we may have in view in our action, or their effects regarded as ends and incentives of the will, cannot give to actions any unconditional or moral worth. In what, then, can their worth lie if it is not to consist in the will in reference to its expected effect? It cannot lie anywhere but in the *principle of the will* without regard to the ends which can be attained by the action. For the will stands between its *a priori* principle, which is formal, and its *a posteriori* incentive, which is material,[11] as between two roads, and as

it must be determined by something, it follows that it must be determined by the formal principle of volition when an action is done from duty, in which case every material principle has been withdrawn from it.

The third proposition, which is a consequence of the two preceding, I would express thus: *Duty is the necessity of acting from respect for the law.* I may have *inclination* for an object as the effect of my proposed action, but *never respect* for it, just because it is an effect and not an activity of will. Similarly, I cannot have respect for inclination, whether my own or another's; I can at most, if my own, approve it; if another's, sometimes even love it, that is, look on it as favorable to my own interest. It is only what is connected with my will as a principle, by no means as an effect—what does not serve my inclination, but outweighs it, or at least in case of choice excludes it from its calculation—in other words, simply the law of itself, which can be an object of respect, and hence a command. Now an action done from duty must wholly exclude the influence of inclination, and with it every object of the will, so that nothing remains which can determine the will except objectively the *law*, and subjectively *pure respect* for this practical law, and consequently the maxim[12] that I should follow this law even to the thwarting of all my inclinations.

Thus the moral worth of an action does not lie in the effect expected from it, nor in any principle of action which needs to borrow its motive from this expected effect. For all these effects—agreeableness of one's condition, and even the promotion of the happiness of others—could have been also brought

---

9   Based on practical reason.

10   Kant means simply motives and actions arising from feeling or bodily impulses. No suggestion of abnormality or disease is intended.

11   *A priori* means "prior to experience": a proposition is *a priori* if it can be known to be true prior to, or

independently of, any specific empirical events. By contrast, something is *a posteriori* if it must be derived from experience. "1 + 1 = 2" is an *a priori* claim whilst "The sky is blue" is *a posteriori*. In order to know the first, one need not have had any particular experience of the external world, but to know that the second is true, you (or some reliable source) must have seen the sky.

12   [Author's note] A maxim is the subjective principle of volition. The objective principle (i.e., that which would serve all rational beings also subjectively as a practical principle if reason had full power over the faculty of desire) is the practical law.

about by other causes, so that for this there would have been no need of the will of a rational being; whereas it is in this alone that the supreme and unconditional good can be found. The pre-eminent good which we call moral can therefore consist in nothing else than *the representation of the law* in itself, *which certainly is only possible in a rational being*, insofar as this representation, and not the expected effect, determines the will. This is a good which is already present in the person who acts accordingly, and we need not wait for it to appear first in the result.[13]

But what sort of law can that be, the conception of which must determine the will, even without pay-

---

13   [Author's note] It might be objected that I seek to take refuge in an obscure feeling behind the word "respect," instead of clearly resolving the question with a concept of reason. But though respect is a feeling, it is not one received through any [outer] influence but is self-wrought by a rational concept; thus it differs specifically from all feelings of the former kind which may be referred to inclination or fear. What I recognize directly as a law for myself I recognize with respect, which means merely the consciousness of the submission of my will to a law without the intervention of other influences on my mind. The direct determination of the will by law and the consciousness of this determination is respect; thus respect can be regarded as the effect of the law on the subject and not as the cause of the law. Respect is properly the conception of a worth which thwarts my self-love. Thus it is regarded as an object neither of inclination nor of fear, though it has something analogous to both. The only object of respect is law, and indeed only the law which we impose on ourselves and yet recognize as necessary in itself. As a law we are subject to it without consulting self-love; as imposed on us by ourselves, it is a consequence of our will. In the former respect it is analogous to fear and in the latter to inclination. All respect for a person is only respect for the law (of righteousness, etc.) of which the person provides an example. Because we see the improvement of our talents as a duty, we think of a person of talent as the example of a law, as it were (the law that we should by practice become like him in his talents), and that constitutes our respect. All so-called moral interest consists solely in respect for the law.

ing any regard to the effect experienced from it, in order that this will may be called good absolutely and without qualification? As I have deprived the will of every impulse which could arise for it from obedience to any particular law, there remains nothing but the universal conformity of its actions to law in general, which alone is to serve the will as a principle, that is, I am never to act otherwise than so *that I could also will that my maxim should become a universal law*. Here, now, it is the simple lawfulness in general, without assuming any particular law applicable to certain actions, that serves the will as its principle, and must so serve it if duty is not to be a vain delusion and a chimerical notion. The common reason of human beings in its practical judgments perfectly coincides with this, and always has in view the principle here suggested.

Let the question be, for example: May I when in distress make a promise with the intention not to keep it? I readily distinguish here between the two significations which the question may have: whether it is prudent or whether it is right to make such a false promise. The former may undoubtedly often be the case. I see clearly indeed that it is not enough to extricate myself from a present difficulty by means of this subterfuge, but it must be well considered whether there may not hereafter spring from this lie much greater inconvenience than that from which I now seek to free myself, and as, with all my supposed *cunning*, the consequences cannot be so easily foreseen but that credit once lost may be much more injurious to me than any mischief which I seek to avoid at present, it should be considered whether it would not be *more prudent* to act herein according to a universal maxim, and to make it a habit to promise nothing except with the intention of keeping it. But it is soon clear to me that such a maxim will still only be based on the fear of consequences. Now it is a wholly different thing to be truthful from duty than to be so from apprehension of injurious consequences. In the first case, the very notion of the action already implies a law for me; in the second case, I must first look about elsewhere to see what results may be combined with it which would affect myself. For to deviate from the principle of duty is beyond all doubt evil; but to be unfaithful to my maxim of prudence may often be very advantageous to me, although to abide by it is certainly safer. The shortest way, however, and an unerring one, to discover the answer to this question whether a lying promise is consistent with duty, is to ask myself: Would I be content that my maxim (to extricate myself from difficulty by a false promise) should hold as a universal law, for myself as well as for others? And would I be able to say to myself, "Everyone may make a deceitful promise when he finds himself in a difficulty from which he cannot otherwise extricate himself"? Then I presently become aware that, while I can will the lie, I can by no means will that lying become a universal law. For with such a law there would be no promises at all, since it would be in vain to profess my intention in regard to my future actions to those who would not believe this profession, or if they over-hastily did so, would pay me back in my own coin. Hence my maxim, as soon as it should be made a universal law, would necessarily destroy itself.

I do not, therefore, need any far-reaching penetration to discern what I have to do in order that my volition may be morally good. Inexperienced in the course of the world, incapable of being prepared for all its contingencies, I only ask myself: Can you also will that your maxim should be a universal law? If not, then it must be rejected, and that not because of a disadvantage accruing from it to myself or even to others, but because it cannot enter as a principle into a possible universal legislation, and reason extorts from me immediate respect for such legislation. I do not indeed as yet *discern* on what this respect is based (this the philosopher may inquire), but at least I understand this—that it is an estimation of the worth which far outweighs all worth of what is recommended by inclination, and that the necessity of acting from *pure* respect for the practical law is what constitutes duty, to which every other motive must give place because it is the condition of a will that is good *in itself*, and the worth of such a will is above everything.

Thus, then, without quitting the moral cognition of common human reason, we have arrived at its principle. And although, no doubt, common human reason does not conceive it in such an abstract and universal form, yet it really always has it before its eyes and uses it as the standard of judgment. Here it would be easy to show how, with this compass in hand, common human reason is well able to distinguish, in every case that occurs, what is good, what evil, conformably to duty or inconsistent with it, if, without in the least teaching it anything new, we only, like Socrates,[14] direct its attention to the principle it itself employs; and that, therefore, we do not need science and philosophy to know what we should do to be honest and good, yes, even to be wise and virtuous. Indeed we might well have conjectured beforehand that the acquaintance with what every human being is obligated to do, and therefore also to know, would be within the reach of every human being, even the commonest. Here we cannot withhold admiration when we see how great an advantage practical judgment has over the theoretical in the common human understanding. In the latter, if common reason ventures to depart from the laws of experience and from the perceptions of the senses, it falls into mere inconceivabilities and self-contradictions, at least into a chaos of uncertainty, obscurity, and instability. But in the practical sphere it is just when the common understanding excludes all sensible incentives from practical laws that its power of judgment begins to show itself to advantage. It then becomes even subtle, whether it be that it quibbles with its own conscience or with other claims regarding what is to be called right, or whether it desires for its own instruction to determine honestly the worth of its actions; and, in the latter case, it may even have as good a hope of hitting the mark as any philosopher whatever can promise himself. Indeed it is almost more sure of doing so, because the philosopher cannot have any other principle, while he may easily perplex his judgment by a multitude of considerations foreign to the matter, and so turn aside from the right way. Would it not therefore be wiser in moral concerns

---

14 This ancient Athenian is famous for (among other things) a technique of teaching—today called the "Socratic method"—in which the master, instead of imparting knowledge, asks a sequence of questions to prompt the pupil to reflect on their own ideas and to uncover knowledge they already have within themselves. Because of this technique, Socrates compared himself to a midwife helping people give birth to philosophical ideas.

to acquiesce in the judgment of common reason, or at most only to call in philosophy for the purpose of rendering the system of morals more complete and intelligible, and its rules more convenient for use (especially disputation), but not so as to draw off the common understanding from its happy simplicity, or bring it by means of philosophy into a new path of inquiry and instruction?

Innocence is indeed a glorious thing; but, on the other hand, it is very sad that it cannot well maintain itself, and is easily seduced. On this account even wisdom—which otherwise consists more in conduct than in knowledge—still has need of science, not in order to learn from it, but to secure for its precepts admission and permanence. Against all the commands of duty which reason represents to the human being as so deserving of respect, he feels in himself a powerful counterweight in his needs and inclinations, the entire satisfaction of which he sums up under the name of happiness. Now reason issues commands unyieldingly, without promising anything to the inclinations, and, as it were, with disregard and contempt for these claims, which are so impetuous and at the same time so plausible, and which will not allow themselves to be suppressed by any command. Hence there arises a *natural dialectic*,[15] that is, a disposition to argue against these strict laws of duty and to question their validity, or at least their purity and strictness; and if possible, to make them more compatible with our wishes and inclinations, that is to say, to corrupt them at their very source and entirely destroy their worth[16]—a thing which even common practical reason cannot ultimately approve.

Thus is the *common human reason* compelled to go out of its sphere and to take a step into the field of *practical philosophy*, not to satisfy any speculative need (which never occurs to it as long as it is content to be mere sound reason), but rather on practical grounds, in order to attain in it information and clear instruction respecting the source of its principle, and the correct determination of it in opposition to the maxims which are based on wants and inclinations, so that it may escape from the perplexity of opposite claims, and not run the risk of losing all genuine moral principles through the equivocation into which it easily falls. Thus, when practical reason cultivates itself, there insensibly arises in it a dialectic which forces it to seek aid in philosophy, just as happens to it in its theoretical use; and in this case, therefore, as well as in the other, it will find rest nowhere but in a thorough critical examination of our reason.

Second Section

Transition from Popular Moral Philosophy to the Metaphysics of Morals

If we have so far drawn our notion of duty from the common use of our practical reason, it is by no means to be inferred that we have treated it as an empirical concept. On the contrary, if we attend to the experience of human conduct, we meet frequent and, as we ourselves allow, just complaints that one cannot find a single, certain example of the disposition to act from pure duty. Although many things are done *in conformity with* what *duty* prescribes, it is nevertheless always doubtful whether they are done strictly *from duty*, and so have moral worth. Hence there have at all times been philosophers who have altogether denied that this disposition actually exists at all in human actions, and have ascribed everything to a more or less refined self-love. Not that they have on that account questioned the soundness of the conception of morality; on the contrary, they spoke with sincere regret of the frailty and impurity of human nature, which, though noble enough to take as its rule an idea so worthy of respect, is yet too weak to follow it; and employs reason, which ought to give it the law, only for the purpose of providing for the interest of the inclinations, whether singly or at the best in the greatest possible harmony with one another.

In fact, it is absolutely impossible to make out by experience with complete certainty a single case in which the maxim of an action, however right in itself, rested simply on moral grounds and on the representation of duty. Sometimes it happens that with the sharpest self-examination we can find nothing beside the

---

15   In Kant's special usage, a dialectic is the "logic of illusion," a process of fallacious or misleading reasoning.

16   For Kant, "dignity" is a technical term meaning something like *intrinsic worth*.

moral principle of duty which could have been power-ful enough to move us to this or that action and to so great a sacrifice; yet we cannot from this infer with certainty that it was not really some secret impulse of self-love, under the false appearance of duty, that was the actual determining cause of the will. We like then to flatter ourselves by falsely taking credit for a more noble motive; whereas in fact we can never, even by the strictest examination, get completely behind the secret incentives, since, when the question is of moral worth, it is not with the actions which we see that we are concerned, but with those inward principles of them which we do not see.

Moreover, we cannot better serve the wishes of those who ridicule all morality as mere chimera of human imagination overstepping itself from vanity, than by conceding to them that concepts of duty must be drawn only from experience (as, from indolence, people are ready to think is the case with all other con-cepts also); for this is to prepare for them a certain tri-umph. I am willing to admit out of love for humanity that even most of our actions are in conformity with duty; but if we look closer at them we everywhere come upon the dear self which is always prominent; and it is this they have in view, and not the strict com-mand of duty, which would often require self-denial. Without being an enemy of virtue, a cool observer, one that does not mistake the wish for good, however lively, for its reality, may sometimes doubt whether true virtue is actually found anywhere in the world, and this especially as years increase and the judgment is partly made wiser by experience, and partly also more acute in observation. This being so, nothing can secure us from falling away altogether from our ideas of duty, or maintain in the soul a well-grounded respect for its law, but the clear conviction that al-though there should never have been actions which really sprang from such pure sources, yet whether this or that takes place is not at all the question; but that reason itself, independent of all experience, ordains what ought to take place, that accordingly actions of which perhaps the world has so far never given an example, the feasibility even of which might be very much doubted by one who founds everything on ex-perience, are nevertheless inflexibly commanded by reason; that, for example, even though there might

never have been a sincere friend, yet not a whit less is pure sincerity in friendship required of everyone, because, prior to all experience, this duty is involved (as duty in general) in the idea of a reason determining the will by *a priori* principles.

When we add further that, unless we deny that the notion of morality has any truth or reference to any possible object, we must admit that its law must be valid, not merely for human beings, but for all *rational beings as such*, not merely under certain contingent conditions or with exceptions, but with *absolute necessity*, then it is clear that no experience could enable us to infer even the possibility of such apodictic[17] laws. For with what right could we bring into unbounded respect as a universal precept for all rational nature that which perhaps holds only under the contingent conditions of humanity? Or how could laws of the determination of *our* will be regarded as laws of the determination of the will of rational beings as such, and for us only as such, if they were merely empirical and did not take their origin wholly *a priori* from pure but practical reason?

Nor could anything be more fatal to morality than that we should wish to derive it from examples. For every example of it that is set before me must first it-self be judged by principles of morality, as to whether it is worthy to serve as an original example, that is, as a model; but by no means can it authoritatively furnish the conception of morality. Even the Holy One of the Gospels[18] must first be compared with our ideal of moral perfection before we can recog-nize Him as such; and so He says of Himself, "Why do you call Me (whom you see) good; none is good (the model of good) but God only (whom you do not see)?"[19] But whence have we the conception of God as the supreme good? Simply from the *idea* of moral perfection, which reason frames *a priori* and connects inseparably with the notion of a free will. Imitation finds no place at all in morality, and examples serve only for encouragement, that is, they put beyond all doubt the feasibility of what the law commands, they make visible that which the practical rule expresses

---

17   Necessarily true, clearly demonstrated or established.
18   Jesus Christ.
19   Matthew 19:17.

more generally, but they can never authorize us to set aside the true original which lies in reason, and to guide ourselves by examples.

If there is no genuine supreme principle of morality but what must rest simply on pure reason, independent on all experience, I think it is not necessary even to ask the question whether it is good to exhibit these concepts in their generality (*in abstracto*[20]) as they are established *a priori* along with the principles belonging to them, if our knowledge is to be distinguished from the *common* and to be called philosophical. In our times indeed this might perhaps be necessary; for if we collected votes, whether pure rational knowledge separated from everything empirical, that is to say, a metaphysics of morals, or whether popular practical philosophy is to be preferred, it is easy to guess which side would predominate.

This descending to popular notions is certainly very commendable if the ascent to the principles of pure reason has first taken place and been satisfactorily accomplished. This implies that we first *ground* the doctrine of morals on metaphysics, and then, when it is firmly established, procure *entry* for it by giving it a popular character. But it is quite absurd to try to be popular in the first inquiry, on which the soundness of the principles depends. It is not only that this procedure can never lay claim to the very rare merit of a true *philosophical popularity*, since there is no art in being intelligible if one renounces all thoroughness of insight; but also it produces a disgusting medley of compiled observations and half-reasoned principles. Shallow minds enjoy this because it can be used for everyday chat, but the sagacious find in it only confusion, and being unsatisfied and unable to help themselves, they turn away their eyes, while philosophers, who see quite well through this delusion, are little listened to when they call people off for a time from this pretended popularity in order that they might be rightfully popular after they have attained a definite insight.

We need only to look at the attempts of moralists in that favorite fashion, and we will find at one time the special constitution of human nature (including, however, the idea of a rational nature generally), at one time perfection, at another time happiness, here moral sense, there fear of God, a little of this and a little of that, in marvelous mixture, without its occurring to them to ask whether the principles of morality are to be sought in the knowledge of human nature at all (which we can have only from experience); and, if this is not so—if these principles are to be found altogether *a priori*, free from everything empirical, in pure rational concepts only, and nowhere else, not even in the smallest degree—then rather to adopt the method of making this a separate inquiry, as pure practical philosophy, or (if one may use a name so decried) as metaphysics[21] of morals, to bring it by itself to completeness, and to require the public, which wishes for popular treatment, to await the outcome of this undertaking.

Such a metaphysics of morals, completely isolated, not mixed with any anthropology, theology, physics, or hyperphysics, or still less with occult qualities (which we might call hypophysical),[22] is not only an indispensable substratum of all sound theoretical knowledge of duties, but is at the same time a desideratum[23] of the highest importance to the actual fulfilment of their precepts. For the pure thought of duty, unmixed with any foreign addition of empirical attractions, and, in a word, the thought of the moral law, exercises on the human heart, by way of reason alone (which first becomes aware with this that it can of itself be practical), an influence so

---

20   "In the abstract."

21   [Author's note] If one wishes, the pure philosophy (metaphysics) of morals can be distinguished from the applied (i.e., applied to human nature), just as pure mathematics and pure logic are distinguished from applied mathematics and applied logic. By this designation one is immediately reminded that moral principles are not founded on the peculiarities of human nature but must stand of themselves *a priori*, and that from such principles practical rules for every rational nature, and accordingly for man, must be derivable.

22   Hyperphysics is that which goes beyond physics. The term is usually used in a similar way as "paranormal" or "supernatural." "Hypophysics" is a coinage meaning that which lies *below* physics.

23   Something very much needed or desired.

much more powerful than all other incentives[24] which may be derived from the field of experience that in the consciousness of its dignity it despises the latter, and can by degrees become their master; whereas a mixed doctrine of morals, compounded partly of incentives drawn from feelings and inclinations, and partly also of conceptions of reason, must make the mind waver between motives which cannot be brought under any principle, which lead to good only by mere accident, and very often also to evil.

From what has been said, it is clear that all moral concepts have their seat and origin completely *a priori* in reason, and that, moreover, in the commonest reason just as truly as in that which is in the highest degree speculative; that they cannot be obtained by abstraction from any empirical, and therefore merely contingent, cognitions; that it is just this purity of their origin that makes them worthy to serve as our supreme practical principle, and that just in proportion as we add anything empirical, we detract from their genuine influence and from the absolute value of actions; that it is not only of the greatest necessity, in a purely speculative point of view, but is also

of the greatest practical importance, to derive these concepts and laws from pure reason, to present them pure and unmixed, and even to determine the compass of this practical or pure rational cognition, that is, to determine the whole faculty of pure practical reason; and, in doing so, we must not make its principles dependent on the particular nature of human reason, though in speculative philosophy this may be permitted, or may even at times be necessary; but since moral laws ought to hold good for every rational being, we must derive them from the universal concept of a rational being. In this way, although for its *application* to human beings morality has need of anthropology, yet, in the first instance, we must treat it in itself (a thing which in such distinct branches of science is easily done); knowing well that, unless we are in possession of this, it would not only be vain to determine the moral element of duty in right actions for purposes of speculative criticism, but it would be impossible to base morals on their genuine principles, even for common practical purposes, especially for moral instruction, so as to produce pure moral dispositions, and to engraft them on people's minds to the promotion of the greatest possible good in the world.

But in order that in this study we may not merely advance by the natural steps from the common moral judgment (in this case very worthy of respect) to the philosophical, as has been already done, but also from a popular philosophy, which goes no further than it can reach by groping with the help of examples, to metaphysics (which does not allow itself to be checked by anything empirical and, as it must measure the whole extent of this kind of rational knowledge, goes as far as ideal conceptions, where even examples fail us), we must follow and clearly describe the practical faculty of reason, from the general rules of its determination to the point where the concept of duty springs from it.

Everything in nature works according to laws. Rational beings alone have the capacity to act *in accordance with the representation* of laws—that is, according to principles, that is, have a *will*. Since the deduction of actions from principles requires *reason*, the will is nothing but practical reason. If reason infallibly determines the will, then the actions of such a

---

24 [Author's note] I have a letter from the late excellent Sulzer [Johann Georg Sulzer (1720–1790), translator of Hume into German and director of the philosophical division of the Berlin Academy] in which he asks me why the theories of virtue accomplish so little even though they contain so much that is convincing to reason. My answer was delayed in order that I might make it complete. The answer is only that the teachers themselves have not completely clarified their concepts, and when they wish to make up for this by hunting in every quarter for motives to the morally good so as to make their physic right strong, they spoil it. For the commonest observation shows that if we imagine an act of honesty performed with a steadfast soul and sundered from all view to any advantage in this or another world and even under the greatest temptations of need or allurement, it far surpasses and eclipses any similar action which was affected in the least by any foreign incentive; it elevates the soul and arouses the wish to be able to act in this way. Even moderately young children feel this impression, and one should never represent duties to them in any other way.

being which are recognized as objectively necessary[25] are subjectively necessary also, that is, the will is a capacity to choose *that only* which reason independent of inclination recognizes as practically necessary, that is, as good. But if reason of itself does not sufficiently determine the will, if the latter is subject also to subjective conditions (particular incentives) which do not always coincide with the objective conditions, in a word, if the will does not *in itself* completely accord with reason (which is actually the case with human beings), then the actions which objectively are recognized as necessary are subjectively contingent, and the determination of such a will according to objective laws is *necessitation*, that is to say, the relation of the objective laws to a will that is not thoroughly good is conceived as the determination of the will of a rational being by principles of reason, but which the will from its nature does not necessarily follow.

The conception of an objective principle, in so far as it is obligatory for a will, is called a command (of reason), and the formula of the command is called an **imperative**.

All imperatives are expressed through an *ought*, and thereby indicate the relation of an objective law of reason to a will which from its subjective constitution is not necessarily determined by it (a necessitation). They say that something would be good to do or to forbear, but they say it to a will which does not always do a thing because it is represented to be good to do it. That is *practically good*, however, which determines the will by means of the representations of reason, and consequently not from subjective causes, but objectively, that is, on principles which are valid for every rational being as such. It is distinguished from the agreeable as that which influences the will only by means of feeling from merely subjective causes, valid only for the senses of this or that one, and not as a principle of reason which holds for everyone.[26]

A perfectly good will would therefore be equally subject to objective laws (viz. laws of good), but could not be conceived as *necessitated* thereby to act lawfully, because of itself from its subjective constitution it can only be determined by the conception of good. Therefore no imperatives hold for the Divine will, or in general for a *holy* will; *ought* is here out of place because the volition is already of itself necessarily in unison with the law. Therefore imperatives are only formulae to express the relation of objective laws of all volition to the subjective imperfection of the will of this or that rational being, for example, a human will.

Now all imperatives command either *hypothetically* or *categorically*. The former represent the practical necessity of a possible action as means to something else that is willed (or at least which one might possibly will). The categorical imperative would be that which represented an action as necessary of itself without reference to another end, that is, as objectively necessary.

Since every practical law represents a possible action as good, and on this account, for a subject who is practically determinable by reason, as necessary, all imperatives are formulae determining an action which is necessary according to the principle of a will good in some respects. If now the action is good only as a means *to something else*, then the imperative is

---

25   As determined by the objective principles of rationality.

26   [Author's note] The dependence of the faculty of desire on sensations is called inclination, and inclination always indicates a need. The dependence of a contingently determinable will on principles of reason, however, is called interest. An interest is present only in a dependent will which is not of itself always in accord with reason; in the divine will we cannot conceive of an interest. But even the human will can take an interest in something without thereby acting from interest. The former means the practical interest in the action; the latter, the pathological interest in the object of the action. The former indicates only the dependence of the will on principles of reason in themselves, while the latter indicates dependence on the principles of reason for the purpose of inclination, since reason gives only the practical rule by which the needs of inclination are to be aided. In the former case the action interests me, and in the latter the object of the action (so far as it is pleasant for me) interests me. In the First Section we have seen that, in the case of an action done from duty, no regard must be given to the interest in the object, but merely to the action itself and its principle in reason (i.e., the law).

hypothetical; if it is conceived as good *in itself* and consequently as being necessarily the principle of a will which of itself conforms to reason, then it is *categorical*.

Thus the imperative declares what action possible by me would be good, and presents the practical rule in relation to a will which does not forthwith perform an action simply because it is good, whether because the subject does not always know that it is good, or because, even if it know this, yet its maxims might be opposed to the objective principles of practical reason.

Accordingly the hypothetical imperative only says that the action is good for some purpose, *possible* or *actual*. In the first case, it is a **problematic**, in the second an **assertoric**, practical principle. The categorical imperative which declares an action to be objectively necessary in itself without reference to any purpose, without any other end, is valid as an **apodictic** (practical) principle.

Whatever is possible only by the power of some rational being may also be conceived as a possible purpose of some will; and therefore the principles of action as regards the means necessary to attain some possible purpose are in fact infinitely numerous. All sciences have a practical part consisting of problems expressing that some end is possible for us, and of imperatives directing how it may be attained. These may, therefore, be called in general imperatives of **skill**. Here there is no question whether the end is rational and good, but only what one must do in order to attain it. The precepts for the physician to make his patient thoroughly healthy, and for a poisoner to ensure certain death, are of equal value in this respect, that each serves to effect its purpose perfectly. Since in early youth it cannot be known what ends are likely to occur to us in the course of life, parents seek to have their children taught a *great many things*, and provide for their *skill* in the use of means for all sorts of *discretionary* ends, of none of which can they determine whether it may not perhaps hereafter be an object to their pupil, but which it is at all events *possible* that he might aim at; and this anxiety is so great that they commonly neglect to form and correct their children's judgment of the value of the things which may be chosen as ends.

There is *one* end, however, which may be assumed to be actually such to all rational beings (so far as imperatives apply to them, viz. as dependent beings), and therefore, one purpose which they not merely *may* have, but which we may with certainty assume that they all actually *do have* by a natural necessity, and this is *happiness*. The hypothetical imperative which expresses the practical necessity of an action as means to the advancement of happiness is *assertoric*. We are not to present it as necessary for an uncertain and merely possible purpose, but for a purpose which we may presuppose with certainty and *a priori* in every human being, because it belongs to his being. Now skill in the choice of means to his own greatest well-being may be called *prudence*,[27] in the narrowest sense. And thus the imperative which refers to the choice of means to one's own happiness, that is, the precept of prudence, is still always *hypothetical*; the action is not commanded absolutely, but only as means to another purpose.

Finally, there is an imperative which commands a certain conduct immediately, without having as its condition any other purpose to be attained by it. This imperative is **categorical**. It concerns not the matter of the action, or its intended result, but its form and the principle of which it is itself a result; and what is essentially good in it consists in the mental disposition, let the consequence be what it may. This imperative may be called that of **morality**.

There is a marked distinction also between the volitions on these three sorts of principles in the *dissimilarity* of the necessitation of the will. In order to mark this difference more clearly, I think they would be most suitably named in their order if we said they

---

27 [Author's note] The word "prudence" may be taken in two senses, and it may bear the names of prudence with reference to things of the world and private prudence. The former sense means the skill of a man in having an influence on others so as to use them for his own purposes. The latter is the ability to unite all these purposes to his own lasting advantage. The worth of the first is finally reduced to the latter, and of one who is prudent in the former sense but not in the latter we might better say that he is clever and cunning yet, on the whole, imprudent.

are either *rules* of skill, or *counsels* of prudence, or *commands* (*laws*) of morality. For it is law only that involves the concept of an *unconditional* and objective necessity, which is consequently universally valid; and commands are laws which must be obeyed, that is, must be followed, even in opposition to inclination. *Counsels*, indeed, involve necessity, but one which can only hold under a contingent subjective condition, viz., they depend on whether this or that human being counts this or that as part of his happiness; the categorical imperative, on the contrary, is not limited by any condition, and as being absolutely, although practically, necessary may be quite properly called a command. We might also call the first kind of imperatives *technical* (belonging to art), the second *pragmatic*[28] (belonging to welfare), and the third *moral* (belonging to free conduct as such, that is, to morals).

Now arises the question, how are all these imperatives possible? This question does not seek to know how we can conceive the performance of the action which the imperative ordains, but merely how we can conceive the necessitation of the will which the imperative expresses. No special explanation is needed to show how an imperative of skill is possible. Whoever wills the end wills also (so far as reason has decisive influence on his action) the means in his power which are indispensably necessary to it. This proposition is, as regards the volition, analytic;[29]

for in willing an object as my effect there is already thought the causality of myself as an acting cause, that is to say, the use of the means; and the imperative educes from the concept of a volition of an end the concept of actions necessary to this end. Synthetic propositions must no doubt be employed in defining the means to a proposed end; but they do not concern the principle, the act of the will, but the object and its realization. For example, that in order to bisect a line on an unerring principle I must draw from its extremities two intersecting arcs; this no doubt is taught by mathematics only in synthetic propositions; but if I know that it is only by this process that the intended operation can be performed, then to say that if I fully will the operation, I also will the action required for it, is an analytic proposition; for it is one and the same thing to represent something as an effect which I can produce in a certain way, and to represent myself as acting in this way.

If it were only equally easy to give a definite conception of happiness, the imperatives of prudence would correspond exactly with those of skill, and would likewise be analytic. For in this case as in that, it could be said whoever wills the end wills also (necessarily in accordance with reason) the indispensable means thereto which are in his power. But, unfortunately, the notion of happiness is so indeterminate that although every human being wishes to attain it, yet he never can say definitely and consistently what it is that he really wishes and wills. The reason for this is that all the elements which belong to the concept of happiness are altogether empirical, that is, they must be borrowed from experience, and nevertheless the idea of happiness requires an absolute whole, a maximum of welfare in my present and all future circumstances. Now it is impossible that the most clear-sighted and at the same time most powerful being (supposed finite) should frame for himself a definite conception of what he really wills in this. If he wills riches, how much anxiety, envy, and snares might he not thereby draw upon his shoulders? If he wills knowledge and discernment, perhaps it might prove to be only an eye

28   [Author's note] It seems to me that the proper meaning of the word "pragmatic" could be most accurately defined in this way. For sanctions which properly flow not from the law of states as necessary statutes but from provision for the general welfare are called pragmatic. A history is pragmatically composed when it teaches prudence (i.e., instructs the world how it could provide for its interest better than, or at least as well as, has been done in the past).

29   Something is analytically true if it is true in virtue of the meanings involved, particularly in cases where, as Kant put it, the concept of the predicate is "contained in" the concept of the subject (e.g., "All aunts are female" or "This poodle is a dog"). Synthetic propositions, according to Kant, are simply propositions that are not analytic: thus, in synthetic propositions, the

predicate provides *new* information about the subject (e.g., "My aunt is called Dora" or "Poodles come in many colors").

so much sharper to show him so much the more fearfully the evils that are now concealed from him and that cannot be avoided, or to impose more wants on his desires, which already give him concern enough. Would he have long life? Who guarantees to him that it would not be a long misery? Would he at least have health? How often has uneasiness of the body restrained from excesses into which perfect health would have allowed one to fall, and so on? In short, he is unable, on any principle, to determine with certainty what would make him truly happy; because to do so he would need to be omniscient. We cannot therefore act on any definite principles to secure happiness, but only on empirical counsels, for example, of regimen, frugality, courtesy, reserve, etc., which experience teaches do, on the average, most promote well-being. Hence it follows that the imperatives of prudence do not, strictly speaking, command at all, that is, they cannot present actions objectively as practically *necessary*; that they are rather to be regarded as counsels (*consilia*) than precepts (*praecepta*) of reason, that the problem to determine certainly and universally what action would promote the happiness of a rational being is completely insoluble, and consequently no imperative respecting it is possible which would, in the strict sense, command him to do what makes him happy; because happiness is not an ideal of reason but of imagination, resting solely on empirical grounds, and it is vain to expect that these should determine an action by which one could attain the totality of a series of consequences which is really endless. This imperative of prudence would, however, be an analytic proposition if we assume that the means to happiness could be certainly assigned; for it is distinguished from the imperative of skill only by this, that in the latter the end is merely *possible*, in the former it is *given*; as, however, both only ordain the means to that which we suppose to be willed as an end, it follows that the imperative which ordains the willing of the means to him who wills the end is in both cases analytic. Thus there is no difficulty in regard to the possibility of an imperative of this kind either.

On the other hand, the question, how the imperative of *morality* is possible, is undoubtedly one, the only one, demanding a solution, as this is not at all hypothetical, and the objective necessity which it presents cannot rest on any hypothesis, as is the case with the hypothetical imperatives. Only here we must never leave out of consideration that we *cannot* make out *by means of any example*, in other words, empirically, whether there is such an imperative at all; but it is rather to be feared that all those which seem to be categorical may yet be at bottom hypothetical. For instance, when the precept is: "You ought not to promise deceitfully," and it is assumed that the necessity of this is not a mere counsel to avoid some other ill, so that it should mean: "You shall not make a lying promise, lest if it become known you should destroy your credit," but that an action of this kind must be regarded as evil in itself, so that the imperative of the prohibition is categorical; then we cannot show with certainty in any example that the will was determined merely by the law, without any other incentives, although it may appear to be so. For it is always possible that fear of disgrace, perhaps also obscure dread of other dangers, may have a secret influence on the will. Who can prove by experience the non-existence of a cause when all that experience tells us is that we do not perceive it? But in such a case the so-called moral imperative, which as such appears to be categorical and unconditional, would in reality be only a pragmatic precept, drawing our attention to our own interests, and merely teaching us to take these into consideration.

We will therefore have to investigate *a priori* the possibility of a *categorical* imperative, as we have not in this case the advantage of its reality being given in experience, so that [the elucidation of]its possibility should be requisite only for its explanation, not for its establishment. In the meantime it may be discerned beforehand that the categorical imperative alone has the purport of a practical law; and the rest may indeed be called *principles* of the will but not laws, since whatever is only necessary for the attainment of some discretionary purpose may be considered as in itself contingent, and we can at any time be free from the precept if we give up the purpose; on the contrary, the unconditional command leaves the will no liberty to choose the opposite, consequently it alone carries with it that necessity which we require of a law.

Secondly, in the case of this categorical imperative or law of morality, the difficulty (of describing its possibility) is a very profound one. It is an *a priori* synthetic practical proposition;[30] and as there is so much difficulty in discerning the possibility of speculative propositions of this kind, it may readily be supposed that the difficulty will be no less with the practical.

In this problem we will first inquire whether the mere concept of a categorical imperative may not perhaps supply us also with the formula of it, containing the proposition which alone can be a categorical imperative; for even if we know the tenor of such an absolute command, yet how it is possible will require further special and laborious study, which we postpone to the last section.

When I conceive a hypothetical imperative, in general I do not know beforehand what it will contain until I am given the condition. But when I conceive a categorical imperative, I know at once what it contains. For as the imperative contains besides the law only the necessity that the maxims[31] shall conform to this law, while the law contains no conditions restricting it, there remains nothing but the general statement that the maxim of the action should conform to universal law, and it is this conformity alone that the imperative properly represents as necessary.

There is therefore but one categorical imperative, namely, this: *Act only on that maxim whereby you can at the same time will that it become a universal law.*[32]

Now if all imperatives of duty can be deduced from this one imperative as their principle, then, although it should remain undecided whether what is called duty is not merely a vain notion, yet at least we shall be able to show what we understand by it and what this notion means.

Since the universality of the law according to which effects are produced constitutes what is properly called *nature* in the most general sense (as to form)—that is, the existence of things so far as it is determined by general laws—the imperative of duty may be expressed thus: *Act as if the maxim of your action were to become by your will a **universal law of nature**.*[33]

We will now enumerate a few duties, adopting the usual division of them into duties to ourselves and duties to others, and into perfect and imperfect duties.[34]

1. Someone reduced to despair by a series of misfortunes feels wearied of life, but is still so far in possession of his reason that he can ask himself whether it would not be contrary to his duty to himself take his own life. Now he inquires whether the maxim of his action could become a universal law of nature. His maxim is: From self love I adopt it as my principle to shorten my life when its longer duration is likely to bring more ill than satisfaction. It is asked then

---

30 [Author's note] I connect a priori, and hence necessarily, the action with the will without supposing as a condition that there is any inclination [to the action] (though I do so only objectively, i.e., under the Idea of a reason which would have complete power over all subjective motives). This is, therefore, a practical proposition which does not analytically derive the willing of an action from some other volition already presupposed (for we do not have such a perfect will); it rather connects it directly with the concept of the will of a rational being as something which is not contained within it.

31 [Author's note] A maxim is the subjective principle of acting and must be distinguished from the objective principle (i.e., the practical law). The former contains the practical rule which reason determines according to the conditions of the subject (often his ignorance or inclinations) and is thus the principle according to which the subject acts. The law, on the other hand, is the objective principle valid for every rational being, and the principle by which it ought to act, i.e., an imperative.

32 This formulation of the categorical imperative is often called the Formula of Universal Law.

33 This is often called the Formula of the Law of Nature.

34 [Author's note] It must be noted here that I reserve the division of duties for a future *Metaphysics of Morals* and that the division here stands as only an arbitrary one (chosen in order to arrange my examples). For the rest, by a perfect duty I here understand a duty which permits no exception in the interest of inclination; thus I have not merely outer but also inner perfect duties. This runs contrary to the usage adopted in the schools, but I am not disposed to defend it here because it is all one to my purpose whether this is conceded or not.

simply whether this principle founded on self-love can become a universal law of nature. Now we can see at once that a system of nature of which it should be a law to destroy life by means of the very feeling whose vocation it is to impel to the improvement of life would contradict itself, and therefore could not exist as a system of nature; hence that maxim cannot possibly exist as a universal law of nature, and consequently would be wholly inconsistent with the supreme principle of all duty.

2. Another finds himself forced by necessity to borrow money. He knows that he will not be able to repay it, but sees also that nothing will be lent to him unless he promises firmly to repay it within in a determinate time. He wants to make this promise, but he has still so much conscience as to ask himself: Is it not unlawful and inconsistent with duty to get out of a difficulty this way? Suppose, however, that he resolves to do so, then the maxim of his action would be expressed thus: When I think myself in want of money, I will borrow money and promise to repay it, although I know that I never can do so. Now this principle of self-love or of one's own advantage may perhaps be consistent with my whole future welfare; but the question now is, Is it right? I change then the suggestion of self-love into a universal law, and state the question thus: How would it be if my maxim were a universal law? Then I see at once that it could never hold as a universal law of nature, but would necessarily contradict itself. For supposing it to be a universal law that everyone when he thinks himself in a difficulty should be able to promise whatever he pleases, with the purpose of not keeping his promise, the promise itself would become impossible, as well as the end that he might have in view in it, since no one would consider that anything was promised to him, but would ridicule all such statements as vain pretenses.

3. A third finds in himself a talent which with the help of some culture might make him a useful human being in many respects. But he finds himself in comfortable circumstances and prefers to indulge in pleasure rather than to take pain in enlarging and improving his fortunate natural predispositions. He asks, however, whether his maxim of neglect of his natural gifts, besides agreeing with his inclination to indulgence, agrees also with what is called duty. He

sees then that a system of nature could indeed subsist with such a universal law, although human beings (like the South Sea islanders[35]) should let their talents rust and resolve to devote their lives merely to idleness, amusement, and propagation of their species—in a word, to enjoyment; but he cannot possibly **will** that this should be a universal law of nature, or be implanted in us as such by a natural instinct. For as a rational being, he necessarily wills that his faculties be developed, since they serve him, and have been given him, for all sorts of purposes.

4. Yet a fourth, who is in prosperity, while he sees that others have to contend with great wretchedness and that he could help them, thinks: What concern is it of mine? Let everyone be as happy as heaven pleases, or as he can make himself; I will take nothing from him nor even envy him, only I do not wish to contribute anything to his welfare or to his assistance in need! Now no doubt, if such a mode of thinking were a universal law, the human race might very well subsist, and doubtless even better than in a state in which everyone talks of sympathy and good-will, or even takes care occasionally to put it into practice, but, on the other side, also cheats when he can, betrays the rights of human beings, or otherwise violates them. But although it is possible that a universal law of nature might exist in accordance with that maxim, it is impossible to **will** that such a principle should have the universal validity of a law of nature. For a will which resolved this would contradict itself, inasmuch as many cases might occur in which one would have need of the love and sympathy of others, and in which, by such a law of nature, sprung from his own will, he would deprive himself of all hope of the aid he desires.

These are a few of the many actual duties, or at least what we regard as such, which obviously fall into two classes on the one principle that we have laid down. We must *be able to will* that a maxim of our action should be a universal law. This is the canon of the moral judgment of the action generally. Some actions are of such a character that their maxim cannot without contradiction be even *conceived* as a universal law of nature, far from it being possible that we should

---

35 The inhabitants of the islands of the southern Pacific, such as Polynesia and Micronesia.

will that it *should* be so. In others, this intrinsic impossibility is not found, but still it is impossible to *will* that their maxim should be raised to the universality of a law of nature, since such a will would contradict itself. It is easily seen that the former violate strict or rigorous (inflexible) duty; the latter only wide (meritorious) duty. Thus it has been completely shown by these examples how all duties depend as regards the nature of the obligation (not the object of the action) on the same principle.

If now we attend to ourselves on occasion of any transgression of duty, we will find that we in fact do not will that our maxim should be a universal law, for that is impossible for us; on the contrary, we will that the opposite should remain a universal law, only we assume the liberty of making an *exception* in our own favor or (just for this time only) in favor of our inclination. Consequently, if we considered all cases from one and the same point of view, namely, that of reason, we should find a contradiction in our own will, namely, that a certain principle should be objectively necessary as a universal law, and yet subjectively should not be universal, but admit of exceptions. As, however, we at one moment regard our action from the point of view of a will wholly conformed to reason, and then again look at the same action from the point of view of a will affected by inclination, there is not really any contradiction, but an opposition (*antagonismus*) of inclination to the precept of reason, whereby the universality (*universalitas*) of the principle is changed into a mere generality (*generalitas*), so that the practical principle of reason shall meet the maxim half way. Now, although this cannot be justified in our own impartial judgment, yet it proves that we do really recognize the validity of the categorical imperative and (with all respect for it) only allow ourselves a few exceptions which we think unimportant and forced upon us.

We have thus established at least this much—that if duty is a conception which is to have any import and real legislative authority for our actions, it can only be expressed in categorical, and not at all in hypothetical, imperatives. We have also, which is of great importance, exhibited clearly and definitely for every practical application the content of the categorical imperative, which must contain the principle of all duty if there is such a thing at all. We have not yet, however, advanced so far as to prove *a priori* that there actually is such an imperative, that there is a practical law which commands absolutely of itself and without any other incentive, and that the following of this law is duty.

With the view of attaining to this it is of extreme importance to remember that we must not allow ourselves to think of deducing the reality of this principle from the *particular attributes of human nature*. For duty is to be a practical, unconditional necessity of action; it must therefore hold for all rational beings (to whom an imperative can apply at all), and *for this reason only* be also a law for all human wills. On the contrary, whatever is deduced from the particular natural characteristics of humanity, from certain feelings and propensities, or even, if possible, from any particular tendency proper to human reason, and which need not necessarily hold for the will of every rational being—this may indeed supply us with a maxim but not with a law; with a subjective principle on which we may have a propensity and inclination to act, but not with an objective principle on which we should be *enjoined* to act, even though all our propensities, inclinations, and natural dispositions were opposed to it. In fact, the sublimity and intrinsic dignity of the command in duty are so much the more evident, the less the subjective impulses favor it and the more they oppose it, without being able in the slightest degree to weaken the obligation of the law or to diminish its validity.

Here then we see philosophy brought to a critical position, since it has to be firmly fixed, notwithstanding that it has nothing to support it in heaven or on earth. Here it must show its purity as absolute director of its own laws, not the herald of those which are whispered to it by an implanted sense or who knows what tutelary nature. Although these may be better than nothing, yet they can never afford principles dictated by reason, which must have their source wholly *a priori* and, at the same time, their commanding authority from this, expecting everything from the supremacy of the law and the due respect for it, nothing from inclination, or else condemning the human being to self-contempt and inward abhorrence.

Thus every empirical element is not only quite incapable of being an aid to the principle of morality, but is even highly prejudicial to the purity of morals; for the proper and inestimable worth of an absolutely good will consists just in this, that the principle of action is free from all influence of contingent grounds, which alone experience can furnish. We cannot too much or too often repeat our warning against this lax and even mean habit of thought which seeks for its principle among empirical motives and laws; for human reason in its weariness is glad to rest on this pillow, and in a dream of sweet illusions (in which, instead of Juno, it embraces a cloud[36]) it substitutes for morality a bastard patched up from limbs of various derivation, which looks like anything one chooses to see in it; only not like virtue to one who has once beheld her in her true form.[37]

The question then is this: Is it a necessary law *for all rational beings* that they should always judge their actions by maxims of which they can themselves will that they should serve as universal laws? If there is such a law, then it must be connected (altogether *a priori*) with the very concept of the will of a rational being as such. But in order to discover this connection we must, however reluctantly, take a step into metaphysics, although into a domain of it which is distinct from speculative philosophy—namely, the metaphysics of morals. In a practical philosophy, where it is not the grounds of what *happens* that we have to ascertain, but the laws of what *ought to happen*, even though it never does, that is, objective practical laws, there it is not necessary to inquire into the grounds why anything pleases or displeases, how the pleasure of mere sensation differs from taste, and whether the latter is distinct from a general satisfaction of reason; on what the feeling of pleasure or pain rests, and how from it desires and inclinations arise, and from these again maxims by the cooperation of reason; for all this belongs to an empirical psychology, which would constitute the second part of the doctrine of nature, if we regard physics as the *philosophy of nature*, so far as it is based *on empirical laws*. But there we are concerned with objective practical laws, and consequently with the relation of the will to itself so far as it is determined by reason alone, in which case whatever has reference to anything empirical is necessarily excluded; since if *reason of itself alone* determines the conduct (and it is the possibility of this that we are now investigating), it must necessarily do so *a priori*.

The will is conceived as a capacity of determining itself to action in accordance with the *representation of certain laws*. And such a capacity can be found only in rational beings. Now that which serves the will as the objective ground of its self-determination is the *end*, and if this is assigned by reason alone, it must hold for all rational beings. On the other hand, that which merely contains the ground of possibility of the action of which the effect is the end, this is called the *means*. The subjective ground of the desire is the *incentive*, the objective ground of the volition is the *motive*; hence the distinction between subjective ends which rest on incentives, and objective ends which depend on motives valid for every rational being. Practical principles are *formal* when they abstract from all subjective ends; they are *material* when they assume these, and therefore particular incentives. The ends which a rational being proposes to himself at pleasure as *effects* of his actions (material ends) are all only relative, for it is only their relation to the particular desires of the subject that gives them their worth, which therefore cannot furnish principles universal and necessary for all rational beings and for every volition, that is to say, practical laws. Hence all these relative ends can give rise only to hypothetical imperatives.

---

36 Juno is the Roman name for the Greek goddess Hera, wife and sister of the god Zeus. The human king Ixion was tricked into making love to a cloud, mistaking it for Juno, and so became the father of the "bastard" race of centaurs, half horse and half human. (Ixion was later punished for his attempted seduction by being pinned for eternity to a burning, revolving wheel in Hades.)

37 [Author's note] To behold virtue in her proper form is nothing else than to exhibit morality stripped of all admixture of sensuous things and of every spurious adornment of reward or self-love. How much she then eclipses everything which appears charming to the senses can easily be seen by everyone with the least effort of his reason, if it be not spoiled for all abstraction.

Supposing, however, that there were something *whose existence* has *in itself* an absolute worth, something which, being *an end in itself*, could be a source of definite laws, then in this and this alone would lie the source of a possible categorical imperative, that is, a practical law.

Now I say: the human being and in general every rational being exists as an end[38] in itself, *not merely as a means* to be arbitrarily used by this or that will, but in all his actions, whether they concern himself or other rational beings, must be always regarded at the same time as an end. All objects of the inclinations have only a conditional worth; for if the inclinations and the needs founded on them did not exist, then their object would be without any value. But the inclinations themselves, being sources of needs, are so far from having an absolute worth for which they should be desired that, on the contrary, it must be the universal wish of every rational being to be wholly free from them. Thus the worth of any object which is *to be acquired* by our action is always conditional. Beings whose existence depends not on our will but on nature's, have nevertheless, if they are nonrational beings, only a relative value as means, and are therefore called *things*; rational beings, on the contrary, are called *persons*, because their very nature restricts all choice (and is an object of respect). These, therefore, are not merely subjective ends whose existence has a worth *for us* as an effect of our action, but *objective ends*, that is, things whose existence is an end in itself—an end, moreover, for which no other can be substituted, to which they should serve *merely* as means, for otherwise nothing whatever would possess *absolute worth*; but if all worth were conditioned and therefore contingent, then there would be no supreme practical principle of reason whatever.

If then there is a supreme practical principle or, with respect to the human will, a categorical imperative, it must be one which, being drawn from the conception of that which is necessarily an end for everyone because it is *an end in itself*, constitutes an *objective* principle of will, and can therefore serve as a universal practical law. The foundation of this principle is: *rational nature exists as an end in itself*.

The human being necessarily conceives of his own existence as being so; so far then this is a *subjective* principle of human actions. But every other rational being regards its existence similarly, just on the same rational principle that holds for me;[39] so that it is at the same time an objective principle from which as a supreme practical law all laws of the will must be capable of being deduced. Accordingly the practical imperative will be as follows: *So act as to treat humanity, whether in your own person or in that of any other, in every case at the same time as an end, never as a means only*.[40] We will now inquire whether this can be practically carried out.

To abide by the previous examples:

First, under the head of necessary duty to oneself: Someone who contemplates suicide should ask himself whether his action can be consistent with the idea of humanity *as an end in itself*. If he destroys himself in order to escape from painful circumstances, he uses a person merely as a *means* to maintain a tolerable condition up to the end of life. But a human being is not a thing, that is to say, something which can be used merely as a means, but must in all his actions be always considered as an end in itself. I cannot, therefore, dispose in any way of a human being in my own person by mutilating, damaging, or killing him. (It belongs to morals proper to define this principle more precisely, so as to avoid all misunderstanding, for example, as to the amputation of the limbs in order to preserve myself; as to exposing my life to danger with a view to preserve it, etc. This question is therefore omitted here.)

Second, as regards necessary duties, or those of strict obligation, towards others: He who is thinking of making a lying promise to others will see at once that he would be using another human being *merely as a means*, without the latter at the same time containing in himself the end. For he whom I propose by such a promise to use for my own purposes cannot possibly assent to my mode of acting toward him,

---

38   A source of value and meaning, a goal or purpose.

39   [Author's note] Here I present this proposition as a postulate, but in the last Section grounds for it will be found.

40   This is often called the Formula of Humanity as End in Itself.

and therefore cannot himself contain the end of this action. This violation of the principle of humanity in other human beings is more obvious if we take in examples of attacks on the freedom and property of others. For then it is clear that he who transgresses the rights of human beings intends to use the person of others merely as means, without considering that as rational beings they ought always to be esteemed also as ends, that is, as beings who must be capable of containing in themselves the end of the very same action.[41]

Third, as regards contingent (meritorious) duties to oneself: It is not enough that the action does not violate humanity in our own person as an end in itself, it must also *harmonize with* it. Now there are in humanity capacities of greater perfection which belong to the end that nature has in view with regard to humanity in ourselves as the subject; to neglect these might perhaps be consistent with the *maintenance* of humanity as an end in itself, but not with the *advancement* of this end.

Fourth, as regards meritorious duties toward others: The natural end which all human beings have is their own happiness. Now humanity might indeed subsist although no one should contribute anything to the happiness of others, provided he did not intentionally withdraw anything from it; but after all, this would only harmonize negatively, not positively, with *humanity as an end in itself*, if everyone does not also endeavor, as far as he can, to forward the ends of others. For the ends of any subject which is an end

in itself ought as far as possible to be *my* ends also, if that conception is to have its *full* effect in me.

This principle that humanity and generally every rational nature is *an end in itself* (which is the supreme limiting condition of every human being's freedom of action), is not borrowed from experience, *first*, because it is universal, applying as it does to all rational beings whatever, and experience is not capable of determining anything about them; *second*, because it does not present humanity as an end to human beings (subjectively), that is, as an object which human beings do of themselves actually adopt as an end; but as an objective end which must as a law constitute the supreme limiting condition of all our subjective ends, let them be what they will; it must therefore spring from pure reason. In fact the ground of all practical legislation lies (according to the first principle) *objectively in the rule* and its form of universality which makes it capable of being a law (say, for example, a law of nature); but *subjectively* in the *end*; now by the second principle, the subject of all ends is each rational being inasmuch as it is an end in itself. From this follows the third practical principle of the will, which is the ultimate condition of its harmony with the universal practical reason, viz., the idea of *the will of every rational being as a will giving universal law*.[42]

On this principle all maxims are rejected which are inconsistent with the will being itself universal legislator. Thus the will is not merely subject to the law, but subject to it so that it must be regarded *as itself giving the law*, and on this ground only subject to the law (of which it can regard itself as the author).

In the previous imperatives, namely, that based on the conception of the conformity of actions to general laws, as in a *system of nature*, and that based on the universal *prerogative* of rational beings as *ends* in themselves—these imperatives just because they were conceived as categorical excluded from any share in their authority all admixture of any interest as an incentive; they were, however, only *assumed* to be categorical, because such an assumption was necessary to explain the conception of duty. But we

---

41 [Author's note] Let it not be thought that the banal "what you do not wish to be done to you…" could here serve as guide or principle, for it is only derived from the principle and is restricted by various limitations. It cannot be a universal law, because it contains the ground neither of duties to one's self nor of the benevolent duties to others (for many a man would gladly consent that others should not benefit him, provided only that he might be excused from showing benevolence to them). Nor does it contain the ground of obligatory duties to another, for the criminal would argue on this ground against the judge who sentences him. And so on.

---

42 This is sometimes called the Formula of Autonomy.

could not prove independently that there are practical propositions which command categorically, nor can it be proved in this section; one thing, however, could be done, namely, to indicate in the imperative itself, by some determinate expression, that in the case of volition from duty all interest is renounced, which is the specific criterion of categorical as distinguished from hypothetical imperatives. This is done in the present third formula of the principle, namely, in the idea of the will of every rational being as a *will giving universal law*.

For although a will *which is subject to laws* may be attached to this law by means of an interest, yet a will which is itself a supreme lawgiver, so far as it is such, cannot possibly depend on any interest, since a will so dependent would itself still need another law restricting the interest of its self-love by the condition that it should be valid as universal law.

Thus the *principle* of every human will as *a will which in all its maxims*[43] *gives universal laws*, provided it be otherwise correct, would be very *well suited* to be the categorical imperative in this respect, namely, that just because of the idea of universal legislation it is *not based on any interest*, and therefore it alone among all possible imperatives can be *unconditional*. Or still better, converting the proposition, if there is a categorical imperative (that is, a law for the will of every rational being), it can only command that everything be done from maxims of one's will regarded as a will which could at the same time will that it should itself give universal laws, for in that case only the practical principle and the imperative which it obeys are unconditional, since they cannot be based on any interest.

Looking back now on all previous attempts to discover the principle of morality, we need not wonder why they all failed. It was seen that the human being is bound to laws by duty, but it was not observed that the laws to which he is subject are *only those of his own giving*, though at the same time they are *universal*, and that he is only bound to act in conformity with his own

will—a will, however, which is designed by nature to give universal laws. For when one has conceived the human being only as subject to a law (no matter what), then this law required some interest, either by way of attraction or constraint, since it did not originate as a law from *his own* will, but this will was according to a law obliged by *something else* to act in a certain manner. Now by this necessary consequence all the labor spent in finding a supreme principle of *duty* was irrevocably lost. For one never elicited duty, but only a necessity of acting from a certain interest. Whether this interest was private or otherwise, in any case the imperative had to be conditional, and could not by any means be capable of being a moral command. I will therefore call this the principle of **autonomy** of the will, in contrast with every other which I accordingly count under **heteronomy**.

The concept of every rational being as one which must consider itself as giving in all the maxims of its will universal laws, so as to judge itself and its actions from this point of view—this concept leads to another which depends on it and is very fruitful, namely, that of a *kingdom of ends*.

By a *kingdom* I understand the systematic union of different rational beings through common laws. Now since it is by laws that the universal validity of ends are determined, hence, if we abstract from the personal differences of rational beings, and likewise from all the content of their private ends, we shall be able to conceive all ends combined in a systematic whole (including both rational beings as ends in themselves, and also the special ends which each may propose to himself), that is to say, we can conceive a kingdom of ends, which on the preceding principles is possible.

For all rational beings come under the *law* that each of them must treat itself and all others *never merely as means*, but in every case *at the same time as ends in themselves*. From this results a systematic union of rational beings through common objective laws, that is, a kingdom which may be called a kingdom of ends, since what these laws have in view is just the relation of these beings to one another as ends and means. It is certainly only an ideal.

A rational being belongs as a *member* to the kingdom of ends when, although giving universal laws in it, he is also himself subject to these laws. He belongs

---

43   [Author's note] I may be excused from citing examples to elucidate this principle, for those that have already illustrated the categorical imperative and its formula can here serve the same purpose.

to it *as sovereign* when, while giving laws, he is not subject to the will of any other.

A rational being must always regard himself as giving laws either as member or as sovereign in a kingdom of ends which is rendered possible by the freedom of will. He cannot, however, maintain the latter position merely by maxims of his will, but only in case he is a completely independent being without needs and with unrestricted power adequate to his will.

Morality consists then in the reference of all action to the legislation which alone can render a kingdom of ends possible.[44] This legislation must be capable of existing in every rational being, and of emanating from his will, so that the principle of this will is never to act on any maxim which could not without contradiction be also a universal law, and accordingly always so to act that *the will could at the same time regard itself as giving through its maxims universal laws*. If now the maxims of rational beings are not by their own nature coincident with this objective principle, then the necessity of acting on it is called practical necessitation, that is, *duty*. Duty does not apply to the sovereign in the kingdom of ends, but it does apply to every member of it and to all in the same degree.

The practical necessity of acting on this principle, that is, duty, does not rest at all on feelings, impulses, or inclinations, but solely on the relation of rational beings to one another, a relation in which the will of a rational being must always be regarded as *legislative*, since otherwise it could not be regarded as *an end in itself*. Reason then refers every maxim of the will, regarding it as legislative universally, to every other will and also to every action towards oneself; and this not on account of any other practical motive or any future advantage, but from the idea of the *dignity* of a rational being, obeying no law but that which he himself also gives.

In the kingdom of ends everything has either *price* or *dignity*. Whatever has price can be replaced by something else which is *equivalent*; whatever, on the other hand, is above all price, and therefore admits of no equivalent, has a dignity.

Whatever has reference to the general inclinations and wants of humankind has a *market price*; whatever, without presupposing a need, corresponds to a certain taste, that is, to a delight in the mere purposeless play of our faculties, has a *fancy price*; but that which constitutes the condition under which alone anything can be an end in itself, this has not merely relative worth, that is, price, but an inner worth, that is, *dignity*.

Now morality is the condition under which alone a rational being can be an end in himself, since by this alone it is possible that he should be a legislating member in the kingdom of ends. Thus morality, and humanity, insofar as it is capable of morality, is that which alone has dignity. Skill and diligence in labor have a market price; wit, lively imagination, and humor have a fancy price; on the other hand, fidelity to promises, benevolence from principle (not from instinct), have an inner worth. Neither nature nor art contains anything which in default of these it could put in their place, for their worth consists not in the effects which spring from them, not in the use and advantage which they secure, but in the disposition, that is, the maxims of the will which are ready to manifest themselves in such actions, even if they do not have the desired effect. These actions also need no recommendation from any subjective taste or sentiment, that they may be looked upon with immediate favor and delight; they need no immediate propensity or feeling for them; they exhibit the will that performs them as an object of an immediate respect, and nothing but reason is required to *impose* them on the will; not to *flatter* it into them, which, in the case of duties, would be a contradiction. This estimation therefore shows that the worth of such a disposition is dignity, and places it infinitely above all price, with which it cannot for a moment be brought into comparison or competition without as it were violating its sanctity.

What then is it which justifies virtue or the morally good disposition, in making such lofty claims? It is nothing less than the *privilege* it secures to the rational being of participating *in the giving of*

---

44 This is sometimes called the Formula of the Kingdom of Ends.

universal laws, by which it qualifies him to be a member of a possible kingdom of ends, a privilege to which he was already destined by his own nature as being an end in itself, and on that account legislating in the kingdom of ends; free as regards all laws of nature, and obeying only those laws which he himself gives, and by which his maxims can belong to a system of universal law to which at the same time he submits himself. For nothing has any worth except what the law assigns it. Now the legislation itself which assigns the worth of everything must for that very reason possess dignity, that is, an unconditional incomparable worth; and the word *respect*[45] alone supplies a becoming expression for the esteem which a rational being must have for it. *Autonomy* then is the basis of the dignity of human nature and of every rational nature.

The three modes of presenting the principle of morality that have been adduced are at bottom only so many formulae of the very same law, and each unites in itself the other two. There is, however, a difference among them, but it is subjectively rather than objectively practical, intended, namely, to bring an idea of reason nearer to intuition (by means of a certain analogy), and thereby nearer to feeling. All maxims, in fact, have—

1. A *form*, consisting in universality; and in this view the formula of the moral imperative is expressed thus, that the maxims must be so chosen as if they were to serve as universal laws of nature.

2. A *matter*, namely, an end, and here the formula says that the rational being, as it is an end by its own nature and therefore an end in itself, must in every maxim serve as the condition limiting all merely relative and arbitrary ends.

3. A *complete determination* of all maxims by means of that formula, namely, that all maxims ought, by their own legislation, to harmonize with a possible kingdom of ends as with a kingdom of nature.[46] There is a progression here in the order of the categories of *unity* of the form of the will (its universality), *plurality* of the matter (the objects, that is, the ends), and *totality* of the system of these. In forming our moral *judgment* of actions it is better to proceed always on the strict method, and start from the universal formula of the categorical imperative: *Act according to a maxim which can at the same time make itself a universal law*. If, however, we wish to gain an *entrance* for the moral law, it is very useful to bring one and the same action under the three specified conceptions, and thereby as far as possible to bring it nearer to intuition.

---

45   Other translators have preferred the English word "reverence." The German word is *Achtung*, which in this context has religious overtones of awe before the sublimity of the moral law.

46   [Author's note] Teleology considers nature as a realm of ends; morals regards a possible realm of ends as a realm of nature. In the former the realm of ends is a theoretical Idea for the explanation of what actually is. In the latter it is a practical Idea for bringing about that which does not exist but which can become actual through our conduct and for making it conform with this Idea.

JOHN STUART MILL
Utilitarianism

Who Was John Stuart Mill?

John Stuart Mill, the most important British philosopher of the nineteenth century, was born in London in 1806, the eldest son of Scottish utilitarian philosopher and political radical James Mill. His childhood was shaped—some might say, misshaped—by his father's fervent belief in the importance of education. James Mill held that every variation in the talents and capacities of individual human beings could be explained by their education and experiences, and thus that a proper educational regime, beginning more or less from birth, could train any child to be an almost superhuman intellect. To prove these theories, James Mill brought up his first son, John Stuart, to be the British radical movement's secret weapon—a prodigious intellect who would be a living demonstration of what could be achieved through properly scientific educational methods, and who would go out into the world to spread the secular gospel of utilitarianism and liberalism.

His father took sole charge of little John Stuart's education from the time when he was a toddler, keeping him isolated from other children (who might be harmful influences) and even from other adults who were not Mill's own philosophical compatriots. John was therefore kept out of schools—which his father believed reinforced ignorant and immoral social attitudes—and educated at home, learning Greek and Latin in the same large study where his father was hard at work on a monumental history of India (and, since no English-Greek dictionary had yet been written, frequently interrupting his father to ask questions about vocabulary). In his autobiography, Mill wrote, "I have no remembrance of the time when I began to learn Greek. I have been told that it was when I was three years old." By the time he was 8—the age at which he began to learn Latin and arithmetic—he had studied much of Greek literature in the original, including all of Herodotus's *Histories* and six dialogues by Plato. At 12 he started on logic and the serious study of philosophy; political economy at 13; and at 20 he was sent to France for a year to become fluent in that language and to study chemistry and mathematics.[1]

Despite these prodigious achievements, Mill's early life seems not to have been a happy one. He had no toys or children's books—not so much, apparently, because his father forbade them as simply because it never occurred to him to provide them—and John Stuart later remarked that he had never learned to play. Until he was 14 he never really mixed with children his own age at all. An early draft of his autobiography contained the following passage, deleted before publication:

---

1   At around this time Mill was offered a place at Cambridge University. His father refused it for him saying he already knew more than Cambridge could ever teach him.

I believe there is less personal affection in England than in any other country of which I know anything, and I give my father's family not as peculiar in this respect but only as a faithful exemplification of the ordinary fact. That rarity in England, a really warm hearted mother, would in the first place have made the children grow up loving and being loved. But my mother with the very best intentions, only knew how to pass her life in drudging for them … but to make herself loved, looked up to, or even obeyed, required qualities which she unfortunately did not possess. I thus grew up in the absence of love and in the presence of fear: and many and indelible are the effects of this bringing-up, in the stunting of my moral growth.

At the age of 22 Mill suffered a nervous breakdown and was plunged into suicidal despair. The trigger—according to his autobiography—was a sudden realization that living the life for which his father had trained him could not make him happy:

> … [I]t occurred to me to put the question directly to myself, "Suppose that all your objects in life were realized; that all the changes in institutions and opinions which you are looking forward to, could be completely effected this very instant: would this be a great joy and happiness to you?" And an irrepressible self-consciousness distinctly answered, "No!" At this my heart sank within me: the whole foundation on which my life was constructed fell down. All my happiness was to have been found in the continual pursuit of this end. The end had ceased to charm, and how could there ever again be any interest in the means? I seemed to have nothing left to live for.

Mill's response to this crisis was not to *abandon* utilitarianism and the radical philosophy of his father, but instead to *modify* the theories by which he had been brought up. He came to adopt the view that "those only are happy … who have their minds fixed on some object other than their own happiness": that is, true happiness—which, as his father had taught him, is the measure of all action—comes not from the pursuit of one's own happiness in itself, but from living a life filled with concern for the happiness of others and with a love of other things, such as poetry and music, for their own sake. Mill, in fact, claimed his sanity was saved by his discovery of Romantic poetry—especially that of William Wordsworth, Samuel Taylor Coleridge, and Johann Wolfgang von Goethe—and he later placed great emphasis on the proper development of the emotional and sentimental side of one's character, as well as one's intellect.

In 1830, at 24, Mill began a deeply passionate (but non-sexual) love affair with a beautiful, vivacious, but married woman, Harriet Hardy Taylor, the wife of John Taylor, a merchant. Mill's relationship with Harriet Taylor was central to his life, and she had a great influence on his writings. For fifteen years, between 1834 and John Taylor's death in 1849, Harriet and the two Johns lived out a curiously Victorian compromise. Harriet and Mill agreed never to be seen in "society" as a couple—which would cause a scandal—but were allowed by Harriet's husband to go on frequent holidays together. In 1851, two years after her husband's death, Harriet and Mill were finally able to marry, but in 1858, Harriet died of tuberculosis—a disease she probably caught from her new husband, who in turn had probably caught it from his father (James Mill died of TB in 1836).

Mill never held an academic position, but spent 35 years working as an administrator for the British East India Company in London. The East India Company, which had also employed Mill's father, was a private trading company formed in 1600 which, by the end of the eighteenth century, had its own army and political service and was effectively administering the sub-continent of India on behalf of the British Government. Mill started his career in 1823, at 17, as a clerk in the office of the Examiner of India Correspondence; by 1856 he had become Chief Examiner of India Correspondence, as his father had been before him. In 1858 the East India Company was taken over by the British Crown following the Indian Mutiny of 1857, and Mill retired with a substantial pension.

Mill's work for the company left him plenty of time for his writing, and he was also very active in public life. In 1823 he was arrested for distributing birth-control pamphlets, and in 1825 he helped to found the London Debating Society. In 1824 James Mill had founded the *Westminster Review*, a quarterly magazine advocating a radically liberal political and social agenda, and John Stuart Mill—only 18 years old at the time—was a frequent and enthusiastic contributor of articles during its early years. In 1835 John Stuart started his own radical periodical, the *London Review*, which soon became the influential *London and Westminster Review* and ran, under his editorship, until 1840. Between 1865 and 1868 Mill was the Liberal Member of Parliament for Westminster, and in 1866 he secured a law guaranteeing freedom of speech in London's Hyde Park.[2] In 1867 he tried, but failed, to amend the second Reform Bill to introduce proportional representation and the vote for women. In 1866—by now something of a "grand old man" of English society—he was made Rector of the University of St. Andrew's in Scotland. In 1872 he became 'godfather' to the newborn Bertrand Russell.

Mill died suddenly, from a fever, in 1873 at Aix-en-Provence, France. From about 1860 until 1870 he had been at the peak of his powers and influence. The moral philosopher Henry Sidgwick wrote in 1873, "from about 1860–1865 or thereabouts he ruled England in the region of thought as very few men ever did. I do not expect to see anything like it again." A few decades later the former Prime Minister James Arthur Balfour noted that the authority of Mill's thought in English universities had been "comparable to that wielded … by Hegel in Germany and in the middle ages by Aristotle." By the First World War, however, Mill's reputation as a philosopher had suffered a precipitous decline, and he remained in ill-favor in the English-speaking philosophical world until the early 1970s, when new scholarship and changing philosophical fashions made possible a gradual increase in the appreciation of Mill as a major philosophical figure—the finest flowering of nineteenth-century British philosophy, and a precursor for the "naturalist" philosophers of the second half of the twentieth century.

---

2 This is the location, since that date, of London's famous Speakers' Corner—a place where "soapbox orators" can say whatever they like with legal impunity.

What Was Mill's Overall Philosophical Project?

Mill is important less for the *originality* of his philosophic thought than for its brilliant *synthesis* of several major strands in nineteenth-century (and especially British) thought into a single, compelling, well-developed picture. The main ingredients for his world-view were empiricism, associationism, utilitarianism, and elements of German Romanticism. Together, these elements became what John Skorupski has called Mill's "liberal naturalism."

The bedrock of Mill's philosophy was empiricism: he believed all human knowledge comes ultimately from sense-experience, and his most substantial intellectual project was the attempt to construct a system of empirical knowledge that could underpin not just science but also moral and social affairs. One of his main interests was in showing that empiricism need not lead to skepticism, such as that espoused by the eighteenth-century Scottish philosopher David Hume. Mill's main discussion of the foundation of knowledge and the principles of inference is the massive *System of Logic*, published in six volumes in 1843. In this work he discussed both deductive inference (including mathematics, which Mill argued was—like all human knowledge—reducible to a set of generalizations of relations among sense-experiences) and inductive inference in the natural sciences. He also tried to show how these methods could be applied in politics and the social sciences. Social phenomena, he argued, are just as much the result of causal laws as are natural events, and thus the social sciences—though they will never make us perfectly able to predict human behavior—are capable of putting social policy on an objective footing which goes beyond the mere "intuitions" of conservative common sense.

His prescriptions for scientific practice—today called "Mill's methods"—were highly influential in the development of the philosophy of science in the twentieth century, and his work is still the foundation of modern methodologies for discovering causal laws. The key engine of science, for Mill, is simply *enumerative induction* or generalization from experience. Crudely put, once we have observed a sequence of events which all obey some regularity—ravens which are black, say, or moving magnetic fields being accompanied by an electrical current—we are justified in inferring that all future events of that type will follow the same law.

Mill's work was also a precursor of what is today called "naturalized epistemology." He proposed that all the phenomena of the human mind, including rationality, be treated as the upshot of the operation of psychological laws acting upon the data of experience. This psychological theory is called "associationism"—since it holds that ideas arise from the psychological *associations* between sensations—and was particularly defended by Mill in his *Examination of Sir William Hamilton's Philosophy* (1865).

In his own time, Mill was for many years most widely known for his *Principles of Political Economy* (1848), which tried to show that the science of economics—criticized in his day as a "dismal science" that could only predict disaster and starvation—could be reformulated as a progressive force for social progress. Mill pointed out the mismatch between what economics measures and what human beings really value, and this led him to argue for limiting economic growth for the sake of the environment, controlling populations in order to allow an adequate standard of living for everyone, and for what he considered the economically ideal form of society—a system of worker-owned cooperatives.

Mill's main ethical position, of course, is utilitarianism, which he sets out in the selection reprinted here. As he wrote in his autobiography, of reading Jeremy Bentham's work on utilitarianism (at the age of 15), "it gave unity to my conceptions of things. I now had opinions; a creed, a doctrine, a philosophy; in one among all the best senses of the word, a religion; the inculcation and diffusion of which could be made the principal outward purpose of a life." Mill was also concerned to apply this moral theory to wider questions of social policy. Of all social institutions—including both formal institutions such as laws and churches, and informal ones like social norms—Mill wants to ask: does this institution contribute to human welfare, and does it do so better than any of the alternatives? If the answer was "No," Mill argued, then that institution should (gradually and non-violently) be changed for the better.

Mill's *On Liberty* (1859)—which, during his lifetime, was probably his most notorious writing—is a classic defence of the freedom of thought and discussion, arguing that "the only purpose for which power can be rightfully exercised over any member of a civilized community, against his will, is to prevent harm to others. His own good, either physical or moral, is not a sufficient warrant." This essay—sections of which are reprinted in Chapter 3—was sparked partly by Mill's growing fear of the middle-class conformism (which he saw in America and detected increasing signs of in Britain) which he thought dangerously stifled originality and the critical consideration of ideas. Central to these concerns is Mill's view of human nature as "progressive," and the importance of individuality and autonomy. These themes, with their emphasis on the power and importance of the human spirit, were part of what he took from the European Romantic movement.

One of Mill's last works, *The Subjection of Women* (1869), is a classic statement of liberal feminism. Mill argues that women should have just as much freedom as men, and attacks the conservative view that women and men have different "natures" which suit them for different spheres of life by arguing that no one could possibly know this—since all knowledge comes only from experience—unless women were first allowed to throw off their oppression and, over several generations, to *try* and do all the things that men were allowed to do.

What Is the Structure of This Reading?

Utilitarianism was not written as a scholarly treatise but as a sequence of articles, published in a monthly magazine, and intended for the general educated reader: consequently, although *Utilitarianism* is philosophically weighty and—just below the surface—often quite difficult, its overall structure is pretty straightforward. Mill begins by making some general remarks in the first chapter, attacking moral intuitionism and suggesting, among other things, that the principle of utilitarianism has always had a major tacit influence on moral beliefs. In Chapter 2 he defines utilitarianism, attempts to head off several common misunderstandings of the doctrine, and raises and responds to about ten possible objections to the theory (such as that utilitarianism is a godless morality worthy only of pigs, or alternatively that it sets an impracticably high standard which can never be attained by mere mortal human beings). In the third chapter, Mill considers the question of moral motivation, and discusses how people might come to feel themselves morally bound by the principles of utilitarianism, arguing that utilitarianism is grounded in the natural social feelings of humanity. In Chapter 4 Mill sets out to give a positive "proof" (insofar as that is possible) for the claim that utilitarianism is the correct moral theory: he argues, first, that one's own happiness is desirable to oneself; second that it follows that happiness is simply desirable in itself, no matter whose it is; and third that *only* happiness is intrinsically desirable. It is this third stage in the argument which takes up most of the chapter. The final chapter of *Utilitarianism*, which is not reprinted here, is a long discussion dealing with the relationship between utilitarianism and justice.

Some Useful Background Information

1. Mill frames much of *Utilitarianism* in terms of a debate between two basic positions on the nature of morality: the "intuitive" school versus the "inductive" school. The intuitionists, whom Mill attacks, believed that ethical facts—though as real and as objectively true as any others—are *non-empirical*: that is, moral truths cannot be detected or confirmed using the five senses, but instead are known through the special faculty of "moral intuition." This philosophical position was represented in Mill's time by, among others, Sir William Hamilton (1788–1856) and William Whewell (1794–1866), and Mill's frequent criticism of the notion of "transcendental" moral facts is directed at intuitionists such as these. Mill considered intuitionism to be not only false but also a serious obstacle to social and moral progress. He thought the claim that (educated) human beings can 'just tell' which moral principles are true, without needing or being able to cite *evidence for these beliefs*, tended to act as a disguise for prejudice and social conservatism.

Mill's own moral methodology, by contrast, was what he called "inductive": he believed *all* human knowledge, including ethical knowledge, comes ultimately from sense experience, and thus that moral judgments must be explained and defended by showing their connections to actual human experience.

2. The notion of *happiness* is a very important part of Mill's moral philosophy, so it is useful to be clear about exactly what his theory of happiness was. Because of Mill's empiricist and associationist philosophical upbringing, it was most natural for him to adopt a kind of *hedonistic* view of happiness. In keeping with his emphasis on sense experience as the key to understanding knowledge and the mind, Mill thinks of happiness as a kind of *pleasurable mental state* (*hēdonē* is the classical Greek word for "pleasure"). For Mill, a happy life is, roughly, one filled with as many pleasurable sensations as possible, and as few painful ones.

Mill followed his philosophical predecessors in thinking that pleasurable experiences can be classified according to their duration and their intensity: thus rational people seeking their own happiness will aim to arrange their lives so that, over time, they will have more longer-lasting pleasures than short-lived ones, and more intense pleasures than dilute ones. For example, the initial painfulness of learning the violin, might be more than off-set by the intense and long-lasting pleasure of playing it well.[3] In addition, however, Mill distinguished

---

3 Mill's mentor Jeremy Bentham even proposed what he called a "felicific calculus": a mathematical system for measuring the total net quantity of pleasure to be expected from a given course of action. (Roughly, calculate the balance of pleasure and pain that would accompany a particular outcome of your actions—taking into account their intensity and duration—and then multiply this number by the probability of that outcome actually occurring. This yields what Bentham called the "expected utility" of an action. The rational agent—according to Bentham—acts in a way which has the greatest expected utility.)

between different *qualities* of pleasure. For Mill (unlike, say, Bentham), pleasure is not just one type of mental sensation but comes in "higher" and "lower" varieties. For example, according to Mill, the pleasant feeling that accompanies advanced intellectual or creative activity is a more valuable kind of pleasure—even if it is no more intense or long-lasting—than that which comes from physical satisfactions like eating and sex.

3. One of Mill's philosophical presuppositions which is significant for his moral and social philosophy is *individualism*. Mill assumed that individual persons are the basic unit of political analysis—that social structures are nothing more than constructions out of these individuals and are nothing over and above particular people and the relations between them. It follows that the analysis of social phenomena must be approached through a study of the actions and intentions of individuals, and similarly that social change is only possible through a large number of changes to individual people. What mattered to Mill was not "the general happiness" in some abstract sense, but the happiness of large numbers of individual human beings. Social institutions were seen as merely *instruments* for benefiting all these people. Furthermore, for Mill (influenced, as he was, by European Romanticism), there is a special kind of *value* in individuality: the particular uniqueness of each person is a thing to be treasured in itself.

Some Common Misconceptions

1. For Mill, mere *exemption* from pain is not itself a good. He holds that pleasure is the only good, and pain the only bad, and the overall goodness of states of affairs consists in the *balance* of pleasure over pain. The absence of pain is thus merely morally neutral, unless it is accompanied by the positive presence of pleasure.

2. Mill is not arguing that people already *do* act in order to produce the greatest happiness of the greatest number: he is arguing that we *should*.

He is not merely describing an already prevalent moral psychology, but arguing for a certain set of moral attitudes which he thinks we ought to cultivate in ourselves and in society in general.

3. Utilitarianism is a theory of actions and not motives. It does not require that people *intend* to maximize utility, just that their behavior, in fact, does so. Mill insists the criterion for what makes an action right is that it maximize utility; it does not follow from this that all our actions must have the conscious goal of maximizing utility. In fact, there is a good case to be made that a community where everyone is *trying* to maximize utility all the time would actually be self-defeating and a much less happy society than it would be if people acted from other motivations. If this is right, it would follow that, according to utilitarianism itself, it would be immoral to be always consciously trying to maximize utility. This is not a paradox or a problem for the theory, however; it simply shows there is a difference between the criterion of right action and the best advice one can give moral agents for actually meeting that criterion.

Actions, according to Mill, include within themselves two parts: an *intention* (which is different from a motive—it is not *why* the action is done but *what* the action is intended to achieve), and the action's *effects*. Mill sometimes appeals to differences of intention to distinguish between kinds of actions (as in his Chapter 3 footnote about a tyrant rescuing a drowning man), but, strictly speaking, only the *effects* or consequences of an action can be morally relevant to the utilitarian.

4. One common complaint against utilitarianism is that it makes *every* action, no matter how trivial, a moral issue: pretty much everything we do (e.g., getting a haircut) will have *some* effect on someone's pleasure and pain, and so it appears we have a moral duty to ensure we *always* act in such a way as to maximize the general happiness—and this, to say the least, would seem to put a bit of a strain on everyday life. However, even if this, in fact, is an implica-

tion of Mill's utilitarian theory, he did not intend to commit us to such an onerous regime. Here is a quote from another of Mill's works (*Auguste Comte and Positivism*): "It is not good that persons should be bound, by other people's opinion, to do everything that they would deserve praise for doing. There is a standard of altruism to which all should be required to come up, and a degree beyond which it is not obligatory, but meritorious."

5. Despite the way *Utilitarianism* can strike us today, in the aftermath of the grand and often massively destructive social engineering projects of the twentieth century, Mill was actually a bitter foe of what might be called "social constructivism." He emphatically did *not* see society as merely a machine built to help human beings to live together, a machine which can be broken into bits and reconstructed if it is not working optimally, and one where the rational, technical vision of collective planners should override individual initiative in the public good. On the contrary, Mill was very much an *individualist* and a humanist. He saw society as built from the actions of separate individual human beings and held that it is a kind of historical "consensus" which has created traditions and cultural practices that are continually but gradually evolving over time. Mill's vision for the reform of society, then, was not the imposition of central planning, but instead the gradual construction of a set of cultural norms—including, especially, a progressive educational system—to create human beings with the best possible moral character.

How Important and Influential Is This Passage?

John Stuart Mill did not *invent* utilitarianism (and never pretended to have done so). Indeed, he was brought up by people who already considered themselves utilitarians. Mill's importance to utilitarianism is that he gave it what is arguably its single greatest and most influential formulation, in the essay *Utilitarianism*. It is this work which, ever since it was written,

has been the starting point for both defenders and foes of utilitarianism. Furthermore, utilitarianism is itself a very important and influential moral theory. Along with Marxism, it was arguably the most prevalent moral theory among philosophers, economists, political scientists, and other social theorists for much of the twentieth century (completely eclipsing—or in some cases, like G.E. Moore's moral philosophy, absorbing—the moral "intuitionism" which Mill saw as his theory's main competitor in 1861). Utilitarianism's influence has waned since the 1970s and it has been subjected to several damaging philosophical attacks, but it is still, uncontroversially, one of the three or four main moral theories.

Suggestions for Critical Reflection

1. One of the attractions of utilitarianism, it is often supposed, is that it is 'scientific' or objective in a way that "intuitionism" (or even Kantianism, or virtue theory) is not. The Greatest Happiness Principle apparently provides a quasi-mathematical, bias-free, and theoretically motivated way of working out what we ought to do in literally any moral situation. But is this really so? For example, can the pleasures and pains of sentient creatures really be 'objectively' measured and compared, in order to calculate the net effect of my actions on utility? Even if pleasures and pains are measurable, do you think *all* the consequences of an action can be properly predicted and measured? How serious are these problems for utilitarianism?

2. Does Mill's notion of "higher" or more "noble" pleasure make sense? How could the "nobility" of an experience add to the pleasure of it? Why couldn't an experience be noble but not pleasant? In that case, would Mill have to say that it is still valuable? In other words, is Mill *really* a hedonist?

3. An influential criticism of the hedonistic component of utilitarianism was invented by philosopher Robert Nozick and is called the "experience machine." The experience machine is a fictional device which keeps your body alive in a tank of fluids, for a normal human

life-span, all the while stimulating your brain so that you continuously feel as if you are having the most pleasant and satisfying experiences imaginable. Since—properly designed—this would be an utterly reliable way of maximizing the quality and number of pleasant sensations during your lifetime, it seems that the utilitarian is forced to conclude that it would be our *moral duty* to plug ourselves into one of these machines (especially if they are such reliable and long-lasting devices that nearly *everyone* can be plugged in at the same time). But Nozick argues that this result is clearly unsatisfactory: surely there is more to a valuable life than a mere succession of pleasant experiences, and so utilitarianism must be a faulty moral theory. What do you think about Nozick's argument? What exactly does it suggest is wrong with utilitarianism (or at least Mill's version of the theory)? Could this problem—if it is a problem—be fixed?

4. The third paragraph of the fourth chapter of *Utilitarianism* has been called "the most notorious [passage] in Mill's writings" (Roger Crisp). In it Mill compares desirability with visibility, in an effort to argue that desire is a faculty which reveals what we morally ought to do. The most famous and apparently devastating criticism of this argument came from G.E. Moore in 1903: "The fact is that 'desirable' does not mean 'able to be desired' as 'visible' means 'able to be seen.' The desirable means simply what *ought* to be desired or deserves to be desired." How does Moore's complaint cause problems for Mill's argument? Does Mill really make the mistake Moore is suggesting? If Mill's own arguments fail to show that we *ought* to desire happiness, is there any other way a utilitarian could consistently argue for this claim? Does utilitarianism *need* to provide arguments for it?

5. How well does Mill refute moral egoism? That is, does his argument show that I ought to care about *everyone's* happiness, and not just my own? Does he have an *argument* for the "impartiality" component of utilitarianism? Does he need one?

6. Is Mill right that we *only* desire happiness—is his claim, "to desire anything, except in proportion as the idea of it is pleasant, is a physical and metaphysical impossibility," a plausible one? If he is wrong, how seriously does this undercut his argument for the truth of utilitarianism? For example, what about Mill's own example of virtue: is he right in arguing that we value our own virtue only as a kind or "part" of our happiness?

7. Utilitarianism is a kind of moral theory which is sometimes called "welfarist": for such theories, the only thing of intrinsic value is the welfare of moral agents (according to Mill, sentient beings). One consequence of welfarism is that *nothing else* is of intrinsic value. Thus, for example, the beauty of art and nature, ecological sustainability, scientific knowledge, justice, equality, loyalty, kindness, or self-sacrifice—none of these things have any value in themselves, but are valuable *only* insofar as they increase the welfare of sentient creatures (and are actually *immoral* if they reduce this welfare). Does this seem to be an acceptable consequence of a moral theory?

8. Utilitarianism is often accused of being an extremely demanding moral theory. According to utilitarianism, a certain unit of pleasure or pain should matter *equally* to me whether it belongs to me, to a member of my family, to a stranger half-way across the world, or even to an animal. Utilitarianism requires us to maximize happiness generally, and does not allow us to think of the happiness of ourselves and our friends as being especially important. If you or I were to spend all of our free time, and use almost all of our money, working to help victims of famine and other natural disasters around the world, this might well produce more overall utility than the lives we currently lead. If so, then utilitarianism commits us to a moral *duty* to behave in this way, and we are being flat-out *immoral* in spending time with our families or watching movies. Is this acceptable? If not, what is wrong with it?

9. According to utilitarianism, should we be morally responsible for all the consequences of our

actions, including the unforeseen ones? What would Mill say? Are we just as responsible for *not* doing things that could have prevented great pain? For example, according to utilitarianism, am I equally morally deficient if I fail to give money to charity as I am if I send poisoned food to famine-stricken areas (supposing the outcomes in terms of human death and suffering would be the same)?

10. Act (or "direct") utilitarianism is the view that one should act in any circumstance so as to produce the greatest overall balance of pleasure over pain. (You would have a moral duty to break an important promise to your best friend if it would increase overall utility by even a tiny amount, for example.) Rule (or "indirect") utilitarianism, on the other hand, is the view that one should act in accordance with certain moral rules, rules fixed as those which, over time, can be expected to maximize utility if they are generally followed. (For example, you should never break an important promise, even if you can foresee that keeping it, in a particular case, will cause far more pain than pleasure.) Is Mill an act or rule utilitarian? Which is the better theory? Is *either* version attractive and, if not, can you think of a third option for utilitarianism?

11. According to utilitarianism, *how* should we maximize utility? Should we aim to maximize the *total* utility of the world, the *average* utility, or what? (For example, if we chose to maximize total utility, we might be morally obliged to aim for an extremely large population, even if each member has only a low level of happiness; on the other hand, if we opt for the highest possible average utility we might be committed to keeping the population small and select, perhaps killing, before birth, people who look as though they might drag the average down.) What would Mill say?

12. Mill thought utilitarianism to be the one true fundamental moral theory, and to be consistent with (what is right in) the moral theories of Aristotle and Kant. If you have read the selections by those thinkers in this chapter, you might want to think about whether utilitarianism *is* in fact consistent with the views of Aristotle and Kant. For example, could Kant accept that consequences are what is morally important about our actions?

Suggestions for Further Reading

Mill's writings have been published as *The Collected Works of John Stuart Mill*, under the general editorship of John Robson (33 volumes, University of Toronto Press, 1963–91). A very good edition of Mill's *Utilitarianism* is by Roger Crisp (ed.) in the Oxford Philosophical Texts series (Oxford University Press, 1998); it is also widely available in other editions (such as that published by Penguin Books in 1987). Mill's *Autobiography* is available from Penguin (1990), and a good edition of his *On Liberty*, with interesting supplemental material, was edited by Edward Alexander and published by Broadview Press (1999). Jeremy Bentham's *Introduction to the Principles of Morals and Legislation*, J.H. Burns and H.L.A. Hart (eds.) (Oxford University Press, 1996) is also essential reading for any serious student of Mill's *Utilitarianism*.

Three worthwhile books about Mill's philosophy as a whole are Alan Ryan's *J.S. Mill* (Routledge & Kegan Paul, 1974) and *The Philosophy of John Stuart Mill* (Prometheus Books, 1990), and John Skorupski's *John Stuart Mill* (Routledge, 1989). Roger Crisp has written a *Routledge Philosophical Guidebook to Mill on Utilitarianism* (Routledge, 1997), and there are a number of good books on Mill's moral theory, including: Fred Berger, *Happiness, Justice, and Freedom: The Moral and Political Philosophy of John Stuart Mill* (University of California Press, 1984); Wendy Donner, *The Liberal Self: John Stuart Mill's Moral and Political Philosophy* (Cornell University Press, 1992); David Lyons, *Rights, Welfare, and Mill's Moral Theory* (Oxford University Press, 1994); and Bernard Semmel, *John Stuart Mill and the Pursuit of Virtue* (Yale University Press, 1984).

G.E. Moore's attack on Mill's argument for utilitarianism appears in *Principia Ethica*, Thomas Baldwin (ed.) (Cambridge University Press, 1994, originally published 1903). An early defense of Mill against this attack is James Seth's "The Alleged Fallacies in Mill's 'Utilitarianism,'" *Philosophical Review* 17 (1908); more recently, Necip Fikri Alican has written a book called

Mill's Principle of Utility: A Defense of John Stuart Mill's Notorious Proof (Rodopi, 1994).

Three useful collections of essays about Mill are J.B. Schneewind (ed.), *Mill: A Collection of Critical Essays* (Doubleday, 1968); David Lyons (ed.), *Mill's 'Utilitarianism': Critical Essays* (Rowman and Littlefield, 1997); and John Skorupski (ed.), *The Cambridge Companion to Mill* (Cambridge University Press, 1998). Other useful articles include: J.O. Urmson, "The Interpretation of the Moral Philosophy of J.S. Mill," *Philosophical Quarterly* 3 (1953); Rex Martin, "A Defence of Mill's Qualitative Hedonism," *Philosophy* 47 (1972); R.M. Adams, "Motive Utilitarianism," *Journal of Philosophy* 73 (1976); Henry R. West, "Mill's Qualitative Hedonism," *Philosophy* 51 (1976); Roger Crisp, "Utilitarianism and the Life of Virtue," *Philosophical Quarterly* 42 (1992); and L.W. Sumner, "Welfare, Happiness and Pleasure," *Utilitas* 4 (1992).

Finally, there is a substantial literature on the moral theory of utilitarianism in its own right. Perhaps the best starting point is J.J.C. Smart and Bernard Williams, *Utilitarianism: For and Against* (Cambridge University Press, 1973). James Griffin's "Modern Utilitarianism," *Revue Internationale de Philosophie* 141 (1982) is a very useful review of the modern development of the theory. The following books are also valuable: Richard Brandt, *Morality, Utilitarianism, and Rights* (Cambridge University Press, 1992); David Lyons, *Forms and Limits of Utilitarianism* (Oxford University Press, 1965); Derek Parfit, *Reasons and Persons* (Oxford University Press, 1986); Anthony Quinton, *Utilitarian Ethics* (Open Court, 1989); Geoffrey Scarre, *Utilitarianism* (Routledge, 1996); Samuel Scheffler (ed.), *Consequentialism and Its Critics* (Oxford University Press, 1988); Samuel Scheffler, *The Rejection of Consequentialism* (Oxford University Press, 1994); Amartya Sen and Bernard Williams (eds.), *Utilitarianism and Beyond* (Cambridge University Press, 1982); and William Shaw, *Contemporary Ethics: Taking Account of Utilitarianism* (Blackwell, 1999).

Utilitarianism[4]

Chapter 1: General Remarks

There are few circumstances among those which make up the present condition of human knowledge, more unlike what might have been expected, or more significant of the backward state in which speculation on the most important subjects still lingers, than the little progress which has been made in the decision of the controversy respecting the criterion of right and wrong. From the dawn of philosophy, the question concerning the *summum bonum*,[5] or, what is the same thing, concerning the foundation of morality, has been accounted the main problem in speculative thought, has occupied the most gifted intellects, and divided them into sects and schools, carrying on a vigorous warfare against one another. And after more than two thousand years the same discussions continue, philosophers are still ranged under the same contending banners, and neither thinkers nor mankind at large seem nearer to being unanimous on the subject, than when the youth Socrates[6] listened to the old Protagoras,[7]

---

4   *Utilitarianism* was first published in 1861 as a series of three essays in volume 64 of *Fraser's Magazine*. It was first published as a book in 1863; this text is from the fourth edition, published in 1871 (by Longmans, Green, Reader, and Dyer), the last to be printed in Mill's lifetime.

5   "The highest good": that thing which is an end-in-itself, which gives everything else its value, and the achievement of which is (arguably) the goal of an ethical system. Candidates for the "highest good" might be—indeed, historically have been—pleasure, human flourishing, the rational comprehension of reality, or God.

6   Socrates (469–399 BCE) was a highly influential philosopher from Athens, in Greece, who—particularly through his great impact on Plato—is often thought to be the main originator of the western philosophical tradition. He wrote nothing himself, but appears as a character in nearly all of Plato's dialogues.

7   Protagoras (c. 490–c. 420 BCE) was the greatest of the Sophist philosophers—itinerant teachers of rhetoric and practical philosophy—and is most famous for his doctrine that "Man is the measure of all things," which is usually interpreted as an extreme form of relativism.

and asserted (if Plato's dialogue be grounded on a real conversation[8]) the theory of utilitarianism against the popular morality of the so-called sophist.

It is true that similar confusion and uncertainty, and in some cases similar discordance, exist respecting the first principles of all the sciences, not excepting that which is deemed the most certain of them, mathematics; without much impairing, generally indeed without impairing at all, the trustworthiness of the conclusions of those sciences. An apparent anomaly, the explanation of which is, that the detailed doctrines of a science are not usually deduced from, nor depend for their evidence upon, what are called its first principles. Were it not so, there would be no science more precarious, or whose conclusions were more insufficiently made out, than algebra; which derives none of its certainty from what are commonly taught to learners as its elements, since these, as laid down by some of its most eminent teachers, are as full of fictions as English law, and of mysteries as theology. The truths which are ultimately accepted as the first principles of a science, are really the last results of metaphysical analysis, practised on the elementary notions with which the science is conversant; and their relation to the science is not that of foundations to an edifice, but of roots to a tree, which may perform their office equally well though they be never dug down to and exposed to light. But though in science the particular truths precede the general theory, the contrary might be expected to be the case with a practical art, such as morals or legislation. All action is for the sake of some end, and rules of action, it seems natural to suppose, must take their whole character and colour from the end to which they are subservient. When

we engage in a pursuit, a clear and precise conception of what we are pursuing would seem to be the first thing we need, instead of the last we are to look forward to. A test of right and wrong must be the means, one would think, of ascertaining what is right or wrong, and not a consequence of having already ascertained it.

The difficulty is not avoided by having recourse to the popular theory of a natural faculty, a sense or instinct, informing us of right and wrong. For—besides that the existence of such a moral instinct is itself one of the matters in dispute—those believers in it who have any pretensions to philosophy, have been obliged to abandon the idea that it discerns what is right or wrong in the particular case in hand, as our other senses discern the sight or sound actually present. Our moral faculty, according to all those of its interpreters who are entitled to the name of thinkers, supplies us only with the general principles of moral judgments; it is a branch of our reason, not of our sensitive faculty;[9] and must be looked to for the abstract doctrines of morality, not for perception of it in the concrete. The intuitive, no less than what may be termed the inductive, school of ethics, insists on the necessity of general laws. They both agree that the morality of an individual action is not a question of direct perception, but of the application of a law to an individual case. They recognise also, to a great extent, the same moral laws; but differ as to their evidence, and the source from which they derive their authority. According to the one opinion, the principles of morals are evident *a priori*,[10] requiring nothing to command assent, except that the meaning of the terms be understood. According to the other doctrine, right and wrong, as well as truth and falsehood, are questions of observation and experience. But both hold equally that morality must be deduced from principles; and the intuitive school affirm as strongly as the inductive, that there is a science of morals. Yet they seldom attempt to make out a list of the *a priori* principles which are to serve as the premises of the science; still more rarely do they make any effort to

---

8   Mill first read this dialogue—called the *Protagoras*—during the "more advanced" period of his education (after he had reached the age of 12). It is questionable whether Socrates does indeed put forward utilitarianism in that dialogue (and almost certain that he was not himself a utilitarian). Mill, however, was always anxious to portray utilitarianism as a doctrine already widespread in the history of philosophy (and especially in ancient Greek philosophy: in *On Liberty,* for example, he describes Aristotle's ethics as "judicious utilitarianism").

---

9   Mill means our faculty of sensation.
10   Obviously true, independently of any actual experience. ("*A priori*" means knowable prior to experience.)

reduce those various principles to one first principle, or common ground of obligation. They either assume the ordinary precepts[11] of morals as of *a priori* authority, or they lay down as the common groundwork of those maxims, some generality much less obviously authoritative than the maxims themselves, and which has never succeeded in gaining popular acceptance. Yet to support their pretensions there ought either to be some one fundamental principle or law, at the root of all morality, or if there be several, there should be a determinate order of precedence among them; and the one principle, or the rule for deciding between the various principles when they conflict, ought to be self-evident.

To inquire how far the bad effects of this deficiency have been mitigated in practice, or to what extent the moral beliefs of mankind have been vitiated or made uncertain by the absence of any distinct recognition of an ultimate standard, would imply a complete survey and criticism, of past and present ethical doctrine. It would, however, be easy to show that whatever steadiness or consistency these moral beliefs have attained, has been mainly due to the tacit influence of a standard not recognised. Although the non-existence of an acknowledged first principle has made ethics not so much a guide as a consecration of men's actual sentiments, still, as men's sentiments, both of favour and of aversion, are greatly influenced by what they suppose to be the effects of things upon their happiness, the principle of utility, or as Bentham[12] latterly called it,

the greatest happiness principle, has had a large share in forming the moral doctrines even of those who most scornfully reject its authority. Nor is there any school of thought which refuses to admit that the influence of actions on happiness is a most material and even predominant consideration in many of the details of morals, however unwilling to acknowledge it as the fundamental principle of morality, and the source of moral obligation. I might go much further, and say that to all those *a priori* moralists who deem it necessary to argue at all, utilitarian arguments are indispensable. It is not my present purpose to criticise these thinkers; but I cannot help referring, for illustration, to a systematic treatise by one of the most illustrious of them, the *Metaphysics of Ethics*, by Kant.[13] This remarkable man, whose system of thought will long remain one of the landmarks in the history of philosophical speculation, does, in the treatise in question, lay down a universal first principle as the origin and ground of moral obligation; it is this: "So act, that the rule on which thou actest would admit of being adopted as a law by all rational beings." But when he begins to deduce from this precept any of the actual duties of morality, he fails, almost grotesquely, to show that there would be any contradiction, any logical (not to say physical) impossibility, in the adoption by all rational beings of the most outrageously immoral rules of conduct. All he shows is that the *consequences* of their universal adoption would be such as no one would choose to incur.

On the present occasion, I shall, without further discussion of the other theories, attempt to contribute something towards the understanding and appreciation of the Utilitarian or Happiness theory, and towards such proof as it is susceptible of. It is evident that this cannot be proof in the ordinary and popular meaning of the term. Questions of ultimate ends are not amenable to direct proof. Whatever can be proved to be good, must be so by being shown to be a means to something

---

11   A precept is an instruction or command prescribing a particular course of action (such as, "always tell the truth" or "do not commit adultery").

12   Jeremy Bentham (1748–1832) was an English philosopher of law and ethics who is usually thought of as the founder of utilitarianism, which he intended as a coherent and sensible foundation for the large-scale reform of social and legal policy. His main theoretical work was *An Introduction to the Principles of Morals and Legislation*, published in 1789, and it is in this book that the Greatest Happiness Principle was first clearly formulated and defended. It was while reading a French edition of Bentham's *Principles of Morals* in 1821 that, according to Mill's autobiography, he was permanently "converted" to utilitarianism. (Bentham

is also the founder of University College London, and his embalmed body, topped with a wax death mask, is still preserved there in a glass box which is wheeled out for special occasions.)

13   Mill is actually thinking of Kant's *Foundations of the Metaphysics of Morals* (see the previous reading).

admitted to be good without proof. The medical art is proved to be good by its conducing to health; but how is it possible to prove that health is good? The art of music is good, for the reason, among others, that it produces pleasure; but what proof is it possible to give that pleasure is good? If, then, it is asserted that there is a comprehensive formula, including all things which are in themselves good, and that whatever else is good, is not so as an end, but as a mean, the formula may be accepted or rejected, but is not a subject of what is commonly understood by proof. We are not, however, to infer that its acceptance or rejection must depend on blind impulse, or arbitrary choice. There is a larger meaning of the word proof, in which this question is as amenable to it as any other of the disputed questions of philosophy. The subject is within the cognisance[14] of the rational faculty; and neither does that faculty deal with it solely in the way of intuition. Considerations may be presented capable of determining the intellect either to give or withhold its assent to the doctrine; and this is equivalent to proof.

We shall examine presently of what nature are these considerations; in what manner they apply to the case, and what rational grounds, therefore, can be given for accepting or rejecting the utilitarian formula. But it is a preliminary condition of rational acceptance or rejection, that the formula should be correctly understood. I believe that the very imperfect notion ordinarily formed of its meaning, is the chief obstacle which impedes its reception; and that could it be cleared, even from only the grosser misconceptions, the question would be greatly simplified, and a large proportion of its difficulties removed. Before, therefore, I attempt to enter into the philosophical grounds which can be given for assenting to the utilitarian standard, I shall offer some illustrations of the doctrine itself; with the view of showing more clearly what it is, distinguishing it from what it is not, and disposing of such of the practical objections to it as either originate in, or are closely connected with, mistaken interpretations of its meaning. Having thus prepared the ground, I shall afterwards endeavour to throw such light as I can upon the question, considered as one of philosophical theory.

---

14   Sphere of concern or awareness.

Chapter 2: What Utilitarianism Is.

A passing remark is all that needs be given to the ignorant blunder of supposing that those who stand up for utility as the test of right and wrong, use the term in that restricted and merely colloquial sense in which utility is opposed to pleasure. An apology is due to the philosophical opponents of utilitarianism, for even the momentary appearance of confounding them with any one capable of so absurd a misconception; which is the more extraordinary, inasmuch as the contrary accusation, of referring everything to pleasure, and that too in its grossest form, is another of the common charges against utilitarianism: and, as has been pointedly remarked by an able writer,[15] the same sort of persons, and often the very same persons, denounce the theory "as impracticably dry when the word utility precedes the word pleasure, and as too practicably voluptuous when the word pleasure precedes the word utility." Those who know anything about the matter are aware that every writer, from Epicurus[16] to Bentham, who maintained the theory of utility, meant by it, not something to be contradistinguished from pleasure, but pleasure itself, together with exemption from pain; and instead of opposing the useful to the agreeable or the ornamental, have always declared that the useful means these, among other things. Yet the common herd, including the herd of writers, not only in newspapers and periodicals, but in books of weight and pretension, are perpetually falling into

---

15   The identity of this writer remains mysterious.

16   Epicurus (341–270 BCE) was a Greek philosopher and founder of the loosely-knit school of thought called Epicureanism. A central plank of this doctrine is—as the modern connotations of the word "epicurean" suggest—that the good life is one filled with pleasure. Indeed, for Epicurus, the only rational goal in life is one's own pleasure. However, contrary to the popular association of "Epicureanism" with mere sensual self-indulgence, Epicurus placed much greater emphasis on stable, non-sensory pleasures (say, the pleasures of friendship and psychological contentment), and also stressed the importance of dispensing with unnecessary desires, harmful fears (such as the fear of death), and hollow gratifications.

this shallow mistake. Having caught up the word utilitarian, while knowing nothing whatever about it but its sound, they habitually express by it the rejection, or the neglect, of pleasure in some of its forms; of beauty, of ornament, or of amusement. Nor is the term thus ignorantly misapplied solely in disparagement, but occasionally in compliment; as though it implied superiority to frivolity and the mere pleasures of the moment. And this perverted use is the only one in which the word is popularly known, and the one from which the new generation are acquiring their sole notion of its meaning. Those who introduced the word, but who had for many years discontinued it as a distinctive appellation, may well feel themselves called upon to resume it, if by doing so they can hope to contribute anything towards rescuing it from this utter degradation.[17]

The creed which accepts as the foundation of morals, Utility, or the Greatest Happiness Principle, holds that actions are right in proportion as they tend to promote happiness, wrong as they tend to produce the reverse of happiness. By happiness is intended pleasure, and the absence of pain; by unhappiness, pain, and the privation of pleasure. To give a clear view of the moral standard set up by the theory, much more requires to be said; in particular, what things it includes in the ideas of pain and pleasure; and to what extent this is left an open question. But these supplementary explanations do not affect the theory of life on which this theory of morality is grounded—namely, that pleasure, and freedom from pain, are the only things desirable as ends; and that all desirable things (which are as numerous in the utilitarian as in any other scheme) are desirable either for the pleasure inherent in themselves, or as means to the promotion of pleasure and the prevention of pain.

Now, such a theory of life excites in many minds, and among them in some of the most estimable in feeling and purpose, inveterate dislike. To suppose that life has (as they express it) no higher end than pleasure—no better and nobler object of desire and pursuit—they designate as utterly mean and grovelling; as a doctrine worthy only of swine, to whom the followers of Epicurus were, at a very early period, contemptuously likened;[18] and modern holders of the doctrine are occasionally made the subject of equally polite comparisons by its German, French, and English assailants.

When thus attacked, the Epicureans have always answered, that it is not they, but their accusers, who represent human nature in a degrading light; since the accusation supposes human beings to be capable of no pleasures except those of which swine are capable. If this supposition were true, the charge could not be gainsaid, but would then be no longer an imputation; for if the sources of pleasure were precisely the same to human beings and to swine, the rule of life which is good enough for the one would be good enough for the other. The comparison of the Epicurean life to that of beasts is felt as degrading, precisely because a beast's pleasures do not satisfy a human being's conceptions of happiness. Human beings have faculties more elevated than the animal appetites, and when once made conscious of them, do not regard anything as happiness which does not include their gratification. I do not, indeed, consider the Epicureans to have been by any means faultless in drawing out their scheme of consequences from the utilitarian principle. To do this in any sufficient manner, many Stoic,[19] as well as Christian elements require to be

---

17   [Author's note] The author of this essay has reason for believing himself to be the first person who brought the word utilitarian into use. He did not invent it, but adopted it from a passing expression in Mr. Galt's *Annals of the Parish*. After using it as a designation for several years, he and others abandoned it from a growing dislike to anything resembling a badge or watchword of sectarian distinction. But as a name for one single opinion, not a set of opinions—to denote the recognition of utility as a standard, not any particular way of applying it—the term supplies a want in the language, and offers, in many cases, a convenient mode of avoiding tiresome circumlocution.

18   For example, in Diogenes Laertius' *Lives of Eminent Philosophers*, written in about 230 CE.

19   Stoicism was, with Epicureanism, one of the two main strands of "Hellenistic" philosophy (roughly, that associated with Greek culture during the 300 years after the death of Alexander the Great in 323 BCE). Its main ethical doctrine was that the wise and virtuous man

included. But there is no known Epicurean theory of life which does not assign to the pleasures of the intellect, of the feelings and imagination, and of the moral sentiments, a much higher value as pleasures than to those of mere sensation. It must be admitted, however, that utilitarian writers in general have placed the superiority of mental over bodily pleasures chiefly in the greater permanency, safety, uncostliness, etc., of the former—that is, in their circumstantial advantages rather than in their intrinsic nature. And on all these points utilitarians have fully proved their case; but they might have taken the other, and, as it may be called, higher ground, with entire consistency. It is quite compatible with the principle of utility to recognise the fact, that some *kinds* of pleasure are more desirable and more valuable than others. It would be absurd that while, in estimating all other things, quality is considered as well as quantity, the estimation of pleasures should be supposed to depend on quantity alone.

If I am asked, what I mean by difference of quality in pleasures, or what makes one pleasure more valuable than another, merely as a pleasure, except its being greater in amount, there is but one possible answer. Of two pleasures, if there be one to which all or almost all who have experience of both give a decided preference, irrespective of any feeling of moral obligation to prefer it, that is the more desirable pleasure. If one of the two is, by those who are competently acquainted with both, placed so far above the other that they prefer it, even though knowing it to be attended with a greater amount of discontent, and would not resign it for any quantity of the other pleasure which their nature is capable of, we are justified in ascribing to the preferred enjoyment a superiority in quality, so far outweighing quantity as to render it, in comparison, of small account.

Now it is an unquestionable fact that those who are equally acquainted with, and equally capable of appreciating and enjoying, both, do give a most

marked preference to the manner of existence which employs their higher faculties. Few human creatures would consent to be changed into any of the lower animals, for a promise of the fullest allowance of a beast's pleasures; no intelligent human being would consent to be a fool, no instructed person would be an ignoramus, no person of feeling and conscience would be selfish and base, even though they should be persuaded that the fool, the dunce, or the rascal is better satisfied with his lot than they are with theirs. They would not resign what they possess more than he for the most complete satisfaction of all the desires which they have in common with him. If they ever fancy they would, it is only in cases of unhappiness so extreme, that to escape from it they would exchange their lot for almost any other, however undesirable in their own eyes. A being of higher faculties requires more to make him happy, is capable probably of more acute suffering, and certainly accessible to it at more points, than one of an inferior type; but in spite of these liabilities, he can never really wish to sink into what he feels to be a lower grade of existence. We may give what explanation we please of this unwillingness; we may attribute it to pride, a name which is given indiscriminately to some of the most and to some of the least estimable feelings of which mankind are capable: we may refer it to the love of liberty and personal independence, an appeal to which was with the Stoics one of the most effective means for the inculcation of it; to the love of power, or to the love of excitement, both of which do really enter into and contribute to it: but its most appropriate appellation is a sense of dignity, which all human beings possess in one form or other, and in some, though by no means in exact, proportion to their higher faculties, and which is so essential a part of the happiness of those in whom it is strong, that nothing which conflicts with it could be, otherwise than momentarily, an object of desire to them. Whoever supposes that this preference takes place at a sacrifice of happiness—that the superior being, in anything like equal circumstances, is not happier than the inferior—confounds the two very different ideas, of happiness, and content. It is indisputable that the being whose capacities of enjoyment are low, has the greatest chance of having them fully satisfied; and a highly endowed being will always

accepts, with calm indifference, his place in the impartial, rational, inevitable order of the universe—even if it is his fate to suffer hardship or painful death—but also works dutifully to foster a social order that mirrors the rational order of the cosmos.

feel that any happiness which he can look for, as the world is constituted, is imperfect. But he can learn to bear its imperfections, if they are at all bearable; and they will not make him envy the being who is indeed unconscious of the imperfections, but only because he feels not at all the good which those imperfections qualify. It is better to be a human being dissatisfied than a pig satisfied; better to be Socrates dissatisfied than a fool satisfied. And if the fool, or the pig, are of a different opinion, it is because they only know their own side of the question. The other party to the comparison knows both sides.

It may be objected, that many who are capable of the higher pleasures, occasionally, under the influence of temptation, postpone them to the lower. But this is quite compatible with a full appreciation of the intrinsic superiority of the higher. Men often, from infirmity of character, make their election for[20] the nearer good, though they know it to be the less valuable; and this no less when the choice is between two bodily pleasures, than when it is between bodily and mental. They pursue sensual indulgences to the injury of health, though perfectly aware that health is the greater good.

It may be further objected, that many who begin with youthful enthusiasm for everything noble, as they advance in years sink into indolence and selfishness. But I do not believe that those who undergo this very common change, voluntarily choose the lower description of pleasures in preference to the higher. I believe that before they devote themselves exclusively to the one, they have already become incapable of the other. Capacity for the nobler feelings is in most natures a very tender plant, easily killed, not only by hostile influences, but by mere want of sustenance; and in the majority of young persons it speedily dies away if the occupations to which their position in life has devoted them, and the society into which it has thrown them, are not favourable to keeping that higher capacity in exercise. Men lose their high aspirations as they lose their intellectual tastes, because they have not time or opportunity for indulging them; and they addict themselves to inferior pleasures, not because they deliberately prefer them, but because they are

either the only ones to which they have access, or the only ones which they are any longer capable of enjoying. It may be questioned whether any one who has remained equally susceptible to both classes of pleasures, ever knowingly and calmly preferred the lower; though many, in all ages, have broken down in an ineffectual attempt to combine both.

From this verdict of the only competent judges, I apprehend there can be no appeal. On a question which is the best worth having of two pleasures, or which of two modes of existence is the most grateful to the feelings, apart from its moral attributes and from its consequences, the judgment of those who are qualified by knowledge of both, or, if they differ, that of the majority among them, must be admitted as final. And there needs be the less hesitation to accept this judgment respecting the quality of pleasures, since there is no other tribunal to be referred to even on the question of quantity. What means are there of determining which is the acutest of two pains, or the intensest of two pleasurable sensations, except the general suffrage[21] of those who are familiar with both? Neither pains nor pleasures are homogeneous, and pain is always heterogeneous with pleasure. What is there to decide whether a particular pleasure is worth purchasing at the cost of a particular pain, except the feelings and judgment of the experienced? When, therefore, those feelings and judgment declare the pleasures derived from the higher faculties to be preferable *in kind*, apart from the question of intensity, to those of which the animal nature, disjoined from the higher faculties, is susceptible, they are entitled on this subject to the same regard.

I have dwelt on this point, as being a necessary part of a perfectly just conception of Utility or Happiness, considered as the directive rule of human conduct. But it is by no means an indispensable condition to the acceptance of the utilitarian standard; for that standard is not the agent's own greatest happiness, but the greatest amount of happiness altogether; and if it may possibly be doubted whether a noble character is always the happier for its nobleness, there can be no doubt that it makes other people happier, and that

---

20　Choose.

21　A view expressed by voting (or the right to make such a vote).

the world in general is immensely a gainer by it. Utilitarianism, therefore, could only attain its end by the general cultivation of nobleness of character, even if each individual were only benefited by the nobleness of others, and his own, so far as happiness is concerned, were a sheer deduction[22] from the benefit. But the bare enunciation of such an absurdity as this last, renders refutation superfluous.

According to the Greatest Happiness Principle, as above explained, the ultimate end, with reference to and for the sake of which all other things are desirable (whether we are considering our own good or that of other people), is an existence exempt as far as possible from pain, and as rich as possible in enjoyments, both in point of quantity and quality; the test of quality, and the rule for measuring it against quantity, being the preference felt by those who in their opportunities of experience, to which must be added their habits of self-consciousness and self-observation, are best furnished with the means of comparison. This, being, according to the utilitarian opinion, the end of human action, is necessarily also the standard of morality; which may accordingly be defined, the rules and precepts for human conduct, by the observance of which an existence such as has been described might be, to the greatest extent possible, secured to all mankind; and not to them only, but, so far as the nature of things admits, to the whole sentient creation.[23]

Against this doctrine, however, arises another class of objectors, who say that happiness, in any form, cannot be the rational purpose of human life and action; because, in the first place, it is unattainable: and they contemptuously ask, what right hast thou to be happy? a question which Mr. Carlyle[24] clenches by the addition, What right, a short time ago, hadst thou even *to be*? Next, they say, that men can do *without* happiness; that all noble human beings have felt this, and could not have become noble but by learning the lesson of Entsagen,[25] or renunciation; which lesson, thoroughly learnt and submitted to, they affirm to be the beginning and necessary condition of all virtue.

The first of these objections would go to the root of the matter were it well founded; for if no happiness is to be had at all by human beings, the attainment of it cannot be the end of morality, or of any rational conduct. Though, even in that case, something might still be said for the utilitarian theory; since utility includes not solely the pursuit of happiness, but the prevention or mitigation of unhappiness; and if the former aim be chimerical,[26] there will be all the greater scope and more imperative need for the latter, so long at least as mankind think fit to live, and do not take refuge in the simultaneous act of suicide recommended under certain conditions by Novalis.[27] When, however, it is thus positively asserted to be impossible that human life should be happy, the assertion, if not something like a verbal quibble, is at least an exaggeration. If by happiness be meant a continuity of highly pleasurable excitement, it is evident enough that this is impossible. A state of exalted pleasure lasts only moments, or in some cases, and with some intermissions, hours or days, and is the occasional brilliant flash of enjoy-

---

22 Subtraction (as opposed to an inference).

23 To all creatures capable of sensation (and thus of feeling pleasure and pain).

24 Thomas Carlyle (1795–1881) was a popular Scottish writer and (somewhat reactionary) social critic. This quote is from his 1836 book, *Sartor Resartus*. As a young man Mill was heavily influenced by Carlyle's allegiance to German Romanticism, but once Carlyle began to realize that Mill did not see himself as one of his disciples their relationship took a sharp turn for the worse. (The fact that Mill's maid accidentally used the only manuscript copy of Carlyle's *History of the French Revolution* to light a fire when Carlyle was visiting him—forcing Carlyle to rewrite all of Volume I—cannot have helped.) *Utilitarianism* is largely intended as a response to criticisms of Mill's moral theories leveled by Carlyle and others.

25 German for "to renounce or abjure." The idea it is supposed to capture is that moral behavior must be painful or difficult to be genuinely virtuous.

26 Unrealistic, fanciful.

27 Novalis was the pseudonym of an early German poet and philosopher in the "Romantic" movement, Friedrich von Hardenberg (1772–1801). His most famous poem, "Hymns to the Night," was written after the death of his young fiancée from tuberculosis in 1799. Just months after its publication, von Hardenberg also succumbed to the disease.

ment, not its permanent and steady flame. Of this the philosophers who have taught that happiness is the end of life were as fully aware as those who taunt them. The happiness which they meant was not a life of rapture; but moments of such, in an existence made up of few and transitory pains, many and various pleasures, with a decided predominance of the active over the passive, and having as the foundation of the whole, not to expect more from life than it is capable of bestowing. A life thus composed, to those who have been fortunate enough to obtain it, has always appeared worthy of the name of happiness. And such an existence is even now the lot of many, during some considerable portion of their lives. The present wretched education, and wretched social arrangements, are the only real hindrance to its being attainable by almost all.

The objectors perhaps may doubt whether human beings, if taught to consider happiness as the end of life, would be satisfied with such a moderate share of it. But great numbers of mankind have been satisfied with much less. The main constituents of a satisfied life appear to be two, either of which by itself is often found sufficient for the purpose: tranquillity, and excitement. With much tranquillity, many find that they can be content with very little pleasure: with much excitement, many can reconcile themselves to a considerable quantity of pain. There is assuredly no inherent impossibility in enabling even the mass of mankind to unite both; since the two are so far from being incompatible that they are in natural alliance, the prolongation of either being a preparation for, and exciting a wish for, the other. It is only those in whom indolence amounts to a vice, that do not desire excitement after an interval of repose: it is only those in whom the need of excitement is a disease, that feel the tranquillity which follows excitement dull and insipid, instead of pleasurable in direct proportion to the excitement which preceded it. When people who are tolerably fortunate in their outward lot do not find in life sufficient enjoyment to make it valuable to them, the cause generally is, caring for nobody but themselves. To those who have neither public nor private affections, the excitements of life are much curtailed, and in any case dwindle in value as the time approaches when all selfish interests must be terminated by death: while those who leave after them objects of personal affection, and especially those who have also cultivated a fellow-feeling with the collective interests of mankind, retain as lively an interest in life on the eve of death as in the vigour of youth and health. Next to selfishness, the principal cause which makes life unsatisfactory is want[28] of mental cultivation. A cultivated mind—I do not mean that of a philosopher, but any mind to which the fountains of knowledge have been opened, and which has been taught, in any tolerable degree, to exercise its faculties—finds sources of inexhaustible interest in all that surrounds it; in the objects of nature, the achievements of art, the imaginations of poetry, the incidents of history, the ways of mankind, past and present, and their prospects in the future. It is possible, indeed, to become indifferent to all this, and that too without having exhausted a thousandth part of it; but only when one has had from the beginning no moral or human interest in these things, and has sought in them only the gratification of curiosity.

Now there is absolutely no reason in the nature of things why an amount of mental culture sufficient to give an intelligent interest in these objects of contemplation, should not be the inheritance of every one born in a civilised country. As little is there an inherent necessity that any human being should be a selfish egotist, devoid of every feeling or care but those which centre in his own miserable individuality. Something far superior to this is sufficiently common even now, to give ample earnest of what the human species may be made. Genuine private affections and a sincere interest in the public good, are possible, though in unequal degrees, to every rightly brought up human being. In a world in which there is so much to interest, so much to enjoy, and so much also to correct and improve, every one who has this moderate amount of moral and intellectual requisites is capable of an existence which may be called enviable; and unless such a person, through bad laws, or subjection to the will of others, is denied the liberty to use the sources of happiness within his reach, he will not fail to find this enviable existence, if he escape the positive evils of life, the great sources of physical and mental suffer-

---

28   Lack.

ing—such as indigence, disease, and the unkindness, worthlessness, or premature loss of objects of affection. The main stress of the problem lies, therefore, in the contest with these calamities, from which it is a rare good fortune entirely to escape; which, as things now are, cannot be obviated, and often cannot be in any material degree mitigated. Yet no one whose opinion deserves a moment's consideration can doubt that most of the great positive evils of the world are in themselves removable, and will, if human affairs continue to improve, be in the end reduced within narrow limits. Poverty, in any sense implying suffering, may be completely extinguished by the wisdom of society, combined with the good sense and providence of individuals. Even that most intractable of enemies, disease, may be indefinitely reduced in dimensions by good physical and moral education, and proper control of noxious influences; while the progress of science holds out a promise for the future of still more direct conquests over this detestable foe. And every advance in that direction relieves us from some, not only of the chances which cut short our own lives, but, what concerns us still more, which deprive us of those in whom our happiness is wrapt up.[29] As for vicissitudes of fortune, and other disappointments connected with worldly circumstances, these are principally the effect either of gross imprudence, of ill-regulated desires, or of bad or imperfect social institutions. All the grand sources, in short, of human suffering are in a great degree, many of them almost entirely, conquerable by human care and effort; and though their removal is grievously slow—though a long succession of generations will perish in the breach before the conquest is completed, and this world becomes all that, if will and knowledge were not wanting, it might easily be made—yet every mind sufficiently intelligent and generous to bear a part, however small and unconspicuous, in the endeavour, will draw a noble enjoyment from the contest itself, which he would not for any bribe in the form of selfish indulgence consent to be without.

And this leads to the true estimation of what is said by the objectors concerning the possibility, and the obligation, of learning to do without happiness. Unquestionably it is possible to do without happiness; it is done involuntarily by nineteen-twentieths of mankind, even in those parts of our present world which are least deep in barbarism; and it often has to be done voluntarily by the hero or the martyr, for the sake of something which he prizes more than his individual happiness. But this something, what is it, unless the happiness of others or some of the requisites of happiness? It is noble to be capable of resigning entirely one's own portion of happiness, or chances of it: but, after all, this self-sacrifice must be for some end; it is not its own end; and if we are told that its end is not happiness, but virtue, which is better than happiness, I ask, would the sacrifice be made if the hero or martyr did not believe that it would earn for others immunity from similar sacrifices? Would it be made if he thought that his renunciation of happiness for himself would produce no fruit for any of his fellow creatures, but to make their lot like his, and place them also in the condition of persons who have renounced happiness? All honour to those who can abnegate for themselves the personal enjoyment of life, when by such renunciation they contribute worthily to increase the amount of happiness in the world; but he who does it, or professes to do it, for any other purpose, is no more deserving of admiration than the ascetic mounted on his pillar.[30] He may be an inspiriting proof of what men *can* do, but assuredly not an example of what they *should*.

Though it is only in a very imperfect state of the world's arrangements that any one can best serve the happiness of others by the absolute sacrifice of his own, yet so long as the world is in that imperfect state, I fully acknowledge that the readiness to make such a sacrifice is the highest virtue which can be found in man. I will add, that in this condition of the world, paradoxical as the assertion may be, the conscious ability to do without happiness gives the best prospect of realising such happiness as is attainable. For nothing except that consciousness can raise a person

29 For example, Mill's wife Harriet Taylor, who died of "pulmonary congestion" in 1858.

30 Mill is probably thinking of St. Simeon Stylites (c. 390–459), a Syrian ascetic who spent more than thirty years living at the top of various pillars, the highest of which was twenty meters tall.

above the chances of life, by making him feel that, let fate and fortune do their worst, they have not power to subdue him: which, once felt, frees him from excess of anxiety concerning the evils of life, and enables him, like many a Stoic in the worst times of the Roman Empire,[31] to cultivate in tranquillity the sources of satisfaction accessible to him, without concerning himself about the uncertainty of their duration, any more than about their inevitable end.

Meanwhile, let utilitarians never cease to claim the morality of self-devotion as a possession which belongs by as good a right to them, as either to the Stoic or to the Transcendentalist.[32] The utilitarian morality does recognise in human beings the power of sacrificing their own greatest good for the good of others. It only refuses to admit that the sacrifice is itself a good. A sacrifice which does not increase, or tend to increase, the sum total of happiness, it considers as wasted. The only self-renunciation which it applauds, is devotion to the happiness, or to some of the means of happiness, of others; either of mankind collectively, or of individuals within the limits imposed by the collective interests of mankind.

I must again repeat, what the assailants of utilitarianism seldom have the justice to acknowledge, that the happiness which forms the utilitarian standard of what is right in conduct, is not the agent's own happiness, but that of all concerned. As between his own happiness and that of others, utilitarianism requires him to be as strictly impartial as a disinterested[33] and benevolent spectator. In the golden rule of Jesus of Nazareth, we read the complete spirit of the ethics of utility. To do as you would be done by, and to love your neighbour as yourself, constitute the ideal perfection of utilitarian morality. As the means of making the nearest approach to this ideal, utility would enjoin, first, that laws and social arrangements should place the happiness, or (as speaking practically it may be called) the interest, of every individual, as nearly as

possible in harmony with the interest of the whole; and secondly, that education and opinion, which have so vast a power over human character, should so use that power as to establish in the mind of every individual an indissoluble association between his own happiness and the good of the whole; especially between his own happiness and the practice of such modes of conduct, negative and positive, as regard for the universal happiness prescribes; so that not only he may be unable to conceive the possibility of happiness to himself, consistently with conduct opposed to the general good, but also that a direct impulse to promote the general good may be in every individual one of the habitual motives of action, and the sentiments connected therewith may fill a large and prominent place in every human being's sentient existence. If the impugners of the utilitarian morality represented it to their own minds in this, its true character, I know not what recommendation possessed by any other morality they could possibly affirm to be wanting to it; what more beautiful or more exalted developments of human nature any other ethical system can be supposed to foster, or what springs of action, not accessible to the utilitarian, such systems rely on for giving effect to their mandates.

The objectors to utilitarianism cannot always be charged with representing it in a discreditable light. On the contrary, those among them who entertain anything like a just idea of its disinterested character, sometimes find fault with its standard as being too high for humanity. They say it is exacting too much to require that people shall always act from the inducement of promoting the general interests of society. But this is to mistake the very meaning of a standard of morals, and confound the rule of action with the motive of it. It is the business of ethics to tell us what are our duties, or by what test we may know them; but no system of ethics requires that the sole motive of all we do shall be a feeling of duty; on the contrary, ninety-nine hundredths of all our actions are done from other motives, and rightly so done, if the rule of duty does not condemn them. It is the more unjust to utilitarianism that this particular misapprehension should be made a ground of objection to it, inasmuch as utilitarian moralists have gone beyond almost all others in affirming

---

31   Many Stoics were punished or killed for opposition to dictatorial Roman emperors.

32   Those—such as Kant—who think the evidence for moral truths "transcends" human sense experience.

33   Free from bias or self-interest (not *un*interested or bored!).

that the motive has nothing to do with the morality of the action, though much with the worth of the agent. He who saves a fellow creature from drowning does what is morally right, whether his motive be duty, or the hope of being paid for his trouble; he who betrays the friend that trusts him, is guilty of a crime, even if his object be to serve another friend to whom he is under greater obligations.[34]

---

34 [Author's note] An opponent, whose intellectual and moral fairness it is a pleasure to acknowledge (the Rev. J. Llewellyn Davies), has objected to this passage, saying, "Surely the rightness or wrongness of saving a man from drowning does depend very much upon the motive with which it is done. Suppose that a tyrant, when his enemy jumped into the sea to escape from him, saved him from drowning simply in order that he might inflict upon him more exquisite tortures, would it tend to clearness to speak of that action as 'a morally right action'? Or suppose again, according to one of the stock illustrations of ethical inquiries, that a man betrayed a trust received from a friend, because the discharge of it would fatally injure that friend himself or some one belonging to him, would utilitarianism compel one to call the betrayal 'a crime' as much as if it had been done from the meanest motive?"

I submit, that he who saves another from drowning in order to kill him by torture afterwards, does not differ only in motive from him who does the same thing from duty or benevolence; the act itself is different. The rescue of the man is, in the case supposed, only the necessary first step of an act far more atrocious than leaving him to drown would have been. Had Mr. Davies said, "the rightness of wrongness of saving a man from drowning does depend very much"—not upon the motive but—"upon the *intention*," no utilitarian would have differed from him. Mr. Davies, by an oversight too common not to be quite venial, has in this case confounded the very different ideas of Motive and Intention. There is no point at which utilitarian thinkers (and Bentham pre-eminently) have taken more pains to illustrate than this. The morality of the action depends entirely upon the intention—that is, upon what the agent *wills to do*. But the motive, that is, the feeling which makes him will to do so, when it makes no difference to the act, makes none in the morality: though it

But to speak only of actions done from the motive of duty, and in direct obedience to principle: it is a misapprehension of the utilitarian mode of thought, to conceive it as implying that people should fix their minds upon so wide a generality as the world, or society at large. The great majority of good actions are intended not for the benefit of the world, but for that of individuals, of which the good of the world is made up; and the thoughts of the most virtuous man need not on these occasions travel beyond the particular persons concerned, except so far as is necessary to assure himself that in benefiting them he is not violating the rights—that is, the legitimate and authorised expectations—of any one else. The multiplication of happiness is, according to the utilitarian ethics, the object of virtue: the occasions on which any person (except one in a thousand) has it in his power to do this on an extended scale, in other words to be a public benefactor, are but exceptional; and on these occasions alone is he called on to consider public utility; in every other case, private utility, the interest or happiness of some few persons, is all he has to attend to. Those alone the influence of whose actions extends to society in general, need concern themselves habitually about so large an object. In the case of abstinences indeed—of things which people forbear to do from moral considerations, though the consequences in the particular case might be beneficial—it would be unworthy of an intelligent agent not to be consciously aware that the action is of a class which, if practised generally, would be generally injurious, and that this is the ground of the obligation to abstain from it. The amount of regard for the public interest implied in this recognition, is no greater than is demanded by every system of morals, for they all enjoin to abstain from whatever is manifestly pernicious to society.

The same considerations dispose of another reproach against the doctrine of utility, founded on a still grosser misconception of the purpose of a standard of

---

makes a great difference in our moral estimation of the agent, especially if it indicates a good or a bad habitual *disposition*—a bent of character from which useful, or from which hurtful actions are likely to arise.

morality, and of the very meaning of the words right and wrong. It is often affirmed[35] that utilitarianism renders men cold and unsympathising; that it chills their moral feelings towards individuals; that it makes them regard only the dry and hard consideration of the consequences of actions, not taking into their moral estimate the qualities from which those actions emanate. If the assertion means that they do not allow their judgment respecting the rightness or wrongness of an action to be influenced by their opinion of the qualities of the person who does it, this is a complaint not against utilitarianism, but against having any standard of morality at all; for certainly no known ethical standard decides an action to be good or bad because it is done by a good or a bad man, still less because done by an amiable, a brave, or a benevolent man, or the contrary. These considerations are relevant, not to the estimation of actions, but of persons; and there is nothing in the utilitarian theory inconsistent with the fact that there are other things which interest us in persons besides the rightness and wrongness of their actions. The Stoics, indeed, with the paradoxical misuse of language which was part of their system, and by which they strove to raise themselves above all concern about anything but virtue, were fond of saying that he who has that has everything; that he, and only he, is rich, is beautiful, is a king. But no claim of this description is made for the virtuous man by the utilitarian doctrine. Utilitarians are quite aware that there are other desirable possessions and qualities besides virtue, and are perfectly willing to allow to all of them their full worth. They are also aware that a right action does not necessarily indicate a virtuous character, and that actions which are blameable, often proceed from qualities entitled to praise. When this is apparent in any particular case, it modifies their estimation, not certainly of the act, but of the agent. I grant that they are, notwithstanding, of opinion, that in the long run the best proof of a good character is good actions; and resolutely refuse to consider any mental disposition as good, of which the predominant tendency is to produce bad conduct. This makes them

unpopular with many people; but it is an unpopularity which they must share with every one who regards the distinction between right and wrong in a serious light; and the reproach is not one which a conscientious utilitarian need be anxious to repel.

If no more be meant by the objection than that many utilitarians look on the morality of actions, as measured by the utilitarian standard, with too exclusive a regard, and do not lay sufficient stress upon the other beauties of character which go towards making a human being lovable or admirable, this may be admitted. Utilitarians who have cultivated their moral feelings, but not their sympathies nor their artistic perceptions, do fall into this mistake; and so do all other moralists under the same conditions. What can be said in excuse for other moralists is equally available for them, namely, that, if there is to be any error, it is better that it should be on that side. As a matter of fact, we may affirm that among utilitarians as among adherents of other systems, there is every imaginable degree of rigidity and of laxity in the application of their standard: some are even puritanically rigorous, while others are as indulgent as can possibly be desired by sinner or by sentimentalist. But on the whole, a doctrine which brings prominently forward the interest that mankind have in the repression and prevention of conduct which violates the moral law, is likely to be inferior to no other in turning the sanctions of opinion again such violations. It is true, the question, What does violate the moral law? is one on which those who recognise different standards of morality are likely now and then to differ. But difference of opinion on moral questions was not first introduced into the world by utilitarianism, while that doctrine does supply, if not always an easy, at all events a tangible and intelligible mode of deciding such differences.

It may not be superfluous to notice a few more of the common misapprehensions of utilitarian ethics, even those which are so obvious and gross that it might appear impossible for any person of candour and intelligence to fall into them; since persons, even of considerable mental endowments, often give themselves so little trouble to understand the bearings of any opinion against which they entertain a prejudice, and men are in general so little conscious of this

---

35   For example, in Charles Dickens's novel *Hard Times* (1854), especially through the character of Gradgrind.

voluntary ignorance as a defect, that the vulgarest misunderstandings of ethical doctrines are continually met with in the deliberate writings of persons of the greatest pretensions both to high principle and to philosophy. We not uncommonly hear the doctrine of utility inveighed against as a *godless* doctrine. If it be necessary to say anything at all against so mere an assumption, we may say that the question depends upon what idea we have formed of the moral character of the Deity. If it be a true belief that God desires, above all things, the happiness of his creatures, and that this was his purpose in their creation, utility is not only not a godless doctrine, but more profoundly religious than any other. If it be meant that utilitarianism does not recognise the revealed will of God as the supreme law of morals, I answer, that a utilitarian who believes in the perfect goodness and wisdom of God, necessarily believes that whatever God has thought fit to reveal on the subject of morals, must fulfil the requirements of utility in a supreme degree. But others besides utilitarians have been of opinion that the Christian revelation was intended, and is fitted, to inform the hearts and minds of mankind with a spirit which should enable them to find for themselves what is right, and incline them to do it when found, rather than to tell them, except in a very general way, what it is; and that we need a doctrine of ethics, carefully followed out, to *interpret* to us the will God. Whether this opinion is correct or not, it is superfluous here to discuss; since whatever aid religion, either natural or revealed, can afford to ethical investigation, is as open to the utilitarian moralist as to any other. He can use it as the testimony of God to the usefulness or hurtfulness of any given course of action, by as good a right as others can use it for the indication of a transcendental law, having no connection with usefulness or with happiness.

Again, Utility is often summarily stigmatised as an immoral doctrine by giving it the name of Expediency, and taking advantage of the popular use of that term to contrast it with Principle. But the Expedient, in the sense in which it is opposed to the Right, generally means that which is expedient for the particular interest of the agent himself; as when a minister sacrifices the interests of his country to keep himself in place. When it means anything better than this, it means that

which is expedient for some immediate object, some temporary purpose, but which violates a rule whose observance is expedient in a much higher degree. The Expedient, in this sense, instead of being the same thing with the useful, is a branch of the hurtful. Thus, it would often be expedient, for the purpose of getting over some momentary embarrassment, or attaining some object immediately useful to ourselves or others, to tell a lie. But inasmuch as the cultivation in ourselves of a sensitive feeling on the subject of veracity, is one of the most useful, and the enfeeblement of that feeling one of the most hurtful, things to which our conduct can be instrumental; and inasmuch as any, even unintentional, deviation from truth, does that much towards weakening the trustworthiness of human assertion, which is not only the principal support of all present social well-being, but the insufficiency of which does more than any one thing that can be named to keep back civilisation, virtue, everything on which human happiness on the largest scale depends; we feel that the violation, for a present advantage, of a rule of such transcendant expediency, is not expedient, and that he who, for the sake of a convenience to himself or to some other individual, does what depends on him to deprive mankind of the good, and inflict upon them the evil, involved in the greater or less reliance which they can place in each other's word, acts the part of one of their worst enemies. Yet that even this rule, sacred as it is, admits of possible exceptions, is acknowledged by all moralists; the chief of which is when the withholding of some fact (as of information from a malefactor, or of bad news from a person dangerously ill) would save an individual (especially an individual other than oneself) from great and unmerited evil, and when the withholding can only be effected by denial. But in order that the exception may not extend itself beyond the need, and may have the least possible effect in weakening reliance on veracity, it ought to be recognised, and, if possible, its limits defined; and if the principle of utility is good for anything, it must be good for weighing these conflicting utilities against one another, and marking out the region within which one or the other preponderates.

Again, defenders of utility often find themselves called upon to reply to such objections as this—that there is not time, previous to action, for calculating and weighing the effects of any line of conduct on the general happiness. This is exactly as if any one were to say that it is impossible to guide our conduct by Christianity, because there is not time, on every occasion on which anything has to be done, to read through the Old and New Testaments. The answer to the objection is, that there has been ample time, namely, the whole past duration of the human species. During all that time, mankind have been learning by experience the tendencies of actions; on which experience all the prudence, as well as all the morality of life, are dependent. People talk as if the commencement of this course of experience had hitherto been put off, and as if, at the moment when some man feels tempted to meddle with the property or life of another, he had to begin considering for the first time whether murder and theft are injurious to human happiness. Even then I do not think that he would find the question very puzzling; but, at all events, the matter is now done to his hand. It is truly a whimsical supposition that, if mankind were agreed in considering utility to be the test of morality, they would remain without any agreement as to what *is* useful, and would take no measures for having their notions on the subject taught to the young, and enforced by law and opinion. There is no difficulty in proving any ethical standard whatever to work ill, if we suppose universal idiocy to be conjoined with it; but on any hypothesis short of that, mankind must by this time have acquired positive beliefs as to the effects of some actions on their happiness; and the beliefs which have thus come down are the rules of morality for the multitude, and for the philosopher until he has succeeded in finding better. That philosophers might easily do this, even now, on many subjects; that the received code of ethics is by no means of divine right; and that mankind have still much to learn as to the effects of actions on the general happiness, I admit, or rather, earnestly maintain. The corollaries from the principle of utility, like the precepts of every practical art, admit of indefinite improvement, and, in a progressive state of the human mind, their improvement is perpetually going on. But to consider the rules of morality as improvable, is one thing; to pass over the intermediate generalisations entirely, and endeavour to test each individual action

directly by the first principle, is another. It is a strange notion that the acknowledgment of a first principle is inconsistent with the admission of secondary ones. To inform a traveller respecting the place of his ultimate destination, is not to forbid the use of landmarks and direction-posts on the way. The proposition that happiness is the end and aim of morality, does not mean that no road ought to be laid down to that goal, or that persons going thither should not be advised to take one direction rather than another. Men really ought to leave off talking a kind of nonsense on this subject, which they would neither talk nor listen to on other matters of practical concernment. Nobody argues that the art of navigation is not founded on astronomy, because sailors cannot wait to calculate the Nautical Almanack.[36] Being rational creatures, they go to sea with it ready calculated; and all rational creatures go out upon the sea of life with their minds made up on the common questions of right and wrong, as well as on many of the far more difficult questions of wise and foolish. And this, as long as foresight is a human quality, it is to be presumed they will continue to do. Whatever we adopt as the fundamental principle of morality, we require subordinate principles to apply it by; the impossibility of doing without them, being common to all systems, can afford no argument against any one in particular; but gravely to argue as if no such secondary principles could be had, and as if mankind had remained till now, and always must remain, without drawing any general conclusions from the experience of human life, is as high a pitch, I think, as absurdity has ever reached in philosophical controversy.

The remainder of the stock arguments against utilitarianism mostly consist in laying to its charge the common infirmities of human nature, and the general difficulties which embarrass conscientious

---

36   An annual government publication that tabulates the astronomical data required for maritime navigation. (For example, the almanac might give the coordinates of the constellation Orion as it would be seen at the horizon on a particular date from various places on the earth's surface: observation of Orion at certain coordinates on that date will therefore tell you where you are.)

persons in shaping their course through life. We are told that a utilitarian will be apt to make his own particular case an exception to moral rules, and, when under temptation, will see a utility in the breach of a rule, greater than he will see in its observance. But is utility the only creed which is able to furnish us with excuses for evil doing, and means of cheating our own conscience? They are afforded in abundance by all doctrines which recognise as a fact in morals the existence of conflicting considerations; which all doctrines do, that have been believed by sane persons. It is not the fault of any creed, but of the complicated nature of human affairs, that rules of conduct cannot be so framed as to require no exceptions, and that hardly any kind of action can safely be laid down as either always obligatory or always condemnable. There is no ethical creed which does not temper the rigidity of its laws, by giving a certain latitude, under the moral responsibility of the agent, for accommodation to peculiarities of circumstances; and under every creed, at the opening thus made, self-deception and dishonest casuistry[37] get in. There exists no moral system under which there do not arise unequivocal cases of conflicting obligation. These are the real difficulties, the knotty points both in the theory of ethics, and in the conscientious guidance of personal conduct. They are overcome practically, with greater or with less success, according to the intellect and virtue of the individual; but it can hardly be pretended that any one will be the less qualified for dealing with them, from possessing an ultimate standard to which conflicting rights and duties can be referred. If utility is the ultimate source of moral obligations, utility may be invoked to decide between them when their demands are incompatible. Though the application of the standard may be difficult, it is better than none at all: while in other systems, the moral laws all claiming independent authority, there is no common umpire entitled to interfere between them; their claims to precedence one over another rest on little better than sophistry,[38] and unless determined, as they generally are, by the unacknowledged influence of considerations of utility, afford a free scope for the action of personal desires

and partialities. We must remember that only in these cases of conflict between secondary principles is it requisite that first principles should be appealed to. There is no case of moral obligation in which some secondary principle is not involved; and if only one, there can seldom be any real doubt which one it is, in the mind of any person by whom the principle itself is recognised.

Chapter 3: Of the Ultimate Sanction[39] of the Principle of Utility.

The question is often asked, and properly so, in regard to any supposed moral standard—What is its sanction? what are the motives to obey it? or more specifically, what is the source of its obligation? whence does it derive its binding force? It is a necessary part of moral philosophy to provide the answer to this question; which, though frequently assuming the shape of an objection to the utilitarian morality, as if it had some special applicability to that above others, really arises in regard to all standards. It arises, in fact, whenever a person is called on to *adopt* a standard, or refer morality to any basis on which he has not been accustomed to rest it. For the customary morality, that which education and opinion have consecrated, is the only one which presents itself to the mind with the feeling of being *in itself* obligatory; and when a person is asked to believe that this morality *derives* its obligation from some general principle round which custom has not thrown the same halo, the assertion is to him a paradox; the supposed corollaries seem to have a more binding force than the original theorem; the superstructure seems to stand better without, than with, what is represented as its foundation. He says to

---

37 Specious rationalizing.

38 Plausible but misleading argument.

39 "Sanction" was a technical term in eighteenth- and nineteenth-century philosophy. Sanctions are the *sources* of the pleasures and pains which motivate people to act. For example, Bentham—in his *Introduction to the Principles of Morals and Legislation*—distinguished between four different types of sanction: "physical" sanctions (e.g., hunger or sexual desire), "political" sanctions (e.g., prison), "religious" sanctions (e.g., heaven and hell), and "moral" sanctions (e.g., social disapproval).

himself, I feel that I am bound not to rob or murder, betray or deceive; but why am I bound to promote the general happiness? If my own happiness lies in something else, why may I not give that the preference?

If the view adopted by the utilitarian philosophy of the nature of the moral sense be correct, this difficulty will always present itself, until the influences which form moral character have taken the same hold of the principle which they have taken of some of the consequences—until, by the improvement of education, the feeling of unity with our fellow-creatures shall be (what it cannot be denied that Christ intended it to be) as deeply rooted in our character, and to our own consciousness as completely a part of our nature, as the horror of crime is in an ordinarily well brought up young person. In the meantime, however, the difficulty has no peculiar application to the doctrine of utility, but is inherent in every attempt to analyse morality and reduce it to principles; which, unless the principle is already in men's minds invested with as much sacredness as any of its applications, always seems to divest them of a part of their sanctity.

The principle of utility either has, or there is no reason why it might not have, all the sanctions which belong to any other system of morals. Those sanctions are either external or internal. Of the external sanctions it is not necessary to speak at any length. They are, the hope of favour and the fear of displeasure, from our fellow creatures or from the Ruler of the Universe, along with whatever we may have of sympathy or affection for them, or of love and awe of Him, inclining us to do his will independently of selfish consequences. There is evidently no reason why all these motives for observance should not attach themselves to the utilitarian morality, as completely and as powerfully as to any other. Indeed, those of them which refer to our fellow creatures are sure to do so, in proportion to the amount of general intelligence; for whether there be any other ground of moral obligation than the general happiness or not, men do desire happiness; and however imperfect may be their own practice, they desire and commend all conduct in others towards themselves, by which they think their happiness is promoted. With regard to the religious motive, if men believe, as most profess to do, in the

goodness of God, those who think that conduciveness to the general happiness is the essence, or even only the criterion of good, must necessarily believe that it is also that which God approves. The whole force therefore of external reward and punishment, whether physical or moral, and whether proceeding from God or from our fellow men, together with all that the capacities of human nature admit of disinterested devotion to either, become available to enforce the utilitarian morality, in proportion as that morality is recognised; and the more powerfully, the more the appliances of education and general cultivation are bent to the purpose.

So far as to external sanctions. The internal sanction of duty, whatever our standard of duty may be, is one and the same—a feeling in our own mind; a pain, more or less intense, attendant on violation of duty, which in properly cultivated moral natures rises, in the more serious cases, into shrinking from it as an impossibility. This feeling, when disinterested, and connecting itself with the pure idea of duty, and not with some particular form of it, or with any of the merely accessory circumstances, is the essence of Conscience; though in that complex phenomenon as it actually exists, the simple fact is in general all encrusted over with collateral associations, derived from sympathy, from love, and still more from fear; from all the forms of religious feeling; from the recollections of childhood and of all our past life; from self-esteem, desire of the esteem of others, and occasionally even self-abasement. This extreme complication is, I apprehend, the origin of the sort of mystical character which, by a tendency of the human mind of which there are many other examples, is apt to be attributed to the idea of moral obligation, and which leads people to believe that the idea cannot possibly attach itself to any other objects than those which, by a supposed mysterious law, are found in our present experience to excite it. Its binding force, however, consists in the existence of a mass of feeling which must be broken through in order to do what violates our standard of right, and which, if we do nevertheless violate that standard, will probably have to be encountered afterwards in the form of remorse. Whatever theory we have of the nature or origin of conscience, this is what essentially constitutes it.

The ultimate sanction, therefore, of all morality (external motives apart) being a subjective feeling in our own minds, I see nothing embarrassing to those whose standard is utility, in the question, what is the sanction of that particular standard? We may answer, the same as of all other moral standards—the conscientious feelings of mankind. Undoubtedly this sanction has no binding efficacy on those who do not possess the feelings it appeals to; but neither will these persons be more obedient to any other moral principle than to the utilitarian one. On them morality of any kind has no hold but through the external sanctions. Meanwhile the feelings exist, a fact in human nature, the reality of which, and the great power with which they are capable of acting on those in whom they have been duly cultivated, are proved by experience. No reason has ever been shown why they may not be cultivated to as great intensity in connection with the utilitarian, as with any other rule of morals.

There is, I am aware, a disposition to believe that a person who sees in moral obligation a transcendental fact, an objective reality belonging to the province of "Things in themselves," is likely to be more obedient to it than one who believes it to be entirely subjective, having its seat in human consciousness only. But whatever a person's opinion may be on this point of Ontology,[40] the force he is really urged by is his own subjective feeling, and is exactly measured by its strength. No one's belief that duty is an objective reality is stronger than the belief that God is so; yet the belief in God, apart from the expectation of actual reward and punishment, only operates on conduct through, and in proportion to, the subjective religious feeling. The sanction, so far as it is disinterested, is always in the mind itself, and the notion therefore of the transcendental moralists must be, that this sanction will not exist *in* the mind unless it is believed to have its root out of the mind; and that if a person is able to say to himself, This which is restraining me, and which is called my conscience, is only a feeling in my own mind, he may possibly draw the conclusion that when the feeling ceases the obligation ceases, and that if he find the feeling inconvenient, he may disregard it, and endeavour to get rid of it. But is this danger confined to the utilitarian morality? Does the belief that moral obligation has its seat outside the mind make the feeling of it too strong to be got rid of? The fact is so far otherwise, that all moralists admit and lament the ease with which, in the generality of minds, conscience can be silenced or stifled. The question, Need I obey my conscience? is quite as often put to themselves by persons who never heard of the principle of utility, as by its adherents. Those whose conscientious feelings are so weak as to allow of their asking this question, if they answer it affirmatively, will not do so because they believe in the transcendental theory, but because of the external sanctions.

It is not necessary, for the present purpose, to decide whether the feeling of duty is innate[41] or implanted. Assuming it to be innate, it is an open question to what objects it naturally attaches itself, for the philosophic supporters of that theory are now agreed that the intuitive perception is of principles of morality and not of the details. If there be anything innate in the matter, I see no reason why the feeling which is innate should not be that of regard to the pleasures and pains of others. If there is any principle of morals which is intuitively obligatory, I should say it must be that. If so, the intuitive ethics would coincide with the utilitarian, and there would be no further quarrel between them. Even as it is, the intuitive moralists, though they believe that there are other intuitive moral obligations, do already believe this to be one; for they unanimously hold that a large *portion* of morality turns upon the consideration due to the interests of our fellow-creatures. Therefore, if the belief in the transcendental origin of moral obligation gives any additional efficacy to the internal sanction, it appears to me that the utilitarian principle has already the benefit of it.

On the other hand, if, as is my own belief, the moral feelings are not innate, but acquired, they are

---

40 Ontology is the study of what exists or of the nature of 'being' itself (*on* is Greek for "being"). Questions about the reality of numbers, of fictional characters, or of theoretical entities (such as quarks or genes) are ontological questions. The particular ontological question Mill has in mind here, is the existence of transcendent moral laws.

---

41 Inborn, possessed at birth.

not for that reason the less natural. It is natural to man to speak, to reason, to build cities, to cultivate the ground, though these are acquired faculties. The moral feelings are not indeed a part of our nature, in the sense of being in any perceptible degree present in all of us; but this, unhappily, is a fact admitted by those who believe the most strenuously in their transcendental origin. Like the other acquired capacities above referred to, the moral faculty, if not a part of our nature, is a natural outgrowth from it; capable, like them, in a certain small degree, of springing up spontaneously; and susceptible of being brought by cultivation to a high degree of development. Unhappily it is also susceptible, by a sufficient use of the external sanctions and of the force of early impressions, of being cultivated in almost any direction: so that there is hardly anything so absurd or so mischievous that it may not, by means of these influences, be made to act on the human mind with all the authority of conscience. To doubt that the same potency might be given by the same means to the principle of utility, even if it had no foundation in human nature, would be flying in the face of all experience.

But moral associations which are wholly of artificial creation, when intellectual culture goes on, yield by degrees to the dissolving force of analysis: and if the feeling of duty, when associated with utility, would appear equally arbitrary; if there were no leading department of our nature, no powerful class of sentiments, with which that association would harmonise, which would make us feel it congenial, and incline us not only to foster it in others (for which we have abundant interested motives), but also to cherish it in ourselves; if there were not, in short, a natural basis of sentiment for utilitarian morality, it might well happen that this association also, even after it had been implanted by education, might be analysed away.

But there *is* this basis of powerful natural sentiment; and this it is which, when once the general happiness is recognised as the ethical standard, will constitute the strength of the utilitarian morality. This firm foundation is that of the social feelings of mankind; the desire to be in unity with our fellow creatures, which is already a powerful principle in human nature, and happily one of those which tend to become stronger,

even without express inculcation,[42] from the influences of advancing civilisation. The social state is at once so natural, so necessary, and so habitual to man, that, except in some unusual circumstances or by an effort of voluntary abstraction, he never conceives himself otherwise than as a member of a body; and this association is riveted more and more, as mankind are further removed from the state of savage independence. Any condition, therefore, which is essential to a state of society, becomes more and more an inseparable part of every person's conception of the state of things which he is born into, and which is the destiny of a human being. Now, society between human beings, except in the relation of master and slave, is manifestly impossible on any other footing than that the interests of all are to be consulted. Society between equals can only exist on the understanding that the interests of all are to be regarded equally. And since in all states of civilisation, every person, except an absolute monarch, has equals, every one is obliged to live on these terms with somebody; and in every age some advance is made towards a state in which it will be impossible to live permanently on other terms with anybody. In this way people grow up unable to conceive as possible to them a state of total disregard of other people's interests. They are under a necessity of conceiving themselves as at least abstaining from all the grosser injuries, and (if only for their own protection) living in a state of constant protest against them. They are also familiar with the fact of co-operating with others and proposing to themselves a collective, not an individual interest as the aim (at least for the time being) of their actions. So long as they are co-operating, their ends are identified with those of others; there is at least a temporary feeling that the interests of others are their own interests. Not only does all strengthening of social ties, and all healthy growth of society, give to each individual a stronger personal interest in practically consulting the welfare of others; it also leads him to identify his *feelings* more and more with their good, or at least with an even greater degree of practical consideration for it. He comes, as though instinctively, to be conscious of himself as a being who *of course* pays regard to oth-

---

42   Frequent repetition or instruction, intended to firmly impress something in someone's mind.

ers. The good of others becomes to him a thing naturally and necessarily to be attended to, like any of the physical conditions of our existence. Now, whatever amount of this feeling a person has, he is urged by the strongest motives both of interest and of sympathy to demonstrate it, and to the utmost of his power encourage it in others; and even if he has none of it himself, he is as greatly interested as any one else that others should have it. Consequently the smallest germs of the feeling are laid hold of and nourished by the contagion of sympathy and the influences of education; and a complete web of corroborative association is woven round it, by the powerful agency of the external sanctions. This mode of conceiving ourselves and human life, as civilisation goes on, is felt to be more and more natural. Every step in political improvement renders it more so, by removing the sources of opposition of interest, and levelling those inequalities of legal privilege between individuals or classes, owing to which there are large portions of mankind whose happiness it is still practicable to disregard. In an improving state of the human mind, the influences are constantly on the increase, which tend to generate in each individual a feeling of unity with all the rest; which, if perfect, would make him never think of, or desire, any beneficial condition for himself, in the benefits of which they are not included. If we now suppose this feeling of unity to be taught as a religion, and the whole force of education, of institutions, and of opinion, directed, as it once was in the case of religion, to make every person grow up from infancy surrounded on all sides both by the profession and the practice of it, I think that no one, who can realise this conception, will feel any misgiving about the sufficiency of the ultimate sanction for the Happiness morality. To any ethical student who finds the realisation difficult, I recommend, as a means of facilitating it, the second of M. Comte's two principle works, the *Système de Politique Positive*.[43] I entertain the strongest objections to the system of

43   This 1854 book by French political philosopher and sociologist Auguste Comte (1798–1857) advocated a capitalist dictatorship based on science as the ideal form of society, and urged that theistic conceptions of religion be replaced by a scientific "religion of humanity."

politics and morals set forth in that treatise; but I think it has superabundantly shown the possibility of giving to the service of humanity, even without the aid of belief in a Providence, both the psychical power and the social efficacy of a religion; making it take hold of human life, and colour all thought, feeling, and action, in a manner of which the greatest ascendancy ever exercised by any religion may be but a type and foretaste; and of which the danger is, not that it should be insufficient but that it should be so excessive as to interfere unduly with human freedom and individuality.

Neither is it necessary to the feeling which constitutes the binding force of the utilitarian morality on those who recognise it, to wait for those social influences which would make its obligation felt by mankind at large. In the comparatively early state of human advancement in which we now live, a person cannot indeed feel that entireness of sympathy with all others, which would make any real discordance in the general direction of their conduct in life impossible; but already a person in whom the social feeling is at all developed, cannot bring himself to think of the rest of his fellow creatures as struggling rivals with him for the means of happiness, whom he must desire to see defeated in their object in order that he may succeed in his. The deeply rooted conception which every individual even now has of himself as a social being, tends to make him feel it one of his natural wants that there should be harmony between his feelings and aims and those of his fellow creatures. If differences of opinion and of mental culture make it impossible for him to share many of their actual feelings—perhaps make him denounce and defy those feelings—he still needs to be conscious that his real aim and theirs do not conflict; that he is not opposing himself to what they really wish for, namely their own good, but is, on the contrary, promoting it. This feeling in most individuals is much inferior in strength to their selfish feelings, and is often wanting altogether. But to those who have it, it possesses all the characters of a natural feeling. It does not present itself to their minds as a superstition of education, or a law despotically imposed by the power of society, but as an attribute which it would not be well for them to be without. This conviction is the ultimate sanction of the greatest happiness morality. This it is which makes any mind, of well-developed feelings, work with, and not against, the outward motives to care for others, afforded by what I have called the external sanctions; and when those sanctions are wanting, or act in an opposite direction, constitutes in itself a powerful internal binding force, in proportion to the sensitiveness and thoughtfulness of the character; since few but those whose mind is a moral blank, could bear to lay out their course of life on the plan of paying no regard to others except so far as their own private interest compels.

Chapter 4: Of what Sort of Proof the Principle of Utility is Susceptible.

It has already been remarked, that questions of ultimate ends do not admit of proof, in the ordinary acceptation of the term. To be incapable of proof by reasoning is common to all first principles; to the first premises of our knowledge,[44] as well as to those of our conduct. But the former, being matters of fact, may be the subject of a direct appeal to the faculties which judge of fact—namely, our senses, and our internal consciousness.[45] Can an appeal be made to the same faculties on questions of practical ends? Or by what other faculty is cognisance taken of them?

Questions about ends are, in other words, questions about what things are desirable. The utilitarian doctrine is, that happiness is desirable, and the only thing desirable, as an end; all other things being only desirable as means to that end. What ought to be required of this doctrine—what conditions is it requisite that the doctrine should fulfil—to make good its claim to be believed?

The only proof capable of being given that an object is visible, is that people actually see it. The only proof that a sound is audible, is that people hear it: and so of the other sources of our experience. In like manner, I apprehend, the sole evidence it is possible to produce that anything is desirable, is that people do actually desire it. If the end which the utilitarian doctrine proposes to itself were not, in theory and in practice, acknowledged to be an end, nothing could

---

44   Sense experience.
45   Mill means the memory of something previously experienced.

ever convince any person that it was so. No reason can be given why the general happiness is desirable, except that each person, so far as he believes it to be attainable, desires his own happiness. This, however, being a fact, we have not only all the proof which the case admits of, but all which it is possible to require, that happiness is a good: that each person's happiness is a good to that person, and the general happiness, therefore, a good to the aggregate of all persons. Happiness has made out its title as *one* of the ends of conduct, and consequently one of the criteria of morality.

But it has not, by this alone, proved itself to be the sole criterion. To do that, it would seem, by the same rule, necessary to show, not only that people desire happiness, but that they never desire anything else. Now it is palpable that they do desire things which, in common language, are decidedly distinguished from happiness. They desire, for example, virtue, and the absence of vice, no less really than pleasure and the absence of pain. The desire of virtue is not as universal, but it is as authentic a fact, as the desire of happiness. And hence the opponents of the utilitarian standard deem that they have a right to infer that there are other ends of human action besides happiness, and that happiness is not the standard of approbation and disapprobation.

But does the utilitarian doctrine deny that people desire virtue, or maintain that virtue is not a thing to be desired? The very reverse. It maintains not only that virtue is to be desired, but that it is to be desired disinterestedly, for itself. Whatever may be the opinion of utilitarian moralists as to the original conditions by which virtue is made virtue; however they may believe (as they do) that actions and dispositions are only virtuous because they promote another end than virtue; yet this being granted, and it having been decided, from considerations of this description, what is virtuous, they not only place virtue at the very head of the things which are good as means to the ultimate end, but they also recognise as a psychological fact the possibility of its being, to the individual, a good in itself, without looking to any end beyond it; and hold, that the mind is not in a right state, not in a state conformable to Utility, not in the state most conducive to the general happiness, unless it does love virtue in this manner—as a thing desirable in itself, even although, in the individual instance, it should not produce those other desirable consequences which it tends to produce, and on account of which it is held to be virtue. This opinion is not, in the smallest degree, a departure from the Happiness principle. The ingredients of happiness are very various, and each of them is desirable in itself, and not merely when considered as swelling an aggregate. The principle of utility does not mean that any given pleasure, as music, for instance, or any given exemption from pain, as for example health, is to be looked upon as means to a collective something termed happiness, and to be desired on that account. They are desired and desirable in and for themselves; besides being means, they are a part of the end. Virtue, according to the utilitarian doctrine, is not naturally and originally part of the end, but it is capable of becoming so; and in those who love it disinterestedly it has become so, and is desired and cherished, not as a means to happiness, but as a part of their happiness.

To illustrate this farther, we may remember that virtue is not the only thing, originally a means, and which if it were not a means to anything else, would be and remain indifferent, but which by association with what it is a means to, comes to be desired for itself, and that too with the utmost intensity. What, for example, shall we say of the love of money? There is nothing originally more desirable about money than about any heap of glittering pebbles. Its worth is solely that of the things which it will buy; the desires for other things than itself, which it is a means of gratifying. Yet the love of money is not only one of the strongest moving forces of human life, but money is, in many cases, desired in and for itself, the desire to possess it is often stronger than the desire to use it, and goes on increasing when all the desires which point to ends beyond it, to be compassed by it, are falling off. It may, then, be said truly, that money is desired not for the sake of an end, but as part of the end. From being a means to happiness, it has come to be itself a principal ingredient of the individual's conception of happiness. The same may be said of the majority of the great objects of human life—power, for example, or fame; except that to each of these there is a certain amount of immediate pleasure annexed, which has at least the semblance of being naturally inherent in them; a

thing which cannot be said of money. Still, however, the strongest natural attraction, both of power and of fame, is the immense aid they give to the attainment of our other wishes; and it is the strong association thus generated between them and all our objects of desire, which gives to the direct desire of them the intensity it often assumes, so as in some characters to surpass in strength all other desires. In these cases the means have become a part of the end, and a more important part of it than any of the things which they are means to. What was once desired as an instrument for the attainment of happiness, has come to be desired for its own sake. In being desired for its own sake it is, however, desired as *part* of happiness. The person is made, or thinks he would be made, happy by its mere possession; and is made unhappy by failure to obtain it. The desire of it is not a different thing from the desire of happiness, any more than the love of music, or the desire of health. They are included in happiness. They are some of the elements of which the desire of happiness is made up. Happiness is not an abstract idea, but a concrete whole; and these are some of its parts. And the utilitarian standard sanctions and approves their being so. Life would be a poor thing, very ill provided with sources of happiness, if there were not this provision of nature, by which things originally indifferent, but conducive to, or otherwise associated with, the satisfaction of our primitive desires, become in themselves sources of pleasure more valuable than the primitive pleasures, both in permanency, in the space of human existence that they are capable of covering, and even in intensity.

Virtue, according to the utilitarian conception, is a good of this description. There was no original desire of it, or motive to it, save its conduciveness to pleasure, and especially to protection from pain. But through the association thus formed, it may be felt a good in itself, and desired as such with as great intensity as any other good; and with this difference between it and the love of money, of power, or of fame, that all of these may, and often do, render the individual noxious to the other members of the society to which he belongs, whereas there is nothing which makes him so much a blessing to them as the cultivation of the disinterested love of virtue. And consequently, the utilitarian standard, while it tolerates and approves those other acquired desires, up to the point beyond which they would be more injurious to the general happiness than promotive of it, enjoins and requires the cultivation of the love of virtue up to the greatest strength possible, as being above all things important to the general happiness.

It results from the preceding considerations, that there is in reality nothing desired except happiness. Whatever is desired otherwise than as a means to some end beyond itself, and ultimately to happiness, is desired as itself a part of happiness, and is not desired for itself until it has become so. Those who desire virtue for its own sake, desire it either because the consciousness of it is a pleasure, or because the consciousness of being without it is a pain, or for both reasons united; as in truth the pleasure and pain seldom exist separately, but almost always together, the same person feeling pleasure in the degree of virtue attained, and pain in not having attained more. If one of these gave him no pleasure, and the other no pain, he would not love or desire virtue, or would desire it only for the other benefits which it might produce to himself or to persons whom he cared for.

We have now, then, an answer to the question, of what sort of proof the principle of utility is susceptible. If the opinion which I have now stated is psychologically true—if human nature is so constituted as to desire nothing which is not either a part of happiness or a means of happiness, we can have no other proof, and we require no other, that these are the only things desirable. If so, happiness is the sole end of human action, and the promotion of it the test by which to judge of all human conduct; from whence it necessarily follows that it must be the criterion of morality, since a part is included in the whole.

And now to decide whether this is really so; whether mankind do desire nothing for itself but that which is a pleasure to them, or of which the absence is a pain; we have evidently arrived at a question of fact and experience, dependent, like all similar questions, upon evidence. It can only be determined by practised self-consciousness and self-observation, assisted by observation of others. I believe that these sources of evidence, impartially consulted, will declare that desiring a thing and finding it pleasant, aversion to it and thinking of it as painful, are phenomena entirely inseparable, or rather two parts of the same phenomenon; in strictness of language, two different modes of naming the same psychological fact: that to think of an object as desirable (unless for the sake of its consequences), and to think of it as pleasant, are one and the same thing; and that to desire anything, except in proportion as the idea of it is pleasant, is a physical and metaphysical[46] impossibility.

So obvious does this appear to me, that I expect it will hardly be disputed: and the objection made will be, not that desire can possibly be directed to anything ultimately except pleasure and exemption from pain, but that the will is a different thing from desire; that a person of confirmed virtue, or any other person whose purposes are fixed, carries out his purposes without any thought of the pleasure he has in contemplating them, or expects to derive from their fulfilment; and persists in acting on them, even though these pleasures are much diminished, by changes in his character or decay of his passive sensibilities, or are outweighed by the pains which the pursuit of the purposes may bring upon him. All this I fully admit, and have stated it elsewhere, as positively and emphatically as any one. Will, the active phenomenon, is a different thing from desire, the state of passive sensibility, and though originally an offshoot from it, may in time take root and detach itself from the parent stock; so much so, that in the case of an habitual purpose, instead of willing the thing because we desire it, we often desire it only because we will it. This, however, is but an instance of that familiar fact, the power of habit, and is nowise confined to the case of virtuous actions. Many indifferent things, which men originally did from a motive of some sort, they continue to do from habit. Sometimes this is done unconsciously, the consciousness coming only after the action: at other times with conscious volition, but volition which has become habitual, and is put in operation by the force of habit, in opposition perhaps

---

46   Mill probably means "psychological." In his view, not only do human beings actually desire things "in proportion as the idea of it is pleasant," but there is no possible human psychology which would be otherwise.

to the deliberate preference, as often happens with those who have contracted habits of vicious or hurtful indulgence. Third and last comes the case in which the habitual act of will in the individual instance is not in contradiction to the general intention prevailing at other times, but in fulfilment of it; as in the case of the person of confirmed virtue, and of all who pursue deliberately and consistently any determinate end. The distinction between will and desire thus understood is an authentic and highly important psychological fact; but the fact consists solely in this—that will, like all other parts of our constitution, is amenable to habit, and that we may will from habit what we no longer desire for itself or desire only because we will it. It is not the less true that will, in the beginning, is entirely produced by desire; including in that term the repelling influence of pain as well as the attractive one of pleasure. Let us take into consideration, no longer the person who has a confirmed will to do right, but him in whom that virtuous will is still feeble, conquerable by temptation, and not to be fully relied on; by what means can it be strengthened? How can the will to be virtuous, where it does not exist in sufficient force, be implanted or awakened? Only by making the person *desire* virtue—by making him think of it in a pleasurable light, or of its absence in a painful one. It is by associating the doing right with pleasure, or the doing wrong with pain, or by eliciting and impressing and

bringing home to the person's experience the pleasure naturally involved in the one or the pain in the other, that it is possible to call forth that will to be virtuous, which, when confirmed, acts without any thought of either pleasure or pain. Will is the child of desire, and passes out of the dominion of its parent only to come under that of habit. That which is the result of habit affords no presumption of being intrinsically good; and there would be no reason for wishing that the purpose of virtue should become independent of pleasure and pain, were it not that the influence of the pleasurable and painful associations which prompt to virtue is not sufficiently to be depended on for unerring constancy of action until it has acquired the support of habit. Both in feeling and in conduct, habit is the only thing which imparts certainty; and it is because of the importance to others of being able to rely absolutely on one's feelings and conduct, and to oneself of being able to rely on one's own, that the will to do right ought to be cultivated into this habitual independence. In other words, this state of the will is a means to good, not intrinsically a good; and does not contradict the doctrine that nothing is a good to human beings but in so far as it is either itself pleasurable, or a means of attaining pleasure or averting pain.

But if this doctrine be true, the principle of utility is proved. Whether it is so or not, must now be left to the consideration of the thoughtful reader.

FRIEDRICH NIETZSCHE
Beyond Good and Evil

In the end, what is there for it? There is no other means to bring philosophy again into honor: one must first hang all moralists.

(Friedrich Nietzsche)

Who Was Friedrich Nietzsche?

Friedrich Wilhelm Nietzsche was one of the most original, important, and—belatedly—influential voices of the nineteenth century, and is (arguably) among the greatest of the German-speaking philosophers since Kant. He was born in 1844, on the birthday of King Friedrich Wilhelm IV of Prussia (after whom he was named), in the village of Röcken near Leipzig in the region of Saxony. His father and both grandfathers were Lutheran ministers. Nietzsche's father, Carl Ludwig, died of a head injury before he was five and Nietzsche's younger brother died the next year, and so he and his sister Elisabeth were brought up by their mother, Franziska, and two aunts. As a young boy he struggled with his schoolwork, but persevered, rising at 5 A.M. to begin his school day and then studying extra hours in the evening to keep up with his Greek. He spent much of his free time playing the piano—Nietzsche was a skilled pianist—and, beginning before the age of ten and continuing throughout his life, composed many pieces of music and wrote a great deal of poetry.

In 1858 Nietzsche was admitted to Schulpforta, one of Germany's oldest and most prestigious private boarding schools. The fourteen-year-old Nietzsche found the transition to the school's rigorous, almost monastic, regime hard, but again he persevered and played an energetic role in the school's intellectual, musical, and cultural life. By 1861, however, he was beginning to be plagued by headaches, fevers, eyestrain, and weakness—the first signs of the ill health from which he would suffer for the rest of his life. In 1864 Nietzsche graduated, and although his grades were patchy he had already shown signs of great intellectual promise, especially in the study of languages.

After a brief stint as a theology student at the University of Bonn, Nietzsche enrolled at the university in Leipzig and began work in classical philology— studying the linguistic, interpretative, and historical aspects of Greek and Roman literature. At this time, he discovered the work of philosopher Arthur Schopenhauer (1788–1860), a pessimistic German philosopher who saw the world as an irrational, godless sequence of ceaseless striving and suffering. He also met and became friends with the composer Richard Wagner (1813–1883), a creative genius who revolutionized opera with his concept of "music drama" which fused music, poetry, drama, and legend, culminating with his famous

Ring cycle. Both these men would greatly influence Nietzsche's philosophical thought.

Even before he had completed his studies and at the unprecedentedly young age of 24, Nietzsche was invited to take up a post as professor of classical philology at the University of Basel in Switzerland. Leipzig University hastily gave him a doctorate, not even bothering with the formality of an examination. Nietzsche began work at Basel in 1869, after renouncing his Prussian citizenship, and in 1870 was promoted to the rank of full professor. In that same year, the French parliament declared war on Prussia and Nietzsche volunteered for military service but, because of Switzerland's neutrality, he was allowed only to serve as a medical orderly. He was on the front lines for approximately a week before he fell ill—of diphtheria—and spent most of the rest of the short Franco-Prussian war (Paris surrendered in January 1871) recuperating and continuing his academic work.

His first book, *The Birth of Tragedy out of the Spirit of Music*, appeared in 1872 and was expected to secure his reputation as a brilliant young scholar. Instead, it caused a small tempest of academic controversy, a battle which Nietzsche was deemed by his professional contemporaries to have lost. Rather than publishing a traditional work of classical scholarship, Nietzsche presented a rhapsodic, free-flowing essay which attempted to apply Schopenhauer's philosophical ideas to an interpretation of the origins of Greek tragedy, and which argued that the spirit of Greek tragedy was reborn in the music-dramas of Richard Wagner. Nietzsche hoped this work would establish him as a philosopher (and allow him to transfer to the philosophy department at Basel), but it did not resemble a traditional work of philosophy either. Nietzsche's reputation as a professional scholar was irreparably damaged.

Nietzsche continued to teach philology at Basel—where, for several years after the publication of *The Birth of Tragedy* he was generally shunned by the students—until 1879. In that year he resigned due to ill health: by this time he could hardly see to read and write, and was beset with headaches and other pains. He was given a pension of two-thirds his salary, not quite enough money for Nietzsche to live comfort-ably, but this freed him to devote all his time to his real love—the writing of philosophy.

Disliking the increasingly nationalist climate of Bismarck's "Second Reich," Nietzsche spent most of the next decade, from 1880 until 1889, in self-imposed exile from Germany, wandering around Europe (France, Italy, Switzerland) staying with various friends. In 1882, in Rome, Nietzsche met the bewitching Lou von Andreas-Salomé, fell madly in love with her, and within two months asked her to marry him; she refused. A month later, in Lucerne, he proposed again, and was again rejected. Nevertheless, Nietzsche, Salomé, and their mutual friend Paul Rée became, for a time, firm companions, traveling together and calling themselves the *Dreieinigkeit* or "trinity" of free spirits. The capricious Salomé, however, was not warmly received by Nietzsche's possessive mother and sister—eventually his mother refused to have Lou in the house. This caused such family bickering that Nietzsche, upset and depressed, broke off his relations with Rée and Salomé and also ceased his correspondence with his mother and sister for a few months. On his (rather bumpy) reconciliation with his sister Elisabeth, she began a campaign to turn Nietzsche decisively against Rée and Salomé, and was quickly successful in making the split between Nietzsche and his former friends irrevocable.

Despite this and various other emotional upsets, Nietzsche produced several substantial philosophical books during the first few years of his "wandering" decade: *Human, All Too Human: A Book for Free Spirits* (1878–1880), *Daybreak: Thoughts on the Prejudices of Morality* (1881), *The Gay Science* (1882), and *Thus Spake Zarathustra* (1883–1885). They sold so few copies, however, that by the time he came to write *Beyond Good and Evil* (1886) he was having great difficulty finding publishers and was rapidly running out of money. The late 1880s were lonely, worried years: his health was very bad, he had little money, he had destroyed his relationships with most of his friends (including Wagner and his circle), and his philosophical work was falling on deaf ears.

In 1887 Nietzsche published *On the Genealogy of Morals* and, at long last, in 1888 began to see the first signs of public recognition—for example, public lectures on his work were held in Copenhagen. However, by this time Nietzsche, never a modest man, was starting to show signs of full-blown megalomania, referring to himself in letters as, for example, "the first spirit of the age" and "a genius of the Truth." Yet in this final year of his sanity he managed to write no fewer than five new books: *The Case of Wagner*, *Twilight of the Idols (or How to Philosophize with a Hammer)*, *The Anti-Christ: Curse on Christianity*, *Ecce Homo*, and *Nietzsche Contra Wagner*. By January of 1889, however, his communications were so bizarre—they are the so-called *Wahnbriefe*, or "mad letters"—that his remaining friends became concerned and called in the director of the Psychiatric Clinic in Basel, Dr. Ludwig Wille.

Nietzsche, by now completely insane, was tracked down in Turin and (with the help of a local dentist named Dr. Bettmann) was brought back to Basel and quickly transferred to a psychiatric clinic in the central German city of Jena. He was only 44. The doctors quickly agreed that the prospects for recovery were slim, even after Nietzsche's condition improved somewhat with confinement and treatment. They reported that he

> speaks more coherently and … the episodes with screaming are more seldom. Different delirious notions appear continually, and auditory hallucinations still occur…. He recognizes his environment only partially, e.g., he calls the chief orderly Prince Bismarck etc. He does not know exactly where he is.

In 1890, Nietzsche was released into the care of his mother and his mental health declined into a kind of permanent apathy and, gradually, paralysis.

Meanwhile, his sister Elisabeth seized control of Nietzsche's literary remains.[1] She created a Nietzsche Archive in Naumburg, near Leipzig, in 1894 and quick-

ly turned out a biography of her brother in which she presented herself as his major influence and closest friend. She even hired a tutor, Rudolf Steiner, to teach her about her brother's philosophy, but after a few months Steiner resigned in disgust, declaring it was impossible to teach her anything about philosophy. After much legal wrangling, editions of many of Nietzsche's previously unpublished works were released, several of his books were translated into English and other languages, and (partly because of his sister's energetic, if self-serving, proselytizing) Nietzsche's intellectual influence began to increase. However, despite her role in publicizing Nietzsche's philosophy, it is now widely agreed that Elisabeth's appalling editing practices caused great harm to Nietzsche's reputation for many years after his death. She had twisted his thoughts to fit her virulent German nationalism and anti-Semitism, and even her own fervent Christianity.

Nietzsche finally died[2] on August 25, 1900, in the German city of Weimar where Elisabeth had relocated the Nietzsche Archive and her helpless brother. For some time before his death, his sister—who was still enthusiastically encouraging a "Nietzsche cult"—had taken to dressing the half-paralyzed Nietzsche in ridiculous "holy" outfits and propping him up on the balcony of his home for adoring groups below to witness, an indignity which Nietzsche would have loathed.

What Was Nietzsche's Overall Philosophical Project?

Nietzsche's philosophical project was essentially a critique of all previous philosophical projects. He held that all philosophers before him, although they may have *believed* that they sought the pure and objective truth, were in fact merely laying out and defending *their own prejudices*—their philosophical theories were really nothing more than a personal statement, "a rarefied and abstract version of their heart's desire." They were often tricked into sincerely believing in

---

1   She and her racist husband Bernhard Förster (whom Nietzsche detested) had been living in Paraguay, South America, where Förster was attempting to establish the pure Aryan colony of "New Germany." However Förster committed suicide in 1889 and, after unsuccessfully trying for a few months to hold the colony together, Elisabeth returned to Germany.

---

2   Although there is still controversy, most commentators agree that he probably suffered from and succumbed to syphilis.

their own objectivity, through the apparent simplicity and clarity of their statements (such as Descartes'"I think, therefore I am") but this, according to Nietzsche, is a form of deception built into the very nature of language. For example, the claim "I think" is not *at all* clear and simple when one considers it carefully: the concept of thinking is not clear, and even if it could be *made* clear it would (in Nietzsche's view) fail to capture the reality of things. The world itself has no sharp edges and is not divided sharply into thinking and non-thinking things, for example, but instead contains subtle gradations and complexities. In fact, for Nietzsche, there is no stable, enduring, fixed reality lying behind the endless flux of experience; there is only experience and the human attempt to impose an individual perspective upon it.

The result of all this, for Nietzsche, is that the proper business of philosophy has been misunderstood. The point is not to scrutinize our most fundamental concepts, in order to come closer to a 'true description of reality'; the point is to ask what *function* our concepts have—to ask why we have adopted them, whether they are life-enhancing or destructive, whether it is necessary for us to have them at all. The goal is to affirm life, to live it free from superstitious illusions.

In urging this change, Nietzsche (probably[3]) does not simply *give up* on the whole project of acquiring 'knowledge,' but he does radically recast it. His philosophers of the future will realize that there is no such thing as 'objective,' non-perspectival knowledge, since this requires the defunct assumption of a 'real' world underlying our ever-changing experience. Instead they will take a *multi*-perspectival approach to understanding reality; roughly, since *all there is* is a set of different individual perspectives on the world, the

best way to achieve as full a comprehension of reality as possible is simply to strive to adopt *as many perspectives as possible* (through art, metaphor, construction of dramatic personas, and so on). Clearly, this is a task which can never be completed; there can never be a 'final understanding' of the world, and we should not look for such a thing, since there will always be a new perspective around the next corner not previously encountered.

Nietzsche's term for his new breed of philosopher was "free spirits" (*freien Geistes*), and he believed that these free spirits would be superior human beings who would assume a place of authority in a future social and intellectual hierarchy. Nietzsche's free spirits disdain democracy, equality, and social convention; and are "*delivered* from the crowd, the multitude, the majority, where he is allowed to forget the rule of 'humanity,' being the exception to it." Instead of toiling for 'objectivity' and consensus, they will revel in their subjectivity and strive for the *extraordinary*. They will be in touch with their own instinctual life—their "will to power"—and will rise beyond, or "overcome," traditional morality and religion.[4] Traditional ethical systems are merely historical creations, according to Nietzsche, that serve the self-interested purposes of their creators and artificially constrain the horizons of human possibility.

The kind of future morality Nietzsche envisages for his "free spirits" is rather elusive. All his mature life, Nietzsche planned a great work, to be called *The Revaluation of All Values*, which would fill in all of the details, but he never seems to have felt able to get beyond the first step of this project. Furthermore, Nietzsche had a deep distrust of systematization: in his view, the desire to make everything "fit together" and "make sense" is really a desire for death and the end of creativity. As he writes in *Beyond Good and Evil* (section 32):

> The overcoming of morality, or even (in a certain sense) the self-overcoming of morality: let

---

3   It should be pointed out that the interpretation of Nietzsche is a tricky business. His philosophical approach is highly unusual, with no sustained arguments or clear statements of philosophical conclusions, and his writing style is more often polemical or metaphorical than analytic. As a result, even more so than for other philosophers, it is more or less impossible to present a summary of 'Nietzsche's views' with which some commentators will not disagree strongly (and this attempt will be no exception).

---

4   One of Nietzsche's most famous aphorisms occurs in *The Gay Science*, where he proclaims, "God is dead" (Book 3, Section 125). In *Beyond Good and Evil* he calls Christianity "an ongoing suicide of reason."

that be the name for the long, clandestine work that was kept in reserve for the most subtle and honest (and also the most malicious) people of conscience today, living touchstones of the human heart.

Nevertheless, there are things that can be said about Nietzsche's positive view of morality (or, as he might have put it, the value system that lies *beyond* morality). First, Nietzsche approaches morality *naturalistically*. He treats it as a natural phenomenon, observable in certain living things such as human beings, and not as something rooted in a supernatural or metaphysical 'other world.' The emergence of value is to be explained in a roughly Darwinian fashion, as the result of human evolution. The "free spirits" or *Übermensch* (supermen) of our future, with their "revalued" values, will not somehow escape this evolutionary progress, but will be the next stage in the development of the human race.

Second, for Nietzsche, genuine moral worth is not a matter of our conscious intentions or rational choices; it's not a matter of following the right rules. Instead, moral value is somehow built into our unconscious, non-autonomous, non-rational "inner nature"—the *noble spirit*. For Nietzsche, there is a natural hierarchy (*Rangordnung*) among human beings, a natural division between those with "noble" souls and the lesser creatures of the "herd." Only a value-system which recognizes this, he thought, is biologically natural, life-affirming, creative, and vital.

Finally, another famous thesis of Nietzsche's which is morally relevant (though it does not appear in *Beyond Good and Evil*) is the notion of "eternal recurrence": the idea that time is cyclical, repeating itself in an endless loop over and over again. It is not fully clear whether Nietzsche actually *believed* this cosmological claim, but he did use it as a way of expressing what he thought of as a more positive attitude to life than the moral or Christian one. Instead of the value of one's life being judged *at its end*, Nietzsche suggests that we should see our lives as being subject to eternal recurrence, and thus that we should strive to make *each moment* of life one that we would want to repeat over and over again for eternity.

What Is the Structure of This Reading?

Despite its title, *Beyond Good and Evil* is not only—or even primarily—about moral philosophy. It is a general statement of much of Nietzsche's philosophical thought, including reflections on religion, epistemology, art, and politics. Its central theme is that philosophers must strip themselves of their preconceptions and contingently existing values, and become perfectly non-dogmatic; only then can they begin a "philosophy of the future" which will, for the first time in history, approach the truth. One of Nietzsche's central concerns in this work, as in much of his philosophy, is to persuade us to abandon previously accepted 'truths' inherited both from philosophy and religion. He is much less interested in laying out a new moral system with which to replace them.

Beyond Good and Evil is structured as a set of loosely connected aphorisms—tersely phrased statements, each dealing with a single focussed claim. The aphorisms (numbered 1 through 296) are self-standing, and each has its own point to make: but together—like threads in a tapestry or notes in a piece of music—they combine to form an overall picture. Ideally, the book needs to be read as a whole to get its full effect. Nietzsche arranged the aphorisms into nine chapters, eight of which are designed to pursue a particular theme:

1. On the Prejudices of the Philosophers
2. The Free Spirit
3. The Religious Disposition
4. Epigrams and Interludes
5. Towards a Natural History of Morals
6. We Scholars
7. Our Virtues
8. Peoples and Fatherlands
9. What is Noble?

The book concludes with a poem—in the style of a Greek ode—called "From High Mountains."

The three aphorisms reprinted here are from the final chapter, What is Noble? Aphorism 259 urges the "exploitative character" of all living things, 260 describes a distinction, very important for Nietzsche's philosophy, between "master moralities" and "slave moralities," and 261, while primarily a rumination on the nature of vanity, also contains important comments on the *source* of value—juxtaposed with 260 it gives further insight into the nature of "slave morality."

Some Useful Background Information

One of the central concepts in Nietzsche's philosophy is the *will to power*. According to Nietzsche, the will to power is the basic disposition of all life, including human life—it is the principle which provides the ultimate motive force for everything that happens in the natural (or at least the biological) world. Thus, every organic phenomenon—such as plant growth, animal predation, or the establishment of a religion—can be understood, according to Nietzsche, as being brought about by an underlying set of power relationships, where each term of the relation is exerting a "force of will" which strives, with varying success, to expand towards and transform the other terms. For example, a hunting lioness is driven by her will to power to kill antelope, whilst the will to power of her prey impels them to attempt to frustrate her.

Some Common Misconceptions

1. Though Nietzsche makes it amply clear in his text that he admires master morality more than slave morality, there is nevertheless controversy over whether Nietzsche actually *endorsed* master morality. (The textual evidence on this is mixed. For example, in a later book called *The Antichrist* Nietzsche asserts: "When the exceptional human being treats the mediocre more tenderly than himself and his peers, this is not mere courtesy of the heart—it is simply his *duty*.") The revalued values of free spirits might have more in common with master morality than slave morality, but might nevertheless supersede *both* types and be a third form of 'morality' entirely.

2. Nietzsche's "master" and "slave" moralities are ideal types, and cannot be identified in the modern world—where types of morality are jumbled—by simply looking at what contemporary people say and do. Instead, clear paradigms can only be found in the distant historical past: perhaps Homer's *Iliad* as an illustration of master morality, and the *New Testament* to exemplify slave morality.

3. Nietzsche called himself an "immoralist," and was (on the surface at least) centrally concerned with *attacking* morality, but this does not mean Nietzsche encourages people to *behave immorally*—he is certainly not saying that people should do the opposite of what traditional moral systems prescribe. In one of his earlier works, *Daybreak* (1881), he firmly asserts:

   > it goes without saying that I do not deny, presupposing I am no fool, that many actions called immoral ought to be avoided and resisted, or that many called moral ought to be done and encouraged—but *for different reasons than formerly*.

4. Although not a philosophical point, it may be worth mentioning that—although Nietzsche certainly did equate the rise of Judeo-Christianity with the ascendance of "slave morality"—his notorious so-called anti-Semitism, and supposed sympathy for what became ideological themes of the Nazi party, are largely a *myth* created by misunderstandings and deliberate distortions of his work during the fifty years after his death. In fact, Nietzsche had difficulty finding a publisher for *Beyond Good and Evil* because he had split from the publisher of his previous books, Ernst Schmeitzner, in part because Nietzsche *objected* to Schmeitzner's close association with the anti-Semitic movement in Germany and did not want it to seem that he had similar racist sympathies.[5] (On the other hand, it *does* seem that Nietzsche, at least late in his life, was avowedly—and very unpleas-

---

5   In the end, Nietzsche had to pay for printing *Beyond Good and Evil* himself. He needed to sell 300 copies to cover his costs, but after a year only 114 had been purchased (and 66 given away to reviewers). As Nietzsche mournfully put it, "I—may no longer afford the luxury of print."

antly—misogynist, and a fierce opponent of the first wave of tentative female emancipation then moving across Germany.[6])

How Important and Influential Is This Passage?

Beyond Good and Evil is widely considered to be the work which best introduces and encapsulates many of the themes of Nietzsche's mature philosophy. Like the rest of his writings, it had little influence during his sane lifetime, and from 1930 to 1960 Nietzsche (tarred by his supposed association with fascism) was hardly considered worthy of study at all. However, since revisionist scholarship on his work began in earnest in the 1960s, Nietzsche's philosophical reputation has been in the ascendant (especially on the European continent), and *Beyond Good and Evil* has now come to be recognized as one of the most important books of the nineteenth century. As Walter Kaufmann, a leading Nietzsche translator and commentator since 1950, puts it:

> It is possible to say briefly what makes this book great: the prophetic independence of its spirit; the hundreds of doors it opens for the mind, revealing new vistas, problems, and relationships; and what it contributes to our understanding of much of recent thought and literature and history.

The particular sections excerpted here, though merely a small part of the book and not in any way a 'summary' of the whole, are especially interesting for the introduction of Nietzsche's notorious distinction between "master" and "slave" moralities, and for some hints as to the connection of this distinction with his concept of a "will to power."

---

6   On the other, other hand, Nietzsche was one of the minority of University of Basel faculty members who voted in *favor* of allowing women to be admitted to doctoral programs in 1874. Clearly, Nietzsche was a complex character.

Suggestions for Critical Reflection

1. Why could "good manners" never be an adequate basic principle of society? What does Nietzsche mean when he says that this would be to "deny life"? How plausible do you find his reasons for saying so?

2. Nietzsche distinguishes between two possible understandings of the difference between good and bad: "noble" vs. "despicable," and "good" vs. "evil." How important is this difference? Are they both really *moral* distinctions, or is one of them dealing with a different sort of value altogether? If they are different kinds of value, does this hurt Nietzsche's argument or help it?

3. "It is obvious that moral value distinctions everywhere are first attributed to *people* and only later and in a derivative fashion applied to *actions*." Is it? If this claim *is* true, then what does it show about the nature of morality?

4. How *historically* and *psychologically* plausible do you find Nietzsche's description of the difference between the moral outlooks of the powerful and their 'slaves'? If it is plausible as a *description* of moral attitudes, what implications should this have (if any) for the moral views we *ought* to hold? What implications would Nietzsche think it has?

5. "Within a slave mentality a good person must in any event be *harmless*." What do you think of this claim?

6. What do Nietzsche's claims about the nature of vanity reveal about his views on the way we, as individuals, come to *endorse* or *reject* particular values? Are these views plausible?

7. What do you think Nietzsche's view of democracy is? What reasons might he have for his views?

8. What is your judgment of Nietzsche's style: do you think that it is 'philosophical' in the right way? For example, is it a productive way of pursuing the truth (if that is indeed the proper goal of philosophy), or is it in the end (merely?) a sophisticated kind of creative writing?

Suggestions for Further Reading

A readable modern translation of *Beyond Good and Evil*, from which this excerpt is taken, is that by Marion Faber in the Oxford World's Classics series (Oxford University Press, 1998). Two older, well-established translations are those by Walter Kaufmann (Random House, 1966) and R.J. Hollingdale (Penguin, 1973). Nietzsche's famous book *Thus Spake Zarathustra* (published between 1883 and 1885) also lays out the central tenets of his mature philosophy—and thus covers much of the same ground as *Beyond Good and Evil*—but does so in a series of enigmatic parables, in a style intended to parody the Bible. Nietzsche's *On the Genealogy of Morality* (1887) was intended as a "supplement and clarification" of *Beyond Good and Evil*. Meanwhile, *Human, All Too Human* (1878–80), *Daybreak* (1881), and *The Gay Science* (1882) are earlier works in which Nietzsche developed his naturalistic approach to morality. Standard translations of Nietzsche's works are by Walter Kaufmann, but other good ones are available. It is also interesting to consult Arthur Schopenhauer's *The World as Will and Representation* (trans. E.F. Payne, 2 vols., Dover, 1969), a book which had a big influence on Nietzsche's philosophical development. (One can also, incidentally, buy recordings of Nietzsche's musical compositions: for example, *The Music of Friedrich Nietzsche*, Atma Records, 1999.)

There is a vast secondary literature on Nietzsche, but its quality is rather uneven. General accounts of Nietzsche's life and work appear in R.J. Hollingdale's *Nietzsche: The Man and His Philosophy* (Cambridge University Press, 2001), Michael Tanner's *Nietzsche* (Oxford University Press, 1994), and Ronald Hayman's *Nietzsche: A Critical Life* (Oxford University Press, 1980). Nietzsche also published an autobiographical work (published posthumously in 1908) called *Ecce Homo* ("Behold the Man"). Other high-quality, comprehensive works on Nietzsche's philosophy include: Walter Kaufmann, *Nietzsche: Philosopher, Psychologist, Antichrist* (Princeton University Press, 1974); Gilles Deleuze, *Nietzsche and Philosophy* (Cambridge University Press, 1983); Alexander Nehamas, *Nietzsche: Life as Literature* (Harvard University Press, 1985); Richard Schacht, *Nietzsche* (Routledge and Kegan Paul, 1983) and *Making Sense of Nietzsche* (University of Illinois Press, 1994); and David Allison, *Reading the New Nietzsche* (Rowman and Littlefield, 2001). Also helpful are Maudemarie Clark's *Nietzsche on Truth and Philosophy* (Cambridge University Press, 1990), Geoff Waite, *Nietzsche's Corps/e* (Duke University Press, 1996), and Peter Berkowitz, *Nietzsche: The Ethics of an Immoralist* (Harvard University Press, 1995). A *Routledge Philosophy Guidebook to Nietzsche on Morality* by Brian Leiter was published in 2002.

There are also several good collections of articles, including: Richardson and Leiter (eds.), *Nietzsche* (Oxford University Press, 2001); Magnus and Higgins (eds.), *The Cambridge Companion to Nietzsche* (Cambridge University Press, 1996); Peter Sedgwick (ed.), *Nietzsche: A Critical Reader* (Blackwell, 1995); Richard Schacht (ed.), *Nietzsche, Genealogy, Morality* (University of California Press, 1994); Solomon and Higgins (eds.), *Reading Nietzsche* (Oxford University Press, 1990); David Allison (ed.), *The New Nietzsche* (MIT Press, 1985); and Robert Solomon (ed.), *Nietzsche: A Collection of Critical Essays* (University of Notre Dame Press, 1980).

Beyond Good and Evil
§§259–261[7]

259

To refrain from injuring, abusing, or exploiting one another; to equate another person's will with our own: in a certain crude sense this can develop into good manners between individuals, if the preconditions are in place (that is, if the individuals have truly similar strength and standards and if they are united within one single social body). But if we were to try to take this principle further and possibly even make it the *basic principle of society*, it would immediately be revealed for what it is: a will to *deny* life, a principle for dissolution and decline. We must think through

---

7   *Jenseits von Gut und Böse: Vorspiel einer Philosophie der Zukunft* [*Beyond Good and Evil: Prelude to a Philosophy of the Future*] was first published in Leipzig in 1886. This excerpt is reprinted from *Friedrich Nietzsche: Beyond Good and Evil*, a new translation by Marion Faber (Oxford World's Classics, 1998). Copyright © 1998. Reprinted by permission of Oxford University Press.

the reasons for this and resist all sentimental frailty: life itself *in its essence* means appropriating, injuring, overpowering those who are foreign and weaker; oppression, harshness, forcing one's own forms on others, incorporation, and at the very least, at the very mildest, exploitation—but why should we keep using this kind of language, that has from time immemorial been infused with a slanderous intent? Even that social body whose individuals, as we have just assumed above, treat one another as equals (this happens in every healthy aristocracy) must itself, if the body is vital and not moribund, do to other bodies everything that the individuals within it refrain from doing to one another: it will have to be the will to power incarnate, it will want to grow, to reach out around itself, pull towards itself, gain the upper hand—not out of some morality or immorality, but because it is *alive*, and because life simply *is* the will to power. This, however, more than anything else, is what the common European consciousness resists learning; people everywhere are rhapsodizing, even under the guise of science, about future social conditions that will have lost their 'exploitative character'—to my ear that sounds as if they were promising to invent a life form that would refrain from all organic functions. 'Exploitation' is not part of a decadent or imperfect, primitive society: it is part of the *fundamental nature* of living things, as its fundamental organic function; it is a consequence of the true will to power, which is simply the will to life.

Assuming that this is innovative as theory—as reality it is the *original fact* of all history: let us at least be this honest with ourselves!

260

While perusing the many subtler and cruder moral codes that have prevailed or still prevail on earth thus far, I found that certain traits regularly recurred in combination, linked to one another—until finally two basic types were revealed and a fundamental difference leapt out at me. There are *master moralities* and *slave moralities*.[8] I would add at once that in all higher and more complex cultures, there are also apparent attempts to mediate between the two moralities, and even more often a confusion of the two and a mutual misunderstanding, indeed sometimes even their violent juxtaposition—even in the same person, within one single breast. Moral value distinctions have emerged either from among a masterful kind, pleasantly aware of how it differed from those whom it mastered, or else from among the mastered, those who were to varying degrees slaves or dependants. In the first case, when it is the masters who define the concept 'good', it is the proud, exalted states of soul that are thought to distinguish and define the hierarchy. The noble person keeps away from those beings who express the opposite of these elevated, proud inner states: he despises them. Let us note immediately that in this first kind of morality the opposition 'good' and 'bad' means about the same thing as 'noble' and 'despicable'—the opposition 'good' and '*evil*' has a different origin. The person who is cowardly, or anxious or petty or concerned with narrow utility is despised; likewise the distrustful person with his constrained gaze, the self-disparager, the craven kind of person who endures maltreatment, the importunate flatterer, and above all the liar: all aristocrats hold the fundamental conviction that the common people are liars. 'We truthful ones'—that is what the ancient Greek nobility called themselves. It is obvious that moral value distinctions everywhere are first attributed to *people* and only later and in a derivative fashion applied to *actions*: for that reason moral historians commit a crass error by starting with questions such as: 'Why do we praise an empathetic action?' The noble type of person feels *himself* as determining value—he does not need approval, he judges that 'what is harmful to me is harmful per se,'[9] he knows that he is the one who causes things to be revered in the first place, he *creates values*. Everything that he knows of himself he reveres: this kind of moral code is self-glorifying. In the foreground is a feeling of fullness, of overflowing power, of happiness in great tension, an awareness of a wealth that

---

8   This distinction was first introduced—though not given these now-famous names—in Nietzsche's *Human, All Too Human* (1878), and plays an important role in Es-

say One of his next book, *On the Genealogy of Morals* (1887).

9   *Per se* is Latin for "in itself" or "intrinsically."

would like to bestow and share—the noble person will also help the unfortunate, but not, or not entirely, out of pity, but rather from the urgency created by an excess of power. The noble person reveres the power in himself, and also his power over himself, his ability to speak and to be silent, to enjoy the practice of severity and harshness towards himself and to respect everything that is severe and harsh. 'Wotan[10] placed a harsh heart within my breast,' goes a line in an old Scandinavian saga: that is how it is written from the heart of a proud Viking—and rightly so. For this kind of a person is proud *not* to be made for pity; and so the hero of the saga adds a warning: 'If your heart is not harsh when you are young, it will never become harsh.' The noble and brave people who think like this are the most removed from that other moral code which sees the sign of morality in pity or altruistic behaviour or *désintéressement*;[11] belief in ourselves, pride in ourselves, a fundamental hostility and irony towards 'selflessness'—these are as surely a part of a noble morality as caution and a slight disdain towards empathetic feelings and 'warm hearts'.

It is the powerful who *understand* how to revere, it is their art form, their realm of invention. Great reverence for old age and for origins (all law is based upon this twofold reverence), belief in ancestors and prejudice in their favour and to the disadvantage of the next generation—these are typical in the morality of the powerful; and if, conversely, people of 'modern ideas' believe in progress and 'the future' almost by instinct and show an increasing lack of respect for old age, that alone suffices to reveal the ignoble origin of these 'ideas'. Most of all, however, the master morality is foreign and embarrassing to current taste because of the severity of its fundamental principle: that we have duties only towards our peers, and that we may treat those of lower rank, anything foreign, as we think best or 'as our heart dictates' or in any event

'beyond good and evil'[12]—pity and the like should be thought of in this context. The ability and duty to feel enduring gratitude or vengefulness (both only within a circle of equals), subtlety in the forms of retribution, a refined concept of friendship, a certain need for enemies (as drainage channels for the emotions of envy, combativeness, arrogance—in essence, in order to be a good *friend*): these are the typical signs of a noble morality, which, as we have suggested, is not the morality of 'modern ideas' and is therefore difficult to sympathize with these days, also difficult to dig out and uncover.

It is different with the second type of morality, *slave morality*. Assuming that the raped, the oppressed, the suffering, the shackled, the weary, the insecure engage in moralizing, what will their moral value judgements have in common? They will probably express a pessimistic suspicion about the whole human condition, and they might condemn the human being along with his condition. The slave's eye does not readily apprehend the virtues of the powerful: he is sceptical and distrustful, he is *keenly* distrustful of everything that the powerful revere as 'good'—he would like to convince himself that even their happiness is not genuine. Conversely, those qualities that serve to relieve the sufferers' existence are brought into relief and bathed in light: this is where pity, a kind, helpful hand, a warm heart, patience, diligence, humility, friendliness are revered—for in this context, these qualities are most useful and practically the only means of enduring an oppressive existence. Slave morality is essentially a morality of utility. It is upon this hearth that the famous opposition 'good' and '*evil*' originates—power and dangerousness, a certain fear-inducing, subtle strength that keeps contempt from surfacing, are translated by experience into evil. According to slave morality, then, the 'evil' person evokes fear; according to master morality, it is exactly the 'good' person who evokes fear and wants to evoke it, while the 'bad' person is felt to be despicable. The opposition comes to a head when, in terms of slave morality, a hint of condescension (it may be slight and well intentioned) clings even to

---

10   Also called Odin, Wotan was the supreme god of Scandinavian and German mythology: creator of the world and god of war, wisdom, poetry, magic, and the dead. He was usually depicted as a one-eyed, wise old man, accompanied by two great ravens. Wednesday— "Wotan's day"—is named for him.

11   French—"disinterestedness."

12   This phrase, in German, has religious as well as moral overtones. *Jenseits* not only means "beyond" but also refers to the afterlife.

those whom this morality designates as 'good', since within a slave mentality a good person must in any event be *harmless*: he is good-natured, easily deceived, perhaps a bit stupid, a *bonhomme*.[13] Wherever slave morality gains the upper hand, language shows a tendency to make a closer association of the words 'good' and 'stupid'.

A last fundamental difference: the longing for *freedom*, an instinct for the happiness and nuances of feeling free, is as necessarily a part of slave morals and morality as artistic, rapturous reverence and devotion invariably signal an aristocratic mentality and judgement.

From this we can immediately understand why *passionate* love (our European speciality) absolutely must have a noble origin: the Provençal poet-knights are acknowledged to have invented it, those splendid, inventive people of the '*gai saber*'[14] to whom Europe owes so much—virtually its very self.

261

Among the things that a noble person finds most difficult to understand is vanity: he will be tempted to deny its existence, even when a different kind of person thinks that he grasps it with both hands. He has trouble imagining beings who would try to elicit a good opinion about themselves that they themselves do not hold (and thus do not 'deserve', either) and who then themselves nevertheless *believe* this good opinion. To him, that seems in part so tasteless and irreverent towards one's self, and in part so grotesquely irrational that he would prefer to consider vanity an anomaly and in most of the cases when it is mentioned, doubt that it exists. He will say, for example: 'I may be

---

13   French—a simple, good man.

14   "Gay science" or "joyful art" in the dialect of Provence, in south-eastern France. One of Nietzsche's earlier books is called *The Gay Science* (1882). The phrase was coined in the early fourteenth century to refer to the art of the troubadours: lyric poets and musicians— mostly noblemen, and sometimes even kings—who flourished in southern France, northern Italy, and eastern Spain from the end of the eleventh to the close of the thirteenth century. Their songs typically dealt with themes of chivalry and courtly love.

wrong about my worth, but on the other hand require that others recognize the worth that I assign—but that is not vanity (rather it is arrogance, or more often what is called "humility", and also "modesty").' Or he will say: 'There are many reasons to be glad about other people's good opinion of me, perhaps because I revere and love them and am happy about every one of their joys, or else perhaps because their good opinion underscores and strengthens my belief in my own private good opinion, or perhaps because the good opinion of others, even in the cases where I do not share it, is nevertheless useful or promises to be useful to me—but none of that is vanity.' It takes compulsion, particularly with the help of history, for the noble person to realize that in every sort of dependent social class, from time immemorial, a common person *was* only what he was *thought to be*—completely unused to determining values himself, he also attributed to himself no other value than what his masters attributed to him (creating values is truly the *master's privilege*). We may understand it as the result of a tremendous atavism[15] that even now, the ordinary person first *waits* for someone else to have an opinion about him, and then instinctively submits to it—and by no means merely to 'good' opinions, but also to bad or improper ones (just think, for example, how most pious women esteem or under-esteem themselves in accordance with what they have learned from their father confessors, or what pious Christians in general learn from their Church). Now, in fact, in conformity with the slow emergence of a democratic order of things (this in turn caused by mixing the blood of masters and slaves), the originally noble and rare impulse to ascribe one's own value to oneself and to 'think well' of oneself, is more and more encouraged and widespread: but always working against it is an older, broader, and more thoroughly entrenched tendency—and when it comes to 'vanity', this older tendency becomes master of the newer. The vain person takes pleasure in e*very* good opinion that he hears about himself (quite irrespective of any prospect of its

---

15   A throwback: a trait which resembles those possessed by remote ancestors, and which has returned after being absent for many generations. (The word comes from *atavus*, which is Latin for one's great-grandfather's grandfather.)

utility, and likewise irrespective of truth or falsehood), just as he suffers at any bad opinion: for he submits himself to both, he *feels* submissive to both, from that old submissive instinct that breaks out in him.

It is the 'slave' in the blood of the vain person, a remnant of the slave's craftiness (and how much of the 'slave' is still left, for example, in women today!) that tries to *seduce* him to good opinions of himself; and it is likewise the slave who straightway kneels down before these opinions, as if he himself were not the one who had called them forth.

So I repeat: vanity is an atavism.

VIRGINIA HELD

"Feminist Transformations of Moral Theory"

Who Is Virginia Held?

Virginia P. Held received her PhD from Columbia University and is now a Distinguished Professor in the philosophy program of the Graduate Center at the City University of New York. She is the author of three books—*Feminist Morality: Transforming Culture, Society and Politics* (University of Chicago Press, 1993), *Rights and Goods: Justifying Social Action* (Free Press, 1984), and *The Public Interest and Individual Interests* (Basic Books, 1972)—and many articles on social and political philosophy, ethics, and feminist philosophy.

What Is the Structure of This Reading?

Held begins her article by arguing that, historically, all ethical theories have been built upon assumptions biased in favor of men and against women. She illustrates this by exploring the implications of the historically important dichotomies of reason vs. emotion and public vs. private, and by discussing the history of our concept of the self or personhood. She then goes on, in the next three sections, to discuss feminist approaches to the transformation of each of these three conceptual areas. In particular, she emphasizes a feminist re-valuing of *emotional responses* in ethics, the importance of *mothering* (which breaks through the public-private distinction), and the notion of the self as being importantly constituted by its *relations* to others.

Suggestions for Critical Reflection

1. Do you agree with Held that there has historically been a characteristically 'male point of view'? Do you think there is today? If so, what does this show about ethics? (Similarly, do you think there is a characteristically *female* point of view, and what would that show?) Do you think it is possible to remove the male bias from ethical philosophy without merely replacing it with a female bias?

2. Held argues that the male bias in the history of ethics requires, for its correction, a *wholesale transformation* of ethical theory: she does not think women should want "simply to be accorded entry as equals into the enterprise of morality as so far developed." How persuasively does Held make this case? If—unlike Held—you think traditional ethical theory might be repaired rather than transformed, how might one go about removing the gender bias that Held detects in, for example, utilitarianism or Kantian ethics?

3. Held writes, "The associations between … philosophical concepts and gender cannot be merely dropped, and the concepts retained regardless of gender, because gender has been built into them in such a way that without it, they will have to be different concepts." What do you make of this argument? What implications does it have for philosophy today?

4. Held suggests that our very concept of *human* has historically been infected with male-biased assumptions. Does this seem plausible? If so, how important a philosophical discovery is this? In what ways should the existing concept be changed (or with what sort of concept should it be replaced)?

5. Should "a mother's sacrifice for her child" be considered an act of moral super-erogation (something it is good to do but not a moral duty)? Why, or why not? What implications, if any, does this have for ethical theory?

6. Do you think Held's portrayal of the history of philosophy is, on the whole, accurate?

7. Held draws a contrast between an "ethic of care" and an "ethic of justice," and suggests the former is more appropriate to women's experience than the latter. Does this claim seem right to you? If so, in what ways—if any—does that make an ethic of care a *better moral theory* than an ethic of justice? What potential benefits and pitfalls can you see in the notion of an ethic of care?

8. Held argues that women are no more biologically determined than men, and, in particular, that the activity of mothering is no less 'human' than, say, politics or trade. What implications does this have for our view of human relationships, and for morality?

9. Feminist ethicists often pay particular attention to a domain of people intermediate between the self and 'everyone': i.e., they focus on our moral relationships to "particular others," our friends, family, and other individuals with whom we have personal relationships. How important, and how defensible, is this shift in focus? *Do* we have special moral responsibilities to particular people—which we do not have to others—just because, for example, they are our friends? If so, is feminist ethics the only theory able to accommodate this insight?

10. Held describes a model of the self which treats it as at least partly constituted by its *relationships* with other people. Does Held mean to suggest that only *women* have a "relational self" or that men do as well? If this model is correct, what are its implications for ethics? For example, how does it affect the problem of moral motivation? What would it do to our conception of justice, rights, and duties? How does it change the nature and value of human autonomy?

Suggestions for Further Reading

In addition to the books mentioned above, several of Held's articles are on topics related to issues she discusses in "Feminist Transformations of Moral Theory": for example, "On the Meaning of Trust," *Ethics* 78 (1968); "Can a Random Collection of Individuals Be Morally Responsible?" *Journal of Philosophy* 67 (1970); "Egalitarianism and Relevance," *Ethics* 81 (1971); "Feminism and Moral Theory," in Eva Feder Kittay (ed.), *Women and Moral Theory* (Rowman and

Littlefield, 1987); "Birth and Death," *Ethics* 99 (1989); "The Meshing of Care and Justice," *Hypatia* 10 (1995); "Feminist Reconceptualizations in Ethics," in Janet Kourany (ed.), *Philosophy in a Feminist Voice* (Princeton University Press, 1998); and "Feminist Ethical Theory," in Klaus Brinkmann (ed.), *Proceedings of the Twentieth World Congress of Philosophy, Volume 1: Ethics* (Philosophy Documentation Center, 1999). There is also a book of specially written essays on Held's work called *Norms and Values: Essays on the Work of Virginia Held*, edited by Joram Haber and Mark Halfon (Rowman and Littlefield, 1998).

On feminist ethics generally, the following collections of articles are a useful starting point: *On Feminist Ethics and Politics*, ed. Claudia Card (University of Kansas Press, 1999); *Justice and Care: Essential Readings in Feminist Ethics*, ed. Virginia Held (Westview Press, 1995); *Explorations in Feminist Ethics*, ed. Cole and Coultrap-McQuinn (Indiana University Press, 1992); *Feminist Ethics*, ed. Claudia Card (University of Kansas Press, 1991); and *Science, Morality and Feminist Theory*, ed. Hanen and Nielsen (University of Calgary Press, 1987). Other interesting articles include: Samantha Brennan, "Recent Work in Feminist Ethics," *Ethics* 109 (1999); Cheshire Calhoun, "Justice, Care, Gender Bias," *Journal of Philosophy* 85 (1988); Monique Deveaux, "New Directions in Feminist Ethics," *European Journal of Philosophy* 3 (1995); Christine James, "Feminist Ethics, Mothering, and Caring," *Kinesis* 22 (1995); Kuhse, Singer, and Rickard, "Reconciling Impartial Morality and a Feminist Ethic of Care," *Journal of Value Inquiry* 32 (1998); Alison Jaggar, "Feminist Ethics: Some Issues for the Nineties," *Journal of Social Philosophy* 20 (1989); Alison Jaggar, "Globalizing Feminist Ethics," *Hypatia* 13 (1998); and Margaret Walker, "Moral Understandings: Alternative 'Epistemology' for a Feminist Ethics," *Hypatia* 4 (1989).

Finally, some books: *Care, Autonomy, and Justice: Feminism and the Ethic of Care*, by Grace Clement (Westview Press, 1999); *Caring: Gender-Sensitive Ethics*, by Peta Bowden (Routledge, 1997); *Moral Understanding: A Feminist Study in Ethics*, by Margaret Walker (Routledge, 1997); *Feminine and Feminist Ethics*, by Rosemarie Tong (Wadsworth, 1993); *Justice, Gender and the Family*, by Susan Moller Okin (Basic Books, 1989); *Caring: A Feminine Approach to Ethics and Moral Education*, by Nel Noddings (University of California Press, 1984); and *In A Different Voice: Psychological Theory and Women's Development*, by Carol Gilligan (Harvard University Press, 1982).

"Feminist Transformations of Moral Theory"[1]

The history of philosophy, including the history of ethics, has been constructed from male points of view, and has been built on assumptions and concepts that are by no means gender-neutral.[2] Feminists characteristically begin with different concerns and give different emphases to the issues we consider than do nonfeminist approaches. And, as Lorraine Code expresses it, "starting points and focal points shape the impact of theoretical discussion."[3] Within philosophy, feminists often start with, and focus on, quite different issues than those found in standard philosophy and ethics, however "standard" is understood. Far from providing mere additional insights which can be incorporated into traditional theory, feminist explorations often require radical transformations of existing fields of inquiry and theory.[4] From a feminist point of view, moral theory along with almost all theory will have to be transformed to take adequate account of the experience of women.

I shall in this paper begin with a brief examination of how various fundamental aspects of the history

---

1   This article was originally published in *Philosophy and Phenomenological Research*, Volume 50 (Supplement Autumn 1990), pp. 321–344. Reproduced with permission of Wiley-Blackwell Inc.

2   [Author's note] See e.g., Cheshire Calhoun, "Justice, Care, Gender Bias," *The Journal of Philosophy* 85 (September, 1988): 451–63.

3   [Author's note] Lorraine Code, "Second Persons," in *Science, Morality and Feminist Theory*, ed. Marsha Hanen and Kai Nielsen (Calgary: University of Calgary Press, 1987), p. 360.

4   [Author's note] See e.g., *Revolutions in Knowledge: Feminism in the Social Sciences*, ed. Sue Rosenberg Zalk and Janice Gordon-Kelter (Boulder: Westview Press, forthcoming).

of ethics have not been gender-neutral. And I shall discuss three issues where feminist rethinking is transforming moral concepts and theories.

The History of Ethics

Consider the ideals embodied in the phrase "the man of reason." As Genevieve Lloyd has told the story, what has been taken to characterize the man of reason may have changed from historical period to historical period, but in each, the character ideal of the man of reason has been constructed in conjunction with a rejection of whatever has been taken to be characteristic of the feminine. "Rationality," Lloyd writes, "has been conceived as transcendence of the 'feminine,' and the 'feminine' itself has been partly constituted by its occurrence within this structure."[5]

This has of course fundamentally affected the history of philosophy and of ethics. The split between reason and emotion is one of the most familiar of philosophical conceptions. And the advocacy of reason "controlling" unruly emotion, of rationality guiding responsible human action against the blindness of passion, has a long and highly influential history, almost as familiar to non-philosophers as to philosophers. We should certainly now be alert to the ways in which reason has been associated with male endeavor, emotion with female weakness, and the ways in which this is of course not an accidental association. As Lloyd writes, "From the beginnings of philosophical thought, femaleness was symbolically associated with what Reason supposedly left behind—the dark powers of the earth goddesses, immersion in unknown forces associated with mysterious female powers. The early Greeks saw women's capacity to conceive as connecting them with the fertility of Nature. As Plato later expressed the thought, women 'imitate the earth.'"[6]

Reason, in asserting its claims and winning its status in human history, was thought to have to conquer the female forces of Unreason. Reason and clarity of thought were early associated with maleness, and as Lloyd notes, "what had to be shed in develop-

ing culturally prized rationality was, from the start, symbolically associated with femaleness."[7] In later Greek philosophical thought, the form/matter distinction was articulated,[8] and with a similar hierarchical and gendered association. Maleness was aligned with active, determinate, and defining form; femaleness with mere passive, indeterminate, and inferior matter. Plato, in the *Timaeus*,[9] compared the defining aspect of form with the father, and indefinite matter with the mother; Aristotle also compared the form/matter distinction with the male/female distinction. To quote Lloyd again, "This comparison ... meant that the very nature of knowledge was implicitly associated with the extrusion of what was symbolically associated with the feminine."[10]

The associations, between Reason, form, knowledge, and maleness, have persisted in various guises, and have permeated what has been thought to be moral knowledge as well as what has been thought to be scientific knowledge, and what has been thought to be the practice of morality. The associations between the philosophical concepts and gender cannot be merely dropped, and the concepts retained regardless of gender, because gender has

---

5   [Author's note] Genevieve Lloyd, *The Man of Reason: 'Male' and 'Female' in Western Philosophy* (Minneapolis: University of Minnesota Press, 1984), p. 104.

6   [Author's note] Ibid., p. 2.

7   [Author's note] Ibid., p. 3.

8   For Plato and Aristotle, the matter of something (roughly) is the stuff it is made of, while its form is the organization, shape, or pattern which gives that thing its particular nature. A simple example would be a clay bowl, where the matter—a lump of clay—has been given the form of a bowl by the potter.

9   A dialogue by Plato (427–347 BCE), which describes how a divine (though not omnipotent) craftsman transformed the chaotic materials of the universe into an ordered and harmonious cosmos by consulting the unchanging Forms and using them as his template for the construction of (rather shoddily inadequate and fluctuating) earthly images of those paradigms. See the Plato reading in this chapter for more information on the Forms.

10   [Author's note] Ibid., p. 4. For a feminist view of how reason and emotion in the search for knowledge might be reevaluated, see Alison M. Jaggar, "Love and Knowledge: Emotion in Feminist Epistemology," *Inquiry* 32 (June, 1989): 151–76.

been built into them in such a way that without it, they will have to be different concepts. As feminists repeatedly show, if the concept of "human" were built on what we think about "woman" rather than what we think about "man," it would be a very different concept. Ethics, thus, has not been a search for universal, or truly human guidance, but a gender-biased enterprise.

Other distinctions and associations have supplemented and reinforced the identification of reason with maleness, and of the irrational with the female; on this and other grounds "man" has been associated with the human, "woman" with the natural. Prominent among distinctions reinforcing the latter view has been that between the public and the private, because of the way they have been interpreted. Again, these provide as familiar and entrenched a framework as do reason and emotion, and they have been as influential for non-philosophers as for philosophers. It has been supposed that in the public realm, man transcends his animal nature and creates human history. As citizen, he creates government and law; as warrior, he protects society by his willingness to risk death; and as artist or philosopher, he overcomes his human mortality. Here, in the public realm, morality should guide human decision. In the household, in contrast, it has been supposed that women merely "reproduce" life as natural, biological matter. Within the household, the "natural" needs of man for food and shelter are served, and new instances of the biological creature that man is are brought into being. But what is distinctively human, and what transcends any given level of development to create human progress, are thought to occur elsewhere.

This contrast was made highly explicit in Aristotle's conceptions of polis[11] and household; it has continued to affect the basic assumptions of a remarkably broad swath of thought ever since. In ancient Athens, women were confined to the household; the public sphere was literally a male domain. In more recent history, though women have been permitted to venture into public space, the associations of the public, historically male sphere with the distinctively human, and of the household, historically a female sphere, with the merely natural and repetitious, have persisted. These associations have deeply affected moral theory, which has often supposed the transcendent, public domain to be relevant to the foundations of morality in ways that the natural behavior of women in the household could not be. To take some recent and representative examples, David Heyd, in his discussion of supererogation,[12] dismisses a mother's sacrifice for her child as an example of the supererogatory because it belongs, in his view, to "the sphere of natural relationships and instinctive feelings (which lie outside morality)."[13] J.O. Urmson had earlier taken a similar position. In his discussion of supererogation, Urmson said, "Let us be clear that we are not now considering cases of natural affection, such as the sacrifice made by a mother for her child; such cases may be said with some justice not to fall under the concept of morality...."[14] And in a recent article called "Distrusting Economics," Alan Ryan argues persuasively about the questionableness of economics and other branches of the social sciences built on the assumption that human beings are ra-

---

11   The *polis* is the ancient Greek city-state. See the Aristotle reading in this chapter for more on his interwoven views on politics and society.

12   "Supererogation" means acting in a way which is not strictly required by moral duty but which goes beyond it, as in cases of exceptional generosity or heroism (from Latin—"beyond what is asked"). The key idea is that a supererogatory act is morally good, but to fail to perform it would not be morally bad. Such acts are of interest partly because several major moral theories— such as utilitarianism, Kantianism, and some versions of Protestantism—appear to be unable to recognize the existence of supererogation.

13   [Author's note] David Heyd, *Supererogation: Its Status in Ethical Theory* (New York: Cambridge University Press, 1982), p. 134.

14   [Author's note] J.O. Urmson, "Saints and Heroes," in *Essays in Moral Philosophy*, ed. A.I. Melden (Seattle: University of Washington Press, 1958), p. 202. I am indebted to Marcia Baron for pointing out this and the previous example in her "Kantian Ethics and Supererogation," *The Journal of Philosophy* 84 (May, 1987): 137–62.

tional, self-interested calculators; he discusses various examples of non-self-interested behavior, such as of men in wartime, which show the assumption to be false, but nowhere in the article is there any mention of the activity of mothering, which would seem to be a fertile locus for doubts about the usual picture of rational man.[15] Although Ryan does not provide the kind of explicit reason offered by Heyd and Urmson for omitting the context of mothering from consideration as relevant to his discussion, it is difficult to understand the omission without a comparable assumption being implicit here, as it so often is elsewhere. Without feminist insistence on the relevance for morality of the experience in mothering, this context is largely ignored by moral theorists. And yet, from a gender-neutral point of view, how can this vast and fundamental domain of human experience possibly be imagined to lie "outside morality"?

The result of the public/private distinction, as usually formulated, has been to privilege the points of view of men in the public domains of state and law, and later in the marketplace, and to discount the experience of women. Mothering has been conceptualized as a primarily biological activity, even when performed by humans, and virtually no moral theory in the history of ethics has taken mothering, as experienced by women, seriously as a source of moral insight, until feminists in recent years have begun to.[16] Women have been seen as emotional rather than as rational beings, and thus as incapable of full moral personhood. Women's behavior has been interpreted as either "natural" and driven by instinct, and thus as irrelevant to morality and to the construction of moral principles, or it has been interpreted as, at best, in need

of instruction and supervision by males better able to know what morality requires and better able to live up to its demands.

The Hobbesian[17] conception of reason is very different from the Platonic or Aristotelian conceptions before it, and from the conceptions of Rousseau or Kant or Hegel later; all have in common that they ignore and disparage the experience and reality of women. Consider Hobbes' account of man in the state of nature contracting with other men to establish society. These men hypothetically come into existence fully formed and independent of one another, and decide on entering or staying outside of civil society. As Christine Di Stefano writes, "What we find in Hobbes's account of human nature and political order is a vital concern with the survival of a self conceived in masculine terms.... This masculine dimension of Hobbes's atomistic egoism is powerfully underscored in his state of nature, which is effectively built on the foundation of denied maternity."[18] In *The Citizen*, where Hobbes gave his first systematic exposition of the state of nature, he asks us to "consider men as if but even now sprung out of the earth, and suddenly, like mushrooms, come to full maturity, without all kind of engagement with each other."[19] As Di Stefano says, it is a most incredible and problematic feature of Hobbes's state of nature that the men in it "are not born of, much less nurtured by, women, or anyone else."[20] To abstract from the complex web of human reality an abstract man for rational perusal, Hobbes has, Di Stefano continues, "expunged human reproduction and early nurturance, two of the most basic

---

15   [Author's note] Alan Ryan, "Distrusting Economics," *New York Review of Books* (May 18, 1989): 25–27. For a different treatment, see *Beyond Self-Interest*, ed. Jane Mansbridge (Chicago: University of Chicago Press, 1990).

16   [Author's note] See especially *Mothering: Essays in Feminist Theory*, ed. Joyce Trebilcot (Totowa, New Jersey: Rowman and Allanheld, 1984); and Sara Ruddick, *Maternal Thinking: Toward a Politics of Peace* (Boston: Beacon Press, 1989).

17   That found in the philosophy of Thomas Hobbes (1588–1679). See the notes to the selection from Hobbes in Chapter 3.

18   [Author's note] Christine Di Stefano, "Masculinity as Ideology in Political Theory: Hobbesian Man Considered," *Women's Studies International Forum* (Special Issue: *Hypatia*), Vol. 6, No. 6 (1983): 633–44, p. 637.

19   [Author's note] Thomas Hobbes, *The Citizen: Philosophical Rudiments Concerning Government and Society*, ed. B. Gert (Garden City, New York: Doubleday, 1972 (1651)), p. 205.

20   [Author's note] Di Stefano, op. cit., p. 638.

and typically female-identified features of distinctively human life, from his account of basic human nature. Such a strategy ensures that he can present a thoroughly atomistic subject...."[21] From the point of view of women's experience, such a subject or self is unbelievable and misleading, even as a theoretical construct. The Leviathan,[22] Di Stefano writes, "is effectively comprised of a body politic of orphans who have reared themselves, whose desires are situated within and reflect nothing but independently generated movement.... These essential elements are natural human beings conceived along masculine lines."[23]

Rousseau, and Kant, and Hegel, paid homage to the emotional power, the aesthetic sensibility, and the familial concerns, respectively, of women. But since in their views morality must be based on rational principle, and women were incapable of full rationality, or a degree or kind of rationality comparable to that of men, women were deemed, in the view of these moralists, to be inherently wanting in morality. For Rousseau,[24] women must be trained from childhood to submit to the will of men lest their sexual power lead both men and women to disaster. For Kant,[25] women were thought incapable of achieving full moral personhood, and women lose all charm if they try to behave like men by engaging in rational pursuits. For Hegel,[26] women's moral concern for their

families could be admirable in its proper place, but is a threat to the more universal aims to which men, as members of the state, should aspire.[27]

These images, of the feminine as what must be overcome if knowledge and morality are to be achieved, of female experience as naturally irrelevant to morality, and of women as inherently deficient moral creatures, are built into the history of ethics. Feminists examine these images, and see that they are not the incidental or merely idiosyncratic suppositions of a few philosophers whose views on many topics depart far from the ordinary anyway. Such views are the nearly uniform reflection in philosophical and ethical theory of patriarchal attitudes pervasive throughout human history. Or they are exaggerations even of ordinary male experience, which exaggerations then reinforce rather than temper other patriarchal conceptions and institutions. They distort the actual experience and aspirations of many men as well as of women. Annette Baier recently speculated about why it is that moral philosophy has so seriously overlooked the trust between human beings that in her view is an utterly central aspect of moral life. She noted that "the great moral theorists in our tradition not only are all men, they are mostly men who had minimal adult dealings with (and so were then minimally influenced by) women."[28] They were for the most part "clerics, misogynists, and puritan bachelors," and thus it is not surprising that they focus their philosophical attention

---

21   [Author's note] Ibid.

22   Hobbes's term for the state, in his book *Leviathan* (1651). A leviathan is something monstrously large and powerful—from the name of a sea monster in the Old Testament—and the term was in part supposed to reflect the state's absolute power over its citizens.

23   [Author's note] Ibid., p. 639.

24   Jean-Jacques Rousseau (1712–1778) was a French-speaking philosopher, born in Geneva, whose early-Romantic writings on human nature were highly influential in the eighteenth and nineteenth centuries; perhaps his most famous work is *The Social Contract* (1762).

25   Immanuel Kant (1724–1804); see the selections in this chapter for more on his philosophy.

26   Georg Wilhelm Friedrich Hegel (1770–1831), who had a huge influence on nineteenth-century German

philosophy and who saw history as progressing towards a fully self-conscious and rationally-organized community or state.

27   [Author's note] For examples of relevant passages, see *Philosophy of Woman: Classical to Current Concepts*, ed. Mary Mahowald (Indianapolis: Hackett, 1978); and *Visions of Women*, ed. Linda Bell (Clifton, New Jersey: Humana, 1985). For discussion, see Susan Moller Okin, *Women in Western Political Thought* (Princeton, New Jersey: Princeton University Press, 1979); and Lorenne Clark and Lynda Lange, eds., *The Sexism of Social and Political Theory* (Toronto: University of Toronto Press, 1979).

28   [Author's note] Annette Baier, "Trust and Anti-Trust," *Ethics* 96 (1986): 231–60, pp. 247–48.

"so single-mindedly on cool, distanced relations between more or less free and equal adult strangers...."[29]

As feminists, we deplore the patriarchal attitudes that so much of philosophy and moral theory reflect. But we recognize that the problem is more serious even than changing those attitudes. For moral theory as so far developed is incapable of correcting itself without an almost total transformation. It cannot simply absorb the gender that has been "left behind," even if both genders would want it to. To continue to build morality on rational principles opposed to the emotions and to include women among the rational will leave no one to reflect the promptings of the heart, which promptings can be moral rather than merely instinctive. To simply bring women into the public and male domain of the polis will leave no one to speak for the household. Its values have been hitherto unrecognized, but they are often moral values. Or to continue to seek contractual restraints on the pursuits of self-interest by atomistic individuals, and to have women join men in devotion to these pursuits, will leave no one involved in the nurturance of children and cultivation of social relations, which nurturance and cultivation can be of greatest moral import.

There are very good reasons for women not to want simply to be accorded entry as equals into the enterprise of morality as so far developed. In a recent survey of types of feminist moral theory, Kathryn Morgan notes that "many women who engage in philosophical reflection are acutely aware of the masculine nature of the profession and tradition, and feel their own moral concerns as women silenced or trivialized in virtually all the official settings that define the practice."[30] Women should clearly not agree, as the price of admission to the masculine realm of traditional morality, to abandon our own moral concerns as women.

And so we are groping to shape new moral theory. Understandably, we do not yet have fully worked out feminist moral theories to offer. But we can suggest some directions our project of developing such theories is taking. As Kathryn Morgan points out, there is not likely to be a "star" feminist moral theorist on the order of a Rawls or Nozick:[31] "There will be no individual singled out for two reasons. One reason is that vital moral and theoretical conversations are taking place on a large dialectical scale as the feminist community struggles to develop a feminist ethic. The second reason is that this community of feminist theoreticians is calling into question the very model of the individualized autonomous self presupposed by a star-centered male-dominated tradition.... We experience it as a common labour, a common task."[32]

The dialogues that are enabling feminist approaches to moral theory to develop are proceeding. As Alison Jaggar makes clear in her useful overview of them, there is no unitary view of ethics that can be identified as "feminist ethics." Feminist approaches to ethics share a commitment to "rethinking ethics with a view to correcting whatever forms of male bias it may contain."[33] While those who develop these approaches are "united by a shared project, they diverge widely in their views as to how this project is to be accomplished."[34]

Not all feminists, by any means, agree that there are distinctive feminist virtues or values. Some are especially skeptical of the attempt to give positive value to such traditional "feminine virtues" as a willingness to nurture, or an affinity with caring, or reluctance to seek independence. They see this approach as playing into the hands of those who would confine women to traditional roles.[35] Other feminists are skeptical

29   [Author's note] Ibid.

30   [Author's note] Kathryn Pauly Morgan, "Strangers in a Strange Land: Feminists Visit Relativists" in *Perspectives on Relativism*, ed. D. Odegaard and Carole Stewart (Toronto: Agathon Press, 1990).

31   John Rawls, Robert Nozick: see Chapter 3 for information on these contemporary philosophers.

32   [Author's note] Kathryn Morgan, "Women and Moral Madness," in *Science, Morality and Feminist Theory*, ed. Hanen and Nielsen, p. 223.

33   [Author's note] Alison M. Jaggar, "Feminist Ethics: Some Issues for the Nineties," *Journal of Social Philosophy* 20 (Spring/Fall 1989), p. 91.

34   [Author's note] Ibid.

35   [Author's note] One well-argued statement of this position is Barbara Houston, "Rescuing Womanly Virtues: Some Dangers of Moral Reclamation," in *Science, Morality and Feminist Theory*, ed. Hanen and Nielsen.

of all claims about women as such, emphasizing that women are divided by class and race and sexual orientation in ways that make any conclusions drawn from "women's experience" dubious.[36]

Still, it is possible, I think, to discern various important focal points evident in current feminist attempts to transform ethics into a theoretical and practical activity that could be acceptable from a feminist point of view. In the glimpse I have presented of bias in the history of ethics, I focused on what, from a feminist point of view, are three of its most questionable aspects: 1) the split between reason and emotion and the devaluation of emotion; 2) the public/private distinction and the relegation of the private to the natural; and 3) the concept of the self as constructed from a male point of view. In the remainder of this article, I shall consider further how some feminists are exploring these topics. We are showing how their previous treatment has been distorted, and we are trying to reenvision the realities and recommendations with which these aspects of moral theorizing do and should try to deal.

I. Reason and Emotion

In the area of moral theory in the modern era, the priority accorded to reason has taken two major forms. A) On the one hand has been the Kantian, or Kantian-inspired search for very general, abstract, deontological,[37] universal moral principles by which rational beings should be guided. Kant's Categorical Imperative is a foremost example: it suggests that all moral problems can be handled by applying an impartial, pure, rational principle to particular cases. It requires that we try to see what the general features of the problem before us are, and that we apply an abstract principle, or rules derivable from it, to this problem. On this view, this procedure should be adequate for all moral decisions. We should thus be able to act as reason recommends, and resist yielding to emotional inclinations and desires in conflict with our rational wills.

B) On the other hand, the priority accorded to reason in the modern era has taken a Utilitarian form. The Utilitarian approach, reflected in rational choice theory, recognizes that persons have desires and interests, and suggests rules of rational choice for maximizing the satisfaction of these. While some philosophers in this tradition espouse egoism,[38] especially of an intelligent and long-term kind, many do not. They begin, however, with assumptions that what are morally relevant are gains and losses of utility to theoretically isolatable individuals, and that the outcome at which morality should aim is the maximization of the utility of individuals. Rational calculation about such an outcome will, in this view, provide moral recommendations to guide all our choices. As with the Kantian approach, the Utilitarian approach relies on abstract general principles or rules to be applied to particular cases. And it holds that although emotion is, in fact, the source of our desires for certain objectives, the task of morality should be to instruct us on how to pursue those objectives most rationally. Emotional attitudes toward moral issues themselves interfere with rationality and should be disregarded. Among the questions Utilitarians can ask can be questions about which emotions to cultivate, and which desires to try to change, but these questions are to be handled in the terms of rational calculation, not of what our feelings suggest.

Although the conceptions of what the judgments of morality should be based on, and of how reason should guide moral decision, are different in Kantian and in Utilitarian approaches, both share a reliance on a highly abstract, universal principle as the appropriate source of moral guidance, and both share the view that moral problems are to be solved by the application of such an abstract principle to particular cases. Both share an admiration for the rules of reason

---

36   [Author's note] See e.g., Elizabeth V. Spelman, *Inessential Woman: Problems of Exclusion in Feminist Thought* (Boston: Beacon Press, 1988). See also Sarah Lucia Hoagland, *Lesbian Ethics: Toward New Value* (Palo Alto, California: Institute of Lesbian Studies, 1989); and Katie Geneva Cannon, *Black Womanist Ethics* (Atlanta, Georgia: Scholars Press, 1988).

37   Based on the notion of a duty or a right (rather than on the value of some kind of state of affairs or type of character).

---

38   That one either is, or ought to be, exclusively motivated by self-interest.

to be appealed to in moral contexts, and both denigrate emotional responses to moral issues.

Many feminist philosophers have questioned whether the reliance on abstract rules, rather than the adoption of more context-respectful approaches, can possibly be adequate for dealing with moral problems, especially as women experience them.[39] Though Kantians may hold that complex rules can be elaborated for specific contexts, there is nevertheless an assumption in this approach that the more abstract the reasoning applied to a moral problem, the more satisfactory. And Utilitarians suppose that one highly abstract principle, The Principle of Utility, can be applied to every moral problem no matter what the context.

A genuinely universal or gender-neutral moral theory would be one which would take account of the experience and concerns of women as fully as it would take account of the experience and concerns of men. When we focus on the experience of women, however, we seem to be able to see a set of moral concerns becoming salient that differs from those of traditional or standard moral theory. Women's experience of moral problems seems to lead us to be especially concerned with actual relationships between embodied persons, and with what these relationships seem to require. Women are often inclined to attend to rather than to dismiss the particularities of the context in which a moral problem arises. And we often pay attention to feelings of empathy and caring to suggest what we ought to do rather than relying as fully as possible on abstract rules of reason.

Margaret Walker, for instance, contrasts feminist moral "understanding" with traditional moral "knowledge." She sees the components of the former as involving "attention, contextual and narrative appreciation, and communication in the event of moral deliberation."[40] This alternative moral epistemology holds that "the adequacy of moral understanding decreases as its form approaches generality through abstraction."[41]

The work of psychologists such as Carol Gilligan and others has led to a clarification of what may be thought of as tendencies among women to approach moral issues differently. Rather than interpreting moral problems in terms of what could be handled by applying abstract rules of justice to particular cases, many of the women studied by Gilligan tended to be more concerned with preserving actual human relationships, and with expressing care for those for whom they felt responsible. Their moral reasoning was typically more embedded in a context of particular others than was the reasoning of a comparable group of men.[42] One should not equate tendencies women in fact display with feminist views, since the former may well be the result of the sexist, oppressive conditions in which women's lives have been lived. But many feminists see our own consciously considered experience as lending confirmation to the view that what has come to be called "an ethic of care" needs to be developed. Some think it should supercede "the ethic of justice" of traditional or standard moral theory. Others think it should be integrated with the ethic of justice and rules.

In any case, feminist philosophers are in the process of reevaluating the place of emotion in morality in at least two respects. First, many think morality requires the development of the moral emotions, in contrast to moral theories emphasizing the primacy of reason. As Annette Baier notes, the rationalism typical of traditional moral theory will be challenged when we pay attention to the role of parent. "It might be

39   [Author's note] For an approach to social and political as well as moral issues that attempts to be context-respectful, see Virginia Held, *Rights and Goods. Justifying Social Action* (Chicago: University of Chicago Press, 1989).

40   [Author's note] Margaret Urban Walker, "Moral Understandings: Alternative 'Epistemology' for a Feminist Ethics," *Hypatia* 4 (Summer, 1989): 15–28, p. 19.

41   [Author's note] Ibid., p. 20. See also Iris Marion Young, "Impartiality and the Civic Public. Some Implications of Feminist Critiques of Moral and Political Theory," in Seyla Benhabib and Drucilla Cornell, *Feminism as Critique* (Minneapolis: University of Minnesota Press, 1987).

42   [Author's note] See especially Carol Gilligan, *In a Different Voice. Psychological Theory and Women's Development* (Cambridge, Massachusetts: Harvard University Press, 1988); and Eva Feder Kittay and Diana T. Meyers eds., *Women and Moral Theory* (Totowa, New Jersey: Rowman and Allanheld, 1987).

important," she writes, "for father figures to have rational control over their violent urges to beat to death the children whose screams enrage them, but more than control of such nasty passions seems needed in the mother or primary parent, or parent-substitute, by most psychological theories. They need to love their children, not just to control their irritation."[43] So the emphasis in many traditional theories on rational control over the emotions, "rather than on cultivating desirable forms of emotion,"[44] is challenged by feminist approaches to ethics.

Secondly, emotion will be respected rather than dismissed by many feminist moral philosophers in the process of gaining moral understanding. The experience and practice out of which feminist moral theory can be expected to be developed will include embodied feeling as well as thought. In a recent overview of a vast amount of writing, Kathryn Morgan states that "feminist theorists begin ethical theorizing with embodied, gendered subjects who have particular histories, particular communities, particular allegiances, and particular visions of human flourishing. The starting point involves valorizing what has frequently been most mistrusted and despised in the western philosophical tradition...."[45] Among the elements being reevaluated are feminine emotions. The "care" of the alternative feminist approach to morality appreciates rather than rejects emotion. The caring relationships important to feminist morality cannot be understood in terms of abstract rules or moral reasoning. And the "weighing" so often needed between the conflicting claims of some relationships and others cannot be settled by deduction or rational calculation. A feminist ethic will not just acknowledge emotion, as do Utilitarians, as giving us the objectives toward which moral rationality can direct us. It will embrace emotion as providing at least a partial basis for morality itself, and for moral understanding.

Annette Baier stresses the centrality of trust for an adequate morality.[46] Achieving and maintaining trusting, caring relationships is quite different from acting in accord with rational principles, or satisfying the individual desires of either self or other. Caring, empathy, feeling with others, being sensitive to each other's feelings, all may be better guides to what morality requires in actual contexts than may abstract rules of reason, or rational calculation, or at least they may be necessary components of an adequate morality.

The fear that a feminist ethic will be a relativistic "situation ethic" is misplaced. Some feelings can be as widely shared as are rational beliefs, and feminists do not see their views as reducible to "just another attitude."[47] In her discussion of the differences between feminist medical ethics and nonfeminist medical ethics, Susan Sherwin gives an example of how feminists reject the mere case by case approach that has come to predominate in nonfeminist medical ethics. The latter also rejects the excessive reliance on abstract rules characteristic of standard ethics, and in this way resembles feminist ethics. But the very focus on cases in isolation from one another deprives this approach from attending to general features in the institutions and practices of medicine that, among other faults, systematically contribute to the oppression of women.[48] The difference of approach can be seen in the treatment of issues in the new reproductive technologies, where feminists consider how the new technologies may further decrease the control of women over reproduction.

This difference might be thought to be one of substance rather than of method, but Sherwin shows the implications for method also. With respect to reproductive technologies one can see especially clearly the deficiencies of the case by case approach: what needs to be considered is not only choice in the purely individualistic interpretation of the case by case approach, but control at a more general level and how it affects the structure of gender in society. Thus, a

---

43   [Author's note] Annette Baier, "The Need for More Than Justice," in *Science, Morality and Feminist Theory*, ed. Hanen and Nielsen, p. 55.

44   [Author's note] Ibid.

45   [Author's note] Kathryn Pauly Morgan, "Strangers in a Strange Land...," p. 2.

46   [Author's note] Annette Baier, "Trust and Anti-Trust."

47   [Author's note] See especially Kathryn Pauly Morgan, "Strangers in a Strange Land...."

48   [Author's note] Susan Sherwin, "Feminist and Medical Ethics: Two Different Approaches to Contextual Ethics," *Hypatia* 4 (Summer, 1989): 57–72.

feminist perspective does not always counsel attention to specific case vs. appeal to general considerations, as some sort of methodological rule. But the general considerations are often not the purely abstract ones of traditional and standard moral theory, they are the general features and judgments to be made about cases in actual (which means, so far, patriarchal) societies. A feminist evaluation of a moral problem should never omit the political elements involved; and it is likely to recognize that political issues cannot be dealt with adequately in purely abstract terms any more than can moral issues.

The liberal tradition in social and moral philosophy argues that in pluralistic society[49] and even more clearly in a pluralistic world, we cannot agree on our visions of the good life, on what is the best kind of life for humans, but we can hope to agree on the minimal conditions for justice, for coexistence within a framework allowing us to pursue our visions of the good life.[50] Many feminists contend that the commitment to justice needed for agreement *in actual conditions* on even minimal requirements of justice is as likely to demand relational feelings as a rational recognition of abstract principles. Human beings can and do care, and are capable of caring far more than at present, about the sufferings of children quite distant from them, about the prospects for future generations, and about the well-being of the globe. The liberal tradition's mutually disinterested rational individualists would seem unlikely to care enough to take the actions needed to achieve moral decency at a global level, or environmental sanity for decades hence, as they would seem unable to represent caring relationships within the family and among friends. As Annette Baier puts it, "A moral theory, it can plausibly be claimed, cannot regard concern for new and future persons as

an optional charity left for those with a taste for it. If the morality the theory endorses is to sustain itself, it must provide for its own continuers, not just take out a loan on a carefully encouraged maternal instinct or on the enthusiasm of a self-selected group of environmentalists, who make it their business or hobby to be concerned with what we are doing to mother earth."[51]

The possibilities as well as the problems (and we are well aware of some of them) in a feminist reenvisioning of emotion and reason need to be further developed, but we can already see that the views of nonfeminist moral theory are unsatisfactory.

II. The Public and the Private

The second questionable aspect of the history of ethics on which I focused was its conception of the distinction between the public and the private. As with the split between reason and emotion, feminists are showing how gender-bias has distorted previous conceptions of these spheres, and we are trying to offer more appropriate understandings of "private" morality and "public" life.

Part of what feminists have criticized has been the way the distinction has been accompanied by a supposition that what occurs in the household occurs as if on an island beyond politics, whereas the personal is highly affected by the political power beyond, from legislation about abortion to the greater earning power of men, to the interconnected division of labor by gender both within and beyond the household, to the lack of adequate social protection for women against domestic violence.[52] Of course we recognize that the family is not identical to the state, and we need concepts for thinking about the private or personal, and

---

49   A society which values (or at least tolerates) a range of different, and even mutually incompatible, views among its members of what constitutes a "good life." For example, toleration of different religions and sexual orientations is a form of pluralism.

50   [Author's note] See especially the work of John Rawls and Ronald Dworkin; see also Charles Larmore, *Patterns of Moral Complexity* (Cambridge: Cambridge University Press, 1987).

51   [Author's note] Annette Baier, "The Need for More Than Justice," pp. 53–54.

52   [Author's note] See e.g., Linda Nicholson, *Gender and History. The Limits of Social Theory in the Age of the Family* (New York: Columbia University Press, 1986); and Jean Bethke Elshtain, *Public Man, Private Woman* (Princeton, New Jersey: Princeton University Press, 1981). See also Carole Pateman, *The Sexual Contract* (Stanford, California: Stanford University Press, 1988).

the public or political. But they will have to be very different from the traditional concepts.

Feminists have also criticized deeper assumptions about what is distinctively human and what is "natural" in the public and private aspects of human life, and what is meant by "natural" in connection with women.[53] Consider the associations that have traditionally been built up: the public realm is seen as the distinctively human realm in which man transcends his animal nature, while the private realm of the household is seen as the natural region in which women merely reproduce the species.[54] These associations are extraordinarily pervasive in standard concepts and theories, in art and thought and cultural ideals, and especially in politics.

Dominant patterns of thought have seen women as primarily mothers, and mothering as the performance of a primarily biological function. Then it has been supposed that while engaging in political life is a specifically human activity, women are engaged in an activity which is not specifically human. Women accordingly have been thought to be closer to nature than men,[55] to be enmeshed in a biological function involving processes more like those in which other animals are involved than like the rational discussion of the citizen in the polis, or the glorious battles of noble soldiers, or the trading and rational contracting of "economic man." The total or relative exclusion of women from the domain of public life has then been seen as either inevitable or appropriate.

---

53 [Author's note] See e.g., Susan Moller Okin, *Women in Western Political Thought*. See also Alison M. Jaggar, *Feminist Politics and Human Nature* (Totowa, New Jersey: Rowman and Allanheld, 1983).

54 [Author's note] So entrenched is this way of thinking that it was even reflected in Simone de Beauvoir's pathbreaking feminist text *The Second Sex*, published in 1949. Here, as elsewhere, feminists have had to transcend our own early searches for our own perspectives.

55 [Author's note] See e.g., Sherry B. Ortner, "Is Female to Male as Nature is to Culture?" in *Woman, Culture, and Society*, ed. Michelle Z. Rosaldo and Louise Lamphere (Stanford: Stanford University Press, 1974).

The view that women are more determined by biology than are men is still extraordinarily prevalent. It is as questionable from a feminist perspective as many other traditional misinterpretations of women's experience. Human mothering is an extremely different activity from the mothering engaged in by other animals. The work and speech of men is recognized as very different from what might be thought of as the "work" and "speech" of other animals. Human mothering is fully as different from animal mothering. Of course all human beings are animal as well as human. But to whatever extent it is appropriate to recognize a difference between "man" and other animals, so would it be appropriate to recognize a comparable difference between "woman" and other animals, and between the activities—including mothering—engaged in by women and the behavior of other animals.

Human mothering shapes language and culture, it forms human social personhood, it develops morality. Animal behavior can be highly impressive and complex, but it does not have built into it any of the consciously chosen aims of morality. In creating human social persons, human mothering is different in kind from merely propagating a species. And human mothering can be fully as creative an activity as those activities traditionally thought of as distinctively human, because to create *new* persons, and new types of *persons*, can surely be as creative as to make new objects, products, or institutions. *Human* mothering is no more "natural" or "primarily biological" than is any other human activity.

Consider nursing an infant, often thought of as the epitome of a biological process with which mothering is associated and women are identified. There is no reason to think of human nursing as any more simply biological than there is to think of, say, a businessmen's lunch this way. Eating is a biological process, but what and how and with whom we eat are thoroughly cultural. Whether and how long and with whom a woman nurses an infant, are also human, cultural matters. If men transcend the natural by conquering new territory and trading with their neighbors and making deals over lunch to do so, women can transcend the natural by choosing not to nurse their children when they could, or choosing to nurse them when their culture tells them not to, or singing songs to their infants as they nurse, or nursing in restaurants to overcome the prejudices against doing so, or thinking human thoughts as they nurse, and so forth. Human culture surrounds and characterizes the activity of nursing as it does the activities of eating, or governing, or writing, or thinking.

We are continually being presented with images of the humanly new and creative as occurring in the public realm of the polis, or the realms of marketplace or of art and science outside the household. The very term 'reproduction' suggests mere repetition, the "natural" bringing into existence of repeated instances of the same human animal. But human reproduction is not repetition.[56] This is not to suggest that bringing up children in the interstices[57] of patriarchal society, in society structured by institutions supporting male dominance, can achieve the potential of transformation latent in the activity of human mothering. But the activity of creating new social persons and new kinds of persons is potentially the most transformative human activity of all. And it suggests that morality should concern itself first of all with this activity, with what its norms and practices ought to be, and with how the institutions and arrangements throughout society and the world ought to be structured to facilitate the right kinds of development of the best kinds of new persons. The flourishing of children ought to be at the very center of moral and social and political and economic and legal thought, rather than, as at present, at the periphery, if attended to at all.

Revised conceptions of public and private have significant implications for our conceptions of human beings and relationships between them. Some feminists suggest that instead of seeing human relationships in terms of the impersonal ones of the "public" sphere, as standard political and moral theory has so often done, we might consider seeing human relationships in terms of those experienced in the sphere of the "private," or of what these relationships could

be imagined to be like in post-patriarchal society.[58] The traditional approach is illustrated by those who generalize, to other regions of human life than the economic, assumptions about "economic man" in contractual relations with other men. It sees such impersonal, contractual relations as paradigmatic, even, on some views, for moral theory. Many feminists, in contrast, consider the realm of what has been misconstrued as the "private" as offering guidance to what human beings and their relationships should be like even in regions beyond those of family and friendship. Sara Ruddick looks at the implications of the practice of mothering for the conduct of peace politics.[59] Marilyn Friedman and Lorraine Code consider friendship, especially as women understand it, as a possible model for human relationships.[60] Others see society as non-contractual rather than as contractual.

Clearly, a reconceptualization is needed of the ways in which every human life is entwined with personal and with social components. Feminist theorists are contributing imaginative work to this project.

III. The Concept of Self

Let me turn now to the third aspect of the history of ethics which I discussed and which feminists are re-envisioning: the concept of self. One of the most important emphases in a feminist approach to morality is the recognition that more attention must be paid to the domain between, on the one hand, the self as ego, as self-interested individual, and, on the other hand, the universal, everyone, others in general.[61] Traditionally, ethics has dealt with these poles of individual self and universal all. Usually, it has called for impartiality against the partiality of the egoistic self; sometimes

---

56   [Author's note] For further discussion and an examination of surrounding associations, see Virginia Held, "Birth and Death," in *Ethics* 99 (January 1989): 362–88.

57   Intervening spaces, cracks.

58   [Author's note] See e.g., Virginia Held, "Non-contractual Society: A Feminist View," in *Science, Morality and Feminist Theory*, ed. Hanen and Nielsen.

59   [Author's note] Sara Ruddick, *Maternal Thinking*.

60   [Author's note] See Marilyn Friedman, "Feminism and Modern Friendship: Dislocating the Community," *Ethics* 99 (January 1989): 275–90; and Lorraine Code, "Second Persons."

61   [Author's note] See Virginia Held, "Feminism and Moral Theory," in *Women and Moral Theory*, ed. Kittay and Meyers.

it has defended egoism against claims for a universal perspective. But most standard moral theory has hardly noticed as morally significant the intermediate realm of family relations and relations of friendship, of group ties and neighborhood concerns, especially from the point of view of women. When it has noticed this intermediate realm it has often seen its attachments as threatening to the aspirations of the Man of Reason, or as subversive of "true" morality. In seeing the problems of ethics as problems of reconciling the interests of the self with what would be right or best for "everyone," standard ethics has neglected the moral aspects of the concern and sympathy which people actually feel for particular others, and what moral experience in this intermediate realm suggests for an adequate morality.

The region of "particular others" is a distinct domain, where what can be seen to be artificial and problematic are the very egoistic "self" and the universal "all others" of standard moral theory. In the domain of particular others, the self is already constituted to an important degree by relations with others, and these relations may be much more salient and significant than the interests of any individual self in isolation.[62] The "others" in the picture, however, are not the "all others," or "everyone," of traditional moral theory; they are not what a universal point of view or a view from nowhere could provide.[63] They are, characteristically, actual flesh and blood other human beings for whom we have actual feelings and with whom we have real ties.

From the point of view of much feminist theory, the individualistic assumptions of liberal theory and of most standard moral theory are suspect. Even if we would be freed from the debilitating aspects of dominating male power to "be ourselves" and to pursue our own interests, we would, as persons, still have ties to other persons, and we would at least in part be constituted by such ties. Such ties would be part of what we inherently are. We are, for instance, the daughter or son of given parents, or the mother or father of given children, and we carry with us at least some ties to the racial or ethnic or national group within which we developed into the persons we are.

If we look, for instance, at the realities of the relation between mothering person (who can be female or male) and child, we can see that what we value in the relation cannot be broken down into individual gains and losses for the individual members in the relation. Nor can it be understood in universalistic terms. Self-development apart from the relation may be much less important than the satisfactory development of the relation. What matters may often be the health and growth of and the development of the relation-and-its-members in ways that cannot be understood in the individualistic terms of standard moral theories designed to maximize the satisfaction of self-interest. The universalistic terms of moral theories grounded in what would be right for "all rational beings" or "everyone" cannot handle, either, what has moral value in the relation between mothering person and child.

Feminism is of course not the only locus of criticism of the individualistic and abstractly universalistic features of liberalism and of standard moral theory. Marxists[64] and communitarians[65] also see the self as

---

62   [Author's note] See Seyla Benhabib, "The Generalized and the Concrete Other. The Kohlberg-Gilligan Controversy and Moral Theory," in *Women and Moral Theory*, ed. Kittay and Meyers. See also Caroline Whitbeck, "Feminist Ontology: A Different Reality," in *Beyond Domination*, ed. Carol Gould (Totowa, New Jersey: Rowman and Allanheld, 1983).

63   [Author's note] See Thomas Nagel, *The View from Nowhere* (New York: Oxford University Press, 1986). For a feminist critique, see Susan Bordo, "Feminism, Postmodernism, and Gender-Skepticism," in *Feminism/Postmodernism*, ed. Linda Nicholson (New York: Routledge, 1989).

64   See Chapter 3 for more on Marx.

65   Communitarian political theories tend to stress the social role of a shared sense of common purpose and tradition and mutual ties of kinship and affection, as opposed to the typically "liberal" conception of society as constructed out of a set of contractual relations between otherwise unattached individuals. In North America, communitarianism is especially associated with a wave of criticism of liberalism in the 1980s, spearheaded by such philosophers as Alasdair MacIntyre, Michael Sandel, Charles Taylor, and Michael Walzer.

constituted by its social relations. But in their usual form, Marxist and communitarian criticisms pay no more attention than liberalism and standard moral theory to the experience of women, to the context of mothering, or to friendship as women experience it.[66] Some recent nonfeminist criticisms, such as offered by Bernard Williams, of the impartiality required by standard moral theory, stress how a person's identity may be formed by personal projects in ways that do not satisfy universal norms, yet ought to be admired. Such views still interpret morality from the point of view of an individual and his project, not a social relationship such as that between mothering person and child. And recent nonfeminist criticisms in terms of traditional communities and their moral practices, as seen for instance in the work of Stuart Hampshire and Alasdair MacIntyre, often take traditional gender roles as given, or provide no basis for a radical critique of them.[67] There is no substitute, then, for feminist exploration of the area between ego and universal, as women experience this area, or for the development of a refocused concept of relational self that could be acceptable from a feminist point of view.

Relationships can be evaluated as trusting or mistrustful, mutually considerate or selfish, harmonious or stressful, and so forth. Where trust and considera-tion are appropriate, which is not always, we can find ways to foster them. But understanding and evaluating relationships, and encouraging them to be what they can be at their best, require us to look at relationships between actual persons, and to see what both standard moral theories and their nonfeminist critics often miss. To be adequate, moral theories must pay attention to the neglected realm of particular others in the actual relationships and actual contexts of women's experi-ence. In doing so, problems of individual self-interest vs. universal rules may recede to a region more like background, out-of-focus insolubility or relative un-importance. The salient problems may then be seen to be how we ought best to guide or to maintain or to reshape the relationships, both close and more distant, that we have, or might have, with actual other human beings. Particular others can be actual children in need in distant continents, or the anticipated children of generations not yet even close to being born. But they are not "all rational beings" or "the greatest number," and the self that is in relationships with particular others and is composed to a significant degree by such relations is not a self whose ego must be pitted against abstract, universal claims. Developing the needed guidance for maintaining and reshaping rela-tionships presents enormous problems, but a first step is to recognize how traditional and nonfeminist moral theory of both an individualistic and communitarian kind falls short in providing it.

The concept of the relational self which is evolv-ing within feminist thought is leading to interesting inquiry in many fields. An example is the work be-ing done at the Stone Center at Wellesley College.[68]

---

66 [Author's note] On Marxist theory, see e.g., *Women and Revolution*, ed. Lydia Sargent (Boston: South End Press, 1981); Alison Jaggar, *Feminist Politics and Human Nature*; and Ann Ferguson, *Blood at the Root. Motherhood, Sexuality and Male Dominance* (London: Pandora, 1989). On communitarian theory, see Marilyn Friedman, "Feminism and Modern Friendship...," and also her paper "The Social Self and the Partial-ity Debates," presented at the Society for Women in Philosophy meeting in New Orleans, April 1990.

67 [Author's note] Bernard Williams, *Moral Luck* (Cam-bridge: Cambridge University Press, 1981); *Public and Private Morality*, ed. Stuart Hampshire (Cambridge: Cambridge University Press, 1978); Alasdair Ma-cIntyre, *After Virtue. A Study in Moral Theory* (Notre Dame, Indiana: University of Notre Dame Press, 1981). For discussion see Susan Moller Okin, *Justice, Gender, and the Family* (New York: Basic Books, 1989).

68 [Author's note] On the Stone Center concept of the self see especially Jean Baker Miller, "The Development of Women's Sense of Self," Wellesley, Massachusetts: Stone Center Working Paper No. 12; Janet Surrey, "The 'Self-in-Relation': A Theory of Women's Develop-ment" (Wellesley, Massachusetts: Stone Center Work-ing Paper No. 13); and Judith Jordan, "The Meaning of Mutuality" (Wellesley, Massachusetts: Stone Center Working Paper No. 23). For a feminist but critical view of this work, see Marcia Westkott, "Female Re-lationality and the Idealized Self," *American Journal of Psychoanalysis* 49 (September, 1989): 239–50.

Psychologists there have posited a self-in-relation theory and are conducting empirical inquiries to try to establish how the female self develops. They are working with a theory that a female relational self develops through a mutually empathetic mother-daughter bond.

The work has been influenced by Jean Baker Miller's re-evaluation of women's psychological qualities as strengths rather than weaknesses. In her book *Toward a New Psychology of Women*, published in 1976, Miller identified women's "great desire for affiliation" as one such strength.[69] Nancy Chodorow's *The Reproduction of Mothering*, published in 1978, has also had a significant influence on the work done at the Stone Center, as it has on much feminist inquiry.[70] Chodorow argued that a female affiliative self is reproduced by a structure of parenting in which mothers are the primary caretakers, and sons and daughters develop differently in relation to a parent of the same sex, or a parent of different sex, as primary caretaker. Daughters develop a sense of self by identifying themselves with the mother; they come to define themselves as connected to or in relation with others. Sons, in contrast, develop a sense of self by differentiating themselves from the mother; they come to define themselves as separate from or unconnected to others. An implication often drawn from Chodorow's work is that parenting should be shared equally by fathers and mothers so that children of either sex can develop with caretakers of both same and different sex.

In 1982, Carol Gilligan, building on both Miller and Chodorow, offered her view of the "different voice" with which girls and women express their understanding of moral problems.[71] Like Miller and Chodorow, Gilligan valued tendencies found especially in women to affiliate with others and to interpret their moral responsibilities in terms of their relationships with others. In all, the valuing of autonomy and individual independence over care and concern for relationships, was seen as an expression of male bias. The Stone Center has tried to elaborate and to study a feminist conception of the relational self. In a series of Working Papers, researchers and clinicians have explored the implications of this conception for various issues in women's psychology (e.g., power, anger, work inhibitions, violence, eating patterns) and for therapy.

The self as conceptualized in these studies is seen as having both a need for recognition and a need to understand the other, and these needs are seen as compatible. They are created in the context of mother-child interaction, and are satisfied in a mutually empathetic relationship. This does not require a loss of self, but a relationship of mutuality in which self and other both express intersubjectivity. Both give and take in a way that not only contributes to the satisfaction of their needs as individuals, but also affirms the "larger relational unit" they compose.[72] Maintaining this larger relational unit then becomes a goal, and maturity is seen not in terms of individual autonomy but in terms of competence in creating and sustaining relations of empathy and mutual intersubjectivity.

The Stone Center psychologists contend that the goal of mutuality is rarely achieved in adult male-female relationships because of the traditional gender system. The gender system leads men to seek autonomy and power over others, and to undervalue the caring and relational connectedness that is expected of women. Women rarely receive the nurturing and empathetic support they provide. Accordingly, these psychologists look to the interaction that occurs in mother-daughter relationships as the best source of insight into the promotion of the healthy, relational self. This research provides an example of exploration into a refocused, feminist conception of the self, and into empirical questions about its development and implications.

In a quite different field, that of legal theory, a refocused concept of self is leading to reexamina-

---

69   [Author's note] Jean Baker Miller, *Toward a New Psychology of Women* (Boston: Beacon Press, 1976).

70   [Author's note] Nancy Chodorow, *The Reproduction of Mothering: Psychoanalysis and the Sociology of Gender* (Berkeley: University of California Press, 1978).

71   [Author's note] Carol Gilligan, *In a Different Voice*.

72   [Author's note] J. V. Jordan, "The Meaning of Mutuality," p. 2.

tions of such concepts as property and autonomy and the role these have played in political theory and in constitutional law. For instance, the legal theorist Jennifer Nedelsky questions the imagery that is dominant in constitutional law and in our conceptions of property: the imagery of a bounded self, a self contained within boundaries and having rights to property within a wall allowing it to exclude others and to exclude government. The boundary metaphor, she argues, obscures and distorts our thinking about human relationships and what is valuable in them. "The boundedness of selves," Nedelsky writes, "may seem to be a self-evident truth, but I think it is a wrong-headed and destructive way of conceiving of the human creatures law and government are created for."[73] In the domain of the self's relation to the state, the central problem, she argues, is not "maintaining a sphere into which the state cannot penetrate, but fostering autonomy when people are already within the sphere of state control or responsibility."[74] What we can from a feminist perspective think of as the male "separative self" seems on an endless quest for security behind such walls of protection as those of property. Property focuses the quest for security "in ways that are paradigmatic of the efforts of separative selves to protect themselves through boundaries...."[75] But of course property is a social construction, not a thing; it requires the involvement of the state to define what it is and to defend it. What will provide what it seeks to offer will not be boundaries and exclusions, but constructive relationships.

In an article on autonomy, Nedelsky examines the deficiencies in the concept of self with which so much of our political and legal thinking about autonomy has been developed. She well recognizes that of course feminists are centrally concerned with freedom and autonomy, with enabling women to live our own lives. But we need a language with which to express these concerns which will also reflect "the equally important feminist precept that any good theorizing will start with people in their social contexts. And the notion of social context must take seriously its constitutive quality; social context cannot simply mean that individuals will, of course, encounter one another."[76] The problem, then, is how to combine the claim of the constitutiveness of social relations with the value of self-determination. Liberalism has been the source of our language of freedom and self-determination, but it lacks the ability to express comprehension of "the reality we know: the centrality of relationships in constituting the self."[77]

In developing a new conception of autonomy that avoids positing self-sufficient and thus highly artificial individuals, Nedelsky points out first that "the capacity to find one's own law can develop only in the context of relations with others (both intimate and more broadly social) that nurture this capacity, and second, that the 'content' of one's own law is comprehensible only with reference to shared social norms, values, and concepts."[78] She sees the traditional liberal view of the self as implying that the most perfectly autonomous man is the most perfectly isolated, and finds this pathological.

Instead of developing autonomy through images of walls around one's property, as does the Western liberal tradition and as does U.S. constitutional law, Nedelsky suggests that "the most promising model, symbol, or metaphor for autonomy is not property, but childrearing. There we have encapsulated the emergence of autonomy through relationship with others.... Interdependence [is] a constant component of autonomy."[79] And she goes on to examine how

---

73   [Author's note] Jennifer Nedelsky, "Law, Boundaries, and the Bounded Self," *Representations* 30 (Spring, 1990): 162–89, at 167.

74   [Author's note] Ibid., p. 169.

75   [Author's note] Ibid., p. 181.

76   [Author's note] Jennifer Nedelsky, "Reconceiving Autonomy: Sources, Thoughts and Possibilities," *Yale Journal of Law and Feminism* 1 (Spring, 1989): 7–36, p. 9. See also Diana T. Meyers, *Self, Society, and Personal Choice* (New York: Columbia University Press, 1989).

77   [Author's note] Ibid.

78   [Author's note] Ibid, p. 11.

79   [Author's note] Ibid., p. 12. See also Mari J. Matsuda, "Liberal Jurisprudence and Abstracted Visions of Human Nature," *New Mexico Law Review* 16 (Fall, 1986): 613–30.

law and bureaucracies can foster autonomy within relationships between citizen and government. This does not entail extrapolating from intimate relations to largescale ones; rather, the insights gained from experience with the context of childrearing allow us to recognize the relational aspects of autonomy. In work such as Nedelsky's we can see how feminist reconceptualizations of the self can lead to the rethinking of fundamental concepts even in terrains such as law, thought by many to be quite distant from such disturbances.

To argue for a view of the self as relational does not mean that women need to remain enmeshed in the ties by which they are constituted. In recent decades, especially, women have been breaking free of relationships with parents, with the communities in which they grew up, and with men, relationships in which they defined themselves through the traditional and often stifling expectations of others.[80] These quests for self have often involved wrenching instability and painful insecurity. But the quest has been for a new and more satisfactory relational self, not for the self-sufficient individual of liberal

theory. Many might share the concerns expressed by Alison Jaggar that disconnecting ourselves from particular others, as ideals of individual autonomy seem to presuppose we should, might make us incapable of morality, rather than capable of it, if, as so many feminists think, "an ineliminable part of morality consists in responding emotionally to particular others."[81]

I have examined three topics on which feminist philosophers and feminists in other fields are thinking anew about where we should start and how we should focus our attention in ethics. Feminist reconceptualizations and recommendations concerning the relation between reason and emotion, the distinction between public and private, and the concept of the self, are providing insights deeply challenging to standard moral theory. The implications of this work are that we need an almost total reconstruction of social and political and economic and legal theory in all their traditional forms as well as a reconstruction of moral theory and practice at more comprehensive, or fundamental, levels.[82]

---

80   [Author's note] See e.g., *Women's Ways of Knowing. The Development of Self, Voice, and Mind*, by Mary Field Belenky, Blyth McVicker Clinchy, Nancy Rule Goldberger, and Jill Mattuck Tarule (New York: Basic Books, 1986).

81   [Author's note] Alison Jaggar, "Feminist Ethics: Some Issues for the Nineties," p. 11.

82   [Author's note] This paper is based in part on my Truax Lectures on "The Prospect of Feminist Morality" at Hamilton College on November 2 and 9, 1989. Early versions were also presented at Colgate University; at Queen's University in Kingston, Ontario; at the University of Kentucky; and at the New School for Social Research. I am grateful to all who made possible these occasions and commented on the paper at these times, and to Alison Jaggar, Laura Purdy, and Sara Ruddick for additional discussion.

MARY MIDGLEY
"Is a Dolphin a Person?"

Who Is Mary Midgley?

Mary Midgley (1919–) is a moral philosopher, renowned for her no-nonsense, highly practical approach to fundamental human issues. She writes mainly on religion, science, and ethics. Formerly a professor of philosophy at the University of Newcastle (now retired), she is one of Britain's most popular and well-known philosophical figures. Fiercely combative, she has been described as possibly "the most frightening philosopher in the country: the one before whom it is least pleasant to appear a fool."

Midgley studied Classics at Somerville College, Oxford, but never completed a PhD. (In 2005 she published a newspaper article called "Proud not to be a doctor," in which she argued that a PhD may give you the skills of a lawyer, but it can also obscure the big issues in a mass of detail.) She wrote her first book in her fifties, after raising a family,[1] but has since produced more than a dozen volumes including *Beast and Man* (revised edition, Routledge, 1995); *Animals and Why They Matter* (reprint edition, University of Georgia Press, 1998); *Wickedness* (revised edition, Routledge, 2001); *Evolution as a Religion* (revised edition, Routledge, 2002); *The Ethical Primate* (Routledge, 1994); and *Science and Poetry* (Routledge, 2001). Between 1979 and 1983 Midgley was involved in a highly public, very heated exchange of articles after she attacked Richard Dawkins' "selfish gene" thesis.

The article reprinted here, "Is a Dolphin a Person?" is included in her book *Utopias, Dolphins and Computers* (Routledge, 1996). In it, she argues that we need to develop a more flexible notion of moral personhood that will allow us to treat animals as morally important in their own right.

How Important and Influential Is This Passage?

This article represents the vastly increased attention that has been paid by professional philosophers in recent decades to the possibility that human beings *have moral obligations to the natural environment* and, in particular, to non-human animals. Though certainly not a new idea, the notion that the so-called 'lower' animals might have moral claims upon us, and that our species might have a moral duty to care for and preserve the planet's various ecosystems, is today playing an unprecedentedly significant role in mainstream moral theorizing.

Suggestions for Critical Reflection

1. Can non-humans be persons? Are all humans persons? How do we decide who is a person and what isn't?
2. What, if anything, is *special* about human beings?
3. What makes cruelty immoral? Is there a moral difference between cruelty to people and cruelty to animals?
4. How far should we allow human interests to be overridden by those of non-humans? Should these considerations affect what we eat or wear? How we farm? The economic and cultural practices of some cultures (such as those that, for example, hunt seals or whales)? When, if ever, should we sacrifice human comfort, health or even life for non-humans?
5. What is the relationship between law and morality? What should it be?

---

1   As she once put it: "I wrote no books until I was a good 50, and I'm jolly glad because I didn't know what I thought before then."

Suggestions for Further Reading

Midgley has published a memoir, *The Owl of Minerva* (Routledge, 2005). Her article "Proud not to be a doctor," is in *The Guardian*, October 3, 2005. In addition to her books listed above, her articles that address the moral status of animals include "Towards a More Humane View of the Beasts?" in *The Environment in Question: Ethics and Global Issues*, ed. David E. Cooper (Routledge, 1992), and "Beasts Versus the Biosphere?" *Environmental Values* 1 (1992).

A good overview of the question of animals in ethics is provided by Angus Taylor's *Animals and Ethics* (Broadview Press, 2009). Rosalind Hursthouse, *Ethics, Humans and Other Animals* (Routledge, 2000) is another introduction which includes a collection of readings, and there is also Armstrong and Botzler, eds., *The Animal Ethics Reader* (Routledge, 2008). Peter Singer's *Animal Liberation* (Harper Perennial, 2009) is a very famous defense of the view that animals have substantial moral claims on us; see also Tom Regan's "The Case for Animal Rights" in a collection edited by Singer, *In Defence of Animals* (Basil Blackwell, 1985)—see also Regan's book also called *The Case for Animal Rights* (University of California Press, 2004). Robert Nozick responded to Singer in a section of his *Anarchy, State and Utopia* (Basic Books, 1974), pp. 34–42.

Decent introductions to philosophy of the environment include Zimmerman et al. (eds.), *Environmental Philosophy: From Animal Rights to Radical Ecology* (Prentice Hall, 2004) and Andrew Light and Holmes Rolston III (eds.), *Environmental Ethics: An Anthology* (Blackwell, 2002).

"Is a Dolphin a Person?"[2]

The Undoubting Judge

This question came up during the trial of the two people who, in May 1977, set free two bottle-nosed dolphins used for experimental purposes by the University of Hawaii's Institute of Marine Biology. It is an interesting question for a number of reasons,

and I want to use most of this discussion in interpreting it, and tracing its connexion with several others which may already be of concern to us. I shall not go into details of the actual case, but shall rely on the very clear and thoughtful account which Gavin Daws gives in his paper, '"Animal Liberation" as Crime'.[3]

Kenneth le Vasseur, the first of the two men to be tried, attempted through his counsel what is called a 'choice of evils' defence. In principle the law allows this in cases where an act, otherwise objectionable, is necessary to avoid a greater evil. For this defence to succeed, the act has to be (as far as the defendant knows) the only way of avoiding an imminent, and more serious, harm or evil to himself or to 'another'.

Le Vasseur, who had been involved in the care of the dolphins, believed that their captivity, with

---

2   This article was first published under the title "Persons and Non-Persons" in *In Defence of Animals*, edited by Peter Singer (Oxford: Basil Blackwell, 1985). Copyright © 1985, pp. 52-62. The version reprinted here appeared as Chapter Nine of *Utopias, Dolphins and Computers* (London: Routledge, 1996). Reprinted with permission of Wiley-Blackwell Inc.

3   [Author's note] Gavin Daws, '"Animal Liberation' as Crime" in Harlan B. Miller and William H. Williams (eds.), *Ethics and Animals* (Totowa, NJ: Humana Press, 1983).

the conditions then prevailing in it, actually endangered their lives. His counsel, in his opening statement for the defence, spoke of the exceptional nature of dolphins as animals; bad and rapidly deteriorating physical conditions at the laboratory; a punishing regimen for the dolphins, involving overwork, reductions in their food rations, the total isolation they endured, deprived of the company of other dolphins, even of contact with humans in the tank, deprived of all toys which they had formerly enjoyed playing with—to the point where Puka, having refused to take part consistently in experimental sessions, developed self-destructive behaviours symptomatic of deep disturbance, and finally became lethargic—'comatose'. Le Vasseur, seeing this, fearing that death would be the outcome, and knowing that there was no law that he could turn to, believed himself authorized, in the interests of the dolphins' well-being, to release them. The release was not a theft in that Le Vasseur did not intend to gain anything for himself. It was intended to highlight conditions in the laboratory. (Daws: 356–67)

But was a dolphin 'another'? The judge thought not. He said that 'another' would have to be another person, and he defined dolphins as property, not as persons, as a matter of law. A dolphin could not be 'another person' under the penal code. The defence tried and failed to get the judge disqualified for prejudice. It then asked leave to go to Federal Court in order to claim that Thirteenth Amendment rights in respect of involuntary servitude might be extended to dolphins. This plea the judge rejected:

Judge Doi said, 'We get to dolphins, we get to orangutans, chimpanzees, dogs, cats. I don't know at what level you say intelligence is insufficient to have that animal or thing, or whatever you want to call it, a human being under the penal code. I'm saying that they're not under the penal code and that's my answer.' (Daws: 365)

At this point—which determined the whole outcome of the trial—something seemed perfectly obvious to the judge about the meaning of the words 'other' and 'person'. What was it? And how obvious is it to everybody else? In the answer just given, he raises the possibility that it might be a matter of intelligence, but he rejects it. That consideration, he says, is not needed. The question is quite a simple one; no tests are called for. The word 'person' just means a human being.

What Are Persons?

I think that this is a very natural view, but not actually a true one, and the complications which we find when we look into the use of this interesting word are instructive. In the first place, there are several well-established and indeed venerable precedents for calling non-human beings 'persons'.

One concerns the persons of the Trinity, and indeed the personhood of God. Another is the case of 'legal persons'—corporate bodies such as cities or colleges, which count as persons for various purposes, such as sueing and being sued. As Blackstone says, these 'corporations or bodies politic ... are formed and created by human laws for the purposes of society and government'; unlike 'natural persons', who can only be created by God.[4] The law, then, can if it chooses create persons; it is not a mere passive recorder of their presence (as indeed Judge Doi implied in making his ruling a matter of law and not of fact). Thirdly, what may look nearer to the dolphins, the word is used by zoologists to describe the individual members of a compound or colonial organism, such as jellyfish or coral, each having (as the dictionary reasonably puts it) 'a more or less independent life'.[5]

There is nothing stretched or paradoxical about these uses, for the word does not in origin mean 'human being' or anything like it. It means a mask, and its basic general sense comes from the drama. The

4   Sir William Blackstone's *Commentaries on the Laws of England*, published in four volumes between 1765 and 1767, codified the common law—law based on judicial custom and precedent—which today forms a major part of the law of many countries which were once British territories or colonies.

5   [Author's note] It is also interesting that 'personal identity' is commonly held to belong to continuity of consciousness rather than of bodily form, in stories where the two diverge. Science fiction strongly supports this view, which was first mooted by John Locke, *Essay Concerning Human Understanding*, bk. 2, ch. 27, sect. 15.

'masks' in a play are the characters who appear in it. Thus, to quote the Oxford Dictionary again, after 'a mask', it means 'a character or personage acted, one who plays or performs any part, a character, relation or capacity in which one acts, a being having legal rights, a juridical person'.

The last two meanings throw a sharp light on the difference between this notion and that of being human. Not all human beings need be persons. The word *persona* in Latin does not apply to slaves, though it does apply to the State as a corporate person. Slaves have, so to speak, no speaking part in the drama; they do not figure in it; they are extras.

There are some entertaining similar examples about women. Thus:

> One case, brought before the US Supreme Court in the 1890s, concerned Virginia's exclusion of a woman from the practice of the law, although the pertinent statute was worded in terms of 'persons'. The Court argued that it was indeed up to the State's Supreme Court '*to determine whether the word 'person' as used (in the Statute) is confined to males*, and whether women are admitted to practise law in that Commonwealth'. The issue of whether women must be understood as included by the word 'persons' continued even into the twentieth century ... In a Massachusetts case in 1931 ... women were denied eligibility for jury service, although the statute stated that every 'person qualified to vote' was so eligible. The Massachusetts Supreme Court asserted: 'No intention to include women can be deduced from the omission of the word male.'[6]

Finding the Right Drama

What is going on here? We shall not understand it, I think, unless we grasp how deeply drama is interwoven with our thinking, how intimately its categories shape our ideas. People who talk like this have a clear notion of the drama which they think is going on around them. They know who is supposed to count in

it and who is not. Attempts to introduce fresh characters irritate them. They are inclined to dismiss these attempts sharply as obviously absurd and paradoxical. The question who is and who is not a person seems at this point a quite simple and clear-cut one. Bertie Wooster simply is not a character in *Macbeth* and that is the end of the matter.

It is my main business here to point out that this attitude is too crude. The question is actually a very complex one, much more like 'who is important?' than 'who has got two legs?' If we asked 'who is important?' we would know that we needed to ask further questions, beginning with 'important for what?' Life does not contain just one purpose or one drama, but many interwoven ones. Different characters matter in different ways. Beings figure in some who are absent from others, and we all play different parts in different scripts.

Even in ordinary human life, it is fatal to ignore this. To insist on reducing all relationships to those prescribed by a single drama—such, for instance, as the Social Contract[7]—is disastrous. Intellectuals are prone to such errors, and need to watch out for them. But when we come to harder cases, where the variation is greater—cases such as abortion, euthanasia or the treatment of other species—this sort of mistake is still more paralysing. That is why these cases are so helpful in illuminating the more central ones.

It is clear that, over women, those who limited the use of the concept 'person' felt this difficulty. They did not want to deny altogether that women were persons, since in the dramas of private life women figured prominently. Public life, however, was a different stage, whose rules and conventions excluded them (queens apart) as completely as elephants or angels. The fact that private life often impinges on public

---

6   [Author's note] Susan Möller Okin, *Women in Western Political Thought* (Princeton, NJ, 1979), p. 251.

7   The idea of a *social contract* is typically appealed to in order to justify constraints on people's individual freedom, on the basis that people voluntarily agree (or would agree, or ought to agree) to these restrictions because in the long run they make everybody better off. For example, one might argue, we tacitly agree to submit appropriately to the authority of the police because we are better off living in a society where there is a police force than one where there is not.

was an informal matter and could not affect this ruling. Similarly at Rome, it is clear that slaves actually played a considerable part in life. In Greek and Roman comedy ingenious slaves, both male and female, often figure as central characters, organizing the intrigue and supplying the brains which the hero and heroine themselves unfortunately lack. This, however, was not going to get them legal rights. The boundaries of particular situations and institutions served to compartmentalize thought and to stop people raising questions about the rights and status of those who were for central purposes currently disregarded.

I think it will be helpful here to follow out a little further the accepted lines of usage for the word person. How complete is its link with the human bodily form? What, for instance, about intelligent alien beings? Could we call them persons? If not, then contact with them—which is certainly conceivable—would surely require us to coin a new word to do the quite subtle moral job which is done at present by 'person'. The idea of a person in the almost technical sense required by morality today is the one worked out by Kant.[8] It is the idea of a rational being, capable of choice and therefore endowed with dignity, worthy of respect, having rights; one that must be regarded always as an end in itself, not only as a means to the ends of others.

Because this definition deals solely with rational qualities, it makes no mention of human form or human descent, and the spirit behind it would certainly not license us to exclude intelligent aliens, any more than disembodied spirits. The moral implications of the word 'person' would therefore, on our current Kantian principles, surely still have to attach to whatever word we might coin to include aliens. C.S. Lewis, describing a planet where there are three distinct rational species, has them use the word *hnau* for the condition which they all share, and this term is naturally central to the morality of all of them.[9]

Now if intelligence is really so important to the issue, a certain vertigo descends when we ask 'where do we draw the line?' because intelligence is a matter of degree. Some inhabitants of our own planet, including whales and dolphins, have turned out to be a lot brighter than was once thought. Quite how bright they are is not yet really clear to us. Indeed it may never become so, because of the difference in the kind of brightness appropriate to beings with very different sorts of life. How can we deal with such a situation?

Attending to the Middle Ground

The first thing needed is undoubtedly to get away from the single, simple, black-and-white antithesis with which Kant started, the antithesis between persons and things. Most of Kant's argument is occupied with this, and while it remains so he does not need to make finer distinctions. *Things* (he says) can properly be used as means to human ends in a way in which *people* cannot. Things have no aims of their own; they are not subjects but objects.

Thing-treatment given to people is exploitation and oppression. It is an outrage, because, as Kant exclaims, 'a man is not a thing'. Masters sell slaves; rulers deceive and manipulate their subjects; employers treat their secretaries as part of the wallpaper. By dwelling on the simple, stark contrast involved here, Kant was able to make some splendid moral points which are still vital to us today, about the thoroughgoing respect which is due to every free and rational human being. But the harsh, bright light which he turned on these situations entirely obscured the intermediate cases. A mouse is not a thing either, before we even start to think about a dolphin.

I find it interesting that, just as the American courts could not quite bring themselves to say that women were not persons, so Kant cannot quite get around to saying what his theory certainly implies, that animals are things. He does say that they 'are not self-conscious and are there merely as a means to an end',[10] that end being ours. But he does not

---

8   [Author's note] See Immanuel Kant, *Foundations of the Metaphysics of Morals* (tr. Lewis White Beck, Bobbs-Merrill, 1959), sect. 428–432, p. 46. In the UK a more available translation is that called *The Moral Law* (tr. H.J. Paton, Hutchinson, 1948), pp. 90–92.

9   [Author's note] C.S. Lewis, *Out of the Silent Planet* (London, John Lane, 1938).

10   [Author's note] Immanuel Kant, 'Duties towards Animals and Spirits' in his *Lectures on Ethics* (tr. Louis Infield, Methuen, London, 1930), p. 239.

actually call them things, nor does he write off their interests. In fact he emphatically condemns cruel and mean treatment of them. But, like many other humane people who have got stuck with an inadequate moral theory, he gives ingeniously unconvincing reasons for this. He says—what has gone on being said ever since—that it is only because cruelty to animals may lead on to cruelty to humans, or degrade us, or be a sign of a bad moral character, that we have to avoid it.

This means that if we can show that, for instance, venting our ill-temper on the dog will prevent our doing it on our families, or if we can produce certificates to show that we are in general people of firm moral character, not easily degraded, we can go ahead with a clear conscience. Dog-bashing, properly managed, could count as a legitimate form of therapy, along with gardening, pottery and raffia-work. In no case would the physical materials involved be directly considered, because all equally would be only objects, not subject. And there is nothing degrading about simply hitting an object.

In spite of the appalling cruelty which human beings show towards animals the world over, it does not seem likely that anyone regards them consistently in this light, as objects. Spasms of regard, tenderness, comradeship and even veneration, alternating with unthinking callousness, seem to make up the typical human attitude to them. And towards fellow-human-beings too, a rather similar alternation is often found. So this cannot really be an attitude confined to things. Actually even cruelty itself, when it is deliberate, seems to require that its objects should not be mere physical objects, but should be capable of minding what is done to them, of responding as separate characters in the drama.

More widely, the appeal of hunting, and also of sports such as bullfighting, seems to depend on the sense of outwitting and defeating a conscious quarry or opponent, 'another', able to be one's opposite in the game or drama. The script distinctly requires non-human characters, who can play their parts well or badly. Moby Dick is not an extra. And the degradingness of deliberate cruelty itself surely requires this other-regarding element. 'Another' is not always another human being.

Indirect Justifications

The degradingness of cruelty is of course widely admitted, and le Vasseur's counsel used this admission as the ground of an alternative defence. He drew attention to his client's status as a state employee, which conferred authority on him to act as he did in coming to the defence of 'another', in this case the United States, whose social values were injured by what was being done to the dolphins. This argument was rejected, on the ground that, in the eyes of the law, cruelty to animals is merely a misdemeanour, whereas theft is a felony. Accordingly the choice of evils could not properly be resolved in such a way as to make theft the less serious offence. It is interesting that this argument makes no objection to treating the United States as 'another' or 'another person'—it does not insist that a person simply means a human being—but rests instead on contending that this 'other' finds its values more seriously attacked by theft than by cruelty to dolphins.

This sort of argument is not easy to come to grips with, even in the case of an ordinary individual person, still less in that of a nation. How serious an evil is cruelty? Once it is conceded that the victim's point of view does not count, that the injury is only to the offender or some body of which he is part, we seem to be cut off from the key considerations of the argument and forced to conduct it in a strained manner, from grounds which are not really central. Is cruelty necessarily depraving? On this approach, that seems partly to be a factual question about how easily people are depraved, and partly perhaps an aesthetic one about how far cruel acts are necessarily disgusting and repellent.

These acts seem to be assimilated now to others which are repellent without being clearly immoral, such as eating the bodies of people whom one has not killed, or watching atrocities over which one has no control. The topic becomes a neighbour of pornography rather than of abortion and euthanasia. (In the disputes about permissiveness in the 1960s, an overlap actually developed here at times, as when a London art gallery organized a happening in which some fish were to be electrocuted as part of the show, and efforts to ban this were attacked as censorious manifestations of aesthetic narrow-mindedness.)

Something seems to have gone wrong with the thinking here. The distinctive feature of actions attacked on purely aesthetic grounds should surely be that their effects are confined to those who actually perform them. No other sentient being is harmed by them. That is why they pose problems for libertarians, when bystanders object to them. But cruelty does not pose this kind of problem, since the presence of 'another' who is harmed is essential to it. In our case it is the dolphin, who does seem to be 'another'. Can we avoid thinking of it in this way? Can the central objection to cruelty really be something rather indirect, such as its being in bad taste?

Moral Change and the Law

The law seems to have ruled thus here. And in doing this, the law shows itself to be in a not uncommon difficulty, one that arises when public opinion is changing. Legal standards are not altogether independent of moral standards. They flow from them and crystallize in ways designed to express certain selected moral insights. When those insights change deeply enough, the law changes. But there are often jolts and discrepancies here, because the pace of change is different. New moral perceptions require the crystals to be broken up and reformed, and this process takes time. Changes of this kind have repeatedly altered the rules surrounding the central crux which concerns us here; the stark division of the world into persons and property. Changing attitudes to slavery are a central case, to which we must come back in a minute. But it is worth noticing first that plain factual discoveries too can make a difference.

When our civilization formed the views on the species barrier which it still largely holds, all the most highly-developed non-human animals were simply unknown. Legend apart, it was assumed that whales and dolphins were much like fish. The great apes were not even discovered till the eighteenth century and no real knowledge of their way of living was acquired until within the last few decades. About better-known creatures too, there was a very general ignorance and unthinking dismissal of available evidence; their sociality was not noticed or believed in. The central official intellectual tradition of our culture never expected to be forced to subtilize its crude, extreme, unshaded dichotomy between man and beast. In spite of the efforts of many concerned thinkers, from Plutarch to Montaigne and from Blake to John Stuart Mill, it did not develop other categories.[11]

If alien beings landed tomorrow, lawyers, philosophers and social scientists would certainly have to do some very quick thinking. (I don't expect the aliens myself, but they are part of the imaginative furniture of our age, and it is legitimate to use them to roust us from our dogmatic slumbers.) Science fiction, though sometimes helpful, has far too often side-tracked the problem by making its aliens just scientists with green antennae—beings whose 'intelligence' is of a kind to be instantly accepted at the Massachusetts Institute of Technology, only of course a little greater. Since neither dolphins nor gorillas write doctoral theses, this would still let us out as far as terrestrial non-human creatures were concerned. 'Persons' and their appropriate rights could still go on being defined in terms of this sort of intelligence, and we could quietly continue to poison the pigeons in the park any time that we felt like it.

The question is, why should this kind of intelligence be so important, and determine the limits of our moral concern? It is often assumed that we can only owe duties to beings capable of speech. Why this should be thought is not altogether clear. At a simple level, Bentham[12] surely got it right: 'The question is not *can they talk*? Nor *can they reason*? But *can they suffer*?'[13] With chimps, gorillas and dolphins, however, there is now a further problem, because people have been trying, apparently with some degree of success, to teach them certain kinds of language.

---

11   Plutarch lived in Greece around 100 CE and Michel de Montaigne was born in France in 1533; both were famous essayists. William Blake, a British Romantic poet, died in 1827 and the philosopher Mill in 1873.

12   Jeremy Bentham, an English philosopher and advocate of legal reform, was an influential formulator of the principle of 'utilitarianism'—the principle that actions are right insofar as they contribute to general happiness, and wrong insofar as they contribute to unhappiness—and was a great influence on John Stuart Mill.

13   [Author's note] Jeremy Bentham, *Introduction to the Principles of Morals and Legislation*, ch. 17.

This project might have taught us a great deal about just what new categories we need in our attempt to classify beings more subtly. But unluckily it has been largely obscured by furious opposition from people who still have just the two categories, and who see the whole proceeding as an illicit attempt to smuggle contraband from one to the other.

This reaction is extremely interesting. What is the threat? Articulate apes and cetaceans[14] are scarcely likely to take over the government. What might happen, however, is that it would become much harder to exclude them from moral consideration. In particular, their use as experimental subjects might begin to look very different. Can the frontier be defended by a resolute and unbreakable refusal to admit that these animals can talk?

The Meaning of Fellowship

It is understandable that people have thought so, but this surely cannot really be the issue. What makes creatures our fellow-beings, entitled to basic consideration, is not intellectual capacity, but emotional fellowship. And if we ask what powers can give a higher claim, bringing some creatures nearer to the degree of consideration which is due to humans, what is most relevant seems to be sensibility, social and emotional complexity of the kind which is expressed by the forming of deep, subtle and lasting relationships. The gift of imitating certain intellectual skills which are important to humans is no doubt an indicator of this, but it cannot be central. We already know that both apes and dolphins have this kind of social and emotional complexity.

If we ask what elements in 'persons' are central in entitling them to moral consideration, we can, I think, get some light on the point by contrasting the claim of these sensitive social creatures with that of a computer of the present generation, programmed in a manner which entitles it, by current controversial usage, to be called 'intelligent' and certainly able to perform calculations impossible to human beings. That computer does not trouble our sleep with any moral claims, and would not do so however much more 'intelligent' it

became, unless it eventually seemed to be conscious, sensitive and endowed with emotions.

If it did seem so, we should have the Frankenstein problem in an acute form. (The extraordinary eagerness with which Frankenstein drove his researches to this disastrous point is something which contemporary monster-makers might like to ponder.) But those who at present emphasize the intelligence of computers do not see any reason to want to call them persons, nor to allow for them as members of the moral community. Speech alone, then, would scarcely do this job for the apes. What is at issue is the already glaring fact, which speech would make it finally impossible to deny, that they mind what happens to them—that they are highly sensitive social beings.

These considerations are not, I think, ones confined to cranks or extremists. They seem fairly widespread today, and probably occur at times to all of us, however uncertain we may be what to do about them. If so, and if the law really allows them no possible weight, then we seem to have reached the situation where the law will have to be changed, because it shocks morality. There is an obvious precedent, to which the dolphin-liberators tried to appeal:

> When the dolphins were taken from the tanks, a message was left behind identifying the releasers as the 'Undersea Railroad', a reference to the Underground Railroad, the Abolitionists' slave-freeing network of pre–Civil War days. Along the Underground Railroad in the 1850s, it sometimes happened that juries refused to convict people charged with smuggling slaves to freedom. That was the kind of vindication le Vasseur and Sipman were looking for ... They did not consider themselves to be criminals. In fact they took the view that, if there was a crime, it was the crime of keeping dolphins—intelligent, highly aware creatures with no criminal record of their own—in solitary confinement, in small, concrete tanks, made to do repetitive experiments, for life. (Daws: 362)

If we go back to the alien beings for a moment and consider whether even the most intelligent of them would have the right to keep any visiting human be-

---

14   Whales, dolphins, and porpoises.

ings, however stupid, in these conditions, even those of us least partial to astronauts may begin to see the point which le Vasseur and Sipman were making. It surely cannot be dismissed merely by entrenching the law round the definition of the word 'person'. We need new thinking, new concepts and new words, not (of course) just about animals but about our whole relation to the non-human world. We are not less capable of providing these than people were in the 1850s, so we should get on with it.

CHAPTER 3

Social/Political Philosophy—What Is Justice?

INTRODUCTION TO THE QUESTION

Social and political philosophy is made up of our attempts to understand and map the basic categories of social life, and to ethically evaluate different forms of social organization. It has three closely interwoven strands: *conceptual analysis* of various important social dimensions, *normative assessment* of the ways society ought to be structured along these dimensions, and *empirical investigation* of issues relevant to the implementation of these social ideals. It includes social philosophy, political philosophy, philosophy of law, and philosophy of the social sciences (such as economics and sociology).

Among the central concepts studied within social and political philosophy are society, culture, human nature, political obligation, power, democracy, toleration, rights, equality, autonomy or freedom, justice, merit, welfare, property, social class, public interest, and social stability. Different analyses of these notions, and different emphases on some ideas (e.g., equality) over others (e.g., autonomy), give rise to differing political philosophies—differing ideological stances as to what the ideal society should look like, and thus different views on how current societies should be modified in order to move them closer to this ideal. Some of the main social-political ideologies (not all of which are mutually exclusive) are:

- *Anarchism*, which denies that any coercive government institutions are ever justified;
- *Libertarianism* (or 'classical liberalism'), which holds that government infringements on individual liberty are always inappropriate, but accepts that a 'minimal' state is consistent with

this; libertarians also hold that failing to help people in need is not an infringement on their liberty, and that the state therefore has no duty to provide this form of support for its citizens;
- *Liberalism* (or 'welfare liberalism'), which is also concerned with promoting individual liberty but holds that a guaranteed social minimum standard of living and enforced equal opportunity are necessary to provide citizens with genuinely substantive autonomy;
- *Communitarianism*, which denies that the rights of individuals are basic and asserts that collectives (states, cultures, communities) have moral claims that are prior to, and sometimes even opposed to, the rights which liberals ascribe to individuals; usually, this is because communitarians hold some version of the thesis that individual identity is constituted by one's social setting, and thus that the liberal notion of an 'isolated individual' who exists independently of society is a mere myth;
- *Fascism*, which is an extreme communitarian view stressing the overriding importance of national culture and giving the state authority to control almost all aspects of social life;
- *Socialism*, which takes neither individual liberty nor community to be a fundamental ideal, but instead emphasizes the value of equality, and justifies coercive social institutions insofar as they promote social equality;
- *Communism*, which advocates a society in which private property is abolished in favor of communal ownership of all goods, in the belief

that it is only in such conditions that human beings can truly flourish;

- *Conservatism*, which distrusts naked political
  power and is skeptical of social planning, and
  which therefore seeks to channel and constrain
  government within historically-evolved, time-
  tested social institutions and relationships; and
- *Feminism*, which advocates social reform (e.g.,
  to the institution of the family) in order to take
  better account of the fact that women have the
  same basic social rights as men.

In addition to conceptual and ethical analysis,
there are also many substantive empirical questions
which have an important bearing on the choice and
implementation of social philosophies. For example,
once a set of principles of distributive justice have
been decided on, it is still a substantial empirical
problem to decide which social and economic arrangements will best instantiate those principles. A
sampling of other important questions: What checks
and balances on government power will be most effective without being inefficient? How can the self-interest of individuals best be harnessed for the public
good? What is the most effective body of legislation
for fostering social stability? Can equality of opportunity be preserved without infringing on personal
autonomy (e.g., on people's choices about who to hire
or rent to)? Which forms of punishment are the most
effective deterrent of crime? How much is human nature shaped and changed by social circumstances?
What is the relationship between free economic markets and democratic political structures? And so on.

The particular social-political issue which is the
focus of this chapter is the problem of justice. The
readings approach the topic in all three of the inter-
connected ways identified above: they deal with
the philosophical analysis of the concept of justice,
make claims about how society should be organized
in order to take proper account of justice, and touch
on some of the empirical data relevant to the construction of a just society. They also deal with some
of the different *aspects* of justice: justice as a property of a political system, a set of social relationships,
of actions, or of individuals; and justice considered
as a problem of specifying how social benefits and

burdens should be distributed among the members
of that society (*distributive justice*), and the problem
of determining the appropriate way to correct injustices or compensate for illegitimate inequalities (*rectificatory justice*).

Aristotle provides an influential initial analysis of
the notion of justice which sets some of the terms for
the following debate. The reading from Hobbes pursues similar questions and also introduces an additional theme: the pressing problem of justifying (and
defining the limits of) coercive state power over individuals. Hobbes, famously, answers this question with
the device of a 'social contract,' by which rationally
self-interested individuals agree to leave the 'state of
nature' and submit themselves to the authority of
the state. Mill is also, in the reading reprinted here,
concerned with the question of the justice of government intervention in the lives of citizens, and he
formulates and defends the classical liberal position
which limits government action to the prevention of
harm. Three of the following readings then present
three of the most important twentieth-century political ideologies on justice, and particularly distributive justice. Marx and Engels argue for the inevitable
ascendance of communism; Rawls carefully lays out
the most influential contemporary version of welfare
liberalism; and Nozick attempts to rebut Rawls with
a lively and fast-moving defense of libertarianism.
There are also two readings representing another
very important social-political movement, feminism:
Simone de Beauvoir criticizes the historical domination of society by males, while the more recent writer
Susan Moller Okin presents a feminist critique of contemporary liberal theory.

There are a number of good books which will
take you deeper into social and political philosophy.
Perhaps the best place to start is with Will Kymlicka's
excellent *Contemporary Political Philosophy* (Oxford
University Press 2001). Also good are Arthur and
Shaw (eds.), *Social and Political Philosophy* (Prentice
Hall 1992); Benn and Peters, *The Principles of Political
Thought* (Free Press 1965); Carl Cohen, *Communism,
Fascism, and Democracy: The Theoretical Foundations*
(McGraw-Hill 1997); Iain Hampsher-Monk, *A History
of Modern Political Thought, Major Political Thinkers
from Hobbes to Marx* (Blackwell 1992); J.R. Lucas, *The*

Principles of Politics (Oxford University Press, 1986); Gerald MacCallum, *Political Philosophy* (Prentice Hall, 1987); George Sher, *Social and Political Philosophy* (Wadsworth, 1999); and Jonathan Wolff, *An Introduction to Political Philosophy* (Oxford University Press, 2006). Goodin and Pettit (eds.), *A Companion to Contemporary Political Philosophy* (Blackwell, 1996) and Robert Simon (ed.), *The Blackwell Guide to Social and Political Philosophy* (Blackwell, 2002) are both well worth consulting.

The modern literature on justice is rich and extensive. Here are some relevant books (focussing mainly on books not already included in the Further Reading sections of the selections in this chapter): Brian Barry, *Theories of Justice*, Volume 1 (University of California Press, 1991); G.A. Cohen, *Self-Ownership, Freedom, and Equality* (Cambridge University Press, 1995); Ronald Dworkin, *Taking Rights Seriously* (Harvard University Press, 1978); Friedrich A. Hayek, *The Constitution of Liberty* (Routledge and Kegan Paul, 1960); David Miller, *Principles of Social Justice* (Harvard University Press, 2001); Stephen Nathanson, *Economic Justice* (Prentice Hall, 1998); D.D. Raphael, *Concepts of Justice* (Oxford University Press, 2001); John Roemer, *Theories of Distributive Justice* (Harvard University Press, 1996); Michael Sandel, *Liberalism and the Limits of Justice* (Cambridge University Press, 1998) and *Justice* (Farrar, Straus and Giroux, 2009); Amartya Sen, *The Idea of Justice* (Harvard University Press, 2009); Arthur and Shaw (eds.), *Justice and Economic Distribution* (Prentice Hall, 1991); and Michael Walzer, *Spheres of Justice* (Basic Books, 1984).

ARISTOTLE
The Nicomachean Ethics

For information on Aristotle's life and his overall philosophical project, please see Chapter 2.

What Is the Structure of This Reading?

The overall structure of the *Nicomachean Ethics* is described in the notes in Chapter 2. Book V, in which Aristotle discusses justice, comes after discussions of various moral virtues, such as courage, temperance, generosity, good temper, and truthfulness. It is fairly clear that Aristotle thinks justice is a particularly important virtue, however, since it is the one to which he devotes by far the most space.

The first five sections of Book V are reprinted here. After distinguishing between the particular virtue of justice and "universal justice," Aristotle goes on, in section two, to divide particular justice into two types: distributive justice and rectificatory justice. In the next three sections, however, he discusses, in turn, *three* varieties of justice—distributive justice in section three, rectificatory justice in section four, and "justice in exchange" in section five. The rest of Book V, which is not included here, deals with the difference between natural and legal justice and emphasizes the role of choice in the virtue of justice (roughly, that people are unjust, according to Aristotle, only if they deliberately *choose* to take unfair advantage of others).

Some Useful Background Information

1. The Greek words for "just" and "unjust" (*dikaios* and *adikos*) are ambiguous in a way which is much less evident in their English counterparts, and Aristotle commences by discussing this ambiguity. The Greek words apply not only to people or actions that we would call just or unjust—i.e., roughly, those that are fair or unfair—but also to moral rightness or wrongness *in general*. Thus

what Aristotle calls "particular justice" is one virtue (albeit a particularly important one) among others, while "universal justice" corresponds to moral virtue in general (or at least, "complete virtue … in relation to our neighbor").

2. For Aristotle, justice is not primarily a state of affairs (such as an even distribution of wealth) or a framework of social rules (such as a fair taxation system). Instead, justice is a *virtue*, just as courage and truthfulness are virtues—justice is, at bottom, a sort of *character trait*. Just actions, then, are (roughly) those performed by just people; a just society is one which is governed by just people; and just laws are those which prescribe moral virtue, and especially the particular virtue of justice.

3. Furthermore, the virtue of justice, for Aristotle, is defined not merely by one's disposition to *behave* in certain ways, but also by one's *motive* for that behavior. That is, unjust people, according to Aristotle, are motivated by what he calls *pleonexia,* usually translated as being "grasping," "greedy," or "overreaching." Literally, it means desiring to have more than other people or wanting more than one's share. (People who possess the particular virtue of justice, presumably, are those who are *not* motivated by *pleonexia*.)

4. At one point Aristotle refers to "those who have a share in the constitution," and this is a significant indicator of his view of the political dimension of distributive justice. For Aristotle, and in ancient Greek thought generally, the free citizens of a political state were like *shareholders* or *partners* in the state. Public property (such as the land of a new colony) or public rewards and honors (such as political office) were to be divided up among citizens in accordance with their merit (i.e., their wealth, nobility, or virtue). The question of just distribution of rewards was therefore, for Aristotle, fundamentally a question about how social goods should be divided up among the (free, male, land-owning) members of the society—that is, of how people should fairly be rewarded for their contribution to a common political enterprise.

A Common Misconception

Aristotle's focus is on *acting* justly or unjustly, rather than on what it is to be *treated* justly or not. Thus, for example, in his discussion of rectificatory justice, his main focus is on how the judge or arbiter should act, and not on the 'injustice' of the state of affairs which the judge is concerned to redress. To put it another way, for Aristotle, justice is a virtue, and since being treated fairly or unfairly manifests neither virtue nor vice, Aristotle's real interest is in those who *do the treating*.

How Important and Influential Is This Passage?

The huge influence of Aristotle's *Nicomachean Ethics* as a whole has already been discussed in notes to the Aristotle reading in the previous chapter. Furthermore, many concepts introduced in Book V specifically have also been particularly influential. For example, the distinction between the just *distribution and exchange of goods* and justice considered as *the redressing of wrongs*, has become a standard part of debates about justice since Aristotle's time. Also, Aristotle's analysis of reciprocal justice is one of the first discussions of political economy and is often hailed as an example of his visionary analytic genius. On the other hand, Aristotle's actual theories of justice—such as that distributive justice is a matter of geometrical proportion—are usually considered useful *starting points* for discussion but are often criticized as being too unsophisticated to be taken seriously today as complete accounts of justice.

Suggestions for Critical Reflection

1. Aristotle seems to suggest the law does (or at least, should) forbid any behavior that conflicts with the virtues—that a good system of law prescribes universal justice. Is Aristotle right about this? For example, should the laws of the state attempt to ensure that I am exactly as generous, even-tempered, courageous, friendly, witty, truthful (and so on) as I ought to be?

2. Do you think people can behave unjustly even if they are not motivated by greed (*pleonexia*)?

If so, can Aristotle take account of this, or is it a problem for his view of justice? Do you think he is entirely consistent throughout this reading in his view that injustice is always connected to *pleonexia*?

3. How adequate is Aristotle's account of distributive justice? If Aristotle is mainly thinking of the fairness of the distribution of goods *by the state*, can his theory of distributive justice work for other forms of distribution (e.g., by a parent to her children, or an employer to her staff)? Are all fair ways of dividing things up connected to the *worth* or *merit* of those receiving shares, as Aristotle seems to think? If so, should more worthy people get a bigger share of *every* good—more money, more food, more respect, and so on—than their less worthy counterparts?

4. How adequately can Aristotle's account of distributive justice deal with cases of goods that cannot be shared (such as, say, a political office like the Presidency of the United States)? Do cases like this cause problems for his theory?

5. Aristotle points out that people disagree about the sort of merit that is relevant to distributive justice: "democrats identify it with the status of freeman, supporters of oligarchy with wealth (or with noble birth), and supporters of aristocracy with excellence." What does Aristotle have to say about the *proper* kind of merit? Do you think he has a view on this? If more than one kind of merit is relevant, does this cause problems for Aristotle's account of distributive justice?

6. How adequate is Aristotle's account of rectificatory justice? For example, is it always possible to take from the offender what has been stolen and restore it to the victim? (What about, for example, cases of adultery or murder?) Is it even *sufficient* merely to restore the situation to the previous status quo? For example, is it an adequate response to theft merely to require the thief to return exactly what has been stolen (no more and no less)?

7. How adequate is Aristotle's account of justice in exchange? How close to modern economic theory is Aristotle's analysis? (For example, how

does modern economics square with Aristotle's view of justice as a kind of *character trait*?) What do you think Aristotle means by "demand"?

8. What is the relationship between justice in exchange and the other two kinds of justice Aristotle deals with? Why do you think Aristotle announces there are *two* kinds of justice and then, apparently, describes three?

9. Does Aristotle have a theory of *criminal* justice (i.e., of just punishment for crimes)? If so, which of the three types of justice does it belong to? If not, then *why* do you think Aristotle neglects this sphere of justice?

10. How does Aristotle's account of the virtue of "particular justice" fit in with his general account of virtue (as presented in the selection from *Nicomachean Ethics* in Chapter 2)? For example, is the virtue of justice really a mean between two vices?

Suggestions for Further Reading

References to Aristotle's works are given in the Aristotle selection in Chapter 2. As well as reading more from Aristotle's *Nicomachean Ethics* and *Politics*, it is also illuminating to compare Plato's *Republic*, especially the section reprinted in Chapter 2. Many of the books recommended in Chapter 2 are also of value in thinking about Aristotle on justice, particularly W.F.R. Hardie's *Aristotle's Ethical Theory* (Oxford University Press, 1980), Terence Irwin's *Aristotle's First Principles* (Oxford University Press, 1990), and David Bostock's *Aristotle's Ethics* (Oxford University Press, 2000). There is also an old but useful commentary by Henry Jackson, *Peri Dikaiosunes: The Fifth Book of the Nicomachean Ethics of Aristotle* (Cambridge University Press, 1879). Wolfgang von Leyden's *Aristotle on Equality and Justice* (Macmillan, 1985) is also worth looking at.

A seminal article on Aristotelian justice is Bernard Williams's "Justice as a Virtue," which appears in Amelie O. Rorty (ed.), *Essays on Aristotle's Ethics* (University of California Press, 1981). David O'Connor responded to Williams's critique in "Aristotelian Justice as a Personal Virtue," *Midwest Studies in Philosophy* 13 (1988). Other interesting articles on Book V of the *Nicomachean Ethics* include Renford Bambrough, "Aristotle on Justice, a

Paradigm of Philosophy," in Renford Bambrough (ed.), *New Essays on Plato and Aristotle* (Humanities Press, 1965); M.I. Finley, "Aristotle and Economic Analysis," *Past and Present* 47 (1970); A.R.W. Harrison, "Aristotle's *Nicomachean Ethics*, Book V, and the Law of Athens," *Journal of Hellenic Studies* 77 (1957); Lindsay Judson, "Aristotle on Fair Exchange," *Oxford Studies in Ancient Philosophy* 15 (1997); Hans Kelsen, "Aristotle's Doctrine of Justice," in Walsh and Shapiro (eds.), *Aristotle's Ethics* (1967); Paul Keyser, "A Proposed Diagram in Aristotle, *EN* V 3, 1131a24–b20 for Distributive Justice in Proportion," *Apeiron* 25 (1992); David Keyt, "Aristotle's Theory of Distributive Justice," in Keyt and Miller (eds.), *A Companion to Aristotle's Politics* (Blackwell, 1991); Konrad Marc-Wogau, "Aristotle's Theory of Corrective Justice and Reciprocity," in his *Philosophical Essays* (Lund, Gleerup, 1967); Stanley Rosen, "The Political Context of Aristotle's Theories of Justice," *Phronesis* 20 (1975); and Ernest Weinrib, "Aristotle's Forms of Justice," in Spiro Panagiotou (ed.), *Justice, Law, and Method in Plato and Aristotle* (Academic, 1987).

The Nicomachean Ethics[1]

Book V, Sections 1-5

1: The just as the lawful (universal justice) and the just as the fair and equal (particular justice): the former considered.

With regard to justice and injustice we must consider (1) what kind of actions they are concerned with, (2) what sort of mean justice is, and (3) between what extremes the just act is intermediate. Our investigation shall follow the same course as the preceding discussions.

---

1   The *Nicomachean Ethics* was probably written as a series of lecture notes, which would have undergone frequent revision, some time between 334 and 322 BCE. This selection is reprinted from *Aristotle: The Nicomachean Ethics*, translated with an Introduction by David Ross [W.D. Ross], revised by J.O. Urmson and J.L. Ackrill (Oxford World's Classics, 1998), by permission of Oxford University Press. The section headings are not Aristotle's own, but supplied by the translators.

We see that all men mean by justice that kind of state of character which makes people disposed to do what is just and makes them act justly and wish for what is just; and similarly by injustice that state which makes them act unjustly and wish for what is unjust. Let us too, then, lay this down as a general basis. For the same is not true of the sciences and the faculties[2] as of states of character. A faculty or a science which is one and the same is held to relate to contrary objects,[3] but a state of character which is one of two contraries does *not* produce the contrary results; e.g., as a result of health we do not do what is the opposite of healthy, but only what is healthy; for we say a man walks healthily, when he walks as a healthy man would.

Now often one contrary state is recognized from its contrary, and often states are recognized from the subjects that exhibit them; for (A) if good condition is known, bad condition also becomes known, and (B) good condition is known from the things that are in good condition, and they from it. If good condition is firmness of flesh, it is necessary both that bad condition should be flabbiness of flesh and that the wholesome should be that which causes firmness in flesh. And it follows for the most part that if one contrary is ambiguous the other also will be ambiguous; e.g., if 'just' is so, that 'unjust' will be so too.

Now 'justice' and 'injustice' seem to be ambiguous, but because their different meanings approach near to one another the ambiguity escapes notice and is not obvious as it is, comparatively, when the meanings are far apart, e.g., (for here the difference in outward form is great) as the ambiguity in the use of *kleis* for the collar-bone of an animal and for that with which we lock a door. Let us take as a starting-point, then, the various meanings of 'an unjust man'. Both the lawless man and the grasping and unfair man are thought to be unjust, so that evidently both the law-abiding and the fair man will be just. The just, then, is the lawful and the fair, the unjust the unlawful and the unfair.

---

2   Sciences are structured bodies of knowledge. Faculties are capacities or skills.

3   For example, medicine deals with disease as well as health; an engineer has the skill necessary to either build or destroy a bridge.

Since the unjust man is grasping, he must be concerned with goods—not all goods, but those with which prosperity and adversity have to do, which taken absolutely are always good, but for a particular person are not always good.[4] Now men pray for and pursue these things; but they should not, but should pray that the things that are good absolutely may also be good for them, and should choose the things that *are* good for them. The unjust man does not always choose the greater, but also the less—in the case of things bad absolutely; but because the lesser evil is itself thought to be in a sense good, and graspingness is directed at the good, therefore he is thought to be grasping. And he is unfair; for this contains and is common to both.

Since the lawless man was seen to be unjust and the law-abiding man just, evidently all lawful acts are in a sense just acts; for the acts laid down by the legislative art are lawful, and each of these, we say, is just. Now the laws in their enactments on all subjects aim at the common advantage either of all or of the best or of those who hold power, or something of the sort; so that in one sense we call those acts just that tend to produce and preserve happiness and its components for the political society. And the law bids us do both the acts of a brave man (e.g., not to desert our post nor take to flight nor throw away our arms), and those of a temperate man (e.g., not to commit adultery nor to gratify one's lust), and those of a good-tempered man (e.g., not to strike another nor to speak evil), and similarly with regard to the other virtues and forms of wickedness, commanding some acts and forbidding others; and the rightly-framed law does this rightly, and the hastily conceived one less well.

This form of justice, then, is complete virtue, although not without qualification, but in relation to our neighbour. And therefore justice is often thought to be the greatest of virtues, and 'neither evening nor morning star' is so wonderful;[5] and proverbially 'in justice is every virtue comprehended'.[6] And it is complete virtue in its fullest sense, because it is the actual exercise of complete virtue. It is complete because he who possesses it can exercise his virtue not only in himself but towards his neighbour also; for many men can exercise virtue in their own affairs, but not in their relations to their neighbour. This is why the saying of Bias[7] is thought to be true, that 'rule will show the man'; for a ruler is necessarily in relation to other men and a member of a society. For this same reason justice, alone of the virtues, is thought to be 'another's good', because it is related to our neighbour; for it does what is advantageous to another, either a ruler or a co-partner. Now the worst man is he who exercises his wickedness both towards himself and towards his friends, and the best man is not he who exercises his virtue towards himself but he who exercises it towards another; for this is a difficult task. Justice in this sense, then, is not part of virtue but virtue entire, nor is the contrary injustice a part of vice but vice entire. What the difference is between virtue and justice in this sense is plain from what we have said; they are the same but their essence is not the same; what, as a relation to one's neighbour, is justice is, as a certain kind of state without qualification, virtue.

2: The just as the fair and the equal: divided into distributive and rectificatory justice.

But at all events what we are investigating is the justice which is a *part* of virtue; for there is a justice of this kind, as we maintain. Similarly it is with injustice in the particular sense that we are concerned.

That there is such a thing is indicated by the fact that while the man who exhibits in action the other forms of wickedness acts wrongly indeed, but not graspingly (e.g., the man who throws away his shield through cowardice or speaks harshly through bad temper or

---

4   For example, wealth is something which can always contribute to a good life, but for people with defective characters—i.e., those who do not use money wisely—it can make them less happy.

5   According to some ancient commentaries, this is a quotation from Euripides' lost play *Melanippe* (of which just a fragment remains today).

6   This saying is attributed to the poet Theognis of Megara and to another poet called Phocylides (both of whom lived around the middle of the sixth century BCE).

7   Bias of Priene (who lived in the sixth century BCE) was one of the Seven Sages—a group of seventh- and sixth-century Greek politicians and philosophers renowned in later ages for their practical wisdom.

fails to help a friend with money through meanness), when a man acts graspingly he often exhibits none of these vices—no, nor all together, but certainly wickedness of some kind (for we blame him) and injustice. There is, then, another kind of injustice which is a part of injustice in the wide sense, and a use of the word 'unjust' which answers to a part of what is unjust in the wide sense of 'contrary to the law'. Again if one man commits adultery for the sake of gain and makes money by it, while another does so at the bidding of appetite though he loses money and is penalized for it, the latter would be held to be self-indulgent rather than grasping, but the former is unjust, but not self-indulgent; evidently, therefore, he is unjust by reason of his making gain by his act. Again, all other unjust acts are ascribed invariably to some particular kind of wickedness, e.g., adultery to self-indulgence, the desertion of a comrade in battle to cowardice, physical violence to anger; but if a man makes gain, his action is ascribed to no form of wickedness but injustice. Evidently, therefore, there is apart from injustice in the wide sense another, 'particular', injustice which shares the name and nature of the first, because its definition falls within the same genus; for the significance of both consists in a relation to one's neighbour, but the one is concerned with honour or money or safety—or that which includes all these, if we had a single name for it—and its motive is the pleasure that arises from gain; while the other is concerned with all the objects with which the good man is concerned.

It is clear, then, that there is more than one kind of justice, and that there is one which is distinct from virtue entire; we must try to grasp its genus and differentia.[8]

The unjust has been divided into the unlawful and the unfair, and the just into the lawful and the fair. To the unlawful answers the aforementioned sense of injustice. But since the unfair and the unlawful are not the same, but are different as a part is from its whole (for all that is unfair is unlawful, but not all that is unlawful is unfair), the unjust and injustice in the sense of the unfair are not the same as but different from the former kind, as part from whole; for injustice

in this sense is a part of injustice in the wide sense, and similarly justice in the one sense of justice in the other. Therefore we must speak also about particular justice and particular injustice and similarly about the just and the unjust. The justice, then, which answers to the whole of virtue, and the corresponding injustice, one being the exercise of virtue as a whole, and the other that of vice as a whole, towards one's neighbour, we may leave on one side. And how the meanings of 'just' and 'unjust' which answer to these are to be distinguished is evident; for practically the majority of the acts commanded by the law are those which are prescribed from the point of view of virtue taken as a whole; for the law bids us practise every virtue and forbids us to practise any vice. And the things that tend to produce virtue taken as a whole are those of the acts prescribed by the law which have been prescribed with a view to education for the common good. But with regard to the education of the individual as such, which makes him without qualification a good *man*, we must determine later whether this is the function of the political art or of another; for perhaps it is not the same to be a good man and a good citizen of any state taken at random.

Of particular justice and that which is just in the corresponding sense, (A) one kind is that which is manifested in distributions of honour or money or the other things that fall to be divided among those who have a share in the constitution[9] (for in these it is possible for one man to have a share either unequal or equal[10] to that of another), and (B) one is that which plays a rectifying part in transactions between man and man. Of this there are two divisions; of transactions (1) some are voluntary and (2) others involuntary—voluntary such transactions as sale, purchase, loan for consumption, pledging, loan for use, depositing, letting (they are called voluntary because the *origin* of these transactions is voluntary), while of the involuntary (a) some are clandestine, such as theft, adultery, poisoning, procuring, enticement of slaves,

---

8   That is, its overall type (genus) and the particular kinds which make up that type (differentia).

9   The political system, public life.

10   The Greek words *anisos* and *isos,* translated here as "unequal" and "equal," have a wider meaning than their English equivalents. In particular, they can also be rendered as "unfair" and "fair."

assassination, false witness, and (*b*) others are violent, such as assault, imprisonment, murder, robbery with violence, mutilation, abuse, insult.

3: Distributive justice, in accordance with geometrical proportion.

(A) We have shown that both the unjust man and the unjust act are unfair or unequal; now it is clear that there is also an intermediate between the two un-equals involved in either case. And this is the equal; for in any kind of action in which there's a more and a less there is also what is equal. If, then, the unjust is unequal, the just is equal, as all men suppose it to be, even apart from argument. And since the equal is intermediate, the just will be an intermediate. Now equality implies at least two things. The just, then, must be both intermediate and equal and relative (i.e., for certain persons). And *qua*[11] intermediate it must be between certain things (which are respectively greater and less); *qua* equal, it involves *two* things; *qua* just, it is for certain people. The just, therefore, involves at least four terms; for the persons for whom it is in fact just are two, and the things in which it is manifested, the objects distributed, are two. And the same equality will exist between the persons and between the things concerned; for as the latter—the things concerned—are related, so are the former; if they are not equal, they will not have what is equal, but this is the origin of quarrels and complaints—when either equals have and are awarded unequal shares, or unequals equal shares. Further, this is plain from the fact that awards should be 'according to merit'; for all men agree that what is just in distribution must be according to merit in some sense, though they do not all specify the same sort of merit, but democrats identify it with the status of freeman, supporters of oligarchy with wealth (or with noble birth), and supporters of aristocracy with excellence.

The just, then, is a species of the proportionate (proportion being not a property only of the kind of number which consists of abstract units, but of number in general[12]). For proportion is equality of ratios, and involves four terms at least (that discrete proportion involves four terms is plain, but so does continuous proportion,[13] for it uses one term as two and mentions it twice; e.g., 'as the line A is to the line B, so is the line B to the line C'; the line B, then, has been mentioned twice, so that if the line B be assumed twice, the proportional terms will be four); and the just, too, involves at least four terms, and the ratio between one pair is the same as that between the other pair; for there is a similar distinction between the persons and between the things. As the term A, then, is to B, so will C be to D, and therefore, *alternando*,[14] as A is to C, B will be to D. Therefore also the whole is in the same ratio to the whole;[15] and this coupling the distribution effects, and, if the terms are so combined, effects justly. The conjunction, then, of the term A with C and of B with D is what is just in distribution, and this species of the just is intermediate, and the unjust is what violates the proportion; for the proportional is intermediate, and the just is proportional. (Mathematicians call this kind of proportion geometrical; for it is in geometrical proportion that it follows that the whole is to the whole as either part is to the corresponding part.) This proportion is not

---

11   "*Qua* such-and-such" means "considered as being such-and-such," "in the capacity of such-and-such." For example, Queen Elizabeth II might be thought of *qua* monarch, *qua* mother or *qua* Canadian head of state.

12   The contrast here is, roughly, between numbers considered as mathematical entities and numbers of *things*—between *the number two* and *two apples*, for example.

13   An example of "discrete proportion" would be $A : B = C : D$. An example of "continuous proportion" would be $A : B = B : C$. (Note that Aristotle uses the terms "discrete" and "continuous" in a way unrelated to their meanings in modern mathematics.)

14   By alternation, taking them alternately.

15   Suppose that A and B are people, and C and D are goods. The idea Aristotle expresses here is that if the ratios of A to B and C to D are the same, then the ratios of A to C and B to D will be the same, and therefore the ratio of $(A + C)$ to $(B + D)$ will be the same as that of A to B. In other words, the goods will be divided according to the same ratio as the difference in merit between the people.

continuous; for we cannot get a single term standing for a person and a thing.

This, then, is what the just is—the proportional; the unjust is what violates the proportion. Hence one term becomes too great, the other too small, as indeed happens in practice; for the man who acts unjustly has too much, and the man who is unjustly treated too little, of what is good. In the case of evil the reverse is true; for the lesser evil is reckoned a good in comparison with the greater evil, since the lesser evil is rather to be chosen than the greater, and what is worthy of choice is good, and what is worthier of choice a greater good.

This, then, is one species of the just.

4: Rectificatory justice, in accordance with arithmetical proportion.

(B) The remaining one is the rectificatory, which arises in connexion with transactions both voluntary and involuntary. This form of the just has a different specific character from the former. For the justice which distributes common possessions is always in accordance with the kind of proportion mentioned above (for in the case also in which the distribution is made from the common funds of a partnership it will be according to the same ratio which the funds put into the business by the partners bear to one another); and the injustice opposed to this kind of justice is that which violates the proportion. But the justice in transactions between man and man is a sort of equality indeed, and the injustice a sort of inequality; not according to that kind of proportion, however, but according to arithmetical proportion.[16] For it makes no difference whether a good man has defrauded a bad man or a bad man a good one, nor whether it is a good or a bad man that has committed adultery; the law looks only to the distinctive character of the injury, and treats the parties as equal, if one is in the wrong and the other is being wronged, and if one inflicted injury and the other has received it. Therefore, this kind of injustice being an inequality, the judge tries to equalize it; for in the case also in which one has received and the other has inflicted a wound, or one has slain and the other been slain, the suffering and the action have been unequally distributed; but the judge tries to equalize by means of the penalty, taking away from the gain of the assailant. For the term 'gain' is applied generally to such cases—even if it be not a term appropriate to certain cases, e.g., to the person who inflicts a wound—and 'loss' to the sufferer; at all events when the suffering has been estimated, the one is called loss and the other gain. Therefore the equal is intermediate between the greater and the less, but the gain and the loss are respectively greater and less in contrary ways; more of the good and less of the evil are gain, and the contrary is loss; intermediate between them is, as we saw, the equal, which we say is just; therefore corrective justice will be the intermediate between loss and gain. This is why, when people dispute, they take refuge in the judge; and to go to the judge is to go to justice; for the nature of the judge is to be a sort of animate justice; and they seek the judge as an intermediate, and in some states[17] they call judges mediators, on the assumption that if they get what is intermediate they will get what is just. The just, then, is an intermediate, since the judge is so. Now the judge restores equality; it is as though there were a line divided into unequal parts, and he took away that by which the greater segment exceeds the half, and added it to the smaller segment. And when the whole has been equally divided, then they say they have 'their own'—i.e., when they have got what is equal. The equal is intermediate between the greater and the lesser line according to arithmetical proportion. It is for this reason also that it is called just (*dikaion*), because it is a division into two equal parts (*dikhā*), just as if one were to call it *dikāion*; and the judge (*dikastes*) is one who bisects (*dikhastes*).[18] For

---

16   An arithmetical proportion is, actually, not so much what we would call a "proportion" at all, but a series in a particular sort of mathematical progression. In such a series, the first term is larger than the second by the same amount by which the third term is larger than the fourth (and so on); thus, $A - B = C - D$. For example, the series 8, 6, 4, 2 would be an arithmetical proportion, since $8 - 6 = 4 - 2$. Aristotle calls this "a sort of equality" because in an arithmetical proportion the sum of the extremes is equal to the sum of the means, i.e., $A + D = B + C$.

17   Such as Larissa (eastern Greece) or Abydos (on the Dardanelles Strait).

18   This is not the actual etymology of these words (Aris-

when something is subtracted from one of two equals and added to the other, the other is in excess by these two; since if what was taken from the one had not been added to the other, the latter would have been in excess by one only. It therefore exceeds the intermediate by one, and the intermediate exceeds by one that from which something was taken. By this, then, we shall recognize both what we must subtract from that which has more, and what we must add to that which has less; we must add to the latter that by which the intermediate exceeds it, and subtract from the greatest that by which it exceeds the intermediate. Let the lines AA', BB', CC' be equal to one another; from the line AA' let the segment AE have been subtracted, and to the line CC' let the segment CD[19] have been added, so that the whole line DCC' exceeds the line EA' by the segment CD and the segment CF;[20] therefore it exceeds the line BB' by the segment CD.

These names, both loss and gain, have come from voluntary exchange; for to have more than one's own is called gaining, and to have less than one's original share is called losing, e.g., in buying and selling and in all other matters in which the law has left people free to make their own terms; but when they get neither more nor less but just what belongs to themselves, they say that they have their own and that they neither lose nor gain.

Therefore the just is intermediate between a sort of gain and a sort of loss, viz. those which are involuntary; it consists in having an equal amount before and after the transaction.

5: Justice in exchange, reciprocity in accordance with proportion.

Some think that *reciprocity*[21] is without qualification just, as the Pythagoreans[22] said; for they defined

justice without qualification as reciprocity. Now 'reciprocity' fits neither distributive nor rectificatory justice—yet people *want* even the justice of Rhadamanthus[23] to mean this:

> Should a man suffer what he did, right justice would be done

—for in many cases reciprocity and rectificatory justice are not in accord; e.g., (1) if an official has inflicted a wound, he should not be wounded in return, and if someone has wounded an official, he ought not to be wounded only but punished in addition. Further (2) there is a great difference between a voluntary and an involuntary act. But in associations for exchange this sort of justice does hold men together—reciprocity in accordance with a proportion and not on the basis of precisely equal return. For it is by proportionate requital that the city holds together. Men seek to return either evil for evil—and if they cannot do so, think their position mere slavery—or good for good—and if they cannot do so there is no exchange, but it is by exchange that they hold together. This is why they give a prominent place to the temple of the Graces[24]—to promote the requital of services; for this is characteristic of grace[25]—we should serve in return one who has shown grace to us, and should another time take the initiative in showing it.

Now proportionate return is secured by cross-conjunction. Let A be a builder, B a shoemaker, C a house, D a shoe. The builder, then, must get from the shoemaker the latter's work, and must himself give him in return his own. If, then, first there is proportionate equality of goods, and then reciprocal action takes place, the result we mention will be effected. If

---

totle was mistaken if he thought it was).

19 For the example to work, CD must be equal in length to AE. Aristotle would have used a diagram to make this clear.

20 Which must also be equal in length to AE.

21 The Greek term—*antipeponthos*—literally means "suffering in return for one's action."

22 The followers of Pythagoras (c. 570–495 BCE), a philosopher who believed in reincarnation and defended

the view that all of reality could be understood in numerical terms (*harmonia*).

23 A mythical king of the Minoans, said to be the son of Zeus and Europa. He was famous for his uncompromising sense of justice and as a reward he was made immortal and transported to Hades, the Greek afterworld, where he judges the souls of the dead. The quotation on the next line is probably from Hesiod.

24 The three goddesses of joy, charm, and beauty.

25 *Charis*, Greek for "grace," also suggests the notions of "gratitude" and "favor."

not, the bargain is not equal, and does not hold; for there is nothing to prevent the work of the one being better than that of the other; they must therefore be equated. (And this is true of the other arts also; for they would have been destroyed if what the patient suffered had not been just what the agent did, and of the same amount and kind.) For it is not two doctors that associate for exchange, but a doctor and a farmer, or in general people who are different and unequal; but these must be equated. This is why all things that are exchanged must be somehow comparable. It is for this end that money has been introduced, and it becomes in a sense an intermediate; for it measures all things, and therefore the excess and the defect— how many shoes are equal to a house or to a given amount of food. The number of shoes exchanged for a house [or for a given amount of food] must therefore correspond to the ratio of builder to shoemaker. For if this be not so, there will be no exchange and no intercourse. And this proportion will not be effected unless the goods are somehow equal. All goods must therefore be measured by some one thing, as we said before. Now this unit is in truth demand,[26] which holds all things together (for if men did not need one another's goods at all, or did not need them equally, there would be either no exchange or not the same exchange); but money has become by convention a sort of representative of demand; and this is why it has the name 'money' (*nomisma*)—because it exists not by nature but by law (*nomos*) and it is in our power to change it and make it useless. There will, then, be reciprocity when the terms have been equated so that as farmer is to shoemaker, the amount of the shoe-maker's work is to that of the farmer's work for which it exchanges. But we must not bring them into a figure of proportion when they have already exchanged (otherwise one extreme will have both excesses), but when they still have their own goods. Thus they are equals and associates just because this equality can be effected in their case. Let A be a farmer, C food, B a shoemaker, D his product equated to C. If it had not been possible for reciprocity to be thus effected, there would have been no association of the parties. That

demand holds things together as a single unit is shown by the fact that when men do not need one another, i.e., when neither needs the other or one does not need the other, they do not exchange, as we do when some one wants what one has oneself, e.g., when people permit the exportation of corn in exchange for wine. This equation therefore must be established. And for the future exchange—that if we do not need a thing now we shall have it if ever we do need it—money is as it were our surety; for it must be possible for us to get what we want by bringing the money. Now the same thing happens to money itself as to goods—it is not always worth the same; yet it tends to be steadier. This is why all goods must have a price set on them; for then there will always be exchange, and if so, association of man with man. Money, then, acting as a measure, makes goods commensurate and equates them; for neither would there have been association if there were not exchange, nor exchange if there were not equality, nor equality if there were not commensurability. Now in truth it is impossible that things differing so much should become commensurate, but with reference to demand they may become so sufficiently. There must, then, be a unit, and that fixed by agreement (for which reason it is called money); for it is this that makes all things commensurate, since all things are measured by money. Let A be a house, B ten minae,[27] C a bed. A is half of B, if the house is worth five minae or equal to them; the bed, C, is a tenth of B; it is plain, then, how many beds are equal to a house, viz. five. That exchange took place thus before there was money is plain; for it makes no difference whether it is five beds that exchange for a house, or the money value of five beds.

We have now defined the unjust and the just. These having been marked off from each other, it is plain that just action is intermediate between acting unjustly and being unjustly treated; for the one is to have too much and the other to have too little. Justice is a kind of mean, but not in the same way as the other virtues, but because it relates to an intermediate amount, while injustice relates to the extremes. And justice is that in virtue of which the just man is said to be a doer, by

---

26 Greek—*chreia*—often translated as "need" rather than "demand."

27 A unit of currency. One mina was worth 100 ancient drachmae.

choice, of that which is just, and one who will distribute either between himself and another or between two others not so as to give more of what is desirable to himself and less to his neighbour (and conversely with what is harmful), but so as to give what is equal in accordance with proportion; and similarly in distributing between two other persons. Injustice on the other hand is similarly related to the unjust, which is excess and defect, contrary to proportion, of the useful or hurtful. For which reason injustice is excess and defect, viz.

because it is productive of excess and defect—in one's own case excess of what is in its own nature useful and defect of what is hurtful, while in the case of others it is as a whole like what it is in one's own case, but proportion may be violated in either direction. In the unjust act to have too little is to be unjustly treated; to have too much is to act unjustly.

Let this be taken as our account of the nature of justice and injustice, and similarly of the just and the unjust in general.

THOMAS HOBBES
Leviathan

Who Was Thomas Hobbes?

Thomas Hobbes was born, prematurely, in 1588[1] in the village of Westport near the small town of Malmesbury, in the southern English county of Wiltshire. Though several relatives had grown wealthy in the family's cloth-making business, Hobbes's father was a poor, ill-educated country clergyman, who frequently ran into trouble with the church authorities for disobedience and volatility. Young Thomas was apparently a studious, unhealthy, rather melancholy boy, who loved music. Because of his black hair, he was nicknamed "Crow" by his schoolfellows. When Hobbes was 16, his father's long-running feud with a nearby

vicar, whom he had publicly slandered as "a knave and an arrant knave and a drunken knave," came to a head when (probably drunk) he encountered his enemy in the churchyard at Malmesbury and set about him with his fists. Any act of violence in a church or churchyard was an excommunicable offense at that time, and laying hands on a clergyman was an even more serious crime, subject to corporal punishment and imprisonment. Hobbes's father was forced to flee. It is not known whether Thomas ever again saw his father, who died "in obscurity beyond London."

By the time of his father's disappearance, however, young Hobbes had already been plucked out of his family situation and sent off to Oxford (an education paid for by his uncle Francis, a prosperous glover). There, Hobbes attended Magdalen Hall, one of the poorer foundations at Oxford and one which was renowned for its religious Puritanism.[2] He does not

---

1   This was the year that the Catholic monarch of Spain, Philip II, dispatched a massive fleet of ships—the Armada—to invade Protestant England. Hobbes later wrote, in an autobiographical poem, that "hereupon it was my mother dear / Did bring forth twins at once, both me and fear," and used to joke that this explained his timid nature. (In the event, however, the Armada was decisively defeated in the English Channel before it could rendezvous with the Spanish invasion force waiting in the Spanish Netherlands, an area comprising modern Belgium, Luxembourg, and part of northern France.)

2   The Puritans were a group of English Protestants who regarded the Protestant Reformation under Elizabeth I (1558–1603) as incomplete. Influenced by Protestant teachings from continental Europe, such as Calvinism, they advocated strict religious discipline and simplification of the ceremonies and creeds of the Church of England.

seem to have been impressed by the quality of the education he received. Later in life he was dismissive of the Aristotelian logic and metaphysics he was taught and claimed that, at the time, he was more interested in reading about explorations of newly-discovered lands and poring over maps of the world and the stars, than in studying traditional philosophy.

As soon as Hobbes completed his BA, in 1608, he was lucky enough to be offered a job as tutor to the eldest son of William Cavendish, a rich and powerful Derbyshire landowner who owned the great stately home at Chatsworth (and who became the first Earl of Devonshire in 1618). Cavendish's son, also called William, was only a few years younger than Hobbes himself, and Hobbes's position quickly became that of a servant, secretary, and friend, rather than tutor. In 1614, Hobbes and Cavendish toured France and Italy, where they both learned Italian and encountered some of the currents of Italian intellectual thought, including the fiercely anti-Papal writings of several Venetian authors.

William Cavendish succeeded his father as the Earl of Devonshire in 1626, but died of disease just two years later. Hobbes, now 40 years old, signed on as tutor to the son of another rich landowner, Sir Gervase Clifton. During this period, he accompanied his charge on another trip to the continent (France and Switzerland), and it was in Geneva that he picked up a copy of Euclid's *Elements* and fell in love with its method of deductive reasoning. A contemporary biographer wrote of the incident:

> Being in a gentleman's library, Euclid's *Elements* lay open, and 'twas the 47th Prop. of Book I. He read the proposition. "By G—," said he (he would now and then swear, by way of emphasis), "this is impossible!" So he reads the demonstration of it, which referred him back to such a proposition; which proposition he read. That referred him back to another, which he also read. And so on, until at last he was demonstratively convinced of that truth. This made him in love with geometry.

After his return to England, Hobbes agreed to re-enter the service of the widowed countess of Devonshire as tutor to her 13-year-old son, the third earl. The 1630s were important years for Hobbes's intellectual development. His secure, and relatively undemanding, position allowed him time to develop both the main outlines of his political philosophy and also to pursue his interest in science (especially optics). His connection to a great noble house also gave him contacts with other intellectuals clustered around noble patrons, such as the mathematicians and scientists supported by the earl of Newcastle, and the theologians, lawyers, and poets associated with the Viscount Falkland.

In 1634, Hobbes embarked on another European tour with his pupil, and spent over a year living in Paris where he met French scientists and mathematicians—and especially the influential and well-connected Marin Mersenne—and became finally and fully gripped by the intellectual excitement of the age. "The extreme pleasure I take in study overcomes in me all other appetites," he wrote at this time in a letter. By 1636, when Hobbes had returned to England, he was devoting as much of his energies as possible to philosophical and scientific work: the third earl turned 18 in 1637, so—although Hobbes remained in his service—he was no longer needed as a tutor and his time was largely his own.

His earliest surviving work is a treatise on the science of optics, in part of which Hobbes attacks Descartes' *Discourse on the Method* (published in 1637). Hobbes accused Descartes of inconsistency and of not taking seriously enough his own mechanistic physics. Since perception is caused entirely by physical motions or pressures, then the mind—that which does the perceiving—must also be a physical object, capable of being affected by motion, Hobbes argued.[3] Hobbes, therefore, in his very earliest philosophical writing rejected the dualism of matter and spirit in favor of a purely mechanical view of the world.

Hobbes's philosophical work was pushed in a different direction at the end of the 1630s, as political events unfolded in England. As the country moved towards civil war, during the final years of the so-called "personal rule" of King Charles I,[4] there was an intense public debate about the degree of absoluteness of the power of the sovereign. The main issue was whether there were any limits to the power of the king at all. It was recognized that the monarch could exceed his normal powers during exceptional circumstances—but the king, himself, claimed to be the judge of which circumstances were exceptional, and this essentially allowed him to exceed his "normal" powers whenever he chose. In 1640, after the Scots invaded and occupied northern England, the King recalled Parliament to grant him extra taxes to raise an army. They refused, and what became known as the "Short Parliament" was abruptly dissolved. In the same year, Hobbes wrote and circulated an unabashedly pro-royalist work called *The Elements of Law*, which attempted to justify the nature and extent of sovereign power from philosophical first principles. By the end of that year, facing a backlash from anti-royalist parliamentarians as tensions grew, Hobbes called in all his investments and left England for Paris.

In Paris, Hobbes was quickly reabsorbed into the intellectual life of the great city, and his reputation was established by the 1642 publication of *De Cive*, a remodeled version of *The Elements of Law*. After this, Hobbes returned to the study of scientific philosophy and theology, and spent several years working on a substantial book on logic, metaphysics, and physics, which was eventually published in 1655 as *De Corpore*. However, his work was frequently interrupted, once by a serious illness from which he nearly died (in 1647), and repeatedly by visitors from England, including royalist exiles from the English Civil War (which had erupted in 1642 and dragged on until 1648). In 1646, Hobbes was made mathematical tutor to the young Prince Charles, now in exile in Paris. This turned Hobbes's thoughts back to politics, and—secretively and rapidly—he completed the major work *Leviathan* between the autumn of 1649 and the spring of 1651.

By this time, Hobbes was keen to return to England. The war had been won by the Parliamentarians (Charles I was beheaded in 1649, the monarchy and House of Lords abolished, and a Commonwealth, led by Oliver Cromwell, set up) and *Leviathan*—which Hobbes took care to ensure was published in London—was partly intended to ease his passage back home. Hobbes did not abandon, or even substantially modify, the central arguments of his earlier, royalist writings, but in *Leviathan* he does emphasize that his project is to justify *political authority* generally (and not necessarily just that of a monarch). He also discusses extensively the question—which at that time was of vital interest to the former aristocratic supporters of the old king—of when it is legitimate to shift allegiance from one ruler to another. Hobbes later said he had written *Leviathan* on behalf of "those many and faithful servants and subjects of His Majesty," who had fought on the royalist side and lost, and who were now in the position of negotiating with the new Parliamentary rulers for their old lands and titles. "They that had done their utmost endeavor to perform their obligation to the King, had done all that they could be obliged unto; and were consequently at liberty to seek the safety of their lives and livelihood wheresover, and without treachery."

---

3   "Since vision is formally and really nothing but motion, it follows that that which sees is also formally and strictly speaking nothing other than that which is moved; for nothing other than a body … can be moved." (*Tractatus opticus*, p. 207. This translation is by Noel Malcolm.)

4   In 1629, after a series of clashes with Parliament, Charles dissolved the legislative body permanently and began an eleven-year period of ruling alone, as an absolute monarch.

Hobbes probably did not expect his work to cause offense among the court-in-exile of the young Charles II in Paris,[5] and he presented a hand-written copy to the king in 1651. However, because he denied that kings ruled by a divine right handed down directly from God, Hobbes was perceived as turning against the monarchy. Furthermore, the attack on organized religion, and especially Catholicism, that *Leviathan* contained provoked fury among Charles's courtiers. Hobbes was banned from the court, and shortly afterwards the French clergy attempted to have him arrested; Hobbes quickly fled back to England.

There he settled back into the employ of the Earl of Devonshire, and resumed a quiet bachelor life of light secretarial work and intellectual discussion. However, the notoriety of *Leviathan* slowly grew, and—because of its bitter attacks on religion and the universities—Hobbes made enemies of many influential groups. For example, when the Royal Society was formed in 1660, Hobbes was pointedly *not* invited to become a member, partly because his fellow exponents of the new "mechanical philosophy" were highly wary of being associated with atheism and reacted by violently attacking Hobbes's supposedly "atheistic" new world-view. Throughout the 1660s and 1670s, Hobbes and his works were denounced from pulpits all over England for what was said to be his godlessness and denial of objective moral values. There were even rumors that Hobbes—a.k.a. the "Beast of Malmesbury"—was to be charged for heresy (which could, even then, have resulted in his being burned at the stake, though the last people to be executed for heresy in England died in 1612). In contrast with the general public vilification Hobbes faced in his own country, in France and Holland his reputation was soaring and (after the death of acclaimed scientist Pierre Gassendi in 1655) he was widely regarded by French scientists and men of letters as the greatest living philosopher.

Hobbes, though now well into old age (and suffering severely from Parkinson's disease), continued to write prolifically, including several public defenses of *Leviathan*, several treatises on mathematics, a debate with Robert Boyle about the experimental evidence for vacuums, a short book on six problems in physics, a polemical church history in Latin verse, translations of Homer's *Iliad* and *Odyssey* into English verse, and a history of the English civil war entitled *Behemoth*. When Hobbes died, shortly after suffering a severe stroke in December 1679, he was 91 years old.

What Was Hobbes's Overall Philosophical Project?

Hobbes thought of himself as primarily a scientist. Not only was he interested in what we would, today, think of as science (optics, physics, geometry), he was also concerned to place the study of human beings—especially psychology, ethics, and politics—on what he considered a *scientific* footing. Hobbes was deeply conscious that he was living during a period of intellectual revolution—a time when the old Aristotelian assumptions were being stripped away by the new mechanical and mathematical science which Hobbes enthusiastically endorsed—as well as during an era of political and religious revolution. He wanted to play a significant role in both these movements.

Since Hobbes considered himself a scientist, his view of what *constitutes* science is particularly significant. Hobbes's scheme of the sciences changes somewhat throughout his writings, but its most stable core looks something like this. The most fundamental science is what Hobbes (like Aristotle) called "first philosophy," and it consists in "universal definitions"—of *body*, *motion*, *time*, *place*, *cause*, and so on—and their logical consequences. Thus the most basic kind of science, for Hobbes, is more purely rational than it is experimental. After first philosophy, comes geometry, which (for Hobbes) was the science of the simple motions of bodies. For example, Hobbes rejected the view that geometry is the study of abstract objects and their relations, but instead insisted that it concerns itself with the movements of concrete objects in real space. The next step in the ladder of the sciences is mechanics, which investigates the more complex motions due to whole bodies working together, and this is followed by physics, the study of the invisible motions of the parts of bodies (including the effects on the human senses of the motions of external bodies). Then comes moral philosophy, which Hobbes

---

5   Charles II was eventually restored to the throne, by a vote of Parliament, in 1660.

thought of as primarily the investigation of passion and volition, which he considered the internal effects of sensation on the human mind. Finally, civil philosophy—the science of politics—formulates the laws of conduct that will ensure peace and self-preservation for communities of creatures with our particular internal psychological constitution.

A central—and at the time infamous—plank of Hobbes's scientific world-view was his unrelenting *materialism*. According to the new "mechanical" philosophy which had caught Hobbes up in its sweep across the thinkers of Europe, all physical phenomena are ultimately to be explained in terms of the motions and interactions of large numbers of tiny, material bodies. Hobbes enthusiastically accepted this view, and was one of the earliest thinkers to extend it to phenomena his peers generally did not think of as "physical." In particular, Hobbes declared that *mental* phenomena ought to be just as susceptible to mechanical explanation as anything else in nature. For Hobbes, then, the natural world did not contain both matter and spirit (minds): it was entirely made up of material bodies, and human beings were to be viewed as nothing more than very complex material objects, like sophisticated robots or automata.

Along similar lines, Hobbes was very skeptical of claims to religious knowledge, and this was one among several reasons why he devoted so much energy to attacks on the authority of the church. According to Hobbes's theory of language, words have meaning only if they express thoughts, and thoughts are nothing more than the residue in our minds of sensations produced by the action of external objects upon our bodies. Since God is supposed to be an infinite, transcendent being, beyond our powers to perceive, Hobbes—although it is not at all clear that he was actually an atheist—was led to assert we can have no meaningful thoughts about God, and thus can say nothing positive about him. Furthermore, according to Hobbes's materialism, the notion of an "incorporeal substance" is simply incoherent, and so, if God exists at all, he must exist as a *material* body (which Hobbes claimed, in fact, to believe).

Like Descartes, Hobbes saw himself as developing the foundations for a completely new and radical philosophy which was to decisively change the way his contemporaries saw the world. Furthermore, Hobbes did not see moral and political philosophy as a purely intellectual exercise. He firmly believed the great and tragic upheaval of the English Civil War was directly caused by the promulgation of false and dangerous moral ideas, and could have been avoided by proper appreciation of the moral truth. In *Leviathan*, then, Hobbes's project was to place social and political philosophy on a *scientific* basis for the first time (and he thought doing so would be of immense service to humanity). His model for this was geometry: he begins with a sequence of axiomatic definitions—such as "justice," "obligation," "right of nature," and "law of nature"—and then tries to show that his philosophical results are rationally derivable from these basic assumptions. His goal was to derive and prove universal political laws—rather like the laws of physics—from which infallible judgments about particular cases can be made.[6]

What Is the Structure of This Reading?

Leviathan is divided into four parts: "Of Man," which deals primarily with human psychology and the state of nature; "Of Commonwealth," which discusses the formation of political states and the powers of their sovereigns; "Of a Christian Commonwealth," which examines the relationship between secular and religious law; and "Of the Kingdom of Darkness," which is a vitriolic attack on certain kinds of organized religion, and especially Catholicism. The excerpts given here come from Parts I and II.

First, there is a sequence of three chapters which come nearly at the end of Part I. In these Hobbes describes the unhappy "state of nature" for human beings and argues that several (nineteen) moral "laws of nature" or "theorems" arise as "convenient articles of peace upon which men may be drawn to agreement." Included in this discussion, at the end of Chap-

---

6   On the other hand, it is important to note that, unlike physics, politics is a *normative* science. It does not simply describe what people do do, but in some sense prescribes what they *ought* to do. In this respect, Hobbes's political science resembles modern economics more than mathematics or experimental science.

ter XIV, is an examination of the way in which natural rights can be transferred or renounced (through contracts, covenants, or free gifts). There is also (near the beginning of Chapter XV) a lengthy discussion of the nature of justice, "*that men perform their covenants made.*" Then we jump to the first two chapters of "Of Commonwealth," in which Hobbes discusses how political states arise and argues that state sovereigns are entitled to almost absolute power over their subjects.

Some Useful Background Information

1. *Leviathan* was published just forty years after the first "King James" English translation of the Bible; hence Hobbes's writing style, dating from the same period, is what, today, we might think of as "biblical." This makes Hobbes all the more interesting to read, but can impose something of a barrier for modern audiences. Here is a short glossary of some words in the reading which might be unfamiliar or used in an unfamiliar or archaic way.

Acception: Favoritism, corrupt preference for one person over another.

Anticipate: To forestall—to prevent someone else's action by acting first.

Asperity: Roughness, difficulty.

Attainted (of): Convicted or condemned for something (especially treason).

Beholding (to): Bound to, under obligation to.

But: Only.

Caution: Security, confident lack of anxiety.

Commodious: Convenient, pleasant. (Hence, an *incommodity* is an inconvenience.)

Commonwealth: An autonomous community or nation—especially a republic—in which supreme political power is derived from the people.

Concord: Agreement, harmony.

Conduce: To lead or contribute to (some result).

Confederacy: An alliance or league formed for the purpose of joint action or mutual support.

Conform: To mold together, bring into agreement, regulate.

Consent (in): To agree to.

Consequent: A thing that follows or is the result of something.

Constitute: To enact, set up, establish.

Contemn: To treat with contempt, scorn, or disdain.

Contumely: Insolent insult or rudeness.

Defect: Lack.

Delectation: Delight, pleasure.

Despoil: To rob or plunder.

Detain: To hold or keep back (especially something that is due).

Diffidence: Distrust (as opposed to the more modern sense, timidity).

Dissociate: To separate.

Distracted: Pulled in different directions.

Dominion: The right to control or possess something.

Emergent: Unexpectedly arising.

Emulation: Ambitious rivalry for power or honor, the desire to excel over another.

Endamage: Injure, cause harm to.

Except: Unless.

Froward: Perverse, difficult to deal with.

Husbandry: Farming, or the careful management of one's resources.

Ignominy: Disgrace, dishonor.

Incommunicable: Not capable of being shared.

Industry: Diligence or energy.

Iniquity: Wickedness.

Invention: Discovery.

Irregular: Unregulated.

List: To desire, to wish.

Lust: Desire, pleasure, relish.

Machination: The act of plotting or scheming.

Manner: Customary mode of behavior.

Moment: Importance, significance.

Obnoxious (to): Exposed to, liable to.

Original: The origin or source of something; coming first, or preceding all others in time.

Own: To recognize or claim as one's own.

Partiality: Bias or prejudice.

Patience: Forbearance.

Peradventure: Perhaps.

Perfect: Complete, lacking nothing.

Plurality: Majority.

Presently: Immediately.

Pressure: Burden, weight.

Pretend: To lay claim to or profess (not necessarily deceitfully).

Propriety: Property, ownership (as opposed to the modern sense, suitableness).

Rapine: Plunder, taking the property of others by force.

Redound (to): Make a large contribution to, or have a great effect on, someone's reputation or advantage.

Restrain: Restrict.

Sensible: Readily perceived or appreciated.

Sentence: Judgment.

Several: Separate.

Soever: To any extent, in any way (e.g., "how great soever it may be").

Specious: Misleadingly attractive or plausible.

Translation: Transfer.

Want: Need, lack.

Wit: Intelligence.

Withal: With.

2. The fundamental political problem for Hobbes, and the issue *Leviathan* primarily sets out to address, was the following: How can any political system unambiguously and indisputably determine the answer to the question *What is the law?* How can universally, uncontroversially acceptable rules of conduct by which the citizens of a state must lead their public lives be determined? A precondition, Hobbes thought, was for there to be only a *single* source of law, and for that source to be *absolute* in the sense that whatever the legislator declared as law *was* law. Any other kind of political system, Hobbes believed, would descend inevitably into factionalism, insecurity, and civil war.

3. Hobbes was quite self-conscious in rejecting the Aristotelian view of *human nature* which had been passed down to his day. For Aristotle, human beings are naturally social animals, our natural situation is as active members of a political community, and our highest good is the sort of happiness, or flourishing, for which our biological species is best suited. Furthermore, according to Aristotle, there is a natural hierarchy among human beings, with some people being inherently more noble than others. These inequalities are not *created* by society, on the Aristotelian picture, but ideally should be *mirrored* in the social order.

For Hobbes, by contrast, human beings are *not* naturally social animals, and furthermore there is no single conception of happiness tied to the human 'essence.' Instead, according to Hobbes, human happiness is a matter of the continual satisfaction of desires or appetites, and since individual human beings differ in their particular desires, so too will what makes people happy. Because people's desires often come into conflict—especially when several people compete for the same scarce resource, such as land, money, or honor—human beings are naturally *anti*-social. Furthermore, even when civil society has been established, according to Hobbes, most of its citizens will not, and should not, be active participants in political life, but will simply lead private lives, out of the public sphere, within the constraints of their obedience to the commands of the sovereign. Finally, it was Hobbes's view that human beings, in the state of nature, are in a state of radical equality, where no one is substantially any better (or worse) than anyone else; similarly, in civil society, although there will be gradations of honor among men, everyone is fundamentally equal under the sovereign.

4. Like Aristotle, however, Hobbes sees justice, and morality generally, as applying to character traits—what Hobbes calls "manners"—rather than primarily to states of affairs or types of action. For Hobbes, moral virtues are those habits which it is rational for all people to praise; that is, they are those dispositions which contribute to the preservation, not merely of the individual, but of *everyone* in the community by contributing to peace and stable society.

Some Common Misconceptions

1. When Hobbes talks about "the state of nature" he is referring *neither* to a particular historical period in human history (such as the age

of hunter-gatherers) *nor* to a mere theoretical possibility (a time that never actually occurred). What Hobbes has in mind is any situation, at any time or place, where there is no effective government capable of imposing order on the local population. Thus primitive or prehistoric societies may (or may not) be in the state of nature; but so may modern societies locked in a civil war, destroyed by conflict with other countries, or simply experiencing a constitutional crisis. Likewise, the international community of nations (then, as now) is in a state of nature, lacking any overarching world government capable of determining and enforcing international law. (Hence, as he points out in the text, when Hobbes describes the state of nature as being "a condition of war" he does not mean it will necessarily involve constant fighting and bloodshed, but rather that no one can feel *secure* against the threat of force.)

2. Hobbes is not the "immoralist" he is sometimes taken to be. Far from arguing *against* the existence of universal moral principles, Hobbes is concerned to *combat* the kind of moral relativism which holds that all laws, including moral laws, are mere matters of arbitrary human convention. Hobbes adopts the assumption of the moral skeptic that the only fundamental, universal moral principle is self-interest, but he then argues that, from the skeptic's *own assumption*, certain "natural" laws of justice follow deductively. In this way, he tries to show there can be laws without a lawgiver: moral principles based, not in divine or human command, but in human nature itself. (On the other hand, Hobbes does stress, we are bound by these laws only if we can be sure others will obey them too—that is, on the whole, only once we have agreed to form a civil society. To that extent, at least, the principles of justice remain, for Hobbes, a matter of *convention*.)

3. A mainspring of Hobbes's political philosophy is the claim that human beings seek their own self-preservation. There is textual evidence that Hobbes saw this desire for self-preservation not as merely a non-rational desire, even one

which all human beings naturally share, but as actually being a *primary goal of reason*. That is, one of the dictates *of rationality*, for Hobbes, is that we should take all measures necessary for our self-preservation, and so the ethical laws Hobbes generates out of this principle are not merely *hypothetical* commands ("Do this if you care more about your self-preservation than anything else") but are dictates that all rational creatures should recognize as binding.

4. Though Hobbes is, legitimately, often said to be rather pessimistic about human nature, this can be overstated. His view, essentially, is not that *everyone* is selfish, but that *enough* people are fundamentally selfish that it would be unwise to construct a civil society on the assumption that people are generally benevolent. According to Hobbes, children are born concerned only with themselves and, though they can learn to care for others, this can be brought about only with proper moral education. Unfortunately, he believed not very many children are actually brought up in this way, and so most of the citizens of a commonwealth will, in fact, care primarily for themselves and their families and not be much moved by the interests of strangers.

5. Hobbes did not think that people *in fact* always act to preserve themselves: his claim is not that people always behave in a way which is optimal in avoiding hardship or death for themselves—on the contrary, Hobbes was convinced that people are often rash and vainglorious and prone to irrational quarrels—but that it is always *reasonable* or *rational* for people to seek self-preservation, and furthermore that this fact is so universally recognized by human beings that it is capable of serving as a solid basis for civil society. (Contrary to popular belief, then, Hobbes is not quite what is technically called a "psychological egoist": someone who believes that all people, as a matter of psychological necessity, always act only in their own self-interest.)

6. Although Hobbes is frequently thought of as a *social contract theorist*, he actually does not

see the foundation of the state as involving a contract or covenant between *all* members of that society, but instead as a kind of *free gift* by the citizens to their sovereign. That is, people in the state of nature (covenant together to) freely turn over their right of nature to a sovereign power, in the hope that this sovereign will protect them and allow them to live in greater security. (Importantly, this means the sovereign cannot *break a covenant* if he or she fails to protect her subjects, though she does come to be bound by the law of nature prohibiting ingratitude, and so must "endeavour that he which giveth [a gift] have no reasonable cause to repent him of his good will.")

7. Hobbes thought that his new political science could conclusively demonstrate that all states need a sovereign (an absolute dispenser of law). He did not, however, insist that this sovereign must be a *monarch*; he was quite ready to recognize that a republic, led by an assembly of senators for example, could be an equally effective form of government.

How Important and Influential Is This Passage?

Hobbes's *Leviathan* is arguably the most important work of political philosophy in English before the twentieth century, even though the work's *conclusions* have been widely rejected from Hobbes's day to this. The project of justifying and delimiting the extent of the state's power over its subjects, without appeal to such supernatural mechanisms as the divine right of kings, is an immensely important one, and it can be said that Hobbes gave this question its first great answer in modern times. The selections reprinted here include several themes for which Hobbes is most notorious: the doctrine that life in a state of nature is "solitary, poor, nasty, brutish, and short"; the attempt to ground universal principles of justice in the essential selfishness of human nature; the notion that the institution of a political state consists in a kind of "contract" between its members; and the claim that the power of a sovereign is absolute.

Suggestions for Critical Reflection

1. Hobbes argues that, in the state of nature, everybody is fundamentally equal in ability and in rights. Is he right about this? If he is, does this mean all *social* inequalities are based on nothing more than convention?

2. Hobbes argues that human beings, in the state of nature, are in a continual state of "war of every one against every one." How good are his arguments for this claim? Are there any real-world examples of groups of people who are in the state of nature (as Hobbes defines it) but *not* at war with each other? If Hobbes incorrectly equates the state of nature with a condition of warfare, how seriously does this affect his subsequent arguments?

3. "By *liberty* is understood, according to the proper signification of the word, the absence of external impediments." Is this a fully adequate definition? Is Hobbes's view of liberty significant for the political theory that he develops? (For example, would someone who took a different view of freedom be happy with Hobbes's view of sovereign power?)

4. At one point, Hobbes suggests injustice is a kind of absurdity or inconsistency, and thus to be unjust is simply to be irrational. Is Hobbes right (in the terms of his own theory)? If so, does this show something about Hobbes's *definition* of injustice? Is injustice really nothing more or less than "*the not performance of covenant*"?

5. "Of the voluntary acts of every man, the object is some *good to himself*." Is this true? Is it a realistic assumption, or is Hobbes being excessively pessimistic about human nature? (Taken in the wider context of this reading, does it seem that Hobbes means to describe how human beings invariably *do* behave, or to state how people *should* behave if they are being rational? Does the way his claim is understood make a difference to Hobbes's argument?)

6. Hobbes argues that, in the state of nature, there is no justice. If Hobbes is right about this, does it follow that all human beings are *immoral* by nature?

7. Does Hobbes reconcile morality and self-interest? That is, does he successfully show that they are *the same thing*? (Is this, in fact, what he is trying to do?)

8. Hobbes formulates his principles of justice, in part, as a reaction to Aristotle's moral theory. If you have read the previous selection, you might want to think about the differences and similarities between, and the relative merits of, Hobbes and Aristotle.

9. "Whatsoever is done to a man, conformable to his own will signified to the doer, is not injury to him." Does this follow logically from Hobbes's assumptions? If it does, is this a problem for those assumptions?

10. Since there is no mechanism for enforcing agreements in the state of nature, how can people in that state first contract together to form a commonwealth? How can this first crucial covenant be made *before* there exists a power to enforce covenants?

11. "The power of the mighty hath no foundation but in the opinion and belief of the people…. If men know not their duty, what is there that can force them to obey the laws? An army, you will say? But what shall force the army?" (Hobbes, *Behemoth*). Since this is the case, and since the absolute authority of sovereigns rests on their power to protect their subjects and enforce covenants between them, then how can people in a state of nature agree to set up a sovereign? How can some single individual simply be *given* absolute power?

12. Hobbes argues that, once a commonwealth has been set up, every member of the commonwealth must treat the sovereign's actions as being *their own* actions—must "*authorize* all the actions and judgments of that man, or assembly of men, in the same manner as if they were his own"—even if those actions cause them personal hardship. (So, for example, if the state puts you in prison it is no different than if you had voluntarily locked yourself up.) Does this seem reasonable? Is it a crucial part of Hobbes's political theory, or could he have adopted a weaker position on this point?

13. What view do you think Hobbes would take of the notion of *democratically elected* government? What would be his view of civil disobedience or protest movements?

Suggestions for Further Reading

Various editions of Hobbes's *Leviathan* are available. The edition by Edwin Curley (Hackett, 1994), includes a useful introduction and some entertaining biographical material, including Hobbes's verse autobiography. There is also a Penguin edition (1982), edited and with an introduction by C.B. Macpherson; an edition with an introduction by Richard Tuck (Cambridge University Press, 1996); and a Norton Critical Edition, edited by Flathman and Johnson, which includes a great selection of background and interpretive material (W.W. Norton, 1996). It is also well worth looking at Hobbes's *De Cive*, which Hobbes, himself, thought of as his most "scientific" statement of his political philosophy. It is available, edited by Bernard Gert, from Hackett (1991).

Useful books on the political background to Hobbes's work are Quentin Skinner's *The Foundations of Modern Political Thought* (Cambridge University Press, 1978) and David Wootton's *Divine Right and Democracy* (Penguin, 1986). An entertaining account of the hostile contemporary reaction to Hobbes's philosophy is by Samuel Mintz, *The Hunting of Leviathan* (Cambridge University Press, 1962); and a fascinating book on one of Hobbes's forays into experimental science is Shapin and Schaffer's *Leviathan and the Air-Pump* (Princeton University Press, 1985).

Three books which describe Hobbes's philosophy as a whole are R.S. Peters, *Hobbes* (Penguin, 1956), Tom Sorrell, *Hobbes* (Routledge, 1986), and Richard Tuck, *Hobbes* (Oxford University Press, 1989). There are also many books specifically on Hobbes's political philosophy; some of the best are: Deborah Baumgold, *Hobbes's Political Theory* (Cambridge University Press, 1988); David Gauthier, *The Logic of Leviathan* (Oxford University Press, 1969); Jean Hampton, *Hobbes and the Social Contract Tradition* (Cambridge University Press, 1986); David Johnston, *The Rhetoric of Leviathan* (Princeton University Press, 1986); Gregory Kavka, *Hobbesian Moral and Political Theory* (Princeton University

Press, 1986); S.A. Lloyd, *Ideals as Interests in Hobbes's Leviathan* (Cambridge University Press, 1992); A.P. Martinich, *The Two Gods of Leviathan* (Cambridge University Press, 1992); Michael Oakeshott, *Hobbes on Civil Association* (Oxford University Press, 1975); Johann Sommerville, *Thomas Hobbes: Political Ideas in Historical Context* (Palgrave, 1992); Leo Strauss, *The Political Philosophy of Thomas Hobbes* (University of Chicago Press, 1952); and Howard Warrender, *The Political Philosophy of Hobbes* (Oxford University Press, 1957).

Three useful collections of articles on Hobbes are Mary Dietz (ed.), *Thomas Hobbes and Political Theory* (University Press of Kansas, 1990); G.A.J. Rogers and A. Ryan (eds.), *Perspectives on Thomas Hobbes* (Oxford University Press, 1991); and Tom Sorrell (ed.), *The Cambridge Companion to Hobbes* (Cambridge University Press, 1996). There is also *A Hobbes Dictionary* by A.P. Martinich (Blackwell, 1995).

from *Leviathan*[7]
Part I: Of Man

Chapter XIII: Of the Natural Condition of Mankind as Concerning their Felicity and Misery

Nature hath made men so equal in the faculties of body and mind as that, though there be found one man sometimes manifestly stronger in body or of quicker mind than another, yet when all is reckoned together the difference between man and man is not so considerable as that one man can thereupon claim to himself any benefit to which another may not pretend as well as he. For as to the strength of body, the weakest has strength enough to kill the strongest, either by secret machination or by confederacy with others that are in the same danger with himself.

---

7   *Leviathan* was first published, in London, in 1651; the excerpts reprinted here are from that edition (with modernized spelling, and partly modernized punctuation). As well as his English version, Hobbes also prepared an edition in Latin (much of which was probably written before the English version), first published in Amsterdam in 1681.

And as to the faculties of the mind—setting aside the arts grounded upon words, and especially that skill of proceeding upon general and infallible rules, called science, which very few have and but in few things, as being not a native faculty born with us, nor attained, as prudence, while we look after somewhat else—I find yet a greater equality amongst men than that of strength. For prudence is but experience, which equal time equally bestows on all men in those things they equally apply themselves unto. That which may perhaps make such equality incredible is but a vain conceit of one's own wisdom, which almost all men think they have in a greater degree than the vulgar; that is, than all men but themselves, and a few others, whom by fame, or for concurring with themselves, they approve. For such is the nature of men that howsoever they may acknowledge many others to be more witty, or more eloquent, or more learned, yet they will hardly believe there be many so wise as themselves; for they see their own wit at hand, and other men's at a distance. But this proveth rather that men are in that point equal, than unequal. For there is not ordinarily a greater sign of the equal distribution of anything than that every man is contented with his share.

From this equality of ability ariseth equality of hope in the attaining of our ends. And therefore if any two men desire the same thing, which nevertheless they cannot both enjoy, they become enemies; and in the way to their end (which is principally their own conservation, and sometimes their delectation only) endeavour to destroy or subdue one another. And from hence it comes to pass that where an invader hath no more to fear than another man's single power, if one plant, sow, build, or possess a convenient seat, others may probably be expected to come prepared with forces united to dispossess and deprive him, not only of the fruit of his labour, but also of his life or liberty. And the invader again is in the like danger of another.

And from this diffidence of one another, there is no way for any man to secure himself so reasonable as anticipation; that is, by force, or wiles, to master the persons of all men he can so long till he see no other power great enough to endanger him: and this is no more than his own conservation requireth, and is generally allowed. Also, because there be some that, taking pleasure in contemplating their own power in the acts of conquest, which they pursue farther than their security requires, if others (that otherwise would be glad to be at ease within modest bounds) should not by invasion increase their power, they would not be able, long time, by standing only on their defence, to subsist. And by consequence, such augmentation of dominion over men being necessary to a man's conservation, it ought to be allowed him.

Again, men have no pleasure (but on the contrary a great deal of grief) in keeping company where there is no power able to overawe them all. For every man looketh that his companion should value him at the same rate he sets upon himself, and upon all signs of contempt or undervaluing naturally endeavours, as far as he dares (which amongst them that have no common power to keep them in quiet is far enough to make them destroy each other), to extort a greater value from his contemners, by damage; and from others, by the example.

So that in the nature of man, we find three principal causes of quarrel. First, competition; secondly, diffidence; thirdly, glory.

The first maketh men invade for gain; the second, for safety; and the third, for reputation. The first use violence, to make themselves masters of other men's persons, wives, children, and cattle; the second, to defend them; the third, for trifles, as a word, a smile, a different opinion, and any other sign of undervalue, either direct in their persons or by reflection in their kindred, their friends, their nation, their profession, or their name.

Hereby it is manifest that during the time men live without a common power to keep them all in awe, they are in that condition which is called war; and such a war as is of every man against every man. For war consisteth not in battle only, or the act of fighting, but in a tract of time, wherein the will to contend by battle is sufficiently known: and therefore the notion of *time* is to be considered in the nature of war, as it is in the nature of weather. For as the nature of foul weather lieth not in a shower or two of rain, but in an inclination thereto of many days together: so the nature of war consisteth not in actual fighting, but in the known disposition thereto during all the time there is no assurance to the contrary. All other time is peace.

Whatsoever therefore is consequent to a time of war, where every man is enemy to every man, the same consequent to the time wherein men live without other security than what their own strength and their own invention shall furnish them withal. In such condition there is no place for industry, because the fruit thereof is uncertain: and consequently no culture of the earth; no navigation, nor use of the commodities that may be imported by sea; no commodious building; no instruments of moving and removing such things as require much force; no knowledge of the face of the earth; no account of time; no arts; no letters; no society; and which is worst of all, continual fear, and danger of violent death; and the life of man, solitary, poor, nasty, brutish, and short.

It may seem strange to some man that has not well weighed these things that Nature should thus dissociate and render men apt to invade and destroy one another: and he may therefore, not trusting to this inference, made from the passions, desire perhaps to have the same confirmed by experience. Let him therefore consider with himself: when taking a journey, he arms himself and seeks to go well accompanied; when going to sleep, he locks his doors; when even in his house he locks his chests; and this when he knows there be laws and public officers, armed, to revenge all injuries shall be done him; what opinion he has of his fellow subjects, when he rides armed; of his fellow citizens, when he locks his doors; and of his children, and servants, when he locks his chests. Does he not there as much accuse mankind by his actions as I do by my words? But neither of us accuse man's nature in it. The desires, and other passions of man, are in themselves no sin. No more are the actions that proceed from those passions till they know a law that forbids them; which till laws be made they cannot know, nor can any law be made till they have agreed upon the person that shall make it.

It may peradventure be thought there was never such a time nor condition of war as this; and I believe it was never generally so, over all the world: but there are many places where they live so now. For the savage people in many places of *America* (except the government of small families, the concord whereof dependeth on natural lust) have no government at all, and live at this day in that brutish manner, as I said before. Howsoever, it may be perceived what manner of life there would be, where there were no common power to fear, by the manner of life which men that have formerly lived under a peaceful government use to degenerate into, in a civil war.

But though there had never been any time wherein particular men were in a condition of war one against another, yet in all times kings and persons of sovereign authority, because of their independency, are in continual jealousies, and in the state and posture of gladiators, having their weapons pointing, and their eyes fixed on one another; that is, their forts, garrisons, and guns upon the frontiers of their kingdoms, and continual spies upon their neighbours, which is a posture of war. But because they uphold thereby the industry of their subjects, there does not follow from it that misery which accompanies the liberty of particular men.

To this war of every man against every man, this also is consequent; that nothing can be unjust. The notions of right and wrong, justice and injustice, have there no place. Where there is no common power, there is no law; where no law, no injustice. Force and fraud are in war the two cardinal virtues. Justice and injustice are none of the faculties neither of the body nor mind. If they were, they might be in a man that were alone in the world, as well as[8] his senses and passions. They are qualities that relate to men in society, not in solitude. It is consequent also to the same condition that there be no propriety, no dominion, no *mine* and *thine* distinct; but only that to be every man's that he can get, and for so long as he can keep it. And thus much for the ill condition which man by mere nature is actually placed in; though with a possibility to come out of it, consisting partly in the passions, partly in his reason.

The passions that incline men to peace are: fear of death; desire of such things as are necessary to commodious living; and a hope by their industry to obtain them. And reason suggesteth convenient articles of peace upon which men may be drawn to agreement. These articles are they which otherwise are called the laws of nature, whereof I shall speak more particularly in the two following chapters.

Chapter XIV: Of the First and Second Natural Laws, and of Contracts

The *right of nature*, which writers commonly call *jus naturale*,[9] is the liberty each man hath to use his own power as he will himself for the preservation of his own nature; that is to say, of his own life; and consequently, of doing anything which, in his own judgement and reason, he shall conceive to be the aptest means thereunto.

By *liberty* is understood, according to the proper signification of the word, the absence of external impediments; which impediments may oft take away part of a man's power to do what he would, but cannot hinder him from using the power left him according as his judgement and reason shall dictate to him.

A *law of nature*, *lex naturalis*, is a precept, or general rule, found out by reason, by which a man is forbidden to do that which is destructive of his life, or taketh away the means of preserving the same, and to omit that by which he thinketh it may be best preserved. For though they that speak of this subject use to confound *jus* and *lex*, *right* and *law*, yet they ought to be distinguished, because *right* consisteth in liberty to do, or to forbear; whereas *law* determineth and bindeth to one of them: so that law and right differ as much as obligation and liberty, which in one and the same matter are inconsistent.

And because the condition of man (as hath been declared in the precedent chapter) is a condition of war of every one against every one, in which case every one is governed by his own reason, and there is nothing he can make use of that may not be a help unto him in preserving his life against his enemies; it followeth that in such a condition every man has a right to every thing, even to one another's body. And therefore, as long as this natural right of every man to every thing endureth, there can be no security to any man, how strong or wise soever he be, of living out the time which nature ordinarily alloweth men to live. And consequently it is a precept, or general rule of reason: *that every man ought to endeavour peace, as far as he has hope of obtaining it; and when he cannot obtain it, that he may seek and use all helps and advantages of war*. The first branch of which rule

---

8   Just as much as.

9   Natural right.

containeth the first and fundamental law of nature, which is: *to seek peace and follow it*. The second, the sum of the right of nature, which is: *by all means we can to defend ourselves*.

From this fundamental law of nature, by which men are commanded to endeavour peace, is derived this second law: *that a man be willing, when others are so too, as far forth as for peace and defence of himself he shall think it necessary, to lay down*[10] *this right to all things; and be contented with so much liberty against other men as he would allow other men against himself*. For as long as every man holdeth this right, of doing anything he liketh; so long are all men in the condition of war. But if other men will not lay down their right, as well as he, then there is no reason for anyone to divest himself of his: for that were to expose himself to prey, which no man is bound to, rather than to dispose himself to peace. This is that law of the Gospel: Whatsoever you require that others should do to you, that do ye to them. And that law of all men, *quod tibi fieri non vis, alteri ne feceris*.[11]

To *lay down* a man's *right* to anything is to divest himself of the *liberty* of hindering another of the benefit of his own right to the same. For he that renounceth or passeth away his right giveth not to any other man a right which he had not before, because there is nothing to which every man had not right by nature, but only standeth out of his way that he may enjoy his own original right without hindrance from him, not without hindrance from another. So that the effect which redoundeth to one man by another man's defect of right is but so much diminution of impediments to the use of his own right original.

Right is laid aside, either by simply renouncing it, or by transferring it to another. By *simply* renouncing, when he cares not to whom the benefit thereof redoundeth. By transferring, when he intendeth the benefit thereof to some certain person or persons. And when a man hath in either manner abandoned or granted away his right, then is he said to be *obliged*, or *bound*, not to hinder those to whom such right is granted, or abandoned, from the benefit of it: and

that he *ought*, and it is his *duty*, not to make void that voluntary act of his own: and that such hindrance is *injustice*, and *injury*, as being *sine jure*;[12] the right being before renounced or transferred. So that *injury* or *injustice*, in the controversies of the world, is somewhat like to that which in the disputations of scholars is called absurdity. For as it is there called an *absurdity* to contradict what one maintained in the beginning; so in the world it is called injustice and injury voluntarily to undo that which from the beginning he had voluntarily done. The way by which a man either simply renounceth or transferreth his right is a declaration, or signification, by some voluntary and sufficient sign, or signs, that he doth so renounce or transfer, or hath so renounced or transferred the same, to him that accepteth it. And these signs are either words only, or actions only; or, as it happeneth most often, both words and actions. And the same are the *bonds*, by which men are bound and obliged: bonds that have their strength, not from their own nature (for nothing is more easily broken than a man's word), but from fear of some evil consequence upon the rupture.

Whensoever a man transferreth his right, or renounceth it, it is either in consideration of some right reciprocally transferred to himself, or for some other good he hopeth for thereby. For it is a voluntary act: and of the voluntary acts of every man, the object is some *good to himself*. And therefore there be some rights which no man can be understood by any words, or other signs, to have abandoned or transferred. As, first, a man cannot lay down the right of resisting them that assault him by force to take away his life, because he cannot be understood to aim thereby at any good to himself. The same may be said of wounds, and chains, and imprisonment, both because there is no benefit consequent to such patience, as there is to the patience of suffering another to be wounded or imprisoned, as also because a man cannot tell when he seeth men proceed against him by violence whether they intend his death or not. And lastly the motive and end for which this renouncing and transferring of right is introduced is nothing else but the security of a man's person, in his life, and in the means of so preserving life as not to be weary of it. And therefore if a man

---

10 To give up.

11 "Do not do to others what you would not want done to yourself."

---

12 Without right.

by words, or other signs, seem to despoil himself of the end for which those signs were intended, he is not to be understood as if he meant it, or that it was his will, but that he was ignorant of how such words and actions were to be interpreted.

The mutual transferring of right is that which men call *contract*.

There is difference between transferring of right to the thing, and transferring or tradition,[13] that is, delivery of the thing itself. For the thing may be delivered together with the translation of the right (as in buying and selling with ready money, or exchange of goods or lands), and it may be delivered some time after.

Again, one of the contractors may deliver the thing contracted for on his part, and leave the other to perform his part at some determinate time after, and in the meantime be trusted; and then the contract on his part is called *pact*, or *covenant*: or both parts[14] may contract now to perform hereafter, in which cases he that is to perform in time to come, being trusted, his performance is called *keeping of promise*, or *faith*, and the failing of performance, if it be voluntary, *violation of faith*.

When the transferring of right is not mutual, but one of the parties transferreth in hope to gain thereby friendship or service from another, or from his friends; or in hope to gain the reputation of charity, or magnanimity; or to deliver his mind from the pain of compassion; or in hope of reward in heaven; this is not contract, but *gift*, *free-gift*, *grace*: which words signify one and the same thing.

…

If a covenant be made wherein neither of the parties perform presently, but trust one another, in the condition of mere nature (which is a condition of war of every man against every man) upon any reasonable suspicion, it is void: but if there be a common power set over them both, with right and force sufficient to compel performance, it is not void. For he that performeth first has no assurance the other will perform after, because the bonds of words are too weak

to bridle men's ambition, avarice, anger, and other passions, without the fear of some coercive power; which in the condition of mere nature, where all men are equal, and judges of the justness of their own fears, cannot possibly be supposed. And therefore he which performeth first does but betray himself to his enemy, contrary to the right he can never abandon of defending his life and means of living.

But in a civil estate, where there is a power set up to constrain those that would otherwise violate their faith, that fear is no more reasonable; and for that cause, he which by the covenant is to perform first is obliged so to do.

The cause of fear, which maketh such a covenant invalid, must be always something arising after the covenant made, as some new fact or other sign of the will not to perform, else it cannot make the covenant void. For that which could not hinder a man from promising ought not to be admitted as a hindrance of performing.…

Chapter XV: Of Other Laws of Nature

From that law of nature by which we are obliged to transfer to another such rights as, being retained, hinder the peace of mankind, there followeth a third; which is this: *that men perform their covenants made*; without which covenants are in vain, and but empty words; and the right of all men to all things remaining, we are still in the condition of war.

And in this law of nature consisteth the fountain and original of *justice*. For where no covenant hath preceded, there hath no right been transferred, and every man has right to everything and consequently, no action can be unjust. But when a covenant is made, then to break it is *unjust* and the definition of *injustice* is no other than *the not performance of covenant*. And whatsoever is not unjust is *just*.

But because covenants of mutual trust, where there is a fear of not performance on either part (as hath been said in the former chapter), are invalid, though the original of justice be the making of covenants, yet injustice actually there can be none till the cause of such fear be taken away; which, while men are in the natural condition of war, cannot be done. Therefore before the names of just and unjust can have place, there must be some coercive power to compel men

---

13   As a legal term, "tradition" means the formal delivery of property to another person.
14   Parties (to the covenant).

equally to the performance of their covenants, by the terror of some punishment greater than the benefit they expect by the breach of their covenant, and to make good that propriety which by mutual contract men acquire in recompense of the universal right they abandon: and such power there is none before the erection of a commonwealth. And this is also to be gathered out of the ordinary definition of justice in the Schools,[15] for they say that *justice is the constant will of giving to every man his own*. And therefore where there is no *own*, that is, no propriety, there is no injustice; and where there is no coercive power erected, that is, where there is no commonwealth, there is no propriety, all men having right to all things: therefore where there is no commonwealth, there nothing is unjust. So that the nature of justice consisteth in keeping of valid covenants, but the validity of covenants begins not but with the constitution of a civil power sufficient to compel men to keep them: and then it is also that propriety begins.

The fool hath said in his heart, there is no such thing as justice,[16] and sometimes also with his tongue, seriously alleging that: every man's conservation and contentment being committed to his own care, there could be no reason why every man might not do what he thought conduced thereunto: and therefore also to make, or not make, keep, or not keep, covenants was not against reason when it conduced to one's benefit. He does not therein deny that there be covenants; and that they are sometimes broken, sometimes kept; and that such breach of them may be called injustice, and the observance of them justice: but he questioneth whether injustice, taking away the fear of God (for the same fool hath said in his heart there is no God), not sometimes stand with that reason which dictateth to every man his own good; and particularly then, when it conduceth to such a benefit as shall put a man in a condition to neglect not only the dispraise and revilings, but also the power of other men. The kingdom of God is gotten by violence:[17] but what if it could be gotten by unjust violence? Were it against reason so to get it, when it is impossible to receive hurt by it? And if it be not against reason, it is not against justice: or else justice is not to be approved for good. From such reasoning as this, successful wickedness hath obtained the name of virtue: and some that in all other things have disallowed the violation of faith, yet have allowed it when it is for the getting of a kingdom. And the heathen that believed that *Saturn* was deposed by his son *Jupiter*[18] believed nevertheless the same *Jupiter* to be the avenger of injustice, somewhat like to a piece of law in *Coke's* Commentaries on *Littleton*;[19] where he says if the right heir of the crown be attainted of treason, yet the crown shall descend to him, and *eo instante*[20] the attainder[21] be void: from which instances a man will be very prone to infer that when the heir apparent[22] of a kingdom shall kill him that is in possession, though his father, you may call it injustice, or by what other name you will; yet it can never be against reason, seeing all the voluntary actions of men tend to the benefit of themselves; and those actions are most reasonable that conduce most to their ends. This specious reasoning is nevertheless false.

For the question is not of promises mutual, where there is no security of performance on either side, as when there is no civil power erected over the parties

---

15   The universities or their teachings, the traditional "scholastic" syllabus handed down from the Middle Ages.

16   A paraphrase from Psalm 14 (and Psalm 53) of the Bible: "The Fool has said in his heart, there is no God."

17   Hobbes's fool alludes to a verse in the Gospel of Matthew (11:12): "And from the days of John the Baptist until now, the kingdom of heaven suffereth violence, and the violent take it by force."

18   Saturn was the Roman equivalent of the ancient Greek god Cronus. Jupiter was the chief Roman god, often identified with the Greek Zeus.

19   *The First Part of the Institutes of the Laws of England*, by Edward Coke (1629). It includes Coke's commentary on Thomas Littleton's *Tenures* (1490), the first treatise to be written on English law and a standard text on English property law until the nineteenth century.

20   Immediately.

21   An old legal term for the forfeiture of property and rights suffered as a consequence of being sentenced to death for treason or felony.

22   The person first in line for succession to the throne.

promising; for such promises are no covenants: but either where one of the parties has performed already, or where there is a power to make him perform, there is the question whether it be against reason; that is, against the benefit of the other to perform, or not. And I say it is not against reason. For the manifestation whereof we are to consider: first, that when a man doth a thing which, notwithstanding anything can be foreseen and reckoned on, tendeth to his own destruction (howsoever some accident, which he could not expect, arriving may turn it to his benefit); yet such events do not make it reasonably or wisely done. Secondly, that in a condition of war, wherein every man to every man, for want of a common power to keep them all in awe, is an enemy, there is no man can hope by his own strength, or wit, to defend himself from destruction without the help of confederates (where every one expects the same defence by the confederation that any one else does); and therefore he which declares he thinks it reason to deceive those that help him can in reason expect no other means of safety than what can be had from his own single power. He, therefore, that breaketh his covenant, and consequently declareth that he thinks he may with reason do so, cannot be received into any society that unite themselves for peace and defence but by the error of them that receive him; nor when he is received be retained in it without seeing the danger of their error; which errors a man cannot reasonably reckon upon as the means of his security: and therefore if he be left or cast out of society, he perisheth; and if he live in society, it is by the errors of other men, which he could not foresee nor reckon upon, and consequently against the reason of his preservation; and so, as all men that contribute not to his destruction forbear him only out of ignorance of what is good for themselves.

As for the instance of gaining the secure and perpetual felicity of heaven by any way, it is frivolous; there being but one way imaginable, and that is not breaking, but keeping of covenant.

And for the other instance of attaining sovereignty by rebellion; it is manifest that, though the event follow, yet because it cannot reasonably be expected, but rather the contrary, and because by gaining it so, others are taught to gain the same in like manner, the attempt thereof is against reason. Justice therefore, that is to say, keeping of covenant, is a rule of reason by which we are forbidden to do anything destructive to our life, and consequently a law of nature.

There be some that proceed further and will not have the law of nature to be those rules which conduce to the preservation of man's life on earth, but to the attaining of an eternal felicity after death; to which they think the breach of covenant may conduce, and consequently be just and reasonable; such are they that think it a work of merit to kill, or depose, or rebel against the sovereign power constituted over them by their own consent. But because there is no natural knowledge of man's estate after death, much less of the reward that is then to be given to breach of faith, but only a belief grounded upon other men's saying that they know it supernaturally or that they know those that knew them that knew others that knew it supernaturally, breach of faith cannot be called a precept of reason or nature.

Others, that allow for a law of nature the keeping of faith, do nevertheless make exception of certain persons—as heretics, and such as use not to perform their covenant to others—and this also is against reason. For if any fault of a man be sufficient to discharge our covenant made, the same ought in reason to have been sufficient to have hindered the making of it.

The names of just and unjust when they are attributed to men, signify one thing, and when they are attributed to actions, another. When they are attributed to men, they signify conformity or inconformity of manners to reason. But when they are attributed to action they signify the conformity or inconformity to reason, not of manners, or manner of life, but of particular actions. A just man therefore is he that taketh all the care he can that his actions may be all just; and an unjust man is he that neglecteth it. And such men are more often in our language styled by the names of righteous and unrighteous than just and unjust though the meaning be the same. Therefore a righteous man does not lose that title by one or a few unjust actions that proceed from sudden passion, or mistake of things or persons, nor does an unrighteous man lose his character for such actions as he does, or forbears to do, for fear; because his will is not framed by the justice, but by the apparent benefit of what he is to do. That which gives to human actions the relish of justice is a certain nobleness or gallantness of courage, rarely found, by which a man scorns to be beholding for the contentment of his life to fraud, or breach of promise. This justice of the manners is that which is meant where justice is called a virtue; and injustice, a vice.

But the justice of actions denominates men, not just, but *guiltless*: and the injustice of the same (which is also called injury) gives them but the name of *guilty*.

Again, the injustice of manners is the disposition or aptitude to do injury, and is injustice before it proceed to act, and without supposing any individual person injured. But the injustice of an action (that is to say, injury) supposeth an individual person injured; namely him to whom the covenant was made: and therefore many times the injury is received by one man when the damage redoundeth to another. As when the master commandeth his servant to give money to a stranger; if it be not done, the injury is done to the master, whom he had before covenanted to obey; but the damage redoundeth to the stranger, to whom he had no obligation, and therefore could not injure him. And so also in commonwealths private men may remit to one another their debts, but not robberies or other violences, whereby they are endamaged; because the detaining of debt is an injury to themselves, but robbery and violence are injuries to the person of the commonwealth.

Whatsoever is done to a man, conformable to his own will signified to the doer, is not injury to him. For if he that doeth it hath not passed away his original right to do what he please by some antecedent covenant, there is no breach of covenant, and therefore no injury done him. And if he have, then his will to have it done, being signified, is a release of that covenant, and so again there is no injury done him.

Justice of actions is by writers[23] divided into *commutative* and *distributive*: and the former they say consisteth in proportion arithmetical; the latter in proportion geometrical. Commutative, therefore, they place in the equality of value of the things contracted for; and distributive, in the distribution of equal benefit to men of equal merit. As if it were injustice to sell dearer than we buy, or to give more to a man than he merits. The value of all things contracted for is measured by the appetite of the contractors, and therefore the just value is that which they be contented to give. And merit (besides that which is by covenant, where the performance on one part meriteth the performance of the other part, and falls under justice commutative, not distributive) is not due by justice, but is rewarded of grace only. And therefore this distinction, in the sense wherein it useth to be expounded, is not right. To speak properly, commutative justice is the justice of a contractor; that is, a performance of covenant in buying and selling, hiring and letting to hire, lending and borrowing, exchanging, bartering, and other acts of contract.

And distributive justice, the justice of an arbitrator; that is to say, the act of defining what is just. Wherein, being trusted by them that make him arbitrator, if he perform his trust, he is said to distribute to every man his own: and this is indeed just distribution, and may be called, though improperly, distributive justice, but more properly equity, which also is a law of nature, as shall be shown in due place.

As justice dependeth on antecedent covenant; so does *gratitude* depend on antecedent grace; that is to say, antecedent free-gift; and is the fourth law of nature, which may be conceived in this form: *that a man which receiveth benefit from another of mere grace endeavour that he which giveth it have no reasonable cause to repent him of his good will.* For no man giveth but with intention of good to himself, because gift is voluntary; and of all voluntary acts, the object is to every man his own good; of which if men see they shall be frustrated, there will be no beginning of benevolence or trust, nor consequently of mutual help, nor of reconciliation of one man to another; and therefore they are to remain still in the condition of war, which is contrary to the first and fundamental law of nature which commandeth men to *seek peace*. The breach of this law is called *ingratitude*, and hath the same relation to grace that injustice hath to obligation by covenant.

A fifth law of nature is *complaisance*; that is to say, *that every man strive to accommodate himself to the*

---

23   See the selection from Aristotle in this chapter. A similar distinction would also have been known to Hobbes from Thomas Aquinas's *Summa Theologiae* (the second part of Part II, question 61).

rest. For the understanding whereof we may consider that there is in men's aptness to society a diversity of nature, rising from their diversity of affections, not unlike to that we see in stones brought together for building of an edifice. For as that stone which by the asperity and irregularity of figure takes more room from others than itself fills, and for hardness cannot be easily made plain,[24] and thereby hindereth the building, is by the builders cast away as unprofitable and troublesome: so also, a man that by asperity of nature will strive to retain those things which to himself are superfluous, and to others necessary, and for the stubbornness of his passions cannot be corrected, is to be left or cast out of society as cumbersome thereunto. For seeing every man, not only by right, but also by necessity of nature, is supposed to endeavour all he can to obtain that which is necessary for his conservation, he that shall oppose himself against it for things superfluous is guilty of the war that thereupon is to follow, and therefore doth that which is contrary to the fundamental law of nature, which commandeth to *seek peace*. The observers of this law may be called *sociable* (the Latins call them *commodi*); the contrary, *stubborn, insociable, froward, intractable*.

A sixth law of nature is this: *that upon caution of the future time, a man ought to pardon the offences past of them that, repenting, desire it*. For *pardon* is nothing but granting of peace; which though granted to them that persevere in their hostility, be not peace, but fear; yet not granted to them that give caution of the future time is sign of an aversion to peace, and therefore contrary to the law of nature.

A seventh is: *that in revenges* (that is, retribution of evil for evil), *men look not at the greatness of the evil past, but the greatness of the good to follow*. Whereby we are forbidden to inflict punishment with any other design than for correction of the offender, or direction of others. For this law is consequent to the next before it, that commandeth pardon upon security of the future time. Besides, revenge without respect to the example and profit to come is a triumph, or glorying in the hurt of another, tending to no end (for the end is always somewhat to come); and glorying to no end is vain-glory, and contrary to reason; and to

hurt without reason tendeth to the introduction of war, which is against the law of nature, and is commonly styled by the name of *cruelty*.

And because all signs of hatred, or contempt, provoke to fight; insomuch as most men choose rather to hazard their life than not to be revenged, we may in the eighth place, for a law of nature, set down this precept: *that no man by deed, word, countenance, or gesture, declare hatred or contempt of another*. The breach of which law is commonly called *contumely*.

The question who is the better man has no place in the condition of mere nature, where (as has been shown before) all men are equal. The inequality that now is has been introduced by the laws civil. I know that *Aristotle* in the first book of his Politics, for a foundation of his doctrine, maketh men by nature, some more worthy to command, meaning the wiser sort, such as he thought himself to be for his philosophy; others to serve, meaning those that had strong bodies, but were not philosophers as he; as master and servant were not introduced by consent of men, but by difference of wit: which is not only against reason, but also against experience. For there are very few so foolish that had not rather govern themselves than be governed by others: nor when the wise, in their own conceit, contend by force with them who distrust their own wisdom, do they always, or often, or almost at any time, get the victory. If nature therefore have made men equal, that equality is to be acknowledged: or if nature have made men unequal, yet because men that think themselves equal will not enter into conditions of peace, but upon equal terms, such equality must be admitted. And therefore for the ninth law of nature, I put this: *that every man acknowledge another for his equal by nature*. The breach of this precept is *pride*.

On this law dependeth another: *that at the entrance into conditions of peace, no man require to reserve to himself any right which he is not content should be reserved to every one of the rest*. As it is necessary for all men that seek peace to lay down certain rights of nature; that is to say, not to have liberty to do all they list, so is it necessary for man's life to retain some: as right to govern their own bodies; enjoy air, water, motion, ways to go from place to place; and all things else without which a man cannot live, or

---

24   Smooth.

not live well. If in this case, at the making of peace, men require for themselves that which they would not have to be granted to others, they do contrary to the precedent law that commandeth the acknowledgement of natural equality, and therefore also against the law of nature. The observers of this law are those we call *modest*, and the breakers *arrogant* men. The Greeks call the violation of this law *pleonexia*; that is, a desire of more than their share.

Also, *if a man be trusted to judge between man and man*, it is a precept of the law of nature that *he deal equally between them*. For without that, the controversies of men cannot be determined but by war. He therefore that is partial in judgement, doth what in him lies to deter men from the use of judges and arbitrators, and consequently, against the fundamental law of nature, is the cause of war.

The observance of this law, from the equal distribution to each man of that which in reason belongeth to him, is called *equity*, and (as I have said before) distributive justice: the violation, *acception of persons* (*prosopolepsia*).

And from this followeth another law: *that such things as cannot be divided be enjoyed in common, if it can be; and if the quantity of the thing permit, without stint; otherwise proportionably to the number of them that have right*. For otherwise the distribution is unequal, and contrary to equity.

But some things there be that can neither be divided nor enjoyed in common. Then, the law of nature which prescribeth equity requireth: *that the entire right, or else (making the use alternate) the first possession, be determined by lot*.[25] For equal distribution is of the law of nature; and other means of equal distribution cannot be imagined.

Of *lots* there be two sorts, *arbitrary* and *natural*. Arbitrary is that which is agreed on by the competitors; natural is either *primogeniture*[26] (which the Greek calls *kleronomia*, which signifies, *given by lot*), or *first seizure*.

And therefore those things which cannot be enjoyed in common, nor divided, ought to be adjudged

to the first possessor; and in some cases to the first born, as acquired by lot.

It is also a law of nature: *that all men that mediate peace be allowed safe conduct*. For the law that commandeth peace, as the *end*, commandeth intercession, as the *means*; and to intercession the means is safe conduct.

And because, though men be never so willing to observe these laws, there may nevertheless arise questions concerning a man's action—first, whether it were done, or not done; secondly, if done, whether against the law, or not against the law; the former whereof is called a question *of fact*, the latter a question *of right*—therefore unless the parties to the question covenant mutually to stand to the sentence of another, they are as far from peace as ever. This other, to whose sentence they submit, is called an *arbitrator*. And therefore it is of the law of nature *that they that are at controversy submit their right to the judgement of an arbitrator*.

And seeing every man is presumed to do all things in order to his own benefit, *no man is a fit arbitrator in his own cause*: and if he were never so fit, yet equity allowing to each party equal benefit, if one be admitted to be judge, the other is to be admitted also; and so the controversy, that is, the cause of war, remains, against the law of nature.

For the same reason no man in any cause ought to be received for arbitrator to whom greater profit, or honour, or pleasure apparently ariseth out of the victory of one party than of the other: for he hath taken, though an unavoidable bribe, yet a bribe; and no man can be obliged to trust him. And thus also the controversy and the condition of war remaineth, contrary to the law of nature.

And in a controversy of *fact*, the judge (being to give no more credit to one than to the other, if there be no other arguments) must give credit to a third;[27] or to a third and fourth; or more: for else the question is undecided, and left to force, contrary to the law of nature.

These are the laws of nature, dictating peace, for a means of the conservation of men in multitudes; and which only concern the doctrine of civil society.

---

25   By chance.

26   Rights of inheritance or succession derived from being first-born.

27   Must listen to a neutral witness.

There be other things tending to the destruction of particular men; as drunkenness, and all other parts of intemperance, which may therefore also be reckoned amongst those things which the law of nature hath forbidden, but are not necessary to be mentioned, nor are pertinent enough to this place.

And though this may seem too subtle a deduction of the laws of nature to be taken notice of by all men, whereof the most part are too busy in getting food, and the rest too negligent to understand; yet to leave all men inexcusable, they have been contracted into one easy sum, intelligible even to the meanest capacity; and that is: *Do not that to another which thou wouldest not have done to thyself*, which showeth him that he has no more to do in learning the laws of nature but, when weighing the actions of other men with his own they seem too heavy, to put them into the other part of the balance, and his own into their place, that his own passions and self-love may add nothing to the weight; and then there is none of these laws of nature that will not appear unto him very reasonable.

The laws of nature oblige *in foro interno*;[28] that is to say, they bind to a desire they should take place: but *in foro externo*;[29] that is, to the putting them in act, not always. For he that should be modest and tractable, and perform all he promises in such time and place where no man else should do so, should but make himself a prey to others, and procure his own certain ruin, contrary to the ground of all laws of nature which tend to nature's preservation. And again, he that having sufficient security that others shall observe the same laws towards him, observes them not himself, seeketh not peace, but war, and consequently the destruction of his nature by violence.

And whatsoever laws bind *in foro interno* may be broken, not only by a fact contrary to the law, but also by a fact according to it, in case a man think it contrary. For though his action in this case be according to the law, yet his purpose was against the law; which, where the obligation is *in foro interno*, is a breach.

The laws of nature are immutable and eternal; for injustice, ingratitude, arrogance, pride, iniquity, acception of persons, and the rest can never be made lawful. For it can never be that war shall preserve life, and peace destroy it.

The same laws, because they oblige only to a desire and endeavour (I mean an unfeigned and constant endeavour) are easy to be observed. For in that they require nothing but endeavour, he that endeavoureth their performance fulfilleth them; and he that fulfilleth the law is just.

And the science of them is the true and only moral philosophy. For moral philosophy is nothing else but the science of what is *good* and *evil* in the conversation and society of mankind. *Good* and *evil* are names that signify our appetites and aversions, which in different tempers, customs, and doctrines of men are different: and diverse men differ not only in their judgement on the senses of what is pleasant and unpleasant to the taste, smell, hearing, touch, and sight; but also of what is conformable or disagreeable to reason in the actions of common life. Nay, the same man, in diverse times, differs from himself; and one time praiseth, that is, calleth good, what another time he dispraiseth, and calleth evil: from whence arise disputes, controversies, and at last war. And therefore so long as a man is in the condition of mere nature, which is a condition of war, private appetite is the measure of good and evil: and consequently all men agree on this, that peace is good, and therefore also the way or means of peace, which (as I have shown before) are *justice*, *gratitude*, *modesty*, *equity*, *mercy*, and the rest of the laws of nature, are good; that is to say, *moral virtues*; and their contrary vices, evil. Now the science of virtue and vice is moral philosophy; and therefore the true doctrine of the laws of nature is the true moral philosophy. But the writers of moral philosophy, though they acknowledge the same virtues and vices; yet, not seeing wherein consisted their goodness, nor that they come to be praised as the means of peaceable, sociable, and comfortable living, place them in a mediocrity[30] of passions: as if not the cause, but the degree of daring, made fortitude; or not the cause, but the quantity of a gift, made liberality.

These dictates of reason men used to call by the name of laws, but improperly: for they are but con-

---

28 In the internal domain (literally, the "inner marketplace").

29 In the external domain.

30 A moderate amount, a mean.

clusions or theorems concerning what conduceth to the conservation and defence of themselves; whereas law, properly, is the word of him that by right hath command over others. But yet if we consider the same theorems as delivered in the word of God that by right commandeth all things, then are they properly called laws.

...

Part II: Of Commonwealth

Chapter XVII: Of the Causes, Generation, and Definition of a Commonwealth

The final cause, end, or design of men (who naturally love liberty, and dominion over others) in the introduction of that restraint upon themselves, in which we see them live in commonwealths, is the foresight of their own preservation, and of a more contented life thereby; that is to say, of getting themselves out from that miserable condition of war which is necessarily consequent, as hath been shown, to the natural passions of men when there is no visible power to keep them in awe, and tie them by fear of punishment to the performance of their covenants, and observation of those laws of nature set down in the fourteenth and fifteenth chapters.

For the laws of nature—as *justice*, *equity*, *modesty*, *mercy*, and, in sum, *doing to others as we would be done to*—of themselves, without the terror of some power to cause them to be observed, are contrary to our natural passions, that carry us to partiality, pride, revenge, and the like. And covenants, without the sword, are but words and of no strength to secure a man at all. Therefore, notwithstanding the laws of nature (which every one hath then kept, when he has the will to keep them, when he can do it safely), if there be no power erected, or not great enough for our security, every man will and may lawfully rely on his own strength and art for caution against all other men. And in all places, where men have lived by small families, to rob and spoil one another has been a trade, and so far from being reputed against the law of nature that the greater spoils they gained, the greater was their honour; and men observed no other laws therein but the laws of honour; that is, to abstain from cruelty, leaving to men their lives and instruments of husbandry. And as small families did then; so now do cities and kingdoms, which are but greater families (for their own security), enlarge their dominions upon all pretences of danger, and fear of invasion, or assistance that may be given to invaders; endeavour as much as they can to subdue or weaken their neighbours by open force, and secret arts, for want of other caution, justly; and are remembered for it in after ages with honour.

Nor is it the joining together of a small number of men that gives them this security; because in small numbers, small additions on the one side or the other make the advantage of strength so great as is sufficient to carry the victory, and therefore gives encouragement to an invasion. The multitude sufficient to confide in for our security is not determined by any certain number, but by comparison with the enemy we fear; and is then sufficient when the odds of the enemy[31] is not of so visible and conspicuous moment to determine the event of war, as to move him to attempt.

And be there never so great a multitude; yet if their actions be directed according to their particular judgements, and particular appetites, they can expect thereby no defence, nor protection, neither against a common enemy, nor against the injuries of one another. For being distracted in opinions concerning the best use and application of their strength, they do not help, but hinder one another, and reduce their strength by mutual opposition to nothing: whereby they are easily, not only subdued by a very few that agree together, but also, when there is no common enemy, they make war upon each other for their particular interests. For if we could suppose a great multitude of men to consent in the observation of justice, and other laws of nature, without a common power to keep them all in awe, we might as well suppose all mankind to do the same; and then there neither would be, nor need to be, any civil government or commonwealth at all, because there would be peace without subjection.

_____

31   The ratio of the enemy's strength to that of the defenders'.

Nor is it enough for the security, which men desire should last all the time of their life, that they be governed and directed by one judgement for a limited time; as in one battle, or one war. For though they obtain a victory by their unanimous endeavour against a foreign enemy, yet afterwards, when either they have no common enemy, or he that by one part is held for an enemy is by another part held for a friend, they must needs by the difference of their interests dissolve, and fall again into a war amongst themselves.

It is true that certain living creatures, as bees and ants, live sociably one with another (which are therefore by *Aristotle* numbered amongst political creatures[32]), and yet have no other direction than their particular judgements and appetites; nor speech, whereby one of them can signify to another what he thinks expedient for the common benefit: and therefore some man may perhaps desire to know why mankind cannot do the same. To which I answer,

First, that men are continually in competition for honour and dignity, which these creatures are not; and consequently amongst men there ariseth on that ground, envy, and hatred, and finally war; but amongst these not so.

Secondly, that amongst these creatures the common good differeth not from the private; and being by nature inclined to their private, they procure thereby the common benefit. But man, whose joy consisteth in comparing himself with other men, can relish nothing but what is eminent.

Thirdly, that these creatures, having not, as man, the use of reason, do not see, nor think they see, any fault in the administration of their common business: whereas amongst men there are very many that think themselves wiser and abler to govern the public better than the rest, and these strive to reform and innovate, one this way, another that way; and thereby bring it into distraction and civil war.

Fourthly, that these creatures, though they have some use of voice in making known to one another their desires and other affections, yet they want that art of words by which some men can represent to others that which is good in the likeness of evil; and evil, in the likeness of good; and augment or diminish the apparent greatness of good and evil, discontenting men and troubling their peace at their pleasure.

Fifthly, irrational creatures cannot distinguish between *injury* and *damage*; and therefore as long as they be at ease, they are not offended with their fellows: whereas man is then most troublesome when he is most at ease; for then it is that he loves to show his wisdom, and control the actions of them that govern the commonwealth.

Lastly, the agreement of these creatures is natural; that of men is by covenant only, which is artificial: and therefore it is no wonder if there be somewhat else required, besides covenant, to make their agreement constant and lasting; which is a common power to keep them in awe and to direct their actions to the common benefit.

The only way to erect such a common power, as may be able to defend them from the invasion of foreigners, and the injuries of one another, and thereby to secure them in such sort as that by their own industry and by the fruits of the earth they may nourish themselves and live contentedly, is to confer all their power and strength upon one man, or upon one assembly of men, that may reduce all their wills, by plurality of voices, unto one will: which is as much as to say, to appoint one man, or assembly of men, to bear their person; and every one to own and acknowledge himself to be author of whatsoever he that so beareth their person shall act, or cause to be acted, in those things which concern the common peace and safety; and therein to submit their wills, every one to his will, and their judgements to his judgement. This is more than consent, or concord; it is a real unity of them all in one and the same person, made by covenant of every man with every man, in such manner as if every man should say to every man: *I authorise and give up my right of governing myself to this man, or to this assembly of men, on this condition; that thou give up, thy right to him, and authorise all his actions in like manner.* This done, the multitude so united in

---

32 See Aristotle's *History of Animals* (Book I, section 1). In fact, Aristotle, though he considered such creatures *social* animals, did not think them *political* in the proper sense of the word (as it applies to human beings). His reasons for this distinction were rather similar to those Hobbes goes on to give.

one person is called a *commonwealth*; in Latin, *civitas*. This is the generation of that great *Leviathan*,[33] or rather, to speak more reverently, of that *Mortal God* to which we owe, under the *Immortal God*, our peace and defence. For by this authority, given him by every particular man in the commonwealth, he hath the use of so much power and strength conferred on him that, by terror thereof, he is enabled to form the wills of them all, to peace at home, and mutual aid against their enemies abroad. And in him consisteth the essence of the commonwealth; which, to define it, is: *one person, of whose acts a great multitude, by mutual covenants one with another, have made themselves every one the author, to the end he may use the strength and means of them all as he shall think expedient for their peace and common defence.*

And he that carryeth this person is called sovereign, and said to have *sovereign power*; and every one besides, his subject.

The attaining to this sovereign power is by two ways. One, by natural force: as when a man maketh his children to submit themselves, and their children, to his government, as being able to destroy them if they refuse; or by war subdueth his enemies to his will, giving them their lives on that condition. The other, is when men agree amongst themselves to sub-

mit to some man, or assembly of men, voluntarily, on confidence to be protected by him against all others. This latter may be called a political commonwealth, or commonwealth by *institution*; and the former, a commonwealth by *acquisition*. And first, I shall speak of a commonwealth by institution.

Chapter XVIII: Of the Rights of Sovereigns by Institution

A *commonwealth* is said to be *instituted* when a *multitude* of men do agree, and *covenant, every one with every one*, that to whatsoever *man*, or *assembly of men*, shall be given by the major part the *right* to *present* the person of them all, that is to say, to be their *representative*; every one, as well he that *voted for it* as he that *voted against it*, shall *authorize* all the actions and judgements of that man, or assembly of men, in the same manner as if they were his own, to the end to live peaceably amongst themselves, and be protected against other men.

From this institution of a commonwealth are derived all the *rights* and *faculties* of him, or them, on whom the sovereign power is conferred by the consent of the people assembled.

First, because they covenant, it is to be understood they are not obliged by former covenant to anything repugnant hereunto. And consequently they that have already instituted a commonwealth, being thereby bound by covenant to own the actions and judgements of one, cannot lawfully make a new covenant amongst themselves to be obedient to any other, in anything whatsoever, without his permission. And therefore, they that are subjects to a monarch cannot without his leave cast off monarchy and return to the confusion of a disunited multitude; nor transfer their person from him that beareth it to another man, or other assembly of men: for they are bound, every man to every man, to own and be reputed author of all that he that already is their sovereign shall do and judge fit to be done; so that any one man dissenting, all the rest should break their covenant made to that man, which is injustice: and they have also every man given the sovereignty to him that beareth their person; and therefore if they depose him, they take from him that which is his own, and so again it is injustice. Besides, if he that attempteth to depose his sovereign be killed or pun-

---

33   This is an allusion to the Old Testament book of Job, where Leviathan is described as a fearsome, fire-breathing, many-headed sea monster. Leviathan's symbolic meaning in the Bible is obscure, but it was sometimes associated with the devil by biblical commentators (such as Aquinas). In the book of Revelation, it is written that God's final victory over Leviathan will herald the end of the world. Why Hobbes chose this controversy-inducing label for the state, and even made it the title of his work, is obscure. However, in a later passage (at the end of Chapter XXVIII) Hobbes quotes from Job: "There is nothing on earth to be compared with him. He is made so as not to be afraid. He seeth every high thing below him, and is king of all the children of pride" (Job 41: 33–34). Yet, Hobbes points out, Leviathan "is mortal and subject to decay, as all other earthly creatures are, and … there is that in heaven (though not on earth) that he should stand in fear of, and whose laws he ought to obey."

ished by him for such attempt, he is author of his own punishment, as being, by the institution, author of all his sovereign shall do; and because it is injustice for a man to do anything for which he may be punished by his own authority, he is also upon that title unjust. And whereas some men have pretended for their disobedience to their sovereign a new covenant, made, not with men but with God, this also is unjust: for there is no covenant with God but by mediation of somebody that representeth God's person, which none doth but God's lieutenant who hath the sovereignty under God. But this pretence of covenant with God is so evident a lie, even in the pretenders' own consciences, that it is not only an act of an unjust, but also of a vile and unmanly disposition.

Secondly, because the right of bearing the person of them all is given to him they make sovereign, by covenant only of one to another, and not of him to any of them, there can happen no breach of covenant on the part of the sovereign; and consequently none of his subjects, by any pretence of forfeiture, can be freed from his subjection. That he which is made sovereign maketh no covenant with his subjects beforehand is manifest; because either he must make it with the whole multitude, as one party to the covenant, or he must make a several covenant with every man. With the whole, as one party, it is impossible, because as yet they are not one person: and if he make so many several covenants as there be men, those covenants after he hath the sovereignty are void; because what act soever can be pretended by any one of them for breach thereof is the act both of himself, and of all the rest, because done in the person and by the right of every one of them in particular. Besides, if any one or more of them pretend a breach of the covenant made by the sovereign at his institution, and others or one other of his subjects, or himself alone, pretend there was no such breach, there is in this case no judge to decide the controversy: it returns therefore to the sword again; and every man recovereth the right of protecting himself by his own strength, contrary to the design they had in the institution. It is therefore in vain to grant sovereignty by way of precedent covenant. The opinion that any monarch receiveth his power by covenant, that is to say, on condition, proceedeth from want of understanding this easy truth: that covenants being but words, and breath, have no force to oblige, contain, constrain, or protect any man, but what it has from the public sword; that is, from the untied hands of that man, or assembly of men, that hath the sovereignty, and whose actions are avouched by them all, and performed by the strength of them all, in him united. But when an assembly of men is made sovereign, then no man imagineth any such covenant to have passed in the institution: for no man is so dull as to say, for example, the people of *Rome* made a covenant with the Romans to hold the sovereignty on such or such conditions; which not performed, the Romans might lawfully depose the Roman people. That men see not the reason to be alike in a monarchy and in a popular government proceedeth from the ambition of some that are kinder to the government of an assembly, whereof they may hope to participate, than of monarchy, which they despair to enjoy.

Thirdly, because the major part hath by consenting voices declared a sovereign, he that dissented must now consent with the rest; that is, be contented to avow all the actions he shall do, or else justly be destroyed by the rest. For if he voluntarily entered into the congregation of them that were assembled, he sufficiently declared thereby his will, and therefore tacitly covenanted, to stand to what the major part should ordain: and therefore if he refuse to stand thereto, or make protestation against any of their decrees, he does contrary to his covenant, and therefore unjustly. And whether he be of the congregation or not, and whether his consent be asked or not, he must either submit to their decrees or be left in the condition of war he was in before; wherein he might without injustice be destroyed by any man whatsoever.

Fourthly, because every subject is by this institution author of all the actions and judgements of the sovereign instituted, it follows that whatsoever he doth, can be no injury to any of his subjects; nor ought he to be by any of them accused of injustice. For he that doth anything by authority from another doth therein no injury to him by whose authority he acteth: but by this institution of a commonwealth every particular man is author of all the sovereign doth; and consequently he that complaineth of injury from his sovereign complaineth of that whereof he himself is author, and therefore ought not to accuse any man but himself; no, nor himself of injury, because to do injury to oneself is impossible. It is true that they that have sovereign power may commit iniquity, but not injustice or injury in the proper signification.

Fifthly, and consequently to that which was said last, no man that hath sovereign power can justly be put to death, or otherwise in any manner by his subjects punished. For seeing every subject is author of the actions of his sovereign, he punisheth another for the actions committed by himself.

And because the end of this institution is the peace and defence of them all, and whosoever has right to the end has right to the means, it belongeth of right to whatsoever man or assembly that hath the sovereignty to be judge both of the means of peace and defence, and also of the hindrances and disturbances of the same; and to do whatsoever he shall think necessary to be done, both beforehand (for the preserving of peace and security, by prevention of discord at home, and hostility from abroad) and when peace and security are lost, for the recovery of the same. And therefore,

Sixthly, it is annexed to the sovereignty to be judge of what opinions and doctrines are averse, and what conducing, to peace; and consequently, on what occasions, how far, and what men are to be trusted withal in speaking to multitudes of people; and who shall examine the doctrines of all books before they be published. For the actions of men proceed from their opinions, and in the well-governing of opinions consisteth the well-governing of men's actions in order to their peace and concord. And though in matter of doctrine nothing ought to be regarded but the truth, yet this is not repugnant to regulating of the same by peace. For doctrine repugnant to peace can no more be true, than peace and concord can be against the law of nature. It is true that in a commonwealth, where—by the negligence or unskilfulness of governors and teachers—false doctrines are by time generally received, the contrary truths may be generally offensive: yet the most sudden and rough bustling in of a new truth that can be does never break the peace, but only sometimes awake the war. For those men that are so remissly governed that they dare take up arms to defend or introduce an opinion are still in war; and their condition, not peace, but only a cessation of arms for fear of one another; and they live, as it were, in the precincts of battle continually. It belongeth therefore to him that hath the sovereign power to be judge (or constitute all judges) of opinions and doctrines, as a thing necessary to peace; thereby to prevent discord and civil war.

Seventhly, is annexed to the sovereignty the whole power of prescribing the rules whereby every man may know what goods he may enjoy, and what actions he may do, without being molested by any of his fellow subjects: and this is it men call *propriety*. For before constitution of sovereign power, as hath already been shown, all men had right to all things, which necessarily causeth war: and therefore this propriety, being necessary to peace, and depending on sovereign power, is the act of that power, in order to the public peace. These rules of propriety (or *meum* and *tuum*[34]) and of *good*, *evil*, *lawful*, and *unlawful* in the actions of subjects are the civil laws; that is to say, the laws of each commonwealth in particular; though the name of civil law be now restrained to the ancient civil laws of the city of *Rome*; which being the head of a great part of the world, her laws at that time were in these parts the civil law.

Eighthly, is annexed to the sovereignty the right of *judicature*; that is to say, of hearing and deciding all controversies which may arise concerning law, either civil or natural, or concerning fact. For without the decision of controversies, there is no protection of one subject against the injuries of another; the laws concerning *meum* and *tuum* are in vain, and to every man remaineth, from the natural and necessary appetite of his own conservation, the right of protecting himself by his private strength, which is the condition of war, and contrary to the end for which every commonwealth is instituted.

Ninthly, is annexed to the sovereignty the right of making war and peace with other nations and commonwealths; that is to say, of judging when it is for the public good, and how great forces are to be assembled, armed, and paid for that end, and to levy money upon the subjects to defray the expenses thereof. For the power by which the people are to be defended consisteth in their armies, and the strength of an army in the union of their strength under one

---

34   Mine and yours.

command; which command the sovereign instituted therefore hath, because the command of the *militia*, without other institution, maketh him that hath it sovereign. And therefore, whosoever is made general of an army, he that hath the sovereign power is always generalissimo.[35]

Tenthly, is annexed to the sovereignty the choosing of all counsellors, ministers, magistrates, and officers, both in peace and war. For seeing the sovereign is charged with the end, which is the common peace and defence, he is understood to have power to use such means as he shall think most fit for his discharge.

Eleventhly, to the sovereign is committed the power of rewarding with riches or honour; and of punishing with corporal or pecuniary punishment, or with ignominy, every subject according to the law he hath formerly made; or if there be no law made, according as he shall judge most to conduce to the encouraging of men to serve the commonwealth, or deterring of them from doing disservice to the same.

Lastly, considering what values men are naturally apt to set upon themselves, what respect they look for from others, and how little they value other men; from whence continually arise amongst them, emulation, quarrels, factions, and at last war, to the destroying of one another, and diminution of their strength against a common enemy; it is necessary that there be laws of honour, and a public rate of the worth of such men as have deserved or are able to deserve well of the commonwealth, and that there be force in the hands of some or other to put those laws in execution. But it hath already been shown that not only the whole *militia*, or forces of the commonwealth, but also the judicature of all controversies, is annexed to the sovereignty. To the sovereign therefore it belongeth also to give titles of honour, and to appoint what order of place and dignity each man shall hold, and what signs of respect in public or private meetings they shall give to one another.

These are the rights which make the essence of sovereignty, and which are the marks whereby a man may discern in what man, or assembly of men, the sovereign power is placed and resideth. For these are incommunicable and inseparable. The power to coin money, to dispose of the estate and persons of infant heirs, to have preemption in markets,[36] and all other statute prerogatives may be transferred by the sovereign, and yet the power to protect his subjects be retained. But if he transfer the *militia*, he retains the judicature in vain, for want of execution of the laws; or if he grant away the power of raising money, the *militia* is in vain; or if he give away the government of doctrines, men will be frighted into rebellion with the fear of spirits. And so if we consider any one of the said rights, we shall presently see that the holding of all the rest will produce no effect in the conservation of peace and justice, the end for which all commonwealths are instituted. And this division is it whereof it is said, *a kingdom divided in itself cannot stand*:[37] for unless this division precede, division into opposite armies can never happen. If there had not first been an opinion received of the greatest part of *England* that these powers were divided between the King and the Lords and the House of Commons, the people had never been divided and fallen into this Civil War;[38] first between those that disagreed in politics, and after between the dissenters about the liberty of religion, which have so instructed men in this point of sovereign right that there be few now in *England* that do not see that these rights are inseparable, and will be so generally acknowledged at the next return of peace; and so continue, till their miseries are forgotten, and no longer, except the vulgar be better taught than they have hitherto been.

And because they are essential and inseparable rights, it follows necessarily that in whatsoever words any of them seem to be granted away, yet if the sovereign power itself be not in direct terms renounced and the name of sovereign no more given by the grantees to him that grants them, the grant is void: for when he has granted all he can, if we grant back the sovereignty, all is restored, as inseparably annexed thereunto.

---

35   Supreme commander.

36   The right to make a purchase or appropriation before any one else can.

37   A biblical quote, see Matthew 12:25, Mark 3:24, and Luke 11:17.

38   The English Civil War (1642–1648) between the Parliamentarians and the Royalists.

This great authority being indivisible, and inseparably annexed to the sovereignty, there is little ground for the opinion of them that say of sovereign kings, though they be *singulis majores*,[39] of greater power than every one of their subjects, yet they be *universis minores*,[40] of less power than them all together. For if by *all together*, they mean not the collective body as one person, then *all together* and *every one* signify the same; and the speech is absurd. But if by *all together*, they understand them as one person (which person the sovereign bears), then the power of all together is the same with the sovereign's power; and so again the speech is absurd: which absurdity they see well enough when the sovereignty is in an assembly of the people; but in a monarch they see it not; and yet the power of sovereignty is the same in whomsoever it be placed.

And as the power, so also the honour of the sovereign, ought to be greater than that of any or all the subjects. For in the sovereignty is the fountain of honour. The dignities of lord, earl, duke, and prince are his creatures. As in the presence of the master, the servants are equal, and without any honour at all; so are the subjects, in the presence of the sovereign. And though they shine some more, some less, when they are out of his sight; yet in his presence, they shine no more than the stars in presence of the sun.

But a man may here object that the condition of subjects is very miserable, as being obnoxious to the lusts and other irregular passions of him or them that have so unlimited a power in their hands. And commonly they that live under a monarch think it the fault of monarchy; and they that live under the government of democracy, or other sovereign assembly, attribute all the inconvenience to that form of commonwealth; whereas the power in all forms, if they be perfect enough to protect them, is the same: not considering that the estate of man can never be without some incommodity or other; and that the greatest that in any form of government can possibly happen to the people in general is scarce sensible, in respect of the miseries and horrible calamities that accompany a civil war, or that dissolute condition of masterless men without subjection to laws and a coercive power to tie their hands from rapine and revenge: nor considering that the greatest pressure of sovereign governors proceedeth, not from any delight or profit they can expect in the damage weakening of their subjects, in whose vigour consisteth their own strength and glory, but in the restiveness of themselves that, unwillingly contributing to their own defence, make it necessary for their governors to draw from them what they can in time of peace that they may have means on any emergent occasion, or sudden need, to resist or take advantage on their enemies. For all men are by nature provided of notable multiplying glasses[41] (that is their passions and self-love) through which every little payment appeareth a great grievance, but are destitute of those prospective glasses[42] (namely moral and civil science) to see afar off the miseries that hang over them and cannot without such payments be avoided.

---

39 Greater than the individual.
40 Less than the collective.
41 Magnifying glasses.
42 Telescopes.

JOHN STUART MILL
On Liberty

For some information on Mill's life and his overall philosophical project, please see the notes on Mill in Chapter 2.

What Is the Structure of This Reading?

On Liberty is a short five-chapter book, the first, second, and fourth chapters of which are reprinted here. Mill's topic is the extent to which the state, and society in general, ought to have authority over the lives of individuals. He begins by introducing this issue and distinguishing two forms of the problem, one historical and the other more modern. The problem of setting limits to society's claims upon the individual, Mill asserts, is "the principal question in human affairs" but, he laments, its solution has not yet been put on a properly rational footing. Mill seeks to address this by formulating "one very simple principle"—sometimes today known as the "harm principle"—that should "govern absolutely the dealings of society with the individual in the way of compulsion and control." After some clarificatory remarks about this principle, Mill argues in defense of it beginning, in Chapter II, with the particular case of liberty of thought and discussion.

Mill's argument for the freedom of thought has three parts. He considers, first, the possibility that the received opinions might be false and the heretical ones true; second, the possibility that the received views are completely true and the heresy false; and lastly, a situation where dogma and heresy both contain only a part of the truth. In each case, Mill argues, allowing complete freedom of thought and discussion provides much greater value than harm to society.

In Chapter III (not included here) Mill discusses the importance of individuality to human well-being, describing it as a valuable component of personal happiness and an essential motor of social progress. In Chapter IV, therefore, he goes on to consider the question of the proper borderline between personal individuality and social authority, and uses his "harm principle" to show how this border should be drawn. The final chapter (not included) describes some illustrative applications of the principle to detailed sample cases, such as trade regulation, liquor taxation, and marriage laws.

Some Common Misconceptions

1. In arguing for the freedom of thought and discussion, Mill asserts we can never be *completely sure* that views which oppose our own, and which we might want to suppress, are not true (and thus we can never be completely sure that our own views are not false). However, he stresses that he does not mean that we should never feel certain of our own views, or that we should never act on them, or even that we should not attempt to persuade others of their truth. Mill is by no means a skeptic about the possibility of human knowledge and certainty. Rather, Mill argues that we should not *force* others to adopt our views by preventing them from hearing or thinking about alternative positions.

2. In arguing for firm limits on the authority of society over the individual, Mill is not arguing for the kind of a *laissez-faire* system in which everyone is assumed to be fundamentally self-interested, and where individuals are thought to have no moral duties towards their fellow-citizens except those arising from their own self-interest. On the contrary, he claims "[h]uman beings owe to each other help to distinguish the better from the worse, and encouragement to choose the former and avoid the latter," and he thought it was very much society's role to provide opportunities and incentives for self-improvement to its citizens.

Similarly, Mill is not simply claiming that society should interfere with individuals as little as possible—that, for example, the coercion of individuals by the state is always a bad thing and should be resorted to only when necessary. By contrast, he thinks there is a sphere in which society should not interfere with its members but also a sphere in which it *ought* to do so: individuals do have duties to the other members of the societies of which they are a part, and society has the right to force people to perform those duties.

How Important and Influential Is This Passage?

Mill's *On Liberty* has been a 'classic' since it was first published. To his great satisfaction, it immediately inspired intense debate between fervent supporters of the views expressed in the book and sharp critics of them, and—though many of the ideas it contains have now become quite familiar—the work is still the focus of substantial controversy today. *On Liberty* is generally considered to be one of the central statements of classical liberalism, and one of the finest defenses of individualism and freedom of thought ever written.

Suggestions for Critical Reflection

1. Mill suggests that, in modern democratic societies, the question of individual liberty requires "a different and more fundamental treatment" than it has historically been given, since in the past people were governed by an independent ruler while in a democracy it is "the people" themselves who exercise power. What exactly is the difference that democracy makes to the question of individual liberty, according to Mill? Do you think Mill might say—or should have said—that the rise of democracy, ironically, makes it *harder* for individuals to be free of illegitimate social interference?

2. Mill asserts (famously) that "the only purpose for which power can be rightfully exercised over any member of a civilized community, against his will, is to prevent harm to others." Given this principle, it is obviously crucial to specify what constitutes "harm." Does Mill ever do so adequately? What is the best way of cashing out this crucial concept? Will it require drawing a distinction between *real* harms and what people merely *perceive* to be a harm to them (such as, say, witnessing a homosexual couple kissing)? If so, how can these 'real' harms be distinguished from the merely apparent ones? *Is* there a way of doing so that supports all the conclusions Mill wants to draw?

3. Before he begins his defense of his "harm principle," Mill notes that "I regard utility as the ultimate appeal on all ethical questions." If you have read the selection from Mill's *Utilitarianism* in Chapter 2, you might want to consider how much of his subsequent reasoning is rooted in utilitarianism … or indeed, whether the principle he defends in *On Liberty* is even *consistent* with Mill's utilitarian theory. What do you think Mill means by "utility in the largest sense, grounded on the permanent interests of man as a progressive being"?

4 "The only freedom which deserves the name, is that of pursuing our own good in our own way…." Is this true, or might there be a deeper, more valuable kind of freedom? What if someone's conception of their own good is importantly limited in some way, or is fallacious (even though it causes no harm to other people)? For example, what if I choose to spend my entire life in a basement watching TV, eating pizza, and growing and smoking (but not buying or selling) marijuana—could this really be an example of "the only freedom which deserves the name"? Further, what if I live this way, not through deliberate choice, but simply because it is how I grew up and is all I have ever experienced, and suppose I would, in fact, be much happier if some social authority were empowered to force me to get out more and make some friends. Must Mill still say I am free *only* if society leaves me alone? If so, is he right about that?

5. Part of Mill's argument in Chapter II involves the claim that "[c]omplete liberty of contradicting and disproving our opinion, is the very condition which justifies us in assuming its truth for purposes of action; and on no other terms can a being with human faculties have any rational assurance of being right." Does Mill really mean that we can have *no* "rational assurance" of being right about anything unless there is *complete* freedom of thought on the issue? If so, does he show that this is a plausible claim? Is there a less black-and-white version of this claim which seems more plausible (and which Mill might really have meant)? If so, does this less extreme version adequately support Mill's conclusions about the value of complete freedom of thought?

6. Mill argues believing something merely on the basis of authority, even if it is true, "is not the way in which truth ought to be held by a rational being." That is, he seems to suggest, believing some claim to be true without first having considered all the available arguments for and against that claim is mere vacant "superstition" and not genuine knowledge. Do Mill's arguments make this claim seem plausible, or does it strike you as too extreme? If he is right, how much of what most people believe could count as genuine knowledge? Is there a less contentious intermediate position? If so, would this weaker claim still support Mill's conclusions about the value of complete freedom of thought?

7. Should people be free to express *any* opinion, whatsoever? Imagine the most morally offensive view you can (involving, for example, the horrible torture of innocent toddlers or the most bizarre and uncomfortable kind of sexual act): should society allow people to, for example, make and distribute movies advocating this view? What if, to your horror, these movies prove highly popular and lots of people start watching them: should they still be allowed? Where, if anywhere, should the line be drawn, and does Mill get this line right?

8. Mill begins Chapter IV by stating "every one who receives the protection of society owes a return for the benefit, and the fact of living in society renders it indispensable that each should be bound to observe a certain line of conduct towards the rest." This, according to Mill, is what justifies society in placing at least *some* limits on the freedom of the individual. Does Mill have an argument for this principle, or it is just an assumption he makes? How philosophically significant is this assumption? For example, do you agree (and does Mill mean) that you have duties to your fellow citizens—such as (according to Mill) the duty to serve in the army in times of war, or to perform jury duty when called upon, or to rescue someone who has fallen into an icy river—*merely* in virtue of your living in a society?

9. Mill tries to distinguish between the "natural" social penalties of having a poor and foolish character, and penalties that might be deliberately inflicted on stupid people to punish them for their stupidity. According to Mill, the former kind of harm is an inevitable and acceptable consequence of one's own choices, while the latter constitutes morally unacceptable social interference. Is the crucial distinction between "natural" and punitive social harms an entirely clear one? (For example, what about repeatedly passing someone over for promotion or preventing them from attending a social organization such as a club or educational institution? Would these be "natural" consequences of someone's unpopularity, or a way of punishing them for being unpopular?) If this distinction is unclear, how serious a problem is this for Mill's position?

10. Mill also distinguishes between "self-regarding" and "social" virtues and vices, and claims only the latter are, properly speaking, *moral* virtues and vices, and that only these are properly within the ambit of social control. Again, is this an entirely clear distinction? For example, is it clear which of your character traits affect only you, personally, and which affect other people as well? If this kind of distinction is unclear or

unworkable, how serious a blow is this for Mill's account of individual liberty?

Suggestions for Further Reading

Mill's works, and much of the secondary literature on his political and ethical writings, are described in the Suggestions for Further Reading for the Mill selection in Chapter 2. There are many editions of Mill's *On Liberty* available: two good ones are edited by Edward Alexander (published by Broadview Press, 1999) and Stefan Collini (published by Cambridge University Press, 1989). Alexis de Toqueville's 1840 book *Democracy in America* (trans. Delba Winthrop, University of Chicago Press, 2000) heavily influenced Mill, and is useful for understanding the concerns that led to his writing of *On Liberty*. A fascinating snapshot of the debate Mill unleashed with the publication of *On Liberty* can be found in Andrew Pyle (ed.), *Liberty: Contemporary Responses to John Stuart Mill* (Thoemmes Press, 1994).

In addition to works listed in Chapter 2, there are several helpful books which are specifically about Mill's *On Liberty*, including John Gray, *Mill on Liberty: A Defence* (Routledge, 1996); John C. Rees, *John Stuart Mill's "On Liberty"* (Oxford University Press, 1985); Jonathan Riley, *The Routledge Philosophy Guidebook to Mill On Liberty* (Routledge, 1998); and C.L. Ten, *Mill on Liberty* (Oxford University Press, 1980). Three collections of articles about the book are: Gerald Dworkin (ed.), *Mill's "On Liberty"* (Rowman & Littlefield, 1997); Gray and Smith (eds.), *J.S. Mill's On Liberty In Focus* (Routledge, 1991); and Peter Radcliffe (ed.), *Limits of Liberty: Studies of Mill's On Liberty* (Wadsworth, 1966).

More general books containing valuable discussions relevant to Mill's concerns in *On Liberty* include Isaiah Berlin, *Four Essays on Liberty* (Oxford University Press, 1969); Joel Feinberg, *Harm to Others: Moral Limits of Criminal Law*, Volume 1 (Oxford University Press, 1984); and Rolf Sartorius, *Individual Conduct and Social Norms* (Wadsworth, 1975).

Finally, of the many articles written about *On Liberty*, the following are recommended: D.G. Brown, "Mill on Harm to Others' Interests," *Political Studies* 26 (1978); Richard Freedman, "A New Exploration of Mill's Essay *On Liberty*," *Political Studies* 14 (1966); Ted Honderich, "The Worth of J.S. Mill on Liberty," *Political Studies* 22 (1974); Ted Honderich, "*On Liberty* and Morality—Dependent Harms," *Political Studies* 30 (1982); Jonathan Riley, "One Very Simple Principle," *Utilitas* 3 (1991); Mark Strasser, "Mill and the Utility of Liberty," *Philosophical Quarterly* 34 (1984); Jeremy Waldron, "Mill and the Value of Moral Distress," *Political Studies* 35 (1987); Geraint Williams, "Mill's Principle of Liberty," *Political Studies* 24 (1976); and Richard Wollheim, "John Stuart Mill and the Limits of State Action," *Social Research* 40 (1973).

from *On Liberty*[1]

Chapter I: Introductory

The subject of this Essay is not the so-called Liberty of the Will, so unfortunately opposed to the misnamed doctrine of Philosophical Necessity, but Civil, or Social Liberty: the nature and limits of the power which can be legitimately exercised by society over the individual. A question seldom stated, and hardly ever discussed, in general terms, but which profoundly influences the practical controversies of the age by its latent presence, and is likely soon to make itself recognized as the vital question of the future. It is so far from being new, that, in a certain sense, it has divided mankind, almost from the remotest ages, but in the stage of progress into which the more civilized portions of the species have now entered, it presents itself under new conditions, and requires a different and more fundamental treatment.

The struggle between Liberty and Authority is the most conspicuous feature in the portions of history with which we are earliest familiar, particularly in that of Greece, Rome, and England. But in old times this contest was between subjects, or some classes of subjects, and the government. By liberty, was meant protection against the tyranny of the political rulers. The rulers were conceived (except in some of the popular governments of Greece) as in a necessarily antagonistic position to the people whom they ruled. They consisted of a governing One, or a govern-

---

1   *On Liberty* was first published in London in 1859.

ing tribe or caste, who derived their authority from inheritance or conquest; who, at all events, did not hold it at the pleasure of the governed, and whose supremacy men did not venture, perhaps did not desire, to contest, whatever precautions might be taken against its oppressive exercise. Their power was regarded as necessary, but also as highly dangerous; as a weapon which they would attempt to use against their subjects, no less than against external enemies. To prevent the weaker members of the community from being preyed upon by innumerable vultures, it was needful that there should be an animal of prey stronger than the rest, commissioned to keep them down. But as the king of the vultures would be no less bent upon preying upon the flock than any of the minor harpies, it was indispensable to be in a perpetual attitude of defence against his beak and claws. The aim, therefore, of patriots, was to set limits to the power which the ruler should be suffered to exercise over the community; and this limitation was what they meant by liberty. It was attempted in two ways. First, by obtaining a recognition of certain immunities, called political liberties or rights, which it was to be regarded as a breach of duty in the ruler to infringe, and which, if he did infringe, specific resistance, or general rebellion, was held to be justifiable. A second, and generally a later expedient, was the establishment of constitutional checks; by which the consent of the community, or of a body of some sort supposed to represent its interests, was made a necessary condition to some of the more important acts of the governing power. To the first of these modes of limitation, the ruling power, in most European countries, was compelled, more or less, to submit. It was not so with the second; and to attain this, or when already in some degree possessed, to attain it more completely, became everywhere the principal object of the lovers of liberty. And so long as mankind were content to combat one enemy by another, and to be ruled by a master, on condition of being guaranteed more or less efficaciously against his tyranny, they did not carry their aspirations beyond this point.

A time, however, came in the progress of human affairs, when men ceased to think it a necessity of nature that their governors should be an independent power, opposed in interest to themselves. It appeared to them much better that the various magistrates of the State should be their tenants or delegates, revocable at their pleasure. In that way alone, it seemed, could they have complete security that the powers of government would never be abused to their disadvantage. By degrees, this new demand for elective and temporary rulers became the prominent object of the exertions of the popular party, wherever any such party existed; and superseded, to a considerable extent, the previous efforts to limit the power of rulers. As the struggle proceeded for making the ruling power emanate from the periodical choice of the ruled, some persons began to think that too much importance had been attached to the limitation of the power itself. That (it might seem) was a resource against rulers whose interests were habitually opposed to those of the people. What was now wanted was, that the rulers should be identified with the people; that their interest and will should be the interest and will of the nation. The nation did not need to be protected against its own will. There was no fear of its tyrannizing over itself. Let the rulers be effectually responsible to it, promptly removable by it, and it could afford to trust them with power of which it could itself dictate the use to be made. Their power was but the nation's own power, concentrated, and in a form convenient for exercise. This mode of thought, or rather perhaps of feeling, was common among the last generation of European liberalism, in the Continental section of which, it still apparently predominates. Those who admit any limit to what a government may do, except in the case of such governments as they think ought not to exist, stand out as brilliant exceptions among the political thinkers of the Continent. A similar tone of sentiment might by this time have been prevalent in our own country, if the circumstances which for a time encouraged it had continued unaltered.

But, in political and philosophical theories, as well as in persons, success discloses faults and infirmities which failure might have concealed from observation. The notion, that the people have no need to limit their power over themselves, might seem axiomatic, when popular government was a thing only dreamed about, or read of as having existed at some distant period of the past. Neither was that notion necessarily disturbed by such temporary aberrations as those of the French

Revolution,[2] the worst of which were the work of an usurping few, and which, in any case, belonged, not to the permanent working of popular institutions, but to a sudden and convulsive outbreak against monarchical and aristocratic despotism. In time, however, a democratic republic[3] came to occupy a large portion of the earth's surface, and made itself felt as one of the most powerful members of the community of nations; and elective and responsible government became subject to the observations and criticisms which wait upon a great existing fact. It was now perceived that such phrases as "self-government," and "the power of the people over themselves," do not express the true state of the case. The "people" who exercise the power, are not always the same people with those over whom it is exercised, and the "self-government" spoken of, is not the government of each by himself, but of each by all the rest. The will of the people, moreover, practically means, the will of the most numerous or the most active *part* of the people; the majority, or those who succeed in making themselves accepted as the majority; the people, consequently, *may* desire to oppress a part of their number; and precautions are as much needed against this, as against any other abuse of power. The limitation, therefore, of the power of government over individuals, loses none of its importance when the holders of power are regularly accountable to the community, that is, to the strongest party therein. This view of things, recommending itself equally to the intelligence of thinkers and to the inclination of those important classes in European society to whose real or supposed interests democracy is adverse, has had no difficulty in establishing itself; and in political speculations "the tyranny of the majority" is now generally included among the evils against which society requires to be on its guard.

---

2   The French Revolution, which began with the storming of the Bastille prison in 1789, toppled the Bourbon monarchy—King Louis XVI was executed in 1793—but failed to produce a stable form of republican government and, after a period of ruthless extremism known as the Reign of Terror (1793–1794), was eventually replaced by Napoleon Bonaparte's imperial reign in 1799.

3   The United States of America.

Like other tyrannies, the tyranny of the majority was at first, and is still vulgarly,[4] held in dread, chiefly as operating through the acts of the public authorities. But reflecting persons perceived that when society is itself the tyrant—society collectively, over the separate individuals who compose it—its means of tyrannizing are not restricted to the acts which it may do by the hands of its political functionaries. Society can and does execute its own mandates: and if it issues wrong mandates instead of right, or any mandates at all in things with which it ought not to meddle, it practises a social tyranny more formidable than many kinds of political oppression, since, though not usually upheld by such extreme penalties, it leaves fewer means of escape, penetrating much more deeply into the details of life, and enslaving the soul itself. Protection, therefore, against the tyranny of the magistrate is not enough; there needs protection also against the tyranny of the prevailing opinion and feeling; against the tendency of society to impose, by other means than civil penalties, its own ideas and practices as rules of conduct on those who dissent from them; to fetter the development, and, if possible, prevent the formation, of any individuality not in harmony with its ways, and compel all characters to fashion themselves upon the model of its own. There is a limit to the legitimate interference of collective opinion with individual independence; and to find that limit, and maintain it against encroachment, is as indispensable to a good condition of human affairs, as protection against political despotism.

But though this proposition is not likely to be contested in general terms, the practical question, where to place the limit—how to make the fitting adjustment between individual independence and social control—is a subject on which nearly everything remains to be done. All that makes existence valuable to any one, depends on the enforcement of restraints upon the actions of other people. Some rules of conduct, therefore, must be imposed, by law in the first place, and by opinion on many things which are not fit subjects for the operation of law. What these rules should be, is the principal question in human affairs; but if we except a few of the most obvious

---

4   Commonly, popularly.

cases, it is one of those which least progress has been made in resolving. No two ages, and scarcely any two countries, have decided it alike; and the decision of one age or country is a wonder to another. Yet the people of any given age and country no more suspect any difficulty in it, than if it were a subject on which mankind had always been agreed. The rules which obtain among themselves appear to them self-evident and self-justifying. This all but universal illusion is one of the examples of the magical influence of custom, which is not only, as the proverb says a second nature, but is continually mistaken for the first. The effect of custom, in preventing any misgiving respecting the rules of conduct which mankind impose on one another, is all the more complete because the subject is one on which it is not generally considered necessary that reasons should be given, either by one person to others, or by each to himself. People are accustomed to believe and have been encouraged in the belief by some who aspire to the character of philosophers, that their feelings, on subjects of this nature, are better than reasons, and render reasons unnecessary. The practical principle which guides them to their opinions on the regulation of human conduct, is the feeling in each person's mind that everybody should be required to act as he, and those with whom he sympathizes, would like them to act. No one, indeed, acknowledges to himself that his standard of judgment is his own liking; but an opinion on a point of conduct, not supported by reasons, can only count as one person's preference; and if the reasons, when given, are a mere appeal to a similar preference felt by other people, it is still only many people's liking instead of one. To an ordinary man, however, his own preference, thus supported, is not only a perfectly satisfactory reason, but the only one he generally has for any of his notions of morality, taste, or propriety, which are not expressly written in his religious creed; and his chief guide in the interpretation even of that. Men's opinions, accordingly, on what is laudable or blameable, are affected by all the multifarious causes which influence their wishes in regard to the conduct of others, and which are as numerous as those which determine their wishes on any other subject. Sometimes their reason—at other times their prejudices or superstitions: often their social affections, not seldom

their anti-social ones, their envy or jealousy, their arrogance or contemptuousness: but most commonly, their desires or fears for themselves—their legitimate or illegitimate self-interest. Wherever there is an ascendant class, a large portion of the morality of the country emanates from its class interests, and its feelings of class superiority. The morality between Spartans and Helots,[5] between planters and negroes, between princes and subjects, between nobles and roturiers,[6] between men and women, has been for the most part the creation of these class interests and feelings: and the sentiments thus generated, react in turn upon the moral feelings of the members of the ascendant class, in their relations among themselves. Where, on the other hand, a class, formerly ascendant, has lost its ascendancy, or where its ascendancy is unpopular, the prevailing moral sentiments frequently bear the impress of an impatient dislike of superiority. Another grand determining principle of the rules of conduct, both in act and forbearance which have been enforced by law or opinion, has been the servility of mankind towards the supposed preferences or aversions of their temporal masters, or of their gods. This servility though essentially selfish, is not hypocrisy; it gives rise to perfectly genuine sentiments of abhorrence; it made men burn magicians and heretics. Among so many baser influences, the general and obvious interests of society have of course had a share, and a large one, in the direction of the moral sentiments: less, however, as a matter of reason, and on their own account, than as a consequence of the sympathies and antipathies which grew out of them: and sympathies and antipathies which had little or nothing to do with the interests of society, have made themselves felt in the establishment of moralities with quite as great force.

The likings and dislikings of society, or of some powerful portion of it, are thus the main thing which has practically determined the rules laid down for gen-

---

5   Sparta, a city-state in ancient Greece, was renowned for its militarism and social and political rigidity. Helots were a class of Spartan serfs, a rank that came between slaves and free citizens.

6   Roturiers are commoners, people of no aristocratic rank, holding land through the payment of rent.

eral observance, under the penalties of law or opinion. And in general, those who have been in advance of society in thought and feeling, have left this condition of things unassailed in principle, however they may have come into conflict with it in some of its details. They have occupied themselves rather in inquiring what things society ought to like or dislike, than in questioning whether its likings or dislikings should be a law to individuals. They preferred endeavouring to alter the feelings of mankind on the particular points on which they were themselves heretical, rather than make common cause in defence of freedom, with heretics generally. The only case in which the higher ground has been taken on principle and maintained with consistency, by any but an individual here and there, is that of religious belief: a case instructive in many ways, and not least so as forming a most striking instance of the fallibility of what is called the moral sense: for the *odium theologicum*,[7] in a sincere bigot, is one of the most unequivocal cases of moral feeling. Those who first broke the yoke of what called itself the Universal Church,[8] were in general as little willing to permit difference of religious opinion as that church itself. But when the heat of the conflict was over, without giving a complete victory to any party, and each church or sect was reduced to limit its hopes to retaining possession of the ground it already occupied; minorities, seeing that they had no chance of becoming majorities, were under the necessity of pleading to those whom they could not convert, for permission to differ. It is accordingly on this battle-field, almost solely, that the rights of the individual against society have been asserted on broad grounds of principle, and the claim of society to exercise authority over dissentients[9] openly controverted. The great writers to whom the world owes what religious liberty it possesses, have mostly asserted freedom of conscience as an indefeasible right, and denied absolutely that a human being is accountable to others for his religious belief. Yet so natural to mankind is intolerance in whatever they really care about, that

religious freedom has hardly anywhere been practically realized, except where religious indifference, which dislikes to have its peace disturbed by theological quarrels, has added its weight to the scale. In the minds of almost all religious persons, even in the most tolerant countries, the duty of toleration is admitted with tacit reserves. One person will bear with dissent in matters of church government, but not of dogma; another can tolerate everybody, short of a Papist[10] or an Unitarian;[11] another, every one who believes in revealed religion;[12] a few extend their charity a little further, but stop at the belief in a God and in a future state.[13] Wherever the sentiment of the majority is still genuine and intense, it is found to have abated little of its claim to be obeyed.

In England, from the peculiar circumstances of our political history, though the yoke of opinion is perhaps heavier, that of law is lighter, than in most other countries of Europe; and there is considerable jealousy of[14] direct interference, by the legislative or the executive power with private conduct; not so much from any just regard for the independence of the individual, as from the still subsisting habit of looking on the government as representing an opposite interest to the public. The majority have not yet learnt to feel the power of the government their power, or its opinions their opinions. When they do so, individual liberty will probably be as much exposed to invasion from the government, as it already is from public opinion. But, as yet, there is a considerable amount of feeling ready to be called forth against any attempt of the law to control individuals in things in which they have not hitherto been accustomed to be controlled by it; and

---

7 Animosity or prejudice generated by religious differences.

8 Catholicism (from the Greek *katholikos*—"universal").

9 Those who dissent, who disagree with a majority view.

10 A Roman Catholic, i.e., a follower of the Pope. (The term is generally considered offensive today.)

11 Unitarianism is a form of Christianity that rejects the doctrines of the Trinity—holding that God is an undivided unity—and thus denies the divinity of Jesus Christ. Unitarians, typically, also reject such doctrines as original sin and eternal punishment.

12 Religion based primarily on the revelations of God to humankind, as in a set of holy scriptures.

13 An afterlife in which people will be rewarded or punished for their behavior on earth.

14 Suspicion or resentment of.

this with very little discrimination as to whether the matter is, or is not, within the legitimate sphere of legal control; insomuch that the feeling, highly salutary on the whole, is perhaps quite as often misplaced as well grounded in the particular instances of its application. There is, in fact, no recognized principle by which the propriety or impropriety of government interference is customarily tested. People decide according to their personal preferences. Some, whenever they see any good to be done, or evil to be remedied, would willingly instigate the government to undertake the business; while others prefer to bear almost any amount of social evil, rather than add one to the departments of human interests amenable to governmental control. And men range themselves on one or the other side in any particular case, according to this general direction of their sentiments; or according to the degree of interest which they feel in the particular thing which it is proposed that the government should do; or according to the belief they entertain that the government would, or would not, do it in the manner they prefer; but very rarely on account of any opinion to which they consistently adhere, as to what things are fit to be done by a government. And it seems to me that, in consequence of this absence of rule or principle, one side is at present as often wrong as the other; the interference of government is, with about equal frequency, improperly invoked and improperly condemned.

The object of this Essay is to assert one very simple principle, as entitled to govern absolutely the dealings of society with the individual in the way of compulsion and control, whether the means used be physical force in the form of legal penalties, or the moral coercion of public opinion. That principle is, that the sole end for which mankind are warranted, individually or collectively in interfering with the liberty of action of any of their number, is self-protection. That the only purpose for which power can be rightfully exercised over any member of a civilized community, against his will, is to prevent harm to others. His own good, either physical or moral, is not a sufficient warrant. He cannot rightfully be compelled to do or forbear because it will be better for him to do so, because it will make him happier, because, in the opinions of others, to do so would be wise, or even right. These

are good reasons for remonstrating with him, or reasoning with him, or persuading him, or entreating him, but not for compelling him, or visiting him with any evil, in case he do otherwise. To justify that, the conduct from which it is desired to deter him must be calculated to produce evil to some one else. The only part of the conduct of any one, for which he is amenable to society, is that which concerns others. In the part which merely concerns himself, his independence is, of right, absolute. Over himself, over his own body and mind, the individual is sovereign.

It is, perhaps, hardly necessary to say that this doctrine is meant to apply only to human beings in the maturity of their faculties. We are not speaking of children, or of young persons below the age which the law may fix as that of manhood or womanhood. Those who are still in a state to require being taken care of by others, must be protected against their own actions as well as against external injury. For the same reason, we may leave out of consideration those backward states of society in which the race itself may be considered as in its nonage.[15] The early difficulties in the way of spontaneous progress are so great, that there is seldom any choice of means for overcoming them; and a ruler full of the spirit of improvement is warranted in the use of any expedients that will attain an end, perhaps otherwise unattainable. Despotism is a legitimate mode of government in dealing with barbarians, provided the end be their improvement, and the means justified by actually effecting that end. Liberty, as a principle, has no application to any state of things anterior to the time when mankind have become capable of being improved by free and equal discussion. Until then, there is nothing for them but implicit obedience to an Akbar or a Charlemagne,[16]

---

15   A period of immaturity, being underage.

16   Akbar the Great was Mogul emperor of northern India from 1556 until 1605. He is generally considered the founder of the Mogul empire, and was famous for implementing an effective administrative system, imposing religious tolerance, and making his court a center for art and literature. Charlemagne ("Charles the Great") was king of the Franks from 768 until 814. His armies conquered much of central and western Europe—including parts of Spain, Italy, Saxony, Bavaria,

if they are so fortunate as to find one. But as soon as mankind have attained the capacity of being guided to their own improvement by conviction or persuasion (a period long since reached in all nations with whom we need here concern ourselves), compulsion, either in the direct form or in that of pains and penalties for non-compliance, is no longer admissible as a means to their own good, and justifiable only for the security of others.

It is proper to state that I forego any advantage which could be derived to my argument from the idea of abstract right as a thing independent of utility. I regard utility as the ultimate appeal on all ethical questions; but it must be utility in the largest sense, grounded on the permanent interests of man as a progressive being. Those interests, I contend, authorize the subjection of individual spontaneity to external control, only in respect to those actions of each, which concern the interest of other people. If any one does an act hurtful to others, there is a *prima facie*[17] case for punishing him, by law, or, where legal penalties are not safely applicable, by general disapprobation.[18] There are also many positive acts for the benefit of others, which he may rightfully be compelled to perform; such as, to give evidence in a court of justice; to bear his fair share in the common defence, or in any other joint work necessary to the interest of the society of which he enjoys the protection; and to perform certain acts of individual beneficence, such as saving a fellow-creature's life, or interposing to protect the defenceless against ill-usage, things which whenever it is obviously a man's duty to do, he may rightfully be made responsible to society for not doing. A person may cause evil to others not only by his actions but by his inaction, and in either case he is justly accountable to them for the injury. The latter case, it is true, requires a much more cautious exercise of compulsion

than the former. To make any one answerable for doing evil to others, is the rule; to make him answerable for not preventing evil, is, comparatively speaking, the exception. Yet there are many cases clear enough and grave enough to justify that exception. In all things which regard the external relations of the individual, he is *de jure*[19] amenable to those whose interests are concerned, and if need be, to society as their protector. There are often good reasons for not holding him to the responsibility; but these reasons must arise from the special expediencies of the case: either because it is a kind of case in which he is on the whole likely to act better, when left to his own discretion, than when controlled in any way in which society have it in their power to control him; or because the attempt to exercise control would produce other evils, greater than those which it would prevent. When such reasons as these preclude the enforcement of responsibility, the conscience of the agent himself should step into the vacant judgment-seat, and protect those interests of others which have no external protection; judging himself all the more rigidly, because the case does not admit of his being made accountable to the judgment of his fellow-creatures.

But there is a sphere of action in which society, as distinguished from the individual, has, if any, only an indirect interest; comprehending all that portion of a person's life and conduct which affects only himself, or, if it also affects others, only with their free, voluntary, and undeceived consent and participation. When I say only himself, I mean directly, and in the first instance: for whatever affects himself, may affect others through himself; and the objection which may be grounded on this contingency, will receive consideration in the sequel. This, then, is the appropriate region of human liberty. It comprises, first, the inward domain of consciousness; demanding liberty of conscience, in the most comprehensive sense; liberty of thought and feeling; absolute freedom of opinion and sentiment on all subjects, practical or speculative, scientific, moral, or theological. The liberty of expressing and publishing opinions may seem to fall under a different principle, since it belongs to that part of the conduct of an individual which concerns other

---

Austria, and Hungary—and, in 800, he was anointed the first Holy Roman Emperor by Pope Leo III. Like Akbar, Charlemagne is known for making his court a great center of culture and scholarship, and for imposing an effective legal and administrative structure on his dominions.

17 At first sight, on first impression.

18 Strong (moral) disapproval.

19 By law, rightfully.

people; but, being almost of as much importance as the liberty of thought itself, and resting in great part on the same reasons, is practically inseparable from it. Secondly, the principle requires liberty of tastes and pursuits; of framing the plan of our life to suit our own character; of doing as we like, subject to such consequences as may follow; without impediment from our fellow-creatures, so long as what we do does not harm them even though they should think our conduct foolish, perverse, or wrong. Thirdly, from this liberty of each individual, follows the liberty, within the same limits, of combination among individuals; freedom to unite, for any purpose not involving harm to others: the persons combining being supposed to be of full age, and not forced or deceived.

No society in which these liberties are not, on the whole, respected, is free, whatever may be its form of government; and none is completely free in which they do not exist absolute and unqualified. The only freedom which deserves the name, is that of pursuing our own good in our own way, so long as we do not attempt to deprive others of theirs, or impede their efforts to obtain it. Each is the proper guardian of his own health, whether bodily, or mental or spiritual. Mankind are greater gainers by suffering each other to live as seems good to themselves, than by compelling each to live as seems good to the rest.

Though this doctrine is anything but new, and, to some persons, may have the air of a truism, there is no doctrine which stands more directly opposed to the general tendency of existing opinion and practice. Society has expended fully as much effort in the attempt (according to its lights) to compel people to conform to its notions of personal, as of social excellence. The ancient commonwealths thought themselves entitled to practise, and the ancient philosophers countenanced, the regulation of every part of private conduct by public authority, on the ground that the State had a deep interest in the whole bodily and mental discipline of every one of its citizens, a mode of thinking which may have been admissible in small republics surrounded by powerful enemies, in constant peril of being subverted by foreign attack or internal commotion, and to which even a short interval of relaxed energy and self-command might so easily be fatal, that they could not afford to wait

for the salutary permanent effects of freedom. In the modern world, the greater size of political communities, and above all, the separation between the spiritual and temporal authority (which placed the direction of men's consciences in other hands than those which controlled their worldly affairs), prevented so great an interference by law in the details of private life; but the engines of moral repression have been wielded more strenuously against divergence from the reigning opinion in self-regarding, than even in social matters; religion, the most powerful of the elements which have entered into the formation of moral feeling, having almost always been governed either by the ambition of a hierarchy, seeking control over every department of human conduct, or by the spirit of Puritanism. And some of those modern reformers who have placed themselves in strongest opposition to the religions of the past, have been noway behind either churches or sects in their assertion of the right of spiritual domination: M. Comte, in particular, whose social system, as unfolded in his *Système de Politique Positive*,[20] aims at establishing (though by moral more than by legal appliances) a despotism of society over the individual, surpassing anything contemplated in the political ideal of the most rigid disciplinarian among the ancient philosophers.

Apart from the peculiar tenets of individual thinkers, there is also in the world at large an increasing inclination to stretch unduly the powers of society over the individual, both by the force of opinion and even by that of legislation: and as the tendency of all the changes taking place in the world is to strengthen society, and diminish the power of the individual, this encroachment is not one of the evils which tend spontaneously to disappear, but, on the contrary, to grow more and more formidable. The disposition of mankind, whether as rulers or as fellow-citizens, to impose their own opinions and inclinations as a rule of conduct on others, is so energetically supported by some of the best and by some of the worst feelings

---

20   Auguste Comte (1789–1857), a French philosopher, social theorist, and founder of positivism, published *Système de Politique Positive* [*The System of Positive Polity*] in 1851–54. Mill later wrote a book on his work, *Auguste Comte and Positivism* (1865).

incident to human nature, that it is hardly ever kept under restraint by anything but want of power; and as the power is not declining, but growing, unless a strong barrier of moral conviction can be raised against the mischief, we must expect, in the present circumstances of the world, to see it increase.

It will be convenient for the argument, if, instead of at once entering upon the general thesis, we confine ourselves in the first instance to a single branch of it, on which the principle here stated is, if not fully, yet to a certain point, recognized by the current opinions. This one branch is the Liberty of Thought: from which it is impossible to separate the cognate liberty of speaking and of writing. Although these liberties, to some considerable amount, form part of the political morality of all countries which profess religious toleration and free institutions, the grounds, both philosophical and practical, on which they rest, are perhaps not so familiar to the general mind, nor so thoroughly appreciated by many even of the leaders of opinion, as might have been expected. Those grounds, when rightly understood, are of much wider application than to only one division of the subject, and a thorough consideration of this part of the question will be found the best introduction to the remainder. Those to whom nothing which I am about to say will be new, may therefore, I hope, excuse me, if on a subject which for now three centuries has been so often discussed, I venture on one discussion more.

Chapter II: Of the Liberty of Thought and Discussion

The time, it is to be hoped, is gone by when any defence would be necessary of the "liberty of the press" as one of the securities against corrupt or tyrannical government. No argument, we may suppose, can now be needed, against permitting a legislature or an executive, not identified in interest with the people, to prescribe opinions to them, and determine what doctrines or what arguments they shall be allowed to hear. This aspect of the question, besides, has been so often and so triumphantly enforced by preceding writers, that it needs not be specially insisted on in this place. Though the law of England, on the subject of the press, is as servile to this day as it was in the time

of the Tudors,[21] there is little danger of its being actually put in force against political discussion, except during some temporary panic, when fear of insurrection drives ministers and judges from their propriety;[22] and, speaking generally, it is not, in constitutional

---

21   The royal dynasty ruling England from 1485 to 1603 (Henry VII–Elizabeth I).

22   [Author's note] These words had scarcely been written, when, as if to give them an emphatic contradiction, occurred the Government Press Prosecutions of 1858. That ill-judged interference with the liberty of public discussion has not, however, induced me to alter a single word in the text, nor has it at all weakened my conviction that, moments of panic excepted, the era of pains and penalties for political discussion has, in our own country, passed away. For, in the first place, the prosecutions were not persisted in; and in the second, they were never, properly speaking, political prosecutions. The offence charged was not that of criticizing institutions, or the acts or persons of rulers, but of circulating what was deemed an immoral doctrine, the lawfulness of Tyrannicide.

If the arguments of the present chapter are of any validity, there ought to exist the fullest liberty of professing and discussing, as a matter of ethical conviction, any doctrine, however immoral it may be considered. It would, therefore, be irrelevant and out of place to examine here, whether the doctrine of Tyrannicide deserves that title. I shall content myself with saying, that the subject has been at all times one of the open questions of morals, that the act of a private citizen in striking down a criminal, who, by raising himself above the law, has placed himself beyond the reach of legal punishment or control, has been accounted by whole nations, and by some of the best and wisest of men, not a crime, but an act of exalted virtue and that, right or wrong, it is not of the nature of assassination but of civil war. As such, I hold that the instigation to it, in a specific case, may be a proper subject of punishment, but only if an overt act has followed, and at least a probable connection can be established between the act and the instigation. Even then it is not a foreign government, but the very government assailed, which alone, in the exercise of self-defence, can legitimately punish attacks directed against its own existence.

countries, to be apprehended that the government, whether completely responsible to the people or not, will often attempt to control the expression of opinion, except when in doing so it makes itself the organ of the general intolerance of the public. Let us suppose, therefore, that the government is entirely at one with the people, and never thinks of exerting any power of coercion unless in agreement with what it conceives to be their voice. But I deny the right of the people to exercise such coercion, either by themselves or by their government. The power itself is illegitimate. The best government has no more title to it than the worst. It is as noxious, or more noxious, when exerted in accordance with public opinion, than when in opposition to it. If all mankind minus one, were of one opinion, and only one person were of the contrary opinion, mankind would be no more justified in silencing that one person, than he, if he had the power, would be justified in silencing mankind. Were an opinion a personal possession of no value except to the owner; if to be obstructed in the enjoyment of it were simply a private injury, it would make some difference whether the injury was inflicted only on a few persons or on many. But the peculiar evil of silencing the expression of an opinion is, that it is robbing the human race; posterity as well as the existing generation; those who dissent from the opinion, still more than those who hold it. If the opinion is right, they are deprived of the opportunity of exchanging error for truth: if wrong, they lose, what is almost as great a benefit, the clearer perception and livelier impression of truth, produced by its collision with error.

It is necessary to consider separately these two hypotheses, each of which has a distinct branch of the argument corresponding to it. We can never be sure that the opinion we are endeavouring to stifle is a false opinion; and if we were sure, stifling it would be an evil still.

First: the opinion which it is attempted to suppress by authority may possibly be true. Those who desire to suppress it, of course deny its truth; but they are not infallible. They have no authority to decide the question for all mankind, and exclude every other person from the means of judging. To refuse a hearing to an opinion, because they are sure that it is false, is to assume that *their* certainty is the same thing as *absolute*

certainty. All silencing of discussion is an assumption of infallibility. Its condemnation may be allowed to rest on this common argument, not the worse for being common.

Unfortunately for the good sense of mankind, the fact of their fallibility is far from carrying the weight in their practical judgment, which is always allowed to it in theory; for while every one well knows himself to be fallible, few think it necessary to take any precautions against their own fallibility, or admit the supposition that any opinion of which they feel very certain, may be one of the examples of the error to which they acknowledge themselves to be liable. Absolute princes, or others who are accustomed to unlimited deference, usually feel this complete confidence in their own opinions on nearly all subjects. People more happily situated, who sometimes hear their opinions disputed, and are not wholly unused to be set right when they are wrong, place the same unbounded reliance only on such of their opinions as are shared by all who surround them, or to whom they habitually defer: for in proportion to a man's want of confidence in his own solitary judgment, does he usually repose, with implicit trust, on the infallibility of "the world" in general. And the world, to each individual, means the part of it with which he comes in contact; his party, his sect, his church, his class of society: the man may be called, by comparison, almost liberal and large-minded to whom it means anything so comprehensive as his own country or his own age. Nor is his faith in this collective authority at all shaken by his being aware that other ages, countries, sects, churches, classes, and parties have thought, and even now think, the exact reverse. He devolves upon his own world the responsibility of being in the right against the dissentient worlds of other people; and it never troubles him that mere accident has decided which of these numerous worlds is the object of his reliance, and that the same causes which make him a Churchman in London, would have made him a Buddhist or a Confucian in Pekin.[23] Yet it is as evident in itself as any amount of argument can make it, that ages are no more infallible than individuals; every age having held many opinions which subsequent

---

23 Peking (today called Beijing), the capital of China.

ages have deemed not only false but absurd; and it is as certain that many opinions, now general, will be rejected by future ages, as it is that many, once general, are rejected by the present.

The objection likely to be made to this argument, would probably take some such form as the following. There is no greater assumption of infallibility in forbidding the propagation of error, than in any other thing which is done by public authority on its own judgment and responsibility. Judgment is given to men that they may use it. Because it may be used erroneously, are men to be told that they ought not to use it at all? To prohibit what they think pernicious, is not claiming exemption from error, but fulfilling the duty incumbent on them, although fallible, of acting on their conscientious conviction. If we were never to act on our opinions, because those opinions may be wrong, we should leave all our interests uncared for, and all our duties unperformed. An objection which applies to all conduct can be no valid objection to any conduct in particular. It is the duty of governments, and of individuals, to form the truest opinions they can; to form them carefully, and never impose them upon others unless they are quite sure of being right. But when they are sure (such reasoners may say), it is not conscientiousness but cowardice to shrink from acting on their opinions, and allow doctrines which they honestly think dangerous to the welfare of mankind, either in this life or in another, to be scattered abroad without restraint, because other people, in less enlightened times, have persecuted opinions now believed to be true. Let us take care, it may be said, not to make the same mistake: but governments and nations have made mistakes in other things, which are not denied to be fit subjects for the exercise of authority: they have laid on bad taxes, made unjust wars. Ought we therefore to lay on no taxes, and, under whatever provocation, make no wars? Men, and governments, must act to the best of their ability. There is no such thing as absolute certainty, but there is assurance sufficient for the purposes of human life. We may, and must, assume our opinion to be true for the guidance of our own conduct: and it is assuming no more when we forbid bad men to pervert society by the propagation of opinions which we regard as false and pernicious.

I answer, that it is assuming very much more. There is the greatest difference between presuming an opinion to be true, because, with every opportunity for contesting it, it has not been refuted, and assuming its truth for the purpose of not permitting its refutation. Complete liberty of contradicting and disproving our opinion, is the very condition which justifies us in assuming its truth for purposes of action; and on no other terms can a being with human faculties have any rational assurance of being right.

When we consider either the history of opinion, or the ordinary conduct of human life, to what is it to be ascribed that the one and the other are no worse than they are? Not certainly to the inherent force of the human understanding; for, on any matter not self-evident, there are ninety-nine persons totally incapable of judging of it, for one who is capable; and the capacity of the hundredth person is only comparative; for the majority of the eminent men of every past generation held many opinions now known to be erroneous, and did or approved numerous things which no one will now justify. Why is it, then, that there is on the whole a preponderance among mankind of rational opinions and rational conduct? If there really is this preponderance—which there must be, unless human affairs are, and have always been, in an almost desperate state—it is owing to a quality of the human mind, the source of everything respectable in man, either as an intellectual or as a moral being, namely, that his errors are corrigible.[24] He is capable of rectifying his mistakes by discussion and experience. Not by experience alone. There must be discussion, to show how experience is to be interpreted. Wrong opinions and practices gradually yield to fact and argument: but facts and arguments, to produce any effect on the mind, must be brought before it. Very few facts are able to tell their own story, without comments to bring out their meaning. The whole strength and value, then, of human judgment, depending on the one property, that it can be set right when it is wrong, reliance can be placed on it only when the means of setting it right are kept constantly at hand. In the case of any person whose judgment is really deserving of confidence, how has it become so? Because he has kept his mind open to

_____

24   Correctable.

criticism of his opinions and conduct. Because it has been his practice to listen to all that could be said against him; to profit by as much of it as was just, and expound to himself, and upon occasion to others, the fallacy of what was fallacious. Because he has felt, that the only way in which a human being can make some approach to knowing the whole of a subject, is by hearing what can be said about it by persons of every variety of opinion, and studying all modes in which it can be looked at by every character of mind. No wise man ever acquired his wisdom in any mode but this; nor is it in the nature of human intellect to become wise in any other manner. The steady habit of correcting and completing his own opinion by collating it with those of others, so far from causing doubt and hesitation in carrying it into practice, is the only stable foundation for a just reliance on it: for, being cognizant of all that can, at least obviously, be said against him, and having taken up his position against all gainsayers knowing that he has sought for objections and difficulties, instead of avoiding them, and has shut out no light which can be thrown upon the subject from any quarter— he has a right to think his judgment better than that of any person, or any multitude, who have not gone through a similar process.

It is not too much to require that what the wisest of mankind, those who are best entitled to trust their own judgment, find necessary to warrant their relying on it, should be submitted to by that miscellaneous collection of a few wise and many foolish individuals, called the public. The most intolerant of churches, the Roman Catholic Church, even at the canonization of a saint, admits, and listens patiently to, a "devil's advocate." The holiest of men, it appears, cannot be admitted to posthumous honours, until all that the devil could say against him is known and weighed. If even the Newtonian philosophy were not permitted to be questioned, mankind could not feel as complete assurance of its truth as they now do. The beliefs which we have most warrant for, have no safeguard to rest on, but a standing invitation to the whole world to prove them unfounded. If the challenge is not accepted, or is accepted and the attempt fails, we are far enough from certainty still; but we have done the best that the existing state of human reason admits of; we have neglected nothing that could give the truth

a chance of reaching us: if the lists[25] are kept open, we may hope that if there be a better truth, it will be found when the human mind is capable of receiving it; and in the meantime we may rely on having attained such approach to truth, as is possible in our own day. This is the amount of certainty attainable by a fallible being, and this the sole way of attaining it.

Strange it is, that men should admit the validity of the arguments for free discussion, but object to their being "pushed to an extreme;" not seeing that unless the reasons are good for an extreme case, they are not good for any case. Strange that they should imagine that they are not assuming infallibility when they acknowledge that there should be free discussion on all subjects which can possibly be doubtful, but think that some particular principle or doctrine should be forbidden to be questioned because it is so *certain*, that is, because *they are certain* that it is certain. To call any proposition certain, while there is any one who would deny its certainty if permitted, but who is not permitted, is to assume that we ourselves, and those who agree with us, are the judges of certainty, and judges without hearing the other side.

In the present age—which has been described as "destitute of faith, but terrified at scepticism"[26]— in which people feel sure, not so much that their opinions are true, as that they should not know what to do without them—the claims of an opinion to be protected from public attack are rested not so much on its truth, as on its importance to society. There are, it is alleged, certain beliefs, so useful, not to say indispensable to well-being, that it is as much the duty of governments to uphold those beliefs, as to protect any other of the interests of society. In a case of such necessity, and so directly in the line of their duty, something less than infallibility may, it is maintained, warrant, and even bind, governments, to act on their own opinion, confirmed by the general opinion of mankind. It is also often argued, and still oftener thought, that none but bad men would desire

---

25 An arena for jousting and other tournaments and thus, metaphorically, an area of controversy.

26 Mill is quoting the contemporary essayist Thomas Carlyle (from his "Memoirs of the Life of Scott," *London and Westminster Review*, January 1838).

to weaken these salutary beliefs; and there can be nothing wrong, it is thought, in restraining bad men, and prohibiting what only such men would wish to practise. This mode of thinking makes the justification of restraints on discussion not a question of the truth of doctrines, but of their usefulness; and flatters itself by that means to escape the responsibility of claiming to be an infallible judge of opinions. But those who thus satisfy themselves, do not perceive that the assumption of infallibility is merely shifted from one point to another. The usefulness of an opinion is itself matter of opinion: as disputable, as open to discussion and requiring discussion as much, as the opinion itself. There is the same need of an infallible judge of opinions to decide an opinion to be noxious, as to decide it to be false, unless the opinion condemned has full opportunity of defending itself. And it will not do to say that the heretic may be allowed to maintain the utility or harmlessness of his opinion, though forbidden to maintain its truth. The truth of an opinion is part of its utility. If we would know whether or not it is desirable that a proposition should be believed, is it possible to exclude the consideration of whether or not it is true? In the opinion, not of bad men, but of the best men, no belief which is contrary to truth can be really useful: and can you prevent such men from urging that plea, when they are charged with culpability for denying some doctrine which they are told is useful, but which they believe to be false? Those who are on the side of received opinions, never fail to take all possible advantage of this plea; you do not find *them* handling the question of utility as if it could be completely abstracted from that of truth: on the contrary, it is, above all, because their doctrine is "the truth," that the knowledge or the belief of it is held to be so indispensable. There can be no fair discussion of the question of usefulness, when an argument so vital may be employed on one side, but not on the other. And in point of fact, when law or public feeling do not permit the truth of an opinion to be disputed, they are just as little tolerant of a denial of its usefulness. The utmost they allow is an extenuation of its absolute necessity or of the positive guilt of rejecting it.

In order more fully to illustrate the mischief of denying a hearing to opinions because we, in our own judgment, have condemned them, it will be desirable to fix down the discussion to a concrete case; and I choose, by preference, the cases which are least favourable to me—in which the argument against freedom of opinion, both on the score of truth and on that of utility, is considered the strongest. Let the opinions impugned be the belief in a God and in a future state, or any of the commonly received doctrines of morality. To fight the battle on such ground, gives a great advantage to an unfair antagonist; since he will be sure to say (and many who have no desire to be unfair will say it internally), Are these the doctrines which you do not deem sufficiently certain to be taken under the protection of law? Is the belief in a God one of the opinions, to feel sure of which, you hold to be assuming infallibility? But I must be permitted to observe, that it is not the feeling sure of a doctrine (be it what it may) which I call an assumption of infallibility. It is the undertaking to decide that question *for others*, without allowing them to hear what can be said on the contrary side. And I denounce and reprobate this pretension not the less, if put forth on the side of my most solemn convictions. However positive any one's persuasion may be, not only of the falsity, but of the pernicious consequences—not only of the pernicious consequences, but (to adopt expressions which I altogether condemn) the immorality and impiety of an opinion; yet if, in pursuance of that private judgment, though backed by the public judgment of his country or his contemporaries, he prevents the opinion from being heard in its defence, he assumes infallibility. And so far from the assumption being less objectionable or less dangerous because the opinion is called immoral or impious, this is the case of all others in which it is most fatal. These are exactly the occasions on which the men of one generation commit those dreadful mistakes which excite the astonishment and horror of posterity. It is among such that we find the instances memorable in history, when the arm of the law has been employed to root out the best men and the noblest doctrines; with deplorable success as to the men, though some of the doctrines have survived to be (as if in mockery) invoked, in defence of similar conduct towards those who dissent from *them*, or from their received interpretation.

Mankind can hardly be too often reminded, that there was once a man named Socrates, between whom and the legal authorities and public opinion of his time, there took place a memorable collision. Born in an age and country abounding in individual greatness,[27] this man has been handed down to us by those who best knew both him and the age, as the most virtuous man in it; while we know him as the head and prototype of all subsequent teachers of virtue, the source equally of the lofty inspiration of Plato and the judicious utilitarianism of Aristotle, "*i maestri di color che sanno*,"[28] the two headsprings of ethical as of all other philosophy. This acknowledged master of all the eminent thinkers who have since lived—whose fame, still growing after more than two thousand years, all but outweighs the whole remainder of the names which make his native city illustrious—was put to death by his countrymen, after a judicial conviction, for impiety and immorality. Impiety, in denying the gods recognized by the State; indeed his accuser asserted (see the "Apologia"[29]) that he believed in no gods at all. Immorality, in being, by his doctrines and instructions, a "corrupter of youth." Of these charges the tribunal, there is every ground for believing, honestly found him guilty, and condemned the man who probably of all then born had deserved best of mankind, to be put to death as a criminal.

To pass from this to the only other instance of judicial iniquity, the mention of which, after the condemnation of Socrates, would not be an anti-climax: the event which took place on Calvary[30] rather more than eighteen hundred years ago. The man who left on the memory of those who witnessed his life and conversation, such an impression of his moral grandeur, that eighteen subsequent centuries have done homage to him as the Almighty in person, was ignominiously put to death, as what? As a blasphemer. Men did not merely mistake their benefactor; they mistook him

for the exact contrary of what he was, and treated him as that prodigy of impiety, which they themselves are now held to be, for their treatment of him. The feelings with which mankind now regard these lamentable transactions, especially the latter of the two, render them extremely unjust in their judgment of the unhappy actors. These were, to all appearance, not bad men—not worse than men most commonly are, but rather the contrary; men who possessed in a full, or somewhat more than a full measure, the religious, moral, and patriotic feelings of their time and people: the very kind of men who, in all times, our own included, have every chance of passing through life blameless and respected. The high-priest who rent his garments when the words were pronounced,[31] which, according to all the ideas of his country, constituted the blackest guilt, was in all probability quite as sincere in his horror and indignation, as the generality of respectable and pious men now are in the religious and moral sentiments they profess; and most of those who now shudder at his conduct, if they had lived in his time and been born Jews, would have acted precisely as he did. Orthodox Christians who are tempted to think that those who stoned to death the first martyrs must have been worse men than they themselves are, ought to remember that one of those persecutors was Saint Paul.

Let us add one more example, the most striking of all, if the impressiveness of an error is measured by the wisdom and virtue of him who falls into it. If ever any one, possessed of power, had grounds for thinking himself the best and most enlightened among his contemporaries, it was the Emperor Marcus Aurelius.[32] Absolute monarch of the whole civilized world, he preserved through life not only the most unblemished justice, but what was less to be expected from his Stoical breeding, the tenderest heart. The few failings which are attributed to him, were all on the side

---

27   Socrates lived in the Greek city-state of Athens in the fifth century BCE.

28   "The masters of those who know," an adaptation of a line from Dante's *Inferno* (Canto IV, 131), where Dante refers, in the singular, to Aristotle.

29   A dialogue by Plato—*The Apology*—which describes Socrates' trial.

30   The crucifixion of Jesus Christ; Calvary is the name of the hill outside Jerusalem where this took place.

31   Caiaphas. This scene is described in Matthew 26:65.

32   Marcus Aurelius (121–180 CE) was a Stoic philosopher and emperor of Rome from 161 to 180. His *Meditations* were an important formulation of Stoicism, a deterministic, rationalistic philosophy which held that the four main virtues are wisdom, courage, justice, and temperance.

of indulgence: while his writings, the highest ethical product of the ancient mind, differ scarcely perceptibly, if they differ at all, from the most characteristic teachings of Christ. This man, a better Christian in all but the dogmatic sense of the word, than almost any of the ostensibly Christian sovereigns who have since reigned, persecuted Christianity. Placed at the summit of all the previous attainments of humanity, with an open, unfettered intellect, and a character which led him of himself to embody in his moral writings the Christian ideal, he yet failed to see that Christianity was to be a good and not an evil to the world, with his duties to which he was so deeply penetrated. Existing society he knew to be in a deplorable state. But such as it was, he saw or thought he saw, that it was held together and prevented from being worse, by belief and reverence of the received divinities. As a ruler of mankind, he deemed it his duty not to suffer society to fall in pieces; and saw not how, if its existing ties were removed, any others could be formed which could again knit it together. The new religion openly aimed at dissolving these ties: unless, therefore, it was his duty to adopt that religion, it seemed to be his duty to put it down. Inasmuch then as the theology of Christianity did not appear to him true or of divine origin; inasmuch as this strange history of a crucified God was not credible to him, and a system which purported to rest entirely upon a foundation to him so wholly unbelievable, could not be foreseen by him to be that renovating agency which, after all abatements, it has in fact proved to be; the gentlest and most amiable of philosophers and rulers, under a solemn sense of duty, authorized the persecution of Christianity. To my mind this is one of the most tragical facts in all history. It is a bitter thought, how different a thing the Christianity of the world might have been, if the Christian faith had been adopted as the religion of the empire under the auspices of Marcus Aurelius instead of those of Constantine.[33] But it would be equally unjust to him and false to truth, to deny, that no one plea which can be urged for punishing anti-Christian teaching, was

wanting to Marcus Aurelius for punishing, as he did, the propagation of Christianity. No Christian more firmly believes that Atheism is false, and tends to the dissolution of society, than Marcus Aurelius believed the same things of Christianity; he who, of all men then living, might have been thought the most capable of appreciating it. Unless any one who approves of punishment for the promulgation of opinions, flatters himself that he is a wiser and better man than Marcus Aurelius—more deeply versed in the wisdom of his time, more elevated in his intellect above it—more earnest in his search for truth, or more single-minded in his devotion to it when found;—let him abstain from that assumption of the joint infallibility of himself and the multitude, which the great Antoninus[34] made with so unfortunate a result.

Aware of the impossibility of defending the use of punishment for restraining irreligious opinions, by any argument which will not justify Marcus Antoninus, the enemies of religious freedom, when hard pressed, occasionally accept this consequence, and say, with Dr. Johnson, that the persecutors of Christianity were in the right;[35] that persecution is an ordeal through which truth ought to pass, and always passes successfully, legal penalties being, in the end, powerless against truth, though sometimes beneficially effective against mischievous errors. This is a form of the argument for religious intolerance, sufficiently remarkable not to be passed without notice.

A theory which maintains that truth may justifiably be persecuted because persecution cannot possibly do it any harm, cannot be charged with being intentionally hostile to the reception of new truths; but we cannot commend the generosity of its dealing with the persons to whom mankind are indebted for them. To discover to[36] the world something which deeply concerns it, and of which it was previously ignorant; to prove to it that it had been mistaken on some vital point of temporal or spiritual interest, is as important a service as a human being can render to his fellow-

---

33   Constantine I, emperor of Rome from 306 to 337, adopted the Christian faith (because he thought it brought him victory in a battle) and suspended the persecution of Christians in 313.

34   Antoninus was Marcus Aurelius's family name.

35   This sentiment of writer and lexicographer Samuel Johnson can be found recorded in James Boswell's *Life of Johnson* (1791), Volume II, entry for May 7, 1773.

36   Expose, reveal to.

creatures, and in certain cases, as in those of the early Christians and of the Reformers,[37] those who think with Dr. Johnson believe it to have been the most precious gift which could be bestowed on mankind. That the authors of such splendid benefits should be requited by martyrdom; that their reward should be to be dealt with as the vilest of criminals, is not, upon this theory, a deplorable error and misfortune, for which humanity should mourn in sackcloth and ashes, but the normal and justifiable state of things. The propounder of a new truth, according to this doctrine, should stand, as stood, in the legislation of the Locrians,[38] the proposer of a new law, with a halter round his neck, to be instantly tightened if the public assembly did not, on hearing his reasons, then and there adopt his proposition.

People who defend this mode of treating benefactors, can not be supposed to set much value on the benefit; and I believe this view of the subject is mostly confined to the sort of persons who think that new truths may have been desirable once, but that we have had enough of them now.

But, indeed, the dictum that truth always triumphs over persecution, is one of those pleasant falsehoods which men repeat after one another till they pass into commonplaces, but which all experience refutes. History teems with instances of truth put down by persecution. If not suppressed forever, it may be thrown back for centuries. To speak only of religious opinions: the Reformation broke out at least twenty times before Luther,[39] and was put down. Arnold of Brescia was put down. Fra Dolcino was put down. Savonarola was put down. The Albigeois were put down. The Vaudois were put down. The Lollards were put down. The Hussites were put down.[40] Even after the era of Luther, wherever persecution was persisted in, it was successful. In Spain, Italy, Flanders, the Austrian empire, Protestantism was rooted out; and, most likely, would have been so in England, had Queen Mary lived, or Queen Elizabeth died. Persecution has always succeeded, save where the heretics were too strong a party to be effectually persecuted. No reasonable person can doubt that Christianity might have been extirpated in the Roman empire. It spread, and became predominant, because the persecutions were only occasional, lasting but a short time, and separated by long intervals of almost undisturbed propagandism. It is a piece of idle sentimentality that truth, merely as truth, has any inherent power denied to error, of prevailing against the dungeon and the stake. Men are not more zealous for truth than they often are for error, and a sufficient application of legal or even of social penalties will generally succeed in stopping the propagation of either. The real advantage which truth has, consists in this, that when an opinion is true, it may be extinguished once, twice, or many times, but in the course of ages there will generally be found persons to rediscover it, until some one of its reappearances falls on a time when from favourable circumstances it escapes persecution until it has made such head as to withstand all subsequent attempts to suppress it.

It will be said, that we do not now put to death the introducers of new opinions: we are not like our fathers who slew the prophets, we even build sep-

---

37   Protestant Reformers, such as Martin Luther and John Calvin, who challenged the doctrines and authority of the Catholic Church in the sixteenth century.

38   Locris was a minor state in ancient Greece, and among the first to adopt a written code of law (in about 660 BCE). Its regulations were severe: in addition to the principle mentioned in the text, it also enshrined the *lex talionis*, the law of retaliation (of taking an eye for an eye, a tooth for a tooth).

39   Martin Luther (1483–1546) was a German theologian who initiated the Protestant Reformation in 1517.

40   Arnold of Brescia was executed as a heretic in 1155; Fra Dolcino of Novara was tortured to death in 1307; Savonarola Girolamo was burned to death in 1498. The Albigeois, or Albigenses, tried to establish a church independent of Roman Catholicism and were exterminated by the Inquisition in the thirteenth century. The Vaudois, or Waldenses, also attempted to break free of Catholicism in the late twelfth century and, though greatly weakened by the oppression of the Inquisition, survived to join the Calvinist movement in the sixteenth century. The Lollards were followers of John Wycliffe (1320–1384) and the Hussites of John Huss (1369–1415). Both movements revolted against the authority of the Church, and both were vigorously suppressed.

ulchres to them. It is true we no longer put heretics to death; and the amount of penal infliction which modern feeling would probably tolerate, even against the most obnoxious opinions, is not sufficient to extirpate them. But let us not flatter ourselves that we are yet free from the stain even of legal persecution. Penalties for opinion, or at least for its expression, still exist by law; and their enforcement is not, even in these times, so unexampled as to make it at all incredible that they may some day be revived in full force. In the year 1857, at the summer assizes of the county of Cornwall, an unfortunate man,[41] said to be of unexceptionable conduct in all relations of life, was sentenced to twenty-one months imprisonment, for uttering, and writing on a gate, some offensive words concerning Christianity. Within a month of the same time, at the Old Bailey, two persons, on two separate occasions,[42] were rejected as jurymen, and one of them grossly insulted by the judge and one of the counsel, because they honestly declared that they had no theological belief; and a third, a foreigner,[43] for the same reason, was denied justice against a thief. This refusal of redress took place in virtue of the legal doctrine, that no person can be allowed to give evidence in a court of justice, who does not profess belief in a God (any god is sufficient) and in a future state; which is equivalent to declaring such persons to be outlaws, excluded from the protection of the tribunals; who may not only be robbed or assaulted with impunity, if no one but themselves, or persons of similar opinions, be present, but any one else may be robbed or assaulted with impunity, if the proof of the fact depends on their evidence. The assumption on which this is grounded, is that the oath is worthless, of a person who does not believe in a future state; a proposition which betokens much ignorance of history in those who assent to it (since it is historically true that a large proportion of infidels in all ages have been

persons of distinguished integrity and honour); and would be maintained by no one who had the smallest conception how many of the persons in greatest repute with the world, both for virtues and for attainments, are well known, at least to their intimates, to be unbelievers. The rule, besides, is suicidal, and cuts away its own foundation. Under pretence that atheists must be liars, it admits the testimony of all atheists who are willing to lie, and rejects only those who brave the obloquy[44] of publicly confessing a detested creed rather than affirm a falsehood. A rule thus self-convicted of absurdity so far as regards its professed purpose, can be kept in force only as a badge of hatred, a relic of persecution; a persecution, too, having the peculiarity that the qualification for undergoing it is the being clearly proved not to deserve it. The rule, and the theory it implies, are hardly less insulting to believers than to infidels. For if he who does not believe in a future state necessarily lies, it follows that they who do believe are only prevented from lying, if prevented they are, by the fear of hell. We will not do the authors and abettors of the rule the injury of supposing, that the conception which they have formed of Christian virtue is drawn from their own consciousness.

These, indeed, are but rags and remnants of persecution, and may be thought to be not so much an indication of the wish to persecute, as an example of that very frequent infirmity of English minds, which makes them take a preposterous pleasure in the assertion of a bad principle, when they are no longer bad enough to desire to carry it really into practice. But unhappily there is no security in the state of the public mind, that the suspension of worse forms of legal persecution, which has lasted for about the space of a generation, will continue. In this age the quiet surface of routine is as often ruffled by attempts to resuscitate past evils, as to introduce new benefits. What is boasted of at the present time as the revival of religion, is always, in narrow and uncultivated minds, at least as much the revival of bigotry; and where there is the strongest permanent leaven[45] of intolerance in

---

41   [Author's note] Thomas Pooley, Bodmin Assizes, July 31, 1857. In December following, he received a free pardon from the Crown.

42   [Author's note] George Jacob Holyoake, August 17, 1857; Edward Truelove, July, 1857.

43   [Author's note] Baron de Gleichen, Marlborough Street Police Court, August 4, 1857.

44   Disgrace, the state of being generally ill-spoken of or abused.

45   A pervasive element that works subtly to modify a whole.

the feelings of a people, which at all times abides in the middle classes of this country, it needs but little to provoke them into actively persecuting those whom they have never ceased to think proper objects of persecution.[46] For it is this—it is the opinions men entertain, and the feelings they cherish, respecting those who disown the beliefs they deem important, which makes this country not a place of mental freedom. For a long time past, the chief mischief of the legal penalties is that they strengthen the social stigma. It is that stigma which is really effective, and so effective is it, that the

profession of opinions which are under the ban of society is much less common in England, than is, in many other countries, the avowal of those which incur risk of judicial punishment. In respect to all persons but those whose pecuniary[47] circumstances make them independent of the good will of other people, opinion, on this subject, is as efficacious as law; men might as well be imprisoned, as excluded from the means of earning their bread. Those whose bread is already secured, and who desire no favours from men in power, or from bodies of men, or from the public, have nothing to fear from the open avowal of any opinions, but to be ill-thought of and ill-spoken of, and this it ought not to require a very heroic mould to enable them to bear. There is no room for any appeal *ad misericordiam*[48] in behalf of such persons. But though we do not now inflict so much evil on those who think differently from us, as it was formerly our custom to do, it may be that we do ourselves as much evil as ever by our treatment of them. Socrates was put to death, but the Socratic philosophy rose like the sun in heaven, and spread its illumination over the whole intellectual firmament. Christians were cast to the lions, but the Christian Church grew up a stately and spreading tree, overtopping the older and less vigorous growths, and stifling them by its shade. Our merely social intolerance, kills no one, roots out no opinions, but induces men to disguise them, or to abstain from any active effort for their diffusion. With us, heretical opinions do not perceptibly gain or even lose, ground in each decade or generation; they never blaze out far and wide, but continue to smoulder in the narrow circles of thinking and studious persons among whom they originate, without ever lighting up the general affairs of mankind with either a true or a deceptive light. And thus is kept up a state of things very satisfactory to some minds, because, without the unpleasant process of fining or imprisoning anybody, it maintains all prevailing opinions outwardly undisturbed, while it does not absolutely interdict[49] the exercise of reason by

---

46 [Author's note] Ample warning may be drawn from the large infusion of the passions of a persecutor, which mingled with the general display of the worst parts of our national character on the occasion of the Sepoy insurrection. The ravings of fanatics or charlatans from the pulpit may be unworthy of notice; but the heads of the Evangelical party have announced as their principle, for the government of Hindoos and Mahomedans, that no schools be supported by public money in which the Bible is not taught, and by necessary consequence that no public employment be given to any but real or pretended Christians. An Under-Secretary of State, in a speech delivered to his constituents on the 12th of November, 1857, is reported to have said: "Toleration of their faith" (the faith of a hundred millions of British subjects), "the superstition which they called religion, by the British Government, had had the effect of retarding the ascendency of the British name, and preventing the salutary growth of Christianity.... Toleration was the great corner-stone of the religious liberties of this country; but do not let them abuse that precious word toleration. As he understood it, it meant the complete liberty to all, freedom of worship, *among Christians, who worshipped upon the same foundation*. It meant toleration of all sects and denominations *of Christians* who believed in the one mediation." I desire to call attention to the fact, that a man who has been deemed fit to fill a high office in the government of this country, under a liberal Ministry, maintains the doctrine that all who do not believe in the divinity of Christ are beyond the pale of toleration. Who, after this imbecile display, can indulge the illusion that religious persecution has passed away, never to return?

47 Financial.
48 To pity.
49 Forbid.

dissentients afflicted with the malady of thought. A convenient plan for having peace in the intellectual world, and keeping all things going on therein very much as they do already. But the price paid for this sort of intellectual pacification, is the sacrifice of the entire moral courage of the human mind. A state of things in which a large portion of the most active and inquiring intellects find it advisable to keep the genuine principles and grounds of their convictions within their own breasts, and attempt, in what they address to the public, to fit as much as they can of their own conclusions to premises which they have internally renounced, cannot send forth the open, fearless characters, and logical, consistent intellects who once adorned the thinking world. The sort of men who can be looked for under it, are either mere conformers to commonplace, or time-servers for truth whose arguments on all great subjects are meant for their hearers, and are not those which have convinced themselves. Those who avoid this alternative, do so by narrowing their thoughts and interests to things which can be spoken of without venturing within the region of principles, that is, to small practical matters, which would come right of themselves, if but the minds of mankind were strengthened and enlarged, and which will never be made effectually right until then; while that which would strengthen and enlarge men's minds, free and daring speculation on the highest subjects, is abandoned.

Those in whose eyes this reticence on the part of heretics is no evil, should consider in the first place, that in consequence of it there is never any fair and thorough discussion of heretical opinions; and that such of them as could not stand such a discussion, though they may be prevented from spreading, do not disappear. But it is not the minds of heretics that are deteriorated most, by the ban placed on all inquiry which does not end in the orthodox conclusions. The greatest harm done is to those who are not heretics, and whose whole mental development is cramped, and their reason cowed, by the fear of heresy. Who can compute what the world loses in the multitude of promising intellects combined with timid characters, who dare not follow out any bold, vigorous, independent train of thought, lest it

should land them in something which would admit of being considered irreligious or immoral? Among them we may occasionally see some man of deep conscientiousness, and subtile[50] and refined understanding, who spends a life in sophisticating with an intellect which he cannot silence, and exhausts the resources of ingenuity in attempting to reconcile the promptings of his conscience and reason with orthodoxy, which yet he does not, perhaps, to the end succeed in doing. No one can be a great thinker who does not recognize, that as a thinker it is his first duty to follow his intellect to whatever conclusions it may lead. Truth gains more even by the errors of one who, with due study and preparation, thinks for himself, than by the true opinions of those who only hold them because they do not suffer themselves to think. Not that it is solely, or chiefly, to form great thinkers, that freedom of thinking is required. On the contrary, it is as much, and even more indispensable, to enable average human beings to attain the mental stature which they are capable of. There have been, and may again be, great individual thinkers, in a general atmosphere of mental slavery. But there never has been, nor ever will be, in that atmosphere, an intellectually active people. Where any people has made a temporary approach to such a character, it has been because the dread of heterodox speculation was for a time suspended. Where there is a tacit convention that principles are not to be disputed; where the discussion of the greatest questions which can occupy humanity is considered to be closed, we cannot hope to find that generally high scale of mental activity which has made some periods of history so remarkable. Never when controversy avoided the subjects which are large and important enough to kindle enthusiasm, was the mind of a people stirred up from its foundations, and the impulse given which raised even persons of the most ordinary intellect to something of the dignity of thinking beings. Of such we have had an example in the condition of Europe during the times immediately following the Reformation; another, though limited to the Continent and to a more cultivated class, in the speculative movement of the

---

50 Subtle.

latter half of the eighteenth century;[51] and a third, of still briefer duration, in the intellectual fermentation of Germany during the Goethian and Fichtean period.[52] These periods differed widely in the particular opinions which they developed; but were alike in this, that during all three the yoke of authority was broken. In each, an old mental despotism had been thrown off, and no new one had yet taken its place. The impulse given at these three periods has made Europe what it now is. Every single improvement which has taken place either in the human mind or in institutions, may be traced distinctly to one or other of them. Appearances have for some time indicated that all three impulses are well-nigh spent; and we can expect no fresh start, until we again assert our mental freedom.

Let us now pass to the second division of the argument, and dismissing the supposition that any of the received opinions may be false, let us assume them to be true, and examine into the worth of the manner in which they are likely to be held, when their truth is not freely and openly canvassed. However unwillingly a person who has a strong opinion may admit the possibility that his opinion may be false, he ought to be moved by the consideration that however true it may be, if it is not fully, frequently, and fearlessly discussed, it will be held as a dead dogma, not a living truth.

There is a class of persons (happily not quite so numerous as formerly) who think it enough if a person assents undoubtingly to what they think true, though he has no knowledge whatever of the grounds of the opinion, and could not make a tenable defence of it against the most superficial objections. Such persons, if they can once get their creed taught from authority, naturally think that no good, and some harm, comes of its being allowed to

be questioned. Where their influence prevails, they make it nearly impossible for the received opinion to be rejected wisely and considerately, though it may still be rejected rashly and ignorantly; for to shut out discussion entirely is seldom possible, and when it once gets in, beliefs not grounded on conviction are apt to give way before the slightest semblance of an argument. Waiving, however, this possibility—assuming that the true opinion abides in the mind, but abides as a prejudice, a belief independent of, and proof against, argument—this is not the way in which truth ought to be held by a rational being. This is not knowing the truth. Truth, thus held, is but one superstition the more, accidentally clinging to the words which enunciate a truth.

If the intellect and judgment of mankind ought to be cultivated, a thing which Protestants at least do not deny, on what can these faculties be more appropriately exercised by any one, than on the things which concern him so much that it is considered necessary for him to hold opinions on them? If the cultivation of the understanding consists in one thing more than in another, it is surely in learning the grounds of one's own opinions. Whatever people believe, on subjects on which it is of the first importance to believe rightly, they ought to be able to defend against at least the common objections. But, some one may say, "Let them be *taught* the grounds of their opinions. It does not follow that opinions must be merely parroted because they are never heard controverted. Persons who learn geometry do not simply commit the theorems to memory, but understand and learn likewise the demonstrations; and it would be absurd to say that they remain ignorant of the grounds of geometrical truths, because they never hear any one deny, and attempt to disprove them." Undoubtedly: and such teaching suffices on a subject like mathematics, where there is nothing at all to be said on the wrong side of the question. The peculiarity of the evidence of mathematical truths is, that all the argument is on one side. There are no objections, and no answers to objections. But on every subject on which difference of opinion is possible, the truth depends on a balance to be struck between two sets of conflicting reasons. Even in natural philosophy, there is always some other explanation possible of the same facts; some geocentric theory

---

51   The Enlightenment, a philosophical and cultural movement that emphasized individualism and the use of reason to question previously accepted doctrines.

52   Johann Wolfgang von Goethe (1749–1832) was a writer, poet, and philosopher-scientist. Johann Gottlieb Fichte (1762–1814) was an influential idealist philosopher. Both figures were important in sparking the Romantic movement of the late eighteenth century.

instead of heliocentric,[53] some phlogiston[54] instead of oxygen; and it has to be shown why that other theory cannot be the true one: and until this is shown and until we know how it is shown, we do not understand the grounds of our opinion. But when we turn to subjects infinitely more complicated, to morals, religion, politics, social relations, and the business of life, three-fourths of the arguments for every disputed opinion consist in dispelling the appearances which favour some opinion different from it. The greatest orator, save one, of antiquity,[55] has left it on record that he always studied his adversary's case with as great, if not with still greater, intensity than even his own. What Cicero practised as the means of forensic[56] success, requires to be imitated by all who study any subject in order to arrive at the truth. He who knows only his own side of the case, knows little of that. His reasons may be good, and no one may have been able to refute them. But if he is equally unable to refute the reasons on the opposite side; if he does not so much as know what they are, he has no ground for preferring either opinion. The rational position for him would be suspension of judgment, and unless he contents himself with that, he is either led by authority, or adopts, like the generality of the world, the side to which he feels most inclination. Nor is it enough that he should hear the arguments of adversaries from his own teachers, presented as they state them, and accompanied by what they offer as refutations. This is not the way to do justice to the arguments, or bring them into real contact with his own mind. He must be able to hear them from persons who actually believe them; who defend them in earnest, and do their very utmost for them. He must know them in their most plausible and persuasive form; he must feel the whole force of the difficulty which the true view of the subject has to encounter and dispose of, else he will never really possess himself of the portion of truth which meets and removes that difficulty. Ninety-nine in a hundred of what are called educated men are in this condition, even of those who can argue fluently for their opinions. Their conclusion may be true, but it might be false for anything they know: they have never thrown themselves into the mental position of those who think differently from them, and considered what such persons may have to say; and consequently they do not, in any proper sense of the word, know the doctrine which they themselves profess. They do not know those parts of it which explain and justify the remainder; the considerations which show that a fact which seemingly conflicts with another is reconcilable with it, or that, of two apparently strong reasons, one and not the other ought to be preferred. All that part of the truth which turns the scale, and decides the judgment of a completely informed mind, they are strangers to; nor is it ever really known, but to those who have attended equally and impartially to both sides, and endeavoured to see the reasons of both in the strongest light. So essential is this discipline to a real understanding of moral and human subjects, that if opponents of all important truths do not exist, it is indispensable to imagine them and supply them with the strongest arguments which the most skilful devil's advocate can conjure up.

To abate the force of these considerations, an enemy of free discussion may be supposed to say, that there is no necessity for mankind in general to know and understand all that can be said against or for their opinions by philosophers and theologians. That it is not needful for common men to be able to expose all the misstatements or fallacies of an ingenious opponent. That it is enough if there is always somebody capable of answering them, so that nothing likely to mislead uninstructed persons remains unrefuted. That simple minds, having been taught the obvious grounds of the truths inculcated on them, may trust to authority for the rest, and being aware that they have neither knowledge nor talent to resolve every difficulty which can be raised, may repose in the assurance that all

---

53   On the geocentric theory, the sun, planets, and other heavenly bodies circle the Earth. According to heliocentric accounts, the planets orbit the Sun.

54   Phlogiston is a mythical substance, once thought to be a volatile constituent of all combustible substances, released as flame in combustion. It is now known that combustion is, in general, a chemical interaction with oxygen.

55   The greatest orator of antiquity was said to be Demosthenes, and the second greatest was Cicero.

56   Relating to debate or argument, especially in a court of law or public discussion.

those which have been raised have been or can be answered, by those who are specially trained to the task.

Conceding to this view of the subject the utmost that can be claimed for it by those most easily satisfied with the amount of understanding of truth which ought to accompany the belief of it; even so, the argument for free discussion is no way weakened. For even this doctrine acknowledges that mankind ought to have a rational assurance that all objections have been satisfactorily answered; and how are they to be answered if that which requires to be answered is not spoken? or how can the answer be known to be satisfactory, if the objectors have no opportunity of showing that it is unsatisfactory? If not the public, at least the philosophers and theologians who are to resolve the difficulties, must make themselves familiar with those difficulties in their most puzzling form; and this cannot be accomplished unless they are freely stated, and placed in the most advantageous light which they admit of. The Catholic Church has its own way of dealing with this embarrassing problem. It makes a broad separation between those who can be permitted to receive its doctrines on conviction, and those who must accept them on trust. Neither, indeed, are allowed any choice as to what they will accept; but the clergy, such at least as can be fully confided in, may admissibly and meritoriously make themselves acquainted with the arguments of opponents, in order to answer them, and may, therefore, read heretical books; the laity, not unless by special permission, hard to be obtained. This discipline recognizes a knowledge of the enemy's case as beneficial to the teachers, but finds means, consistent with this, of denying it to the rest of the world: thus giving to the elite more mental culture, though not more mental freedom, than it allows to the mass. By this device it succeeds in obtaining the kind of mental superiority which its purposes require; for though culture without freedom never made a large and liberal mind, it can make a clever *nisi prius*[57] advocate of a cause. But in

countries professing Protestantism, this resource is denied; since Protestants hold, at least in theory, that the responsibility for the choice of a religion must be borne by each for himself, and cannot be thrown off upon teachers. Besides, in the present state of the world, it is practically impossible that writings which are read by the instructed can be kept from the uninstructed. If the teachers of mankind are to be cognizant of all that they ought to know, everything must be free to be written and published without restraint.

If, however, the mischievous operation of the absence of free discussion, when the received opinions are true, were confined to leaving men ignorant of the grounds of those opinions, it might be thought that this, if an intellectual, is no moral evil, and does not affect the worth of the opinions, regarded in their influence on the character. The fact, however, is, that not only the grounds of the opinion are forgotten in the absence of discussion, but too often the meaning of the opinion itself. The words which convey it, cease to suggest ideas, or suggest only a small portion of those they were originally employed to communicate. Instead of a vivid conception and a living belief, there remain only a few phrases retained by rote; or, if any part, the shell and husk only of the meaning is retained, the finer essence being lost. The great chapter in human history which this fact occupies and fills, cannot be too earnestly studied and meditated on.

It is illustrated in the experience of almost all ethical doctrines and religious creeds. They are all full of meaning and vitality to those who originate them, and to the direct disciples of the originators. Their meaning continues to be felt in undiminished strength, and is perhaps brought out into even fuller consciousness, so long as the struggle lasts to give the doctrine or creed an ascendancy over other creeds. At last it either prevails, and becomes the general opinion, or its progress stops; it keeps possession of the ground it has gained, but ceases to spread further. When either of these results has become apparent, controversy on the subject flags, and gradually dies away. The doctrine has taken its place, if not as a received opinion, as one of the admitted sects or divisions of opinion: those

---

57   Latin for "unless previously," most commonly a legal term for a type of court. However, by a "*nisi prius* advocate" Mill probably means someone who can make a case for something only by refuting all potential

objections to it—someone who argues on the grounds that a position is sound unless shown to be unsound.

who hold it have generally inherited, not adopted it; and conversion from one of these doctrines to another, being now an exceptional fact, occupies little place in the thoughts of their professors. Instead of being, as at first, constantly on the alert either to defend themselves against the world, or to bring the world over to them, they have subsided into acquiescence, and neither listen, when they can help it, to arguments against their creed, nor trouble dissentients (if there be such) with arguments in its favour. From this time may usually be dated the decline in the living power of the doctrine. We often hear the teachers of all creeds lamenting the difficulty of keeping up in the minds of believers a lively apprehension of the truth which they nominally recognize, so that it may penetrate the feelings, and acquire a real mastery over the conduct. No such difficulty is complained of while the creed is still fighting for its existence: even the weaker combatants then know and feel what they are fighting for, and the difference between it and other doctrines; and in that period of every creed's existence, not a few persons may be found, who have realized its fundamental principles in all the forms of thought, have weighed and considered them in all their important bearings, and have experienced the full effect on the character, which belief in that creed ought to produce in a mind thoroughly imbued with it. But when it has come to be an hereditary creed, and to be received passively, not actively—when the mind is no longer compelled, in the same degree as at first, to exercise its vital powers on the questions which its belief presents to it, there is a progressive tendency to forget all of the belief except the formularies, or to give it a dull and torpid assent, as if accepting it on trust dispensed with the necessity of realizing it in consciousness, or testing it by personal experience; until it almost ceases to connect itself at all with the inner life of the human being. Then are seen the cases, so frequent in this age of the world as almost to form the majority, in which the creed remains as it were outside the mind, encrusting and petrifying it against all other influences addressed to the higher parts of our nature; manifesting its power by not suffering any fresh and living conviction to get in, but itself doing nothing for the mind or heart, except standing sentinel over them to keep them vacant.

To what an extent doctrines intrinsically fitted to make the deepest impression upon the mind may remain in it as dead beliefs, without being ever realized in the imagination, the feelings, or the understanding, is exemplified by the manner in which the majority of believers hold the doctrines of Christianity. By Christianity I here mean what is accounted such by all churches and sects—the maxims and precepts contained in the New Testament. These are considered sacred, and accepted as laws, by all professing Christians. Yet it is scarcely too much to say that not one Christian in a thousand guides or tests his individual conduct by reference to those laws. The standard to which he does refer it, is the custom of his nation, his class, or his religious profession. He has thus, on the one hand, a collection of ethical maxims, which he believes to have been vouchsafed to him by infallible wisdom as rules for his government; and on the other, a set of every-day judgments and practices, which go a certain length with some of those maxims, not so great a length with others, stand in direct opposition to some, and are, on the whole, a compromise between the Christian creed and the interests and suggestions of worldly life. To the first of these standards he gives his homage; to the other his real allegiance. All Christians believe that the blessed are the poor and humble, and those who are ill-used by the world; that it is easier for a camel to pass through the eye of a needle than for a rich man to enter the kingdom of heaven; that they should judge not, lest they be judged; that they should swear not at all; that they should love their neighbour as themselves; that if one take their cloak, they should give him their coat also; that they should take no thought for the morrow; that if they would be perfect, they should sell all that they have and give it to the poor.[58] They are not insincere when they say that they believe these things. They do believe them, as people believe what they have always heard lauded and never discussed. But in the sense of that living belief which regulates conduct, they believe these doctrines just up to the point to which it is usual to act upon them. The doctrines in their integrity are serviceable to pelt adversaries with; and it is understood

---

58   All these principles appear in the Gospel of Matthew, except the first, which appears in Luke.

that they are to be put forward (when possible) as the reasons for whatever people do that they think laudable. But any one who reminded them that the maxims require an infinity of things which they never even think of doing would gain nothing but to be classed among those very unpopular characters who affect to be better than other people. The doctrines have no hold on ordinary believers—are not a power in their minds. They have an habitual respect for the sound of them, but no feeling which spreads from the words to the things signified, and forces the mind to take them in, and make them conform to the formula. Whenever conduct is concerned, they look round for Mr. A and B to direct them how far to go in obeying Christ.

Now we may be well assured that the case was not thus, but far otherwise, with the early Christians. Had it been thus, Christianity never would have expanded from an obscure sect of the despised Hebrews into the religion of the Roman empire. When their enemies said, "See how these Christians love one another"[59] (a remark not likely to be made by anybody now), they assuredly had a much livelier feeling of the meaning of their creed than they have ever had since. And to this cause, probably, it is chiefly owing that Christianity now makes so little progress in extending its domain, and after eighteen centuries, is still nearly confined to Europeans and the descendants of Europeans. Even with the strictly religious, who are much in earnest about their doctrines, and attach a greater amount of meaning to many of them than people in general, it commonly happens that the part which is thus comparatively active in their minds is that which was made by Calvin, or Knox,[60] or some such person much nearer in character to themselves. The sayings of Christ coexist passively in their minds, producing hardly any effect beyond what is caused by mere listening to words so amiable and bland. There are

many reasons, doubtless, why doctrines which are the badge of a sect retain more of their vitality than those common to all recognized sects, and why more pains are taken by teachers to keep their meaning alive; but one reason certainly is, that the peculiar doctrines are more questioned, and have to be oftener defended against open gainsayers. Both teachers and learners go to sleep at their post, as soon as there is no enemy in the field.

The same thing holds true, generally speaking, of all traditional doctrines—those of prudence and knowledge of life, as well as of morals or religion. All languages and literatures are full of general observations on life, both as to what it is, and how to conduct oneself in it; observations which everybody knows, which everybody repeats, or hears with acquiescence, which are received as truisms, yet of which most people first truly learn the meaning, when experience, generally of a painful kind, has made it a reality to them. How often, when smarting under some unforeseen misfortune or disappointment, does a person call to mind some proverb or common saying familiar to him all his life, the meaning of which, if he had ever before felt it as he does now, would have saved him from the calamity. There are indeed reasons for this, other than the absence of discussion: there are many truths of which the full meaning *cannot* be realized, until personal experience has brought it home. But much more of the meaning even of these would have been understood, and what was understood would have been far more deeply impressed on the mind, if the man had been accustomed to hear it argued *pro* and *con* by people who did understand it. The fatal tendency of mankind to leave off thinking about a thing when it is no longer doubtful, is the cause of half their errors. A contemporary author has well spoken of "the deep slumber of a decided opinion."[61]

But what! (it may be asked) Is the absence of unanimity an indispensable condition of true knowledge? Is it necessary that some part of mankind should persist in error, to enable any to realize the truth? Does a belief cease to be real and vital as soon as it is generally received—and is a proposition never thoroughly

---

59 Said by Tertullian, a Roman lawyer who converted to Christianity in about 195 and was one of the first Christian theologians to write in Latin. The quote comes from his *Apologeticus* (written in 197).

60 John Calvin (1509–1564), a French-born Swiss Protestant reformer; John Knox (1505–1572), a Scottish religious reformer. Both were important in the foundation of Presbyterianism.

---

61 Sir Arthur Helps, in *Thoughts in the Cloister and the Crowd* (1835).

understood and felt unless some doubt of it remains? As soon as mankind have unanimously accepted a truth, does the truth perish within them? The highest aim and best result of improved intelligence, it has hitherto been thought, is to unite mankind more and more in the acknowledgment of all important truths: and does the intelligence only last as long as it has not achieved its object? Do the fruits of conquest perish by the very completeness of the victory?

I affirm no such thing. As mankind improve, the number of doctrines which are no longer disputed or doubted will be constantly on the increase: and the well-being of mankind may almost be measured by the number and gravity of the truths which have reached the point of being uncontested. The cessation, on one question after another, of serious controversy, is one of the necessary incidents of the consolidation of opinion; a consolidation as salutary in the case of true opinions, as it is dangerous and noxious when the opinions are erroneous. But though this gradual narrowing of the bounds of diversity of opinion is necessary in both senses of the term, being at once inevitable and indispensable, we are not therefore obliged to conclude that all its consequences must be beneficial. The loss of so important an aid to the intelligent and living apprehension of a truth, as is afforded by the necessity of explaining it to, or defending it against, opponents, though not sufficient to outweigh, is no trifling drawback from, the benefit of its universal recognition. Where this advantage can no longer be had, I confess I should like to see the teachers of mankind endeavouring to provide a substitute for it; some contrivance for making the difficulties of the question as present to the learner's consciousness, as if they were pressed upon him by a dissentient champion, eager for his conversion.

But instead of seeking contrivances for this purpose, they have lost those they formerly had. The Socratic dialectics, so magnificently exemplified in the dialogues of Plato, were a contrivance of this description. They were essentially a negative discussion of the great questions of philosophy and life, directed with consummate skill to the purpose of convincing any one who had merely adopted the commonplaces of received opinion, that he did not understand the subject—that he as yet attached no definite meaning to the doctrines he professed; in order that, becoming aware of his ignorance, he might be put in the way to attain a stable belief, resting on a clear apprehension both of the meaning of doctrines and of their evidence. The school disputations of the Middle Ages had a somewhat similar object. They were intended to make sure that the pupil understood his own opinion, and (by necessary correlation) the opinion opposed to it, and could enforce the grounds of the one and confute those of the other. These last-mentioned contests had indeed the incurable defect, that the premises appealed to were taken from authority, not from reason; and, as a discipline to the mind, they were in every respect inferior to the powerful dialectics which formed the intellects of the "Socratici viri":[62] but the modern mind owes far more to both than it is generally willing to admit, and the present modes of education contain nothing which in the smallest degree supplies the place either of the one or of the other. A person who derives all his instruction from teachers or books, even if he escape the besetting temptation of contenting himself with cram,[63] is under no compulsion to hear both sides; accordingly it is far from a frequent accomplishment, even among thinkers, to know both sides; and the weakest part of what everybody says in defence of his opinion, is what he intends as a reply to antagonists. It is the fashion of the present time to disparage negative logic—that which points out weaknesses in theory or errors in practice, without establishing positive truths. Such negative criticism would indeed be poor enough as an ultimate result; but as a means to attaining any positive knowledge or conviction worthy the name, it cannot be valued too highly; and until people are again systematically trained to it, there will be few great thinkers, and a low general average of intellect, in any but the mathematical and physical departments of speculation. On any other subject no one's opinions deserve the name of knowledge, except so far as he has either had forced upon him by others, or gone through of himself, the same mental process which would have been required of him in carrying on an active controversy with op-

---

62   The disciples of Socrates.

63   With hasty memorization, rather than true study and understanding.

ponents. That, therefore, which when absent, it is so indispensable, but so difficult, to create, how worse than absurd is it to forego, when spontaneously offering itself! If there are any persons who contest a received opinion, or who will do so if law or opinion will let them, let us thank them for it, open our minds to listen to them, and rejoice that there is some one to do for us what we otherwise ought, if we have any regard for either the certainty or the vitality of our convictions, to do with much greater labour for ourselves.

It still remains to speak of one of the principal causes which make diversity of opinion advantageous, and will continue to do so until mankind shall have entered a stage of intellectual advancement which at present seems at an incalculable distance. We have hitherto considered only two possibilities: that the received opinion may be false, and some other opinion, consequently, true; or that, the received opinion being true, a conflict with the opposite error is essential to a clear apprehension and deep feeling of its truth. But there is a commoner case than either of these; when the conflicting doctrines, instead of being one true and the other false, share the truth between them; and the nonconforming opinion is needed to supply the remainder of the truth, of which the received doctrine embodies only a part. Popular opinions, on subjects not palpable to sense, are often true, but seldom or never the whole truth. They are a part of the truth; sometimes a greater, sometimes a smaller part, but exaggerated, distorted, and disjoined from the truths by which they ought to be accompanied and limited. Heretical opinions, on the other hand, are generally some of these suppressed and neglected truths, bursting the bonds which kept them down, and either seeking reconciliation with the truth contained in the common opinion, or fronting it as enemies, and setting themselves up, with similar exclusiveness, as the whole truth. The latter case is hitherto the most frequent, as, in the human mind, one-sidedness has always been the rule, and many-sidedness the exception. Hence, even in revolutions of opinion, one part of the truth usually sets while another rises. Even progress, which ought to superadd, for the most part only substitutes one partial and incomplete truth for another; improvement consisting chiefly in this, that the new fragment

of truth is more wanted, more adapted to the needs of the time, than that which it displaces. Such being the partial character of prevailing opinions, even when resting on a true foundation; every opinion which embodies somewhat of the portion of truth which the common opinion omits, ought to be considered precious, with whatever amount of error and confusion that truth may be blended. No sober judge of human affairs will feel bound to be indignant because those who force on our notice truths which we should otherwise have overlooked, overlook some of those which we see. Rather, he will think that so long as popular truth is one-sided, it is more desirable than otherwise that unpopular truth should have one-sided asserters too; such being usually the most energetic, and the most likely to compel reluctant attention to the fragment of wisdom which they proclaim as if it were the whole.

Thus, in the eighteenth century, when nearly all the instructed, and all those of the uninstructed who were led by them, were lost in admiration of what is called civilization, and of the marvels of modern science, literature, and philosophy, and while greatly overrating the amount of unlikeness between the men of modern and those of ancient times, indulged the belief that the whole of the difference was in their own favour; with what a salutary shock did the paradoxes of Rousseau[64] explode like bombshells in the midst, dislocating the compact mass of one-sided opinion, and forcing its elements to recombine in a better form and with additional ingredients. Not that the current opinions were on the whole farther from the truth than Rousseau's were; on the contrary, they were nearer to it; they contained more of positive truth, and very much less of error. Nevertheless there lay in Rousseau's doctrine, and has floated down the stream of opinion along with it, a considerable amount of exactly those

---

64 Jean-Jacques Rousseau (1712–1778), a very influential Swiss-born philosopher, argued that the troubles of the human condition derive from the distorting effects of human society and civilization, and that human beings in their natural state are free, independent, innocent, happy, and intuitively wise. His most famous work is *The Social Contract* (1762), which helped lay the ideological groundwork for the French Revolution.

truths which the popular opinion wanted;[65] and these are the deposit which was left behind when the flood subsided. The superior worth of simplicity of life, the enervating and demoralizing effect of the trammels and hypocrisies of artificial society, are ideas which have never been entirely absent from cultivated minds since Rousseau wrote; and they will in time produce their due effect, though at present needing to be asserted as much as ever, and to be asserted by deeds, for words, on this subject, have nearly exhausted their power.

In politics, again, it is almost a commonplace, that a party of order or stability, and a party of progress or reform, are both necessary elements of a healthy state of political life; until the one or the other shall have so enlarged its mental grasp as to be a party equally of order and of progress, knowing and distinguishing what is fit to be preserved from what ought to be swept away. Each of these modes of thinking derives its utility from the deficiencies of the other; but it is in a great measure the opposition of the other that keeps each within the limits of reason and sanity. Unless opinions favourable to democracy and to aristocracy, to property and to equality, to co-operation and to competition, to luxury and to abstinence, to sociality and individuality, to liberty and discipline, and all the other standing antagonisms of practical life, are expressed with equal freedom, and enforced and defended with equal talent and energy, there is no chance of both elements obtaining their due; one scale is sure to go up, and the other down. Truth, in the great practical concerns of life, is so much a question of the reconciling and combining of opposites, that very few have minds sufficiently capacious and impartial to make the adjustment with an approach to correctness, and it has to be made by the rough process of a struggle between combatants fighting under hostile banners. On any of the great open questions just enumerated, if either of the two opinions has a better claim than the other, not merely to be tolerated, but to be encouraged and countenanced, it is the one which happens at the particular time and place to be in a minority. That is the opinion which, for the time being, represents the neglected interests, the side of

human well-being which is in danger of obtaining less than its share. I am aware that there is not, in this country, any intolerance of differences of opinion on most of these topics. They are adduced to show, by admitted and multiplied examples, the universality of the fact, that only through diversity of opinion is there, in the existing state of human intellect, a chance of fair play to all sides of the truth. When there are persons to be found, who form an exception to the apparent unanimity of the world on any subject, even if the world is in the right, it is always probable that dissentients have something worth hearing to say for themselves, and that truth would lose something by their silence.

It may be objected, "But *some* received principles, especially on the highest and most vital subjects, are more than half-truths. The Christian morality, for instance, is the whole truth on that subject and if any one teaches a morality which varies from it, he is wholly in error." As this is of all cases the most important in practice, none can be fitter to test the general maxim. But before pronouncing what Christian morality is or is not, it would be desirable to decide what is meant by Christian morality. If it means the morality of the New Testament, I wonder that any one who derives his knowledge of this from the book itself, can suppose that it was announced, or intended, as a complete doctrine of morals. The Gospel always refers to a pre-existing morality, and confines its precepts to the particulars in which that morality was to be corrected, or superseded by a wider and higher; expressing itself, moreover, in terms most general, often impossible to be interpreted literally, and possessing rather the impressiveness of poetry or eloquence than the precision of legislation. To extract from it a body of ethical doctrine, has never been possible without eking it out from the Old Testament, that is, from a system elaborate indeed, but in many respects barbarous, and intended only for a barbarous people. St. Paul, a declared enemy to this Judaical mode of interpreting the doctrine and filling up the scheme of his Master, equally assumes a pre-existing morality, namely, that of the Greeks and Romans; and his advice to Christians is in a great measure a system of accommodation to that; even to the extent of giving an apparent sanction to slavery. What is called Christian,

---

65   Needed, lacked.

but should rather be termed theological, morality, was not the work of Christ or the Apostles, but is of much later origin, having been gradually built up by the Catholic Church of the first five centuries, and though not implicitly adopted by moderns and Protestants, has been much less modified by them than might have been expected. For the most part, indeed, they have contented themselves with cutting off the additions which had been made to it in the Middle Ages, each sect supplying the place by fresh additions, adapted to its own character and tendencies. That mankind owe a great debt to this morality, and to its early teachers, I should be the last person to deny; but I do not scruple to say of it, that it is, in many important points, incomplete and one-sided, and that unless ideas and feelings, not sanctioned by it, had contributed to the formation of European life and character, human affairs would have been in a worse condition than they now are. Christian morality (so called) has all the characters of a reaction; it is, in great part, a protest against Paganism. Its ideal is negative rather than positive; passive rather than active; Innocence rather than Nobleness; Abstinence from Evil, rather than energetic Pursuit of Good: in its precepts (as has been well said) "thou shalt not" predominates unduly over "thou shalt." In its horror of sensuality, it made an idol of asceticism, which has been gradually compromised away into one of legality. It holds out the hope of heaven and the threat of hell, as the appointed and appropriate motives to a virtuous life: in this falling far below the best of the ancients, and doing what lies in it to give to human morality an essentially selfish character, by disconnecting each man's feelings of duty from the interests of his fellow-creatures, except so far as a self-interested inducement is offered to him for consulting them. It is essentially a doctrine of passive obedience; it inculcates submission to all authorities found established; who indeed are not to be actively obeyed when they command what religion forbids, but who are not to be resisted, far less rebelled against, for any amount of wrong to ourselves. And while, in the morality of the best Pagan nations, duty to the State holds even a disproportionate place, infringing on the just liberty of the individual; in purely Christian ethics that grand department of duty is scarcely noticed or acknowledged. It is in the Koran, not the New Testament, that we read the maxim—"A ruler who appoints any man to an office, when there is in his dominions another man better qualified for it, sins against God and against the State." What little recognition the idea of obligation to the public obtains in modern morality, is derived from Greek and Roman sources, not from Christian; as, even in the morality of private life, whatever exists of magnanimity, high-mindedness, personal dignity, even the sense of honour, is derived from the purely human, not the religious part of our education, and never could have grown out of a standard of ethics in which the only worth, professedly recognized, is that of obedience.

I am as far as any one from pretending that these defects are necessarily inherent in the Christian ethics, in every manner in which it can be conceived, or that the many requisites of a complete moral doctrine which it does not contain, do not admit of being reconciled with it. Far less would I insinuate this of the doctrines and precepts of Christ himself. I believe that the sayings of Christ are all, that I can see any evidence of their having been intended to be; that they are irreconcilable with nothing which a comprehensive morality requires; that everything which is excellent in ethics may be brought within them, with no greater violence to their language than has been done to it by all who have attempted to deduce from them any practical system of conduct whatever. But it is quite consistent with this, to believe that they contain and were meant to contain, only a part of the truth; that many essential elements of the highest morality are among the things which are not provided for, nor intended to be provided for, in the recorded deliverances of the Founder of Christianity, and which have been entirely thrown aside in the system of ethics erected on the basis of those deliverances by the Christian Church. And this being so, I think it a great error to persist in attempting to find in the Christian doctrine that complete rule for our guidance, which its author intended it to sanction and enforce, but only partially to provide. I believe, too, that this narrow theory is becoming a grave practical evil, detracting greatly from the value of the moral training and instruction, which so many well-meaning persons are now at length exerting themselves to promote. I much fear that by attempting to form the mind and feelings on an exclusively religious type, and discarding those secular standards (as for want of a better name they may be called) which heretofore coexisted with and supplemented the Christian ethics, receiving some of its spirit, and infusing into it some of theirs, there will result, and is even now resulting, a low, abject, servile type of character, which, submit itself as it may to what it deems the Supreme Will, is incapable of rising to or sympathizing in the conception of Supreme Goodness. I believe that other ethics than any one which can be evolved from exclusively Christian sources, must exist side by side with Christian ethics to produce the moral regeneration of mankind; and that the Christian system is no exception to the rule that in an imperfect state of the human mind, the interests of truth require a diversity of opinions. It is not necessary that in ceasing to ignore the moral truths not contained in Christianity, men should ignore any of those which it does contain. Such prejudice, or oversight, when it occurs, is altogether an evil; but it is one from which we cannot hope to be always exempt, and must be regarded as the price paid for an inestimable good. The exclusive pretension made by a part of the truth to be the whole, must and ought to be protested against, and if a reactionary impulse should make the protestors unjust in their turn, this one-sidedness, like the other, may be lamented, but must be tolerated. If Christians would teach infidels to be just to Christianity, they should themselves be just to infidelity. It can do truth no service to blink the fact, known to all who have the most ordinary acquaintance with literary history, that a large portion of the noblest and most valuable moral teaching has been the work, not only of men who did not know, but of men who knew and rejected, the Christian faith.

I do not pretend that the most unlimited use of the freedom of enunciating all possible opinions would put an end to the evils of religious or philosophical sectarianism. Every truth which men of narrow capacity are in earnest about, is sure to be asserted, inculcated, and in many ways even acted on, as if no other truth existed in the world, or at all events none that could limit or qualify the first. I acknowledge that the tendency of all opinions to become sectarian is not cured by the freest discussion, but is often heightened and exacerbated thereby; the truth which ought to have been, but was not, seen, being rejected all the more violently because proclaimed by persons regarded as opponents. But it is not on the impassioned partisan, it is on the calmer and more disinterested bystander, that this collision of opinions works its salutary effect. Not the violent conflict between parts of the truth, but the quiet suppression of half of it, is the formidable evil: there is always hope when people are forced to listen to both sides; it is when they attend only to one that errors harden into prejudices, and truth itself ceases to have the effect of truth, by being exaggerated into falsehood. And since there are few mental attributes more rare than that judicial faculty which can sit in intelligent judgment between two sides of a question, of which only one is represented by an advocate before it, truth has no chance but in proportion as every side of it, every opinion which embodies any fraction of the truth, not only finds advocates, but is so advocated as to be listened to.

We have now recognized the necessity to the mental well-being of mankind (on which all their other well-being depends) of freedom of opinion, and freedom of the expression of opinion, on four distinct grounds; which we will now briefly recapitulate.

First, if any opinion is compelled to silence, that opinion may, for aught we can certainly know, be true. To deny this is to assume our own infallibility.

Secondly, though the silenced opinion be an error, it may, and very commonly does, contain a portion of truth; and since the general or prevailing opinion on any object is rarely or never the whole truth, it is only by the collision of adverse opinions that the remainder of the truth has any chance of being supplied.

Thirdly, even if the received opinion be not only true, but the whole truth; unless it is suffered to be, and actually is, vigorously and earnestly contested, it will, by most of those who receive it, be held in the manner of a prejudice, with little comprehension or feeling of its rational grounds. And not only this, but, fourthly, the meaning of the doctrine itself will be in danger of being lost, or enfeebled, and deprived of its vital effect on the character and conduct: the dogma becoming a mere formal profession, inefficacious for good, but cumbering the ground, and preventing the growth of any real and heartfelt conviction, from reason or personal experience.

Before quitting the subject of freedom of opinion, it is fit to take notice of those who say, that the free expression of all opinions should be permitted, on condition that the manner be temperate, and do not pass the bounds of fair discussion. Much might be said on the impossibility of fixing where these supposed bounds are to be placed; for if the test be offence to those whose opinion is attacked, I think experience testifies that this offence is given whenever the attack is telling and powerful, and that every opponent who pushes them hard, and whom they find it difficult to answer, appears to them, if he shows any strong feeling on the subject, an intemperate opponent. But this, though an important consideration in a practical point of view, merges in a more fundamental objection. Undoubtedly the manner of asserting an opinion, even though it be a true one, may be very objectionable, and may justly incur severe censure. But the principal offences of the kind are such as it is mostly impossible, unless by accidental self-betrayal, to bring home to conviction. The gravest of them is, to argue sophistically,[66] to suppress facts or arguments, to misstate the elements of the case, or misrepresent the opposite opinion. But all this, even to the most aggravated degree, is so continually done in perfect good faith, by persons who are not considered, and in many other respects may not deserve to be considered, ignorant or incompetent, that it is rarely possible on adequate grounds conscientiously to stamp the misrepresentation as morally culpable; and still less could law presume to interfere with this kind of controversial misconduct. With regard to what is commonly meant by intemperate discussion, namely, invective, sarcasm, personality, and the like, the denunciation of these weapons would deserve more sympathy if it were ever proposed to interdict them equally to both sides; but it is only desired to restrain the employment of them against the prevailing opinion: against the unprevailing they may not only be used without general disapproval, but will be likely to obtain for him who uses them the praise of honest zeal and righteous indignation. Yet whatever mischief arises from their use, is greatest when they are employed against the comparatively defenceless; and whatever unfair advantage can be derived by any opinion from this mode of asserting it, accrues almost exclusively to received opinions. The worst offence of this kind which can be committed by a polemic, is to stigmatize those who hold the contrary opinion as bad and immoral men. To calumny of this sort, those who hold any unpopular opinion are peculiarly exposed, because they are in general few and uninfluential, and nobody but themselves feels much interest in seeing justice done them; but this weapon is, from the nature of the case, denied to those who attack a prevailing opinion: they can neither use it with safety to themselves, nor if they could, would it do anything but recoil on their own cause. In general, opinions contrary to those commonly received can only obtain a hearing by studied moderation of language, and the most cautious avoidance of unnecessary offence, from which they hardly ever deviate even in a slight degree without losing ground: while unmeasured vituperation[67] employed on the side of the prevailing opinion, really does deter people from professing contrary opinions, and from listening to those who profess them. For the interest, therefore, of truth and justice, it is far more important to restrain this employment of vituperative language than the other; and, for example, if it were necessary to choose, there would be much more need to discourage offensive attacks on infidelity, than on religion. It is, however, obvious that law and authority have no business with restraining either, while opinion ought, in every instance, to determine its verdict by the circumstances of the individual case; condemning every one, on whichever side of the argument he places himself, in whose mode of advocacy either want of candour, or malignity, bigotry or intolerance of feeling manifest themselves, but not inferring these vices from the side which a person takes, though it be the contrary side of the question to our own; and giving merited honour to every one, whatever opinion he may hold, who has calmness to see and honesty to state what his opponents and their opinions really are, exaggerating nothing to their discredit, keeping nothing back which tells, or can be supposed to tell, in their favour. This is the real morality of public discussion; and if often violated, I am happy to think that

---

66   Plausibly but fallaciously.

67   Harsh abuse.

there are many controversialists who to a great extent observe it, and a still greater number who conscientiously strive towards it.

...

Chapter IV: Of the Limits to the Authority of Society over the Individual

What, then, is the rightful limit to the sovereignty of the individual over himself? Where does the authority of society begin? How much of human life should be assigned to individuality, and how much to society?

Each will receive its proper share, if each has that which more particularly concerns it. To individuality should belong the part of life in which it is chiefly the individual that is interested; to society, the part which chiefly interests society.

Though society is not founded on a contract, and though no good purpose is answered by inventing a contract in order to deduce social obligations from it, every one who receives the protection of society owes a return for the benefit, and the fact of living in society renders it indispensable that each should be bound to observe a certain line of conduct towards the rest. This conduct consists, first, in not injuring the interests of one another; or rather certain interests, which, either by express legal provision or by tacit understanding, ought to be considered as rights; and secondly, in each person's bearing his share (to be fixed on some equitable principle) of the labours and sacrifices incurred for defending the society or its members from injury and molestation. These conditions society is justified in enforcing, at all costs to those who endeavour to withhold fulfilment. Nor is this all that society may do. The acts of an individual may be hurtful to others, or wanting in due consideration for their welfare, without going the length of violating any of their constituted rights. The offender may then be justly punished by opinion, though not by law. As soon as any part of a person's conduct affects prejudicially the interests of others, society has jurisdiction over it, and the question whether the general welfare will or will not be promoted by interfering with it, becomes open to discussion. But there is no room for entertaining any such question when a person's conduct affects the interests of no persons besides himself, or needs not affect them unless they like (all the persons concerned

being of full age, and the ordinary amount of understanding). In all such cases there should be perfect freedom, legal and social, to do the action and stand the consequences.

It would be a great misunderstanding of this doctrine, to suppose that it is one of selfish indifference, which pretends that human beings have no business with each other's conduct in life, and that they should not concern themselves about the well-doing or well-being of one another, unless their own interest is involved. Instead of any diminution, there is need of a great increase of disinterested exertion to promote the good of others. But disinterested benevolence can find other instruments to persuade people to their good, than whips and scourges, either of the literal or the metaphorical sort. I am the last person to undervalue the self-regarding virtues; they are only second in importance, if even second, to the social. It is equally the business of education to cultivate both. But even education works by conviction and persuasion as well as by compulsion, and it is by the former only that, when the period of education is past, the self-regarding virtues should be inculcated. Human beings owe to each other help to distinguish the better from the worse, and encouragement to choose the former and avoid the latter. They should be forever stimulating each other to increased exercise of their higher faculties, and increased direction of their feelings and aims towards wise instead of foolish, elevating instead of degrading, objects and contemplations. But neither one person, nor any number of persons, is warranted in saying to another human creature of ripe years, that he shall not do with his life for his own benefit what he chooses to do with it. He is the person most interested in his own well-being, the interest which any other person, except in cases of strong personal attachment, can have in it, is trifling, compared with that which he himself has; the interest which society has in him individually (except as to his conduct to others) is fractional, and altogether indirect: while, with respect to his own feelings and circumstances, the most ordinary man or woman has means of knowledge immeasurably surpassing those that can be possessed by any one else. The interference of society to overrule his judgment and purposes in what only regards himself, must be grounded on general presumptions;

which may be altogether wrong, and even if right, are as likely as not to be misapplied to individual cases, by persons no better acquainted with the circumstances of such cases than those are who look at them merely from without. In this department, therefore, of human affairs, Individuality has its proper field of action. In the conduct of human beings towards one another, it is necessary that general rules should for the most part be observed, in order that people may know what they have to expect; but in each person's own concerns, his individual spontaneity is entitled to free exercise. Considerations to aid his judgment, exhortations to strengthen his will, may be offered to him, even obtruded on him, by others; but he, himself, is the final judge. All errors which he is likely to commit against advice and warning, are far outweighed by the evil of allowing others to constrain him to what they deem his good.

I do not mean that the feelings with which a person is regarded by others, ought not to be in any way affected by his self-regarding qualities or deficiencies. This is neither possible nor desirable. If he is eminent in any of the qualities which conduce to his own good, he is, so far, a proper object of admiration. He is so much the nearer to the ideal perfection of human nature. If he is grossly deficient in those qualities, a sentiment the opposite of admiration will follow. There is a degree of folly, and a degree of what may be called (though the phrase is not unobjectionable) lowness or depravation of taste, which, though it cannot justify doing harm to the person who manifests it, renders him necessarily and properly a subject of distaste, or, in extreme cases, even of contempt: a person could not have the opposite qualities in due strength without entertaining these feelings. Though doing no wrong to any one, a person may so act as to compel us to judge him, and feel to him, as a fool, or as a being of an inferior order: and since this judgment and feeling are a fact which he would prefer to avoid, it is doing him a service to warn him of it beforehand, as of any other disagreeable consequence to which he exposes himself. It would be well, indeed, if this good office were much more freely rendered than the common notions of politeness at present permit, and if one person could honestly point out to another that he thinks him in fault, without being considered unman-

nerly or presuming. We have a right, also, in various ways, to act upon our unfavourable opinion of any one, not to the oppression of his individuality, but in the exercise of ours. We are not bound, for example, to seek his society; we have a right to avoid it (though not to parade the avoidance), for we have a right to choose the society most acceptable to us. We have a right, and it may be our duty, to caution others against him, if we think his example or conversation likely to have a pernicious effect on those with whom he associates. We may give others a preference over him in optional good offices, except those which tend to his improvement. In these various modes a person may suffer very severe penalties at the hands of others, for faults which directly concern only himself; but he suffers these penalties only in so far as they are the natural, and, as it were, the spontaneous consequences of the faults themselves, not because they are purposely inflicted on him for the sake of punishment. A person who shows rashness, obstinacy, self-conceit—who cannot live within moderate means—who cannot restrain himself from hurtful indulgences—who pursues animal pleasures at the expense of those of feeling and intellect—must expect to be lowered in the opinion of others, and to have a less share of their favourable sentiments, but of this he has no right to complain, unless he has merited their favour by special excellence in his social relations, and has thus established a title to their good offices, which is not affected by his demerits towards himself.

What I contend for is, that the inconveniences which are strictly inseparable from the unfavourable judgment of others, are the only ones to which a person should ever be subjected for that portion of his conduct and character which concerns his own good, but which does not affect the interests of others in their relations with him. Acts injurious to others require a totally different treatment. Encroachment on their rights; infliction on them of any loss or damage not justified by his own rights; falsehood or duplicity in dealing with them; unfair or ungenerous use of advantages over them; even selfish abstinence from defending them against injury—these are fit objects of moral reprobation, and, in grave cases, of moral retribution and punishment. And not only these acts, but the dispositions which lead to them, are properly immoral, and fit subjects of disapprobation which may rise to abhorrence. Cruelty of disposition; malice and ill-nature; that most anti-social and odious of all passions, envy; dissimulation and insincerity, irascibility on insufficient cause, and resentment disproportioned to the provocation; the love of domineering over others; the desire to engross more than one's share of advantages (the πλεονεξία[68] of the Greeks); the pride which derives gratification from the abasement of others; the egotism which thinks self and its concerns more important than everything else, and decides all doubtful questions in his own favour;—these are moral vices, and constitute a bad and odious moral character: unlike the self-regarding faults previously mentioned, which are not properly immoralities, and to whatever pitch they may be carried, do not constitute wickedness. They may be proofs of any amount of folly, or want of personal dignity and self-respect; but they are only a subject of moral reprobation when they involve a breach of duty to others, for whose sake the individual is bound to have care for himself. What are called duties to ourselves are not socially obligatory, unless circumstances render them at the same time duties to others. The term duty to oneself, when it means anything more than prudence, means self-respect or self-development; and for none of these is any one accountable to his fellow-creatures, because for none of them is it for the good of mankind that he be held accountable to them.

The distinction between the loss of consideration which a person may rightly incur by defect of prudence or of personal dignity, and the reprobation which is due to him for an offence against the rights of others, is not a merely nominal distinction. It makes a vast difference both in our feelings and in our conduct towards him, whether he displeases us in things in which we think we have a right to control him, or in things in which we know that we have not. If he displeases us, we may express our distaste, and we may stand aloof from a person as well as from a thing that displeases us; but we shall not therefore feel called on to make his life uncomfortable. We shall reflect that he already bears, or will bear, the whole penalty of his error; if he spoils his life by mismanagement, we

shall not, for that reason, desire to spoil it still further: instead of wishing to punish him, we shall rather endeavour to alleviate his punishment, by showing him how he may avoid or cure the evils his conduct tends to bring upon him. He may be to us an object of pity, perhaps of dislike, but not of anger or resentment; we shall not treat him like an enemy of society: the worst we shall think ourselves justified in doing is leaving him to himself, if we do not interfere benevolently by showing interest or concern for him. It is far otherwise if he has infringed the rules necessary for the protection of his fellow-creatures, individually or collectively. The evil consequences of his acts do not then fall on himself, but on others; and society, as the protector of all its members, must retaliate on him; must inflict pain on him for the express purpose of punishment, and must take care that it be sufficiently severe. In the one case, he is an offender at our bar,[69] and we are called on not only to sit in judgment on him, but, in one shape or another, to execute our own sentence: in the other case, it is not our part to inflict any suffering on him, except what may incidentally follow from our using the same liberty in the regulation of our own affairs, which we allow to him in his.

The distinction here pointed out between the part of a person's life which concerns only himself, and that which concerns others, many persons will refuse to admit. How (it may be asked) can any part of the conduct of a member of society be a matter of indifference to the other members? No person is an entirely isolated being; it is impossible for a person to do anything seriously or permanently hurtful to himself, without mischief reaching at least to his near connections, and often far beyond them. If he injures his property, he does harm to those who directly or indirectly derived support from it, and usually diminishes, by a greater or less amount, the general resources of the community. If he deteriorates his bodily or mental faculties, he not only brings evil upon all who depended on him for any portion of their happiness, but disqualifies himself for rendering the services which he owes to his fellow-creatures generally; perhaps becomes a burthen[70] on their affection or

---

68   *Pleonexia*—greediness, graspingness.

69   Tribunal, place of judgment.

70   Burden.

benevolence; and if such conduct were very frequent, hardly any offence that is committed would detract more from the general sum of good. Finally, if by his vices or follies a person does no direct harm to others, he is nevertheless (it may be said) injurious by his example; and ought to be compelled to control himself, for the sake of those whom the sight or knowledge of his conduct might corrupt or mislead.

And even (it will be added) if the consequences of misconduct could be confined to the vicious or thoughtless individual, ought society to abandon to their own guidance those who are manifestly unfit for it? If protection against themselves is confessedly due to children and persons under age, is not society equally bound to afford it to persons of mature years who are equally incapable of self-government? If gambling, or drunkenness, or incontinence,[71] or idleness, or uncleanliness, are as injurious to happiness, and as great a hindrance to improvement, as many or most of the acts prohibited by law, why (it may be asked) should not law, so far as is consistent with practicability and social convenience, endeavour to repress these also? And as a supplement to the unavoidable imperfections of law, ought not opinion at least to organize a powerful police against these vices, and visit rigidly with social penalties those who are known to practise them? There is no question here (it may be said) about restricting individuality, or impeding the trial of new and original experiments in living. The only things it is sought to prevent are things which have been tried and condemned from the beginning of the world until now; things which experience has shown not to be useful or suitable to any person's individuality. There must be some length of time and amount of experience, after which a moral or prudential truth may be regarded as established, and it is merely desired to prevent generation after generation from falling over the same precipice which has been fatal to their predecessors.

I fully admit that the mischief which a person does to himself, may seriously affect, both through their sympathies and their interests, those nearly connected with him, and in a minor degree, society at large. When, by conduct of this sort, a person is led to violate a distinct and assignable obligation to any other person or persons, the case is taken out of the self-regarding class, and becomes amenable to moral disapprobation in the proper sense of the term. If, for example, a man, through intemperance or extravagance, becomes unable to pay his debts, or, having undertaken the moral responsibility of a family, becomes from the same cause incapable of supporting or educating them, he is deservedly reprobated, and might be justly punished; but it is for the breach of duty to his family or creditors, not for the extravagance. If the resources which ought to have been devoted to them, had been diverted from them for the most prudent investment, the moral culpability would have been the same. George Barnwell murdered his uncle to get money for his mistress, but if he had done it to set himself up in business, he would equally have been hanged.[72] Again, in the frequent case of a man who causes grief to his family by addiction to bad habits, he deserves reproach for his unkindness or ingratitude; but so he may for cultivating habits not in themselves vicious, if they are painful to those with whom he passes his life, or who from personal ties are dependent on him for their comfort. Whoever fails in the consideration generally due to the interests and feelings of others, not being compelled by some more imperative duty, or justified by allowable self-preference, is a subject of moral disapprobation for that failure, but not for the cause of it, nor for the errors, merely personal to himself, which may have remotely led to it. In like manner, when a person disables himself, by conduct purely self-regarding, from the performance of some definite duty incumbent on him to the public, he is guilty of a social offence. No person ought to be punished simply for being drunk; but a soldier or a policeman should be punished for being drunk on duty. Whenever, in

---

71   Lack of self-control.

72   This tale was featured in the popular seventeenth-century ballad "George Barnwell," and later formed the subject matter of a play by George Lillo, *The London Merchant, or, the History of George Barnwell* (1731), which was one of the first prose works of domestic tragedy in English. It is the story of a young apprentice's downfall caused by his love for a beautiful, but unfeeling, prostitute.

short, there is a definite damage, or a definite risk of damage, either to an individual or to the public, the case is taken out of the province of liberty, and placed in that of morality or law.

But with regard to the merely contingent or, as it may be called, constructive injury which a person causes to society, by conduct which neither violates any specific duty to the public, nor occasions perceptible hurt to any assignable individual except himself; the inconvenience is one which society can afford to bear, for the sake of the greater good of human freedom. If grown persons are to be punished for not taking proper care of themselves, I would rather it were for their own sake, than under pretence of preventing them from impairing their capacity of rendering to society benefits which society does not pretend it has a right to exact. But I cannot consent to argue the point as if society had no means of bringing its weaker members up to its ordinary standard of rational conduct, except waiting till they do something irrational, and then punishing them, legally or morally, for it. Society has had absolute power over them during all the early portion of their existence: it has had the whole period of childhood and nonage in which to try whether it could make them capable of rational conduct in life. The existing generation is master both of the training and the entire circumstances of the generation to come; it cannot indeed make them perfectly wise and good, because it is itself so lamentably deficient in goodness and wisdom; and its best efforts are not always, in individual cases, its most successful ones; but it is perfectly well able to make the rising generation, as a whole, as good as, and a little better than, itself. If society lets any considerable number of its members grow up mere children, incapable of being acted on by rational consideration of distant motives, society has itself to blame for the consequences. Armed not only with all the powers of education, but with the ascendancy which the authority of a received opinion always exercises over the minds who are least fitted to judge for themselves; and aided by the *natural* penalties which cannot be prevented from falling on those who incur the distaste or the contempt of those who know them; let not society pretend that it needs, besides all this, the power to issue commands and enforce obedience in the personal concerns of individuals, in

which, on all principles of justice and policy, the decision ought to rest with those who are to abide the consequences. Nor is there anything which tends more to discredit and frustrate the better means of influencing conduct, than a resort to the worse. If there be among those whom it is attempted to coerce into prudence or temperance, any of the material of which vigorous and independent characters are made, they will infallibly rebel against the yoke. No such person will ever feel that others have a right to control him in his concerns, such as they have to prevent him from injuring them in theirs; and it easily comes to be considered a mark of spirit and courage to fly in the face of such usurped authority, and do with ostentation the exact opposite of what it enjoins; as in the fashion of grossness which succeeded, in the time of Charles II,[73] to the fanatical moral intolerance of the Puritans. With respect to what is said of the necessity of protecting society from the bad example set to others by the vicious or the self-indulgent; it is true that bad example may have a pernicious effect, especially the example of doing wrong to others with impunity to the wrong-doer. But we are now speaking of conduct which, while it does no wrong to others, is supposed to do great harm to the agent himself: and I do not see how those who believe this, can think otherwise than that the example, on the whole, must be more salutary than hurtful, since, if it displays the misconduct, it displays also the painful or degrading consequences which, if the conduct is justly censured, must be supposed to be in all or most cases attendant on it.

But the strongest of all the arguments against the interference of the public with purely personal conduct, is that when it does interfere, the odds are that it interferes wrongly, and in the wrong place. On questions of social morality, of duty to others, the opinion of the public, that is, of an overruling majority, though often wrong, is likely to be still oftener right; because on such questions they are only required to judge of their own interests; of the manner in which some mode of conduct, if allowed to be practised, would affect themselves. But the opinion of a similar majority, imposed

---

73   Charles II was King of England (1660–1685) immediately following the Restoration of the monarchy after its overthrow during the English Civil War.

as a law on the minority, on questions of self-regarding conduct, is quite as likely to be wrong as right; for in these cases public opinion means, at the best, some people's opinion of what is good or bad for other people; while very often it does not even mean that; the public, with the most perfect indifference, passing over the pleasure or convenience of those whose conduct they censure, and considering only their own preference. There are many who consider as an injury to themselves any conduct which they have a distaste for, and resent it as an outrage to their feelings; as a religious bigot, when charged with disregarding the religious feelings of others, has been known to retort that they disregard his feelings, by persisting in their abominable worship or creed. But there is no parity between the feeling of a person for his own opinion, and the feeling of another who is offended at his holding it; no more than between the desire of a thief to take a purse, and the desire of the right owner to keep it. And a person's taste is as much his own peculiar concern as his opinion or his purse. It is easy for any one to imagine an ideal public, which leaves the freedom and choice of individuals in all uncertain matters undisturbed, and only requires them to abstain from modes of conduct which universal experience has condemned. But where has there been seen a public which set any such limit to its censorship? or when does the public trouble itself about universal experience? In its interferences with personal conduct it is seldom thinking of anything but the enormity of acting or feeling differently from itself; and this standard of judgment, thinly disguised, is held up to mankind as the dictate of religion and philosophy, by nine tenths of all moralists and speculative writers. These teach that things are right because they are right; because we feel them to be so. They tell us to search in our own minds and hearts for laws of conduct binding on ourselves and on all others. What can the poor public do but apply these instructions, and make their own personal feelings of good and evil, if they are tolerably unanimous in them, obligatory on all the world?

The evil here pointed out is not one which exists only in theory; and it may perhaps be expected that I should specify the instances in which the public of this age and country improperly invests its own preferences with the character of moral laws. I am not writing an essay on the aberrations of existing moral feeling. That is too weighty a subject to be discussed parenthetically, and by way of illustration. Yet examples are necessary, to show that the principle I maintain is of serious and practical moment, and that I am not endeavouring to erect a barrier against imaginary evils. And it is not difficult to show, by abundant instances, that to extend the bounds of what may be called moral police, until it encroaches on the most unquestionably legitimate liberty of the individual, is one of the most universal of all human propensities.

As a first instance, consider the antipathies which men cherish on no better grounds than that persons whose religious opinions are different from theirs, do not practise their religious observances, especially their religious abstinences. To cite a rather trivial example, nothing in the creed or practice of Christians does more to envenom the hatred of Mahomedans[74] against them, than the fact of their eating pork. There are few acts which Christians and Europeans regard with more unaffected disgust, than Mussulmans[75] regard this particular mode of satisfying hunger. It is, in the first place, an offence against their religion; but this circumstance by no means explains either the degree or the kind of their repugnance; for wine also is forbidden by their religion, and to partake of it is by all Mussulmans accounted wrong, but not disgusting. Their aversion to the flesh of the "unclean beast" is, on the contrary, of that peculiar character, resembling an instinctive antipathy, which the idea of uncleanness, when once it thoroughly sinks into the feelings, seems always to excite even in those whose personal habits are anything but scrupulously cleanly and of which the sentiment of religious impurity, so intense in the Hindoos, is a remarkable example. Suppose now that in a people, of whom the majority were Mussulmans, that majority should insist upon not permitting pork to be eaten within the limits of the country. This would be nothing new in Mahomedan countries.[76] Would

---

74   Muslims.

75   Also Muslims (archaic form).

76   [Author's note] The case of the Bombay Parsees is a curious instance in point. When this industrious and enterprising tribe, the descendants of the Persian fire-worshippers, flying from their native country before

it be a legitimate exercise of the moral authority of public opinion? and if not, why not? The practice is really revolting to such a public. They also sincerely think that it is forbidden and abhorred by the Deity. Neither could the prohibition be censured as religious persecution. It might be religious in its origin, but it would not be persecution for religion, since nobody's religion makes it a duty to eat pork. The only tenable ground of condemnation would be, that with the personal tastes and self-regarding concerns of individuals the public has no business to interfere.

To come somewhat nearer home: the majority of Spaniards consider it a gross impiety, offensive in the highest degree to the Supreme Being, to worship him in any other manner than the Roman Catholic; and no other public worship is lawful on Spanish soil. The people of all Southern Europe look upon a married clergy as not only irreligious, but unchaste, indecent, gross, disgusting. What do Protestants think of these perfectly sincere feelings, and of the attempt to enforce them against non-Catholics? Yet, if mankind are justified in interfering with each other's liberty in things which do not concern the interests of others, on what principle is it possible consistently to exclude these cases? or who can blame people for desiring to suppress what they regard as a scandal in the sight of God and man? No stronger case can be shown for prohibiting anything which is regarded as a personal immorality, than is made out for suppressing these practices in the eyes of those who regard them as impieties; and unless we are willing to adopt the logic of persecutors, and to say that we may persecute others because we are right, and that they must not persecute us because they are wrong, we must beware

of admitting a principle of which we should resent as a gross injustice the application to ourselves.

The preceding instances may be objected to, although unreasonably, as drawn from contingencies impossible among us: opinion, in this country, not being likely to enforce abstinence from meats, or to interfere with people for worshipping, and for either marrying or not marrying, according to their creed or inclination. The next example, however, shall be taken from an interference with liberty which we have by no means passed all danger of. Wherever the Puritans have been sufficiently powerful, as in New England, and in Great Britain at the time of the Commonwealth, they have endeavoured, with considerable success, to put down all public, and nearly all private, amusements: especially music, dancing, public games, or other assemblages for purposes of diversion, and the theatre. There are still in this country large bodies of persons by whose notions of morality and religion these recreations are condemned; and those persons belonging chiefly to the middle class, who are the ascendant power in the present social and political condition of the kingdom, it is by no means impossible that persons of these sentiments may at some time or other command a majority in Parliament. How will the remaining portion of the community like to have the amusements that shall be permitted to them regulated by the religious and moral sentiments of the stricter Calvinists and Methodists? Would they not, with considerable peremptoriness, desire these intrusively pious members of society to mind their own business? This is precisely what should be said to every government and every public, who have the pretension that no person shall enjoy any pleasure which they think wrong. But if the principle of the pretension be admitted, no one can reasonably object to its being acted on in the sense of the majority, or other preponderating power in the country; and all persons must be ready to conform to the idea of a Christian commonwealth, as understood by the early settlers in New England, if a religious profession similar to theirs should ever succeed in regaining its lost ground, as religions supposed to be declining have so often been known to do.

To imagine another contingency, perhaps more likely to be realized than the one last mentioned. There

---

the Caliphs, arrived in Western India, they were admitted to toleration by the Hindoo sovereigns, on condition of not eating beef. When those regions afterwards fell under the dominion of Mahomedan conquerors, the Parsees obtained from them a continuance of indulgence, on condition of refraining from pork. What was at first obedience to authority became a second nature, and the Parsees to this day abstain both from beef and pork. Though not required by their religion, the double abstinence has had time to grow into a custom of their tribe; and custom, in the East, is a religion.

is confessedly a strong tendency in the modern world towards a democratic constitution of society, accompanied or not by popular political institutions. It is affirmed that in the country where this tendency is most completely realized—where both society and the government are most democratic—the United States—the feeling of the majority, to whom any appearance of a more showy or costly style of living than they can hope to rival is disagreeable, operates as a tolerably effectual sumptuary law,[77] and that in many parts of the Union it is really difficult for a person possessing a very large income, to find any mode of spending it, which will not incur popular disapprobation. Though such statements as these are doubtless much exaggerated as a representation of existing facts, the state of things they describe is not only a conceivable and possible, but a probable result of democratic feeling, combined with the notion that the public has a right to a veto on the manner in which individuals shall spend their incomes. We have only further to suppose a considerable diffusion of Socialist opinions, and it may become infamous in the eyes of the majority to possess more property than some very small amount, or any income not earned by manual labour. Opinions similar in principle to these, already prevail widely among the artisan class, and weigh oppressively on those who are amenable to[78] the opinion chiefly of that class, namely, its own members. It is known that the bad workmen who form the majority of the operatives in many branches of industry, are decidedly of opinion that bad workmen ought to receive the same wages as good, and that no one ought to be allowed, through piecework or otherwise, to earn by superior skill or industry more than others can without it. And they employ a moral police, which occasionally becomes a physical one, to deter skilful workmen from receiving, and employers from giving, a larger remuneration for a more useful service. If the public have any jurisdiction over private concerns, I cannot see that these people are in fault, or that any individual's particular

public can be blamed for asserting the same authority over his individual conduct, which the general public asserts over people in general.

But, without dwelling upon supposititious cases, there are, in our own day, gross usurpations upon the liberty of private life actually practised, and still greater ones threatened with some expectation of success, and opinions proposed which assert an unlimited right in the public not only to prohibit by law everything which it thinks wrong, but in order to get at what it thinks wrong, to prohibit any number of things which it admits to be innocent.

Under the name of preventing intemperance the people of one English colony, and of nearly half the United States,[79] have been interdicted by law from making any use whatever of fermented drinks, except for medical purposes: for prohibition of their sale is in fact, as it is intended to be, prohibition of their use. And though the impracticability of executing the law has caused its repeal in several of the States which had adopted it, including the one from which it derives its name,[80] an attempt has notwithstanding been commenced, and is prosecuted with considerable zeal by many of the professed philanthropists, to agitate for a similar law in this country. The association, or "Alliance" as it terms itself,[81] which has been formed for this purpose, has acquired some notoriety through the publicity given to a correspondence between its Secretary and one of the very few English public men[82] who hold that a politician's opinions ought

---

77 A law regulating or limiting personal expenditures, especially one forbidding great displays of wealth (e.g., building excessively large houses) or expenditures which are judged immoral (e.g., gambling).

78 Accountable to, judged by.

79 New Brunswick (then an English colony; it became one of the four founding provinces of the Dominion of Canada in 1867) and thirteen of the American states.

80 Maine: "Maine Law" was a popular term for prohibition in this period.

81 The "United Kingdom Alliance for the Legislative Suppression of the Sale of Intoxicating Liquors," founded in 1853. This organization energetically continued its fight into the early decades of the twentieth century.

82 Edward John Stanley, a Whig (Liberal) politician who was president of the Board of Trade from 1855 until 1858. In the later years of the nineteenth century the temperance movement became generally associated with the Liberal Party, while the Conservative Party tended to defend the interests of the drink trade.

to be founded on principles. Lord Stanley's share in this correspondence is calculated to strengthen the hopes already built on him, by those who know how rare such qualities as are manifested in some of his public appearances, unhappily, are among those who figure in political life. The organ of the Alliance, who would "deeply deplore the recognition of any principle which could be wrested to justify bigotry and persecution," undertakes to point out the "broad and impassable barrier" which divides such principles from those of the association. "All matters relating to thought, opinion, conscience, appear to me," he says, "to be without the sphere of legislation; all pertaining to social act, habit, relation, subject only to a discretionary power vested in the State itself, and not in the individual, to be within it." No mention is made of a third class, different from either of these, viz., acts and habits which are not social, but individual; although it is to this class, surely, that the act of drinking fermented liquors belongs. Selling fermented liquors, however, is trading, and trading is a social act. But the infringement complained of is not on the liberty of the seller, but on that of the buyer and consumer; since the State might just as well forbid him to drink wine, as purposely make it impossible for him to obtain it. The Secretary, however, says, "I claim, as a citizen, a right to legislate whenever my social rights are invaded by the social act of another." And now for the definition of these "social rights." "If anything invades my social rights, certainly the traffic in strong drink does. It destroys my primary right of security, by constantly creating and stimulating social disorder. It invades my right of equality, by deriving a profit from the creation of a misery I am taxed to support. It impedes my right to free moral and intellectual development, by surrounding my path with dangers, and by weakening and demoralizing society, from which I have a right to claim mutual aid and intercourse." A theory of "social rights," the like of which probably never before found its way into distinct language—being nothing short of this—that it is the absolute social right of every individual, that every other individual shall act in every respect exactly as he ought; that whosoever fails thereof in the smallest particular, violates my social right, and entitles me to demand from the legislature the removal of the grievance. So

monstrous a principle is far more dangerous than any single interference with liberty; there is no violation of liberty which it would not justify; it acknowledges no right to any freedom whatever, except perhaps to that of holding opinions in secret, without ever disclosing them; for the moment an opinion which I consider noxious, passes any one's lips, it invades all the "social rights" attributed to me by the Alliance. The doctrine ascribes to all mankind a vested interest in each other's moral, intellectual, and even physical perfection, to be defined by each claimant according to his own standard.

Another important example of illegitimate interference with the rightful liberty of the individual, not simply threatened, but long since carried into triumphant effect, is Sabbatarian legislation.[83] Without doubt, abstinence on one day in the week, so far as the exigencies of life permit, from the usual daily occupation, though in no respect religiously binding on any except Jews,[84] is a highly beneficial custom. And inasmuch as this custom cannot be observed without a general consent to that effect among the industrious classes, therefore, in so far as some persons by working may impose the same necessity on others, it may be allowable and right that the law should guarantee to each, the observance by others of the custom, by suspending the greater operations of industry on a particular day. But this justification, grounded on the direct interest which others have in each individual's observance of the practice, does not apply to the self-chosen occupations in which a person may think fit to employ his leisure; nor does it hold good, in the smallest degree, for legal restrictions on amusements. It is true that the amusement of some is the day's work of others; but the pleasure, not to say the useful recreation, of many, is worth the labour of a few, provided the occupation is freely chosen, and can be freely resigned. The operatives are perfectly right in thinking that

---

83　Legislation making it unlawful to work or perform other activities on the Sabbath (which, for most Christians, is Sunday).

84　Orthodox Jews are prohibited from work and travel during their Sabbath (sundown Friday until sundown Saturday).

if all worked on Sunday, seven days' work would have to be given for six days' wages: but so long as the great mass of employments are suspended, the small number who for the enjoyment of others must still work, obtain a proportional increase of earnings; and they are not obliged to follow those occupations, if they prefer leisure to emolument.[85] If a further remedy is sought, it might be found in the establishment by custom of a holiday on some other day of the week for those particular classes of persons. The only ground, therefore, on which restrictions on Sunday amusements can be defended, must be that they are religiously wrong; a motive of legislation which never can be too earnestly protested against. "Deorum injuriae Diis curae."[86] It remains to be proved that society or any of its officers holds a commission from on high to avenge any supposed offence to Omnipotence, which is not also a wrong to our fellow-creatures. The notion that it is one man's duty that another should be religious, was the foundation of all the religious persecutions ever perpetrated, and if admitted, would fully justify them. Though the feeling which breaks out in the repeated attempts to stop railway travelling on Sunday, in the resistance to the opening of Museums, and the like, has not the cruelty of the old persecutors, the state of mind indicated by it is fundamentally the same. It is a determination not to tolerate others in doing what is permitted by their religion, because it is not permitted by the persecutor's religion. It is a belief that God not only abominates the act of the misbeliever, but will not hold us guiltless if we leave him unmolested.

I cannot refrain from adding to these examples of the little account commonly made of human liberty, the language of downright persecution which breaks out from the press of this country, whenever it feels called on to notice the remarkable phenomenon of Mormonism. Much might be said on the unexpected and instructive fact, that an alleged new revelation, and a religion, founded on it, the product of palpable imposture,[87] not even supported by the *prestige* of extraordinary qualities in its founder, is believed by hundreds of thousands, and has been made the foundation of a society, in the age of newspapers, railways, and the electric telegraph. What here concerns us is, that this religion, like other and better religions, has its martyrs; that its prophet and founder was, for his teaching, put to death by a mob; that others of its adherents lost their lives by the same lawless violence; that they were forcibly expelled, in a body, from the country in which they first grew up; while, now that they have been chased into a solitary recess in the midst of a desert,[88] many in this country openly declare that it would be right (only that it is not convenient) to send an expedition against them, and compel them by force to conform to the opinions of other people. The article of the Mormonite doctrine which is the chief provocative to the antipathy which thus breaks through the ordinary restraints of religious tolerance, is its sanction of polygamy;[89] which, though permitted to Mahomedans, and Hindoos, and Chinese, seems to excite unquenchable animosity when practised by persons who speak English, and profess to be a kind of Christians. No one has a deeper disapprobation than I have of this Mormon institution; both for other reasons, and because, far from being in any way countenanced by the principle of liberty, it is a direct infraction of that principle, being a mere riveting of

---

85 Compensation, payment.

86 "The gods can avenge their own wrongs"—from the *Annals* (c. 116 CE) of Tacitus, a Roman historian.

87 Obvious deception. The Mormon religion, officially known as the Church of Jesus Christ of Latter-Day Saints, was founded in 1830 in Palmyra, New York by Joseph Smith. He based the religion on the *Book of Mormon*, which he claimed was revealed to him by an angel in 1827. This was a translation of a golden book written in a mysterious hieroglyphic script, buried in a nearby hill, and accessible only through the angel's intervention. The religion has more than eight million members today.

88 Now Salt Lake City, in Utah. The Mormons were this inhospitable area's first permanent, Western settlers. Utah did not become a part of the United States until 1896.

89 Having more than one spouse at the same time: in the case of the Mormons, one man may have several wives.

the chains of one half of the community, and an emancipation of the other from reciprocity of obligation towards them. Still, it must be remembered that this relation is as much voluntary on the part of the women concerned in it, and who may be deemed the sufferers by it, as is the case with any other form of the marriage institution; and however surprising this fact may appear, it has its explanation in the common ideas and customs of the world, which teaching women to think marriage the one thing needful, make it intelligible that many a woman should prefer being one of several wives, to not being a wife at all. Other countries are not asked to recognize such unions, or release any portion of their inhabitants from their own laws on the score of Mormonite opinions. But when the dissentients have conceded to the hostile sentiments of others, far more than could justly be demanded; when they have left the countries to which their doctrines were unacceptable, and established themselves in a remote corner of the earth, which they have been the first to render habitable to human beings; it is difficult to see on what principles but those of tyranny they can be prevented from living there under what laws they please, provided they commit no aggression on other nations, and allow perfect freedom of departure to those who are dissatisfied with their ways. A recent writer, in some respects of considerable merit, proposes (to use his own words,) not a crusade, but a *civilizade*, against this polygamous community, to put an end to what seems to him a retrograde step in civilization. It also appears so to me, but I am not aware that any community has a right to force another to be civilized. So long as the sufferers by the bad law do not invoke assistance from other communities, I cannot admit that persons entirely unconnected with them ought to step in and require that a condition of things with which all who are directly interested appear to be satisfied, should be put an end to because it is a scandal to persons some thousands of miles distant, who have no part or concern in it. Let them send missionaries, if they please, to preach against it; and let them, by any fair means, (of which silencing the teachers is not one,) oppose the progress of similar doctrines among their own people. If civilization has got the better of barbarism when barbarism had the world to itself, it is too much to profess to be afraid lest barbarism, after having been fairly got under, should revive and conquer civilization. A civilization that can thus succumb to its vanquished enemy must first have become so degenerate, that neither its appointed priests and teachers, nor anybody else, has the capacity, or will take the trouble, to stand up for it. If this be so, the sooner such a civilization receives notice to quit, the better. It can only go on from bad to worse, until destroyed and regenerated (like the Western Empire[90]) by energetic barbarians.

---

90   The western part of the Roman Empire, which was broken up by barbarian invaders during the fifth century.

KARL MARX AND FRIEDRICH ENGELS
The Communist Manifesto

The philosophers have only *interpreted* the world in different ways; the point is to *change* it.
(Karl Marx, *Theses on Feuerbach*)

Who Were Karl Marx and Friedrich Engels?

Karl Heinrich Marx was born in 1818 in the town of Trier in the Rhineland, formerly a region of Prussia lying next to the French border that is today part of Germany. Both his parents were Jewish, descended from a long line of rabbis and Jewish intellectuals. They were part of the first generation of German Jews to enjoy equal legal status with Christians and to be granted free choice of residence and profession. The Rhineland had been ruled by the French during the Napoleonic period, from 1792 until 1815, and Marx's father Heinrich had benefited from the relatively enlightened French regime, using the opportunity to forge a successful career as a respected lawyer. However, after Prussian power was restored in Trier in 1815, Marx's father felt obliged to convert himself and his family to Lutheranism in order to protect his career, and so Karl was not brought up as a Jew.

Karl's father wanted him to become a lawyer, but Karl was a rowdy, rebellious child and, as a young man, chose to spend his time studying philosophy and history, dueling, and writing romantic verses to his childhood sweetheart, the daughter of his neighbor, Jenny von Westphalen (whom he married in 1843). From 1835 to 1841 Marx studied at the universities of Bonn (where he spent a year studying law) and Berlin, where he was exposed to, and heavily influenced by, the idealist philosophy of G.W.F. Hegel. Marx's early writings show his preoccupation with the notion of human self-realization through the struggle for freedom and a view of the nature of reality as turbulently changing, themes which find resonance in Hegel. However, like many contemporary "Young Hegelians," Marx found the Hegelian system, as it was then taught in the Prussian universities, to be politically and religiously much too conservative.

In 1841 Marx successfully submitted a doctoral dissertation (on Greek philosophy) to the university of Jena, but—because his political radicalism made him effectively unhireable in the contemporary political climate—he quickly gave up any prospect of an academic

Karl Marx   *Friedrich Engels*

career. Instead, he wrote for a liberal newspaper in Cologne, the *Rheinische Zeitung*, and in short order became its editor. Under Marx, the paper went from cautious criticism of the government to a more radical critique of prevailing conditions, especially issues of economic justice. Inevitably, the paper was first heavily censored and then, in 1843, shut down by the Prussian authorities. At this point Marx and his new wife left for the more bohemian city of Paris, where Marx worked as a journalist for another radical publication, the *Deutsch-Französische Jahrbücher* [*German-French Annals*]. Realizing that he knew little about the economic issues which he saw as so politically significant, Marx threw himself into the study of political economy. Even before these studies began, however, Marx was already—like many of his compatriots—politically left-wing in a way that could loosely be called "communist." He was convinced of the need for "cooperative" rather than individual control of economic resources, and was ferociously concerned about the need to alleviate the living conditions of the swelling numbers of urban poor.

In 1845, pressure from the Prussian government caused Marx to be expelled from France and he and his family moved to Brussels. There he developed a close friendship, begun in France, with Friedrich Engels, the man who was to be Marx's most important intellectual collaborator, supporter, and friend (indeed, the only lasting friend Marx ever had).

Engels was born in 1820 in Barmen, near Düsseldorf. His family were wealthy mill owners in the rapidly-industrializing northwest German Ruhr valley, and although Engels had hoped for a career in literature, his father insisted that he leave school at 17 to work for the family firm. He worked first in a local factory, then in an export office in the port city of Bremen, and finally as an accountant for the English branch of the firm Ermen and Engels. Thus, from the time he was a young man, Engels saw first-hand the profound social changes brought about by the introduction of new methods of production in the textile industry. Although he never formally attended university, he did sit in on lectures at Berlin university during his spell of compulsory military service and, through his exposure to the radical democratic movement, acquired a working knowledge of Hegel-

ian philosophy. He worked for the *Rheinische Zeitung* while Marx was its editor, writing articles from Manchester, England, where, employed by the family firm, he was appalled to witness the living conditions of the English working class. In 1844 he wrote the impassioned *Condition of the Working Classes in England*. He also wrote a critical study of the standard positions in political economy—a work that greatly impressed Marx, and directly intersected with his interests at the time. After Engels's return to Germany in 1844, the two began collaborating on writings, speeches, and debates intended to spread their radical ideas among workers and intellectuals. Their most important publication of this period was the *Communist Manifesto*.

1848, the year the *Communist Manifesto* was published, was a year of revolution in Europe. Most of the countries of Europe, except Britain, Belgium, and Russia, underwent a spasm of social upheaval in which old, aristocratic regimes fell and were replaced (briefly) by bold, new republican governments. Marx and Engels, in their different ways, attempted to play a role in this revolutionary process. Marx, now expelled from Belgium for his activism, returned to Cologne and started up a new radical broadsheet, the *Neue Reinische Zeitung*, his goal being to inspire and educate the revolutionary leaders (along the lines of the *Communist Manifesto*). Meanwhile, Engels was an officer in a short-lived military uprising in the German region of Baden. Within a matter of months, however, the European upheaval was over and, everywhere except France, the new democratic, republican regimes began to collapse and the old order reasserted itself. Marx and his associates were tried in a Cologne court for charges of inciting revolt and, although Marx successfully defended himself in court, he was nevertheless exiled from Prussian territory in 1849. As a result, Marx and Engels emigrated permanently to England: Marx, to live and write in London, and Engels to work for his family firm in Manchester.

Conditions were extremely hard for the Marx family, especially for the first decade of their lives in London. Marx was unwilling to take work that would interfere with his writing, and when he did seek stable employment he was unable to get it. (At one point he applied for a job as a railway clerk, but was unsuccessful because of the—now notorious—illegibility of his handwriting.) He and his family—his wife, her servant, and six children—subsisted on financial gifts from family and friends and on the income from Marx's occasional freelance journalism (mostly as a European correspondent for the *New York Tribune*, which paid £1 per article). Their main financial benefactor was Engels, who sent them grants and allowances taken from his own income and the money from his investments. Nevertheless, the Marx household lived in relative poverty for many years, enduring poor housing and bad food. Three of Marx's children died young, in part because of these hard conditions, and his own health suffered a collapse from which it never fully recovered.[1]

Meanwhile, Marx single-mindedly devoted his life to the cause of ending what he saw as the serious, and increasing, inequalities and exploitation inherent in capitalist society. His role, he thought, was to formulate the theoretical framework that would reveal the true state of things to the masses of workers and, by doing so, would both incite and guide the impending revolutionary replacement of capitalism by communism. He saw himself mainly as an 'ideas man' and a publicist for the communist movement, rather than an organizer or leader (and indeed, during his lifetime, his personal political influence was quite small). He spent ten hours a day, most days, in the Reading Room of the British Museum, conducting research and writing; after returning home, he would often continue to write late into the night. His main work during these years, a massive, wide-ranging, detailed analysis of capitalist society and what Marx saw as the tensions intrinsic to it, was eventually published in three substantial volumes as *Das Kapital* or *Capital*.[2]

Engels, meanwhile, ran his family's cotton mills in Lancashire and became a respected figure in Man-

chester society. He rode two days a week with the aristocratic Cheshire Hunt (valuable training, he claimed, for a future leader of the armies of the revolution), but at heart, Engels was unquestionably a devoted revolutionary, sincerely committed to the cause of communism, and he did his best to support Marx's work. He lived with an Irish factory girl called Mary Burns, and when she died he took in, and eventually married, her sister Lizzie.

In 1864 the International Working Men's Association (otherwise known as the First International) was formed. This was a watershed in the history of the working class movement, and for the next eight years the organization was highly influential in European left-wing politics. Marx was one of its main leaders, and was heavily engaged with its internal politics. By the 1870s he had become the leading theoretician for the radical movement in Europe, especially in Germany, and had become notorious across the continent as the "Red Doctor Marx."

Marx died, of chronic respiratory disease, in London in 1883. (Despite Engels's best efforts: he took him on a tour of France, Switzerland, and Algiers in the hope that a change of climate might help his condition.) He is buried next to his wife in Highgate Cemetery.

After 1870, Engels—who retired at fifty, an independently wealthy man—had devoted all of his time to helping Marx with his research, and after Marx's death he continued the writing of *Capital* from Marx's notes, completing it in 1894, a year before his own death.

In a speech given at Marx's graveside, Engels said

> …Marx was above all else a revolutionist. His real mission in life was to contribute, in one way or another, to the overthrow of capitalist society and of the state institutions which it had brought into being, to contribute to the liberation of the modern proletariat, which *he* was the first to make conscious of its own position and needs, conscious of the conditions of its emancipation. Fighting was his element. And he fought with a passion, a tenacity and a success such as few could rival.

---

1   Despite these hardships, however, Marx's marriage was apparently a very happy one, and he was a devoted husband and father.

2   Marx's mother is said to have commented that it was a shame that her boy merely wrote about capital and never acquired any.

What Was Marx's Overall Philosophical Project?

In 1852, Marx summarized his three most important political ideas in the following way:

1. That social classes are not permanent features of society, but instead are phases in the historical development of the relations of economic production.

2. That the struggle between these classes will necessarily lead to the "dictatorship of the proletariat," in which the working people will forcibly take over political power from the property-owners.

3. That the dictatorship of the proletariat is not an end in itself, but a transition period before the advent of a classless communist society devoted to the free development and flourishing of individuals.

What does Marx mean by these three claims? The first is best approached through Marx's analysis of capitalism. A large proportion of his writing was devoted to this analysis, and it provides the clearest example of how he thought social class divisions were produced and perpetuated by a particular type of economic system.

A society is capitalist, according to Marx, if the production of goods is dominated by the use of wage-labor: that is, by the use of labor power sold, as their only way to make a living, by people who have no significant control over means of production (the proletariat), and bought by other people who do have control over means of production such as raw materials, capital, and machinery (the bourgeoisie). The bourgeoisie make their money mostly by combining the purchased labor power with the means of production they own, and selling the commodities thus produced. Marx held that the relationship between these two classes, bourgeoisie and proletariat, was intrinsically and inescapably *antagonistic*, and he attempted to explain all the main institutional features of capitalist society in terms of this relation. Since, in Marx's view, the main institutions of a capitalist society have the function of preserving the interests of the bourgeoisie, and since these interests are opposed to those of the proletarians, capitalist society is therefore a kind of class rule, or oppression, of the majority by the minority.

Furthermore, for Marx, social structures, such as capitalism, that are based on the oppression of one class by another give rise to what he called *ideologies*. An ideology is a (socially influential) system of beliefs or assumptions that reflects a false perception of reality—a perception of reality distorted by the social forces involved in class oppression. Central examples, for Marx, were systems of religious belief and the capitalist doctrine of the "free market." The dominance of a ruling class, whose members usually make up only a tiny minority of society, cannot be preserved through physical coercion alone: it can only survive as long as most people believe (falsely) that the social status quo is in their own interests, or that there is no realistic alternative to the current system, or in a situation where the oppressed classes are divided against each other (e.g., by nationalism, racism, or sexism) and fail to see their own common interest.

Considerations like these give rise to one of the best-known components of Marx's philosophical system, *historical materialism*: "[t]he mode of production of material life conditions the social, political, and intellectual life-process in general." This is the view that the foundation or "base" of society is its economic structure, which is defined by historical facts about the means of production (for example, facts about the level of agricultural sophistication, industrial technology, trade and transportation networks, and so on). As productive forces change, economic adjustments—changes to the relations of production—give rise to revolutions in society's "superstructure": the political, legal, moral, religious, and philosophical components of culture. In other words, political and social changes do not cause economic change, but the other way around: political and social systems are determined by their economic basis.

Marx's second main political-philosophical idea, in his 1852 summary, was the view that capitalism contains internal tensions which, in time, will inevitably produce the revolutionary overthrow of the bourgeoisie by the workers and usher in a "dictatorship of the proletariat." This view is, in part, the heritage of Marx's early influence by, and reaction to, the philosophical system of Hegel. For Hegel, history is a "dialectical" movement in which a thesis—a principle or idea—is challenged by its antithesis, and from this conflict there emerges a synthesis of the two, a new principle. In time this new principle meets *its* antithesis, and so on (until the ideal, final synthesis is achieved). Thus Hegel was an *idealist*, in the sense that for him the engine of world change was the clash of *Ideas*.[3] In Engels's words, Marx turned the Hegelian system on its head: instead of conflicts between ideas (in the shape of political structures) driving change, Marx held that the world contains its own internal conflicts and that political ideas actually spring up *from* this conflict rather than causing it. These built-in conflicts, the mainspring of historical change, are *economic* in nature, generated by people's attempts to satisfy their material needs—for food, clothing, shelter and so on—and their subsequent pursuit of personal wealth, within the context of their society's particular level of economic development. (Thus, Marx's system is often called *dialectical materialism*, though Marx himself never used this label.)

Marx's diagnosis of the economic conflicts driving capitalism towards revolution is complex and many-faceted. One of its central notions is that of *alienation*, which in turn arises from two other fundamental ideas in Marx's system: his theory of human nature and his "labor theory of value." According to Marx, human beings are essentially *active* and *creative* beings. Human flourishing consists in the continual transformation of one's inherent creative power into objective products, the constant *realization* of one's "subjectivity." Thus, productive activity—that is, work—is an essential component of human well-being. Marx's concern for the poor was never merely concern for their basic "material needs," such as food and housing, but was part of his view of human flourishing as being a matter of "free self-activity," of true self-expression in a social context.

The institution of private property, in Marx's view, stifles the flourishing of the human spirit. Since private property represents the products of labor as if

they were mere *things*, it alienates labor—and thus, human nature—from itself. Workers in a modern economy typically do not experience the economic goods they spend their lives producing as expressions of *themselves*, but merely as things to be sold. Furthermore, capitalism intensifies this process of alienation by treating *labor itself* as a commodity, to be bought and sold. Not only is the product of your creative activity alienated from you, but that very activity, work itself, is alienated—it is no longer *yours*, once you have sold it to an employer.

Furthermore, on Marx's analysis, the capitalist sale of goods for profit is inherently exploitative. According to the labor theory of value, which Marx took over from British economists Adam Smith (1723–1790) and David Ricardo (1772–1823) and developed into his own economic theory, the fair value of anything in a free market is determined by the amount of labor required to produce it. This has two major implications. First it means, according to Marx, that *capital* adds no value to goods over and above the labor taken to produce them, and thus the capitalist, after recompensing his workers for the value of the labor they have expended in his factories, simply appropriates the "surplus value" which is generated as profits. Although not economically "unfair," in Marx's view, this is nevertheless a form of exploitation. Second, when the labor theory of value is applied to a free market for *labor itself*, it has the implication that the working classes will necessarily (and not "unjustly," by the lights of capitalism) be forced into permanent poverty. This is because the labor-value of labor itself is simply the amount necessary to keep the worker healthy and ready to work each day—that is, the minimum amount of food and shelter necessary to sustain the worker. This therefore, no more and no less, is the labor wage in a free capitalist market, and this produces a huge class of workers with no security, no prospects, no savings, no interest in preserving the current social conditions—in short, "nothing to lose but their chains."

Finally, there is the third part of Marx's 1852 summary: communism. Marx actually had relatively little to say about the nature of a future communist society, but it is clear that he saw it as a society in which the tensions inherent in capitalism have annihilated

---

3   This is, of necessity, rather a caricature of Hegel's philosophical system. A good first introduction to Hegel's work is Charles Taylor's *Hegel* (Cambridge University Press, 1977).

themselves and produced an economic system that—because there is no private property or capital—does not generate alienation and exploitation but instead allows for genuine human flourishing as active, creative individuals, self-determined and self-sufficient within a community of other self-determined human beings.

What Is the Structure of This Reading?

The *Communist Manifesto* was written to be a statement of the ideals and aims of the Communist League. The Communist League, an umbrella organization linking the main centers of communist activity in London, Paris, Brussels, and Cologne was formed in June 1847, largely at the instigation of Marx and Engels, and was descended from a shadowy Parisian 'secret society' called the League of the Just. Most of its (few) members were German émigrés, and included several tailors, a few students, a typesetter, a cobbler, a watchmaker, a painter of miniatures, a disgraced Prussian officer, and Marx's aristocratic brother-in-law. A Congress of the League was held in London in November of 1847. To quote the eminent British historian A.J.P. Taylor:

> Marx attended in person. He listened impatiently while the worthy tailors lamented the wickedness of capitalism and preached universal brotherhood. He rose and denounced brotherhood in the name of class war. The tailors were entranced. Where they relied on sentiment, a learned man explained to them how society worked and placed the key to the future in their hands. They invited Marx to write a declaration of principles for them. He agreed.

Engels wrote a first draft—a question-and-answer brief on the main principles of communism—which was then completely rewritten by Marx (who was less than 30 years old at the time) in the space of less than six weeks.

The *Manifesto* has four sections. The first part is a history of society from the Middle Ages to the present day, presented as a succession of class struggles, and predicting the imminent victory of the proletariat over the present ruling class, the bourgeoisie. Part II describes the position of communists with respect to the proletarian class and then goes on to reject a sequence of bourgeois objections to communism. This is followed by a brief characterization of the nature of the forthcoming communist revolution. The third part, not included here, contains an extended criticism of other forms of socialism: reactionary, bourgeois, and utopian. The final section provides a short description of communist tactics toward opposition parties and culminates with a call for proletarian unity.

Some Useful Background Information

For Marx, no external force or random accident is required to topple capitalism. He believed the overthrow of capitalism by socialism was inescapable, that it would come about because of the very nature of capitalism itself. An accurate grasp of the forces that sustain almost all social systems throughout history, Marx thought, would show that they must inevitably, as a result of internal processes, decline and be replaced by a radically different social system. However, *inevitably* does not mean *spontaneously*: the actual overthrow of existing society must be performed by a band of determined revolutionaries, joining the already existing, day-to-day class struggles and introducing revolutionary ideas to combat the ruling ideology, emphasizing the need for unity among the oppressed, and, when the time is ripe, boldly leading the revolution. The key is to follow the course of history *knowingly* by controlling the circumstances that generate it.

Some Common Misconceptions

1. Although Marx believed all the main institutions of society function to preserve the interests of the ruling class, he was not a conspiracy theorist. He did not believe, for example, that leading political figures receive covert orders from the business community. Instead, he held that institutional mechanisms press the actions of successful political figures into reflecting the long-term interests of the bourgeoisie (including the need for social and economic stability

and the suppression of revolution). One especially important mechanism for this, according to Marx, is national debt: governments depend on capitalists to renew huge but routine loans, and these financiers could throw national finances into chaos if their interests are too directly threatened. Another major influence is the pace of investment: if capitalists are displeased, the rate of investment slows and this has serious repercussions for employment rates and income levels. A third major factor is bourgeois ownership of the media (in Marx's time, mass-circulation newspapers), and their consequent ability to manipulate and mould public opinion.

2. Marx's philosophy, as it is found in his writings, is not exactly the same thing as the ideological system often called "Marxism" today. His thought has been built on and interpreted by many other writers, starting with Engels and including several prominent Russian thinkers such as Georgy Plekhanov (1856–1918) and Vladimir Ilich Lenin (1870–1924) who formulated an 'orthodox,' systematic Soviet version of Marxism, and the so-called Western Marxists such as Georg Lukács (1885–1971), Theodor Adorno (1903–1969), and Louis Althusser (1918–1990). Nor is it quite the same thing as communism. The notion of the abolition of private property dates back at least to the early Christians, and was proposed during the French Revolution by a few fringe groups whom even the revolutionaries considered beyond the pale. And of course, the modern association of Communism with the political and economic structures of China and the Soviet Union is a development which occurred after Marx's death (and it is highly unlikely that Marx would have unconditionally approved of those regimes).

How Important and Influential Is This Passage?

The *Communist Manifesto* is the most successful political pamphlet of all time: for a substantial period of the twentieth century, roughly a third of the human race was ruled by governments that claimed allegiance to the ideas expressed in it. Practically, Marx's thought is the chief inspiration for all modern forms of social radicalism. Intellectually, according to the *Blackwell Encyclopedia of Political Thought*, "[o]ver the whole range of the social sciences, Marx has proved probably the most influential figure of the twentieth century." Marx's central ideas—"historical materialism," the labor theory of value, the notion of class struggle—have had an inestimable influence on the development of contemporary economics, history, and sociology, even when they are not widely accepted by most Western intellectuals today.

Suggestions for Critical Reflection

1. "The history of all hitherto existing society is the history of class struggles." What role does this resounding phrase have in Marx's argument? Is it a *true* claim? (How easy would it be for professional historians to show it to be either true or false?) If its historical truth is open to question, how serious a problem is this for Marx's views?

2. Marx's critique of the bourgeoisie has both positive and negative elements. For example, he notes that they have "accomplished wonders far surpassing … Gothic cathedrals," but also claims the bourgeois have reduced the family to "a mere money relation." What is Marx's overall judgment of the bourgeoisie? How far do you agree with it?

3. "The executive of the modern State is but a committee for managing the common affairs of the whole bourgeoisie." How does Marx support this claim? What, exactly, do you think he means by it? What implications does it have, if true?

4. Marx suggests modern bourgeois society contains within it the seeds of its own self-destruction (as did feudal society before it). How compelling are his arguments for this claim?

5. Marx says that, for the proletariat, "[l]aw, morality, religion, are to him so many bourgeois prejudices, behind which lurk in ambush just as many bourgeois interests." What are the im-

plications of this statement? Why do you think Marx says it, and do you think he is justified in doing so?

6. Marx addresses the criticism of communism which says that, if private property and personal wealth are abolished, people will have no incentive to be productive at all "and universal laziness will overtake us." How adequately do you think Marx handles this objection?

7. What do you make of Marx's list of ten components for the dictatorship of the proletariat? How radical or unreasonable do they seem today? How likely would they be to result in the elimination of private property and the emancipation of the proletariat?

8. What, if anything, do historical developments since Marx's death—in particular, the rise and fall of the Soviet Union, and the failure of capitalism to end in revolution in the democratic West—show about the validity of his philosophical thought?

Suggestions for Further Reading

Marx's theoretical masterwork is *Capital*, a massive, detailed and rigorous critical study of the capitalist form of life, a project which involves Marx in descriptions of his views of science, culture, art, religion, and knowledge. (A single-volume version, abridged by David McLellan, is available from Oxford University Press, 2000.) Two shorter works, *Wage-Labour and Capital* and *Value, Price and Profit* were written as lectures to workers and present Marx's critique of capitalist society in simpler terms, while his *Contribution to a Critique of Political Economy* includes a succinct statement of historical materialism in the Preface. Marx's main political writings include *The Eighteenth Brumaire of Louis Napoleon* and *The Civil War in France*, while perhaps his most purely "philosophical" book is *The German Ideology*, though it is not a particularly accessible work for modern readers. A good way to approach Marx's voluminous writings is to use an edited volume of selections from his works. Three of the best such anthologies are *Karl Marx: Selected Writings*, ed. David McLellan (Oxford University Press, 2000), *The Marx-Engels Reader*, ed. Robert Tucker (W.W. Norton,

1978), and *Karl Marx: Selected Writings*, ed. Lawrence Simon (Hackett, 1994).

There are several available editions of *The Communist Manifesto*. The Penguin edition, edited by A.J.P. Taylor (Penguin, 1967), contains a valuable, and entertainingly astringent, introduction. *The Communist Manifesto* edited by John Toews (Bedford/St. Martin's, 1999), contains lots of interesting and useful background material, and there is also a Norton Critical Edition of the *Manifesto*, edited by Frederic Bender (W.W. Norton, 1988).

A good short biography of Marx is Werner Blumenberg's *Karl Marx: An Illustrated Biography* (Verso, 1998); worthwhile longer studies include Isaiah Berlin, *Karl Marx: His Life and Environment* (Oxford University Press, 1978) and David McLellan, *Karl Marx: His Life and Thought* (Harper & Row, 1977).

As one might expect, given Marx's historical importance, there are huge numbers of books about his thought. The reader needs to be somewhat judicious in choosing secondary material, however, as a significant number of works are of relatively low philosophical quality or merely uncritical Marxian apologetics. Though encompassing diverse philosophical viewpoints, the following books are all reliable and valuable: Shlomo Avineri, *The Social and Political Thought of Karl Marx* (Cambridge University Press, 1970); Ball and Farr (eds.), *After Marx* (Cambridge University Press, 1984); Allen Buchanan, *Marx and Justice* (Rowman & Littlefield, 1982); Terrell Carver, *Marx's Social Theory* (Oxford University Press, 1982); G.A. Cohen, *Karl Marx's Theory of History: A Defense* (Princeton University Press, 1978); Jon Elster, *Making Sense of Marx* (Cambridge University Press, 1985); Jon Elster, *An Introduction to Karl Marx* (Cambridge University Press, 1986); Michael Evans, *Karl Marx* (Allen & Unwin, 1975); Richard Heilbroner, *Marxism: For and Against* (Norton, 1980); George Lichtheim, *Marxism: An Historical and Critical Study* (Praeger, 1967); Steven Lukes, *Marxism and Morality* (Oxford University Press, 1984); David McLellan, *The Thought of Karl Marx: An Introduction* (Pan Books, 1995); Richard Miller, *Analyzing Marx: Morality, Power and History* (Princeton University Press, 1984); R.G. Peffer, *Marxism, Morality, and Social Justice* (Princeton University Press, 1990); John Plamenatz, *Karl Marx's Philosophy of Man* (Oxford University Press,

1975); John Roemer (ed.), *Analytical Marxism* (Cambridge University Press, 1986); Richard Schmitt, *Introduction to Marx and Engels* (Westview Press, 1997); Robert Paul Wolff, *Understanding Marx* (Princeton University Press, 1984); and Allen Wood, *Karl Marx* (Routledge & Kegan Paul, 1981).

from *The Communist Manifesto*[4]

A spectre is haunting Europe—the spectre of Communism. All the Powers of old Europe have entered into a holy alliance to exorcise this spectre: Pope and Tsar, Metternich and Guizot,[5] French Radicals and German police-spies.

Where is the party in opposition that has not been decried as Communistic by its opponents in power? Where the Opposition that has not hurled back the branding reproach of Communism, against the more advanced opposition parties, as well as against its reactionary adversaries?

Two things result from this fact:

I.   Communism is already acknowledged by all European Powers to be itself a Power.
II.   It is high time that Communists should openly, in the face of the whole world, publish their views, their aims, their tendencies, and meet this nursery tale of the Spectre of Communism with a Manifesto of the party itself.

To this end, Communists of various nationalities have assembled in London and sketched the follow-

ing Manifesto, to be published in the English, French, German, Italian, Flemish and Danish languages.[6]

I. Bourgeois and Proletarians[7]

The history of all hitherto existing society[8] is the history of class struggles.

Freeman and slave, patrician and plebeian, lord and serf, guild-master[9] and journeyman,[10] in a word, op-

4   *Manifest der Kommunistischen Partei* was first published, in German, in London in 1848. The text reprinted here is the English translation made in 1888 by Samuel Moore, which was edited and authorized by Friedrich Engels. The author's notes in the text are those made by Engels in 1888.

5   Prince Klemens Metternich (1773–1859) was the conservative chancellor of the Austrian empire; he was the dominant figure in European politics at this time, but was soon to be driven from power by the Revolutions of 1848. François Guizot (1787–1874) was the liberal moderate premier of France until he also was overthrown in the political turbulence of 1848.

6   In the event, only one translation—into Swedish—was published in 1848–49, and widespread translation and reprinting of the *Manifesto* did not begin until after 1870.

7   [Author's note] By bourgeoisie is meant the class of modern Capitalists, owners of the means of social production and employers of wage-labour. By proletariat, the class of modern wage-labourers who, having no means of production of their own, are reduced to selling their labour-power in order to live.

8   [Author's note] That is, all *written* history. In 1847, the pre-history of society, the social organization existing previous to recorded history, was all but unknown. Since then, [August von] Haxthausen discovered common ownership of land in Russia, [Georg Ludwig von] Maurer proved it to be the social foundation from which all Teutonic races started in history, and by and by village communities were found to be, or to have been the primitive form of society everywhere from India to Ireland. The inner organization of this primitive Communistic society was laid bare, in its typical form, by [Lewis Henry] Morgan's crowning discovery of the true nature of the *gens* and its relation to the *tribe*. With the dissolution of these primaeval communities society begins to be differentiated into separate and finally antagonistic classes. I have attempted to retrace this dissolution in *Der Ursprung der Familie, des Privateigenthums und des Staats* [*The Origins of the Family, Private Property and the State*], second edition, Stuttgart, 1886.

9   [Author's note] Guild-master, that is, a full member of a guild, a master within, not a head of a guild.

10   A patrician was a member of one of the noble families of the ancient Roman republic, while plebeians were the common people of Rome. The terminology was also used in later ages (e.g., in the medieval free cities of Italy and Germany) to mark a similar distinction. A

pressor and oppressed, stood in constant opposition to one another, carried on an uninterrupted, now hidden, now open fight, a fight that each time ended, either in a revolutionary re-constitution of society at large, or in the common ruin of the contending classes.

In the earlier epochs of history, we find almost everywhere a complicated arrangement of society into various orders, a manifold gradation of social rank. In ancient Rome we have patricians, knights, plebeians, slaves; in the Middle Ages, feudal lords, vassals,[11] guild-masters, journeymen, apprentices, serfs; in almost all of these classes, again, subordinate gradations.

The modern bourgeois society that has sprouted from the ruins of feudal society has not done away with class antagonisms. It has but established new classes, new conditions of oppression, new forms of struggle in place of the old ones.

Our epoch, the epoch of the bourgeoisie, possesses, however, this distinctive feature: it has simplified class antagonisms. Society as a whole is more and more splitting up into two great hostile camps, into two great classes directly facing each other: Bourgeoisie and Proletariat.

From the serfs of the Middle Ages sprang the chartered burghers[12] of the earliest towns. From these burgesses the first elements of the bourgeoisie were developed.

The discovery of America, the rounding of the Cape,[13] opened up fresh ground for the rising bourgeoisie. The East-Indian and Chinese markets, the colonisation of America, trade with the colonies, the increase in the means of exchange and in commodities generally, gave to commerce, to navigation, to industry, an impulse never before known, and thereby, to the revolutionary element in the tottering feudal society, a rapid development.

The feudal system of industry, under which industrial production was monopolized by closed guilds, now no longer sufficed for the growing wants of the new markets. The manufacturing system took its place. The guild-masters were pushed on one side by the manufacturing middle class; division of labour between the different corporate guilds vanished in the face of division of labour in each single workshop.

Meantime the markets kept ever growing, the demand ever rising. Even manufacture no longer sufficed. Thereupon, steam and machinery revolutionized industrial production. The place of manufacture was taken by the giant, Modern Industry, the place of the industrial middle class, by industrial millionaires, the leaders of whole industrial armies, the modern bourgeois.

Modern industry has established the world market, for which the discovery of America paved the way. This market has given an immense development to commerce, to navigation, to communication by land. This development has, in its turn, reacted on the extension of industry; and in proportion as industry, commerce, navigation, railways extended, in the same proportion the bourgeoisie developed, increased its capital, and pushed into the background every class handed down from the Middle Ages.

We see, therefore, how the modern bourgeoisie is itself the product of a long course of development, of a series of revolutions in the modes of production and of exchange.

Each step in the development of the bourgeoisie was accompanied by a corresponding political advance in that class. An oppressed class under the sway of the feudal nobility, an armed and self-governing association in the medieval commune;[14] here inde-

---

serf was a member of a particular feudal class of people in Europe, those bound by law to a particular piece of land and, like the land, owned by a lord. A journeyman is a craftsman who has completed his apprenticeship and is employed at a fixed wage by a master artisan, but who is not yet allowed (by his guild) to work for himself.

11   A vassal received land and protection from a feudal lord, in return for homage and allegiance.

12   Someone who is a citizen of a town in virtue of being a full member of a legally chartered trade association or guild.

13   The Cape of Good Hope, at the southern tip of Africa.

---

14   [Author's note] "Commune" was the name taken, in France, by the nascent towns even before they had conquered from their feudal lords and masters local self-government and political rights as the "Third Estate." Generally speaking, for the economical development

pendent urban republic (as in Italy and Germany), there taxable "third estate" of the monarchy (as in France), afterwards, in the period of manufacture proper, serving either the semi-feudal or the absolute monarchy as a counterpoise against the nobility, and, in fact, cornerstone of the great monarchies in general, the bourgeoisie has at last, since the establishment of Modern Industry and of the world market, conquered for itself, in the modern representative State,[15] exclusive political sway. The executive of the modern State is but a committee for managing the common affairs of the whole bourgeoisie.

The bourgeoisie, historically, has played a most revolutionary part.

The bourgeoisie, wherever it has got the upper hand, has put an end to all feudal, patriarchal, idyllic relations. It has pitilessly torn asunder the motley feudal ties that bound man to his "natural superiors," and has left no other nexus between man and man than naked self-interest, than callous "cash payment." It has drowned out the most heavenly ecstasies of religious fervour, of chivalrous enthusiasm, of philistine sentimentalism, in the icy water of egotistical calculation. It has resolved personal worth into exchange value, and in place of the numberless indefeasible chartered freedoms, has set up that single, unconscionable freedom—Free Trade. In one word, for exploitation, veiled by religious and political illusions, it has substituted naked, shameless, direct, brutal exploitation.

The bourgeoisie has stripped of its halo every occupation hitherto honoured and looked up to with reverent awe. It has converted the physician, the lawyer, the priest, the poet, the man of science, into its paid wage-labourers.

The bourgeoisie has torn away from the family its sentimental veil, and has reduced the family relation to a mere money relation.

---

of the bourgeoisie, England is here taken as the typical country; for its political development, France.

15 A modern, rather than a feudal, state: one whose institutions are based on the political representation of *individuals*, rather than of social corporations (such as towns or guilds) or estates (such as the nobility or the clergy).

The bourgeoisie has disclosed how it came to pass that the brutal display of vigour in the Middle Ages, which Reactionists so much admire, found its fitting complement in the most slothful indolence. It has been the first to show what man's activity can bring about. It has accomplished wonders far surpassing Egyptian pyramids, Roman aqueducts, and Gothic cathedrals; it has conducted expeditions that put in the shade all former Exoduses of nations and crusades.

The bourgeoisie cannot exist without constantly revolutionizing the instruments of production, and thereby the relations of production, and with them the whole relations of society. Conservation of the old modes of production in unaltered form, was, on the contrary, the first condition of existence for all earlier industrial classes. Constant revolutionizing of production, uninterrupted disturbance of all social conditions, everlasting uncertainty and agitation distinguish the bourgeois epoch from all earlier ones. All fixed, fast-frozen relations, with their train of ancient and venerable prejudices and opinions, are swept away, all new-formed ones become antiquated before they can ossify. All that is solid melts into air, all that is holy is profaned, and man is at last compelled to face with sober senses, his real condition of life and his relations with his kind.

The need of a constantly expanding market for its products chases the bourgeoisie over the entire surface of the globe. It must nestle everywhere, settle everywhere, establish connections everywhere.

The bourgeoisie has, through its exploitation of the world market, given a cosmopolitan character to production and consumption in every country. To the great chagrin of Reactionists, it has drawn from under the feet of industry the national ground on which it stood. All old-established national industries have been destroyed or are daily being destroyed. They are dislodged by new industries, whose introduction becomes a life and death question for all civilized nations, by industries that no longer work up indigenous raw material, but raw material drawn from the remotest zones; industries whose products are consumed, not only at home, but in every quarter of the globe. In place of the old wants, satisfied by the production of the country, we find new wants, requiring for their satisfaction the products of distant lands and climes.

In place of the old local and national seclusion and self-sufficiency, we have intercourse in every direction, universal inter-dependence of nations. And as in material, so also in intellectual production. The intellectual creations of individual nations become common property. National one-sidedness and narrow-mindedness become more and more impossible, and from the numerous national and local literatures, there arises a world literature.

The bourgeoisie, by the rapid improvement of all instruments of production, by the immensely facilitated means of communication, draws all, even the most barbarian, nations into civilization. The cheap prices of its commodities are the heavy artillery with which it batters down all Chinese walls, with which it forces the barbarians' intensely obstinate hatred of foreigners to capitulate.[16] It compels all nations, on pain of extinction, to adopt the bourgeois mode of production; it compels them to introduce what it calls civilization into their midst, *i.e.*, to become bourgeois themselves. In one word, it creates a world after its own image.

The bourgeoisie has subjected the country to the rule of the towns. It has created enormous cities, has greatly increased the urban population as compared with the rural, and has thus rescued a considerable part of the population from the idiocy of rural life. Just as it has made the country dependent on the towns, so it has made barbarian and semi-barbarian countries dependent on the civilized ones, nations of peasants on nations of bourgeois, the East on the West.

The bourgeoisie keeps more and more doing away with the scattered state of the population, of the means of production, and of property. It has agglomerated population, centralized means of production, and has concentrated property in a few hands. The necessary consequence of this was political centralization. Independent, or but loosely connected provinces with separate interests, laws, governments and systems of taxation, became lumped together into one nation, with one government, one code of laws, one national class-interest, one frontier, and one customs-tariff.

The bourgeoisie, during its rule of scarce one hundred years, has created more massive and more colossal productive forces than have all preceding generations together. Subjection of Nature's forces to man, machinery, application of chemistry to industry and agriculture, steam-navigation, railways, electric telegraphs, clearing of whole continents for cultivation, canalization of rivers, whole populations conjured out of the ground—what earlier century had even a presentiment that such productive forces slumbered in the lap of social labour?

We see then: the means of production and of exchange, on whose foundation the bourgeoisie built itself up, were generated in feudal society. At a certain stage in the development of these means of production and of exchange, the conditions under which feudal society produced and exchanged, the feudal organization of agriculture and manufacturing industry, in one word, the feudal relations of property became no longer compatible with the already developed productive forces; they became so many fetters. They had to be burst asunder; they were burst asunder.

Into their place stepped free competition, accompanied by a social and political constitution adapted in it, and the economical and political sway of the bourgeois class.

A similar movement is going on before our own eyes. Modern bourgeois society, with its relations of production, of exchange and of property, a society that has conjured up such gigantic means of production and of exchange, is like the sorcerer who is no longer able to control the powers of the nether world whom he has called up by his spells. For many a decade past the history of industry and commerce is but the history of the revolt of modern productive forces against modern conditions of production, against the property relations that are the conditions for the existence of the bourgeois and of its rule. It is enough to mention the commercial crises that by their periodical return put on its trial, each time more threateningly, the existence of the entire bourgeois society. In these crises a great part not only of the existing products, but also of the previously created productive forces, are periodically destroyed. In these crises there breaks

---

16   A reference to the first Opium War in China (1839–1843), which forced the Chinese to cede Hong Kong to the British and to open five of their ports to foreign trade.

out an epidemic that, in all earlier epochs, would have seemed an absurdity—the epidemic of over-production.[17] Society suddenly finds itself put back into a state of momentary barbarism; it appears as if a famine, a universal war of devastation had cut off the supply of every means of subsistence; industry and commerce seem to be destroyed; and why? Because there is too much civilization, too much means of subsistence, too much industry, too much commerce. The productive forces at the disposal of society no longer tend to further the development of the conditions of bourgeois property; on the contrary, they have become too powerful for these conditions, by which they are fettered, and so soon as they overcome these fetters, they bring disorder into the whole of bourgeois society, endanger the existence of bourgeois property. The conditions of bourgeois society are too narrow to comprise the wealth created by them. And how does the bourgeoisie get over these crises? On the one hand by enforced destruction of a mass of productive forces; on the other, by the conquest of new markets, and by the more thorough exploitation of the old ones. That is to say, by paving the way for more extensive and more destructive crises, and by diminishing the means whereby crises are prevented.

The weapons with which the bourgeoisie felled feudalism to the ground are now turned against the bourgeoisie itself.

But not only has the bourgeoisie forged the weapons that bring death to itself; it has also called into existence the men who are to wield those weapons—the modern working class—the proletarians.

In proportion as the bourgeoisie, *i.e.*, capital, is developed, in the same proportion is the proletariat, the modern working class, developed—a class of labourers, who live only so long as they find work, and who find work only so long as their labour increases capital. These labourers, who must sell themselves piecemeal, are a commodity, like every other article of commerce, and are consequently exposed to all the vicissitudes of competition, to all the fluctuations of the market.

Owing to the extensive use of machinery and to division of labour, the work of the proletarians has lost all individual character, and, consequently, all charm for the workman. He becomes an appendage of the machine, and it is only the most simple, most monotonous, and most easily acquired knack, that is required of him. Hence, the cost of production of a workman is restricted, almost entirely, to the means of subsistence that he requires for maintenance, and for the propagation of his race. But the price of a commodity, and therefore also of labour, is equal to its cost of production. In proportion, therefore, as the repulsiveness of the work increases, the wage decreases. Nay more, in proportion as the use of machinery and division of labour increases, in the same proportion the burden of toil also increases, whether by prolongation of the working hours, by the increase of the work exacted in a given time, or by increased speed of the machinery, etc.

Modern industry has converted the little workshop of the patriarchal master into the great factory of the industrial capitalist. Masses of labourers, crowded into the factory, are organized like soldiers. As privates of the industrial army they are placed under the command of a perfect hierarchy of officers and sergeants. Not only are they slaves of the bourgeois class, and of the bourgeois State; they are daily and hourly enslaved by the machine, by the overlooker, and, above all, by the individual bourgeois manufacturer himself. The more openly this despotism proclaims gain to be its end and aim, the more petty, the more hateful and the more embittering it is.

The less the skill and exertion of strength implied in manual labour, in other words, the more modern

17   Such crises occurred regularly in advanced capitalist economies from 1825 until 1939. Periodically, as more and more companies joined a particular industry, firms found themselves facing a glut of their products on the market. This over-supply depressed prices below expected profit levels, and so companies suddenly began to cut back production. Each time, these cutbacks started a vicious chain reaction, as suppliers were also forced to make cutbacks, which increased the unemployment rate, which reduced consumer spending and so increased over-supply, which depressed prices still further, and so on. At the height of the Great Depression of the 1930s, the worst such crisis, unemployment reached 25% in the United States. Marx provided a sophisticated analysis of such crises in *Capital*.

industry becomes developed, the more is the labour of men superseded by that of women. Differences of age and sex have no longer any distinctive social validity for the working class. All are instruments of labour, more or less expensive to use, according to their age and sex.

No sooner is the exploitation of the labourer by the manufacturer, so far, at an end, and he receives his wages in cash, than he is set upon by the other portions of the bourgeoisie, the landlord, the shopkeeper, the pawnbroker, etc.

The lower strata of the middle class—the small tradespeople, shopkeepers, and retired tradesmen generally, the handicraftsmen and peasants—all these sink gradually into the proletariat, partly because their diminutive capital does not suffice for the scale on which Modern Industry is carried on, and is swamped in the competition with the large capitalists, partly because their specialized skill is rendered worthless by new methods of production. Thus, the proletariat is recruited from all classes of the population.

The proletariat goes through various stages of development. With its birth begins its struggle with the bourgeoisie. At first, the contest is carried on by individual labourers, then by the workpeople of a factory, then by the operatives of one trade, in one locality, against the individual bourgeois who directly exploits them. They direct their attacks not against the bourgeois condition of production, but against the instruments of production themselves; they destroy imported wares that compete with their labour, they smash to pieces machinery, they set factories ablaze, they seek to restore by force the vanished status of the workman of the Middle Ages.

At this stage the labourers still form an incoherent mass scattered over the whole country, and broken up by their mutual competition. If anywhere they unite to form more compact bodies, this is not yet the consequence of their own active union, but of the union of the bourgeoisie, which class, in order to attain its own political ends, is compelled to set the whole proletariat in motion, and is moreover yet, for a time, able to do so. At this stage, therefore, the proletarians do not fight their enemies, but the enemies of their enemies, the remnants of absolute monarchy, the landowners, the non-industrial bourgeois, the petty bourgeoisie.[18] Thus, the whole historical movement is concentrated in the hands of the bourgeoisie; every victory so obtained is a victory for the bourgeoisie.

But with the development of industry, the proletariat not only increases in number; it becomes concentrated in greater masses, its strength grows, and it feels that strength more. The various interests and conditions of life within the ranks of the proletariat are more and more equalized, in proportion as machinery obliterates all distinctions of labour, and nearly everywhere reduces wages to the same low level. The growing competition among the bourgeois, and the resulting commercial crises, make the wages of the workers ever more fluctuating. The increasing improvement of machinery, ever more rapidly developing, makes their livelihood more and more precarious; the collisions between individual workmen and individual bourgeois take more and more the character of collisions between two classes. Thereupon, the workers begin to form combinations (Trades' Unions) against the bourgeois; they club together in order to keep up the rate of wages; they found permanent associations in order to make provision beforehand for these occasional revolts. Here and there the contest breaks out into riots.

Now and then the workers are victorious, but only for a time. The real fruit of their battles lies, not in the immediate result, but in the ever expanding union of the workers. This union is helped on by the improved means of communication that are created by modern industry and that place the workers of different localities in contact with one another. It was just this contact that was needed to centralize the numerous local struggles, all of the same character, into one national struggle between classes. But every class struggle is a political struggle. And that union, to attain which the burghers of the Middle Ages, with their miserable highways, required centuries, the modern proletarian, thanks to railways, achieve in a few years.

---

18   The petty bourgeoisie, for Marx, are those who control means of production (like the bourgeoisie) but work them with their own labor (like the proletariat): for example, independent shopkeepers or small farmers.

This organization of the proletarians into a class, and consequently into a political party, is continually being upset again by the competition between the workers themselves. But it ever rises up again, stronger, firmer, mightier. It compels legislative recognition of particular interests of the workers, by taking advantage of the divisions among the bourgeoisie itself. Thus, the ten-hours' bill in England was carried.[19]

Altogether collisions between the classes of the old society further, in many ways, the course of development of the proletariat. The bourgeoisie finds itself involved in a constant battle. At first with the aristocracy; later on, with those portions of the bourgeoisie itself, whose interests have become antagonistic to the progress of industry; at all times, with the bourgeoisie of foreign countries. In all these battles it sees itself compelled to appeal to the proletariat, to ask for its help, and thus, to drag it into the political arena. The bourgeoisie itself, therefore, supplies the proletariat with its own elements of political and general education, in other words, it furnishes the proletariat with weapons for fighting the bourgeoisie.

Further, as we have already seen, entire sections of the ruling class are, by the advance of industry, precipitated into the proletariat, or are at least threatened in their conditions of existence. These also supply the proletariat with fresh elements of enlightenment and progress.

Finally, in times when the class struggle nears the decisive hour, the progress of dissolution going on within the ruling class, in fact within the whole range of old society, assumes such a violent, glaring character, that a small section of the ruling class cuts itself adrift, and joins the revolutionary class, the class that holds the future in its hands. Just as, therefore, at an earlier period, a section of the nobility went over to the bourgeoisie, so now a portion of the bourgeoisie goes over to the proletariat, and in particular, a portion of the bourgeois ideologists, who have raised themselves to the level of comprehending theoretically the historical movement as a whole.

Of all the classes that stand face to face with the bourgeoisie today, the proletariat alone is a genuinely revolutionary class. The other classes decay and finally disappear in the face of Modern Industry; the proletariat is its special and essential product.

The lower middle class, the small manufacturer, the shopkeeper, the artisan, the peasant, all these fight against the bourgeoisie, to save from extinction their existence as fractions of the middle class. They are therefore not revolutionary, but conservative. Nay more, they are reactionary, for they try to roll back the wheel of history. If by chance they are revolutionary, they are only so in view of their impending transfer into the proletariat, they thus defend not their present, but their future interests, they desert their own standpoint to place themselves at that of the proletariat.

The "dangerous class," the social scum,[20] that passively rotting mass thrown off by the lowest layers of the old society may, here and there, be swept into the movement by a proletarian revolution; its conditions of life, however, prepare it far more for the part of a bribed tool of reactionary intrigue.

In the condition of the proletariat, those of old society at large are already virtually swamped. The proletarian is without property; his relation to his wife and children has no longer anything in common with the bourgeois family relations; modern industrial labour, modern subjection to capital, the same in England as in France, in America as in Germany, has stripped him of every trace of national character. Law, morality, religion, are to him so many bourgeois prejudices, behind which lurk in ambush just as many bourgeois interests.

All the preceding classes that got the upper hand sought to fortify their already acquired status by subjecting society at large to their conditions of appropriation. The proletarians cannot become masters of the productive forces of society, except by abolishing their own previous mode of appropriation, and thereby also every other previous mode of appropriation. They

---

19   This law—part of the 1847 Factory Act—limited the daily working hours of women and children to 58 hours a week. It was highly controversial, and was passed by Parliament only because conservative "Old England" landowners opposed the interests of the ever-more-powerful industrialists and mill owners.

20   The original German word here is *Lumpenproletariat*, literally, "proletariat in rags."

have nothing of their own to secure and to fortify; their mission is to destroy all previous securities for, and insurances of, individual property.

All previous historical movements were movements of minorities, or in the interest of minorities. The proletarian movement is the self-conscious, independent movement of the immense majority, in the interest of the immense majority. The proletariat, the lowest stratum of our present society, cannot stir, cannot raise itself up, without the whole superincumbent strata of official society being sprung into the air.

Though not in substance, yet in form, the struggle of the proletariat with the bourgeoisie is at first a national struggle. The proletariat of each country must, of course, first of all settle matters with its own bourgeoisie.

In depicting the most general phases of the development of the proletariat, we traced the more or less veiled civil war, raging within existing society, up to the point where that war breaks out into open revolution, and where the violent overthrow of the bourgeoisie lays the foundation for the sway of the proletariat.

Hitherto, every form of society has been based, as we have already seen, on the antagonism of oppressing and oppressed classes. But in order to oppress a class, certain conditions must be assured to it under which it can, at least, continue its slavish existence. The serf, in the period of serfdom, raised himself to membership in the commune, just as the petty bourgeois, under the yoke of the feudal absolutism, managed to develop into a bourgeois. The modern labourer, on the contrary, instead of rising with the progress of industry, sinks deeper and deeper below the conditions of existence of his own class. He becomes a pauper, and pauperism develops more rapidly than population and wealth. And here it becomes evident that the bourgeoisie is unfit any longer to be the ruling class in society, and to impose its conditions of existence upon society as an over-riding law. It is unfit to rule because it is incompetent to assure an existence to its slave within his slavery, because it cannot help letting him sink into such a state, that it has to feed him, instead of being fed by him. Society can no longer live under this bourgeoisie, in other words, its existence is no longer compatible with society.

The essential condition for the existence, and for the sway of the bourgeois class, is the formation and augmentation of capital; the condition for capital is wage-labour. Wage-labour rests exclusively on competition between the labourers. The advance of industry, whose involuntary promoter is the bourgeoisie, replaces the isolation of the labourers, due to competition, by their revolutionary combination, due to association. The development of Modern Industry, therefore, cuts from under its feet the very foundation on which the bourgeoisie produces and appropriates products. What the bourgeoisie, therefore, produces, above all, is its own grave-diggers. Its fall and the victory of the proletariat are equally inevitable.

II. Proletarians and Communists

In what relation do the Communists stand to the proletarians as a whole?

The Communists do not form a separate party opposed to the other working-class parties.

They have no interests separate and apart from those of the proletariat as a whole.

They do not set up any sectarian principles of their own, by which to shape and mold the proletarian movement.

The Communists are distinguished from the other working-class parties by this only: (1) In the national struggles of the proletarians of the different countries, they point out and bring to the front the common interests of the entire proletariat, independently of all nationality. (2) In the various stages of development which the struggle of the working class against the bourgeoisie has to pass through, they always and everywhere represent the interests of the movement as a whole.

The Communists, therefore, are on the one hand, practically, the most advanced and resolute section of the working-class parties of every country, that section which pushes forward all others; on the other hand, theoretically, they have over the great mass of the proletariat the advantage of clearly understanding the line of march, the conditions, and the ultimate general results of the proletarian movement.

The immediate aim of the Communists is the same as that of all other proletarian parties: formation of the proletariat into a class, overthrow of the bourgeois supremacy, conquest of political power by the proletariat.

The theoretical conclusions of the Communists are in no way based on ideas or principles that have been invented, or discovered, by this or that would-be universal reformer.

They merely express, in general terms, actual relations springing from an existing class struggle, from a historical movement going on under our very eyes. The abolition of existing property relations is not at all a distinctive feature of Communism.

All property relations in the past have continually been subject to historical change consequent upon the change in historical conditions.

The French Revolution, for example, abolished feudal property in favour of bourgeois property.

The distinguishing feature of Communism is not the abolition of property generally, but the abolition of bourgeois property. But modern bourgeois private property is the final and most complete expression of the system of producing and appropriating products, that is based on class antagonisms, on the exploitation of the many by the few.

In this sense, the theory of the Communists may be summed up in the single sentence: Abolition of private property.

We Communists have been reproached with the desire of abolishing the right of personally acquiring property as the fruit of a man's own labour, which property is alleged to be the groundwork of all personal freedom, activity and independence.

Hard-won, self-acquired, self-earned property! Do you mean the property of the petty artisan and of the small peasant, a form of property that preceded the bourgeois form? There is no need to abolish that; the development of industry has to a great extent already destroyed it, and is still destroying it daily.

Or do you mean the modern bourgeois private property?

But does wage-labour create any property for the labourer? Not a bit. It creates capital, *i.e.*, that kind of property which exploits wage-labour, and which cannot increase except upon conditions of begetting a new supply of wage-labour for fresh exploitation. Property, in its present form, is based on the antago-nism of capital and wage-labour. Let us examine both sides of this antagonism.

To be a capitalist, is to have not only a purely personal, but a social *status* in production. Capital is a collective product, and only by the united action of many members, nay, in the last resort, only by the united action of all members of society, can it be set in motion.

Capital is, therefore, not a personal, it is a social power.

When, therefore, capital is converted into common property, into the property of all members of society, personal property is not thereby transformed into social property. It is only the social character of the property that is changed. It loses its class character.

Let us now take wage-labour.

The average price of wage-labour is the minimum wage, *i.e.*, that quantum of the means of subsistence, which is absolutely requisite to keep the labourer in bare existence as a labourer. What, therefore, the wage-labourer appropriates by means of his labour, merely suffices to prolong and reproduce a bare existence. We by no means intend to abolish this personal appropriation of the products of labour, an appropriation that is made for the maintenance and reproduction of human life, and that leaves no surplus wherewith to command the labour of others. All that we want to do away with is the miserable character of this appropriation, under which the labourer lives merely to increase capital, and is allowed to live only in so far as the interest of the ruling class requires it.

In bourgeois society, living labour is but a means to increase accumulated labour. In Communist society, accumulated labour is but a means to widen, to enrich, to promote the existence of the labourer.

In bourgeois society, therefore, the past dominates the present; in Communist society, the present dominates the past. In bourgeois society capital is independent and has individuality, while the living person is dependent and has no individuality.

And the abolition of this state of things is called by the bourgeois abolition of individuality and freedom! And rightly so. The abolition of bourgeois individuality, bourgeois independence, and bourgeois freedom is undoubtedly aimed at.

By freedom is meant, under the present bourgeois conditions of production, free trade, free selling and buying.

But if selling and buying disappears, free selling and buying disappears also. This talk about free selling and buying, and all the other "brave words" of our bourgeoisie about freedom in general, have a meaning, if any, only in contrast with restricted selling and buying, with the fettered traders of the Middle Ages, but have no meaning when opposed to the Communistic abolition of buying and selling, or the bourgeois conditions of production, and of the bourgeoisie itself.

You are horrified at our intending to do away with private property. But in your existing society, private property is already done away with for nine-tenths of the population; its existence for the few is solely due to its non-existence in the hands of those nine-tenths. You reproach us, therefore, with intending to do away with a form of property, the necessary condition for whose existence is the non-existence of any property for the immense majority of society.

In one word, you reproach us with intending to do away with your property. Precisely so; that is just what we intend.

From the moment when labour can no longer be converted into capital, money, or rent, into a social power capable of being monopolized, *i.e.*, from the moment when individual property can no longer be transformed into bourgeois property, into capital, from that moment, you say, individuality vanishes.

You must, therefore, confess that by "individual" you mean no other person than the bourgeois, than the middle-class owner of property. This person must, indeed, be swept out of the way, and made impossible.

Communism deprives no man of the power to appropriate the products of society; all that it does is to deprive him of the power to subjugate the labour of others by means of such appropriation.

It has been objected that upon the abolition of private property all work will cease, and universal laziness will overtake us.

According to this, bourgeois society ought long ago to have gone to the dogs through sheer idleness; for those who work, acquire nothing, and those who acquire anything, do not work. The whole of this ob-jection is but another expression of the tautology: that there can no longer be any wage-labour when there is no longer any capital.

All objections urged against the Communistic mode of producing and appropriating material products, have, in the same way, been urged against the Communistic mode of producing and appropriating intellectual products. Just as, to the bourgeois, the disappearance of class property is the disappearance of production itself, so the disappearance of class culture is to him identical with the disappearance of all culture.

That culture, the loss of which he laments, is, for the enormous majority, a mere training to act as a machine.

But don't wrangle with us so long as you apply, to our intended abolition of bourgeois property, the standard of your bourgeois notions of freedom, culture, law, etc. Your very ideas are but the outgrowth of the conditions of your bourgeois production and bourgeois property, just as your jurisprudence is but the will of your class made into a law for all, a will, whose essential character and direction are determined by the economical conditions of existence of your class.

The selfish misconception that induces you to transform into eternal laws of nature and of reason, the social forms springing from your present mode of production and form of property—historical relations that rise and disappear in the progress of production—this misconception you share with every ruling class that has preceded you. What you see clearly in the case of ancient property, what you admit in the case of feudal property, you are of course forbidden to admit in the case of your own bourgeois form of property.

Abolition of the family! Even the most radical flare up at this infamous proposal of the Communists.

On what foundation is the present family, the bourgeois family, based? On capital, on private gain. In its completely developed form this family exists only among the bourgeoisie. But this state of things finds its complement in the practical absence of the family among proletarians, and in public prostitution.

The bourgeois family will vanish as a matter of course when its complement vanishes, and both will vanish with the vanishing of capital.

Do you charge us with wanting to stop the exploitation of children by their parents? To this crime we plead guilty.

But, you will say, we destroy the most hallowed of relations, when we replace home education by social.

And your education! Is not that also social, and determined by the social conditions under which you educate, by the intervention, direct or indirect, of society, by means of schools, etc.? The Communists have not invented the intervention of society in education; they do but seek to alter the character of that intervention, and to rescue education from the influence of the ruling class.

The bourgeois clap-trap about the family and education, about the hallowed co-relation of parent and child, becomes all the more disgusting, the more, by the action of Modern Industry, all family ties among the proletarians are torn asunder, and their children transformed into simple articles of commerce and instruments of labour.

But you Communists would introduce community of women, screams the bourgeoisie in chorus.

The bourgeois sees his wife a mere instrument of production. He hears that the instruments of production are to be exploited in common, and, naturally, can come to no other conclusion that the lot of being common to all will likewise fall to the women.

He has not even a suspicion that the real point aimed at is to do away with the status of women as mere instruments of production.

For the rest, nothing is more ridiculous than the virtuous indignation of our bourgeois at the community of women which, they pretend, is to be openly and officially established by the Communists. The Communists have no need to introduce community of women; it has existed almost from time immemorial.

Our bourgeois, not content with having the wives and daughters of their proletarians at their disposal, not to speak of common prostitutes, take the greatest pleasure in seducing each other's wives.

Bourgeois marriage is in reality a system of wives in common and thus, at the most, what the Communists might possibly be reproached with is that they desire to introduce, in substitution for a hypocritically concealed, an openly legalized community of women. For the rest, it is self-evident that the abolition of the present system of production must bring with it the abolition of the community of women springing from that system, *i.e.*, of prostitution both public and private.

The Communists are further reproached with desiring to abolish countries and nationality.

The workers have no country. We cannot take from them what they have not got. Since the proletariat must first of all acquire political supremacy, must rise to be the leading class of the nation, must constitute itself *the* nation, it is so far, itself national, though not in the bourgeois sense of the word.

National differences and antagonism between peoples are daily more and more vanishing, owing to the development of the bourgeoisie, to freedom of commerce, to the world market, to uniformity in the mode of production and in the conditions of life corresponding thereto.

The supremacy of the proletariat will cause them to vanish still faster. United action, of the leading civilized countries at least, is one of the first conditions for the emancipation of the proletariat.

In proportion as the exploitation of one individual by another is put an end to, the exploitation of one nation by another will also be put an end to. In proportion as the antagonism between classes within the nation vanishes, the hostility of one nation to another will come to an end.

The charges against Communism made from a religious, a philosophical, and, generally, from an ideological standpoint, are not deserving of serious examination.

Does it require deep intuition to comprehend that man's ideas, views, and conception, in one word, man's consciousness, changes with every change in the conditions of his material existence, in his social relations and in his social life?

What else does the history of ideas prove, than that intellectual production changes its character in proportion as material production is changed? The ruling ideas of each age have ever been the ideas of its ruling class.

When people speak of ideas that revolutionize society, they do but express that fact, that within the old society, the elements of a new one have been created, and that the dissolution of the old ideas keeps even pace with the dissolution of the old conditions of existence.

When the ancient world was in its last throes, the ancient religions were overcome by Christianity. When Christian ideas succumbed in the eighteenth century to rationalist ideas, feudal society fought its death battle with the then revolutionary bourgeoisie. The ideas of religious liberty and freedom of conscience merely gave expression to the sway of free competition within the domain of knowledge.

"Undoubtedly," it will be said, "religious, moral, philosophical, and juridical ideas have been modified in the course of historical development. But religion, morality, philosophy, political science, and law, constantly survived this change.

"There are, besides, eternal truths, such as Freedom, Justice, etc., that are common to all states of society. But Communism abolishes eternal truths, it abolishes all religion and all morality, instead of constituting them on a new basis; it therefore acts in contradiction to all past historical experience."

What does this accusation reduce itself to? The history of all past society has consisted in the development of class antagonisms, antagonisms that assumed different forms at different epochs.

But whatever form they may have taken, one fact is common to all past ages, viz., the exploitation of one part of society by the other. No wonder, then, that the social consciousness of past ages, despite all the multiplicity and variety it displays, moves within certain common forms, or general ideas, which cannot completely vanish except with the total disappearance of class antagonisms.

The Communist revolution is the most radical rupture with traditional relations; no wonder that its development involved the most radical rupture with traditional ideas.

But let us have done with the bourgeois objections to Communism.

We have seen above, that the first step in the revolution by the working class is to raise the proletariat to the position of ruling class, to win the battle of democracy.

The proletariat will use its political supremacy to wrest, by degrees, all capital from the bourgeoisie, to centralize all instruments of production in the hands of the State, i.e., of the proletariat organized as the ruling class; and to increase the total productive forces as rapidly as possible.

Of course, in the beginning, this cannot be effected except by means of despotic inroads on the rights of property, and on the conditions of bourgeois production; by means of measures, therefore, which appear economically insufficient and untenable, but which, in the course of the movement, outstrip themselves, necessitate further inroads upon the old social order, and are unavoidable as a means of entirely revolutionizing the mode of production.

These measures will, of course, be different in different countries.

Nevertheless in most advanced countries, the following will be pretty generally applicable:

1. Abolition of property in land and application of all rents of land to public purposes.

2. A heavy progressive or graduated income tax.

3. Abolition of all right of inheritance.

4. Confiscation of the property of all emigrants and rebels.

5. Centralization of credit in the banks of the State, by means of a national bank with State capital and an exclusive monopoly.

6. Centralization of the means of communication and transport in the hands of the State.

7. Extension of factories and instruments of production owned by the State; the bringing into cultivation of waste-lands, and the improvement of the soil generally in accordance with a common plan.

8. Equal liability of all to labour. Establishment of industrial armies, especially for agriculture.

9. Combination of agriculture with manufacturing industries; gradual abolition of all the distinction between town and country by a more equable distribution of the population over the country.

10. Free education for all children in public schools. Abolition of children's factory labour in its present form. Combination of education with industrial production, etc., etc.

When, in the course of development, class distinctions have disappeared, and all production has been concentrated in the hands of a vast association of the whole nation, the public power will lose its political character. Political power, properly so called, is merely the organized power of one class for oppressing another. If the proletariat during its contest with the bourgeoisie is compelled, by the force of circumstances, to organize itself as a class, if, by means of a revolution, it makes itself the ruling class, and, as such, sweeps away by force the old conditions of production, then it will, along with these conditions, have swept away the conditions for the existence of class antagonisms and of classes generally, and will thereby have abolished its own supremacy as a class.

In place of the old bourgeois society, with its classes and class antagonisms, we shall have an association, in which the free development of each is the condition for the free development of all.

…

IV. Position of the Communists in Relation to the Various Existing Opposition Parties

Section II has made clear the relations of the Communists to the existing working-class parties, such as the Chartists in England and the Agrarian Reformers in America.[21]

The Communists fight for the attainment of the immediate aims, for the enforcement of the momentary interests of the working class; but in the movement of the present, they also represent and take care of the future of that movement. In France the Communists ally with the Social Democrats,[22] against the conservative and radical bourgeoisie, reserving, however, the right to take up a critical position in regard to phases and illusions traditionally handed down from the great Revolution.

In Switzerland, they support the Radicals, without losing sight of the fact that this party consists of antagonistic elements, partly of Democratic Socialists, in the French sense, partly of radical bourgeois.

In Poland, they support the party that insists on an agrarian revolution as the prime condition for national emancipation, that party which fomented the insurrection of Kraków in 1846.[23]

In Germany, they fight with the bourgeoisie whenever it acts in a revolutionary way, against the absolute monarchy, the feudal squirearchy,[24] and the petty bourgeoisie.

But they never cease, for a single instant, to instil into the working class the clearest possible recognition of the hostile antagonism between bourgeoisie and proletariat, in order that the German workers may straightway use, as so many weapons against the bourgeoisie, the social and political conditions that the bourgeoisie must necessarily introduce along with its supremacy, and in order that, after the fall of the reactionary classes in Germany, the fight against the bourgeoisie itself may immediately begin.

The Communists turn their attention chiefly to Germany, because that country is on the eve of a bourgeois revolution that is bound to be carried out under more advanced conditions of European civilization, and with a much more developed proletariat, than that of England was in the seventeenth, and France in the eighteenth century, and because the bourgeois revolution in Germany will be but the prelude to an immediately following proletarian revolution.

In short, the Communists everywhere support every revolutionary movement against the existing social and political order of things.

---

21 Chartism was a popular reformist movement that lasted from 1837 to 1848. Among its demands (outlined in an 1837 "People's Charter") were universal male suffrage, equal electoral districts, abolition of the property qualification for running for Parliament, and annual parliaments. The National Reform Association was founded in 1844 to campaign for free settlement of the landless on public lands, a moratorium on seizure of family farms for non-payment of debt, and establishment of a 160-acre ceiling on land ownership to ensure there would be enough small-holdings to go around.

22 [Author's note] The party then represented in Parliament by Ledru-Rollin, in literature by Louis Blanc, in the daily press by the *Réforme*. The name of Social-Democracy signified, with these its inventors, a section of the Democratic or Republican Party more or less tinged with Socialism.

23 A nationalist, republican uprising in southern Poland against the Russians, Prussians, and Austrians who had jointly occupied it since the collapse of Napoleon's empire in 1815. The rebellion was crushed, and Kraków incorporated into the Austrian empire.

24 Landed gentry.

In all these movements they bring to the front, as the leading question in each, the property question, no matter what its degree of development at the time.

Finally, they labour everywhere for the union and agreement of the democratic parties of all countries.

The Communists disdain to conceal their views and aims. They openly declare that their ends can be attained only by the forcible overthrow of all existing social conditions. Let the ruling classes tremble at a Communist revolution. The proletarians have nothing to lose but their chains. They have a world to win.

WORKING MEN OF ALL COUNTRIES, UNITE!

SIMONE DE BEAUVOIR
"Introduction" to *The Second Sex*

Who Was Simone de Beauvoir?

Born in Paris in 1908, Simone de Beauvoir had become such an important figure in France by the time of her death in 1986 that her funeral was attended by 5000 people, including four former ministers of the Mitterrand government. A headline announcing her death read "Women, you owe her everything!"

De Beauvoir was the eldest of two daughters in a respectable, conservative bourgeois family, and she spent her formative years heatedly reacting against her parents and their values. She became an atheist while still a teenager, and decided early on to devote her life to writing and studying 'rather than' becoming a wife and mother. She studied philosophy at the ancient Parisian university of the Sorbonne and was the youngest person ever to obtain the *agrégation* (a high-level competitive examination for recruiting teachers in France) in philosophy, in 1929.[1] She was 21. In that same year she met the famous existentialist philosopher Jean-Paul Sartre and began an intense relationship with him—the most important of her life—that lasted until his death in 1980.

De Beauvoir and Sartre became notorious throughout France as a couple who were lovers and soul-mates but who maintained an open relationship; both considered themselves highly sexually 'liberated,' and de Beauvoir was openly bisexual. Sartre made what he called a "pact" with de Beauvoir—they could have affairs with other people, but they were required to tell each other everything—and he proceeded to match his actions to this rule. As he put it to de Beauvoir: "What *we* have is an *essential* love; but it is a good idea for us also to experience *contingent* love affairs."

Despite the rotating cast of lovers, de Beauvoir remained devoted to Sartre all her life and always maintained that he was the most brilliant man she had ever known. Indeed, she once declared that, her many books, literary prizes, and social influence notwithstanding, her greatest achievement in life was her relationship with Sartre.

Between 1932 and 1943 de Beauvoir was a high school teacher of philosophy in Rouen, in northwestern France. There, she was subject to official reprimands for her protests about male chauvinism and for her pacifism; finally, a parental complaint made against her for 'corrupting' one of her female students caused her dismissal. For the rest of her life, de Beauvoir lived in Paris and made her living from her writing. At the end of World War II, de Beauvoir became an editor at *Les Temps Modernes*, a new political journal founded by Sartre and other French intellec-

---

1   When the university *agrégation* results came out, Sartre was ranked first in the year and de Beauvoir second. Also, incidentally, 1929 was the year de Beauvoir acquired her lifelong nickname, *le Castor* (the French for beaver, because of the resemblance of her surname to "beaver").

tuals. She used this journal to promote her own work, and several excerpts from *The Second Sex* were first published in it.

Interestingly, part of the impetus to write *The Second Sex* came to her as she gradually realized that, unlike some of her female friends, she did *not* at first feel any sense that she was disadvantaged as a woman, but that this feeling of personal satisfaction and of independence resulted primarily from her relationship with a well-known, influential man—Sartre. When she reflected on this relationship, she realized with astonishment that she was fundamentally different from Sartre "because he was a man and I was only a woman." As she put it, "In writing *The Second Sex* I became aware, for the first time, that I myself was leading a false life, or rather, that I was profiting from this male-oriented society without even knowing it."

She was also influenced by what she saw in America, during a visit in 1947, of the experience of blacks in a segregated society. For example, she was friends with the black American short story writer and novelist Richard Wright, who, with his white wife Ellen, was a tireless advocate for black equality. For de Beauvoir, feminism was part of a larger project of social justice and human rights. From the late 1940s until the 1960s she was a very public left-wing political activist and a vocal supporter of communism (and critic of American-style capitalism).

The Second Sex is an extended examination of the problems women have encountered throughout history and of the possibilities left open to them. After the Introduction (reprinted here), the book is broken into two halves: Book One is a historical overview of "Facts and Myths" about women, and Book Two deals with "Women's Life Today." Book One is divided

into sections describing the "Destiny" of women according to theories of biology, psychoanalysis and Marxist historical materialism; the "History" of women from prehistoric times to the granting of the vote to women in France in 1947; and "Myths" about women in literature. Book Two is more personal, and talks about women in childhood, adolescence, sexual initiation, various forms of mature loving and sexual relationships, and old age. The conclusion of the book is positive and optimistic, as de Beauvoir tries to set out a model of life and action for future generations of women.

Some Useful Background Information

1. The first words of Book Two of *The Second Sex* are "One is not born, but rather becomes, a woman. No biological, psychological or economic fate determines the figure that the human female presents in society; it is civilization as a whole that determines this creature." This is how de Beauvoir most famously expresses an influential central thesis of the book: that 'woman,' as a biological category, is separable from 'feminine,' as a social construction—or more generally, that sex is not the same thing as gender. Thus, woman's status under the patriarchy as the Other is a contingent, socially constructed fact rather than an essential truth about the female gender.

It is important to appreciate that de Beauvoir is not denying that there are biological differences between men and women, nor does she insist that these biological differences must be simply ignored in a properly constituted society. Rather, she is arguing that our *biologi-*

cal constitutions do not determine our *gender* characteristics: such things as 'femininity' or 'masculinity,' being 'nurturing' or 'modest' or 'emotional' or 'delicate'—these things are constructed and constrained purely by *social* influences. Under different social conditions women and men might naturally and freely behave in ways radically different from contemporary social norms.

Thus, according to de Beauvoir, gender is more something we *do*—a way we live—than something we *are*. Gender is constrained by social pressures in large part because social pressures constrain how we can legitimately behave. A woman in, say, Canada in the 1950s could not just decide as an individual to behave like a man—or like someone who is neither masculine nor feminine—and in this way change her gender unilaterally. Even if she were brave enough to attempt the experiment, according to de Beauvoir—and the other existentialists—one cannot possess a certain trait, such as being masculine, unless others recognize one as doing so.

2. This emphasis on the social construction of gender, race, and other aspects of the reality we experience in our day-to-day lives is related to de Beauvoir's commitment to *existentialism*. Central to existentialism is the doctrine that *existence precedes essence*: humans have no pre-given purpose or essence determined for them by God or by biology. According to existentialism, each consciousness faces the world as an isolated individual, and inevitably creates itself—gives itself determinate form—by making choices. These choices are forced by the need to respond to the things around us, including both passive natural objects and other consciousnesses.

De Beauvoir and Sartre see the meeting of one consciousness with another as profoundly disturbing: faced with the gaze of an Other, we recognize a point of view which is necessarily different from our own and so we are required to concede our own incompleteness; furthermore, the opposing consciousness must treat us as an Other, which we feel as a threat to destroy us by turning us into an object.

De Beauvoir's feminism can be seen as a development of this idea: in response to the threat posed by other consciousnesses, according to existentialism, one might retaliate by objectifying and dominating the Other, to be able to control it without destroying it and thus be able to withstand its gaze. Thus, according to de Beauvoir, men have objectified and dominated women as the Other, and succumbing to all-pervasive social pressures women have allowed themselves to be dominated.

3. Towards the end of this essay, de Beauvoir mentions the contrast between being *en-soi* (in-itself) and being *pour-soi* (for-itself). Being for-itself is a mode of existence that is purposive and, as it were, constituted by its own activity; being in-itself, by contrast, is a less fully human kind of existence that is more like being a 'thing'—self-sufficient, non-purposive, driven by merely contingent current conditions.

How Important and Influential Is This Passage?

The Second Sex is often considered the founding work of twentieth-century feminism. It has been called "one of the most important and far-reaching books on women ever published" (Terry Keefe) and "the best book about women ever written" (*The Guardian*, 1999). From the day it was published it was both popular and controversial: twenty-two thousand copies of the first volume were sold in France in the first week, and de Beauvoir received large quantities of hate mail including some from "very active members of the First Sex." "How courageous you are.... You're going to lose a lot of friends!" one of her friends wrote to her. She was accused of writing a pornographic book (because of *The Second Sex*'s discussion of female sexuality), and the Vatican put it on the Index of prohibited books. "Once," de Beauvoir reported in her autobiography, "during an entire dinner at Nos Provinces on the Boulevard Montparnasse, a table of people nearby stared at me and giggled; I didn't like dragging [her lover, Nelson] Algren into a scene, but as I left I gave them a piece of my mind." On the other hand, some of the contemporary reviews were glowing: *The New Yorker* called it "more than a work of scholarship; it is a work of art, with the salt of reckless-ness that makes art sting."

After the initial furor died down, the book was criti-cized by scholars and critics as having too much of a middle-class, distorted viewpoint—as having been written by someone who had no cause to actually feel the pressures that give life to feminism. The poet Stevie Smith wrote, in 1953: "She has written an enor-mous book about women and it is soon clear that she does not like them, nor does she like being a woman." This debate continues today, and arguably it is only recently that *The Second Sex* has come to be appreci-ated seriously as a work of philosophy that stands on its own merits, rather than read solely in terms of de Beauvoir's "biography, relationship with ... Sartre, psy-che, or feminist credentials" (*TLS*, 2005).

De Beauvoir is a pivotal figure in the history of feminist thought from the Renaissance to the twen-ty-first century. In the Renaissance and early mod-ern period, writers that we would today think of as feminist [such as Christine de Pizan (1365–c. 1430) and Mary Astell (1666–1731)] tended to focus on the social asymmetries between women and men. They argued that women have similar innate abil-ities to men and should be granted opportunities equivalent to those their male counterparts enjoyed in certain key areas, especially education, the family, and sometimes work and politics. The eighteenth and nineteenth centuries [in work by writers such as Olympe de Gouges (1745–93), Mary Wollstonecraft (1759–97), Sojourner Truth (1797–1883), John Stuart Mill (1806–73), and Harriet Taylor (1807–58)] saw a greater accumulation of forceful writings against the oppression of women, combined with more explicit (but only gradually successful) political campaigns to have women's equal status with men enshrined in law. It was at the end of the nineteenth century—in France, during the 1890s—that the term 'feminism' first appeared.

Up to this point, feminism can be usefully—albeit simplistically—understood as characterized by a de-mand for equal rights with men. Once women are educated as extensively as men, are given the oppor-tunity to vote, are not forbidden from joining certain professions, and so on, then it was assumed that their innate capacities—in many (though perhaps not all) respects equal to, or even superior to, those of the male sex—would flourish free from oppression. That is, pre-twentieth-century feminism tended to focus on the suppression and distortion of woman's nature by contingent social structures such as laws and institu-tions. De Beauvoir's writings marked a significant shift and deepening in the nature of feminist thought. She denied that there is an inborn 'female nature' that just awaits the opportunity to break free from male op-pression, and insisted that women are dominated by men in *all* aspects of their lives—that their very con-sciousness, the very shape of their minds, is formed by the patriarchal society of which they are a part. Fem-inism cannot aspire simply to change the laws and in-stitutions of a country; this will leave the subordinate position of women essentially untouched. Feminists must fight for much more thoroughgoing change to the basic practices and assumptions of the whole society.

Later twentieth-century feminism, often known as *second-wave feminism* [representatives of which include Susan Moller Okin (1946–2004), Catharine MacKinnon (1946–), Martha Nussbaum (1947–), and Iris Young (1949–)], took up this emphasis on the deep and subtle nature of patriarchal dominance (though often without a very self-conscious sense of the debt to de Beauvoir). The distinction between sex and gender—the notion of gender as a social construct—proved especially significant in making this case. For many feminists, this has evolved into a critique of standards that are taken to have an object-ive and universal status—such as 'rational,' 'true,' and 'right'—but which, feminists argue, in fact reflect par-ticular gender interests. Thus, for example, to argue—as Wollstonecraft did—that women are 'equally rational' as men is to succumb to, rather than combat, one of the hidden patriarchal structures that oppress women.

The so-called *third-wave* (or sometimes, *postmod-ern*) feminism that began in the 1980s can also be seen as having roots in the work of de Beauvoir. Third-wave feminism emphasizes the claim that gender is a social, contingent, rather than a natural category, and adopts an 'anti-essentialist' stance about women: that is, there is nothing that can be usefully said about woman 'as such,' and instead we must focus in an explicitly un-unified way on different conceptions of femininity in particular ethnic, religious, and social groups.

Suggestions for Critical Reflection

1. De Beauvoir begins her book by asking "What is a woman?" How do you think she answers this question?

2. De Beauvoir claims that the terms *masculine* and *feminine* are not symmetrical opposites. What do you make of this claim? How does de Beauvoir develop it? What is its importance?

3. "Throughout history [women] have always been subordinated to men, and hence their dependency is not the result of a historical event or a social change—it was not something that *occurred*." Does this claim seem plausible? How important is it to de Beauvoir's argument?

4. De Beauvoir suggests that for women to renounce their status as an Other would be to abandon "all the advantages conferred upon them by their alliance with the superior caste." What does she mean by this? Is she right? How serious a difficulty is this for feminism?

5. "[T]he dominant class bases its argument on a state of affairs that it has itself created." Does this ring true? How important is it for the social activist, including the feminist, to notice this? How much does this explain the behavior towards women by even well-intentioned men?

6. "We are no longer like our partisan elders; by and large we have won the game." Is de Beauvoir right about this? Is this claim consistent with her general theory of the oppression of women in society?

7. "One is not born, but rather becomes, a woman." Some commentators have argued that, in making this central claim, de Beauvoir herself falls victim to the patriarchal mindset she is criticizing—that she is tacitly assuming that "femaleness is indeed optional and subhuman, and maleness the slipped-from standard." Does

this criticism strike you as plausible? Does it suggest a fundamental problem with de Beauvoir's project, or with the way she carries it out?

Suggestions for Further Reading

De Beauvoir's two most important works of philosophy are *The Second Sex* (1949) and *The Ethics of Ambiguity* (1947; it was translated into English by Bernard Frechtman and published by Citadel Press in 1949). The latter is an excellent introduction to existentialism. De Beauvoir also published four philosophical novels between 1943 and 1954, and in her later years she published several volumes of autobiography and biography, especially exploring her relationship with Sartre and the phenomenon of old age.

There are several biographies of de Beauvoir, including Deirdre Bair, *Simone de Beauvoir: A Biography* (Summit Books, 1990), and Toril Moi, *Simone de Beauvoir: The Making of an Intellectual Woman* (Blackwell, 1994). Useful secondary sources include: Nancy Bauer, *Simone de Beauvoir, Philosophy and Feminism* (Columbia University Press, 2001); Debra Bergoffen, *The Philosophy of Simone de Beauvoir: Gendered Phenomenologies, Erotic Generosities* (SUNY Press, 1996); Claudia Card, ed., *The Cambridge Companion to Simone de Beauvoir* (Cambridge University Press, 2003); Ruth Evans, ed., *Simone de Beauvoir's the Second Sex: New Interdisciplinary Essays* (St. Martin's, 1998); Elizabeth Fallaize, ed., *Simone de Beauvoir: A Critical Reader* (Routledge, 1998); Lori Jo Marso and Patricia Moynagh, eds., *Simone de Beauvoir's Political Thinking* (University of Illinois Press, 2006); Toril Moi, *Feminist Theory and Simone de Beauvoir* (Blackwell, 1990); Fredrika Scarth, *The Other Within* (Rowman & Littlefield, 2004); Margaret Simons, ed., *Feminist Interpretations of Simone de Beauvoir* (Pennsylvania State University Press, 1995); Margaret Simons, *Beauvoir and the Second Sex: Feminism, Race, and the Origins of Existentialism* (Rowman & Littlefield, 1999); and Karen Vintges, *Philosophy as Passion: The Thinking of Simone de Beauvoir* (translated by Anne Lavelle, Indiana University Press, 1996). Volume 72 of *Yale French Studies* (1986) is devoted to articles on Simone de Beauvoir, several of which are valuable.

"Introduction" to *The Second Sex*[2]

For a long time I have hesitated to write a book on woman. The subject is irritating, especially to women; and it is not new. Enough ink has been spilled in the quarreling over feminism, now practically over, and perhaps we should say no more about it. It is still talked about, however, for the voluminous nonsense uttered during the last century seems to have done little to illuminate the problem. After all, is there a problem? And if so, what is it? Are there women, really? Most assuredly the theory of the eternal feminine still has its adherents who will whisper in your ear: "Even in Russia[3] women still are *women*"; and other erudite persons—sometimes the very same—say with a sigh: "Woman is losing her way, woman is lost." One wonders if women still exist, if they will always exist, whether or not it is desirable that they should, what place they occupy in this world, what their place should be. "What has become of women?" was asked recently in an ephemeral magazine.[4]

But first we must ask: what is a woman? "*Tota mulier in utero*,"[5] says one, "woman is a womb." But in speaking of certain women, connoisseurs declare that they are not women, although they are equipped with a uterus like the rest. All agree in recognizing the fact that females exist in the human species; today as always they make up about one half of humanity. And yet we are told that femininity is in danger; we are exhorted to be women, remain women, become women. It would appear, then, that every female human being is not necessarily a woman; to be so considered she must

share in that mysterious and threatened reality known as femininity. Is this attribute something secreted by the ovaries? Or is it a Platonic essence, a product of the philosophic imagination? Is a rustling petticoat enough to bring it down to earth? Although some women try zealously to incarnate this essence, it is hardly patentable. It is frequently described in vague and dazzling terms that seem to have been borrowed from the vocabulary of the seers, and indeed in the times of St. Thomas[6] it was considered an essence as certainly defined as the somniferous virtue[7] of the poppy.

But conceptualism has lost ground. The biological and social sciences no longer admit the existence of unchangeably fixed entities that determine given characteristics, such as those ascribed to woman, the Jew, or the Negro. Science regards any characteristic as a reaction dependent in part upon a *situation*. If today femininity no longer exists, then it never existed. But does the word *woman*, then, have no specific content? This is stoutly affirmed by those who hold to the philosophy of the enlightenment, of rationalism, of nominalism;[8] women, to them, are merely the human beings arbitrarily designated by the word *woman*. Many American women particularly are prepared to think that there is no longer any place for woman as such; if a backward individual still takes herself for a woman, her friends advise her to be psychoanalyzed and thus get rid of this obsession. In regard to a work, *Modern Woman: The Lost Sex*,[9] which in other respects has its irritating features, Dorothy Parker[10] has written: "I cannot be just to books which treat of woman as woman.... My idea is that all of us, men as

---

2   This is the Introduction to *The Second Sex* by Simone de Beauvoir, translated by H.M. Parshley, copyright 1952 and renewed 1980 by Alfred A. Knopf Inc. (It was first published in French in 1949.) Used by permission of Alfred A. Knopf, a division of Random House, Inc.

3   That is, even after the reorganization of society in Russia after the Communist revolution of 1917 (and the upheaval of World War II).

4   [Author's note] *Franchise*, dead today.

5   "The whole woman is in her uterus," or, more snappily, "Woman is a womb." This aphorism dates back to medieval scholastic theology.

6   Aquinas.

7   "Power to induce sleep."

8   Nominalism is the view that only particular things exist, and 'abstract' things—*universals*—such as beauty, redness, or species-membership, are not real. Conceptualism (mentioned above) is the view that abstractions do exist as mental concepts.

9   By Ferdinand Lundberg and Marynia F. Farnham, published in 1947. Among other things, this book proposed that laws be adopted prohibiting single women from working, thus forcing them into marriage.

10   Parker (1893–1967) was an American critic, satirical poet, and short-story writer, famous for her acerbic wit.

well as women, should be regarded as human beings." But nominalism is a rather inadequate doctrine, and the antifemininists have had no trouble in showing that women simply *are not* men. Surely woman is, like man, a human being; but such a declaration is abstract. The fact is that every concrete human being is always a singular, separate individual. To decline to accept such notions as the eternal feminine, the black soul, the Jewish character, is not to deny that Jews, Negroes, women exist today—this denial does not represent a liberation for those concerned, but rather a flight from reality. Some years ago a well-known woman writer refused to permit her portrait to appear in a series of photographs especially devoted to women writers; she wished to be counted among the men. But in order to gain this privilege she made use of her husband's influence! Women who assert that they are men lay claim none the less to masculine consideration and respect. I recall also a young Trotskyite standing on a platform at a boisterous meeting and getting ready to use her fists, in spite of her evident fragility. She was denying her feminine weakness; but it was for love of a militant male whose equal she wished to be. The attitude of defiance of many American women proves that they are haunted by a sense of their femininity. In truth, to go for a walk with one's eyes open is enough to demonstrate that humanity is divided into two classes of individuals whose clothes, faces, bodies, smiles, gaits, interests, and occupations are manifestly different. Perhaps these differences are superficial, perhaps they are destined to disappear. What is certain is that right now they do most obviously exist.

If her functioning as a female is not enough to define woman, if we decline also to explain her through "the eternal feminine," and if nevertheless we admit, provisionally, that women do exist, then we must face the question: what is a woman?

To state the question is, to me, to suggest, at once, a preliminary answer. The fact that I ask it is in itself significant. A man would never get the notion of writing a book on the peculiar situation of the human male.[11] But if I wish to define myself, I must first of all say: "I am a woman"; on this truth must be based all further discussion. A man never begins by presenting himself as an individual of a certain sex; it goes without saying that he is a man. The terms *masculine* and *feminine* are used symmetrically only as a matter of form, as on legal papers. In actuality the relation of the two sexes is not quite like that of two electrical poles, for man represents both the positive and the neutral, as is indicated by the common use of *man* to designate human beings in general; whereas woman represents only the negative, defined by limiting criteria, without reciprocity. In the midst of an abstract discussion it is vexing to hear a man say: "You think thus and so because you are a woman"; but I know that my only defense is to reply: "I think thus and so because it is true," thereby removing my subjective self from the argument. It would be out of the question to reply: "And you think the contrary because you are a man," for it is understood that the fact of being a man is no peculiarity. A man is in the right in being a man; it is the woman who is in the wrong. It amounts to this: just as for the ancients there was an absolute vertical with reference to which the oblique was defined, so there is an absolute human type, the masculine. Woman has ovaries, a uterus; these peculiarities imprison her in her subjectivity, circumscribe her within the limits of her own nature. It is often said that she thinks with her glands. Man superbly ignores the fact that his anatomy also includes glands, such as the testicles, and that they secrete hormones. He thinks of his body as a direct and normal connection with the world, which he believes he apprehends objectively, whereas he regards the body of woman as a hindrance, a prison, weighed down by everything peculiar to it. "The female is a female by virtue of a certain *lack* of qualities," said Aristotle; "we should regard the female nature as afflicted with a natural defectiveness." And St. Thomas for his part pronounced woman to be an "imperfect man," an "incidental" being. This is symbolized in Genesis where Eve is depicted as

---

11   [Author's note] The Kinsey Report [Alfred C. Kinsey and others: *Sexual Behavior in the Human Male* (W.B. Saunders Co., 1948)] is no exception, for it is limited to describing the sexual characteristics of American men, which is quite a different matter.

made from what Bossuet called "a supernumerary bone" of Adam.[12]

Thus humanity is male and man defines woman not in herself but as relative to him; she is not regarded as an autonomous being. Michelet writes: "Woman, the relative being...." And Benda is most positive in his *Rapport d'Uriel*: "The body of man makes sense in itself quite apart from that of woman, whereas the latter seems wanting in significance by itself.... Man can think of himself without woman. She cannot think of herself without man."[13] And she is simply what man decrees; thus she is called "the sex," by which is meant that she appears essentially to the male as a sexual being. For him she is sex—absolute sex, no less. She is defined and differentiated with reference to man and not he with reference to her; she is the incidental, the inessential as opposed to the essential. He is the Subject, he is the Absolute—she is the Other.[14]

---

12 Jacques-Bénigne Bossuet (1627–1704) was a French bishop famous for his brilliant sermons. *Supernumerary* means "superfluous," "exceeding the required number."

13 Jules Michelet (1798–1874) was a French historian. Julien Benda (1867–1956) was a French novelist and critic; *Le rapport d'Uriel* was published in 1946.

14 [Author's note] E. Lévinas expresses this idea most explicitly in his essay *Temps et l'Autre*. "Is there not a case in which otherness, alterity [*altérité*], unquestionably marks the nature of a being, as its essence, an instance of otherness not consisting purely and simply in the opposition of two species of the same genus? I think that the feminine represents the contrary in its absolute sense, this contrariness being in no wise affected by any relation between it and its correlative and thus remaining absolutely other. Sex is not a certain specific difference ... no more is the sexual difference a mere contradiction.... Nor does this difference lie in the duality of two complementary terms, for two complementary terms imply a pre-existing whole.... Otherness reaches its full flowering in the feminine, a term of the same rank as consciousness but of opposite meaning."

I suppose that Lévinas does not forget that woman, too, is aware of her own consciousness, or ego. But it is striking that he deliberately takes a man's point of

The category of the *Other* is as primordial as consciousness itself. In the most primitive societies, in the most ancient mythologies, one finds the expression of a duality—that of the Self and the Other. This duality was not originally attached to the division of the sexes; it was not dependent upon any empirical facts. It is revealed in such works as that of Granet on Chinese thought and those of Dumézil on the East Indies and Rome.[15] The feminine element was at first no more involved in such pairs as Varuna-Mitra, Uranus-Zeus,[16] Sun-Moon, and Day-Night than it was in the contrasts between Good and Evil, lucky and unlucky auspices, right and left, God and Lucifer. Otherness is a fundamental category of human thought.

Thus it is that no group ever sets itself up as the One without at once setting up the Other over against itself. If three travelers chance to occupy the same compartment, that is enough to make vaguely hostile "others" out of all the rest of the passengers on the train. In small-town eyes all persons not belonging to the village are "strangers" and suspect; to the native of a country all who inhabit other countries are "foreigners"; Jews are "different" for the anti-Semite, Negroes are "inferior" for American racists, aborigines are "natives" for colonists, proletarians are the "lower class" for the privileged.

Lévi-Strauss,[17] at the end of a profound work on the various forms of primitive societies, reaches the

---

view, disregarding the reciprocity of subject and object. When he writes that woman is mystery, he implies that she is mystery for man. Thus his description, which is intended to be objective, is in fact an assertion of masculine privilege.

15 Marcel Granet (1884–1940) was a French sociologist, and Georges Dumézil (1898–1986) was a philologist and historian of religions.

16 Varuna and Mitra are Hindu gods (both concerned with upholding law and order), and Uranus and Zeus were Greek gods. One of Dumézil's classic books is *Mitra-Varuna: An Essay on Two Indo-European Representations of Sovereignty* (1948).

17 Claude Lévi-Strauss (1908–2009) was a French anthropologist, famous for developing structuralism as a method of understanding human society and culture (e.g., the structures of kinship systems).

following conclusion: "Passage from the state of Nature to the state of Culture is marked by man's ability to view biological relations as a series of contrasts; duality, alternation, opposition, and symmetry, whether under definite or vague forms, constitute not so much phenomena to be explained as fundamental and immediately given data of social reality."[18] These phenomena would be incomprehensible if in fact human society were simply a *Mitsein*[19] or fellowship based on solidarity and friendliness. Things become clear, on the contrary, if, following Hegel, we find in consciousness itself a fundamental hostility toward every other consciousness; the subject can be posed only in being opposed—he sets himself up as the essential, as opposed to the other, the inessential, the object.

But the other consciousness, the other ego, sets up a reciprocal claim. The native traveling abroad is shocked to find himself in turn regarded as a "stranger" by the natives of neighboring countries. As a matter of fact, wars, festivals, trading, treaties, and contests among tribes, nations, and classes tend to deprive the concept *Other* of its absolute sense and to make manifest its relativity; willy-nilly, individuals and groups are forced to realize the reciprocity of their relations. How is it, then, that this reciprocity has not been recognized between the sexes, that one of the contrasting terms is set up as the sole essential, denying any relativity in regard to its correlative and defining the latter as pure otherness? Why is it that women do not dispute male sovereignty? No subject will readily volunteer to become the object, the inessential; it is not the Other who, in defining himself as the Other, establishes the One. The Other is posed as such by the One in defining himself as the One. But if the Other is not to regain the status of being the One, he must be submissive enough to accept this alien point of view. Whence comes this submission in the case of woman?

There are, to be sure, other cases in which a certain category has been able to dominate another completely for a time. Very often this privilege depends upon inequality of numbers—the majority imposes its rule upon the minority or persecutes it. But women are not a minority, like the American Negroes or the Jews; there are as many women as men on earth. Again, the two groups concerned have often been originally independent; they may have been formerly unaware of each other's existence, or perhaps they recognized each other's autonomy. But a historical event has resulted in the subjugation of the weaker by the stronger. The scattering of the Jews, the introduction of slavery into America, the conquests of imperialism are examples in point. In these cases the oppressed retained at least the memory of former days; they possessed in common a past, a tradition, sometimes a religion or a culture.

The parallel drawn by Bebel[20] between women and the proletariat is valid in that neither ever formed a minority or a separate collective unit of mankind. And instead of a single historical event it is in both cases a historical development that explains their status as a class and accounts for the membership of *particular individuals* in that class. But proletarians have not always existed, whereas there have always been women. They are women in virtue of their anatomy and physiology. Throughout history they have always been subordinated to men, and hence their dependency is not the result of a historical event or a social change—it was not something that *occurred*. The reason why otherness in this case seems to be an absolute is in part that it lacks the contingent or incidental nature of historical facts. A condition brought about at a certain time can be abolished at some other time, as the Negroes of Haiti and others have proved; but it might seem that a natural condition is beyond the possibility of change. In truth, however, the nature

---

18   [Author's note] See C. Lévi-Strauss: *Les Structures élémentaires de la parenté* [1949]. My thanks are due to C. Lévi-Strauss for his kindness in furnishing me with the proofs of his work, which, among others, I have used liberally in Part II.

19   A Hegelian term, literally meaning "being with."

20   August Bebel (1840–1913) was a German Marxist revolutionary. In *Woman and Socialism*, first published in 1879, he argued that the social emancipation of women was a crucial precursor to the overthrow of capitalism. In Marxist theory the proletariat is the lower class of society that does not have ownership of the means of production and must instead work for wages.

of things is no more immutably given, once for all, than is historical reality. If woman seems to be the inessential which never becomes the essential, it is because she herself fails to bring about this change. Proletarians say "We"; Negroes also. Regarding themselves as subjects, they transform the bourgeois, the whites, into "others." But women do not say "We," except at some congress of feminists or similar formal demonstration; men say "women," and women use the same word in referring to themselves. They do not authentically assume a subjective attitude. The proletarians have accomplished the revolution in Russia, the Negroes in Haiti, the Indo-Chinese are battling for it in Indo-China; but the women's effort has never been anything more than a symbolic agitation. They have gained only what men have been willing to grant; they have taken nothing, they have only received.[21]

The reason for this is that women lack concrete means for organizing themselves into a unit which can stand face to face with the correlative unit. They have no past, no history, no religion of their own; and they have no such solidarity of work and interest as that of the proletariat. They are not even promiscuously herded together in the way that creates community feeling among the American Negroes, the ghetto Jews, the workers of Saint-Denis,[22] or the factory hands of Renault. They live dispersed among the males, attached through residence, housework, economic condition, and social standing to certain men—fathers or husbands—more firmly than they are to other women. If they belong to the bourgeoisie, they feel solidarity with men of that class, not with proletarian women; if they are white, their allegiance is to white men, not to Negro women. The proletariat can propose to massacre the ruling class, and a sufficiently fanatical Jew or Negro might dream of getting sole possession of the atomic bomb and making humanity wholly Jewish or black; but woman cannot

even dream of exterminating the males. The bond that unites her to her oppressors is not comparable to any other. The division of the sexes is a biological fact, not an event in human history. Male and female stand opposed within a primordial *Mitsein*, and woman has not broken it. The couple is a fundamental unity with its two halves riveted together, and the cleavage of society along the line of sex is impossible. Here is to be found the basic trait of woman: she is the Other in a totality of which the two components are necessary to one another.

One could suppose that this reciprocity might have facilitated the liberation of woman. When Hercules sat at the feet of Omphale[23] and helped her with her spinning, his desire for her held him captive; but why did she fail to gain a lasting power? To revenge herself on Jason, Medea killed their children;[24] and this grim legend would seem to suggest that she might have obtained a formidable influence over him through his love for his offspring. In *Lysistrata*[25] Aristophanes gaily depicts a band of women who joined

---

21 [Author's note] See Part II, ch. viii [not reprinted here].
22 Saint-Denis is a region including the northern suburbs of Paris and has been the scene of several significant worker uprisings and strikes, including the revolt of 1848 (and others as recently as 2003). Saint-Ouen, in Saint-Denis, was one of the first cities where a factory worker was elected mayor.
23 A queen of Lydia, an ancient kingdom in the region that is today Turkey, who is said to have owned Hercules as her slave for three years. (Hercules was being punished for the murder of his friend Iphitus. The story goes that during his time as a slave he became so weak that he wore women's clothes and did 'women's work,' while the queen wore his lion skin and carried his club.)
24 Medea was a powerful sorceress, the daughter of King Aeëtes of Colchis (at the eastern end of the Black Sea), and the granddaughter of Helios, the sun god. When Jason and the crew of the Argo arrived at Colchis seeking the Golden Fleece, Medea fell in love with Jason and used her magic to help him, in return for Jason's promise to marry her. When Jason later deserted her and married the daughter of Creon, the king of Corinth, Medea took her revenge by killing the new bride with a poisoned robe and crown which burned the flesh from her body (and killed King Creon as well when he tried to embrace his dying daughter), and also murdering the two children she had with Jason.
25 A play, written in about 411 BCE, in which the women of Hellas (ancient Greece) agree to withhold sex from their men folk until they agree to end the long-running war between Athens and Sparta.

forces to gain social ends through the sexual needs of their men; but this is only a play. In the legend of the Sabine women, the latter soon abandoned their plan of remaining sterile to punish their ravishers.[26] In truth woman has not been socially emancipated through man's need—sexual desire and the desire for offspring—which makes the male dependent for satisfaction upon the female.

Master and slave, also, are united by a reciprocal need, in this case economic, which does not liberate the slave. In the relation of master to slave the master does not make a point of the need that he has for the other; he has in his grasp the power of satisfying this need through his own action; whereas the slave, in his dependent condition, his hope and fear, is quite conscious of the need he has for his master. Even if the need is at bottom equally urgent for both, it always works in favor of the oppressor and against the oppressed. That is why the liberation of the working class, for example, has been slow.

Now, woman has always been man's dependent, if not his slave; the two sexes have never shared the world in equality. And even today woman is heavily handicapped, though her situation is beginning to change. Almost nowhere is her legal status the same as man's, and frequently it is much to her disadvantage. Even when her rights are legally recognized in the abstract, long-standing custom prevents their full

expression in the mores.[27] In the economic sphere men and women can almost be said to make up two castes; other things being equal, the former hold the better jobs, get higher wages, and have more opportunity for success than their new competitors. In industry and politics men have a great many more positions and they monopolize the most important posts. In addition to all this, they enjoy a traditional prestige that the education of children tends in every way to support, for the present enshrines the past—and in the past all history has been made by men. At the present time, when women are beginning to take part in the affairs of the world, it is still a world that belongs to men—they have no doubt of it at all and women have scarcely any. To decline to be the Other, to refuse to be a party to the deal—this would be for women to renounce all the advantages conferred upon them by their alliance with the superior caste. Man-the-sovereign will provide woman-the-liege with material protection and will undertake the moral justification of her existence; thus she can evade at once both economic risk and the metaphysical risk of a liberty in which ends and aims must be contrived without assistance. Indeed, along with the ethical urge of each individual to affirm his subjective existence, there is also the temptation to forgo liberty and become a thing. This is an inauspicious road, for he who takes it—passive, lost, ruined—becomes henceforth the creature of another's will, frustrated in his transcendence and deprived of every value. But it is an easy road; on it one avoids the strain involved in undertaking an authentic existence. When man makes of woman the *Other*, he may, then, expect her to manifest deep-seated tendencies toward complicity. Thus, woman may fail to lay claim to the status of subject because she lacks definite resources, because she feels the necessary bond that ties her to man regardless of reciprocity, and because she is often very well pleased with her role as the *Other*.

But it will be asked at once: how did all this begin? It is easy to see that the duality of the sexes, like any duality, gives rise to conflict. And doubtless the winner will assume the status of absolute. But why should man have won from the start? It seems possible that women could have won the victory; or that

---

26 At the beginning of Roman history, according to myth, the newly founded city of Rome needed to increase its population quickly in order to defend itself against its neighbors, but they did not have enough women to sustain their numbers. The Romans therefore invited the neighboring community of the Sabines to a religious celebration in honour of Neptune, and during the party the younger Roman men kidnapped the Sabine women and raped them. The Sabines—some months later!—returned with an army to bring back their women by force, but discovered (according to legend) that their erstwhile wives and daughters had reconciled with their new Roman husbands, and borne their children. The women stopped the battle before it started by placing themselves between the two armies; the Romans and the Sabines made peace, and Rome continued to grow.

27 "Prevailing manners or habits."

the outcome of the conflict might never have been decided. How is it that this world has always belonged to the men and that things have begun to change only recently? Is this change a good thing? Will it bring about an equal sharing of the world between men and women?

These questions are not new, and they have often been answered. But the very fact that woman *is the Other* tends to cast suspicion upon all the justifications that men have ever been able to provide for it. These have all too evidently been dictated by men's interest. A little-known feminist of the seventeenth century, Poulain de la Barre,[28] put it this way: "All that has been written about women by men should be suspect, for the men are at once judge and party to the lawsuit." Everywhere, at all times, the males have displayed their satisfaction in feeling that they are the lords of creation. "Blessed be God ... that He did not make me a woman," say the Jews in their morning prayers, while their wives pray on a note of resignation: "Blessed be the Lord, who created me according to His will." The first among the blessings for which Plato thanked the gods was that he had been created free, not enslaved; the second, a man, not a woman. But the males could not enjoy this privilege fully unless they believed it to be founded on the absolute and the eternal; they sought to make the fact of their supremacy into a right. "Being men, those who have made and compiled the laws have favored their own sex, and jurists have elevated these laws into principles," to quote Poulain de la Barre once more.

Legislators, priests, philosophers, writers, and scientists have striven to show that the subordinate position of woman is willed in heaven and advantageous on earth. The religions invented by men reflect this wish for domination. In the legends of Eve and Pandora men have taken up arms against women. They have made use of philosophy and theology, as the quotations from Aristotle and St. Thomas have shown. Since ancient times satirists and moralists have delighted in showing up the weaknesses of women. We are familiar with the savage indictments hurled against women throughout French literature. Montherlant, for example, follows the tradition of Jean de Meung,[29] though with less gusto. This hostility may at times be well founded, often it is gratuitous; but in truth it more or less successfully conceals a desire for self-justification. As Montaigne[30] says, "It is easier to accuse one sex than to excuse the other." Sometimes what is going on is clear enough. For instance, the Roman law limiting the rights of woman cited "the imbecility, the instability of the sex" just when the weakening of family ties seemed to threaten the interests of male heirs. And in the effort to keep the married woman under guardianship, appeal was made in the sixteenth century to the authority of St. Augustine, who declared that "woman is a creature neither decisive nor constant," at a time when the single woman was thought capable of managing her property. Montaigne understood clearly how arbitrary and unjust was woman's appointed lot: "Women are not in the wrong when they decline to accept the rules laid down for them, since the men make these rules without consulting them. No wonder intrigue and strife abound." But he did not go so far as to champion their cause.

---

28   François Poulain de la Barre, a French Catholic village priest, published three pamphlets urging the equality of the sexes, including "De l'égalité des deux sexes" (1671) from which this quote is taken.

29   Henri de Montherlant (1896–1972) was a French writer, soldier, athlete and bullfighter whose novels glorify force and masculinity. Jean de Meung (c. 1240–c. 1305) was a French poet and alchemist known for his continuation of the *Roman de la rose* (Romance of the Rose), an allegorical poem in the courtly love tradition begun by Guillaume de Lorris in about 1230. His section of the poem is particularly noted for its controversial digressions on a variety of topics, including a quatrain vilifying womankind. (For this offense, it is said, he was cornered by the ladies of the court of Charles VI who tried to have him stripped naked and whipped; only his impish eloquence allowed him to escape.)

30   Michel de Montaigne (1533–1592) was a French courtier and the author of *Essais*, which established, as a new literary form, the essay (a short piece dealing with the author's personal thoughts about a particular subject).

It was only later, in the eighteenth century, that genuinely democratic men began to view the matter objectively. Diderot,[31] among others, strove to show that woman is, like man, a human being. Later John Stuart Mill came fervently to her defense. But these philosophers displayed unusual impartiality. In the nineteenth century the feminist quarrel became again a quarrel of partisans. One of the consequences of the industrial revolution was the entrance of women into productive labor, and it was just here that the claims of the feminists emerged from the realm of theory and acquired an economic basis, while their opponents became the more aggressive. Although landed property lost power to some extent, the bourgeoisie clung to the old morality that found the guarantee of private property in the solidity of the family. Woman was ordered back into the home the more harshly as her emancipation became a real menace. Even within the working class the men endeavored to restrain woman's liberation, because they began to see the women as dangerous competitors—the more so because they were accustomed to work for lower wages.[32]

In proving woman's inferiority, the antifeminists then began to draw not only upon religion, philosophy, and theology, as before, but also upon science—biology, experimental psychology, etc. At most they were willing to grant "equality in difference" to the *other* sex. That profitable formula is most significant; it is precisely like the "equal but separate" formula of the Jim Crow laws[33] aimed at the North American Negroes. As is well known, this so-called equalitarian segregation has resulted only in the most extreme discrimination. The similarity just noted is in no way due to chance, for whether it is a race, a caste, a class, or a sex that is reduced to a position of inferiority, the methods of justification are the same. "The eternal feminine" corresponds to "the black soul" and to "the Jewish character." True, the Jewish problem is on the whole very different from the other two—to the anti-Semite the Jew is not so much an inferior as he is an enemy for whom there is to be granted no place on earth, for whom annihilation is the fate desired. But there are deep similarities between the situation of woman and that of the Negro. Both are being emancipated today from a like paternalism, and the former master class wishes to "keep them in their place"—that is, the place chosen for them. In both cases the former masters lavish more or less sincere eulogies, either on the virtues of "the good Negro" with his dormant, childish, merry soul—the submissive Negro—or on the merits of the woman who is "truly feminine"—that is, frivolous, infantile, irresponsible—the submissive woman. In both cases the dominant class bases its argument on a state of affairs that it has itself created. As George Bernard Shaw[34] puts it, in substance, "The American white relegates the black to the rank of shoeshine boy; and he concludes from this that the black is good for nothing but shining shoes." This vicious circle is met with in all analogous circumstances; when an individual (or a group of individuals) is kept in a situation of inferiority, the fact is that he *is* inferior. But the significance of the verb *to be* must be rightly understood here; it is in bad faith to give it a static value when it really has the dynamic Hegelian sense of "to have become." Yes, women on the whole *are* today inferior to men; that is, their situation affords them fewer possibilities. The question is: should that state of affairs continue?

---

31   Denis Diderot (1713–1784) was a French philosopher best known as the chief editor of *L'Encyclopédie*. Arguably the supreme literary creation of the Age of Enlightenment, *L'Encyclopédie* attempted to present all the achievements of human learning in a single (28 volume) work.

32   [Author's note] See Part II, pp. 115–117 [not reprinted here].

33   From the 1880s until, in many cases, the 1960s, more than half of the US states passed "Jim Crow" laws (so-called after a black character in minstrel shows) to enforce segregation, imposing legal punishments on people for consorting with members of another race. For example, business owners and public institutions were often ordered to keep their black and white clientele separated.

---

34   Shaw (1856–1950) was an Irish playwright and critic, awarded the Nobel Prize in Literature in 1925. In addition to his plays, he is also the author of *The Intelligent Woman's Guide to Socialism and Capitalism* (1928).

Many men hope that it will continue; not all have given up the battle. The conservative bourgeoisie still see in the emancipation of women a menace to their morality and their interests. Some men dread feminine competition. Recently a male student wrote in the *Hebdo-Latin*:[35] "Every woman student who goes into medicine or law robs us of a job." He never questioned his rights in this world. And economic interests are not the only ones concerned. One of the benefits that oppression confers upon the oppressors is that the most humble among them is made to *feel* superior; thus, a "poor white" in the South can console himself with the thought that he is not a "dirty nigger"—and the more prosperous whites cleverly exploit this pride.

Similarly, the most mediocre of males feels himself a demigod as compared with women. It was much easier for M. de Montherlant to think himself a hero when he faced women (and women chosen for his purpose) than when he was obliged to act the man among men—something many women have done better than he, for that matter. And in September 1948, in one of his articles in the *Figaro littéraire*, Claude Mauriac—whose great originality is admired by all—could[36] write regarding woman: "*We* listen on a tone [*sic!*] of polite indifference ... to the most brilliant among them, well knowing that her wit reflects more or less luminously ideas that come from *us*."[37] Evidently the speaker referred to is not reflecting the ideas of Mauriac himself, for no one knows of his having any. It may be that she reflects ideas originating with men, but then, even among men there are those who have been known to appropriate ideas not their own; and one can well ask whether Claude Mauriac might

not find more interesting a conversation reflecting Descartes, Marx, or Gide[38] rather than himself. What is really remarkable is that by using the questionable *we* he identifies himself with St. Paul, Hegel, Lenin, and Nietzsche, and from the lofty eminence of their grandeur looks down disdainfully upon the bevy of women who make bold to converse with him on a footing of equality. In truth, I know of more than one woman who would refuse to suffer with patience Mauriac's "tone of polite indifference."

I have lingered on this example because the masculine attitude is here displayed with disarming ingenuousness. But men profit in many more subtle ways from the otherness, the alterity[39] of woman. Here is miraculous balm for those afflicted with an inferiority complex, and indeed no one is more arrogant toward women, more aggressive or scornful, than the man who is anxious about his virility. Those who are not fear-ridden in the presence of their fellow men are much more disposed to recognize a fellow creature in woman; but even to these the myth of Woman, the Other, is precious for many reasons.[40] They cannot be blamed for not cheerfully relinquishing all the benefits they derive from the myth, for they realize what they

---

35 Like *Franchise*, another ephemeral magazine of the era.

36 [Author's note] Or at least he thought he could.

37 Claude Mauriac (1914–1996) was a French journalist, critic, and avant-garde novelist. Several of his experimental novels (published in the late 1950s and early 1960s) focus on the exploits of a cold-hearted, womanizing egoist named Bertrand Carnéjoux. *Figaro littéraire* is the literary supplement of the French daily newspaper *Le Figaro* (which has been in operation since 1866).

38 André Gide (1869–1951), a French novelist, intellectual, literary critic, and social crusader (for, especially, homosexual rights). He received the Nobel Prize for Literature in 1947.

39 *Alterity* is the state of being different, especially lack of identification with some part of one's personality or community. It has come to be a technical, philosophical term for the principle of exchanging one's own perspective for that of the Other.

40 [Author's note] A significant article on this theme by Michel Carrouges appeared in No. 292 of the *Cahiers du Sud*. He writes indignantly: "Would that there were no woman-myth at all but only a cohort of cooks, matrons, prostitutes, and bluestockings serving functions of pleasure or usefulness!" That is to say, in his view woman has no existence in and for herself; he thinks only of her *function* in the male world. Her reason for existence lies in man. But then, in fact, her poetic "function" as a myth might be more valued than any other. The real problem is precisely to find out why woman should be defined with relation to man.

would lose in relinquishing woman as they fancy her to be, while they fail to realize what they have to gain from the woman of tomorrow. Refusal to pose oneself as the Subject, unique and absolute, requires great self-denial. Furthermore, the vast majority of men make no such claim explicitly. They do not *postulate* woman as inferior, for today they are too thoroughly imbued with the ideal of democracy not to recognize all human beings as equals.

In the bosom of the family, woman seems in the eyes of childhood and youth to be clothed in the same social dignity as the adult males. Later on, the young man, desiring and loving, experiences the resistance, the independence of the woman desired and loved; in marriage, he respects woman as wife and mother, and in the concrete events of conjugal life she stands there before him as a free being. He can therefore feel that social subordination as between the sexes no longer exists and that on the whole, in spite of differences, woman is an equal. As, however, he observes some points of inferiority—the most important being unfitness for the professions—he attributes these to natural causes. When he is in a co-operative and benevolent relation with woman, his theme is the principle of abstract equality, and he does not base his attitude upon such inequality as may exist. But when he is in conflict with her, the situation is reversed: his theme will be the existing inequality, and he will even take it as justification for denying abstract equality.[41]

So it is that many men will affirm as if in good faith that women *are* the equals of man and that they have nothing to clamor for, while *at the same time* they will say that women can never be the equals of man and that their demands are in vain. It is, in point of fact, a difficult matter for man to realize the extreme importance of social discriminations which seem outwardly insignificant but which produce in woman moral and intellectual effects so profound

that they appear to spring from her original nature.[42] The most sympathetic of men never fully comprehend woman's concrete situation. And there is no reason to put much trust in the men when they rush to the defense of privileges whose full extent they can hardly measure. We shall not, then, permit ourselves to be intimidated by the number and violence of the attacks launched against women, nor to be entrapped by the self-seeking eulogies bestowed on the "true woman," nor to profit by the enthusiasm for woman's destiny manifested by men who would not for the world have any part of it.

We should consider the arguments of the feminists with no less suspicion, however, for very often their controversial aim deprives them of all real value. If the "woman question" seems trivial, it is because masculine arrogance has made of it a "quarrel"; and when quarreling one no longer reasons well. People have tirelessly sought to prove that woman is superior, inferior, or equal to man. Some say that, having been created after Adam, she is evidently a secondary being; others say on the contrary that Adam was only a rough draft and that God succeeded in producing the human being in perfection when He created Eve. Woman's brain is smaller; yes, but it is relatively larger. Christ was made a man; yes, but perhaps for his greater humility. Each argument at once suggests its opposite, and both are often fallacious. If we are to gain understanding, we must get out of these ruts; we must discard the vague notions of superiority, inferiority, equality which have hitherto corrupted every discussion of the subject and start afresh.

Very well, but just how shall we pose the question? And, to begin with, who are we to propound it at all? Man is at once judge and party to the case; but so is woman. What we need is an angel—neither man nor woman—but where shall we find one? Still, the angel would be poorly qualified to speak, for an angel is ignorant of all the basic facts involved in the problem. With a hermaphrodite we should be no better off, for here the situation is most peculiar; the hermaphrodite is not really the combination of a whole man and a whole woman, but consists of parts

---

41   [Author's note] For example, a man will say that he considers his wife in no wise degraded because she has no gainful occupation. The profession of housewife is just as lofty, and so on. But when the first quarrel comes he will exclaim: "Why, you couldn't make your living without me!"

---

42   [Author's note] The specific purpose of Book II of this study is to describe this process.

of each and thus is neither. It looks to me as if there are, after all, certain women who are best qualified to elucidate the situation of woman. Let us not be misled by the sophism that because Epimenides was a Cretan he was necessarily a liar;[43] it is not a mysterious essence that compels men and women to act in good or in bad faith, it is their situation that inclines them more or less toward the search for truth. Many of today's women, fortunate in the restoration of all the privileges pertaining to the estate of the human being, can afford the luxury of impartiality—we even recognize its necessity. We are no longer like our partisan elders; by and large we have won the game. In recent debates on the status of women the United Nations has persistently maintained that the equality of the sexes is now becoming a reality, and already some of us have never had to sense in our femininity an inconvenience or an obstacle. Many problems appear to us to be more pressing than those which concern us in particular, and this detachment even allows us to hope that our attitude will be objective. Still, we know the feminine world more intimately than do the men because we have our roots in it, we grasp more immediately than do men what it means to a human being to be feminine; and we are more concerned with such knowledge. I have said that there are more pressing problems, but this does not prevent us from seeing some importance in asking how the fact of being women will affect our lives. What opportunities precisely have been given us and what withheld? What fate awaits our younger sisters, and what directions should they take? It is significant that books by women on women are in general animated in our day less by a wish to demand our rights than by an effort toward clarity and understanding. As we emerge from an era of excessive controversy, this book is offered as one attempt among others to confirm that statement.

But it is doubtless impossible to approach any human problem with a mind free from bias. The way in which questions are put, the points of view assumed, presuppose a relativity of interest; all characteristics imply values, and every objective description, so called, implies an ethical background. Rather than attempt to conceal principles more or less definitely implied, it is better to state them openly at the beginning. This will make it unnecessary to specify on every page in just what sense one uses such words as *superior*, *inferior*, *better*, *worse*, *progress*, *reaction*, and the like. If we survey some of the works on woman, we note that one of the points of view most frequently adopted is that of the public good, the general interest; and one always means by this the benefit of society as one wishes it to be maintained or established. For our part, we hold that the only public good is that which assures the private good of the citizens; we shall pass judgment on institutions according to their effectiveness in giving concrete opportunities to individuals. But we do not confuse the idea of private interest with that of happiness, although that is another common point of view. Are not women of the harem[44] more happy than women voters? Is not the housekeeper happier than the working-woman? It is not too clear just what the word *happy* really means and still less what true values it may mask. There is no possibility of measuring the happiness of others, and it is always easy to describe as happy the situation in which one wishes to place them.

In particular those who are condemned to stagnation are often pronounced happy on the pretext that happiness consists in being at rest. This notion we reject, for our perspective is that of existentialist ethics. Every subject plays his part as such specifically through exploits or projects that serve as a mode of transcendence; he achieves liberty only through a continual reaching out toward other liberties. There is no justification for present existence other than its expansion into an indefinitely open future. Every time transcendence falls back into immanence, stagnation, there is a degradation of existence into the "*en-soi*"— the brutish life of subjection to given conditions—and

---

43   The Cretan philosopher Epimenides of Knossos (who lived around 600 BCE) invented a famous logical paradox by asserting, "Cretans, always liars." That is, since Epimenides himself was a Cretan, if this sentence is true then it must be false; a bit less obviously, if it is false then (arguably) it is true since it says of itself that it is false, which is true.

---

44   The private part of an Arab household, traditionally forbidden to male strangers.

of liberty into constraint and contingence. This down-fall represents a moral fault if the subject consents to it; if it is inflicted upon him, it spells frustration and oppression. In both cases it is an absolute evil. Every individual concerned to justify his existence feels that his existence involves an undefined need to transcend himself, to engage in freely chosen projects.

Now, what peculiarly signalizes the situation of woman is that she—a free and autonomous being like all human creatures—nevertheless finds herself living in a world where men compel her to assume the status of the Other. They propose to stabilize her as object and to doom her to immanence since her transcendence is to be overshadowed and forever transcended by another ego (*conscience*) which is essential and sovereign. The drama of woman lies in this conflict between the fundamental aspirations of every subject (ego)—who always regards the self as the essential—and the compulsions of a situation in which she is the inessential. How can a human being in woman's situation attain fulfillment? What roads are open to her? Which are blocked? How can

independence be recovered in a state of dependency? What circumstances limit woman's liberty and how can they be overcome? These are the fundamental questions on which I would fain throw some light. This means that I am interested in the fortunes of the individual as defined not in terms of happiness but in terms of liberty.

Quite evidently this problem would be without significance if we were to believe that woman's destiny is inevitably determined by physiological, psychological, or economic forces. Hence I shall discuss first of all the light in which woman is viewed by biology, psychoanalysis, and historical materialism. Next I shall try to show exactly how the concept of the "truly feminine" has been fashioned—why woman has been defined as the Other—and what have been the consequences from man's point of view. Then from woman's point of view I shall describe the world in which women must live; and thus we shall be able to envisage the difficulties in their way as, endeavoring to make their escape from the sphere hitherto assigned them, they aspire to full membership in the human race.

JOHN RAWLS

Justice as Fairness: A Restatement

Who Is John Rawls?

John Borden Rawls was, until his death in 2002, perhaps the world's most important contemporary political philosopher, and his 1971 book *A Theory of Justice* is generally regarded as the most significant work of political theory published in the twentieth century. Born in 1921 in Baltimore to an upper-class southern family, Rawls's father was a successful tax lawyer and constitutional expert while his mother was the feminist president of the local League of Women Voters. As a boy, Rawls was sent to Kent, a renowned Episcopalian preparatory school in Connecticut, and then went

on to Princeton for his undergraduate degree. In 1943, he joined the US infantry and served in New Guinea, the Philippines, and Japan (where he witnessed firsthand the aftermath of the atomic bombing of Hiroshima). He turned down the opportunity to become an officer, and left the army as a private in 1946, returning to Princeton to pursue his PhD in philosophy.

After completing the doctorate, he taught at Princeton for two years, visited Oxford University for a year on a Fulbright Fellowship, and was then employed as a professor at Cornell. In 1964 Rawls moved to Harvard University, where he was appointed James Bryant Conant Professor of Philosophy in 1979.

Throughout the eighties and early nineties Rawls was an omnipresent figure in political philosophy, and exerted a great influence on the discipline through his teaching and mentoring of younger academics as well as his writings. Unfortunately, in 1995, Rawls suffered the first of several strokes that seriously impeded his ability to continue working.

Though Rawls was always much more the reclusive academic than a campaigning public figure, his work was nevertheless guided by a deep personal commitment to combating injustice. Because of his family's origins in the American south, one of Rawls's earliest moral concerns was the injustice of black slavery. He was interested in formulating a moral theory that not only showed slavery to be unjust, but described its injustice *in the right way*. For Rawls, the immorality of slavery does not lie merely in the fact that benefits for slaveowners were out-

weighed by harms done to slaves—rather, slavery is the kind of thing that should *never* be imposed on any human being, no matter what overall benefits or efficiencies it might bring about. Thus, Rawls found himself opposed to the then-dominant political morality of utilitarianism, and seeking a new foundation for social justice in the work of Immanuel Kant and social contract theorists such as John Locke and Jean-Jacques Rousseau.[1]

Two guiding assumptions behind Rawls's neo-Kantian project (he calls it "Kantian constructivism") have been, first, that there is such a thing as moral truth—that at least some fundamental moral questions have objectively correct answers, even if it is difficult to discover them—and second, that "the right"

is separate from and prior to "the good." This latter claim is the idea (which is found in Kant) that the morally right thing to do cannot be defined as, and will not always be the same thing as, the maximization of some moral good, such as happiness or equality. There are certain constraints on how people can be treated which always take precedence over the general welfare.

The central doctrine which has informed the resulting political morality is what Rawls calls "justice as fairness." This is the view that social institutions should not confer morally arbitrary long-term advantages on some persons at the expense of others. According to Rawls, one's prospects and opportunities in life are strongly influenced by the circumstances of one's birth—one's place in the social, political, and economic structure defined by the basic institutions of one's society. For example, one might have been born to slaveowners or to slaves, to a wealthy political dynasty in New England or to a poor family in a Philadelphia ghetto, to an Anglophone or to a Francophone family in 1950s Montréal. These important differences are morally arbitrary—a mere matter of luck—not something for which people deserve to be either rewarded or punished. According to Rawls, therefore, the fundamental problem of social justice is to ensure that the basic institutions of our society are set up in such a way that they do not generate and perpetuate morally arbitrary inequalities.

The upshot of this, in Rawls's view, includes the radical result that inequalities in wealth, income, and other "primary social goods" are justified *only* if they are to the advantage of the least well off in society. Rawls's work has thus been widely seen (and criticized) as the philosophical foundation for a particularly egalitarian and left-wing version of the modern welfare state, and also—because of his emphasis

---

1   See Chapter 2 for readings on utilitarianism and Kant's moral theory. Social contract theory is represented by the Hobbes reading in this chapter.

on a set of universal, indefeasible basic rights and liberties—as an important successor to the rich tradition of liberal political thought.

What Is the Structure of This Reading?

The selection reprinted here comes from Rawls's recent book *Justice as Fairness*. In it he sets out to re-present, in their final form, the ideas first laid out in his seminal 1971 work *A Theory of Justice*. The heart of his substantive theory is the so-called "two principles of justice," and his description of these (though not his extended argument for their adequacy) is included here.

In Part I of *Justice as Fairness* Rawls lays out the fundamental ideas underlying his political theory, including the important notion of society as a fair system of co-operation, and the main concepts involved in arguing for his theory of justice as being justified by a "contract" made in the "original position." Some of these basic notions are briefly described in "Some Useful Background Information," below. Part II of the book presents his two principles of justice, and the first two sections of it are reprinted here. In the first section, Rawls summarizes three basic points which inform and constrain his reasoning, and in the second he describes the two principles themselves. In the rest of Part II (not included) he provides more details about the two principles, and in Part III he lays out the argument from the original position. In Part IV he describes some of the institutions of a just basic structure, and finally in Part V he address questions about the political stability of such a society.

Some Useful Background Information

1. Rawls believes democratic societies are always characterized by what he calls "the fact of reasonable pluralism." By this he means "the fact of profound and irreconcilable differences in citizens' reasonable comprehensive religious and philosophical conceptions of the world, and in their views of the moral and aesthetic values to be sought in human life." A consequence of this reasonable pluralism, Rawls believes, is that a democratic society can never genuinely be a *community*—a collection of persons united in affirming and pursuing the same conception of the good life. Rawls therefore proposes that we adopt—in fact, tacitly already have adopted—a different view of contemporary society: one that sees it as *a fair system of co-operation between free and equal citizens*. The task of a theory of justice then becomes one of specifying the fair terms of co-operation (and doing so in a way that is acceptable—that seems fair—even to citizens who have widely divergent conceptions of the good).

2. Rawls assumes the primary subject of this kind of theory of justice will be what he calls the *basic structure* of society. "[T]he basic structure of society is the way in which the main political and social institutions of society fit together into one system of social co-operation, and the way they assign basic rights and duties and regulate the division of advantages that arises from social co-operation over time…. The basic structure is the background social framework within which the activities of associations and individuals take place." Examples of components of the basic structure include the political constitution, the relationship between the judiciary and the government, the structure of the economic system, and the social institution of the family. The kinds of things *not* included in the basic structure—and thus affected only indirectly by Rawls's theory of justice—are the internal arrangements of associations such as churches and universities, particular pieces of non-constitutional legislation or legal decisions, and social relationships between individual citizens.

3. If justice consists in the fair terms of co-operation for society viewed as a system of co-operation, then the question becomes: how are these fair terms of co-operation arrived at? Since the fact of reasonable pluralism precludes appeal to any kind of shared moral authority or outlook, Rawls concludes that the free terms of co-operation must be "settled by an agreement reached by free and equal citizens engaged in co-operation, and made in view of what they

regard as their reciprocal advantage." Furthermore this contract, like any agreement, must be made under conditions which are fair to all the parties involved. Rawls's attempt to specify the circumstances in which agreement on the basic structure of society would be fair is called the *original position*.

In the original position, the parties to the contract are placed behind what Rawls calls a *veil of ignorance*: they are not allowed to know their social positions; their particular comprehensive doctrines of the good; their race, sex, or ethnic group; or their genetic endowments of such things as strength and intelligence. In other words, knowledge of all the contingent or arbitrary aspects of one's place in actual society are removed. On the other hand, the parties in the original position are assumed to be well-informed about such things as economic and political theory and human psychology, and to be rational. In this way, all information which would—in Rawls's view—introduce unfair distortions into the social contract is excluded from the original position and only the data needed to make a fair decision are allowed in: thus, for example, there could be no question of rich people trying to establish a basic social structure which protects their wealth by disadvantaging the poor, since nobody in the original position knows whether they are rich or poor.

Rawls's idea is that whatever contract would be agreed to by representatives in the original position must be a fair one, one that any reasonable citizen could accept no matter what their place in society or their conception of the good. This contract is, of course, merely hypothetical (there was never actually any original position). Rawls's point is not that citizens are actually bound by a historical social contract, but that the thought-experiment of making a contract in the original position is a device for showing what principles of justice *we should accept if we are reasonable*. And, Rawls argues, the principles that would be rationally arrived at in the original position will not be, say, utili-

tarian, or non-egalitarian, but will be something very much like his two principles of justice.

Suggestions for Critical Reflection

1. Rawls restricts the application of his theory of justice to democratic societies. Why do you think he makes this restriction? Is it appropriate to stipulate such preconditions for a philosophical theory of social justice? Could his theory of justice as fairness be recast to apply to *all* kinds of societies, and not just democracies?

2. Rawls argues "the fact of reasonable pluralism" in democratic societies gives rise to a problem of political legitimacy, and offers what he calls a "liberal" solution to that problem via a "political" conception of justice. How plausible is it that democracies really do face the deep problem of political legitimacy which Rawls describes? How adequate and attractive do you find his proposed solution? Is the kind of political conception of justice Rawls describes even *available* in contemporary liberal democratic societies?

3. Rawls appeals several times to "our firmest considered convictions" to help us decide what the basic structure of a just society should look like. Is this kind of appeal to intuition legitimate—or avoidable—in political philosophy?

4. Rawls's theory of justice as fairness is encapsulated in his two principles. How plausible and attractive are they? How radical are they? What kind of implications might they have, if any, which could be controversial? What changes would we have to make to bring our society into accord with these principles (in particular with the second principle, which deals with distributive justice)?

5. The "difference principle" makes a crucial reference to the "least-advantaged members of society." Who exactly is Rawls thinking of here? What difference does it make?

6. The first part of the second principle stipulates "fair equality of opportunity." What does Rawls seem to have in mind? How different is Rawls's idea of fair equality of opportunity from what

one might think of as the "free market" view of equal opportunity?

7. Rawls emphasizes that the question of the justice of social inequalities arises, for his theory, only *after* basic equal liberties and fair equality of opportunity have been secured. Why does he prioritize his principles in this way? Is he right to do so? Does this "lexical ordering" of the principles mean substantial social inequalities could, in fact, be justified in a Rawlsian society?

8. Why does Rawls not consider the second principle of justice a "constitutional essential"? What is the significance of this?

9. Rawls suggests the notion of democratic equality "involves reciprocity at the deepest level," and that this in turn requires "something like the difference principle." Is he right? What kind of argument might he have in mind?

Suggestions for Further Reading

Rawls's main work, and the first place to turn when delving further into Rawls, is *A Theory of Justice* (1971, revised edition Harvard University Press, 1999). Many of these themes are further developed and defended in his book *Political Liberalism* (Columbia University Press, 1995). *Justice as Fairness: A Restatement* (Harvard University Press, 2001) is a useful and accessible presentation of Rawls's mature view. *The Law of Peoples* (Harvard University Press, 1999) applies the Rawlsian outlook to international politics, while his *Collected Papers* (Harvard University Press, 1999) and a series of *Lectures on the History of Moral Philosophy* (Harvard University Press, 2000) have also recently been published.

Some significant critiques and developments of Rawls's justice as fairness are found in: Roberto Alejandro, *The Limits of Rawlsian Justice* (Johns Hopkins University Press, 1998); Brian Barry, *The Liberal Theory of Justice* (Oxford University Press, 1973) and *Theories of Justice* (University of California Press, 1991); Daniel Dombrowski, *Rawls and Religion* (State University of New York Press, 2001); Kukathas and Pettit, *Rawls* (Stanford University Press, 1990); Rex Martin, *Rawls and Rights* (University Press of Kansas, 1985); Robert Nozick, *Anarchy, State, and Utopia* (Basic Books, 1974); A. Pampapathy Rao, *Distributive Justice* (International

Scholars Publications, 1998); Thomas Pogge, *Realizing Rawls* (Cornell University Press, 1989); Michael Sandel, *Liberalism and the Limits of Justice* (Cambridge University Press, 1998); David Lewis Schaefer, *Justice or Tyranny?* (Associated Faculty Press, 1979); and Robert Paul Wolff, *Understanding Rawls* (Princeton University Press, 1977).

Collections of articles on Rawls's philosophy include J. Angelo Corlett (ed.), *Equality and Liberty* (Palgrave, 1991); Norman Daniels (ed.), *Reading Rawls* (Stanford University Press, 1989); and Mulhall and Swift, *Liberals and Communitarians* (Blackwell, 1996). Finally, an excellent overview of the relevant philosophical terrain is Will Kymlicka's *Contemporary Political Philosophy* (Oxford University Press, 2001).

Justice as Fairness: A Restatement[2]
Part II: Principles of Justice, §§ 12–13

§12. Three Basic Points

12.1. In Part II we discuss the content of the two principles of justice that apply to the basic structure, as well as various grounds in favor of them and replies to a number of objections. A more formal and organized argument for these principles is presented in Part III, where we discuss the reasoning that moves the parties in the original position. In that argument the original position serves to keep track of all our assumptions and to bring out their combined force by uniting them into one framework so that we can more easily see their implications.

I begin with three basic points which review some matters discussed in Part I and introduce others we are about to examine. Recall first that justice as fairness is framed for a democratic society. Its principles are meant to answer the question: once we view a demo-

---

2   Reprinted with permission of the publisher from "Three Basic Points" and "Two Principles of Justice" in *Justice as Fairness: A Restatement* by John Rawls, edited by Erin Kelly, pp. 39–50, Cambridge: Mass.: The Belknap Press of Harvard University Press. Copyright © 2001 by the President and Fellows of Harvard College.

cratic society as a fair system of social cooperation between citizens regarded as free and equal, what principles are most appropriate to it? Alternatively: which principles are most appropriate for a democratic society that not only professes but wants to take seriously the idea that citizens are free and equal, and tries to realize that idea in its main institutions? The question of whether a constitutional regime is to be preferred to majoritarian democracy, we postpone until later (Part IV, §44).[3]

12.2. The second point is that justice as fairness takes the primary subject of political justice to be the basic structure of society, that is, its main political and social institutions and how they fit together into one unified system of cooperation (§4). We suppose that citizens are born into society and will normally spend their whole lives within its basic institutions. The nature and role of the basic structure importantly influence social and economic inequalities and enter into determining the appropriate principles of justice.

In particular, let us suppose that the fundamental social and economic inequalities are the differences in citizens' life-prospects (their prospects over a complete life) as these are affected by such things as their social class of origin, their native endowments, their opportunities for education, and their good or ill fortune over the course of life (§16). We ask: by what principles are differences of that kind—differences in life-prospects—made legitimate and consistent with the idea of free and equal citizenship in society seen as a fair system of cooperation?

12.3. The third point is that justice as fairness is a form of political liberalism: it tries to articulate a family of highly significant (moral) values that characteristi-

cally apply to the political and social institutions of the basic structure. It gives an account of these values in the light of certain special features of the political relationship as distinct from other relationships, associational, familial, and personal.

(a) It is a relationship of persons within the basic structure of society, a structure we enter only by birth and exit only by death (or so we may assume for the moment). Political society is closed, as it were; and we do not, and indeed cannot, enter or leave it voluntarily.

(b) Political power is always coercive power applied by the state and its apparatus of enforcement; but in a constitutional regime political power is at the same time the power of free and equal citizens as a collective body. Thus political power is citizens' power, which they impose on themselves and one another as free and equal.

The idea of political liberalism arises as follows. We start from two facts: first, from the fact of reasonable pluralism, the fact that a diversity of reasonable comprehensive doctrines is a permanent feature of a democratic society; and second, from the fact that in a democratic regime political power is regarded as the power of free and equal citizens as a collective body. These two points give rise to a problem of political legitimacy. For if the fact of reasonable pluralism always characterizes democratic societies and if political power is indeed the power of free and equal citizens, in the light of what reasons and values—of what kind of a conception of justice—can citizens legitimately exercise that coercive power over one another?

Political liberalism answers that the conception of justice must be a political conception, as defined in §9.1.[4] Such a conception when satisfied allows us

---

3   In that section, Rawls explains that "[a] constitutional regime is one in which laws and statutes must be consistent with certain fundamental rights and liberties.... There is in effect a constitution (not necessarily written) with a bill of rights specifying those freedoms and interpreted by the courts as constitutional limits on legislation." By contrast, there are no constitutional limits on legislation in a majoritarian democracy, and whatever the majority decides (according to the proper procedures) is law.

4   According to Rawls, a conception of justice is *political* if, a) it applies only to the basic structure of society (and not directly to particular groups of people within those societies); b) it does not presuppose any particular comprehensive conception of the good life; and c) it is formulated, as far as possible, from ideas already implicit in the public political culture of a democratic society.

to say: political power is legitimate only when it is exercised in accordance with a constitution (written or unwritten) the essentials of which all citizens, as reasonable and rational, can endorse in the light of their common human reason. This is the liberal principle of legitimacy. It is a further desideratum[5] that all legislative questions that concern or border on these essentials, or are highly divisive, should also be settled, so far as possible, by guidelines and values that can be similarly endorsed.

In matters of constitutional essentials, as well as on questions of basic justice, we try to appeal only to principles and values each citizen can endorse. A political conception of justice hopes to formulate these values: its shared principles and values make reason public, while freedom of speech and thought in a constitutional regime make it free. In providing a public basis of justification, a political conception of justice provides the framework for the liberal idea of political legitimacy. As noted in §9.4, however, and discussed further in §26, we do not say that a political conception formulates political values that can settle all legislative questions. This is neither possible nor desirable. There are many questions legislatures must consider that can only be settled by voting that is properly influenced by nonpolitical values. Yet at least on constitutional essentials and matters of basic justice we do try for an agreed basis; so long as there is at least rough agreement here, fair social cooperation among citizens can, we hope, be maintained.[6]

12.4. Given these three points, our question is: viewing society as a fair system of cooperation between citizens regarded as free and equal, what principles of justice are most appropriate to specify basic rights and liberties, and to regulate social and economic in-

equalities in citizens' prospects over a complete life? These inequalities are our primary concern.

To find a principle to regulate these inequalities, we look to our firmest considered convictions about equal basic rights and liberties, the fair value of the political liberties as well as fair equality of opportunity. We look outside the sphere of distributive justice more narrowly construed to see whether an appropriate distributive principle is singled out by those firmest convictions once their essential elements are represented in the original position as a device of representation (§6). This device is to assist us in working out which principle, or principles, the representatives of free and equal citizens would select to regulate social and economic inequalities in these prospects over a complete life when they assume that the equal basic liberties and fair opportunities are already secured.

The idea here is to use our firmest considered convictions about the nature of a democratic society as a fair system of cooperation between free and equal citizens—as modeled in the original position—to see whether the combined assertion of those convictions so expressed will help us to identify an appropriate distributive principle for the basic structure with its economic and social inequalities in citizens' life-prospects. Our convictions about principles regulating those inequalities are much less firm and assured; so we look to our firmest convictions for guidance where assurance is lacking and guidance is needed (*Theory*, §§4, 20).

§13. Two Principles of Justice

13.1. To try to answer our question, let us turn to a revised statement of the two principles of justice discussed in *Theory*, §§11–14. They should now read:[7]

---

5   Something which is needed or considered highly desirable.

6   [Author's note] It is not always clear whether a question involves a constitutional essential, as will be mentioned in due course. If there is doubt about this and the question is highly divisive, then citizens have a duty of civility to try to articulate their claims on one another by reference to political values, if that is possible.

7   [Author's note] This section summarizes some points from "The Basic Liberties and Their Priority," *Tanner Lectures on Human Values*, vol. 3, ed. Sterling McMurrin (Salt Lake City: University of Utah Press, 1982), §I, reprinted in *Political Liberalism*. In that essay I try to reply to what I believe are two of the more serious objections to my account of liberty in *Theory* raised by H.L.A. Hart in his splendid critical review essay, "Rawls on Liberty and Its Priority," *University of Chicago Law Review* 40 (Spring 1975): 551–555, re-

(a) Each person has the same indefeasible[8] claim to a fully adequate scheme of equal basic liberties, which scheme is compatible with the same scheme of liberties for all; and

(b) Social and economic inequalities are to satisfy two conditions: first, they are to be attached to offices and positions open to all under conditions of fair equality of opportunity; and second, they are to be to the greatest benefit of the least-advantaged members of society (the difference principle).[9]

As I explain below, the first principle is prior to the second; also, in the second principle fair equality of opportunity is prior to the difference principle. This priority means that in applying a principle (or checking it against test cases) we assume that the prior principles are fully satisfied. We seek a principle of distribution (in the narrower sense) that holds within the setting of background institutions that secure the basic equal liberties (including the fair value of the political liberties)[10] as well as fair equality of opportunity. How far that principle holds outside that setting is a separate question we shall not consider.[11]

13.2. The revisions in the second principle are merely stylistic. But before noting the revisions in the first principle, which are significant,[12] we should attend to the meaning of fair equality of opportunity. This is a difficult and not altogether clear idea; its role is perhaps best gathered from why it is introduced: namely, to correct the defects of formal equality of opportunity—careers open to talents—in the system of natural liberty, so-called (*Theory*, §12: 62ff.; §14).[13] To this end, fair equality of opportunity is said to require not merely that public offices and social positions be open in the formal sense, but that all should have a fair chance to attain them. To specify the idea of a fair chance we say: supposing that there is a distribution of native endowments, those who have the same level

---

printed in his *Essays in Jurisprudence and Philosophy* (Oxford: Oxford University Press, 1983). No changes made in justice as fairness in this restatement are more significant than those forced by Hart's review.

8   One which cannot, under any circumstances, be annulled.

9   [Author's note] Instead of "the difference principle," many writers prefer the term "the maximin principle," or simply "maximin justice," or some such locution. See, for example, Joshua Cohen's very full and accurate account of the difference principle in "Democratic Equality," *Ethics* 99 (July 1989): 727–751. But I still use the term "difference principle" to emphasize first, that this principle and the maximin rule for decision under uncertainty (§28.1) are two very distinct things; and second, that in arguing for the difference principle over other distributive principles (say a restricted principle of (average) utility, which includes a social minimum), there is no appeal at all to the maximin rule for decision under uncertainty. The widespread idea that the argument for the difference principle depends on extreme aversion to uncertainty is a mistake, although a mistake unhappily encouraged by the faults of exposition in *Theory*, faults to be corrected in Part III of this restatement.

10   [Author's note] See *Theory*, §36: 197–199.

11   [Author's note] Some have found this kind of restriction objectionable; they think a political conception should be framed to cover all logically possible cases, or all conceivable cases, and not restricted to cases that can arise only within a specified institutional context. See for example Brian Barry, *The Liberal Theory of Justice* (Oxford: Oxford University Press, 1973), p. 112. In contrast, we seek a principle to govern social and economic inequalities in democratic regimes as we know them, and so we are concerned with inequalities in citizens' life-prospects that may actually arise, given our understanding of how certain institutions work.

12   Rawls's original, 1971 formulation was: "Each person is to have an equal right to the most extensive total system of equal basic liberties compatible with a similar system of liberty for all."

13   The "system of natural liberty," in Rawls's terminology, is one which assumes that, in an economically efficient free market economy, a basic structure "in which positions are open to those able and willing to strive for them will lead to a just distribution" (*A Theory of Justice*, §12), but which makes no effort to correct for arbitrary inequalities in the initial social conditions of the competitors.

of talent and ability and the same willingness to use these gifts should have the same prospects of success regardless of their social class of origin, the class into which they are born and develop until the age of reason. In all parts of society there are to be roughly the same prospects of culture and achievement for those similarly motivated and endowed.

Fair equality of opportunity here means liberal equality. To accomplish its aims, certain requirements must be imposed on the basic structure beyond those of the system of natural liberty. A free market system must be set within a framework of political and legal institutions that adjust the long-run trend of economic forces so as to prevent excessive concentrations of property and wealth, especially those likely to lead to political domination. Society must also establish, among other things, equal opportunities of education for all regardless of family income (§15).[14]

13.3. Consider now the reasons for revising the first principle.[15] One is that the equal basic liberties in this principle are specified by a list as follows: freedom of thought and liberty of conscience; political liberties (for example, the right to vote and to participate in politics) and freedom of association, as well as the rights and liberties specified by the liberty and integrity (physical and psychological) of the person; and finally, the rights and liberties covered by the rule of law. That the basic liberties are specified by a list is quite clear from *Theory*, §11: 61 (1st ed.); but the use of the singular term "basic liberty" in the statement of the principle in *Theory*, §11: 60 (1st ed.), obscures this important feature of these liberties.

This revision brings out that no priority is assigned to liberty as such, as if the exercise of something called "liberty" had a preeminent value and were the main, if not the sole, end of political and social justice. While there is a general presumption against imposing legal and other restrictions on conduct without a sufficient reason, this presumption creates no special priority for any particular liberty. Throughout the history of democratic thought the focus has been on achieving certain specific rights and liberties as well as specific constitutional guarantees, as found, for example, in various bills of rights and declarations of the rights of man. Justice as fairness follows this traditional view.

13.4. A list of basic liberties can be drawn up in two ways. One is historical: we survey various democratic regimes and assemble a list of rights and liberties that seem basic and are securely protected in what seem to be historically the more successful regimes. Of course, the veil of ignorance means that this kind of particular information is not available to the parties in the original position, but it is available to you and me in setting up justice as fairness.[16] We are perfectly free to use it to specify the principles of justice we make available to the parties.

A second way of drawing up a list of basic rights and liberties is analytical: we consider what liberties provide the political and social conditions essential for the adequate development and full exercise of the two moral powers of free and equal persons (§7.1).[17]

---

14 [Author's note] These remarks are the merest sketch of a difficult idea. We come back to it from time to time.

15 [Author's note] This principle may be preceded by a lexically prior principle requiring that basic needs be met, as least insofar as their being met is a necessary condition for citizens to understand and to be able fruitfully to exercise the basic rights and liberties. For a statement of such a principle with further discussion, see R.G. Peffer, *Marxism, Morality, and Social Justice* (Princeton: Princeton University Press, 1990), p.14.

16 [Author's note] Here I should mention that there are three points of view in justice as fairness that it is essential to distinguish: the point of view of the parties in the original position, the point of view of citizens in a well-ordered society, and the point of view of you and me who are setting up justice as fairness as a political conception and trying to use it to organize into one coherent view our considered judgments at all levels of generality. Keep in mind that the parties are, as it were, artificial persons who are part of a procedure of construction that we frame for our philosophical purposes. We may know many things that we keep from them. For these three points of view, see *Political Liberalism*, p. 28.

17 These moral powers are a) the capacity to understand, apply, and act from the principles of political justice,

Following this we say: first, that the equal political liberties and freedom of thought enable citizens to develop and to exercise these powers in judging the justice of the basic structure of society and its social policies; and second, that liberty of conscience and freedom of association enable citizens to develop and exercise their moral powers in forming and revising and in rationally pursuing (individually or, more often, in association with others) their conceptions of the good.

Those basic rights and liberties protect and secure the scope required for the exercise of the two moral powers in the two fundamental cases just mentioned: that is to say, the first fundamental case is the exercise of those powers in judging the justice of basic institutions and social policies; while the second fundamental case is the exercise of those powers in pursuing our conception of the good. To exercise our powers in these ways is essential to us as free and equal citizens.

13.5. Observe that the first principle of justice applies not only to the basic structure (both principles do this) but more specifically to what we think of as the constitution, whether written or unwritten. Observe also that some of these liberties, especially the equal political liberties and freedom of thought and association, are to be guaranteed by a constitution (*Theory*, chap. IV). What we may call "constituent power," as opposed to "ordinary power,"[18] is to be suitably institutionalized in the form of a regime: in the right to vote and to hold office, and in so-called bills of rights, as well as in the procedures for amending the constitution, for example.

These matters belong to the so-called constitutional essentials, these essentials being those crucial matters about which, given the fact of pluralism, working political agreement is most urgent (§9.4). In view of the fundamental nature of the basic rights and liberties, explained in part by the fundamental interests they protect, and given that the power of the people to constitute the form of government is a superior power (distinct from the ordinary power exercised routinely by officers of a regime), the first principle is assigned priority.

This priority means (as we have said) that the second principle (which includes the difference principle as one part) is always to be applied within a setting of background institutions that satisfy the requirements of the first principle (including the requirement of securing the fair value of the political liberties), as by definition they will in a well-ordered society.[19, 20] The fair value of the political liberties ensures that citizens similarly gifted and motivated have roughly an equal chance of influencing the government's policy and of attaining positions of authority irrespective of their economic and social class.[21] To explain the priority of the first principle over the second: this priority rules out exchanges ("trade-offs," as economists say)

---

and b) the capacity to have, revise, and rationally pursue a conception of the good (i.e., what is of value in human life).

18   [Author's note] This distinction is derived from Locke, who speaks of the people's power to constitute the legislative as the first and fundamental law of all commonwealths. John Locke, *Second Treatise of Government*, §§134, 141, 149.

19   [Author's note] It is sometimes objected to the difference principle as a principle of distributive justice that it contains no restrictions on the overall nature of permissible distributions. It is concerned, the objection runs, solely with the least advantaged. But this objection is incorrect: it overlooks the fact that the parts of the two principles of justice are designed to work in tandem and apply as a unit. The requirements of the prior principles have important distributive effects. Consider the effects of fair equality of opportunity as applied to education, say, or the distributive effects of the fair value of the political liberties. We cannot possibly take the difference principle seriously so long as we think of it by itself, apart from its setting within prior principles.

20   By "well-ordered society," Rawls means a society in which the following are true: a) all citizens accept the same political conception of justice, b) its basic structure is publicly known to satisfy those shared principles of justice, and c) citizens have an "effective sense of justice," i.e., they understand and act in accordance with those principles of justice.

21   [Author's note] See *Political Liberalism*, p. 358.

between the basic rights and liberties covered by the first principle and the social and economic advantages regulated by the difference principle. For example, the equal political liberties cannot be denied to certain groups on the grounds that their having these liberties may enable them to block policies needed for economic growth and efficiency.

Nor can we justify a selective service act that grants educational deferments or exemptions to some on the grounds that doing this is a socially efficient way both to maintain the armed forces and to provide incentives to those otherwise subject to conscription to acquire valuable skills by continuing their education. Since conscription is a drastic interference with the basic liberties of equal citizenship, it cannot be justified by any needs less compelling than those of the defense of these equal liberties themselves (*Theory*, §58: 333f.).

A further point about priority: in asserting the priority of the basic rights and liberties, we suppose reasonably favorable conditions to obtain. That is, we suppose historical, economic and social conditions to be such that, provided the political will exists, effective political institutions can be established to give adequate scope for the exercise of those freedoms. These conditions mean that the barriers to constitutional government (if such there are) spring largely from the political culture and existing effective interests, and not from, for instance, a lack of economic means, or education, or the many skills needed to run a democratic regime.[22]

13.6. It is important to note a distinction between the first and second principles of justice. The first principle, as explained by its interpretation, covers the constitutional essentials. The second principle requires fair equality of opportunity and that social and economic inequalities be governed by the difference principle, which we discuss in §§17–19. While some principle of opportunity is a constitutional essential—for example, a principle requiring an open society, one with careers open to talents (to use the eighteenth-century phrase)—fair equality of opportunity requires more than that, and is not counted a constitutional essential. Similarly, although a social minimum providing for the basic needs of all citizens is also a constitutional essential (§38.3–4; §49.5), the difference principle is more demanding and is not so regarded.

The basis for the distinction between the two principles is not that the first expresses political values while the second does not. Both principles express political values. Rather, we see the basic structure of society as having two coordinate roles, the first principle applying to one, the second principle to the other (*Theory*, §11: 53). In one role the basic structure specifies and secures citizens' equal basic liberties (including the fair value of the political liberties (§45)) and establishes a just constitutional regime. In the other role it provides the background institutions of social and economic justice in the form most appropriate to citizens seen as free and equal. The questions involved in the first role concern the acquisition and the exercise of political power. To fulfill the liberal principle of legitimacy (§12.3), we hope to settle at least these questions by appeal to the political values that constitute the basis of free public reason (§26).[23]

The principles of justice are adopted and applied in a four-stage sequence.[24] In the first stage, the parties adopt the principles of justice behind a veil of ignorance. Limitations on knowledge available to the parties are progressively relaxed in the next three stages: the stage of the constitutional convention, the legislative stage in which laws are enacted as the constitution allows and as the principles of justice require and permit, and the final stage in which the

---

22 [Author's note] The priority (or the primacy) of the basic equal liberties does not, contrary to much opinion, presuppose a high level of wealth and income. See Amartya Sen and Jean Dreze, *Hunger and Public Action* (Oxford: Oxford University Press, 1989), chap. 13; and Partha Dasgupta, *An Inquiry into Well-Being and Destitution* (Oxford: Oxford University Press, 1999), chaps. 1–2, 5 and passim.

23 By "free public reason," Rawls means the principles of reasoning and the rules of evidence which are accepted by all the citizens of a well-ordered society (irrespective of their differing conceptions of the good).

24 [Author's note] See *Theory*, §31: 172–176, and *Political Liberalism* pp. 397–398.

rules are applied by administrators and followed by citizens generally and the constitution and laws are interpreted by members of the judiciary. At this last stage, everyone has complete access to all the facts. The first principle applies at the stage of the constitutional convention, and whether the constitutional essentials are assured is more or less visible on the face of the constitution and in its political arrangements and the way these work in practice. By contrast the second principle applies at the legislative stage and it bears on all kinds of social and economic legislation, and on the many kinds of issues arising at this point (*Theory*, §31: 172–176). Whether the aims of the second principle are realized is far more difficult to ascertain. To some degree these matters are always open to reasonable differences of opinion; they depend on inference and judgment in assessing complex social and economic information. Also, we can expect more agreement on constitutional essentials than on issues of distributive justice in the narrower sense.

Thus the grounds for distinguishing the constitutional essentials covered by the first principle and the institutions of distributive justice covered by the second are not that the first principle expresses political values and the second does not. Rather, the grounds of the distinction are four:

(a) The two principles apply to different stages in the application of principles and identify two distinct roles of the basic structure;

(b) It is more urgent to settle the constitutional essentials;

(c) It is far easier to tell whether those essentials are realized; and

(d) It seems possible to gain agreement on what those essentials should be, not in every detail, of course, but in the main outlines.

13.7. One way to see the point of the idea of constitutional essentials is to connect it with the idea of loyal opposition, itself an essential idea of a constitutional regime. The government and its loyal opposition agree on these constitutional essentials. Their so agreeing makes the government legitimate in intention and the opposition loyal in its opposition. Where the loyalty of both is firm and their agreement mutually recognized, a constitutional regime is secure. Differences about the most appropriate principles of distributive justice in the narrower sense, and the ideals that underlie them, can be adjudicated, though not always properly, within the existing political framework.

While the difference principle does not fall under the constitutional essentials, it is nevertheless important to try to identify the idea of equality most appropriate to citizens viewed as free and equal, and as normally and fully cooperating members of society over a complete life. I believe this idea involves reciprocity[25] at the deepest level and thus democratic equality properly understood requires something like the difference principle. (I say "something like," for there may be various nearby possibilities.) The remaining sections of this part (§§14–22) try to clarify the content of this principle and to clear up a number of difficulties.

---

25 [Author's note] As understood in justice as fairness, reciprocity is a relation between citizens expressed by principles of justice that regulate a social world in which all who are engaged in cooperation and do their part as the rules and procedures require are to benefit in an appropriate way as assessed by a suitable benchmark of comparison. The two principles of justice, including the difference principle with its implicit reference to equal division as a benchmark, formulate an idea of reciprocity between citizens. For a fuller discussion of the idea of reciprocity, see *Political Liberalism*, pp. 16–17, and the introduction to the paperback edition, pp. xliv, xlvi, li. The idea of reciprocity also plays an important part in "The Idea of Public Reason Revisited," *University of Chicago Law Review*, 64 (Summer 1997): 765–807, reprinted in *The Law of Peoples* (Cambridge, Mass.: Harvard University Press, 1999) and *Collected Papers*.

ROBERT NOZICK
Anarchy, State, and Utopia

Who Was Robert Nozick?

Robert Nozick was born in 1938 and grew up in Brooklyn, New York. He took his undergraduate degree at Columbia College and his PhD, on theories of rational decision-making, at Princeton. He taught at Princeton from 1962 until 1965, Harvard from 1965 to 1967, Rockefeller University from 1967 until 1969, and then returned to Harvard, a full professor of philosophy, at the tender age of 30. Already well-known in philosophical circles, Nozick's first book, *Anarchy, State, and Utopia* (1974) propelled him into the public eye with its controversial but intellectually dazzling defense of political libertarianism. It won the National Book Award and was named by *The Times Literary Supplement* as one of "The Hundred Most Influential Books Since the War." In 1998, Nozick was made Joseph Pellegrino University Professor at Harvard. Sadly he died of stomach cancer in 2002, at the relatively young age of 63.

As a young man, Nozick was a radical left-winger; he was converted to libertarianism—the view that individual rights should be maximized and the role of the state minimized—as a graduate student, largely through reading *laissez-faire* economists like F.A. Hayek and Milton Friedman. However, he was never fully comfortable with his public reputation as a right-wing ideologue. In a 1978 article in *The New York Times Magazine*, he said, "right-wing people like the pro-free-market argument, but don't like the arguments for individual liberty in cases like gay rights—although I view them as an interconnecting whole."

In the same article, Nozick also described his fresh and lively approach to philosophical writing, noting, "[i]t is as though what philosophers want is a way of saying something that will leave the person they're talking to no escape. Well, why should they be bludgeoning people like that? It's not a nice way to behave."

Nozick's philosophical interests were notably broad. Best known for his work in political philosophy, he also made important contributions to epistemology (especially his notion of knowledge as a kind of "truth tracking"), metaphysics (with his "closest continuer" theory of personal identity), and decision theory (particularly through his introduction of Newcomb's problem to the philosophical literature).

What Is the Structure of This Reading?

In Part I of *Anarchy, State, and Utopia*, Nozick argues that a minimal state is justified; then, in Part II, that no state more powerful or extensive than a minimal state is morally justified. In Part III he argues this is not an unfortunate result, that rather, the minimal state is "a framework for utopia" and "inspiring as well as right." The material reprinted here is from the first section of the first chapter of Part II, where Nozick argues that considerations of distributive justice do not require going beyond the minimal state, and, in fact, on the contrary, a proper account of distributive justice shows that state interference in distributive patterns must violate the rights of individuals.

Nozick first outlines what he considers the correct theory of distributive justice. He calls this the *entitlement theory of justice in holdings*, and presents it as made up of exactly three principles of justice. Nozick goes on to contrast what he calls *historical* theories of justice with *end-state* principles, and explains that the entitlement theory belongs to the former—in his view more plausible—type. He then distinguishes between two possible varieties of historical principles of justice—*patterned* or *non-patterned*—and claims that his entitlement theory belongs to the latter class. In the next section, Nozick argues that all end-state or patterned theories of distributive justice are inconsistent with liberty—i.e., they are committed to the repeated violation of the rights of individuals.

The final two sections deal with what Nozick calls the principle of justice in acquisition. He begins by critiquing John Locke's seventeenth-century theory of just acquisition, but preserves a version of the Lockean proviso that an acquisition is just only if it leaves "enough and as good left in common for others." He then spells out details and implications of such a proviso, including some of the constraints its "historical shadow" places on just transfers of holdings.

Some Useful Background Information

Nozick argues in *Anarchy, State, and Utopia* that only a minimal "night-watchman" state is consistent with individual liberty. A minimal state has a monopoly on the use of force within its boundaries (except for force used in immediate self-defense), and it uses this monopoly to guard its citizens against violence, theft, and fraud, and to enforce compliance with legally-made contracts. Beyond this, however, the minimal state has no legitimate function. For example, in the minimal state there can be no central bank or other form of economic regulation, no department of public works, no public education system, no welfare provisions or state pensions, no social healthcare system, no environmental protection regulations or agencies, and so on.

A Common Misconception

Nozick does not believe it is actually *immoral* to help the poor (or preserve the environment, or provide universal healthcare, or foster the arts ...). He argues that it is immoral to *force* people to do these things—

in other words, that we have no legally enforceable *duty* to do them—but it is perfectly consistent to believe that it would be *morally good* if we were (voluntarily) to contribute to these ends.

Suggestions for Critical Reflection

1. What does Nozick mean when he claims that "[t]he term 'distributive justice' is not a neutral one"? Is the terminology he introduces instead any more "neutral"? What is the significance of this issue (if any) for the arguments that follow?

2. "Whatever arises from a just situation by just steps is itself just." Is this apparently straightforward claim *really* true? Can you think of any reasons to doubt it—for example, can you come up with any plausible counter-examples to this general claim? How significant a part of Nozick's general argument is this assertion? If we accept it, might we then be forced to accept a version of libertarianism, or is there a way of making it consistent with a more extensive state?

3. How plausible do you find Nozick's sketch of a principle of rectification of injustice? Is the goal of such rectifications to return injured parties (such as former slaves or their present-day children) to the position they would have been in had the injustice not occurred, or do we normally think there is more (or less) to it than that?

4. Is the distinction between historical and end-state principles of justice as clear-cut as Nozick presents it? Are most—or even many—theories of justice pure forms of one or the other? How comfortably, if at all, can historical and end-state views of justice be combined in a single theory (for example, an egalitarian theory)?

5. "People want their society to be and to look just. But must the look of justice reside in a resulting pattern rather than in the underlying generating principles?" This is a crucial question for Nozick, and the plausibility of his theory depends upon our willingness to answer, "No." But what if the entitlement theory generates distributive patterns which many people intui-

tively find *unjust*, such as very wide inequalities in wealth, educational opportunities, access to health care, and so on? Would we then want to say that distributive justice *does* place constraints on appropriate patterns of distribution for social goods? If so, what implications would this have for Nozick's theory of justice?

6. What do you think of Nozick's Wilt Chamberlain argument? If it is sound, what are its implications? If you think it is not sound, what, exactly, is wrong with it (bearing in mind that it's not enough to simply disagree with its conclusion)?

7. Nozick argues that distributional patterns "cannot be continuously realized without continuous interference with people's lives." Does this, in itself, show that no adequate principles of justice can be patterned? What ethical assumptions might Nozick be making here? Are these assumptions justified?

8. Does Nozick's "weaker" version of the Lockean proviso seem adequate as an account of justice in acquisition? Are you persuaded by his suggestion that the institution of private property is consistent with such a proviso? How substantial is the "baseline" problem he identifies?

9. How acceptable is Nozick's assertion that "[a] medical researcher who synthesizes a new substance that effectively treats a certain disease and who refuses to sell except on his terms" does not behave unjustly? Does Nozick's principle of justice in acquisition commit him to this position?

10. Nozick claims that the unfettered operations of a free market will be perfectly consistent with his Lockean proviso on justice. Do you agree? What justification might there be for such a claim?

Suggestions for Further Reading

Nozick's books cover a wide philosophical terrain, and each one is a stimulating read. They include: *Anarchy, State, and Utopia* (Basic Books, 1974); *Philosophical Explanations* (Harvard University Press, 1981); *The Examined Life* (Touchstone Books, 1990); *The Nature of Rationality* (Princeton University Press, 1993); *Socratic Puzzles* (Harvard University Press, 1997); and *Invariances: The Structure of the Objective World* (Harvard University Press, 2001). Five useful books explaining and critiquing Nozick's philosophy are: Jeffrey Paul (ed.), *Reading Nozick: Essays on 'Anarchy, State, and Utopia'* (Rowman & Littlefield, 1981); Jonathan Wolff, *Robert Nozick: Property, Justice, and the Minimal State* (Stanford University Press, 1991); Simon Hailwood, *Exploring Nozick: Beyond Anarchy, State, and Utopia* (Avebury, 1996); A.R. Lacey, *Robert Nozick* (Princeton University Press, 2001); and David Schmidtz (ed.), *Robert Nozick* (Cambridge University Press, 2002). Finally, two good sources for exploring libertarianism are David Boaz (ed.), *The Libertarian Reader* (Free Press, 1998) and Jan Narveson, *The Libertarian Idea* (Broadview Press, 2001).

from *Anarchy, State, and Utopia*[1]

The minimal state is the most extensive state that can be justified. Any state more extensive violates people's rights. Yet many persons have put forth reasons purporting to justify a more extensive state. It is impossible within the compass of this book to examine all the reasons that have been put forth. Therefore, I shall focus upon those generally acknowledged to be most weighty and influential, to see precisely wherein they fail. In this chapter we consider the claim that a more extensive state is justified, because necessary (or the best instrument) to achieve distributive justice; in the next chapter we shall take up diverse other claims.

The term "distributive justice" is not a neutral one. Hearing the term "distribution," most people presume that some thing or mechanism uses some principle or criterion to give out a supply of things. Into this process of distributing shares some error may have crept. So it is an open question, at least, whether *re*distribution should take place; whether we should do again what has already been done once,

---

1   From Chapter 7, "Distributive Justice," of *Anarchy, State, and Utopia* by Robert Nozick (New York: Basic Books, 1974), 149–164, 174–182. Copyright © 1974 by Basic Books, Inc. Reprinted by permission of Basic Books, a member of the Perseus Books Group.

though poorly. However, we are not in the position of children who have been given portions of pie by someone who now makes last minute adjustments to rectify careless cutting. There is no *central* distribution, no person or group entitled to control all the resources, jointly deciding how they are to be doled out. What each person gets, he gets from others who give to him in exchange for something, or as a gift. In a free society, diverse persons control different resources, and new holdings arise out of the voluntary exchanges and actions of persons. There is no more a distributing or distribution of shares than there is a distributing of mates in a society in which persons choose whom they shall marry. The total result is the product of many individual decisions which the different individuals involved are entitled to make. Some uses of the term "distribution," it is true, do not imply a previous distributing appropriately judged by some criterion (for example, "probability distribution"); nevertheless, despite the title of this chapter, it would be best to use a terminology that clearly is neutral. We shall speak of people's holdings; a principle of justice in holdings describes (part of) what justice tells us (requires) about holdings. I shall state first what I take to be the correct view about justice in holdings, and then turn to the discussion of alternate views.[2]

Section I:

The Entitlement Theory

The subject of justice in holdings consists of three major topics. The first is the *original acquisition of holdings*, the appropriation of unheld things. This includes the issues of how unheld things may come to be held, the process, or processes, by which unheld things may come to be held, the things that may come to be held by these processes, the extent of what comes to be held by a particular process, and so on. We shall refer to the complicated truth about this topic, which we shall not formulate here, as the principle of justice in acquisition. The second topic concerns the *transfer of holdings* from one person to another. By what processes may a person transfer holdings to another? How may a person acquire a holding from another who holds it? Under this topic come general descriptions of voluntary exchange, and gift and (on the other hand) fraud, as well as reference to particular conventional details fixed upon in a given society. The complicated truth about this subject (with placeholders for conventional details) we shall call the principle of justice in transfer. (And we shall suppose it also includes principles governing how a person may divest himself of a holding, passing it into an unheld state.)

If the world were wholly just, the following inductive definition would exhaustively cover the subject of justice in holdings.

1. A person who acquires a holding in accordance with the principle of justice in acquisition is entitled to that holding.

2. A person who acquires a holding in accordance with the principle of justice in transfer, from someone else entitled to the holding, is entitled to the holding.

3. No one is entitled to a holding except by (repeated) applications of 1 and 2.

The complete principle of distributive justice would say simply that a distribution is just if everyone is entitled to the holdings they possess under the distribution.

A distribution is just if it arises from another just distribution by legitimate means. The legitimate means of moving from one distribution to another are specified by the principle of justice in transfer. The legitimate first "moves" are specified by the principle of justice in acquisition.[3] Whatever arises

---

2   [Author's note] The reader who has looked ahead and seen that the second part of this chapter discusses Rawls' theory mistakenly may think that every remark or argument in the first part against alternative theories of justice is meant to apply to, or anticipate, a criticism of Rawls' theory. This is not so; there are other theories also worth criticizing.

---

3   [Author's note] Applications of the principle of justice in acquisition may also occur as part of the move from one distribution to another. You may find an unheld thing now and appropriate it. Acquisitions also are to be understood as included when, to simplify, I speak only of transitions by transfers.

from a just situation by just steps is itself just. The means of change specified by the principle of justice in transfer preserve justice. As correct rules of inference are truth-preserving, and any conclusion deduced via repeated application of such rules from only true premises is itself true, so the means of transition from one situation to another specified by the principle of justice in transfer are justice-preserving, and any situation actually arising from repeated transitions in accordance with the principle from a just situation is itself just. The parallel between justice-preserving transformations and truth-preserving transformations illuminates where it fails as well as where it holds. That a conclusion could have been deduced by truth-preserving means from premises that are true suffices to show its truth. That from a just situation a situation *could* have arisen via justice-preserving means does *not* suffice to show its justice. The fact that a thief's victims voluntarily *could* have presented him with gifts does not entitle the thief to his ill-gotten gains. Justice in holdings is historical; it depends upon what actually has happened. We shall return to this point later.

Not all actual situations are generated in accordance with the two principles of justice in holdings: the principle of justice in acquisition and the principle of justice in transfer. Some people steal from others, or defraud them, or enslave them, seizing their product and preventing them from living as they choose, or forcibly exclude others from competing in exchanges. None of these are permissible modes of transition from one situation to another. And some persons acquire holdings by means not sanctioned by the principle of justice in acquisition. The existence of past injustice (previous violations of the first two principles of justice in holdings) raises the third major topic under justice in holdings: the rectification of injustice in holdings. If past injustice has shaped present holdings in various ways, some identifiable and some not, what now, if anything, ought to be done to rectify these injustices? What obligations do the performers of injustice have toward those whose position is worse than it would have been had the injustice not been done? Or, than it would have been had compensation been paid promptly? How, if at all, do things

change if the beneficiaries and those made worse off are not the direct parties in the act of injustice, but, for example, their descendants? Is an injustice done to someone whose holding was itself based upon an unrectified injustice? How far back must one go in wiping clean the historical slate of injustices? What may victims of injustice permissibly do in order to rectify the injustices being done to them, including the many injustices done by persons acting through their government? I do not know of a thorough or theoretically sophisticated treatment of such issues.[4] Idealizing greatly, let us suppose theoretical investigation will produce a principle of rectification. This principle uses historical information about previous situations and injustices done in them (as defined by the first two principles of justice and rights against interference), and information about the actual course of events that flowed from these injustices, until the present, and it yields a description (or descriptions) of holdings in the society. The principle of rectification presumably will make use of its best estimate of subjunctive information[5] about what would have occurred (or a probability distribution[6] over what might have occurred, using the expected value) if the injustice had not taken place. If the actual description of holdings turns out not to be one of the descriptions yielded by the principle, then one of the descriptions yielded must be realized.[7]

---

4   [Author's note] See, however, the useful book by Boris Bittker, *The Case for Black Reparations* (New York: Random House, 1973).

5   Information about a hypothetical, non-actual situation.

6   A specification of all possible values of a variable along with the probability that each will occur.

7   [Author's note] If the principle of rectification of violations of the first two principles yields more than one description of holdings, then some choice must be made as to which of these is to be realized. Perhaps the sort of considerations about distributive justice and equality that I argue against play a legitimate role in *this* subsidiary choice. Similarly, there may be room for such considerations in deciding which otherwise arbitrary features a statute will embody, when such features are unavoidable because other considerations do not specify a precise line; yet a line must be drawn.

The general outlines of the theory of justice in holdings are that the holdings of a person are just if he is entitled to them by the principles of justice in acquisition and transfer, or by the principle of rectification of injustice (as specified by the first two principles). If each person's holdings are just, then the total set (distribution) of holdings is just. To turn these general outlines into a specific theory we would have to specify the details of each of the three principles of justice in holdings: the principle of acquisition of holdings, the principle of transfer of holdings, and the principle of rectification of violations of the first two principles. I shall not attempt that task here. (Locke's principle of justice in acquisition is discussed below.)

Historical Principles and the End-Result Principle

The general outlines of the entitlement theory illuminate the nature and defects of other conceptions of distributive justice. The entitlement theory of justice in distribution is *historical*; whether a distribution is just depends upon how it came about. In contrast, *current time-slice principles* of justice hold that the justice of a distribution is determined by how things are distributed (who has what) as judged by some *structural* principle(s) of just distribution. A utilitarian who judges between any two distributions by seeing which has the greater sum of utility and, if the sums tie, applies some fixed equality criterion to choose the more equal distribution, would hold a current time-slice principle of justice. As would someone who had a fixed schedule of trade-offs between the sum of happiness and equality. According to a current time-slice principle, all that needs to be looked at, in judging the justice of a distribution, is who ends up with what; in comparing any two distributions one need look only at the matrix presenting the distributions. No further information need be fed into a principle of justice. It is a consequence of such principles of justice that any two structurally identical distributions are equally just. (Two distributions are structurally identical if they present the same profile, but perhaps have different persons occupying the particular slots. My having ten and your having five, and my having five and your having ten are structurally identical distributions.) Welfare economics is the theory of current time-slice principles of justice. The subject is conceived as operating on matrices representing only current information about distribution. This, as well as some of the usual conditions (for example, the choice of distribution is invariant under relabeling of columns), guarantees that welfare economics will be a current time-slice theory, with all of its inadequacies.

Most persons do not accept current time-slice principles as constituting the whole story about distributive shares. They think it relevant in assessing the justice of a situation to consider not only the distribution it embodies, but also how that distribution came about. If some persons are in prison for murder or war crimes, we do not say that to assess the justice of the distribution in the society we must look only at what this person has, and that person has, and that person has, … at the current time. We think it relevant to ask whether someone did something so that he *deserved* to be punished, deserved to have a lower share. Most will agree to the relevance of further information with regard to punishments and penalties. Consider also desired things. One traditional socialist view is that workers are entitled to the product and full fruits of their labor; they have earned it; a distribution is unjust if it does not give the workers what they are entitled to. Such entitlements are based upon some past history. No socialist holding this view would find it comforting to be told that because the actual distribution *A* happens to coincide structurally with the one he desires *D*, *A* therefore is no less just than *D*; it differs only in that the "parasitic" owners of capital receive under *A* what the workers are entitled to under *D*, and the workers receive under *A* what the owners are entitled to under *D*, namely very little. This socialist rightly, in my view, holds onto the notions of earning, producing, entitlement, desert, and so forth, and he rejects current time-slice principles that look only to the structure of the resulting set of holdings. (The set of holdings resulting from what? Isn't it implausible that how holdings are produced and come to exist has no effect at all on who should hold what?) His mistake lies in his view of what entitlements arise out of what sorts of productive processes.

We construe the position we discuss too narrowly by speaking of *current* time-slice principles. Nothing is changed if structural principles operate upon a time sequence of current time-slice profiles and, for example, give someone more now to counterbalance the less he has had earlier. A utilitarian or an egalitarian or any mixture of the two over time will inherit the difficulties of his more myopic comrades. He is not helped by the fact that *some* of the information others consider relevant in assessing a distribution is reflected, unrecoverably, in past matrices. Henceforth, we shall refer to such unhistorical principles of distributive justice, including the current time-slice principles, as *end-result principles* or *end-state principles*.

In contrast to end-result principles of justice, *historical principles* of justice hold that past circumstances or actions of people can create differential entitlements or differential deserts to things. An injustice can be worked by moving from one distribution to another structurally identical one, for the second, in profile the same, may violate people's entitlements or deserts; it may not fit the actual history.

Patterning

The entitlement principles of justice in holdings that we have sketched are historical principles of justice. To better understand their precise character, we shall distinguish them from another subclass of the historical principles. Consider, as an example, the principle of distribution according to moral merit. This principle requires that total distributive shares vary directly with moral merit; no person should have a greater share than anyone whose moral merit is greater. (If moral merit could be not merely ordered but measured on an interval or ratio scale, stronger principles could be formulated.) Or consider the principle that results by substituting "usefulness to society" for "moral merit" in the previous principle. Or instead of "distribute according to moral merit," or "distribute according to usefulness to society," we might consider "distribute according to the weighted sum[8] of moral merit, usefulness to society, and need," with the weights of the different dimensions equal. Let us call a principle of distribution *patterned* if it specifies that a distribu-

tion is to vary along with some natural dimension, weighted sum of natural dimensions, or lexicographic ordering[9] of natural dimensions. And let us say a distribution is patterned if it accords with some patterned principle. (I speak of natural dimensions, admittedly without a general criterion for them, because for any set of holdings some artificial dimensions can be gimmicked up to vary along with the distribution of the set.) The principle of distribution in accordance with moral merit is a patterned historical principle, which specifies a patterned distribution. "Distribute according to I.Q." is a patterned principle that looks to information not contained in distributional matrices. It is not historical, however, in that it does not look to any past actions creating differential entitlements to evaluate a distribution; it requires only distributional matrices whose columns are labeled by I.Q. scores. The distribution in a society, however, may be composed of such simple patterned distributions, without itself being simply patterned. Different sectors may operate different patterns, or some combination of patterns may operate in different proportions across a society. A distribution composed in this manner, from a small number of patterned distributions, we also shall term "patterned." And we extend the use of "pattern" to include the overall designs put forth by combinations of end-state principles.

Almost every suggested principle of distributive justice is patterned: to each according to his moral merit, or needs, or marginal product,[10] or how hard

_____

8   A weighted sum is obtained by adding terms, each of which is given a certain value (weight) by using a multiplier which reflects their relative importance.

9   Strictly speaking, this means sorting a group of items in the order they would appear if they were listed in a dictionary (i.e., roughly, alphabetically), but listing first all the words made up of only *one* letter, then all the words made up of *two* letters, then all those with *three* letters, and so on. (The main idea here is to impose a useful *order* on an infinite sequence of formulae.) In the philosophical literature on justice, however, the phrase is generally used to mean a strict *prioritizing* of principles: first principle A must be satisfied, and only then should we worry about principle B; only when both A and B are satisfied can we apply principle C; and so on.

10   The contribution that each additional worker makes to total output. Thus, to be rewarded according to one's

he tries, or the weighted sum of the foregoing, and so on. The principle of entitlement we have sketched is not patterned.[11] There is no one natural dimension or weighted sum or combination of a small number of natural dimensions that yields the distributions generated in accordance with the principle of entitlement. The set of holdings that results when some persons receive their marginal products, others win at gambling, others receive a share of their mate's income, others receive gifts from foundations, others receive interest on loans, others receive gifts from admirers, others receive returns on investment, others make for themselves much of what they have, others find things, and so on, will not be patterned. Heavy strands of patterns will run through it; significant portions of the variance in holdings will be accounted for by pattern-variables. If most people most of the time choose to transfer some of their entitlements to others only in exchange for something from them, then a large part of what many people hold will vary with what they held that others wanted. More details are provided by the theory of marginal productivity. But gifts to relatives, charitable donations, bequests to children, and the like, are not best conceived, in the first instance, in this manner. Ignoring the strands of pattern, let us suppose for the moment that a distribution actually arrived at by the operation of the principle of entitlement is random with respect to any pattern. Though the resulting set of holdings will be unpatterned, it will not be incomprehensible, for it can be seen as arising from the operation of a small number of principles. These principles specify how an initial distribution may arise (the principle of acquisition of holdings) and how distributions may be transformed into others (the principle of transfer of holdings). The process whereby the set of holdings is generated will be intelligible, though the set of holdings itself that results from this process will be unpatterned.

The writings of F.A. Hayek[12] focus less than is usually done upon what patterning distributive justice requires. Hayek argues that we cannot know enough about each person's situation to distribute to each according to his moral merit (but would justice demand we do so if we did have this knowledge?); and he goes on to say, "our objection is against all attempts to impress upon society a deliberately chosen pattern of distribution, whether it be an order of equality or of inequality."[13] However, Hayek concludes that in a free society there will be distribution in accordance with value rather than moral merit; that is, in accordance with the perceived value of a person's actions and services to others. Despite his rejection of a patterned conception of distributive justice, Hayek himself suggests a pattern he thinks justifiable: distribution in accordance with the perceived benefits given to others, leaving room for the complaint that a free society does not

---

marginal product is to be paid in proportion to the amount that your contribution has increased output over what it would have been if you hadn't been employed.

11 [Author's note] One might try to squeeze a patterned conception of distributive justice into the framework of the entitlement conception, by formulating a gimmicky obligatory "principle of transfer" that would lead to the pattern. For example, the principle that if one has more than the mean income one must transfer everything one holds above the mean to persons below the mean so as to bring them up to (but not over) the mean. We can formulate a criterion for a "principle of transfer" to rule out such obligatory transfers, or we can say that no correct principle of transfer, no principle of transfer in a free society will be like this. The former is probably the better course, though the latter also is true.

Alternatively, one might think to make the entitlement conception instantiate a pattern, by using matrix entries that express the relative strength of a person's entitlements as measured by some real-valued function. But even if the limitation to natural dimensions failed to exclude this function, the resulting edifice would *not* capture our system of entitlements to *particular* things.

12 Friedrich August Hayek (1899–1992) was an Austrian-British economist and political philosopher best known for his critique of socialism and the welfare state, and defense of extreme *laissez-faire* economic individualism.

13 [Author's note] F.A. Hayek, *The Constitution of Liberty* (Chicago: University of Chicago Press, 1960), p. 87.

realize exactly this pattern. Stating this patterned strand of a free capitalist society more precisely, we get "To each according to how much he benefits others who have the resources for benefiting those who benefit them." This will seem arbitrary unless some acceptable initial set of holdings is specified, or unless it is held that the operation of the system over time washes out any significant effects from the initial set of holdings. As an example of the latter, if almost anyone would have bought a car from Henry Ford, the supposition that it was an arbitrary matter who held the money then (and so bought) would not place Henry Ford's earnings under a cloud. In any event, *his* coming to hold it is not arbitrary. Distribution according to benefits to others *is* a major patterned strand in a free capitalist society, as Hayek correctly points out, but it is only a strand and does not constitute the whole pattern of a system of entitlements (namely, inheritance, gifts for arbitrary reasons, charity, and so on) or a standard that one should insist a society fit. Will people tolerate for long a system yielding distributions that they believe are unpatterned?[14] No doubt people will not long accept a distribution they believe is *unjust*. People want their society to be and to look just. But must the look of justice reside in a resulting pattern rather than in the underlying generating principles? We are in no position to conclude that the inhabitants of a society embodying an entitlement conception of justice in holdings will find it unacceptable. Still, it must be granted that were people's reasons for transferring some of their holdings to others always irrational or arbitrary, we would find this disturbing. (Suppose people always determined what holdings they would transfer, and to whom, by using a random device.) We feel more comfortable upholding the justice of an entitlement system if most of the transfers under it are done for reasons. This does not mean necessarily that all deserve what holdings they receive. It means only that there is a purpose or point to someone's transferring a holding to one person rather than to another; that usually we can see what the transferrer thinks he's gaining, what cause he thinks he's serving, what goals he thinks he's helping to achieve, and so forth. Since in a capitalist society people often transfer holdings to others in accordance with how much they perceive these others benefiting them, the fabric constituted by the individual transactions and transfers is largely reasonable and intelligible.[15] (Gifts to loved ones, bequests to children, charity to the needy also are nonarbitrary components of the fabric.) In stressing the large strand of distribution in accordance with benefit to others, Hayek shows the point of many transfers, and so shows that the system of transfer of entitlements is not just spinning its gears aimlessly. The system of entitlements is defensible when constituted by the individual aims of individual transactions. No overarching aim is needed, no distributional pattern is required.

To think that the task of a theory of distributive justice is to fill in the blank in "to each according to

---

14 [Author's note] This question does not imply that they will tolerate any and every patterned distribution. In discussing Hayek's views, Irving Kristol has recently speculated that people will not long tolerate a system that yields distributions patterned in accordance with value rather than merit. ("'When Virtue Loses All Her Loveliness'—Some Reflections on Capitalism and 'The Free Society,'" *The Public Interest*, Fall 1970, pp. 3–15.) Kristol, following some remarks of Hayek's, equates the merit system with justice. Since some case can be made for the external standard of distribution in accordance with benefit to others, we ask about a weaker (and therefore more plausible) hypothesis.

15 [Author's note] We certainly benefit because great economic incentives operate to get others to spend much time and energy to figure out how to serve us by providing things we will want to pay for. It is not mere paradox mongering to wonder whether capitalism should be criticized for most rewarding and hence encouraging, not individualists like Thoreau who go about their own lives, but people who are occupied with serving others and winning them as customers. But to defend capitalism one need not think businessmen are the finest human types. (I do not mean to join here the general maligning of businessmen, either.) Those who think the finest should acquire the most can try to convince their fellows to transfer resources in accordance with *that* principle.

his _____" is to be predisposed to search for a pattern; and the separate treatment of "from each according to his _____" treats production and distribution as two separate and independent issues. On an entitlement view these are *not* two separate questions. Whoever makes something, having bought or contracted for all other held resources used in the process (transferring some of his holdings for these cooperating factors), is entitled to it. The situation is *not* one of something's getting made, and there being an open question of who is to get it. Things come into the world already attached to people having entitlements over them. From the point of view of the historical entitlement conception of justice in holdings, those who start afresh to complete "to each according to his _____" treat objects as if they appeared from nowhere, out of nothing. A complete theory of justice might cover this limit case as well; perhaps here is a use for the usual conceptions of distributive justice.[16]

So entrenched are maxims of the usual form that perhaps we should present the entitlement conception as a competitor. Ignoring acquisition and rectification, we might say:

> From each according to what he chooses to do, to each according to what he makes for himself (perhaps with the contracted aid of others) and what others choose to do for him and choose to give him of what they've been given previously (under this maxim) and haven't yet expended or transferred.

This, the discerning reader will have noticed, has its defects as a slogan. So as a summary and great simplification (and not as a maxim with any independent meaning) we have:

> *From each as they choose, to each as they are chosen.*

---

16   [Author's note] Varying situations continuously from that limit situation to our own would force us to make explicit the underlying rationale of entitlements and to consider whether entitlement considerations lexicographically precede the considerations of the usual theories of distributive justice, so that the *slightest* strand of entitlement outweighs the considerations of the usual theories of distributive justice.

How Liberty Upsets Patterns

It is not clear how those holding alternative conceptions of distributive justice can reject the entitlement conception of justice in holdings. For suppose a distribution favored by one of these non-entitlement conceptions is realized. Let us suppose it is your favorite one and let us call this distribution D_1; perhaps everyone has an equal share, perhaps shares vary in accordance with some dimension you treasure. Now suppose that Wilt Chamberlain[17] is greatly in demand by basketball teams, being a great gate attraction. (Also suppose contracts run only for a year, with players being free agents.) He signs the following sort of contract with a team: In each home game, twenty-five cents from the price of each ticket of admission goes to him. (We ignore the question of whether he is "gouging" the owners, letting them look out for themselves.) The season starts, and people cheerfully attend his team's games; they buy their tickets, each time dropping a separate twenty-five cents of their admission price into a special box with Chamberlain's name on it. They are excited about seeing him play; it is worth the total admission price to them. Let us suppose that in one season one million persons attend his home games, and Wilt Chamberlain winds up with $250,000, a much larger sum than the average income and larger even than anyone else has.[18] Is he entitled to this income? Is this new distribution D_2, unjust? If so, why? There is *no* question about whether each of the people was entitled to the control over the resources they held in D_1; because that was the distribution (your favorite) that (for the purposes of argument) we assumed was acceptable. Each of these persons *chose* to give twenty-five cents of their money to Chamberlain. They could have spent it on going to the movies, or on candy bars, or on copies of *Dissent* magazine, or of *Monthly Review*. But they all, at least one million of them, converged on giving it to Wilt Chamberlain in exchange for watching him play

---

17   Wilt Chamberlain was a well-known American basketball player during the 1960s. He was seven-time consecutive winner of the National Basketball Association scoring title from 1960 to 1966, and in 1962 he scored a record 100 points in a single game.

18   In 1974, the U.S. average (mean) income was $5,672.

basketball. If D_1 was a just distribution, and people voluntarily moved from it to D_2, transferring parts of their shares they were given under D_1 (what was it for if not to do something with?), isn't D_2 also just? If the people were entitled to dispose of the resources to which they were entitled (under D_1), didn't this include their being entitled to give it to, or exchange it with, Wilt Chamberlain? Can anyone else complain on grounds of justice? Each other person already has his legitimate share under D_1. Under D_1, there is nothing that anyone has that anyone else has a claim of justice against. After someone transfers something to Wilt Chamberlain, third parties *still* have their legitimate shares; *their* shares are not changed. By what process could such a transfer among two persons give rise to a legitimate claim of distributive justice on a portion of what was transferred, by a third party who had no claim of justice on any holding of the others *before* the transfer?[19] To cut off objections irrelevant here, we might imagine the exchanges occurring in a socialist society, after hours. After playing whatever basketball he does in his daily work, or doing whatever other daily work he does, Wilt Chamberlain decides to put in *overtime* to earn additional money. (First his work quota is set; he works time over that.) Or imagine it is a skilled juggler people like to see, who puts on shows after hours.

Why might someone work overtime in a society in which it is assumed their needs are satisfied? Perhaps because they care about things other than needs. I like to write in books that I read, and to have easy access to books for browsing at odd hours. It would be very pleasant and convenient to have the resources of Widener Library[20] in my back yard. No society, I assume, will provide such resources close to each person who would like them as part of his regular allotment (under D_1). Thus, persons either must do without some extra things that they want, or be allowed to do something extra to get some of these things. On what basis could the inequalities that would eventuate be forbidden? Notice also that small factories would spring up in a socialist society, unless forbidden. I melt down some of my personal possessions (under D_1) and build a machine out of the material. I offer you, and others, a philosophy lecture once a week in exchange for your cranking the handle on my machine, whose products I exchange for yet other things, and so on. (The raw materials used by the machine are given to me by others who possess them under D_1, in exchange for hearing lectures.) Each person might participate to gain things over and above their allotment under D_1. Some persons even might want to leave their job in socialist industry and work full time in this private sector. I shall say something more about these issues in the next chapter. Here I wish merely to note how private property even in means of production would occur in a socialist society that did not forbid people to use as they wished some of the resources they are given under the socialist distribution D_1.[21] The social-

---

19   [Author's note] Might not a transfer have instrumental effects on a third party, changing his feasible options? (But what if the two parties to the transfer independently had used their holdings in this fashion?) I discuss this question below, but note here that this question concedes the point for distributions of ultimate intrinsic noninstrumental goods (pure utility experiences, so to speak) that are transferrable. It also might be objected that the transfer might make a third party more envious because it worsens his position relative to someone else. I find it incomprehensible how this can be thought to involve a claim of justice. On envy, see Chapter 8 [of *Anarchy, State and Utopia*].

Here and elsewhere in this chapter, a theory which incorporates elements of pure procedural justice might find what I say acceptable, *if* kept in its proper place; that is, if background institutions exist to ensure the satisfaction of certain conditions on distributive shares. But if these institutions are not themselves the sum or invisible-hand result of people's voluntary (nonaggressive) actions, the constraints they impose require justification. At no point does *our* argument assume any background institutions more extensive than those of the minimal night-watchman state, a state limited to protecting persons against murder, assault, theft, fraud, and so forth.

20   Harvard University's library.

21   [Author's note] See the selection from John Henry MacKay's novel, *The Anarchists*, reprinted in Leonard Krimmerman and Lewis Perry, eds., *Patterns of Anarchy* (New York: Doubleday Anchor Books, 1966), in

ist society would have to forbid capitalist acts between consenting adults.

The general point illustrated by the Wilt Chamberlain example and the example of the entrepreneur in a socialist society is that no end-state principle or distributional patterned principle of justice can be continuously realized without continuous interference with people's lives. Any favored pattern would be transformed into one unfavored by the principle, by people choosing to act in various ways; for example, by people exchanging goods and services with other people, or giving things to other people, things the transferrers are entitled to under the favored distributional pattern. To maintain a pattern one must either continually interfere to stop people from transferring resources as they wish to, or continually (or periodically) interfere to take from some persons resources

that others for some reason chose to transfer to them. (But if some time limit is to be set on how long people may keep resources others voluntarily transfer to them, why let them keep these resources for *any* period of time? Why not have immediate confiscation?) It might be objected that all persons voluntarily will choose to refrain from actions which would upset the pattern. This presupposes unrealistically (1) that all will most want to maintain the pattern (are those who don't, to be "reeducated" or forced to undergo "self-criticism"?), (2) that each can gather enough information about his own actions and the ongoing activities of others to discover which of his actions will upset the pattern, and (3) that diverse and far-flung persons can coordinate their actions to dovetail into the pattern. Compare the manner in which the market is neutral among persons' desires, as it reflects and transmits widely scattered information via prices, and coordinates persons' activities.

It puts things perhaps a bit too strongly to say that every patterned (or end-state) principle is liable to be thwarted by the voluntary actions of the individual parties transferring some of their shares they receive under the principle. For perhaps some *very* weak patterns are not so thwarted.[22] Any distributional pattern

---

which an individualist anarchist presses upon a communist anarchist the following question: "Would you, in the system of society which you call 'free Communism' prevent individuals from exchanging their labour among themselves by means of their own medium of exchange? And further: Would you prevent them from occupying land for the purpose of personal use?" The novel continues: "[the] question was not to be escaped. If he answered 'Yes!' he admitted that society had the right of control over the individual and threw overboard the autonomy of the individual which he had always zealously defended; if on the other hand, he answered 'No!' he admitted the right of private property which he had just denied so emphatically.... Then he answered 'In Anarchy any number of men must have the right of forming a voluntary association, and so realizing their ideas in practice. Nor can I understand how any one could justly be driven from the land and house which he uses and occupies ... every serious man must declare himself: for Socialism, and thereby for force and against liberty, or for Anarchism, and thereby for liberty and against force.'" In contrast, we find Noam Chomsky writing, "Any consistent anarchist must oppose private ownership of the means of production," "the consistent anarchist then ... will be a socialist ... of a particular sort." Introduction to Daniel Guerin, *Anarchism: From Theory to Practice* (New York: Monthly Review Press, 1970), pages xiii, xv.

22 [Author's note] Is the patterned principle stable that requires merely that a distribution be Pareto-optimal? One person might give another a gift or bequest that the second could exchange with a third to their mutual benefit. Before the second makes this exchange, there is not Pareto-optimality. Is a stable pattern presented by a principle choosing that among the Pareto-optimal positions that satisfies some further condition *C*? It may seem that there cannot be a counter-example, for won't any voluntary exchange made away from a situation show that the first situation wasn't Pareto-optimal? (Ignore the implausibility of this last claim for the case of bequests.) But principles are to be satisfied over time, during which new possibilities arise. A distribution that at one time satisfies the criterion of Pareto-optimality might not do so when some new possibilities arise (Wilt Chamberlain grows up and starts playing basketball); and though people's activities will tend to move then to a new Pareto-optimal position, *this* new one need not satisfy the contentful condition

with any egalitarian component is overturnable by the voluntary actions of individual persons over time; as is every patterned condition with sufficient content so as actually to have been proposed as presenting the central core of distributive justice. Still, given the possibility that some weak conditions or patterns may not be unstable in this way, it would be better to formulate an explicit description of the kind of interesting and contentful patterns under discussion, and to prove a theorem about their instability. Since the weaker the patterning, the more likely it is that the entitlement system itself satisfies it, a plausible conjecture is that any patterning either is unstable or is satisfied by the entitlement system.

…

Locke's Theory of Acquisition

Before we turn to consider other theories of justice in detail, we must introduce an additional bit of complexity into the structure of the entitlement theory: This is best approached by considering Locke's[23] attempt to specify a principle of justice in acquisition. Locke views property rights in an unowned object as originating through someone's mixing his labor with it. This gives rise to many questions. What are the boundaries of what labor is mixed with? If a private astronaut clears a place on Mars, has he mixed his labor with (so that he comes to own) the whole planet, the whole uninhabited universe, or just a particular plot? Which plot does an act bring under ownership? The minimal (possibly disconnected) area such that an act decreases entropy in that area, and not elsewhere? Can virgin land (for the purposes of ecological investigation by high-flying airplane) come under ownership by a Lockean process? Building a fence around a territory presumably would make one the owner of only the fence (and the land immediately underneath it).

Why does mixing one's labor with something make one the owner of it? Perhaps because one owns one's labor, and so one comes to own a previously unowned thing that becomes permeated with what one owns. Ownership seeps over into the rest. But why isn't mixing what I own with what I don't own a way of losing what I own rather than a way of gaining what I don't? If I own a can of tomato juice and spill it in the sea so that its molecules (made radioactive, so I can check this) mingle evenly throughout the sea, do I thereby come to own the sea, or have I foolishly dissipated my tomato juice? Perhaps the idea, instead, is that laboring on something improves it and makes it more valuable; and anyone is entitled to own a thing whose value he has created. (Reinforcing this, perhaps, is the view that laboring is unpleasant. If some people made things effortlessly, as the cartoon characters in *The Yellow Submarine*[24] trail flowers in their wake, would they have lesser claim to their own products whose making didn't *cost* them anything?) Ignore the fact that laboring on something may make it less valuable (spraying pink enamel paint on a piece of driftwood that you have found). Why should one's entitlement extend to the whole object rather than just to the *added value* one's labor has produced? (Such reference to value might also serve to delimit the extent of ownership; for example, substitute "increases the value of" for "decreases entropy in" in the above entropy criterion.) No workable or coherent value-added property scheme has yet been devised, and any such scheme presumably would fall to objections (similar to those) that fell to the theory of Henry George.[25]

It will be implausible to view improving an object as giving full ownership to it, if the stock of unowned objects that might be improved is limited. For an object's coming under one person's ownership changes the situation of all others. Whereas previously they

---

C. Continual interference will be needed to insure the continual satisfaction of *C.* (The theoretical possibility of a pattern's being maintained by some invisible-hand process that brings it back to an equilibrium that fits the pattern when deviations occur should be investigated.)

23 English philosopher John Locke (1632–1704). Nozick is referring specifically to Locke's *Two Treatises on Government* (1690).

24 A 1968 animated film by the *Beatles*.

25 Henry George (1839–1897) was a US social philosopher and economist who argued that the economic boom in the American West, brought about by the advent of the railroads, was actually making most people poorer, and only a few richer, and proposed controversial tax reforms (shifting the tax burden from buildings to land) in order to rectify this situation.

were at liberty (in Hohfeld's sense[26]) to use the object, they now no longer are. This change in the situation of others (by removing their liberty to act on a previously unowned object) need not worsen their situation. If I appropriate a grain of sand from Coney Island, no one else may now do as they will with *that* grain of sand. But there are plenty of other grains of sand left for them to do the same with. Or if not grains of sand, then other things. Alternatively, the things I do with the grain of sand I appropriate might improve the position of others, counterbalancing their loss of the liberty to use that grain. The crucial point is whether appropriation of an unowned object worsens the situation of others.

Locke's proviso that there be "enough and as good left in common for others" (sect. 27) is meant to ensure that the situation of others is not worsened. (If this proviso is met is there any motivation for his further condition of nonwaste?) It is often said that this proviso once held but now no longer does. But there appears to be an argument for the conclusion that if the proviso no longer holds, then it cannot ever have held so as to yield permanent and inheritable property rights. Consider the first person Z for whom there is not enough and as good left to appropriate. The last person Y to appropriate left Z without his previous liberty to act on an object, and so worsened Z's situation. So Y's appropriation is not allowed under Locke's proviso. Therefore the next to last person X to appropriate left Y in a worse position, for X's act ended permissible appropriation. Therefore X's appropriation wasn't permissible. But then the appropriator two from last, W, ended permissible appropriation and so, since it worsened X's position, W's appropriation wasn't permissible. And so on back to the first person A to appropriate a permanent property right.

This argument, however, proceeds too quickly. Someone may be made worse off by another's appropriation in two ways: first, by losing the opportunity to improve his situation by a particular appropriation or any one; and second, by no longer being able to use freely (without appropriation) what he previously could. A *stringent* requirement that another not be made worse off by an appropriation would exclude the first way if nothing else counterbalances the diminution in opportunity, as well as the second. A *weaker* requirement would exclude the second way, though not the first. With the weaker requirement, we cannot zip back so quickly from Z to A, as in the above argument; for though person Z can no longer *appropriate*, there may remain some for him to *use* as before. In this case Y's appropriation would not violate the weaker Lockean condition. (With less remaining that people are at liberty to use, users might face more inconvenience, crowding, and so on; in that way the situation of others might be worsened, unless appropriation stopped far short of such a point.) It is arguable that no one legitimately can complain if the weaker provision is satisfied. However, since this is less clear than in the case of the more stringent proviso, Locke may have intended this stringent proviso by "enough and as good" remaining, and perhaps he meant the nonwaste condition to delay the end point from which the argument zips back.

Is the situation of persons who are unable to appropriate (there being no more accessible and useful unowned objects) worsened by a system allowing appropriation and permanent property? Here enter the various familiar social considerations favoring private property: it increases the social product by putting means of production in the hands of those who can use them most efficiently (profitably); experimentation is encouraged, because with separate persons controlling resources, there is no one person or small group whom someone with a new idea must convince to try it out; private property enables people to decide on the pattern and types of risks they wish to bear, leading to specialized types of risk bearing; private property protects future persons by leading some to hold back resources from current consumption for future markets; it provides alternate sources of employment for unpopular persons who don't have to convince any one person or small group to hire them, and so on. These considerations enter a Lockean theory to support the claim that appropriation of private property

---

26   Wesley Newcomb Hohfeld (1879–1918) was an American law professor, best remembered for his influential analysis of a number of basic legal notions, especially the idea of a legal and moral right. Hohfeld's definition of a legal liberty (or privilege) is that one can do X when one does not have a duty (to Y) *not* to do X.

satisfies the intent behind the "enough and as good left over" proviso, *not* as a utilitarian justification of property. They enter to rebut the claim that because the proviso is violated no natural right to private property can arise by a Lockean process. The difficulty in working such an argument to show that the proviso is satisfied is in fixing the appropriate base line for comparison. Lockean appropriation makes people no worse off than they would be *how*?[27] This question of fixing the baseline needs more detailed investigation than we are able to give it here. It would be desirable to have an estimate of the general economic importance of original appropriation in order to see how much leeway there is for differing theories of appropriation and of the location of the baseline. Perhaps this importance can be measured by the percentage of all income that is based upon untransformed raw materials and given resources (rather than upon human actions), mainly rental income representing the unimproved value of land, and the price of raw material *in situ*,[28] and by the percentage of current wealth which represents such income in the past.[29]

We should note that it is not only persons favoring *private* property who need a theory of how property rights legitimately originate. Those believing in collective property, for example those believing that a group of persons living in an area jointly own the territory, or its mineral resources, also must provide a theory of how such property rights arise; they must show why the persons living there have rights to determine what is done with the land and resources there that persons living elsewhere don't have (with regard to the same land and resources).

The Proviso

Whether or not Locke's particular theory of appropriation can be spelled out so as to handle various difficulties, I assume that any adequate theory of justice in acquisition will contain a proviso similar to the weaker of the ones we have attributed to Locke. A process normally giving rise to a permanent bequeathable property right in a previously unowned thing will not do so if the position of others no longer at liberty to use the thing is thereby worsened. It is important to specify *this* particular mode of worsening the situation of others, for the proviso does not encompass other modes. It does not include the worsening due to more limited opportunities to appropriate (the first way above, corresponding to the more stringent condition), and it does not include how I "worsen" a seller's position if I appropriate materials to make some of what he is selling, and then enter into competition with him. Someone whose appropriation otherwise would violate the proviso still may appropriate provided he compensates the others so that their situation is not thereby worsened; unless he does compensate these others, his appropriation will violate the proviso of the principle of justice in acquisition and will be an illegitimate one.[30] A theory of appropriation incorporating this Lockean proviso will handle correctly the cases (objections to the theory lacking the proviso) where

---

27   [Author's note] Compare this with Robert Paul Wolff's "A Refutation of Rawls' Theorem on Justice," *Journal of Philosophy*, March 31, 1966, sect. 2. Wolff's criticism does not apply to Rawls' conception under which the baseline is fixed by the difference principle.

28   In its original position, i.e., not yet extracted or harvested.

29   [Author's note] I have not seen a precise estimate. David Friedman, *The Machinery of Freedom* (N.Y.: Harper & Row, 1973), pp. xiv, xv, discusses this issue and suggests 5 percent of U.S. national income as an upper limit for the first two factors mentioned. However he does not attempt to estimate the percentage of current wealth which is based upon such income in the past. (The vague notion of "based upon" merely indicates a topic needing investigation.)

30   [Author's note] [Charles] Fourier [1772–1837] held that since the process of civilization had deprived the members of society of certain liberties (to gather, pasture, engage in the chase), a socially guaranteed minimum provision for persons was justified as compensation for the loss (Alexander Gray, *The Socialist Tradition* (New York: Harper & Row, 1968), p. 188). But this puts the point too strongly. This compensation would be due those persons, if any, for whom the process of civilization was a *net loss*, for whom the benefits of civilization did not counterbalance being deprived of these particular liberties.

someone appropriates the total supply of something necessary for life.[31]

A theory which includes this proviso in its principle of justice in acquisition must also contain a more complex principle of justice in transfer. Some reflection of the proviso about appropriation constrains later actions. If my appropriating all of a certain substance violates the Lockean proviso, then so does my appropriating some and purchasing all the rest from others who obtained it without otherwise violating the Lockean proviso. If the proviso excludes someone's appropriating all the drinkable water in the world, it also excludes his purchasing it all. (More weakly, and messily, it may exclude his charging certain prices for some of his supply.) This proviso (almost?) never will come into effect; the more someone acquires of a scarce substance which others want, the higher the price of the rest will go, and the more difficult it will become for him to acquire it all. But still, we can imagine, at least, that something like this occurs: someone makes simultaneous secret bids to the separate owners of a substance, each of whom sells assuming he can easily purchase more from the other owners; or some natural catastrophe destroys all of the supply of something except that in one person's possession. The total supply could not be permissibly appropriated by one person at the beginning. His later acquisition of it all does not show that the original appropriation violated the proviso (even by a reverse argument similar to the one above that tried to zip back from *Z* to *A*). Rather, it is the combination of the original appropriation *plus* all the later transfers and actions that violates the Lockean proviso.

Each owner's title to his holding includes the historical shadow of the Lockean proviso on appropriation. This excludes his transferring it into an agglomeration that does violate the Lockean proviso and excludes his using it in a way, in coordination with others or independently of them, so as to violate the proviso by making the situation of others worse than their baseline situation. Once it is known that someone's ownership runs afoul of the Lockean proviso, there are stringent limits on what he may do with (what it is difficult any longer unreservedly to call) "his property." Thus a person may not appropriate the only water hole in a desert and charge what he will. Nor may he charge what he will if he possesses one, and unfortunately it happens that all the water holes in the desert dry up, except for his. This unfortunate circumstance, admittedly no fault of his, brings into operation the Lockean proviso and limits his property rights.[32] Similarly, an owner's property right in the only island in an area does not allow him to order a castaway from a shipwreck off his island as a trespasser, for this would violate the Lockean proviso.

Notice that the theory does not say that owners do have these rights, but that the rights are overridden

31 [Author's note] For example, Rashdall's case of someone who comes upon the only water in the desert several miles ahead of others who also will come to it and appropriates it all. Hastings Rashdall, "The Philosophical Theory of Property," in *Property, Its Duties and Rights* (London: MacMillan, 1915).

We should note Ayn Rand's theory of property rights ("Man's Rights" in *The Virtue of Selfishness* (New York: New American Library, 1964), p. 94), wherein these follow from the right to life, since people need physical things to live. But a right to life is not a right to whatever one needs to live; other people may have rights over these other things (see Chapter 3 of this book). At most, a right to life would be a right to have or strive for whatever one needs to live, provided that having it does not violate anyone else's rights. With regard to material things, the question is whether having it does violate any right of others. (Would appropriation of all unowned things do so? Would appropriating the water hole in Rashdall's example?) Since special considerations (such as the Lockean proviso) may enter with regard to material property, one *first* needs a theory of property rights before one can apply any supposed right to life (as amended above). Therefore the right to life cannot provide the foundation for a theory of property rights.

32 [Author's note] The situation would be different if his water hole didn't dry up, due to special precautions he took to prevent this. Compare our discussion of the case in the text with Hayek, *The Constitution of Liberty*, p. 136; and also with Ronald Hamowy, "Hayek's Concept of Freedom; A Critique," *New Individualist Review*, April 1961, pp. 28–31.

to avoid some catastrophe. (Overridden rights do not disappear; they leave a trace of a sort absent in the cases under discussion.)[33] There is no such external (and *ad hoc*?) overriding. Considerations internal to the theory of property itself, to its theory of acquisition and appropriation, provide the means for handling such cases. The results, however, may be coextensive with some condition about catastrophe, since the baseline for comparison is so low as compared to the productiveness of a society with private appropriation that the question of the Lockean proviso being violated arises only in the case of catastrophe (or a desert-island situation).

The fact that someone owns the total supply of something necessary for others to stay alive does *not* entail that his (or anyone's) appropriation of anything left some people (immediately or later) in a situation worse than the baseline one. A medical researcher who synthesizes a new substance that effectively treats a certain disease and who refuses to sell except on his terms does not worsen the situation of others by depriving them of whatever he has appropriated. The others easily can possess the same materials he appropriated; the researcher's appropriation or purchase of chemicals didn't make those chemicals scarce in a way so as to violate the Lockean proviso. Nor would someone else's purchasing the total supply of the synthesized substance from the medical researcher. The fact that the medical researcher uses easily available chemicals to synthesize the drug no more violates the Lockean proviso than does the fact that the only surgeon able to perform a particular operation eats easily obtainable food in order to stay alive and to have the energy to work. This shows that the Lockean proviso is not an "end-state principle"; it focuses on a particular way that appropriative actions affect others, and not on the structure of the situation that results.[34]

Intermediate between someone who takes all of the public supply and someone who makes the total supply out of easily obtainable substances is someone who appropriates the total supply of something in a way that does not deprive the others of it. For example, someone finds a new substance in an out-of-the-way place. He discovers that it effectively treats a certain disease and appropriates the total supply. He does not worsen the situation of others; if he did not stumble upon the substance no one else would have, and the others would remain without it. However, as time passes, the likelihood increases that others would have come across the substance; upon this fact might be based a limit to his property right in the substance so that others are not below their baseline position; for example, its bequest might be limited. The theme of someone worsening another's situation by depriving him of something he otherwise would possess may also illuminate the example of patents. An inventor's patent does not deprive others of an object which would not exist if not for the inventor. Yet patents would have this effect on others who independently invent the object. Therefore, these independent inventors, upon whom the burden of proving independent discovery may rest, should not be excluded from utilizing their own invention as they wish (including selling it to others). Furthermore, a known inventor drastically lessens the chances of actual independent invention. For persons who know of an invention usually will not try to reinvent it, and the notion of independent discovery here would be murky at best. Yet we may assume that in the absence of the original invention, sometime later someone else would have come up with it. This suggests placing a time limit on patents, as a rough rule of thumb to approximate how long it would have taken, in the absence of knowledge of the invention, for independent discovery.

33   [Author's note] I discuss overriding and its moral traces in "Moral Complications and Moral Structures," *Natural Law Forum*, 1968, p. 1–50.

34   [Author's note] Does the principle of compensation (Chapter 4) introduce patterning considerations? Though it requires compensation for the disadvantages imposed by those seeking security from risks, it is not a patterned principle. For it seeks to remove only those disadvantages which prohibitions inflict on those who might present risks to others, not all disadvantages. It specifies an obligation on those who impose the prohibition, which stems from their own particular acts, to remove a particular complaint those prohibited may make against them.

I believe that the free operation of a market system will not actually run afoul of the Lockean proviso. (Recall that crucial to our story in Part I of how a protective agency becomes dominant and a *de facto* monopoly is the fact that it wields force in situations of conflict, and is not merely in competition, with other agencies. A similar tale cannot be told about other businesses.) If this is correct, the proviso will not play a very important role in the activities of protective agencies and will not provide a significant opportunity for future state action. Indeed, were it not for the effects of previous illegitimate state action, people would not think the possibility of the proviso's being violated as of more interest than any other logical possibility. (Here I make an empirical historical claim; as does someone who disagrees with this.) This completes our indication of the complication in the entitlement theory introduced by the Lockean proviso.

SUSAN MOLLER OKIN
"Justice and Gender"

Who Was Susan Moller Okin?

Susan Moller Okin, "perhaps the best feminist political philosopher in the world,"[1] was born in 1946 in Auckland, New Zealand, and died in 2004 at the age of only 57. At the time of her death she was a professor of political science at Stanford University, and she had previously taught at Auckland, Vassar, Brandeis, and Harvard. Her doctorate, which she received in 1975, was from Harvard.

Okin's main importance as a political philosopher lay in her insistence that gender—the status and position of women—is an issue that lies at the heart of political theory, and is not merely a fringe topic that can be addressed after the main principles of justice have been laid down. As the article reprinted here makes clear, at the time that Okin began writing—in the 1970s—this was a radical view:

one which, it seems fair to say, had not even occurred to the (male) writers who were mainly responsible for carrying on the liberal political tradition. Okin formulated careful and forceful arguments that, in particular, the role and structure of the family—the so-called 'domestic sphere,' that shaped, and still shapes, the opportunities available to women in society—were crucial to any adequate account of social justice. These arguments brought about a sea change in political philosophy, carrying issues surrounding gender roles and the family to the center of the discipline.

Towards the end of her career, Okin's interests shifted towards the situation of women in less developed countries, and she worked on the complex tangle of issues raised by the interaction between gender issues, poverty, and multiculturalism. Once again, she was among the first to identify an issue that at the time was barely on the radar and has since become a main theme in political thought: the potential for conflict between the aim of gender

---

1   Debra Satz, a Stanford philosopher, quoted in Okin's obituary in the *Stanford Report*, March 9, 2004.

equality, and sensitivity to the customs of other cultures and religions. Okin's own view was a provocative defense of the liberal egalitarian position that all citizens in a state should have equal rights and privileges and that this trumps certain oppressive cultural practices, such as forced marriage, polygamy, or female genital mutilation. She became a highly visible supporter of the Global Fund for Women, an international foundation devoted to the support of women's human rights.

Probably Okin's best-known work is the book *Justice, Gender and the Family*, published in 1989. She also wrote two other very influential books—*Women in Western Political Thought* (1979), and *Is Multiculturalism Bad for Women?* (1999)—and many widely-read articles.

What Is the Structure of This Reading?

After introducing the topic "how just is gender?", Okin begins by outlining the role of gender in justifying inequality in the western tradition of political thought, including that of Aristotle, Rousseau, Kant, Hegel, and Bentham. She then asks whether modern political theory fares any better on this front—whether modern theorists are more sensitive to the problem of gender-based inequalities in society—and examines two representative leading writers: John Rawls, the most prominent liberal ideologist; and Michael Walzer, a leading communitarian. Okin concludes that insufficient attention is still being devoted to gender. She argues that, although Walzer appears on the surface to be more sympathetic to feminist concerns, in fact it is the Rawlsian tradition that is best able to accommodate feminism. However, she concludes by suggesting that full consideration of the problem of gender in a theory of social justice will require not only modifying contemporary liberal theory but also, potentially, a radical alteration of gender itself.

Some Useful Background Information

1. In her article, Okin deliberately focuses on a leading representative of liberalism (Rawls) and a leading communitarian (Walzer). Liberalism, as a political ideology, focuses on the rights of the individual, as against the government or other social institutions, and tends to hold that such rights—such as the right to freedom of expression, equality of respect, freedom of religion, and so on—are universally applicable. Communitarianism, by contrast, stresses the manner in which individual self-identity is embedded in, even created by, social ties of kinship, tradition, and common purpose, and hence rejects liberal individualism.

Some Common Misconceptions

1. Although Okin, in this article and elsewhere in her work, attacks liberalism for its historical bias against women, she nevertheless does not reject liberal political theory. On the contrary, her view is that liberalism is an emancipatory doctrine that simply has not been taken far enough. The basic idea of freedom and equality for all citizens is the right one—but in order to apply fully to women (and, indeed, to men), these liberal principles must be applied to the family as well as to the public spheres of government and economics.

Questions for Further Thought

1. Okin writes that, "[i]n one way or another, liberals have assumed that the 'individual' who is the basic subject of their theories is the male head of a patriarchal household." Consider the works from this tradition that you might have read: is Okin right in her judgment? What implications does she draw from this?

2. Is there a difference between the way we should understand justice and equity within families as opposed to in society at large? Does Okin think there should be? Do you?

3. "For the family with its gender structure, female parenting in particular, is clearly a crucial determinant in the different socialization of the two sexes—in how men and women 'get to be what they are.'" Is Okin right about this? What implications does it have?

4. Okin quotes Rawls as apparently assuming "that family institutions are just," and then proceeds to argue that, by Rawls's own lights, the institution of the family cannot be considered just. Does Okin mean by this that it must be considered *unjust*? How effective are Okin's arguments on this point? Do they apply only to Rawls, or do they have wider application?

5. Okin asserts that "a much larger proportion of women's than men's labor is unpaid, and is often not even acknowledged to be labor." What are the implications of this claim for social justice?

6. In her discussion of Walzer, Okin compares gender inequality with hierarchies of caste that exist, or have existed, in some societies (such as nineteenth-century India). How plausible is this comparison? How does Okin use it to critique Walzer? What implication does this comparison have for the place of gender in modern political theory?

7. "The danger of [Walzer's] conception of justice is that what is just depends heavily on what people are persuaded of." What is your assessment of this important criticism by Okin?

8. In the final section of her paper, Okin "raises the question whether, in fact, sex *is* a morally irrelevant and contingent human characteristic, in a society structured by gender." What is the significance of this question? How does Okin answer it?

9. Okin concludes that "gender [is] incompatible with a just society." What does she mean by this? How radical a claim is this? Do you think it is warranted?

10. This article was published in 1987. In your view, has there been any significant change to the attitudes that Okin describes concerning the relevance of gender to justice, or the place of principles of justice within the family?

Suggestions for Further Reading

Okin wrote three books that mark the main stages of the progression of her feminist critique of political science. In *Women in Western Political Thought* (Prince-ton University Press, 1979) she argues that unquestioned assumptions about the 'natural' form of the family have excluded women from public political life throughout western history. Then in *Justice, Gender and the Family* (Basic Books, 1989) Okin applies this critique to contemporary political theorists. *Is Multiculturalism Bad for Women?* (Princeton University Press, 1999) collects together Okin's titular essay with responses from a range of different critical commentators, and a reply from Okin.

Two review essays are useful starting points for critical responses to Okin's views on the family: Joshua Cohen, "Okin on Justice, Gender, and the Family," *The Canadian Journal of Philosophy* 22 (1992), pp. 263–86; and Will Kymlicka, "Rethinking the Family," *Philosophy and Public Affairs* 20 (1991), pp. 77–97.

"Justice and Gender"[2,3]

Theories of justice are centrally concerned with whether, how, and why persons should be treated differently from each other. Which initial or acquired characteristics or positions in society, they ask, legitimize differential treatment of persons by social institutions, laws, and customs? In particular, how should beginnings affect outcomes? The division of humanity into two sexes would seem to provide an obvious subject for such inquiries. We live in a society in whose past the innate characteristic of sex has been regarded as one of the clearest legitimizers of different rights and

---

2 From *Philosophy and Public Affairs*, Vol. 16, No. 1 (Winter, 1987), 42–72. Reproduced by permission of Wiley-Blackwell Inc.

3 [Author's note] An earlier version of this article was presented at the 80th Annual Meeting of the American Political Science Association, August 30–September 2, 1984 in Washington, D.C. I gratefully acknowledge the helpful comments of the following people: Robert Amdur, Peter Euben, Robert Goodin, Anne Harper, Robert Keohane, Carole Pateman, John Rawls, Nancy Rosenblum, Robert Simon, Quentin Skinner, Michael Walzer, Iris Young and the Editors of *Philosophy & Public Affairs*. Thanks also to Lisa Carisella and Elaine Herrmann for typing the manuscript.

restrictions, both formal and informal. While the legal sanctions that uphold male dominance have been to some extent eroded within the past century, and more rapidly in the last twenty years, the heavy weight of tradition, combined with the effects of socialization broadly defined, still work powerfully to reinforce roles for the two sexes that are commonly regarded as of unequal prestige and worth.[4] The sexual division of labor within the family, in particular, is not only a fundamental part of the marriage contract, but so deeply influences us in our most formative years that feminists of both sexes who try to reject it find themselves struggling against it with varying degrees of ambivalence. Based on this linchpin, the deeply entrenched social institutionalization of sex difference, which I will refer to as "the gender system" or simply "gender," still permeates our society.

This gender system has rarely been subjected to the tests of justice. When we turn to the great tradition of Western political thought with questions about the justice of gender in mind, it is to little avail. Bold feminists like Mary Astell, Mary Wollstonecraft, Harriet Taylor, and George Bernard Shaw have occasionally challenged the tradition,[5] often using its own premises and arguments to overturn its justification of the un-

equal treatment of women. But John Stuart Mill is a rare exception to the rule that those who hold central positions in the tradition almost never questioned the justice of the subordination and oppression of women. This phenomenon is undoubtedly due in part to the fact that Aristotle, whose theory of justice has been so influential, relegated women and slaves to a realm of "household justice," whose participants are not fundamentally equal to the free men who participate in political justice, but inferiors whose natural function is to serve those who are more fully human. The liberal tradition, despite its supposed foundation of individual rights and human equality, is more Aristotelian in this respect than is generally acknowledged.[6] In one way or another, liberals have assumed that the "individual" who is the basic subject of their theories is the male head of a patriarchal household.[7] Thus the application of principles of justice to relations between the sexes, or within the household, has frequently been ruled out from the start.

Other assumptions, too, contribute to the widespread belief that neither women nor the family are appropriate subjects for discussions of justice. One is that women, whether because of their essential disorderliness, their enslavement to nature, their private and particularist inclinations, or their oedipal development,[8] are incapable of developing a sense

---

4   [Author's note] On the history of the legal enforcement of traditional sex roles and recent changes therein, see Leo Kanowitz, *Sex Roles in Law and Society* (Albuquerque: University of New Mexico Press, 1973, and 1974 Supplement), esp. pts. 2, 4, 5; also Kenneth M. Davidson, Ruth Bader Ginsburg and Henna Hill Kay, *Sex-Based Discrimination* (St. Paul: West Publishing Co., 1974, and 1978 Supplement by Wendy Williams), esp. chap. 2.

5   Mary Astell (1666–1731) wrote *A Serious Proposal to the Ladies, for the Advancement of Their True and Greatest Interest* (1694) and fought for more equal educational opportunities for women; Mary Wollstonecraft (1759–1797) was the author of *A Vindication of the Rights of Woman* (1792); Harriet Taylor (1807–1858) worked with John Stuart Mill (her second husband) as a key contributor to *On Liberty* (1859); George Bernard Shaw (1856–1950), the playwright, was a prominent socialist and author of *The Intelligent Woman's Guide to Socialism and Capitalism* (1928).

6   [Author's note] See Judith Hicks Stiehm, "The Unit of Political Analysis: Our Aristotelian Hangover," in Sandra Harding and Merrill B. Hintikka, eds., *Discovering Reality: Feminist Perspectives on Epistemology, Metaphysics, Methodology, and Philosophy of Science* (Dordrecht: Reidel, 1983), pp. 31–43.

7   [Author's note] See Carole Pateman and Theresa Brennan, "'Mere Auxiliaries to the Commonwealth'; Women and the Origins of Liberalism," *Political Studies* 27, no. 2 (June 1979): 183–200; also Susan Moller Okin, "Women and the Making of the Sentimental Family," *Philosophy & Public Affairs* 11, no. 1 (Winter 1982): 65–88.

8   That is, according to Freudian psychoanalytic theory, the psychosexual development of children, passing through a period during which they develop the unconscious desire to possess the parent of the opposite sex and eliminate the parent of the same sex. This has

of justice. This notion can be found—sometimes briefly suggested, sometimes developed at greater length—in the works of theorists from Plato to Freud, including Bodin, John Knox,[9] Rousseau, Kant, Hegel and Bentham.[10] The frequent implication is that those who do not possess the qualifications for fully ethical reasoning or action need not have principles of justice applied to them. Finally, in Rousseau (as so often, original) we find the unique claim that woman, being "made to submit to man and even to put up with his injustice," is imbued innately with a capacity to tolerate the unjust treatment with which she is likely to meet.[11]

For those who are not satisfied with these reasons for excluding women and gender from the subject matter of justice, the great tradition has little to offer, directly at least, to our inquiry. When we turn to contemporary theories of justice, however, we can expect to find more illuminating and positive contributions to the subject of gender and justice. I turn to two such theories, John Rawls's *A Theory of Justice* and Michael Walzer's *Spheres of Justice,* to

see what they say or imply in response to the question "How just is gender?"[12]

Justice as Fairness

An ambiguity runs throughout John Rawls's *A Theory of Justice,* continually noticeable to anyone reading it from a feminist perspective. On the one hand, as I shall argue below, a consistent and wholehearted application of Rawls's liberal principles can lead us to challenge fundamentally the gender system of our society. On the other hand, in his own account of his theory, this challenge is barely hinted at, much less developed. The major reason is that throughout most of the argument, it is assumed (as throughout almost the entire liberal tradition) that the appropriate subjects of political theories are heads of families. As a result, although Rawls indicates on several occasions that a person's sex is a morally arbitrary and contingent characteristic, and although he states explicitly that the family itself is one of those basic social institutions to which the principles of justice must apply, his theory of justice fails to develop either of these convictions.

Rawls, like almost all political theorists until very recent years, employs supposedly generic male terms of reference. "Men," "mankind," "he" and "his" are interspersed with nonsexist terms of reference such as "individual" and "moral person." Examples of intergenerational concern are worded in terms of "fathers" and "sons," and the difference principle[13] is said to correspond to "the principle of fraternity."[14] This linguistic usage would perhaps be less significant if it were not for the fact that Rawls is self-consciously a member of a long tradition of moral and political philosophy that has used in its arguments either such

become known as the Oedipus complex.

9   Jean Bodin (1530–1596) was a French legal theorist who argued for the absolute authority of the sovereign; John Knox (c. 1510–1572) was the leading Protestant reformer in Scotland, and author of *The First Blast of the Trumpet Against the Monstrous Regiment of Women* (1558).

10   [Author's note] See Nannerl O. Keohane, "Female Citizenship: The Monstrous Regiment of Women," presented at the Annual Meeting of the Conference for the Study of Political Thought, April 6–8, 1979, on Bodin, John Knox and Rousseau; Carole Pateman, "'The Disorder of Women'; Women, Love, and The Sense of Justice," *Ethics* 81, no. 1 (October 1980): 20–34, on Rousseau and Freud; Susan Moller Okin, "Thinking like a Woman," unpublished ms., 1984, on Plato and Hegel; Terence Ball, "Utilitarianism, Feminism and the Franchise: James Mill and his Critics," *History of Political Thought* 1, no. 1 (Spring 1980): 91–115, on Bentham.

11   [Author's note] Jean-Jacques Rousseau, *Émile,* in *Oeuvres Complètes* 4 (Paris: Pléiade, 1969), pp. 734–35, 750.

12   [Author's note] John Rawls, *A Theory of Justice* (Cambridge, MA: Harvard University Press, 1971), hereafter referred to as *Theory*; Michael L. Walzer, *Spheres of Justice* (New York: Basic Books, 1983), hereafter referred to as *Spheres.*

13   The principle, developed by Rawls, that inequalities in the distribution of goods are justified only if those inequalities benefit the worst-off members of society.

14   [Author's note] *Theory*, pp. 105–106, 208–209, 288–289.

supposedly generic masculine terms, or even more inclusive terms of reference ("human beings," "persons," "all rational beings as such"), only to exclude women from the scope of the conclusions reached. Kant is a clear example.[15] But when Rawls refers to the generality and universality of Kant's ethics, and when he compares the principles chosen in his own original position to those regulative of Kant's kingdom of ends, "acting from [which] expresses our nature as free and equal rational persons,"[16] he does not mention the fact that women were not included in that category of "free and equal rational persons," to which Kant meant his moral theory to apply. Again, in a brief discussion of Freud's account of moral development, Rawls presents Freud's theory of the formation of the male super-ego in largely gender-neutral terms, without mentioning that Freud considered women's moral development to be sadly deficient, on account of their incomplete resolution of the Oedipus complex.[17] Thus there is a certain blindness to the sexism of the tradition in which Rawls is a participant, which tends to render his terms of reference even more ambiguous than they might otherwise be. A feminist reader finds it difficult not to keep asking: "Does this theory of justice apply to women, or not?"

This question is not answered in the important passages that list the characteristics that persons in the original position[18] are not to know about themselves, in order to formulate impartial principles of justice. In a subsequent article, Rawls has made it clear that sex is one of those morally irrelevant contingencies that is to be hidden by the veil of ignorance.[19] But throughout

A *Theory of Justice,* while the list of things unknown by a person in the original position includes

> his place in society, his class position or social status, ... his fortune in the distribution of natural assets and abilities, his intelligence and strength, and the like, ... his conception of the good, the particulars of his rational plan of life, [and] even the special features of his psychology ...[20]

"his" sex is not mentioned. Since the parties also "know the general facts about human society,"[21] presumably including the fact that it is structured along the lines of gender both by custom and by law, one might think that whether or not they knew their sex might matter enough to be mentioned. Perhaps Rawls means to cover it by his phrase "and the like," but it is also possible that he did not consider it significant.

The ambiguity is exacerbated by Rawls's statement that those free and equal moral persons in the original position who formulate the principles of justice are to be thought of not as "single individuals" but as "heads of families" or "representatives of families."[22] He says that it is not necessary to think of the parties as heads of families, but that he will generally do so. The reason he does this, he explains, is to ensure that each person in the original position cares about the well-being of some persons in the next generation. These "ties of sentiment" between generations, which Rawls regards as important in the establishment of his just savings principle, would otherwise constitute a problem, because of the general assumption that the parties in the original position are mutually disinterested. In spite of the ties of sentiment *within* families, then, "as representatives of families their interests are opposed as the circumstances of justice imply."[23]

The head of a family need not necessarily, of course, be a man. The very fact, however, that in com-

---

15 [Author's note] See Okin, "Women and the Making of the Sentimental Family," pp. 78–82.

16 [Author's note] *Theory*, pp. 251, 256.

17 [Author's note] Ibid., p. 459.

18 A hypothetical situation in which people are deprived of all knowledge of their personal and historical circumstances that are irrelevant to justice—they are behind "the veil of ignorance"—in order to ensure that any judgments they make about the proper structure of society will be appopriately impartial.

19 [Author's note] "Fairness to Goodness," *Philosophical Review* 84 (1975): 537. He says: "That we have one conception of the good rather than another is not

relevant from a moral standpoint. In acquiring it we are influenced by the same sort of contingencies that lead us to rule out a knowledge of our sex and class."

20 [Author's note] *Theory*, p. 137; see also p. 12.

21 [Author's note] Ibid., p. 137.

22 [Author's note] Ibid., pp. 128, 146.

23 [Author's note] Ibid., p. 128; see also p. 292.

mon usage the term "female-headed households" is used *only* in reference to households without resident adult males, tends to suggest that it is assumed that any present male adult takes precedence over a female as the household or family head. Rawls does nothing to dispel this impression when he says of those in the original position that "imagining themselves to be fathers, say, they are to ascertain how much they should set aside for their sons by noting what they would believe themselves entitled to claim of their fathers."[24] He makes the "heads of families" assumption only in order to address the problem of savings between generations, and presumably does not intend it to be a sexist assumption. Nevertheless, Rawls is effectively trapped by this assumption into the traditional mode of thinking that life within the family and relations between the sexes are not properly to be regarded as part of the subject matter of a theory of social justice.

Before I go on to argue this, I must first point out that Rawls states at the outset of his theory that the family *is* part of the subject matter of social justice. "For us" he says,

> the primary subject of justice is the basic structure of society, or more exactly, the way in which the major social institutions distribute fundamental rights and duties and determine the division of advantages from social cooperation.[25]

He goes on to specify "the monogamous family" as an example of such major social institutions, together with the political constitution, the legal protection of essential freedoms, competitive markets, and private property. The reason that Rawls makes such institutions the primary subject of his theory of social justice is that they have such profound effects on people's lives from the start, depending on where they find themselves placed in relation to them. He explicitly distinguishes between these major institutions and other "private associations," "less comprehensive social groups," and "various informal conventions and customs of everyday life,"[26] for which the principles

of justice satisfactory for the basic structure might be less appropriate or relevant. There is no doubt, then, that in his initial definition of the sphere of social justice, the family is included.[27] The two principles of justice that Rawls defends in Part I, the principle of equal basic liberty, and the difference principle combined with the requirement of fair equality of opportunity, are intended to apply to the basic structure of society. They are "to govern the assignment of rights and duties and to regulate the distribution of social and economic advantages."[28] Whenever in these basic institutions there are differences in authority, in responsibility, in the distribution of resources such as wealth or leisure, these differences must be both to the greatest benefit of the least advantaged, and attached to positions accessible to all under conditions of fair equality of opportunity.

In Part II, Rawls discusses at some length the application of his principles of justice to almost all of the major social institutions listed at the beginning of the book. The legal protection of freedom of thought and liberty of conscience is defended, as are just democratic constitutional institutions and procedures; competitive markets feature prominently in the discussion of the just distribution of income; the issue of the private or public ownership of the means of production is explicitly left open, since Rawls argues that justice as fairness might be compatible with certain versions of either. But throughout these discussions, the question of whether the monogamous family, in either its traditional or any other form, is a just social institution, is never raised. When Rawls announces that "the sketch of the system of institutions that satisfy the two principles of justice is now complete,"[29] he has still paid no attention at all to the internal justice of the family. The family, in fact, apart from passing references, appears in *A Theory*

---

24   [Author's note] Ibid., p. 289.

25   [Author's note] Ibid., p. 8.

26   [Author's note] Ibid., p. 7.

27   [Author's note] It is interesting to note that in a subsequent paper on the question why the basic structure of society is the primary subject of justice, Rawls does not mention the family as part of the basic structure. "The Basic Structure as Subject," *American Philosophical Quarterly* 14, no. 2 (April 1977): 159.

28   [Author's note] Theory, p. 61.

29   [Author's note] Ibid., p. 303.

of Justice in only three contexts: as the link between generations necessary for the savings principle, as a possible obstacle to fair equality of opportunity—on account of inequalities amongst families—and as the first school of moral development. It is in the third of these contexts that Rawls first specifically mentions the family as a just institution. He mentions it, however, not to *consider* whether or not the family "in some form" is a just institution, but to *assume* it. Clearly regarding it as important, Rawls states as part of his first psychological law of moral development: "given that family institutions are just...."[30]

Clearly, however, by Rawls's own reasoning about the social justice of major institutions, this assumption is unwarranted. For the central tenet of the theory is that justice characterizes institutions whose members could hypothetically have agreed to their structure and rules from a position in which they did not know which place in the structure they were to occupy. The argument of the book is designed to show that the two principles of justice as fairness are those that individuals in such a hypothetical situation would indeed agree upon. But since those in the original position are the heads or representatives of families, they are *not in a position to determine questions of justice within families*.[31] As far as children are concerned, Rawls makes a convincing argument from paternalism for their temporary inequality. But wives (or whichever adult member[s] of a family are *not* its "head") go completely unrepresented in the original position. If

families are just, as Rawls assumes, then they must *get* to be just in some different way (unspecified by Rawls) than other institutions, for it is impossible to see how the viewpoint of their less advantaged members ever gets to be heard.

There are two occasions where Rawls seems either to depart from his assumption that those in the original position are "family heads" or to assume that a "head of a family" is equally likely to be a woman as a man. In the assumption of the basic rights of citizenship, Rawls argues, favoring men over women is "justified by the difference principle ... only if it is to the advantage of women and acceptable from their standpoint."[32] Later, he seems to imply that the injustice and irrationality of racist doctrines are also characteristic of sexist ones.[33] But in spite of these passages, which appear to challenge formal sex discrimination, the discussions of institutions in Part II implicitly rely, in a number of respects, on the assumption that the parties formulating just institutions are (male) heads of (fairly traditional) families, and are therefore not concerned with issues of just distribution within the family. Thus the "head of family" assumption, far from being neutral or innocent, has the effect of banishing a large sphere of human life—and a particularly large sphere of most women's lives—from the scope of the theory.

First, Rawls's discussion of the distribution of wealth seems to assume that all the parties in the original position expect to be, once the veil of ignorance is removed, participants in the paid labor market. Distributive shares are discussed in terms of household income, but reference to "individuals" is interspersed into this discussion as if there were no difference between the advantage or welfare of a household and that of an individual.[34] This confusion obscures the fact that wages are paid to those in the labor force but that in societies characterized by a gender system (all current societies) a much larger proportion of women's than men's labor is unpaid, and is often not even acknowledged to be labor. It obscures the fact that such resulting disparities and the

---

30 [Author's note] *Theory*, p. 490. See Deborah Kearns, "A Theory of Justice—and Love; Rawls on the Family," *Politics* (Australasian Political Studies Association Journal) 18, no. 2 (November 1983): 30–40 for an interesting discussion of the significance of Rawls's failure to address the justice of the family for his theory of moral development.

31 [Author's note] As Jane English says, in a paper that is more centrally concerned with the problems of establishing Rawls's savings principle than with justice within the family *per se*: "By making the parties in the original position heads of families rather than individuals, Rawls makes the family opaque to claims of justice." "Justice between Generations," *Philosophical Studies* 31 (1977): 95.

32 [Author's note] *Theory*, p. 99.

33 [Author's note] Ibid., p. 149.

34 [Author's note] Ibid., pp. 270–274, 304–309.

economic dependence of women on men are likely to affect power relations within the household, as well as access to leisure, prestige, political office, and so on amongst its adult members. Any discussion of justice *within* the family would have to address these issues.

Later, too, in his discussion of the obligations of citizens, Rawls's assumption that justice is the result of agreement amongst heads of families in the original position seems to prevent him from considering an issue of crucial importance to women as citizens—their exemption from the draft. He concludes that military conscription is justifiable in the case of defense against an unjust attack on liberty, so long as institutions "try to make sure that the risks of suffering from these imposed misfortunes are more or less evenly shared by all members of society over the course of their life, and that there is no avoidable *class* bias in selecting those who are called for duty."[35] However, the issue of the exemption of women from this major interference with the basic liberties of equal citizenship is not even mentioned.

In spite of two explicit rejections of the justice of formal sex discrimination in Part I, then, Rawls seems in Part II to be so heavily influenced by his "family heads" assumption that he fails to consider as part of the basic structure of society the greater economic dependence of women and the sexual division of labor within the typical family, or any of the broader social repercussions of this basic gender structure. Moreover, in Part III, where Rawls *assumes* the justice of the family "in some form" as a given, although he has not discussed any alternative forms, he sounds very much as though he is thinking in terms of traditional, gendered family structure. The family, he says, is "a small association, normally characterized by a definite hierarchy, in which each member has certain rights and duties."[36] The family's role as moral teacher is achieved partly through parental expectations of "the virtues of a good son or a good daughter."[37] In the family and in other associations such as schools, neighborhoods, and peer groups, Rawls continues, one learns various moral virtues and ideals, leading

to those adopted in the various statuses, occupations, and family positions of later life. "The content of these ideals is given by the various conceptions of a good wife and husband, a good friend and citizen, and so on."[38] It seems likely, given these unusual departures from the supposedly generic male terms of reference used throughout the rest of the book, that Rawls means to imply that the goodness of daughters is distinct from the goodness of sons, and that of wives from that of husbands. A fairly traditional gender system seems to be assumed.

However, despite this, not only does Rawls, as noted above, "assume that the basic structure of a well-ordered society includes the family *in some form*." He adds to this the comment that "in a broader inquiry the institution of the family might be questioned, and other arrangements might indeed prove to be preferable."[39] But why should it require a broader inquiry than that engaged in *A Theory of Justice,* to ask questions about the institution of the family? Surely Rawls is right at the outset when he names it as one of those basic social institutions that most affects the life chances of individuals. The family is not a private association like a church or a university, which vary considerably in type, and which one can join and leave voluntarily. For although one has some choice (albeit highly constrained) about marrying into a gender-structured family, one has no choice at all about being born into one. Given this, Rawls's failure to subject the structure of the family to his principles of justice is particularly serious in the light of his belief that a theory of justice must take account of "how [individuals] get to be what they are" and "cannot take their final aims and interests, their attitudes to themselves and their life, as given."[40] For the family with its gender structure, female parenting in particular, is clearly a crucial determinant in the different socialization of the two sexes—in how men and women "get to be what they are."

If Rawls were to assume throughout the construction of his theory that all human adults are to be par-

---

35   [Author's note] Ibid., pp. 380–381 (emphasis added).
36   [Author's note] Ibid., p. 467.
37   [Author's note] Ibid., p. 468.

38   [Author's note] Ibid.
39   [Author's note] Ibid., pp. 462–63 (emphasis added).
40   [Author's note] "The Basic Structure as Subject," p. 160.

ticipants in what goes on behind the veil of ignorance, he would have no option but to require that the family, as a major social institution affecting the life chances of individuals, be constructed in accordance with the two principles of justice. I will develop this conclusion in the final section of the paper. But first I will turn to another recent theory of justice which is argued very differently from Rawls's, and poses another set of problems from a feminist point of view.

Justice In Its Separate Spheres

Michael Walzer's *Spheres of Justice* is remarkable amongst contemporary theories of justice for the attention that its author pays to sex- and gender-related issues.[41] From its largely non-sexist language to its insistence that the family constitutes a significant "sphere of justice" and its specific references to power imbalances between the sexes and discrimination, Walzer's theory stands out in contrast to most moral and political philosophers' continued indifference to feminist issues. Viewing the book through the prism of gender, however, accentuates both its strengths and its weaknesses. The theoretical framework of separate spheres that, in a just society, must allow for different inequalities to exist side by side without creating a situation of domination, has considerable force as a tool for feminist criticism. But I will argue that, to the extent that this criticism is developed and emphasized, it calls into question the cultural relativism that is so essential a part of Walzer's theory of justice. And to the extent that the relativism flourishes, it seriously blunts the impact of the theory's feminist potential.

At the beginning of *Spheres of Justice,* Walzer sets out the aims of his theory:

> I want to argue ... that the principles of justice are themselves pluralistic in form; that differ-

ent social goods ought to be distributed for different reasons, in accordance with different procedures, by different agents; and that all these differences derive from different understandings of the social goods themselves—the inevitable product of historical and cultural particularism.[42]

Within this brief summary are contained two criteria for justice, criteria that, I will argue, are not only quite distinct but in serious tension with each other. I will first summarize Walzer's "separate spheres" argument and his relativist or particularist position, and will then show how the conflict between them is readily apparent in the context of issues of gender and their justice or injustice.

It is one of Walzer's fundamental theses that justice does not require the equal distribution of social goods within their respective spheres but, rather, that these spheres of distribution be kept autonomous, in the sense that the inequality that exists within each should not be allowed to translate itself into inequalities within the others. In principle, both the monopoly by one or a few persons of a social good or goods within a single sphere, and the dominance of a good over the command of other goods outside of its sphere, are threats to social justice. But because of his conviction that monopoly is impossible to eliminate without continual state intervention,[43] Walzer concerns himself primarily with the elimination of dominance. His critique of dominance leads to the adoption of the distributive principle that "no social good x should be distributed to men and women who possess some other good y merely because they possess y and without regard to the meaning of x."[44] The result of the adoption of this principle would be a society whose justice consisted in the distribution of "different goods to different companies of men and women for different reasons and in accordance with different procedures."[45]

---

41   Michael Walzer (1935–) is professor emeritus at the Institute for Advanced Study in Princeton. He is a leading representative of the 'communitarian' position in political theory, which holds—in contrast to liberalism—that theories of justice must be grounded in the traditions and culture of particular societies (and hence that no abstract, universal account of justice is possible or desirable).

42   [Author's note] *Spheres*, p. 6.
43   [Author's note] Ibid., pp. 14–17.
44   [Author's note] Ibid., p. 20.
45   [Author's note] Ibid., p. 26.

This conception of justice as depending on the autonomy of the various spheres of distribution is presented by Walzer as "a critical principle—indeed, ... a radical principle."[46] A number of his specific applications of the principle—notably to the issue of worker ownership and control of all but small-scale enterprises[47]—confirm this view, and when we turn to the feminist implications of the separate spheres criterion of justice, we shall see that they, too, can be interpreted as establishing the need for radical social change. Walzer says that the standards for distribution that the criterion establishes

> are often violated, the goods usurped, the spheres invaded, by powerful men and women.
>
> In fact, the violations are systematic.... For all the complexity of their distributive arrangements, most societies are organized on what we might think of as a social version of the gold standard: one good or one set of goods is dominant and determinative of value in all the spheres of distribution. And that good or set of goods is commonly monopolized, its value upheld by the strength and cohesion of its owners.[48]

Having thus indicated the extent to which the "spheres of justice" criterion is commonly violated, Walzer goes on to show how ideology is used to legitimate such violations. Operating in the service of a group's claim to monopolize a dominant good, "its standard form is to connect legitimate possession with some set of personal qualities through the medium of a philosophical principle."[49] But Walzer regards ideologies, like conceptions of justice, as pluralistic. In his view, groups using different ideological principles to justify their dominance "compete with one another, struggling for supremacy. One group wins, and then a different one; or coalitions are worked out, and supremacy is uneasily shared. There is no final victory, nor should there be."[50] If this is an accurate depiction

of the past and present situation in our society, it softens the critical impact of Walzer's first criterion of justice, for it is difficult to see how the dominance and monopoly that he finds characteristic of most societies could coexist with genuinely competing pluralistic ideologies. But before examining it further, we must turn to his second criterion.

Walzer asserts clearly from the start that his theory of justice is highly relativist or, as he puts it, "radically particularist."[51] Beyond rights to life and liberty, he argues, men's and women's rights "do not follow from our common humanity; they follow from shared conceptions of social goods; they are local and particular in character."[52] "Justice" he says, "is relative to social meanings.... A given society is just if its substantive life is lived ... in a way faithful to the shared understandings of the members."[53] And since "social meanings are historical in character, ... distributions, and just and unjust distributions, change over time."[54]

In the course of establishing and emphasizing the cultural relativism of his theory of justice, Walzer takes issue with philosophers who "leave the city [to] fashion ... an objective and universal standpoint."[55] In particular, he argues with Rawls's development of a theory of justice that is not tied to a particular culture, that does not issue from the shared understandings or agreements of actual historical human beings with full knowledge of who they are and where they are situated in society. While he seems not to disagree that things would be decided by rational subjects behind the veil of ignorance much as Rawls concludes, he is unconvinced of the significance or force of the principles of justice agreed upon in such a situation for those same human beings once they are transformed into "ordinary people, with a firm sense of their own identity, with their own goods in their hands, caught up in everyday troubles." Would they "reiterate their hypothetical choice or even recognize it as their own [?]"[56] If conclusions about justice are to have

---

46   [Author's note] Ibid., p. 10.

47   [Author's note] Ibid., pp. 291–303.

48   [Author's note] Ibid., p. 10.

49   [Author's note] Ibid., p. 12.

50   [Author's note] Ibid.

51   [Author's note] Ibid., p. xiv.

52   [Author's note] Ibid., p. xv.

53   [Author's note] Ibid., p. 312–313.

54   [Author's note] Ibid., p. 9.

55   [Author's note] Ibid., p. xiv.

56   [Author's note] Ibid., p. 5; see also p. 79.

"force," they must be principles chosen not in some such hypothetical situation, but in answer to the question:

> What would individuals like us choose, who are situated as we are, who share a culture and are determined to go on sharing it? And this is a question that is readily transformed into, What choices have we already made in the course of our common life? What understandings do we (really) share?[57]

A distinct lack of critical perspective seems to be embodied in this highly relativist criterion for the justice of social arrangements and distributions. If all that Walzer were to mean by a conclusion's or a system's having "force" were that they were more readily *enforceable,* he would undoubtedly be right to reject Rawls's method. But he clearly means more than this. For he says that Rawls's formula for deciding principles of justice behind the veil of ignorance "doesn't help very much in determining what choices people will make, *or what choices they should make,* once they know who and where they are."[58] He means, then, that the principles of justice chosen in a Rawlsian manner do not have any particular *moral* force. To the contrary, it is only "when philosophers ... write out of a respect for the understandings they share with their fellow citizens [that] they pursue justice justly."[59]

A multitude of complexities, however, is contained within Walzer's reliance on "shared understandings." For he does not want to construct a theory of justice that is completely uncritical of whatever distributions take place and are justified within any given society. He says that the social vision he seeks is "*latent* already ... in our shared understandings of social goods," and that "the goal ... is a reflection of a special kind, which picks up *those deeper understandings* of social goods which are not necessarily mirrored in the everyday practice of dominance and monopoly."[60] But how is it to be determined which understandings we "(really) share," deep, latent, and not necessarily mirrored in our practices?

Walzer's reliance on two distinct criteria for justice—"the separate spheres" standard and the "shared understandings" or "social meanings" standard—creates considerable tension within his theory. There seems to be only one way of preventing the two criteria from yielding different conclusions about what is just, and that is to argue that our shared social understandings about issues of justice do in fact satisfy the criterion of "separate spheres." In spite of passages such as that quoted on p. 54 above, Walzer at times appears to believe this to be the case. He says that if a just or egalitarian society "isn't already here—hidden, as it were, in our concepts and categories—we will never know it concretely or realize it in fact," and adds that "our conceptions ... do tend steadily to proscribe the use of things for the purposes of domination."[61]

Walzer's two criteria for justice are subjected to most strain in relation to each other in the case of fundamentally hierarchical societies, those in which "dominance and monopoly are not violations but enactments of meaning, where social goods are conceived in hierarchical terms." He chooses feudal and caste societies, particularly the latter, in order to explore the challenge posed by such societies to his assumption that "social meanings call for the autonomy, or the relative autonomy, of distributive spheres."[62] Such systems, he says, are

> constituted by an extraordinary integration of meanings. Prestige, wealth, knowledge, office, occupation, food, clothing, even the social good of conversation: all are subject to the intellectual as well as to the physical discipline of hierarchy.[63]

The hierarchy itself is determined by a single value—in the case of the caste system, ritual purity, dominated by birth and blood—which dominates over the distribution of all other goods, so that "social meanings overlap and cohere,"[64] losing their autonomy.

---

57   [Author's note] Ibid., p. 5.
58   [Author's note] Ibid., p. 79 (emphasis added).
59   [Author's note] Ibid., p. 320.
60   [Author's note] Ibid., pp. xiv, 26 (emphasis added).

61   [Author's note] Ibid., pp. xiv–xv.
62   [Author's note] Ibid., p. 26.
63   [Author's note] Ibid., p. 27.
64   [Author's note] Ibid.

In such systems, Walzer says, the more perfect the coherence of social meanings, "the less possible it is even to think about complex equality" and "justice will come to the aid of inequality."[65] Nevertheless, as he must in measuring them against his "shared understandings" or "social meanings" criterion for justice, he asserts unambiguously that such societies can meet "(internal) standards of justice."[66] By this criterion, indeed, there are no grounds for concluding that caste societies are any less just than societies that do not discriminate on the basis of inborn status or characteristics.

Walzer writes of caste societies, with their undifferentiated social meanings, as if they were distant from anything that characterizes our culture. It is only on this assumption that he is able to perceive his two criteria for a just society as not seriously in conflict in the contemporary context. But when we read his description of caste society, in which an inborn characteristic determines dominant or subordinate status in relation to social goods over the whole range of spheres, it can be seen to bear strong resemblances to the gender system that our society has only begun to shed formally within the last century, and that it still perpetuates to a large extent through the force of its economic structure and custom, and the ideology inherited from its highly patriarchal past. There seem, in fact, to be only two significant differences between caste and gender hierarchies: one is that women have not been physically segregated from men; the other is that, whereas Walzer says that "political power seems always to have escaped the laws of caste,"[67] it has only rarely escaped the laws of gender. Like the caste hierarchy, the gender hierarchy is determined by a single value—sex—with maleness taking the place of ritual purity. Like the hierarchy of caste, that of gender ascribes roles, responsibilities, rights, and other social goods in accordance with an inborn characteristic that is imbued with tremendous significance. All the social goods listed in Walzer's description of a caste society have been, and many still are, differentially distributed to the members of the two sexes. In the cases of prestige, wealth, knowledge, office, and occupation, this statement is fairly obviously true, although the disparities between the sexes have begun to decline in some of them in recent years. Better and greater amounts of food are often reserved for men in poor classes and cultures, women's clothing has been and still is to a large extent designed either to constrict their movements or to appeal to men rather than for their own comfort and convenience, and women have been excluded from men's conversation in numerous social contexts, from ancient Greece to nineteenth- and twentieth-century after-dinner conversations and men's clubs.[68]

As in caste societies, ideology has played a crucial part in perpetuating the legitimacy of patriarchy. Though Walzer says in the context of caste society that "we should not assume that men and women are ever entirely content with radical inequality,"[69] ideology helps us to comprehend the extent to which they often have been and are content. Taking the gender system as an example, if the family is founded in law and custom on male dominance and female subordination and dependence, if religion inculcates the same hierarchy and enhances it with the mystical and sacred significance of a male god, and if the educational system not only excludes women from its higher reaches but establishes as truth and reason the same intellectual foundations of patriarchy, the opportunity for a competing ideology about sex and gender to arise is seriously limited. In fact, the ideology that is embodied in what has recently been termed "male-stream" thought is undoubtedly one of the most

---

65 [Author's note] Ibid., pp. 27, 313.

66 [Author's note] Ibid., p. 315.

67 [Author's note] Ibid., p. 27.

68 [Author's note] In a passage in which his nonsexist language strains credibility, Walzer says that "in different historical periods," dominant goods such as "physical strength, familial reputation, religious or political office, landed wealth, capital, technical knowledge" have each been "monopolized by some group of men and women" (*Spheres*, p. 11). In fact, men have monopolized these goods to the exclusion of women (and still monopolize some of the most important ones) to at least as great an extent as any group of men and women has monopolized them to the exclusion of any other group.

69 [Author's note] *Spheres*, p. 27.

all-encompassing and pervasive examples of ideology in history.[70]

Walzer relies, for the possibility of social change in general, on the flourishing of dissent. In most societies, even if

> the ideology that justifies the seizure [of social goods] is widely believed to be true, ... resentment and resistance are (almost) as pervasive as belief. There are always some people, and after a time there are a great many, who think the seizure is not justice but usurpation.[71]

But the closer the social system is to a caste system, in which social meanings "overlap and cohere," the less likely is the appearance or development of such dissent. The more thoroughgoing the dominance, and the more pervasive its ideology across the various spheres, the less chance there is that the whole prevailing structure will be questioned or resisted. By arguing that such a system can meet "(internal) standards of justice" if it is really accepted by its members, Walzer admits the paradox that the more *unjust* a system is by one of his criteria (in that dominance is all-pervasive within it) the more likely it is to be able to enshrine the ideology of the ruling group and hence to meet his other criterion (that it is in accord with shared understandings). The danger of his conception of justice is that what is just depends heavily on what people are persuaded of.[72]

Even if the social meanings in a fundamentally hierarchical society were shared, we should surely be wary of concluding, as Walzer clearly does, that the hierarchy was rendered just by the agreement or lack of dissent.[73] But what if the oppressors and the oppressed disagree fundamentally? What if the oppressors claim, as they often have, that aristocrats, or Brahmins,[74] or men are fully human in a way that serfs, or untouchables, or women are not, and that while the rulers institutionalize equal justice amongst themselves, it is just for them to require the other categories of people to perform functions supportive of the fully human existence of those capable of it? And what if the serfs or untouchables or women somehow actually do become convinced (against all the odds) that they too are fully human and that whatever principles of justice apply amongst their oppressors should rightfully be extended to them too? With disagreements this basic, rather than a meaningful debate being joined, there would seem to be two irreconcilable theories of justice. There would be no shared meanings on the most fundamental of questions.

This problem is rendered even more complex if there are fundamental disagreements not only between the oppressors and the oppressed, but even *within* the ranks of the oppressed. Contemporary views about the gender system are a clear example of such disagreement. As studies of feminism and antifeminism have shown, women themselves are deeply divided on the subject of the gender system, with antifeminist women not rejecting it as unjust, but regarding the continued economic dependence of women and the dominance of the world outside the home by men as natural and inevitable, given women's special reproductive functions.[75] Even amongst feminists, there has grown

---

70 [Author's note] This phrase was coined by Mary O'Brien in *The Politics of Reproduction* (London: Routledge and Kegan Paul, 1981).

71 [Author's note] *Spheres*, p. 12.

72 [Author's note] See Bernard Williams, "The Idea of Equality," in *Philosophy, Politics and Society* (Second Series), ed. Peter Laslett and W.G. Runciman (Oxford: Basil Blackwell, 1962), pp. 119–120, for a succinct discussion of social conditioning and the justification of hierarchical societies, critical of a position such as Walzer takes. Norman Daniels has recently criticized Walzer on this issue in a review of *Spheres of Justice,* in *The Philosophical Review* XCIV, no. 1 (January 1985): 145–146.

73 [Author's note] See Ronald Dworkin's review of *Spheres of Justice,* in *New York Review of Books* (April 14, 1983), pp. 4–5, and Walzer's response in *New York Review of Books* (July 21, 1983).

74 The highest caste in Hinduism: the class of educators, lawmakers, scholars, and preachers.

75 [Author's note] For a recent analysis of such attitudes, see Kristin Luker, *Abortion and the Politics of Motherhood* (Berkeley: University of California Press, 1984), esp. chap. 8. Feminists tend to attribute such attitudes in part at least to the influence of patriarchal ideology; it is clear that religion is an important factor. Such an

a rift in recent years between those who see the gender system itself as the problem and look forward to an androgynous society, and those who, celebrating women's unique nature and traditional roles, consider the problem to be not the *existence* of these roles but the *devaluation* of women's qualities and activities by a male-dominated culture.[76] These opposite poles of opinion about the very nature of sex difference and its appropriate social repercussions seem to provide no shared intellectual structure in which to debate distributions. And Walzer's theory of justice provides no criterion for adjudicating between them, aside from an appeal to some deeper, latent understandings which all supposedly hold, beneath their disagreements.

As I pointed out above, the coherence of Walzer's theory of justice depends on the compatibility of his two criteria of justice, which in turn depends upon whether the shared understandings of a society call for the autonomy of different distributive spheres. I have also suggested that contemporary society is still sufficiently pervaded by the caste-like gender system that fully characterized its past that it does not fulfill this condition.

While at times Walzer seems forgetful of our patriarchal history,[77] he sometimes shows clear awareness of its current manifestations. At the beginning of his chapter on recognition, for example, he states that the argument to follow applies only in part to women.

The extent to which women are still designated and defined by their position within the family, he says, is symbolized by the continued use of the titles "Miss" and "Mrs.": "the absence of a universal title suggests the continued exclusion of women, or of many women, from the social universe, the sphere of recognition as it is currently constituted."[78] But this point—that the argument applies only in part to women, or to a few women—is equally applicable to almost all of the other spheres of justice discussed in the book. Political power and office, hard work, money and commodities, security—is any of these things evenly distributed between the two sexes? Surely in each case, the explicit or implicit assignment of women to the functional role of actual or potential wife and mother and, as primary nurturer, to basic dependence upon a man, has a great deal to do with the fact that women are, in general, less benefited by the benefits and more burdened by the burdens, in the distribution of most social goods. While Walzer occasionally extends the feminist perspective he displays in the argument on recognition, and develops briefly a section entitled "The Woman Question," he frequently overlooks its implications.

Introducing his discussion of the oppression of women, Walzer argues that "the real domination of women has less to do with their familial place than with their exclusion from all other places." The family disfavors women by imposing sex-roles upon many activities "to which sex is entirely irrelevant." Liberation from this "political and economic misogyny" begins outside of the family. The market must set "no internal bar to the participation of women."[79] But, as he seems to imply, in the context of the example of nineteenth-century China, it cannot *end* outside: "The family itself must be reformed so that its power no longer reaches into the sphere of office" (or any of the other spheres of distribution, we might add).[80] On a number of occasions, both within his section

---

antifeminist posture becomes increasingly difficult to maintain consistently, once feminist reforms are instituted. For then, female proponents of it are faced with the problem of how they are to be successful in reversing political change while maintaining what they believe to be their proper, politically powerless role.

76   [Author's note] For a fair and lucid account of this division, see Iris Marion Young, "Humanism, Gynocentrism and Feminist Politics," *Hypatia: A Journal of Feminist Philosophy* no. 3, a special issue of *Women's Studies International Forum* 8, no. 3 (1985): 173–83. Gynocentric feminism faces a similar problem to that faced by antifeminism: How *can* women's work, concerns and perspectives come to be properly valued, unless women seek and attain power in the predominant, male realm?

77   [Author's note] See note [68] above.

78   [Author's note] *Spheres*, p. 252. See also William Safire, "On Language," and the Editors' response, *New York Times Magazine*, Sunday, August 5, 1984, pp. 8–10. In 1986, the *New York Times* finally agreed to use the term "Ms." in certain circumstances.

79   [Author's note] *Spheres*, pp. 240–241.

80   [Author's note] Ibid., p. 240.

on "The Woman Question" and elsewhere, Walzer criticizes the operation of the gender system outside of the family. But he pays almost no attention to its continued operation within.

This lacuna is certainly not attributable to a belief that justice is not an appropriate moral virtue for families. For Walzer, although he perceives the family as "a sphere of special relationships,"[81] also asserts plainly that "the sphere of personal relations, domestic life, reproduction, and child-rearing remains ... the focus of enormously important distributions,"[82] and where there are distributions, whether of responsibilities, rights, favors or goods, there is potential for justice and injustice. He does not, however, give this important sphere of distribution the attention it would seem to warrant. While all kinds of hard (undesirable but necessary) work done for wages are discussed at some length, virtually no attention is paid to all the unpaid work, much of it "hard" by his definition, that is done by women at home, and he refers only briefly to the immensely time-consuming activity of child care. If his argument were not in so many respects egalitarian, one might suppose that he accepted, as a less egalitarian thinker might, paid domestic labor for those who could afford it as the solution to these demands on wives and/or mothers who chose to work, to seek recognition, political power or office, and so on, in the outside world. But this is clearly not an acceptable solution, since he regards families with live-in servants as "inevitably ... little tyrann[ies]," and considers domestic service of any sort to be "degraded" work.[83] In an egalitarian society, at any rate, he considers that the market will raise the wages of unskilled workers much closer to those of skilled ones than at present, with the desirable result that workers will be much less likely to take on such degraded work.[84] To compound the problems of working couples with children, he disapproves of the communal care of young children as "likely to result in a great loss of love," except in a small, close-knit society such as the kibbutz.[85] This is reiterated in a passage in which he talks of children being "abandoned to bureaucratic rearing."[86]

How, then, is the unpaid work that is currently done almost entirely by women within the household to be done in a society that regards the family, and relations between the sexes in particular, as an appropriate sphere for the operations of justice? Walzer's answers to this question are so rapidly whisked over, in a clause and a footnote respectively, that they are easily missed. In the chapter on hard work—which is mostly concerned with hard wage work (also, as he points out, largely done by women)—he suggests that the only answer to hard, and particularly to dirty, work in a society of equals is that "at least in some partial and symbolic sense, we will all have to do it."[87] Otherwise, those who do it will be degraded by it and will never be equal members of the political community. "What is required, then, is a kind of domestic *corvée*,[88] not only in households—though it is especially important there—but also in communes, factories, offices, and schools."[89] Thus in a society of equals, "at least in some partial and symbolic sense," housework will be shared, regardless of sex. And, while child care is a different matter, since it hardly meets his negative definition of "hard work" (at least, most of the time), Walzer suggests the same solution. Parenthetically, in a footnote, he asks "(why can't the parents share in social *re*production?)"[90]

---

81   [Author's note] Ibid., p. 229.
82   [Author's note] Ibid., p. 242.
83   [Author's note] Ibid., p. 52.
84   [Author's note] Ibid., pp. 179–180.

85   [Author's note] Ibid., p. 233n.
86   [Author's note] Ibid., p. 238.
87   [Author's note] Ibid., p. 174.
88   *Corvée* is labor that someone can be compelled to perform unless this obligation is commuted in some way (such as by a cash payment). For example, the vassal of a medieval feudal lord might be obliged to work for a certain number of days plowing or harvesting his lord's land, or a nobleman might have to fight for the monarch in a time of war.
89   [Author's note] Ibid., p. 175.
90   [Author's note] Ibid., p. 233n. The importance of shared childrearing for justice between the sexes is not due to its being undesirable work, for in favorable circumstances it can be immensely challenging and pleasurable. It is the immensely time-consuming nature

With one important proviso,[91] I would affirm that these solutions (if the sharing is real and complete rather than symbolic) represent the only way in which the injustices inherent in the traditional gender-structured family can be done away with. Until the unpaid and largely unrecognized work of the household is shared equally by its adult members, women will not have equal opportunities with men either within the family or in any of the other spheres of distribution—from politics to free time, from recognition to security to money. This sharing is necessary if Walzer's separate spheres criterion for justice is to be met—if a society of equal men and women is to distribute its social goods in such a way that what happens within the family is not to dominate over, to invade, all the other spheres of justice. But, on the other hand (and perhaps this is why it is so rapidly brushed past in the argument),

---

of childrearing, and the everpresence of its demands, that make its just distribution essential. While Walzer asserts that free time is not readily convertible into other social goods (p. 184), I would strongly dissent. The kind of free time that one does *not* have when primarily or solely responsible for small children is translatable into many things, including education, career advancement and recognition, the pursuit of political office and wealth, as well as just plain leisure. On the other hand, those who do not share in parenting to a substantial extent could be said to suffer injustice in the sense that they miss out on its own special social rewards, the experiences of intimacy with and nurturing love for a child.

91 [Author's note] Walzer is too quick to dismiss day care for small children as a partial solution. Even a "mass society" does not have to provide "mass" day care. It can provide small-scale, loving day care for all if it cares enough and is prepared to subsidize the full costs for parents unable to afford them. Good day care, besides being a positive experience for the child, also helps to solve two other problems: without it, the shared parenting solution is of no help at all to single parents, of whom there are increasing numbers, mainly women; and good, subsidized day care can help to alleviate the obstacle that the inequality of family situation poses for equality of opportunity.

this solution constitutes a radical break not only from prevailing patterns of behavior but also from widely, though not completely, shared understandings of our society about the social meanings of sex and gender. It constitutes no less than the abolition of gender in its most entrenched bastion, with likely reverberations throughout all social spheres. Only if it could be argued that deep or latent in our shared current understandings lies the justification for the total abolition of gender could Walzer claim that his solution to sex inequality is just by his relativist criterion.

Thus the paradox of Walzer's theory of justice is strikingly exemplified by the theory's feminist implications. Insofar as the reduction of domination requires a thoroughgoing feminism that undermines the very roots of our gendered institutions, it is in considerable tension with the relativist requirement that a just society is one that abides by its shared understandings. And insofar as the latter criterion is applied, the feminist implications of the theory lose their force, on account of the deeply rooted attitudes about sex differences that we have inherited from our past and continue to imbibe from many aspects of our culture.

Women and Justice in Theory and Practice

I have argued that Walzer's requirement that justice be relative to "shared understandings" or "social meanings" tends to conflict with his "separate spheres" criterion of justice. It is also inadequate as a foundation for a moral theory. On some important issues in contemporary society—gender in particular—there are no fully shared understandings. To the extent that understandings are in fact shared in this or any existing society, their influence may be due to the past or present hegemony of certain groups over others. Moreover, divisions between conservative and radical standpoints on such issues may be so deep that they provide little foundation from which the different parties, *situated as they actually are,* can come to any conclusions about what is just. The significance of Rawls's central, brilliant idea of the original position, in which one's characteristics and position in society are not known, is that it forces one to question shared understandings from all points of view, and ensures that the principles of justice chosen are acceptable to everyone, regardless of what position he ends up in.

The problem for a feminist reader of Rawls's theory as stated by Rawls himself however, is encapsulated in that ambiguous "he." As I have shown above, while Rawls briefly rules out formal, legal discrimination on the grounds of sex (as on other grounds that he regards as "morally irrelevant"), he fails entirely to address the justice of the gender system, which—with its roots in the sex roles of the family and with its branches extending into virtually every corner of our lives—is one of the fundamental structures of our society. If, however, we read Rawls taking seriously both the notion that those behind the veil of ignorance are sexless persons, and the requirement that the family and the gender system—as basic social institutions—are to be subject to scrutiny, constructive feminist criticism of these contemporary institutions follows. So, also, do hidden difficulties for a Rawlsian theory of justice in a gendered society.

I will explain each of these points in turn. But first, both the critical perspective and the incipient problems of a feminist reading of Rawls can perhaps be illuminated by a description of a cartoon I saw a few years ago. Three elderly, robed male justices are depicted, looking down with astonishment at their very pregnant bellies. One says to the others, without further elaboration: "Perhaps we'd better reconsider that decision." This illustration points to several things. First, it graphically demonstrates the importance, in thinking about justice, of a concept like Rawls's original position, which makes us put ourselves into the positions of others—especially positions that we ourselves can never be in. Second, it suggests that those thinking in such a way might well conclude that more than formal legal equality of the sexes is required if justice is to be done. As we have seen in recent years, it is quite possible to institutionalize the formal legal equality of the sexes and at the same time to enact laws concerning pregnancy, abortion, maternity leave, and so on, that in effect discriminate against women, not as women *per se,* but as "pregnant persons." The U.S. Supreme Court decided in 1976, for example, that "an exclusion of pregnancy from a disability benefits plan ... providing general coverage

is not a gender-based discrimination at all."[92] One of the virtues of the cartoon is its suggestion that one's thinking on such matters is likely to be affected by the knowledge that one might become a "pregnant person." Finally, however, the illustration suggests the limits of what is possible, in terms of thinking ourselves into the original position, as long as we live in a gender-structured society. While the elderly male justices can, in a sense, imagine *themselves* pregnant, what is much more doubtful is whether, in constructing principles of justice, they can imagine themselves *women.* This raises the question whether, in fact, sex *is* a morally irrelevant and contingent human characteristic, in a society structured by gender.

Let us first assume that sex is contingent in this way, though I will later question this assumption. Let us suppose that it is possible, as Rawls clearly considers that it is, to hypothesize the moral thinking of representative human beings, ignorant of their sex and of all the other things that are hidden by the veil of ignorance. It seems clear that, while Rawls does not do this, we must consistently take the relevant positions of both sexes into account in formulating principles of justice. In particular, those in the original position must take special account of the perspective of women, since their knowledge of "the general facts about human society"[93] must include the knowledge that women have been and continue to be the less advantaged sex in a number of respects. In considering the basic institutions of society, they are more likely to pay special attention to the family than virtually to ignore it, since its unequal assigning of responsibilities and privileges to the two sexes and its socialization of children into sex roles make it, in its current form, a crucial institution for the preservation of sex inequality.

It is impossible to discuss here all the ways in which the principles of justice that Rawls arrives at are inconsistent with a gender-structured society. A general explanation of this point and three examples to illustrate it will have to suffice. The critical impact of a feminist reading of Rawls comes chiefly from his

---

92   [Author's note] *General Electric* vs. *Gilbert,* 429, U.S. 125 (1976).

93   [Author's note] *Theory,* p. 137.

second principle, which requires that inequalities be "to the greatest benefit of the least advantaged" and "attached to offices and positions open to all."[94] This means that if any roles or positions analogous to our current sex roles, including those of husband and wife, mother and father, were to survive the demands of the first requirement, the second requirement would disallow any linkage between these roles and sex. Gender, as I have defined it in this article, with its ascriptive designation of positions and expectations of behavior in accordance with the inborn characteristic of sex, could no longer form a legitimate part of the social structure, whether inside or outside the family. Three illustrations will help to link this conclusion with specific major requirements that Rawls makes of a just or well-ordered society.

First, after the basic political liberties, one of the most essential liberties is "the important liberty of free choice of occupation."[95] It is not difficult to see that this liberty is compromised by the assumption and customary expectation, central to our gender system, that women take far greater responsibility than men for housework and child care, whether or not they also work for wages outside the home. In fact, both the assigning of these responsibilities to women—resulting in their asymmetrical economic dependency on men—and also the related responsibility of husbands to support their wives, compromise the liberty of choice of occupation of both sexes. While Rawls has no objection to some aspects of the division of labor, he asserts that, in a well-ordered society, "no one need be servilely dependent on others and made to choose between monotonous and routine occupations which are deadening to human thought and sensibility" but that work can be "meaningful for all."[96] These conditions are far more likely to be met in a society which does not assign family responsibilities in a way that makes women into a marginal sector of the paid work force and renders likely their economic dependence upon men.

Second, the abolition of gender seems essential for the fulfillment of Rawls's criteria for political

justice. For he argues that not only would equal formal political liberties be espoused by those in the original position, but that any inequalities in the *worth* of these liberties (for example, the effects on them of factors like poverty and ignorance) must be justified by the difference principle. Indeed, "the constitutional process should preserve the equal representation of the original position to the degree that this is practicable."[97] While Rawls discusses this requirement in the context of *class* differences, stating that those who devote themselves to politics should be "drawn more or less equally from all sectors of society,"[98] it is just as clearly applicable to sex differences. And the equal political representation of women and men, especially if they are parents, is clearly inconsistent with our gender system.

Finally, Rawls argues that the rational moral persons in the original position would place a great deal of emphasis on the securing of self-respect or self-esteem. They "would wish to avoid at almost any cost the social conditions that undermine self-respect," which is "perhaps the most important" of all the primary goods.[99] In the interests of this primary value, if those in the original position did not know whether they were to be men or women, they would surely be concerned to establish a thoroughgoing social and economic equality between the sexes that would preserve either from the need to pander to or servilely provide for the pleasures of the other. They would be highly motivated, for example, to find a means of regulating pornography that did not seriously compromise freedom of speech. In general, they would be unlikely to tolerate basic social institutions that asymmetrically either forced or gave strong incentives to members of one sex to become sex objects for the other.

There is, then, implicit in Rawls's theory of justice a potential critique of gender-structured social institutions, which can be made explicit by taking seriously the fact that those formulating the principles of justice

---

94 [Author's note] Ibid., p. 302.

95 [Author's note] Ibid., p. 274.

96 [Author's note] Ibid., p. 529.

97 [Author's note] Ibid., p. 222; see also pp. 202–205, 221–228.

98 [Author's note] Ibid., p. 228.

99 [Author's note] Ibid., pp. 440, 396; see also pp. 178–179.

do not know their sex. At the beginning of my brief discussion of this feminist critique, however, I made an assumption that I said would later be questioned— that a person's sex is, as Rawls at times indicates, a contingent and morally irrelevant characteristic, such that human beings can hypothesize ignorance of this fact about them, imagining themselves as *sexless,* free and equal, rational, moral persons. First, I will explain why, unless this assumption is a reasonable one, there are likely to be further feminist ramifications for a Rawlsian theory of justice, as well as those I have just sketched out. I will then argue that the assumption is very probably not plausible in any society that is structured along the lines of gender. The conclusion I reach is that not only is the disappearance of gender necessary if social justice is to be enjoyed in practice by members of both sexes, but that the disappearance of gender is a prerequisite for the *complete* development of a nonsexist, fully human *theory* of justice.

Although Rawls is clearly aware of the effects on individuals of their different places in the social system, he regards it as possible to hypothesize free and rational moral persons in the original position who, freed from the contingencies of actual characteristics and social circumstances, will adopt the viewpoint of the "representative human being." He is under no illusions about the difficulty of this task, which requires "a great shift in perspective" from the way we think about fairness in everyday life. But with the help of the veil of ignorance, he believes that we can "take up a point of view that everyone can adopt on an equal footing," so that "we share a common standpoint along with others and do not make our judgments from a personal slant."[100] The result of this rational impartiality or objectivity, Rawls argues, is that, all being convinced by the same arguments, agreement about the basic principles of justice will be unanimous.[101] He does not mean that those in the original position will agree about *all* moral or social issues, but that complete agreement will be reached on all basic principles, or "essential understandings."[102] It is a crucial assumption of this argument for una-

nimity, however, that all the parties have similar motivations and psychologies (he assumes mutually disinterested rationality and an absence of envy), and that they have experienced similar patterns of moral development (they are presumed capable of a sense of justice). Rawls regards these assumptions as the kind of "weak stipulations" on which a general theory can safely be founded.[103]

The coherence of Rawls's hypothetical original position, with its unanimity of representative human beings, however, is placed in doubt if the kinds of human beings we actually become in society not only differ in respect of interests, superficial opinions, prejudices, and points of view that we can discard for the purpose of formulating principles of justice, but also differ in their basic psychologies, conceptions of self in relation to others, and experiences of moral development. A number of feminist scholars have argued in recent years that, in a gender-structured society, women's and men's different life experiences in fact affect their respective psychologies, modes of thinking, and patterns of moral development in significant ways.[104] Special attention has been paid to the effects on the psychological and moral development of both sexes of the fact, fundamental to our gendered

---

100 [Author's note] Ibid., pp. 516–517.

101 [Author's note] Ibid., pp. 139–141.

102 [Author's note] Ibid., pp. 516–517.

103 [Author's note] Ibid., p. 149.

104 [Author's note] Major works contributing to this thesis are Jean Baker Miller, *Toward a New Psychology of Women* (Boston: Beacon Press, 1976); Dorothy Dinnerstein, *The Mermaid and the Minotaur* (New York: Harper and Row, 1977); Nancy Chodorow, *The Reproduction of Mothering* (Berkeley: University of California Press, 1978); Carol Gilligan, *In a Different Voice* (Cambridge, MA: Harvard University Press, 1982); Nancy Hartsock, *Money, Sex, and Power* (New York: Longmans, 1983). Two of the more important individual papers are Jane Flax, "The Conflict between Nurturance and Autonomy in Mother-Daughter Relationships and within Feminism," *Feminist Studies* 4, no. 2 (Summer 1978); Sara Ruddick, "Maternal Thinking," *Feminist Studies* 6, no. *2* (Summer 1980). A good summary and discussion of "women's standpoint" is presented in Alison Jaggar, *Feminist Politics and Human Nature* (Totowa, NJ: Rowman and Allanheld, 1983), chap. 11.

society, that children of both sexes are primarily reared by women. It has been argued that the experience of individuation—of separating oneself from the nurturer with whom one is originally psychologically fused—is a very different experience for girls than for boys, leaving the members of each sex with a different perception of themselves and of their relations with others. In addition, it has been argued that the experience of *being* primary nurturers (and of growing up with this expectation) also affects the psychological and moral perspective of women, as does the experience of growing up in a society in which members of one's sex are in many respects subordinate to the other. Feminist theorists' scrutiny and analysis of the different experiences that we encounter as we develop, from our actual lived lives to our absorption of their ideological underpinnings, have in valuable ways filled out de Beauvoir's claim that "one is not born, but rather becomes, a woman."[105]

What is already clearly indicated by these studies, despite their incompleteness so far, is that in a gender-structured society there is such a thing as the distinct standpoint of women, and that this standpoint cannot be adequately taken into account by male philosophers doing the theoretical equivalent of the elderly male justices in the cartoon. The formative influence on small children of female parenting, especially, seems to suggest that sex difference is more likely to affect one's moral psychology, and therefore one's thinking about justice, in a gendered society than, for example, racial difference in a society in which race has social significance or class difference in a class society. The notion of the standpoint of women, while not without its own problems, suggests that a fully human moral theory can be developed only when there is full participation by both sexes in the dialogue that is moral and political philosophy. This will not come to pass until women take their place with men in the enterprise in approximately equal numbers and in positions of comparable influence. In a society structured along the lines of gender, this is most unlikely to happen.

In itself, moreover, it is insufficient for the complete development of a fully human theory of justice. For if principles of justice are to be adopted unanimously by representative human beings ignorant of their particular characteristics and positions in society, they must be persons whose psychological and moral development is in all essentials identical. This means that the social factors influencing the differences presently found between the sexes—from female parenting to all the manifestations of female subordination and dependence—would have to be replaced by genderless institutions and customs. Only when men participate equally in what has been principally women's realm of meeting the daily material and psychological needs of those close to them, and when women participate equally in what have been principally men's realms of larger scale production, government, and intellectual and creative life, will members of both sexes develop a more complete *human* personality than has hitherto been possible. Whereas Rawls and most other philosophers have assumed that human psychology, rationality, moral development and so on are completely represented by the males of the species, this assumption itself is revealed as a part of the male-dominated ideology of our gendered society.

It is not feasible to indicate here at any length what effect the consideration of women's standpoint might have on a theory of justice. I would suggest, however, that in the case of Rawls's theory, it might place in doubt some assumptions and conclusions, while reinforcing others. For example, Rawls's discussion of rational plans of life and primary goods might be focused more on relationships and less exclusively on the complex activities that his "Aristotelian principle" values most highly, if it were to encompass the traditionally more female parts of life.[106] On the other hand, those aspects of Rawls's theory, such as the difference principle, that seem to require a greater capacity to identify with others than is normally characteristic of liberalism, might be strengthened

---

105 [Author's note] Simone de Beauvoir, *The Second Sex* (1949; reprinted., London: New English Library, 1969), p. 9.

106 [Author's note] Brian Barry has made a similar, though more general, criticism of the Aristotelian principle in *The Liberal Theory of Justice* (Oxford: Oxford University Press, 1973), pp. 27–30.

by reference to conceptions of relations between self and others that seem in a gendered society to be more predominantly female.

In the earlier stages of working on this article, I thought mainly in terms of what justice has to say about gender, rather than about the effects of gender on justice. I looked at two recent theories of justice from this perspective, and found that although Walzer's focused far more attention on women's place in society, it was in fact Rawls's that could more consistently yield feminist principles of justice when the standpoint of women was taken into account. But, given the reliance of this latter theory on the agreement of representative human beings about the basic moral principles that are to govern their lives, I conclude that, while we can use it along the way to critique existing inequalities, we cannot complete such a theory of justice until the life experiences of the two sexes become as similar as their biological differences permit. Such a theory, and the society that puts it into practice, will be fundamentally influenced by the participation of both women and men in all spheres of human life. Not only is gender incompatible with a just society but the disappearance of gender is likely to lead in turn to important changes in the theory and practices of justice.

Philosophical Puzzles and Paradoxes

INTRODUCTION

Paradoxes and puzzles have played an important role in philosophy since the beginning of philosophical thought. They make us question our beliefs and pre-suppositions—often very basic ones. They don't always make us reject what we had taken for granted, but they do always subject it to scrutiny from a new and fascinating direction.

A paradox is an argument that appears to derive an absurd or obviously false conclusion by entirely valid reasoning from clearly acceptable premises. Sometimes philosophers argue that a premise is, despite appearances, actually false, or that the reasoning is actually invalid. Sometimes they argue that the premises and reasoning are fine, but the conclusion is true. Sometimes philosophers simply don't know what to do about a paradox. Any of these reactions is surprising, and may be of deep philosophical importance.

Puzzles are questions that seem like they ought to have a satisfying answer—but apparently do not. Philosophical reactions here include arguments for an (unobvious) solution, claims that there's something wrong with the unanswerable question in the first place, or, again, just puzzlement. Again, any of these reactions is surprising and can be instructive.

The puzzles and paradoxes presented here are almost all very well-known and widely discussed in the philosophical literature. We'll often include a brief indication of how, in general, philosophers have reacted. We have not included very much discussion of philosophical reactions, or bibliographies, but you won't have any trouble finding these on the Internet. We have also little to say about philosophical implications. What we aim at here is to give you enough of an introduction to each puzzle or paradox to stimulate your own philosophical intelligence—to get you to think about these brain-twisters on your own—and

we're confident you'll often find this engaging, enlightening, and fun.

BARBER PARADOX

Imagine a town in which there's a (male) barber who shaves all the men who don't shave themselves, and only those men. Does he shave himself? The answer can't be yes—because he doesn't shave men who shave themselves. The answer can't be no—because he does shave all the men who don't shave themselves. This paradox is resolved by concluding that there can't be a town with a barber who is the way we're trying to imagine.

BERTRAND'S BOX PARADOX

Imagine three boxes, each containing two drawers. In one box, both drawers contain a gold coin. (Call this box GG.) In another box, both drawers contain a silver coin. (Call this box SS.) In the third box, one drawer has a gold coin, the other has a silver. (Call this box GS.) You pick a box at random, open one drawer, and find a gold coin. What's the probability the other drawer in that box contains a silver coin? (Stop now and try to answer.)

Here's how most people reason. You've got a gold coin, so that means that the box you picked isn't SS. It's equally likely—50%—to be GG or GS. So the likelihood that the other coin is silver is 50%.

But that's wrong. What you've got might be (1) drawer G of GS; (2) drawer G1 of GG; (3) drawer G2 of GG. The probability of each of these is equal:

33%. So the probability the other drawer has a silver coin is the probability of outcome (1): 33%.

BLACKMAIL PARADOX

It's neither illegal nor immoral to ask somebody for money. It's neither illegal nor immoral to threaten to expose somebody's theft. But it's both illegal and immoral to ask somebody for money, threatening that if you don't get the money, you'll expose their theft.

This is a paradox only if you accept the principle that if it's not illegal (or immoral) to do X, and it's not illegal (or immoral) to do Y, then it's not illegal (immoral) to do X and Y. But that's clearly a false principle. There are plenty of counter-examples. It's not illegal (or immoral) for example to drink, or to drive, but it is illegal to drink-and-drive (and probably immoral too, because of the increased risk of a damaging accident).

What is illegal (and immoral) in the blackmail case is not merely doing both actions—I might threaten to expose your theft, and also, unconnectedly, ask you for money—but to do both with a particular connection between them. What connection? What's the general principle here?

BURIDAN'S ASS

Imagine an ass (come on now, we mean a donkey) who is very hungry and very thirsty, and is placed equidistant between equal quantities of hay and water. If we assume that the ass is determined to choose by a variety of factors (more hungry or thirsty?; which hunger/thirst remover is nearer?; which is larger?), since all these are equal, nothing would cause the ass to go to one or the other; so it would stay stuck in the middle and starve to death.

Some philosophers argue that because this could never happen, decisions (even from an ass) cannot be fully determined in this fashion: there must be an arbitrary—free—element that's at least capable of resolving ties. (This free element is supposedly of primary importance in human decisions.) Others argue, however, that this sort of paralysis between equally attractive options could happen, but rarely does because such perfect equality is so uncommon.

THE CIRCLE THAT'S A STRAIGHT LINE

As the radius of a circle gets larger and larger, the curvature of the circle gets less and less. A circle with infinite radius would thus be a straight line!

Sometimes it's said that we should accept this odd result, and that it's just one of the odd things that happen when infinite magnitudes are imagined. (See, for example, the St. Petersburg Paradox, below.) Others point out that this would be true only if space is Euclidian—which it isn't, in fact.

CURRY'S PARADOX

Consider this sentence, which we'll call 'S':

If S is true, then Santa Claus exists.

Is S true? Well, suppose for the moment it is. Now we have the antecedent of the true conditional statement S, so the consequent follows: Santa Claus exists. When we assume S is true we derive Santa Claus exists, and this is the standard way to prove the truth of a conditional statement. So we've just proven If S is true then Santa Claus exists. But this is Statement S; so it follows that Santa Claus exists.

What's wrong here is not a matter of whether you're a Santa-believer or not. It's that this kind of reasoning can be used to prove any arbitrary proposition. What has gone wrong? Briefly, we can see the problem here as one of many odd consequences of allowing self-referential statements. (Statement S mentions itself.) See also, among others, Grelling's Paradox and The Liar Paradox.

DETERRENCE PARADOX

Think back to when the cold war between the US and the USSR was raging. Both countries had hundreds of nuclear warheads aimed at each other's cities. Each warned the other that the other's first strike would result in massive retaliation, in which hundreds of cities would be devastated and millions of innocent civilians killed and injured.

The aim here on both sides was preventing war, and in hindsight it seems we can say it was an astoundingly successful strategy. It's hard to find any other instances in history in which a face-off between powerful armed enemies did not result in major war.

But there are other moral considerations to raise here besides the morally laudable aim of preventing war. When one side threatens retaliation, it is announcing its intention to commit an absolutely horrible act. Is an intention to commit a hugely immoral act under certain circumstances itself immoral, even though—thankfully—those circumstances never come about?

Imagine that back then accidentally or on purpose the USSR bombed one or more US cities. Then what? The US would have had to choose whether to go forward with its threatened massive and unspeakably horrible retaliation on the USSR. That would have been in itself hugely immoral—it would have made things much worse than they already were, and would have been completely without any possible good effect. (At that point, nobody would have been deterred from anything.) If the US government had had any shred of morality left at that point, it would not have retaliated.

But surely the Soviet planners knew that the US people would have been thinking this way, and in fact would not have retaliated. (And vice versa: the US planners knew this about the Soviets.) If so, everyone would have known that all the threats of retaliation were empty.

To give retaliation-threats some force, in a situation like this, there would have to be some mechanism that unleashed retaliation automatically, no matter what the attacked side wanted to do then. (This is the "Doomsday Machine" imagined in the great movie *Doctor Strangelove*.) But then, having suffered a first strike from side B, horrible, useless, immoral retaliation would be unavoidable, whatever side A did—and they set it up to be this way!

GRELLING'S PARADOX

A couple of definitions:

- an adjective is homological if it describes itself.
- an adjective is heterological if it doesn't.

The adjective 'short' is homological because it's short. The adjective 'German' is heterological: it's not German—it's English.

Now consider the adjective 'heterological.' Which category does it go into? Is it heterological? If it is, then it doesn't describe itself; but if 'heterological' doesn't describe it, then it isn't heterological. So if it is heterological, then it isn't.

Is it then homological? If it is, then it does describe itself, but if 'heterological' describes itself, then it isn't homological. So if it is homological, then it isn't.

Either way, we get a self-contradiction. Another paradox resulting from self-reference; this one was formulated in 1908 by German mathematician Kurt Grelling. (See Russell's Paradox, below, which is analogous.)

GRUE (GOODMAN'S NEW RIDDLE OF INDUCTION)

Definitions:

- Time T is midnight on New Year's Eve at the end of the year 2020.
- X is grue provided that (a) it's T or earlier, and X is green; or (b) it's later than T, and X is blue.
- X is bleen provided that (a) it's T or earlier, and X is blue; or (b) it's later than T, and X is green.

All the emeralds we've seen so far have been green, so (because it's not yet T), they've also been grue. Ordinary scientific reasoning predicts the future on the basis of past observation, so we predict that after T, emeralds will still be green. But this sort of reasoning also predicts that after T emeralds will still be grue. But after T, something that's still green won't be grue any longer—it will have turned bleen overnight! It order to stay grue, it would have to turn blue.

A common reaction to this problem is to try to explain why 'grue' and 'bleen' are illegitimate properties to do science with. But what's wrong with them? The way we have defined them, they seem unlike regular color properties, in that their definitions include mention of time. Scientists who wanted to see whether things stayed grue around time T would have to keep checking their watches. But note that this is just a matter of the way we've been putting things. We could just as well have taken 'grue' and 'bleen' as the real color properties, and defined 'blue' and 'green' in terms of these, plus time T. (See if you can produce these definitions.) And a grue/bleen perceiving scientist would look at an emerald at time T, and might say, without consulting a watch, 'Yep, it stayed grue okay!' or 'Jeez! It suddenly turned bleen!'

HARMING THE DEAD

Imagine your best friend gives you a shirt which you hate, but you wear occasionally when you see her, so as not to insult. If she knew you hated it, she'd be upset, and you don't want that. But now your friend has died. You still think very kindly of her memory, but is it okay to throw away that awful shirt now? The answer seems to be yes. After all, the only morally relevant thing here is that you not hurt her feelings. That would be harming her. But after death, people can't be harmed.

But now consider other things that might be done to "harm the dead." Suppose you maliciously do what you can to destroy the good reputation of someone now dead. A lot of people think that there's something wrong with this. But what? Sometimes it's thought that the morality of actions regarding others isn't all a matter of helping or harming them, because this never applies to the dead. So what other moral considerations are relevant for "dealing with" dead people? and why?

HERACLITUS' PARADOX

The paradox associated with this ancient Greek philosopher is the claim that you can't step into the same river twice. Why not? Because at every instant, the water that makes up this section of the river (or the river as a whole, for that matter), changes.

What this shows, of course, is that identical water is not the basis for the same river. What then is? Note that the same sort of question might be raised with regard to the "same" anything, which (almost) always changes, to some small or large degree, over time.

HOTEL INFINITY
(HILBERT'S HOTEL)

David Hilbert was a pioneer in the mathematical treatment of infinity. He illustrated one way that notion introduces strange results by asking us to imagine a hotel with an infinite number of rooms, all completely booked for the night. A traveler arrives, asking for a room—a request that would be denied by an ordinary completely-booked hotel—but in Hilbert's Hotel, matters are easily solved: the guests in room 1 are asked to move to room 2, while those in room 2, move to room 3, and those in 3 to room 4, and so on. This leaves room 1 empty for the arrivals.

HYPOTHETICAL DESIRE
PARADOX

If you're right-handed, you'd probably assent to this:

If I have to lose an arm, I want to lose my left arm.

Now imagine that, unfortunately, the antecedent of this conditional (hypothetical statement) becomes true: you have to lose one arm. Given the truth of the conditional, it follows by very elementary logic that You want to lose your left arm. But wait! That's hardly true. You don't want to lose either arm! Is this a counter-example to the very basic logical principle called modus ponens: If P then Q; P; therefore Q?

Instead of rejecting modus ponens, it has been suggested, we might understand that original proposition not as "If P then I want X," but rather, "I want: (If P then X)." From P and the latter, X does not follow. But now we need a logic to distinguish hypothetical desires from desires for hypotheticals.

LIAR PARADOX

(EPIMENIDES' PARADOX)

Suppose Fred says, "I'm lying right now." Is he telling the truth? Well, telling the truth isn't lying, so he isn't lying. But what he says is that he is lying, so if he's telling the truth he is lying. On the other hand, if he's not telling the truth, then ... well the same kind of self-negating puzzle emerges. Turns out the assumption that Fred's statement is true and that it's false both imply self-contradictions.

There are many versions of this sort of paradox. Another one frequently seen is the Postcard Paradox: on one side of a postcard, it says, "What's written on the other side is false." On the other side, it says, "What's written on the other side is true." See if you can work out how there isn't any way to assign truth and falsity here.

And another variant is this book title:

There Are Two Errors in the
the Title of this Book

The Liar Paradox is one of the most basic and oldest versions of a self-referential paradox. It's sometimes called the Epimenides' Paradox, after the ancient Cretan philosopher who wrote that all Cretans (probably intending to exclude himself) were liars. There has been a great deal written ever since in the attempt to try to cope with self-reference. One major tack has been to try to find a way in principle to rule out self-reference (without making arbitrary restrictions).

LOTTERY PARADOX

Imagine a lottery that will randomly draw one winning ticket from a million tickets. It's unreasonable to believe that the ticket you hold—number 439,664—will win, and you believe it won't win. But it's also unreasonable to believe that number 439,665 will win, and to believe that 439,666 will win, and so on, for every one of the million tickets. So for each of the tickets, you completely reasonably believe it won't win. But you also believe, completely reasonably again, that one of the million will win. So your set of a million and one completely reasonable beliefs is inconsistent.

One sort of reply points out that ground-floor inconsistency of belief requires a belief that P and a belief that not-P; but that's not what we have here, unless we believe a principle of agglomeration: that if you believe Q and you believe R, then you do (or should) believe (Q and R). Some sort of principle of this type is very attractive, but perhaps needs to yield here.

MONTY HALL PARADOX

Loosely based on the TV gameshow of which Monty Hall was the emcee, the question is this:

You're presented with three doors, and told that one hides a valuable car, the other two each a worthless goat. You pick a door at random. Then Monty, the emcee, knowing what's behind the other two, picks one that hides a goat, and opens it, revealing the contents. Now he asks you: do you want to stick to your door or switch to the contents of the remaining closed door?

This widely-publicized problem got wrong answers from a huge variety of people including many mathematicians. They reasoned: you've picked (say) Door A: Door C is opened to reveal a goat. Now it's 50/50 whether the car is behind your door or behind door B. If there's any advantage to sticking to door A (e.g., you're offered $100 to stay put) you should do so; but otherwise there's no reason to stay put or switch.

The correct (but widely disbelieved) answer is this: there's 1/3 probability that Door A, the one you picked first, has the car, thus 2/3 that the car is behind one of Door B or Door C. Monty knows what's back there, and he picks one of (or the only) door hiding a goat (say Door C) and opens it. But there's still a 2/3 chance that a door you haven't picked—only Door B now—has the car; and a 1/3 chance that Door A has it. So you'll double your chances by switching.

(See also the related Bertrand's Box Paradox, above.)

MORAL LUCK

Fred and Barney are both at a party at Wilma's house, and both of them are drinking way more than they should, given that each will be driving himself home. When the booze runs out and Wilma kicks both of them out, they each get in their cars, and attempt to drive to their homes. They're barely capable of steering effectively, and both frequently swerve onto the wrong side of the road. Fred is stopped by the police half-way home, and is charged (and eventually convicted) of driving under the influence. He pays a large fine, and has his license suspended for a year. Barney is unlucky, however: while driving on the opposite side of the road, his car collides head-on with one coming the other way, killing its driver. Barney is convicted of second-degree murder, and is sentenced to a very long jail term.

What Fred and Barney did was significantly similar. Both drank far too much at the party, given that they intended to drive themselves home. Both drove themselves, at great risk, despite knowing that they had drunk too much. Both were swerving all over the road. The difference was merely a matter of luck: Fred didn't crash into anything, and the property and persons of others were unharmed, but unluckily for Barney, an oncoming car just happened to be there just where he swerved off of his side of the road.

Everyone feels that Barney's more to blame than Fred is, and that his much more severe legal punishment was entirely justified. But the difference between his case and Fred's was entirely out of either's control: one was comparatively lucky, the other wasn't. How can we distribute moral blame and judicial punishment differently on the basis of this sort of luck (or un-luck)? But we do it all the time.

NEWCOMB'S PARADOX

Imagine a really smart computer, able to predict people's responses almost perfectly having been fed information about their personality and background. This computer presents you with a choice involving two boxes, Box A and Box B. You can choose to take either the contents of Box B alone, or else what's in Box A plus what's in Box B. In Box A there is $10,000, and it's transparent, so you can see the big pile of $100 notes sitting inside. The contents of Box B, you're told, however, depends on the computer's prediction of what you're going to do. If it has predicted that you'll take Box B alone, it has already put $1 million in Box B. If it has predicted that you'll take Box A plus Box B, it has put nothing into Box B. Should you take what's in Box B alone, or what's in both boxes? There are two lines of reasoning that attempt to answer this question.

(1) At the time you must decide, the computer has already set up what's in Box B—maybe nothing or maybe $1 million. Anyway, your decision won't cause a change in what's in there. You can take whatever's in Box B alone, or else that plus the $10,000 in Box A. Maybe there's a million in Box B, maybe nothing; either way, you'd get $10,000 more by taking both boxes, so do it.

(2) The computer, remember, is almost always right in its predictions. That means that if you take both boxes, it almost certainly has predicted that, and put nothing in Box B, and you'll get $10,000. But if you take just Box B, it almost certainly has predicted that, and put $1 million in Box B, so you'll get a million. Go with the probabilities. Take just Box B.

This interesting problem has resulted in a lot of response. Reactions are divided between advocating strategy (1) and advocating strategy (2), and there are interesting implications for decision theory about which strategy might be the right one.

OMNISCIENCE PROOF OF GOD'S EXISTENCE

God is often conceived of as omniscient—that is, all-knowing. That means that He knows everything that's the case. Maybe we'd like to express that fact this way:

For all propositions P (P is true if and only if God knows that P).

The trouble is that this seems to presuppose the existence of God, so atheists wouldn't accept it. Let's reformulate it more neutrally:

For all propositions P (P is true if and only if, if God existed, God would know that P).

That sounds unexceptionable. Now, if that's true for all propositions, it's true in particular for the proposition, God exists. So we can infer:

'God exists' is true if and only if, if God existed, God would know that he exists.

Consider the second part of that sentence:

if God existed, God would know that he exists.

Nobody, it seems—atheist or believer—could deny this. After all, if anybody exists, he'd know that he exists, right?

But when you have a true sentence made of two parts connected by 'if and only if,' and when one of those parts is true, it follows that the other is true. So from the truth of the second part of that sentence, we can validly infer the truth of the first part:

'God exists' is true.

Or, putting the same thing more briefly,

God exists.

The reason there has to be something wrong in this reasoning is not that there isn't any God. The reason is that we appear to be pulling a proof of God's existence out of thin air—something atheists and believers alike should be suspicious of. What, exactly, has gone wrong here?

THE PREFACE

If you find out that what you say or believe is inconsistent, you shouldn't rationally continue to say or believe that: you should try to fix it, right? It's irrational to allow to stand what you know is an inconsistent set of statements one makes or beliefs one has, right? Wrong and wrong. Here's why.

Often one finds in the preface of a book the modest statement that the book surely contains errors, but that these are the fault of the author, not of the numerous people thanked for help in writing the book.

Now consider the set of sentences consisting of everything stated in book B, including the statement in its preface, "There's at least one error in here." It's logically impossible that this whole set is true. Here's why. If the preface-statement is true, then there's at least one false statement elsewhere in the set. But if the preface is false, then again the whole set isn't true. That set is what logicians call a logically inconsistent set: one such that it's logically impossible that everything in it is true.

Never mind about books and their prefaces. Everyone who is a clear thinker and who doesn't have inappropriately and ridiculously inflated views about his own omniscience knows that some of his many beliefs—one hopes not many, but some anyway—must be false. This is a rational thing to believe. Rational, but rendering one's whole belief set logically inconsistent.

PRISONER'S DILEMMA

You and your buddy are arrested for a major crime; the police know you both did it, but have evidence only good enough for convictions on a rather trivial charge. So they put you two in separate cells, and offer you a deal: your sentence will depend on whether or not you confess, implicating yourself and the other guy, and on what your buddy does when offered the same deal. The following chart summarizes how this works, specifies the years in jail you will serve under all four eventualities.

	He confesses	He stays silent
You confess	7 years	1 year
You stay silent	10 years	3 years

The best outcome for you is confession—if he stays silent. But he's offered the same deal, so his best deal is confession, while you stay silent. And if both of you confess, you'll both be badly off.

It seems that what's best for both of you would be to both keep quiet; you'd each get your second-best possible outcome, but you'd both avoid other possible disasters. If there were a way of making an enforceable and effective deal that both of you would keep silent, this would be good. But there isn't.

Under the circumstances, then, it seems that the most rational thing for you to do is to confess. Whatever he does, you'll come out better than if you stayed silent. This, however, is the most rational choice for the other guy as well. So if both of you do what's rational, both will get seven years in jail—next to the worst of the four possibilities. It seems that there's something irrational about doing what's most rational.

This little story can be taken as a simplified model for a wide range of social situations: competition vs. cooperation between individuals, and between nations. Psychologists and social and ethical philosophers have had a lot to say about it.

PROTAGORAS' PARADOX

The famous ancient Greek philosopher Protagoras taught law to Euathlus, with the agreement that Euathlus would pay Protagoras tuition fees if he won his first case; but if he lost, he wouldn't have to pay. Euathlus finishes his education, sets himself up as a lawyer, but for some reason takes on no cases. Finally, Protagoras gets fed up, and sues Euathlus for the money.

Protagoras points out that he's suing for the fees, so if he wins, Euthalus would have to pay, and if he loses, Euthalus wouldn't have to. But Euathlus reminds the court of the contract for payment: if he wins his first case, he pays the tuition; if he loses he doesn't. And this, of course, is his first case.

So who is right?

(Also called The Lawyer, Euathlus, the Paradox of the Court.)

THE QUESTION PARADOX

An angel visits the Annual Meetings of the American Philosophical Association, and tells the philosophers there that they will be given the gift of asking God exactly one question, and that God in His omniscience will answer it.

There is a good deal of debate about what is the one question to ask. "What is the meaning of life?" is ruled out as too vague, and as very likely to have an unsatisfying answer. "How do you best remove red wine stains from a light-colored carpet?" is a question whose answer many philosophers have an interest in, but in the end it's thought too trivial for such a great opportunity. There's some enthusiasm for asking "What is the most important question we could ask, and what is its answer?" but there's a worry this might be counted as two questions. A logician suggests they avoid this potential difficulty by converting this to one question: "What is the ordered pair consisting of (a) the most important question that could be asked and (b) the answer to that question?"

The angel appears, is asked this question, and five minutes later returns with God's answer: "The most important question you could ask is 'What is the ordered pair consisting of (a) the most important question that could be asked and (b) the answer to that question?' and the answer to that question is what I'm saying now."

RAVEN PARADOX

This famous paradox challenges two seemingly obvious assumptions: (1) that scientific generalizations are confirmed by observation of instances of them (e.g., that 'All ravens are black' is confirmed a little every time an additional black raven is observed); and (2) that if some observation O confirms generalization G, and G is logically equivalent to H, then O must also confirm H (because, after all, when two statements are logically equivalent, they say the same thing—anything that makes one true (or false) does the same to the other).

G: All non-black things are non-ravens is logically equivalent to H: All ravens are black. The observation of a yellow pencil confirms G, but it surely does not seem to confirm H. (Otherwise H would be confirmed by the uncountable number of observations of non-black non-ravens everyone makes all the time.)

Maybe, on the other hand, you might want to insist that that pencil does confirm (to an extremely tiny degree) the raven generalization. Or else, you might want to explore the idea that scientific confirmation is not at all merely a simple matter of observations of instances of a generalization.

RUSSELL'S PARADOX

Think of a class in the technical sense involved here as a collection of things that share a common attribute. Some classes are not members of themselves: the class of poodles, for example, is not itself a poodle.

Call these classes non-self-inclusive. Some classes are members of themselves: examples are the class of non-poodles (which is itself not a poodle), or the class of things with more than five members, which itself has more than five members. Call these classes self-inclusive.

Now consider the class of non-self-inclusive classes. It contains poodles, planets, and so on, but is it a member of itself? Try two answers:

YES: but since it's the class of non-self-inclusive classes, if it's a member of itself, then it's non-self-inclusive, so it doesn't include itself.

NO: but if it's not in there, it must be in the class of self-inclusive classes; so it does include itself.

Bertrand Russell discovered this paradox in 1901, and shortly thereafter told the great logician Frege about it. Frege realized that this paradox showed that two very basic axioms used in his book on formal logic, about to be published, were inconsistent. There has been a great deal of consideration about the implications of Russell's Paradox ever since. (See Grelling's Paradox, above, which is analogous.)

RUSSELL'S PROOF OF GOD'S EXISTENCE

The next time you're driving around, take a look at the first license plate number you see: it's EJR 036 (or whatever). What are the odds against seeing exactly that license plate number, out of all the possible ones, just then? They're minuscule, one out of several million or more. It's a miracle! God must exist.

This "proof" was cooked up by Bertrand Russell, who was a well-known atheist and of course had his tongue firmly planted in his cheek. Of course this goes no way toward proving God's existence. But the interesting question it raises is: why exactly is seeing that license plate not a hugely unlikely—almost miraculous—event?

SAYING WHAT YOU MEAN

Can you say, "Gloob! Gloob! Gloob!" but mean, It's snowing in Tibet? No? Why not?

SHIP OF THESEUS

According to ancient Greek legend, Theseus kept repairing the ship of which he was captain while at sea, replacing, one at a time, old rotten planks with new sound ones. When this process was complete, there was not a single bit of the ship that was there at the start of the voyage. Is the ship Theseus returned in the same one as the one he started out in? If yes, then how come? If no, then what happened to the old one?

In the seventeenth century, Thomas Hobbes added a wrinkle to this story by imagining further that Theseus kept all the old rotten lumber, and eventually a (pretty useless) ship was constructed out of this. At that point there are two ships: the one made of new, sound lumber, and the one made of rotten old planks. Which is the one Theseus began his voyage in?

SIMPSON'S PARADOX

In basketball, you get two points for a basket shot from closer in, 3 points from further out. The following table lists successes/attempts at 2- and 3-point shots made during a season by two players, Wilt Jordan and Michael Chamberlain:

	Jordan	Chamberlain
2 pt	200 / 400: 50%	440 / 950: 46.3%
3 pt	80 / 320: 25%	30 / 190: 15.8%

As you can see, Jordan's average is better at scoring on attempted 2-point shots and 3-point shots. That implies that Jordan is better at making shots altogether, right? Wrong. Here are the totals:

Jordan	Chamberlain
280 / 720: 38.9%	470 / 1140: 41.2%

Check the arithmetic yourself: there's no trick here. This sort of counterintuitive result is quite common in statistics. It was brought to wide attention by a mathematician named E.H. Simpson.

SORITES' PARADOX

A person 7 feet high is definitely tall. Subtract a ¼ inch from this, and consider a person 6 feet 11¾ inches high: that person is definitely tall too. Now imagine a series of subtractions, each of ¼ inch; is there a height H in this series such that a person of height H is tall, but a person of height (H–¼") is not tall? It seems not. If you think there is, try to specify that height, and see if you can get anyone to agree with you. But if there is no such H, then we can keep subtracting ¼", and still have the height of a tall person; so reach the obviously false conclusion that a person 3 feet high is tall. What has gone wrong here?

There are practical (mis)applications of this fallacious reasoning. Someone considering one more little sip of beer before driving home can believe correctly that one more little sip won't make any difference in his driving ability. But this is true of each little sip in a series in which, at some point, the drinker has become completely disabled.

A lot of thought has been given to how to rethink matters to locate and fix the mistake in reasoning of this sort.

'Sorites', pronounced so-RIGHT-eez, is Greek for heap (another traditional name for this paradox); a very early version imagined starting with one grain of sand—clearly not a heap—and reasoning that adding one additional grain never transformed a non-heap into a heap. Another traditional example reasons that removal of just one hair from a head cannot transform a non-bald head into a bald one.

THE SPECIOUS PRESENT

Your third birthday party does not exist—now. Nothing in the past exists. Neither does anything in the future. All that exists is the present.

Now consider apparently present facts: the cat is on the mat, Cleveland is in Ohio, Jupiter is the largest planet. Each of these has a time span, with a past and (we'd expect) a future component. But the past and future components, as we've seen, don't exist. Well, what about the present component? How long does that last? If it has any non-zero duration, then part of it is non-existent, in the past or in the future. Anything that's completely present must have a zero duration. But here's the problem: something that lasts for zero time is nothing at all. So the supposedly zero-duration present doesn't exist either. It apparently follows that nothing exists.

Obviously this reasoning is mistaken. But it's no easy job to figure out exactly where. In the process of considering this, in any case, we can get clearer on some things we would never otherwise consider, some basic presuppositions about duration and existence.

ST. PETERSBURG PARADOX

When you're playing a game of chance, a fair bet is the amount of money you should pay to play, expecting to come out even in the long run. (Of course, casinos never offer a fair bet in this sense—they need to make a profit on you.)

You calculate a fair bet by summing the products of multiplying the probability of each outcome times the payoff given that outcome. Imagine a coin flip that would pay you $1 for heads, $2 for tails. Each outcome has a probability of .5, so the fair bet is $(.5 \times \$1) + (.5 \times \$2)$. This equals $1.50.

Now consider the St. Petersburg Game. You flip a fair coin counting the number of flips till it comes up tails, when the game ends. Call the number of flips in a finished game n; the payoff is then $\$2^n$. (A run of three heads then a tails would thus have $n = 4$, and a payoff of $16.)

What's the fair bet for St. Petersburg? The probability that $n = 1$ is 1/2; its payoff is $2. The probability that $n = 2$ is 1/4; its payoff is $4. The probability that $n = 3$ is 1/8; its payoff is $8. And so on. You can see where this is going. The sum of $(1/2 \times \$2) + (1/4 \times \$4) + (1/8 \times \$8)$ and so on equals $\$1 + \$1 + \$1 + \$1$ and so on. The fair bet is an infinite amount of money! In other words, any finite amount you pay to play each game will be smaller than your eventual winnings, if you play long enough.

Of course, you'd probably run out of money to bet before you had an enormous win; or the casino would close, or you'd die. This is not a practical plan. But it does, probability theorists think, raise important theoretical questions about the ideas taken for granted in thinking about fair bets on chance events.

THE THOMSON LAMP

This is an imaginary light-fixture. You push a button to turn it on, and in ½ of a minute, it turns itself off; then after another ¼ of a minute, it turns back on again, then after another ⅛ of a minute, it turns back off, and so on. Imagine (contrary, perhaps, to the laws of physics) that it can do this switching an infinite number of times. It doesn't take a great deal of mathematical skill to sum this series, and determine that the whole series will finish exactly one minute after you start it. The question is: at the end of this minute, will the lamp be on or off? (or, bizarrely, neither or both?)

This kind of peculiar event has been treated extensively in the literature, where it's sometimes called a supertask.

THE TIME AND THE PLACE

OF A MURDER

On December 2, 2002, Bob is visiting a tourist attraction, the Four Corners Monument, located at the only point in the US where four states come together and you can stand with one foot overlapping all four states (should that sound exciting to you). Bob notices his enemy Bart standing nearby, pulls out his gun, and shoots Bart in the foot. Police apprehend Bob, and Bart is taken to hospital, and eventually dies of his wound.

Bob is guilty of murder, but where did it take place? Bob was standing in Arizona when he shot Bart, but about eighteen inches of his right arm, with the gun in hand, extended east into New Mexico. Bart was standing north of Bob, in Utah, but his foot, when it was shot, was slightly over the state line, and was in Colorado. Did the murder take place where Bob was? And was that in Arizona or New Mexico (or both)? Or did it take place where Bart was? And was that in Utah or Colorado (or both)? Or maybe the murder took place in all four states?

Bart's medical condition deteriorated despite treatment, and he died in hospital in early January. This raises questions about timing. Did the murder take place when Bart was shot, in December, or when he died, the following January? Or maybe it was a spread-out event, taking about a month to happen? Imagine you're the police officer at the press conference in December, following Bob's apprehension. You're asked, "Was that murder?" What's the answer: "Not yet!" because Bart was still alive? But when he dies in January, does that retroactively transform the shooting, done the previous month, into murder? Or was it murder all along, though given Bart's survival through December, nobody knew it yet?

How these questions are answered may have practical bearing: the location questions if the laws regarding murder are different in each of the four states; the timing question if there's a change in law to take place on January 1. A court may have to decide these answers. Notice however that there don't seem to be any facts that could be discovered that would determine the right answers. We already know all the relevant facts, and they don't add up to any answers. Would the answers to these questions then be a matter of totally arbitrary decision?

TIME TRAVEL

The main paradox involved here involves the question about whether a time traveler could change the past. For example, could you, on Tuesday, go back to Monday, and move that coffee cup away from the edge of the table, so that it didn't get knocked off and break? This is hard to understand. We start by supposing that it's Tuesday, and the coffee cup did break on Monday. Then, supposedly, you go back and prevent this; but then does it happen that on Tuesday that the coffee cup didn't break earlier? Do those pieces of coffee-cup in the trash suddenly disappear? Or were they never there in the first place?

This sort of science-fiction story is familiar: Fred goes back 60 years, finds his grandfather aged 15, and tries to kill him. If Fred succeeds, then he wouldn't have been born, but then who went back in time and killed grandpa? Some philosophers argue that this doesn't show that time travel is inherently self-contradictory, but rather that no matter what else you accomplish when going back in time, you won't kill your grandfather when he was a teenager, because—simply put—it didn't happen!

TRAGEDY OF THE COMMONS

A commons is a piece of land in the center of a town which traditionally was publicly owned and reserved for shared use. Sometimes all the livestock owners in the town were allowed to graze their animals on this land. When grazed by too many animals, however, the grass could not grow back, and the land was ruined for this use.

The problem here is that it's clearly to each individual herder's self-interest to graze as many animals as he could on the commons. It would be highly unlikely that putting just his few animals there would overload an otherwise sustainable grass crop; if the land was already overloaded by general use, and the grass crop was headed for extinction, it would still be to each herder's interest to get as much as he could out of it, before it became useless.

The generalized problem illustrated here is that in many situations, when individuals act in their own undoubted rational self-interest, a shared general resource will ultimately be depleted, contrary to anyone's interest. What's at issue here is very much like the problem raised, above, by the Prisoner's Dilemma.

TREASURE-HUNTER PARADOX

Years ago, the CBC interviewed a historian who was researching treasure-hunting in Nova Scotia, where the numerous islands and hidden coves gave pirates an ideal place to bury their treasure. Of the many attempts to find buried treasure, a few had actually found it; the historian reported that a very large proportion of successful diggers had deepened holes made by previous searchers. The earlier searches had stopped just short of success. So the interviewer asked the historian what advice to give future treasure-hunters, on the basis of this information. The historian hesitated for a moment, then replied that he guessed that they should dig a little deeper than they do.

TRISTRAM SHANDY

This is the name of the hero of the novel bearing his name. In the novel, he has undertaken to write his autobiography, but he writes so slowly that he takes a year to cover only one day of his life. That means, as time goes on, he'll fall more and more behind. Bertrand Russell, however, pointed out in an influential study of infinity, that paradoxically if Shandy would live for an infinite length of time, despite falling further and further behind at any moment, he'd nevertheless be able to finish his work. One of the many paradoxes of infinity.

TROLLEY PROBLEM

You're standing next to trolley tracks, and see an out-of-control trolley fast approaching. Five people are tied to the tracks farther down, and would die when the trolley gets there; but you can throw a switch which would steer the trolley instead on to another track where only one person would die.

Some philosophers react to this story (introduced by Philippa Foot and widely discussed) that one is not morally permitted to throw the switch, because that would amount to killing the one person on the alternate track; one must, then, accept the (nevertheless horrible) outcome of the death of the five, because that's not the result of your wrongdoing. Killing is wrong; allowing to die is under some circumstances permitted.

Other philosophers, however, have the strong reaction that all that's relevant here is that you have the choice of five dying, or just one; so you must throw the switch: they deny that the difference between acting and refraining from acting has any moral significance.

TWO ENVELOPES PARADOX

You're presented with two sealed envelopes, a red and a blue one, and told that one contains twice the amount of money as the other; but you can't tell which is which. You pick the red one, at random. But before opening it, you're offered the option of swapping it for the blue one. Should you take that option?

At first glance, it seems that it's a matter of indifference whether you swap or not. But consider this reasoning: Call the amount of money in the red envelope (whatever that is) M. It's 50% probable that the blue envelope contains $\frac{1}{2} \times M$, and 50% probable it contains $2 \times M$. So it's equiprobable that swapping would increase your payoff by M, or decrease it by $\frac{1}{2}$ M. Swapping is a good bet. It's probably advantageous for you to swap.

Now, imagine that the reasoning convinces you, and you agree to swap, and exchange envelopes. Now you hold the blue envelope. But now you're offered the option of swapping again, back to the red one. You reason this way: Call the amount of money in the blue envelope (whatever that is) N. It's 50% probable that the red envelope contains ½ × N, and 50% probable it contains 2 × N. So it's equiprobable that swapping would increase your payoff by N, or decrease it by ½ N. Swapping is a good bet. It's probably advantageous for you to swap. So you swap again.

But it's clear that something has gone wrong here. It's impossible that this could go on and on, with your reasoning telling you that every time that each swap adds to your advantage. That can't be. Okay, it's clear that somewhere there's a mistake in your reasoning: but where?

There's a variant of the Two-Envelopes Paradox called the Two-Wallet Game. Here's how this works. You and a friend are drinking in a bar, and he suggests this game. You both put your wallets on the table, and whoever's wallet has less money in it gets the money that's in the other's wallet. (Neither of you has any idea of how much is in the others' wallet, or in your own.)

You reason: Call the amount of money in my wallet (whatever it is) A, and call the amount of money in Buddy's wallet B. It's equally likely that A is less than B, or more. So there's a 50% probability that A is more than B, and I'd lose A. But it's 50% probability that I'd win B—if B was larger than A. So if I won, what I'd win is more than what I'd lose if I lost. The game is favorable to me.

Buddy, of course, is reasoning the same way. It can't be that this game is favorable to both players. Both of you have made a mistake, and maybe you have the feeling that it's the same sort of mistake that showed up in the reasoning about the envelope switch.

UNEXPECTED (SURPRISE) HANGING (OR EXAM) PARADOX

On Friday, your algebra teacher announces that there will be a surprise quiz during one of the classes next week—'surprise' meaning that you won't be able to figure out when it will take place before the class starts in which it is given.

You reason: there are classes on Monday, Wednesday, and Friday. If the test were on Friday, we'd know that in advance—after class on Wednesday—because there was no test on Monday or Wednesday, and it had to be on one of those three days. So a Friday quiz wouldn't be a surprise. It can't be on Friday.

So it must be on Monday or Wednesday. But if it were on Wednesday, we'd know that in advance—after class on Monday; as we've already figured out, so since it wasn't on Monday, it would have to be on Wednesday. So a Wednesday quiz wouldn't be a surprise. It can't be on Wednesday.

So it must be on Monday, the only remaining possibility. But we can figure that out—know already that it has to be Monday. But that wouldn't be a surprise then.

So a surprise quiz under these conditions is impossible.

This is a very perplexing paradox because it's perfectly clear that there can be a surprise quiz, and so there has to be an error in the reasoning above. But philosophers have had some trouble finding a persuasive account of what has gone wrong.

Does this addition to the story help you figure out what's wrong? Having done all the reasoning above, you show up in Monday's algebra class, and the teacher hands out the quiz. "But!" you object, "But! But!" The teacher says, "Surprise!!"

(A nastier version of the same story involves the surprise timing of the hanging of a condemned man.)

UNINTERESTING NUMBERS

Consider what we'll call interesting numbers—positive integers with special facts or associations attached to them. 1 is surely an interesting number: it's the number of gods believed in by many religions, the smallest prime number, etc. 2 is also interesting: it's the smallest even number. 3 is the number of blind mice, of little pigs, of bears Goldilocks met, etc. 4 is the July date celebrated as the US national holiday. 5 is the number of fingers on one hand. Probably you can think of something that sets apart 6, 7, 8, 9, 10, and more, and makes them interesting. What then is the smallest uninteresting number? Hard to say, but let's suppose that it's 2,693, a number associated with no facts whatsoever. Oh but wait: there is something that makes this number stand out: it's the smallest uninteresting number, so it's interesting after all. (A contradiction?) Okay, anyway, let's keep looking. How about 2,694 then? If that's the smallest uninteresting number, that's an interesting fact about it. And so on, as high as you care to go. So we've proven that every number is interesting, right?

What's foolish about this reasoning?

VOTER'S PARADOX (1)

In the most common sort of election, the candidate wins who receives more votes than the others; and there are special procedures in the regulations concerning ties.

Voters often want to see their candidate get a large number of votes, win or lose, but we'll ignore this for our purposes, and consider only what's by far the chief motivation for voting: you want your candidate to win. Regarding this motivation, your vote can make a difference if, without it, your candidate would be tied for first place, or if your vote creates a tie.

Now, consider the chances of either of these happening in an election with more than a handful of voters. A statistics professor estimates that a tied congressional election might be expected to occur in the US once approximately every 400 years. It is overwhelmingly unlikely that your vote will make a difference in this and in almost every other sort of election.

So why vote? Your chances of being hit by lightning on the way to the polling station are probably greater than the chance of making a difference.

VOTER'S PARADOX (2)

Confusingly sometimes known by the same name as the one just considered, this one shows that under certain circumstances, voting is not a way to produce a rational general will out of individual preferences.

Consider this simple case: There are three candidates for a position, A, B, and C, and three voters, 1, 2, and 3. The three voters each have preferences among the candidates, in this order:

voter 1: prefers A to B, and B to C

voter 2: prefers B to C, and C to A

voter 3: prefers C to A, and A to B

A simple vote in which each voted for his/her preferred candidate would result in a tie: one vote for each of A, B, and C, and no decision.

Let's try a series of votes to see in general what preferences the voters have when considering only two of the three. Vote first on A and B: 1 and 3 prefer A to B; only 2 disagrees. Good so far. Now let's compare B and C: 1 and 2 prefer B to C.

So now we have majority votes preferring A to B, and B to C. Does that mean that the general will is best served by ranking them in the order A, B, C, giving the victory to A, with C coming in third? To make sure, let's compare A and C: 2 and 3 both prefer A to C. Whoops.

ZENO'S PARADOXES

Zeno of Elea was a fifth-century BCE Greek philosopher who is now known for having created a number of paradoxes involving motion, plurality, and change. Nine of these are known today, on the basis of quotation or discussion by other philosophers; we'll briefly look at the three best-known of them.

On the surface, Zeno's paradoxes seem like silly denials of the obvious, but really they are, in Russell's words, "immeasurably subtle and profound" explorations of problems involved in our presuppositions about time, space, motion, and so on.

Achilles and the Tortoise is the most famous of Zeno's paradoxes. Suppose speedy Achilles is in a race with a tortoise. Achilles can run much faster than the tortoise, so the latter is given a head start, beginning farther down the track than Achilles. The race begins, and Achilles very soon runs to the place the tortoise started from; but by then the tortoise has run (or waddled) on to a point a little further on. So then Achilles continues running till he gets to this second point, but by then the tortoise has gone on to a third point. And so on. No matter how many times Achilles catches up to where the tortoise just left, he hasn't caught up with him. Conclusion: he can never catch up.

This conclusion is obviously false, and modern mathematics (given the figures for the speed of each, and the head-start distance) can tell us exactly when Achilles will catch up—and pass—the tortoise. But then what has gone bad in this reasoning? This is a hard question to answer. (Note, by the way, the connection between this item and what's discussed above in the Thomson Lamp section.)

The Racecourse is closely related to the first Achilles paradox. Here Zeno concentrates simply on Achilles' run down the racecourse, ignoring the tortoise. Can Achilles reach the end of the course? To do so, he must first reach the half-way point; then, having gotten there, he must travel half of the remaining portion, arriving at the point $3/4$ of the way down the field; then he must again cover half the remaining distance, arriving at the $7/8$ point; and so on and so on. There's an endless series of smaller and smaller runs he must make, and at the end of each run in the series there's still some distance to go. So he can never get to the end of the field. (This paradox is also often called The Dichotomy.)

The Arrow. Consider an arrow flying through the air. At any one moment—a dimensionless point in time, with zero duration—it's in exactly one well-defined space, which is not moving. At another moment, it's in another motionless space, not moving. There isn't any moment during its flight when this is not true. So how can it be moving?

APPENDIX 2

Philosophical Lexicon

INTRODUCTION

Philosophy, having been around the longest of any academic discipline, has accumulated what may be the longest list of technical jargon terms. These are useful shorthand for philosophers already familiar with these words, but they can provide stumbling-blocks for students. We've included here a rather minimal dictionary of the more common philosophical terms, including some that occur in the readings in this volume, and others that don't.

This is a revised and severely shortened version of a much more inclusive philosophical lexicon: *The Philosopher's Dictionary*, by Robert M. Martin (Broadview Press).

LEXICON

abstract / concrete entities / ideas Abstract entities are supposed not to be locatable in space or time, not perceptible, without causes or effects, necessarily existing. Putative examples are properties, universals, sets, geometrical figures, and numbers. Something is, by contrast, concrete when it is particular and spatially and temporally locatable—perhaps material. There's a long history of philosophical argument about the reality of certain abstracta. Clearly some of them aren't real, for example, the average American family, with its 2.6 children. Reification is mistakenly taking something to be real that's merely abstract; this sort of reasoning is known as the fallacy of misplaced concreteness.

There's a good deal of historical debate about whether we can even have abstract ideas at all. We experience only particulars, so ab-stract ideas were a problem for the classical empiricists, who thought that every idea was a copy of an experience. Plato and others argued that we must have innate abstract ideas, not originating with sensation, in order to be able to classify the particulars.

act / agent moralities Some moral philosophers think that the basic sort of thing ethics evaluates is the worth of actions people do (act morality); others think that what's basic to moral theory is the worth of the person who acts (agent morality). Kant argued that good actions were those done by people with the right sort of motives, so his ethical theory is one species of agent morality; another species is virtue ethics. The utilitarians held that the basic kind of ethical reasoning evaluates actions (via their consequences), whatever the motives or moral worth of the people who do them, so their ethics is a variety of act morality.

action at a distance The effect that one thing can have on another that it is not touching and to which it is not connected by something in-between. Gravitation is an example. Some philosophers and scientists—e.g., Leibniz—thought that this was impossible. One way they tried to explain gravitation is to suppose that bodies that gravitationally attract each other are connected by some intervening invisible thing that fills the space between them and transfers the gravitational force.

action theory The branch of philosophy that considers questions about action. Examples of these are: What differentiates an action from other movements? Can there be actions that are refrainings from acting? Where does an action end and its consequences begin? What sort of explanation is suitable for actions?

Moral questions (about, for example, acts / omissions) and the questions of free will and responsibility are sometimes included in action theory.

acts / omissions An act is doing something, by contrast with an omission (or refraining), which is merely failing to do something. Some philosophers think that there can be a moral difference between these even when they have the same motives and outcome.

a fortiori (Latin: "from what is stronger") Means 'with even stronger reason', 'even more so'. "You owe thanks to someone who lets you use his car for a day. So a fortiori, you should really be grateful to Fred, who let you have his car for a whole month."

agent An agent is one who can perform a genuine intentional action, and who is thus morally responsible for what he/she does. This excludes people, for example, who are unable to perceive relevant facts, or who can't reason about consequences.

agent / event causation Often it is thought that causes and effects must be events. But if our actions are caused by other events, then how can we be responsible for them? It's sometimes argued that the cause of an action is not an event but rather the agent who did it.

agnosticism is in general the position that one does not, maybe cannot, know the truth or falsity of statements in some area—that there is insufficient reason to believe either. This term is used most frequently regarding religion, to contrast with theism and atheism (which are confident that we know that God does / doesn't exist).

alienation Estrangement, separation. Hegel discussed the possibility of human estrangement from the natural world. The existentialists thought that our alienation from nature and from each other was an important and inevitable part of the human condition. In Marx, 'alienation' means the separation from the products of our labor (as employees, we don't own what we produce) as well as from society and from ourselves.

altruism 1. Generosity. 2. The philosophical position that one ought to act for the benefit of others; contrast with egoism.

analogy / disanalogy An analogy is a similarity of two things. Reasoning from (or by) analogy—'analogical argument'—concludes that because two things share one or more characteristics, they share another; e.g., that because others show external behavior similar to one's own, others must have a similar internal life. A disanalogy is a difference between compared things; disanalogies between things reduce the strength of an argument from analogy.

analysis Some things are capable of being understood in terms of their component parts; analysis takes them apart into their simpler elements. Some twentieth century anglophone philosophers took analysis of concepts to be the job of philosophy. What is to be analyzed is called the analysandum, and what provides the analysis is called the analysans.

analytic / synthetic Kant called a judgment analytic when the "predicate was contained in the subject"; thus, for example, the judgment that all bachelors are unmarried is analytic because the subject ('bachelors') "contains" the predicate ('unmarried'). Later philosophers preferred to make this distinction in terms of sentences and meanings: a sentence is analytic when the meaning of the subject of that sentence contains the meaning of the predicate: 'unmarried' is part of the definition of 'bachelor'. So an analytic sentence is one that is true merely because of the meanings of the words. 'It's snowing or it's not snowing' is true merely because of the meaning of the words 'or' and 'not', so perhaps we should count this as analytic too. But since the relevant words in this case are "logical" words, this sentence is more particularly known as a logical truth. A synthetic truth is a sentence that is true, but not merely because of the meaning of the words. 'Pigs don't fly' is true partially because of the meaning of the words, of course: if 'pigs' meant 'woodpeckers', then that sentence would be false. But since the definition of 'pig' tells us nothing about flying, this sentence is not true merely because of the meaning of the words. One can speak also about analytically false sentences, for example, 'There exists a married bachelor'. Analytic sentences are necessarily true, and may (sometimes) be known a priori; but Kant argued that there are also synthetic a priori statements. Quine argued that the analytic / synthetic distinction is not a good one, because one cannot distinguish between matters of meaning of the words of a sentence and matters of fact.

ancient philosophy Ancient philosophy began in primitive form, we suppose, in prehistory; the earliest Western philosopher of whose work we have a historical account is Thales (c. 580 BCE.). The end of this period is often marked by the beginning of medieval philosophy, with the work of Augustine (about 400 CE).

antecedent conditions The events or states of affairs that come before a given event and that cause it, or are necessary or sufficient (See necessary / sufficient conditions) for it to happen.

a priori / a posteriori Two different ways in which something might be known to be true (or false). It can be known a priori if it can be known before—that is, or independently of—sense-experience of the fact in question. It can be known a posteriori if it can be known after—that is, on the basis of—sense-experience of the fact. One can know that all bachelors are unmarried a priori; one doesn't need to observe even one bachelor to know this is true. In this case (but perhaps not in all cases) a priori knowledge is possible because what's known is a conceptual truth or because the sentence that expresses this truth is analytic or logically true. Kant argued that certain a priori truths (for example, that every event has a cause) were not conceptual or analytic.

argument An argument in ordinary talk is a debate, especially a heated one. But in philosophical usage, an argument is one or more statements (called 'premises'; singular 'premise' or 'premiss') advanced in order to support another statement (the conclusion). Thus philosophers need not get angry when they argue. Premises actually support a conclusion only when there is the appropriate sort of logical connection between the premises and the conclusion. In deductive arguments, the conclusion must be true given the truth of the premises; in an inductive argument, the truth of the premises makes the conclusion more probable. Any deductive argument in which the premises really do have the appropriate logical connection with the conclusion is called a 'valid' argument; in invalid arguments, this connection is lacking. A valid argument may, however, fail to support its conclusion because one or more of its premises is false—for example: All pigs fly. All flying things are lighter than air. Therefore all pigs are lighter than air. This argument is valid, but it fails to convince because both of its premises are false. An argument with at least one false premise is called 'unsound'; a sound argument is a valid argument all of whose premises are true. A sound argument provides a proof of its conclusion (though in logic it's often said that a proof is provided merely when the argument is valid).

argument from illusion / hallucination The argument (against naïve realisms) that the existence of perceptual illusions and hallucinations shows that we really directly perceive only sense-data and not an independent world.

artificial intelligence An area of study in computer science and psychology that involves building (or imagining) machines, or programming computers, to mimic certain complex intelligent human activities. The creation of a program that can play chess at a high level is one of its successes. Artificial intelligence might shed light on what human mentality is like, and its successes and failures enter into arguments about materialism.

artificial / natural language A natural language is one used by some actual group of people, that has developed on its own, culturally and historically. An artificial language is one developed for some purpose—examples are computer languages and symbolic logic.

association of ideas One thought produces another: when you think about shoes, maybe this drags along the thought of socks. Associationism was the view that this sort of thing is at the core of our mental life, and that its laws constitute a scientific cognitive psychology.

atheism Atheists believe that God doesn't exist, and (sometimes) that religious practice is foolish, or that the morality fostered by religion is wrong. Because atheism has been so unpopular, atheistic philosophers have sometimes disguised their views. Lucretius and Hume were probably atheists. Russell was open about his atheism, and got into trouble for it. Not every religion includes the belief in God—Buddhism, for example, is sometimes said to be an atheistic religion. Atheism contrasts with theism, the view that God does exist, and with agnosticism, the view that there isn't any good reason to believe either that God exists or that He doesn't.

atomism The view that things are composed of elementary basic parts. From ancient times onward physics was often atomistic (though what's now called an 'atom' is no longer regarded as a basic component—contemporary physicists think that much smaller parts might be basic).

automata These are (arguably) mindless devices that imitate the intelligent and goal-directed actions of people—robots, for example. Descartes thought that animals were automata—merely physical "mechanisms" without mind.

autonomy / heteronomy Autonomy is self-governance—the ability or right to determine one's own actions and beliefs. Some ethical theories see the respect for autonomy as a central ethical principle. Heteronomy is its opposite: dependence on others.

average / total utilitarianism Utilitarianism needs to specify how to understand the greatest good for the greatest number of people. Is the measure of the worth of a society the average utility of its members, or the total utility?

axiom / postulate / posit An axiom is a statement regarded as obviously true, used as a starting point for deriving other statements. An axiomatic theory is one that is based on axioms. Non-axiomatic theories don't have such basic statements. 'Postulate' (as a noun) is often used to mean the same thing, though sometimes it refers only to such statements within a particular theory, while axioms are basic and obvious statements common to many theories (for example, the basic laws of logic). The verb 'to postulate' means the act of postulation—assumption, often of the existence of something, for theoretical purposes. A posit is an assumption, especially some thing assumed to exist; to posit something is to assume it.

basic statement The truth or falsity of some statements is determined by appeal to some others (by means of logic or scientific method, for example), but some philosophers think that there must be a starting point: basic statements. Whether there are basic statements, what they are, and why they are acceptable, are all controversial questions.

behaviorism Early in the twentieth century, many psychologists decided that introspection was not a good basis for the science of the mind; instead they advocated reliance on subjects' external, observable behavior. Methodological (psychological) behaviorism is the view that only external behavior should be investigated by science. Metaphysical or analytical behaviorism is the philosophical view that public behavior is all there is—that this is what we're talking about when we refer to mental events or characteristics in others, and even in ourselves. This is a form of materialism.

best of all possible worlds A phrase associated with Leibniz, who believed that God, being perfectly good, knowing, and powerful, could not have created anything less than perfect; thus this world (despite how it sometimes appears) is the best of all possible worlds.

bioethics The ethics involved in various sorts of biology-related activities, mostly centering on medical matters, where subjects for debate include, for example, abortion, genetic control, euthanasia, and in vitro fertilization.

biting the bullet What philosophers are said to do when they choose to accept the unlikely counterintuitive consequences of their position, rather than taking them as counterexamples. The phrase supposedly arose because biting down on something would help with the pain of surgery without anaesthetic.

bodily interchange This is what would happen if the same person existed at one time in one body and at another time in another body, for example, through reincarnation, or through a variety of science-fiction techniques such as brain or memory transplant. The topic is important in religious contexts and in thought experiments about personal identity.

bourgeoisie / proletariat Names of the two social /economic classes important in Marx's analysis. The former is the capitalist class—employers, financiers, landlords, etc., though more generally now the bourgeoisie is taken to include middle class wage earners as well. The latter is the working class.

bundle theory In general, the view of classical empiricists who argued that things are nothing more than bundles of properties, and that there is no need to think of substrata (underlying substance). The phrase most often refers to Hume's bundle theory of personal identity: we don't perceive a continuing self, so our self-idea must refer to an introspectible continuously changing "bundle" of different mental events.

burden of proof When there is a disagreement, it's sometimes the case that one side has the burden of proof, that is, it is expected to prove its case, and if it can't, the other wins by default. It may be the side with the position that is surprising, or unorthodox, or that runs counter to other well-accepted beliefs.

calculus An abstract system of symbols, aimed at calculating something. One can call each symbol-system of symbolic logic a 'calculus': for example, the sentential and quantifier calculi. The system for calculating probabilities is called the 'probability calculus'. Some philosophers think of the various sciences as interpreted calculi; a calculus is interpreted (given a "valuation") when its symbols are given meaning by relating them to things in the real world; uninterpreted, it is just a bunch of symbols with syntax but no semantics. 'The calculus' names a branch of mathematics independently developed by Leibniz and Newton during the late seventeenth century.

casuistry The determination of right and wrong by reasoning involving general principles applied to particular cases. Because religious casuists sometimes reasoned in overly complex ways to silly conclusions, this word has come to have disparaging overtones.

categorical / hypothetical imperative Kant's distinction. An imperative is a command. 'Categorical' means absolute—not dependent on particular aims or circumstances; 'hypothetical' means relative to, depending on, particular aims or circumstances. Thus, 'Tell the truth' is a categorical imperative, but 'If it is to everyone's benefit, tell the truth' and 'If you want others to trust you, tell the truth' are hypothetical imperatives. Kant argued that hypothetical imperatives could give useful practical advice, but do not express the standards of morality, which are expressed only by categorical imperatives. He argued further that there is one command central to all morality—the categorical imperative: Act in a way such that the general rule behind your action could consistently be willed to be a universal law. He argued that this was equivalent to saying that others should be treated as ends, never as means only.

category mistake A claim that's absurd because it makes an ascription completely inappropriate to the category of the object in question. To claim that the number 7 is faster than the number 8 is to assert this kind of absurdity. Gilbert Ryle introduced this term arguing that the standard Cartesian view of mind/body dualism committed this kind of mistake.

causal theories A variety of theories that make the notion of cause basic in some way. The causal theory of knowledge proposes, as a condition of 'P knows that x', that P's belief be causally connected in some appropriate way to the fact that x. The causal theory of perception points out that a "blue sensation" is one normally caused by a blue thing, and tries to avoid sense-data by explaining that what is happening when there is no blue thing there is that the sensation is one that would have been caused by a blue thing, were the situation normal. Functionalism is a causal theory of mind. The causal theory of meaning / reference makes the meaning / reference of terms a matter of the causal connections their uses have with the external world.

causation The relation that holds between a cause and its effect. Also called 'causality'. Longstanding philosophical problems are concerned with the nature of cause, and how we find out about it. Hume skeptically argued that we perceive no "power" in causal connections, and that when we say that x causes y, we're only saying that things of x-sort regularly precede things of y-sort. Critics object that this fails to distinguish between causal connections and mere accidental but universal regularities.

cause-of-itself (Latin: causa sui) Narrowly, a thing that causes itself to exist (or to be the way it is). God is commonly thought to be the only thing that is capable of this. But because causes are supposed to precede their effects, a cause-of-itself would (problematically) have to precede its own existence. Thinking of cause in an older way, as explanation, perhaps avoids this difficulty, but has its own problems: how can something provide the explanation for its own existence?

certainty A belief is called 'certain' in ordinary talk when it is believed very strongly, or when one is unable to think, or even imagine, that it might be false. Philosophers often don't want to rely on a subjective and psychological test for certainty, and demand proof that some belief really is beyond rational doubt. Some philosophers think that all our knowledge must have a certain foundation. 'Moral certainty' means sufficiently warranted to justify action;

'metaphysical certainty' means warranted not merely by fallible perception of particulars, but rather by some presumably more reliable reasoning about all being; 'logical certainty' is the extremely strong warrant we get for a proposition which is in some sense a truth of logic.

ceteris paribus (Latin: "other things being equal") This is used in comparing two things while assuming they differ only in the one characteristic under consideration. For example, it could be said that, ceteris paribus, a simple theory is better than a complicated one; though if everything else is not equal—if, for example, the simpler theory has fewer true predictions—then it might not be better.

circular reasoning / definition A definition is (viciously) circular (and thus useless) when the term to be defined, or a version of it, occurs in the definition; for example, the definition of 'free action' as 'action that is freely done'. (Viciously) circular reasoning defends some statement by assuming the truth of that statement; e.g.: "Why do you think what the Bible says is true?" "Because the Bible is the Word of God." "How do you know that it is the Word of God?" "Because it says so in the Bible, and everything there is true." Some philosophers argue that not all circles are vicious, and that some sorts of circular reasoning are acceptable—"virtuously circular"—for example, when the circle is wide enough. A dictionary, for example, must be circular, defining words in terms of other words; but this is okay. Circular reasoning is also known as 'begging the question'. Careless speakers sometimes think that this means 'raising the question'; it doesn't. Begging the question is sometimes called by its Latin name, 'petitio principii'.

cognitive / emotive meaning The former is what a sentence states—what makes it true or false. The latter is its "expressive" content—the speaker's feelings that it communicates, rather than any beliefs. Some theories of ethical statements hold that they have emotive, but no cognitive, meaning.

cognition The operations of the mind; sometimes particularly believing and awareness; sometimes, more particularly, the mental process by which we get knowledge.

cognitive science A recently-developed discipline combining philosophers, psychologists, and computer scientists, devoted to providing theories of cognition.

cognitivism / noncognitivism Cognitivism is the position that something can be known. Ethical cognitivism is the view that ethical statements are statements about (supposed) facts and thus are true or false, and might be known to be true or false. This is opposed to the noncognitivist position that ethical statements are not knowable. A species of ethical noncognitivism is emotivism, which argues that ethical statements are expressions of approval or disapproval (like 'Hooray for that!'), or invitations to action (like 'Please do that!') and are thus neither true nor false, and not knowable.

coherence / incoherence A set of beliefs or sentences is coherent when it fits together in a logical way—that is, when everything in the set is consistent, or when the items in it confirm others in it. A set in which one item would be false, or probably false, given the truth of others is not coherent (is incoherent).

collectively / distributively What applies to a group collectively applies to it as a whole only, i.e., not to its individual members (not distributively). The atoms that constitute a pig collectively, but not distributively, outweigh a fly.

collective responsibility The controversial idea that a group or nation or culture can bear responsibility as a whole for bad acts: for example, the whole German nation for Nazi atrocities.

commensurability / incommensurability Different things are commensurable when they can be measured on the same scale. Utilitarians sometimes assume that different people's different pleasures are commensurable on a common scale of utilites; but it has been argued that there's no way to make sensible quantity comparisons. Another example of supposed incommensurability is in the comparison of science and religion: some philosophers think that it's foolish to criticize religious statements using the criteria of scientific adequacy.

common sense 1. Until the eighteenth century or so, this term named the supposed mental faculty which combined input from different senses to give us a unified idea of an external object, combining, for example, the smell, taste, look and feel of a peach. 2. More recently, it has come to mean the mental faculty which all people are supposed to possess "in common," for knowledge of basic everyday truths. This is sometimes taken to answer skeptical doubts about the obvious truths that there exists an external world, other minds, etc. The eighteenth-century Scottish "common sense philosophers" relied heavily on this notion as a vindication of ordinary views and a refutation of skepticism.

communitarianism Advocates the position in social philosophy that the rights of individuals are not basic—that groups, or society as a whole, can have rights that are not constituted by or based on the individual rights of the members of those groups, and that these group rights may override claims to individual rights. Fascism is a rather extreme example of communitarianism. Communitarianism is a form of holism in social theory; the contrast is with individualism.

compatibilism Any philosophical position that claims that two things are compatible (they can both exist at once), most referring to the view that free will and determinism are compatible—that is, that people's actions are (sometimes) free even though they are fully causally determined. Compatibilists argue that we're not free when we're acting under compulsion (that is, forced to act), but that this is a different thing from the action's being determined or caused.

compulsion An action is said to be done under compulsion (also known as 'constraint' or 'coercion') when it is "forced" by internal or external circumstances, and thus the doer of that action can't be held morally responsible for doing it. If you steal something, for example, because someone is forcing you to do it at gunpoint, or because you are a kleptomaniac, that doesn't make your action any better, but it does mean that you're not to blame. Compatibilists about free will argue that compulsion makes one unfree and not responsible, but that ordinary actions are causally determined but not compelled in this sense.

concept May refer to the ability to categorize things; thus to say that someone has the concept of duck is to say that that person can sort things correctly into ducks and non-ducks. A concept is sometimes distinguished from a percept, which is a particular mental item had while sensing a particular thing. A concept, then, may be thought to be a generalization or abstraction from one or many percepts. Thus a percept is sometimes considered a particular idea, and a concept a general or abstract idea.

conceptual scheme The most general framework of someone's view of the world—a structured system of concepts that divide that person's world into kinds of things. It has sometimes been supposed that two people's conceptual schemes might differ so much that one would never be able to understand or translate what the other said.

conceptual truth A statement that is true merely because of the nature of the concepts that make it up. The fact that all bachelors are unmarried is a conceptual truth, because the concept of being a bachelor involves being unmarried. Compare: snow is white is not a conceptual truth, because being white, despite being true of snow, is not part of the concept of snow. We can imagine, consistent with our concept of snow, that snow is always green. (Substitute 'word' for 'concept' in this definition, and it turns into the definition of 'analytic truth'.)

confirmation / disconfirmation / verification / falsification Confirmation is the collection of evidence for a statement. Because there might be some evidence for a false statement, a statement might be confirmed though false. Collecting evidence that a statement is false is called 'disconfirmation'. 'Verification' means 'confirmation' and 'falsification' means 'disconfirmation', though one tends to speak of a statement as having been verified (or falsified) only if the statement is really true (or false), and has been shown to be so by the evidence. Confirmation theory is the attempt to give a general account of what counts as confirmation.

conscience This is the sense of right and wrong that is sometimes supposed to be a way of knowing moral facts, perhaps through a reliable internal "voice" or moral sense-perception, or a faculty of moral intuition.

consciousness 1. The state that we are in when awake: mental events are going on. 2. Awareness of something. (You aren't usually conscious of the position of your tongue.) 3. = mind (though it might be that the mind exists even while we are asleep or not aware of anything). The fact that we are conscious is supposed by some to distinguish people from machines and other non-living things, and perhaps from (at least the lower) animals.

consequentialism The position that people's actions are right or wrong because of their consequences (their results). This sort of ethical theory also called 'teleological', is contrasted with deontological theories—those that hold that results of actions are morally irrelevant. Thus, for example, a deontologist might think that lying is always wrong just in itself, whereas a consequentialist might think that lying is morally permissible in those circumstances in which the lie results in good consequences overall.

consistency A set of statements is consistent if it is logically possible that all the statements in that set are true. It is inconsistent if this is not possible—if one statement contradicts another, or if a contradiction results from reasoning from the set. The set consisting of this one statement 'It's raining and it's not raining' is inconsistent, because this statement is self-contradictory.

contingency To say that a statement is contingent is to say that it is neither necessary nor impossible. Metaphysical contingency is contrasted with what must be true or false; logical contingency is contrasted with logical truth / falsity.

contra-causal freedom It's sometime argued that a free action— one we're responsible for—could only be one that is not caused by previous events. Libertarians believe that some of our actions are free because contra-causal.

contradiction / contrary Two statements are contradictories when the truth of one logically requires the falsity of the other, and the falsity of one requires the truth of the other—in other words, when it is impossible that both are true, and it is impossible that both are false. 'It's raining' and 'It's not raining' are contradictory: exactly one of them must be true. Two statements are contraries when it is impossible that they are both true, though they might both be false. 'No pigs fly' and 'All pigs fly' are contraries, not contradictories. It is logically impossible that both of them are true, though they both might be false (were it the case that some, but not all, pigs fly). One can also call a self-contradiction a 'contradiction'.

cosmological argument for God's existence Given that every natural event has a cause, an apparently unacceptable infinite chain of past events would follow—unless there were an initial uncaused (supernatural) cause, identified with God. A very commonly encountered argument, with versions dating back at least to Plato. It's also commonly known as the first-cause argument.

counterexample An example intended to show that some general claim is false. Reasoning by counterexample is frequently a useful philosophical tactic for arguing against some position. (Also called 'counterinstance'.)

counterfactual A counterfactual (also called a 'counterfactual conditional' or a 'contrary-to-fact conditional') is a conditional statement whose antecedent is false. The subjunctive is used in English counterfactuals: 'If Fred were here, you wouldn't be doing that'. (This is properly said only when Fred isn't here.) One important and controversial area in modern logic is concerned with the truth-conditions for counterfactuals. A powerful and widely accepted way of understanding counterfactuals uses the notion of possible worlds: a counterfactual is true when the consequent is true in the nearest possible world (i.e., a world as much as possible like ours) in which the antecedent is true.

covering law A general law applying to a particular instance. The covering law theory (or "model") of explanation (also called the 'Deductive-Nomological' or 'D-N' theory) says that a particular event is explained by providing one or more covering laws that, together with particular facts, imply the event. For example, we can explain why a piece of metal rusted by appealing to the covering law that iron rusts when exposed to air and moisture, and the facts that the metal is iron, and was exposed to air and moisture.

criterion A test or standard for the presence of a property, or for the applicability of a word, or for the truth or falsity of a proposition. This word is singular; its plural is 'criteria'.

crucial experiment This is an experiment whose outcome would provide a central or conclusive test for the truth or falsity of some position or scientific hypothesis. Sometimes called, in Latin, 'experimentum crucis'.

decision theory The largely mathematical theory of decision-making. Generally includes some way of evaluating desirability of outcomes and their probabilities when not certain.

deconstructionism A skeptical and frequently anti-intellectual postmodern movement which seeks to interpret texts and the positions held in them by "deconstructing" them—showing their incoherence, the hidden and often contradictory presuppositions, prejudices, motives, and political aims behind them.

de dicto / de re (Latin: "about what's said" / "about a thing") A de re belief is a belief considered with respect to the actual thing that it's about. Thus, if someone mistakenly thinks that the moving thing in the sky he's looking at is a satellite, whereas it's actually a meteor, then he has the de re belief that a meteor is moving in the sky—more clearly: about that meteor, he believes it's moving in the sky above him. But he has the de dicto belief that a satellite is moving in the sky above him. Philosophers speak also of a distinction between de dicto and de re necessity. It is de re necessary of the number of planets that it is larger than five (because nine is necessarily larger than five); but it is de dicto contingent, because there might have been only three planets.

deduction / induction 1. In an outdated way of speaking, deduction is reasoning from the general to the particular, and induction is reasoning from the particular to the general. 2. Nowadays, this distinction between kinds of reasoning is made as follows: correct ("valid") deductive reasoning is reasoning of the sort that if the premises are true, the conclusion must be true; whereas correct inductive reasoning supports the conclusion by showing only that it's more probably true. Examples:

Deduction: No pigs fly; Porky is a pig; therefore, Porky doesn't fly.

Induction: Porky, Petunia, and all the other pigs observed in a wide variety of circumstances don't fly; therefore no pigs fly.

These examples in fact fit definition 1; but here are examples of deduction according to definition 2 that do not fit definition 1:

No pigs fly; therefore all pigs are non-flying things.

Porky doesn't fly; Porky is a pig; therefore not all pigs fly.

A common form of induction works by enumeration: as support for the conclusion that all A's are B's, one lists many examples of A's that are B's.

defeasible Means 'defeatible', in the sense of 'capable of being overruled'. A driver's license confers a defeasible right to drive, for example, because under certain circumstances (e.g., when he is drunk) the holder of a valid license would nevertheless not be allowed to drive. A defeasible proposition is one that can be overturned by future evidence.

definiens / definiendum A definiendum (Latin: "to be defined") is a word or phrase to be defined, and the definition is the definiens (Latin: "defining thing").

degrees of perfection argument for God's existence One of many different forms of this argument: Comparative terms describe degrees of approximation to superlative terms. Nothing would count as falling short of the superlative unless the superlative thing existed. Ordinary things are less than perfect, so there must be something completely perfect; and what is completely perfect is God. Objection: Comparative terms do not imply the existence of a superlative instance. For example, the existence of people who are more or less stupid does not imply that someone exists who is maximally, completely, perfectly stupid.

deism A form of religious belief especially popular during the Enlightenment. Deists practice "natural religion"—that is, they rely on reason, distrusting faith, revelation, and the institutional churches. They believe that God produced the universe with its laws of nature, but then left it alone to operate solely by these laws. Deism seems incompatible with some aspects of conventional religion, for example, with the notion of a loving God, or with the practice of prayer.

denotation / connotation The denotation or reference of a word is what that word refers to—the thing in the world that it "names." The connotation or sense of a word is, by contrast, its meaning. Synonymous with 'extension / intension'. A word can have connotation but no denotation: 'unicorn' has meaning but no reference. Note that the philosophical use of 'connotation' is different from the ordinary one, in which it refers not to what a word means, but to more or less distant associations it has; for example, the word 'roses' may carry the connotation of romance to many people. A connotative definition is one that gives the characteristics shared by all and only the objects to which the term refers; often a definition by genus / species. A denotative definition defines by identifying the denotation—for example, by pointing out or listing several things to which the word applies.

deontic Means 'having to do with obligation'. Deontic logic is that branch of modal logic dealing with connections of sentences saying what one ought to do, must do, is permitted to do, etc.

derivation A method for proving deductive validity, in which one moves from premises to succeeding steps using accepted rules of inference, eventuating at the conclusion. There are other methods of proof; for example, in sentential logic, the truth table.

determinism The view that every event is necessitated by previous causes, so that given its causes, each event must have existed in the form it does. There is some debate about how (and whether) this view can be justified. The view that at least some events are not fully caused is called 'indeterminism'. Determinism is often taken to be a presupposition of science; Kant thought it was necessary; but quantum physics says that it is false. One of the main areas of concern about determinism arises when it is considered in connection with free will.

deterrence A motive for punishment: that threatening punishment can prevent future occurrences of undesirable acts. (Other competing theories of punishment attempt to justify it as retribution or rehabilitation.) So one may try to justify jailing criminals by claiming that the threat of similar jailing will discourage them and others from future crime. One may even successfully deter crime by framing the innocent. Deterrence as a national defense policy attempts to prevent other nations' aggression by threatening them with massive (perhaps nuclear) retaliation. The moral status of deterrence is controversial. Preventing war is of course a good thing, but is threatening deterrence justified when it involves the willingness to go through with really horrible retaliation?

dialectic Sometimes this word refers to a style of philosophical discourse most famously due to Plato, involving dialogue: claims, counterclaims, and logical argument. (A contrasting style is rhetoric.) In Kant, dialectical reasoning fallaciously attributes external existence to objects internal to our minds. In Hegel, Marx, and other Continental philosophers, the Dialectic is the interplay of contradictory forces supposed to be a central principle of metaphysical and social existence and change.

divine command theory The ethical theory which explains morality as what is commanded by God. It is often argued that this has things backwards: God commands it because it is right, not vice versa.

double effect The doctrine of double effect holds that, although it is always wrong to use a bad means to a good end, one may act to bring about a good result when also knowingly bringing about bad results, under the following conditions: 1) The bad result is not caused by the good result—both are caused by the action (thus 'double effect'); (2) there's no way of getting the good result without the bad; 3) the good result is so good that it's worth accepting the bad one.

For example, a dentist is allowed to drill, and thus cause some pain (the bad result) for the sake of dental improvements (the good result), since these conditions hold—most notably (1): the pain doesn't cause the improvement; both are results of the drilling.

This principle is associated with Catholic morality, and has been applied most frequently in contexts of medical ethics. It is disputed by some philosophers, who sometimes argue that the distinction between double effect and bad means / good end is artificial and not morally relevant.

doxastic Means 'pertaining to belief', as in 'doxastic state', 'doxastic principle' (for justifying beliefs).

dualism Dualists hold that there are two sorts of things that exist, neither of which can be understood in terms of the other—often, in particular, mental and physical. Other sorts of dualism distinguish the visible and invisible, the actual and the possible, God and the universe, etc. The contrast here is with monism.

egalitarianism The view that people are equal—that they are entitled to equal rights and treatment in society, or to equal possessions or satisfactions.

egoism, ethical / psychological Psychological egoism is the position that people in fact act only in their own interests. It's sometimes argued that even the most generous act is done for the doer's own satisfaction; but this might simply be a way of saying that even the most generous act is motivated—something nobody would deny. Ethical egoism is the position that I (or people in general) ought to act only in my (their) own interests.

emotivism A position in meta-ethics that holds that ethical utterances are to be understood not as statements of fact that are either true or false, but rather as expressions of approval or disapproval, and invitations to the listener to have the same reactions and to act accordingly. Thus emotivists emphasize the "emotive meaning" of ethical utterances, denying that they have cognitive meaning. Emotivists can nevertheless agree that evaluative utterances have some "descriptive content": when I say this is a good apple, I express my approval, but also describe it as having certain characteristics on which my approval rests: that it is, for example, not worm-infested.

empirical This means having to do with sense-experience and experiment. Empirical knowledge is knowledge we get through experience of the world; thus it is a posteriori. An empirical concept is one that is not innate; it can be developed only through experience.

empiricism The position (usually contrasted with rationalism) that all our concepts and substantive knowledge come from sense experience. Empiricists deny that there are innate concepts. While they grant that certain kinds of trivial knowledge (of conceptual, analytic, and logical truths) can be gained by reason alone, independently of experience, they deny the existence of the synthetic a priori.

end in itself 1. Something sought for its own sake; an intrinsic good. 2. Someone is seen as an end in him / herself when that person's aims are seen as having value just because they are that person's aims. Treating people as ends in themselves is respecting their aims, and refraining from thinking of, or using, that person merely as a means to your aims.

ends / means A long-standing controversy in ethics is whether one might be permitted to use bad means to a good end: does the end justify the means? For example, is it permitted to lie to someone if everyone will be better off in the long run as a result? Extreme opponents of consequentialism sometimes hold that no action that is bad in itself is ever permitted no matter how good the consequences. Notice that this means that telling a little lie would not be justified even if it would prevent the destruction of the earth. A more moderate view merely warns against actions which are so bad in themselves that the good consequences do not overwhelm this badness.

Enlightenment The Enlightenment was a cultural and philosophical movement of the seventeenth and eighteenth centuries whose chief features were a belief in rationality and scientific method, and a tendency to reject conventional religion and other traditions. The Age of Enlightenment is also known as the 'Age of Reason'.

enthymeme An argument with some steps left unstated but understood. All pigs are sloppy eaters, so Porky is a sloppy eater is an enthymeme, leaving unsaid Porky is a pig.

epiphenomenalism A variety of dualism in which mental events are just "by-products" of physical ones: physical events cause mental ones, but not vice versa. Analogy: the noise your car makes is caused by the mechanical goings-on inside, but it has no effect on them.

epistemic Having to do with knowledge. Epistemic logic is that branch of modal logic dealing with relations between sentences involving 'knows', 'believes', etc.

epistemology Theory of knowledge: one of the main branches of philosophy. Among the central questions studied here are: What is the difference between knowledge and mere belief? Is all (or any) knowledge based on sense-perception? How, in general, are our knowledge-claims justified?

essence / accident The essential characteristics of something are the ones that it must have in order to be what it is, or the kind of thing it is. It is essential, for example, for a tree to be a plant—if something was not a plant, it could not be a tree. By contrast, a tree that in fact is thirty-three meters high could still be a tree if it weren't that height; thus this characteristic is accidental. (Note that 'accident' and 'accidental' don't have their ordinary meanings in this philosophical use.) Some philosophers think that the essence / accident distinction does not concern the real characteristics of something, but is only a consequence of the words we apply to them: being a plant is said to be an essential characteristic of a tree only because it's part of the definition of 'tree'. But essentialist philosophers believe in real, objective essences.

ethics The general philosophical study of what makes things good or bad, right or wrong. Often the following areas of study are distinguished within ethics: (1) Descriptive ethics: the discovery of what ethical views particular societies in fact have; and speculative anthropological theorizing about the origin and function of these views; (2) Normative ethics: theorizing about what the basic principles are that might serve systematically to distinguish right from wrong. (3) Applied ethics: the normative ethics of particular areas or disciplines: medical ethics, business ethics, computer ethics ... . (4) Meta-ethics: the study of the meaning of moral language and the possibility of ethical knowledge.

'Morality' and 'ethics' (and 'moral' and 'ethical') are usually used as synonyms, though 'ethics' is more frequently generally used as the name of the philosophical study of these matters. Philosophers usually avoid the tendency in ordinary talk to restrict the word 'ethics' to an official code of acceptable behavior in some area (as in 'professional ethics').

ethnocentric Someone is ethnocentric who regards the views or characteristics of his / her own race or culture as the only correct or important ones. Other "-centric" words have arisen by analogy: eurocentric, logocentric, phallocentric for example.

euthanasia Mercy killing, the intentional bringing-about or hastening the death of someone, presumably for his own good, when his life is judged not to be worth continuing, typically when that person is suffering from an untreatable, fatal illness causing horrible unavoidable pain or suffering. Voluntary euthanasia is done at the expressed wish of that person; this wish is not expressed in the case of involuntary euthanasia (for example, when the person has mentally deteriorated beyond the point of being able to express, or perhaps even to have, coherent wishes). Passive euthanasia involves refraining from providing life-prolonging treatment to someone suffering from a fatal condition; active euthanasia is killing, for example, by administering a fatal injection. Ethical opinion is deeply divided concerning euthanasia. Some who argue in favor of its permissibility would accept it only when voluntary, and/or only when passive.

expected utility / value The expected utility (or expected value) of an action is calculated by multiplying the utility (or value) of each possible result of that action by its probability, and adding up the results. For example, consider this betting game: you get $10 if a random draw from a deck of cards is a spade; and you pay $4 if it's any other suit. Assuming the utility of each dollar is 1, to calculate the expected utility of this game we add: [.25 (probability of a spade) x 10 (the utility if it's a spade)] + [.75

(the probability of a non-spade) x -4 (the utility of a non-spade)]. Since (.25 x 10) + (.75 x -4) = 2.5 - 3 = -.5, the game thus has an expected utility of -.5, so you'll average 50 cents loss per play in the long run. One (controversial) theory for rational decision-making advocates maximizing expected utility, so you should not play this game. (But if you enjoy gambling, this has to be figured in too, and might make it worthwhile.)

explanans / explanandum An explanandum (Latin: "to be explained") is something that is being explained: what does the explaining is the explanans (Latin: "explaining thing").

explanation An explanation answers the question 'Why?' and provides understanding; sometimes it also provides us with the abilities to control, and to predict (and retrodict) the world. This is fairly vague, and philosophers have tried to provide theories of explanation—to give a general account of how explanations work, and what makes some good and some bad. One important account is the covering law model. One (but only one) sort of explanation is causal: we explain something by saying what its causes are. Sometimes, instead, we explain by telling what something is made of, or by giving reasons for human actions, as in some explanations in history.

externalism / internalism A variety of related doctrines. Meta-ethical externalism holds that the fact that something is good does not by itself automatically supply the motivation for someone to do it; in addition, motivation ("external" to the mere belief about goodness) must be supplied; internalism is the view that the judgment that something is good itself guarantees or includes the motivation to do it. As a theory of mind, externalism is the view that to specify the "content" of a belief one must refer to the external facts or objects that the belief is about.

fallacy An argument of a type that may seem correct but in fact is not. (Thus, not just any mistaken argument should be called 'fallacious'.) Formal fallacies are mistakes in reasoning that spring from mistakes in logical form; their persuasiveness springs from their similarity, on first glance, to valid forms. Informal fallacies spring instead from ambiguities in meaning or grammar, or from psychological tendencies to be convinced by reasons that are not good reasons.

fatalism The position that our futures are inevitable, whatever we do—that events are "fated" to happen. It's important to distinguish this from determinism, which claims merely that our futures are determined. A determinist who is not a fatalist thinks that our futures are not inevitable—they depend on what we do.

feminism The name of various philosophical—especially ethical, social, and political—theories and social movements that see elements of our society as unjust to and exploitative of women. Feminists often advocate equality under the law and equal economic status for women; but many go further, arguing in favor of preferential treatment for women to counteract past injustices. Sometimes they find male bias and male patterns of thought in many areas of our personal, social, and intellectual lives. Recent developments are feminist theories of the self, of knowledge, and of science.

formal In philosophy this means pertaining to structure (as opposed to content); or rigorous and rule-governed.

foundationalism The position that there is a particular sort of statement (sometimes thought to be indubitable) from which all other statements comprising a system of belief should be derived. There are foundationalist theories of knowledge, of ethics, etc.

free will To say that we have free will (or freedom) is to say that our decisions and actions are sometimes entirely (or at least partially) "up to us"—not forced or determined by anything internal or external to us. We can then either do or not do—we have alternatives. It seems that this is necessary for responsibility for our actions. But if determinism is true, then our actions and "decisions" are determined by previous causes, themselves determined by still earlier causes, and ultimately whatever we decide or do is determined by events that happened a long time ago, and that are not up to us. Thus, it seems that determinism is incompatible with free will. There are three main responses to this apparent problem: (1) Hard determinists accept determinism, which they take to rule out free will. (2) Libertarians accept free will. They think that this means determinism is false, at least for some human events. Both libertarianism and hard determinism are incompatibilist; that is, they hold that the freedom of an act is incompatible with its being determined. (3) Soft determinists are compatibilists, in that they attack the reasoning above, and argue that our actions might be determined, but also free in some sense—that a determined action might nevertheless be up to the doer, and one that the doer is morally responsible for—when it's determined but not compelled.

functional A functional definition defines by giving the typical use of the kind of thing, or its typical cause-and-effect relations with other things; a functional explanation explains something by its function, for example, telling what use the pancreas is in the body, or a social ritual in a particular society. A functional kind is defined by causes and effects (and not, for example, by shape or physical make-up). Functionalism centrally argues that a kind of thing is a functional kind. In philosophy of mind, functionalists argue that mental kinds are functional kinds.

generalization A statement about a group of things, or about everything in a particular category (contrasted with a 'particular statement / proposition'); or the process of reasoning that arrives at one of these. Inductive logic studies the principles of deriving them from particular instances; the rule in deductive logic for deriving one is called universal generalization. An ethical generalization is a rule everyone should follow; Kant argued that the right action was the one whose maxim could be generalized.

general will What is desired by, or desirable for, society as a whole; sometimes taken to be the appropriate justification for government policy. This notion can be problematic when it is taken to mean something other than what's revealed by majority vote or unanimity.

hedonism The advocacy of pleasure as the basic good; philosophical hedonists often distinguish between the "higher" (sometimes = mental or spiritual) and the "lower" pleasures (the merely sensual), making the former more important. Psychological hedonism claims that people in fact seek only pleasure; ethical hedonism claims that people ought to seek pleasure (or only pleasure).

holism / individualism In philosophical use, holism involves the claim that certain sorts of things are more than merely the sum of their parts—that they can be understood only by examining them as a whole; contrasted with individualism. In social science and history, for example, holists argue that one can't explain events on the basis of individual people's actions, because these get their significance only in a society. Semantic holism insists that words and sentences get their meaning only through their relationships with all other words and sentences. Holism about living things refuses to see them merely as the sum of their non-living parts. Methodological individualism is the method in sociology of investigating social facts by discovering facts about individual people. Individualism in ethics emphasizes individual rights and freedoms, contrasting with communitarianism.

hypothesis A tentative suggestion that may be merely a guess or a hunch, or may be based on some sort of reasoning; in any case it needs further evidence to be rationally acceptable as true. Some philosophers think that all scientific enquiry begins with hypotheses.

idea / impression An "idea" is, in general, any thought or perception in the mind. Platonic forms are sometimes called 'ideas'. In Hume, ideas are the faint imprint left on the mind by impressions, which are the mental events one has as the immediate result of, and while, using one's senses (= sense-data); ideas may be called up later in the absence of sensation. Empiricists believe that all ideas are copies of impressions.

idealism In the philosophical sense of this word, it's the view that only minds and their contents really or basically exist. Its competitors are materialism and dualism.

ideal observer theory A theory of ethics that attempts to explain what is really good as what would be chosen by an ideal observer—that is, someone who would have all the relevant information, and who would not be misled by particular interests or biases.

identity 1. Your identity is what you are—what's important about you, or what makes you different from everyone else. 2. Two different things might be said to be 'identical' when they are exactly alike in some characteristics; this is sometimes called qualitative identity. 3. Object a and object b are said to be (strictly or numerically or quantitatively) identical when a and b are in fact the same thing—when 'a' and 'b' are two different names or ways of referring to exactly the same object. 4. Identity (over time) is the relation between something at one time and that same thing at another time: they are said to be two temporal stages (or time-slices) of the same continuing thing.

identity theory of mind The view that each mental state is really a physical state, probably of the brain. Often identity theorists believe in addition in the type-identity of mental and physical states.

illusion / hallucination / delusion Illusions and hallucinations are "false" perceptual experiences—ones that lead, or could lead, to mistakes about what is out there. A hallucination is the apparent perception of something that does not exist at all (as in dreaming, mirages, drug-induced states). An illusion is the incorrect perception of something that does exist. A delusion is a perception that actually results in a false belief; illusions and hallucinations can delude, but often do not. The argument from illusion draws epistemological conclusions from the existence of these things.

imagination Sometimes philosophers have used this word to refer to the faculty of having images—mental pictures.

immaterialism 1. The view that some things exist that are not material: that are not made of ordinary physical stuff, but of mental or spiritual—immaterial stuff instead. This is the denial of materialism. The most extreme form of immaterialism is the view that no material things exist: this is idealism. 2. The view that objects are merely collections of qualities, without a substratum to hold them together. If one thinks of qualities as essentially mental perceptions, then this is a species of immaterialism in sense 1.

immediate / mediate In its more technical philosophical sense 'immediate' means 'without mediation'—that is, 'directly'. In this sense, for example, philosophers ask whether external things are sensed immediately, or mediated by the sensing of internal images. An immediate inference is one performed in one step, needing only a single use of only one rule, for example, when Q is inferred from (P and Q).

immorality / amorality The first means 'contrary to morality'; the second, 'without morality'. Someone who knows about moral rules but intentionally disobeys them or rejects them is immoral; someone who doesn't know or think about morality is amoral. Amorality is typical of small children; immorality of adults.

incorrigibility / corrigibility 'Corrigibility' means 'correctibility'. Something is incorrigible when it is impossible to correct it, or when it is guaranteed correct. Some philosophers have thought that our beliefs about our own mental states are incorrigible. For example, if you sincerely believe that you are now feeling a pain, how could you be wrong?

indubitability / dubitability 'Dubitable' means 'doubtable'. Dubitable statements are not just ones we are psychologically capable of doubting, but ones about which even highly fanciful and unlikely doubts might be raised, doubts that no one in his/her right mind would seriously have. Thus Descartes thought that because our senses might be fooled, information from them was dubitable. He then went on to try to discover what sort of belief was really indubitable: about which it could be proven that no doubt can be raised.

inference / implication / entailment 1. Implication (also known as entailment) is a logical relation that holds between two statements when the second follows deductively from the first. The first is then said to 'imply' (or 'entail') the second. Be careful not to confuse these with 'inference', which is something that people do, when they reason from one statement to another. A rule of inference is an acceptable procedure for reasoning from one set of statements of a particular form to another statement. 2. Sometimes a sentence 'implies' what it doesn't literally state. For example, if I said "Fred is now not robbing banks," I imply that at one time he was robbing banks. This is sometimes called conversational or contextual implicature, or pragmatic implication, to distinguish it from logical implicature.

infinite regress A sequence (of definition, explanation, justification, cause, etc.) that must continue backwards endlessly. For example, if every event must have a cause, then a present event must be caused by some past event; and this event by another still earlier, and so on infinitely. Sometimes the fact that reasoning leads to an infinite regress shows that it is faulty. One then calls it a vicious regress.

informal / formal logic The latter is that kind of logic that relies heavily on symbols and rigorous procedures much like those in mathematics; it concentrates on reasoning that is correct because of syntax. Only a small fraction of the ordinary sorts of reasoning we do can be explained this way, and there is a vast scope for informal logic, which analyzes good and bad arguments semantically, and relies less heavily on symbols and mathematics-style procedures.

informed consent Agreement based on sufficient knowledge of relevant information; relevant especially to medical ethics. It's widely agreed that informed consent by the patient is necessary for all medical procedures, but problems arise here: how much information is enough? What should be done when the patient is unable to understand the information or to make a rational choice?

innateness A belief, concept, or characteristic is innate when it is inborn—when it doesn't come from experience or education—though experience may be thought necessary to make conscious or actualize something that is given innately. An argument for the innateness of something is that experience is not sufficient to produce it in us.

in principle Contrasted with 'in fact' or 'in practice'. Philosophers talk about things we can do in principle, meaning that we could do them if we had the time or technology, or if other merely practical difficulties did not stand in the way. For example, we can verify the statement 'There is a red pebble lying on the north pole of Mars' in principle, though at the moment we can't test this by observation. In principle, we can count to one trillion, because we know the rules for doing it, though in fact we lack the patience and wouldn't live long enough anyway.

intentionality Sometimes this refers to what's true of things done on purpose—intentionally. But in contemporary usage in philosophy of mind, it usually refers to aboutness—the power of referring to or meaning real or imagined external objects. It's sometimes argued that this is a necessary, unique, and essential characteristic of mental states.

interactionism A form of mind / body dualism. It holds that mind and body can interact—that is, that mental events can cause physical events (e.g., when your decision to touch something causes your physical hand movement) and that physical events can cause mental events (e.g., when a physical stimulation to your body causes a mental feeling of pain). A standard objection to this commonsense position is that it's hard to see how this sort of causal interaction could take place, since the mental and the physical work according to their own laws: how could an electrical impulse in a (physical) nerve cell cause a non-physical pain in a mind?

intrinsic / inherent / instrumental / extrinsic Something has intrinsic value when it is valuable for its own sake and not merely as a means to something else. Pleasure, for example, is intrinsically valuable. Something by contrast has instrumental value when it is valuable as a means to some other end. The value of money is primarily instrumental. An intrinsic or inherent or natural right is one people have permanently or essentially, because of the very nature of a person. An extrinsic right is one people have only temporarily, or one they don't have unless they are granted it.

introspection The capacity for finding things out about oneself by "looking inward"—by direct awareness of one's own mental states. You might find out that you have a headache, for example, by introspection. This is contrasted with the way someone else might find this out, by observing your outward behavior—your groaning, holding your head, etc. Sometimes called 'reflection'.

intuition A belief that comes immediately, without reasoning, argument, evidence; before analysis (thus 'preanalytic'). Some philosophers think that certain intuitions are the reliable, rational basis for knowledge of certain sorts. Some beliefs that arise immediately when we perceive are the basis of our knowledge of the outside world (though perceptual intuitions are not always reliable). Our ethical intuitions are sometimes taken to be the basis and the test of ethical theories. Intuitionism is any theory that holds that intuition is a valid source of knowledge.

is / ought problem Clearly what is is sometimes different from what ought to be; but can one infer the latter from the former? Some philosophers hold that you can't: no matter how detailed an account you have of how things are, they don't imply how things ought to be. But ethical naturalists and other objectivists typically claim that they do, because ethical facts are facts too. The supposed is / ought gap is also known as the fact-value gap.

lawlike statements Statements which have the logical form of laws whether they are true or not. Part of the philosophy of science is the attempt to specify the logic of lawlike statements.

law of the indiscernibility of identicals The supposed law of metaphysics (associated with Leibniz, thus also called 'Leibniz's law') that says that if x and y are identical—that is, if x is y—then x and y are indiscernible (share all the same properties). Distinguish this from its reverse, the law of the identity of indiscernibles: if x and y are indiscernible, then they are identical. Imagine two things that are alike in every detail: they even occupy the same space at the same time. Why then think of them as two? Wouldn't there really be only one thing?

libertarianism 1. The position that some of our actions are free in the sense of not being caused. 2. The political position that people have a strong right to political liberty. Thus libertarians tend to object to restrictive laws, taxes, the welfare state, and state economic control. A more specific variety of (traditional) liberalism, though nowadays this position tends to be espoused by some of those who are called 'conservatives'.

logic Loosely speaking, logic is the process of correct reasoning, and something is logical when it makes sense. Philosophers often reserve this word for reasoning norms covered by various particular theories of inference, justification, and proof. Traditional logic was fairly narrowly restricted, concentrating on the syllogism. Nowadays, symbolic deductive and inductive logics cover a much wider area, but far from the totality of reasoning.

logical form The form of a sentence is its general structure, ignoring the particular content it has. For example, If it's Tuesday, then I'm late for class and If Peru is in Asia, then Porky is a frog have the same overall logical form (if P then Q). The sort of logic that works by exhibiting, often in symbolic notation, the logical form of sentences is called 'formal logic'.

logical positivism A school of philosophy (also known as "logical empiricism"), subscribed to by many twentieth-century English-speaking philosophers. Impressed by empiricism and by the success and rigor of science, the logical positivists advocated that philosophers avoid speculation about matters only science and experience could settle; if a sentence was not scientifically verifiable or a matter of logical truth or conceptual truth, it was nonsense and should be discarded (the verifiability criterion). Ethical statements were thought not verifiable, so without literal meaning: they were sometimes thought merely to be expressions of feelings of approval or disapproval.

logical truth / falsity A sentence is logically true (or false) when it is true (or false) merely because of its logical structure. Examples: All ducks are ducks. Either it's raining or it's not raining. These should be distinguished from analytic truths / falsehoods, which are true / false merely because of the meaning of their words: for example, All fathers are male. Logical truths / falsehoods are also called logically necessary / impossible sentences, but these should also be distinguished from (metaphysically) necessary truths / falsehoods (see necessary / contingent truth): those that must be true or false. 'Tautology' is sometimes used as a synonym for 'logical truth', though in ordinary talk a tautology is something that says the same thing twice. Thus, It's raining and it's raining is a tautology in the ordinary sense, though not in the philosophers' sense (since it might be false). Sentences that are neither logically true nor logically false— that are merely true or false—are said to be logically contingent (or logically indeterminate).

materialism As a philosophical term, this refers to the position that all that exists is physical. (Synonym: physicalism.) Materialists about mind sometimes argue that apparently non-physical things like the soul or mind or thoughts are actually material things. Central-state materialists identify mental events with physical events central in the body (i.e., in the nervous system). Eliminative materialists, however, think that categorizing things as mental is altogether a mistake (like believing in ghosts).

matter of fact / relation of ideas Hume's distinction. He seems to have meant that a matter of fact is a contingent state of affairs, to be discovered a posteriori; a relation of ideas is a conceptual or analytic or logical truth, which can be known a priori.

medieval philosophy The dividing lines between ancient, medieval, and modern philosophy are rough, but it's often said that medieval philosophy starts with Augustine (c. 400), and ends just before Descartes (c. 1600).

meta- This prefix often means 'beyond', or 'about', so thinking about meta-x is (sometimes) thinking about the structure or nature of x. Examples of its use are 'meta-language' and 'meta-ethics'; it is used differently, however, in 'metaphysics'.

metaphysics One of the main branches of philosophy, having to do with the ultimate components of reality, the types of things that exist, the nature of causation, change, time, God, free will.

mind-body problem What is the relation between mental and physical events? Is one sort of event reducible to the other? Are mental events merely a sort of bodily event? Or are they distinct? If so, how are they connected?

modal statements are (roughly speaking) the ones that are not straightforward assertions, and have complexities involved in the logic of their relations (studied in modal logic), their confirmation, etc. The basic kind of modal statements are those affirming necessity and possibility; but also considered in this category are belief, tense, moral, counterfactual, causal, and lawlike statements.

modern philosophy The borderline between medieval philosophy and modern philosophy is rough, but it is usually said that Descartes was the first modern philosopher (around 1600). The era of modern philosophy can be said to extend through the present, though it's often taken to end around the beginning of the nineteenth century, or later with the advent of postmodernism.

monism A monistic metaphysics is the belief that there is one basic kind of thing in existence. Monists about mind deny dualism (belief in two irreducible substances, mind and matter). Nowadays most monists are materialists, but historically, many were idealists (believing that this one kind of stuff was basically mental).

monotheism / polytheism / pantheism Monotheism is the belief in one (and only one) God. Polytheism is the belief in many gods. Pantheism is the belief that God somehow exists in everything, or that everything is God.

moral argument for God's existence One version of this argument: There is a real objective difference between right and wrong, but the only way to make sense of this is to think of it as arising from a divine moral order. So the existence of morality shows that God exists.

moral realism The view that there are real, objective, knowable moral facts.

moral sense theory The idea that we have a way of "sensing" the objective moral properties, on the analogy of the way we can sense the property of redness using our eyes. Moral sensation would clearly be a very different kind of sensation, however; what is the sense organ involved? Is it at all reliable?

mutatis mutandis (Latin: "having changed the things that were to be changed") Philosophers say things like "This case is, mutatis mutandis, like the other," meaning that the two cases are alike except for certain details—that one can derive one case from the other by making the appropriate substitutions or changes.

mutually exclusive / jointly exhaustive Mutually exclusive sets do not overlap each other in membership. For example, each of these sets: mammals, birds, fish, reptiles, amphibians, is exclusive of the others, since nothing belongs to more than one of them. The list is jointly exhaustive of vertebrates, since every vertebrate is included in these categories. It is mutually exclusive and jointly exhaustive because every vertebrate is included in exactly one of these categories.

mystical experience argument for God's existence The existence and nature of the mystical experiences some people have are sometimes taken to show God's existence. One criticism of this argument is that even though having this experience sometimes provides a compelling motivation for belief, it's not reliable evidence.

mysticism A variety of religious practice that relies on direct experience which is often taken to be a union with God or with the divine ground of all being. The content of these experiences is often taken to be ineffable, but we are told that they produce enlightenment or bliss. Mystics often advocate exercises or rituals designed to induce the abnormal psychological states in which these experiences occur.

naïve realism What's supposed to be the ordinary view about perception: that it (usually) reveals external objects to us directly, the way they really are. The implication is that this "naïve" view is overturned by philosophical sophistication. Also called common-sense realism or direct realism.

naturalism This term names the view that everything is a natural entity, and thus to be studied by the usual methods of natural science. Naturalistic or "naturalizing" theories in philosophy try to apply ordinary scientific categories and methods to philosophical problems. Philosophers have proposed naturalized epistemology, philosophy of mind, and ethics.

natural kind Some philosophers think that some of the ways we divide the world into kinds correspond to the way nature really is divided—they "cut nature at the joints." Classically, a natural kind is a kind that things belong to necessarily: thus, human being is a natural kind because Fred is necessarily human; but living within fifty miles of the Empire State Building is not: Fred might move further away; or, if he doesn't he might have. Some contemporary thinkers hold that natural kinds are the ones that support certain modal implications needed in science; but others argue that there are no natural kinds—all kinds are artificial human creations.

natural law There are several philosophically relevant senses of this phrase: 1. A law of nature—i.e., a formulation of a regularity found in the natural world, the sort of thing science discovers. 2. A principle of proper human action or conduct, taken to be God-given, or to be a consequence of "human nature"—our structure or function. In this sense, there are "natural law" theories in ethics and in political philosophy. 3. The view that the validity of the laws of a legal system depends on their coherence with God-given or otherwise objective morality.

necessary / contingent truth A necessary truth is one that could not possibly be false; a contingent truth could be false but isn't, just as a matter of fact. Some philosophers think that the necessity or contingency of some fact is a metaphysical matter—is a matter of the way the external world is—but others hold that this difference is merely a matter of the way we think or talk about the world—that a truth taken to be necessary is merely a conceptual or logical or analytic truth. A necessary truth is also called a necessity, a contingent truth a contingency, and a necessary falsehood an impossibility.

necessary / sufficient condition x is a sufficient condition for y when: if x is true, then y must also be true—that x can't exist without y. This is the same as saying: x can't be without y. x is a necessary condition for y when: if y is true, then x must also be true. In other words, y can't be without x. If you can't have either without the other, then x and y are both necessary and sufficient for each other.

nomic Means 'having to do with law'. A nomic regularity is distinguished from a mere (accidental) regularity or coincidence, in that the first represents a law of nature. One way this difference is explained is by saying that a nomic regularity supports counterfactuals: it's not only the case that all A's are B's, but it's also the case that if something were an A, it would be a B. [synonym: 'nomological']

norm / normative A norm is a standard. 'Normative' means prescribing a norm. When somebody says, "We think abortion is wrong," that statement may be descriptive—informing you what a group's views are, or normative—morally condemning abortion.

obligation Generally, something one morally must do, a synonym for 'duty'. What one must do is perhaps not all there is to morality. Some good things are supererogatory—above and beyond the call of duty—great if you do them, but nobody would blame you if you didn't.

omni- Many (not all) religious thinkers take God to be omnibenevolent—totally, perfectly good; omnipotent—all-powerful, able to do anything; omnipresent—everywhere at once, or influential in everything; and omniscient—all-knowing.

ontological argument for God's existence A variety of arguments that rely on the concept of God to prove His existence. In the best-known version it is supposed that part of the concept of God is that He is perfect: since something would not be perfect if it did not exist, it follows that God exists.

ontology The philosophical study of existence or being. Typical questions are: What basic sorts of things exist? What are the basic things out of which others are composed, and the basic relations between things?

operational definition Defines by giving an account of the procedures or measurements used to apply the word. For example, one might describe weighing procedures and outcomes to define 'weight'.

operationalism / instrumentalism Operationalism is the view that scientific concepts should have operational definitions, and that any terms not definable in this way should be eliminated from science as meaningless. Instrumentalists are operationalists who are explicitly anti-realists about theoretical entities. They say that electrons, for example, don't really exist; electron-talk is about nothing but what's observable.

ordinary language philosophy A branch of twentieth-century philosophy that held that philosophical problems arose because of confusions about, or complexities in, ordinary language, and might be solved (or dissolved) by attention to the subtleties of actual talk.

overdetermination An event is overdetermined when two or more events have happened, each of which is individually a sufficient condition for it. Thus someone's death is overdetermined when he is given a fatal dose of poison and then shot through the heart.

parallelism Because of the difficulties in interactionism some philosophers were led to the belief that mind and body events don't cause each other, but just run along independently; they are coordinated, however, perhaps inexplicably, or maybe because God sets them up in advance (occasionalism) to run in parallel, like two clocks set in advance to chime the hour simultaneously.

Pascal's wager is Blaise Pascal's famous argument for belief in God: Belief in God might result in infinite benefit—eternal salvation—if He exists, while we risk only a little—wasting some time, and foregoing some pleasures forbidden to believers—if He doesn't. Conversely, disbelief might result in infinite harm—eternal damnation—if He exists, or could provide a tiny benefit if we were right. So even if there isn't any evidence one way or the other, it's a very good bet to believe.

paternalism Paternalistic action provides for what is taken to be someone's good, without giving that person responsibility for determining his/her own aims or actions. It arises from a sort of benevolence plus lack of trust in people's ability to decide what's to their own benefit or to act for their own real long-range good. Some critics of paternalism argue that the only way to determine someone's good is to see what that person chooses. Some argue that respect for individual autonomy means that we shouldn't interfere even when someone is

choosing badly. This issue arises most importantly in political theory and medical ethics, since governments and physicians often act paternalistically.

patriarchy Societal and familial institutions are patriarchal when they systematically embody male dominance over women: when they arrange things so that men hold power and women do not. Feminists emphasize the widespread incidence of patriarchal institutions in historical and contemporary families and societies.

perception In its broadest use, this means any sort of mental awareness, but it's more often used to refer to the awareness we get when using the senses.

person Philosophers sometimes use this word in such a way that persons do not necessarily coincide with living human organisms. The idea here is that a person is anything that has special rights (for example, the right to life, or to self-determination) or special dignity or worth. Sometimes it's held that some humans (e.g., those in a permanent coma) are not persons in this sense, or that some higher animals are.

personal identity 1. What makes you you. Is it your body, your mind, your personality, your memories, or something else? 2. What makes this person now the same person as that one, earlier. Is it a continuing body, or mind, or personality, or that this later stage remembers the experiences that happened to the earlier one?

phenomenalism Phenomenalists believe (on the basis, for example, of the argument from illusion) that all we're ever aware of is appearances or sense-data, the mental events we have when using our senses. Accepting the empiricist rule that we're entitled to believe in only what's given by our senses, they deny the existence of external objects independent of perception. Ordinary "objects" like tables and chairs are thus thought to be collections of these appearances—actual and perhaps possible ones.

phenomena / noumena Philosophers sometimes use 'phenomenon' in the ordinary sense, referring merely to something that happens, but often it's used in a more technical way, referring to a way things seem to us—to something as we perceive it. Noumena are, by contrast, things-in-themselves—things as they really are. These are unavailable to the senses, but perhaps rationally comprehensible; though Kant argued that they are unknowable.

pluralism Pluralist theories argue for a multiplicity of basic kinds. To be a pluralist about value is to believe that there are many incompatible, but equally valid, value systems.

positivism The philosophy associated with Auguste Comte, which holds that scientific knowledge is the only valid kind of knowledge, and that anything else is idle speculation. Sometimes this term is loosely used to refer to logical positivism, which is a twentieth-century outgrowth of more general nineteenth-century positivism.

possible worlds This world—the collection of all facts—is the actual world. The set of possible worlds includes the actual world plus non-actual worlds—ones in which one or more things are not as they actually are, but might have been.

postmodernism Various late twentieth-century movements, in general characterized by a rejection of foundationalism, an interest in textual interpretation and deconstruction, antagonism to analytic philosophy, rejection of the goals of the Enlightenment, tendency to perspectivism, denial of the applicability of the concepts of reality, objectivity, truth.

poststructuralism A postmodern view, thought of as a successor to structuralism. Holds in general that the meaning of words is their relation to other words (in a "text"), not their relation to reality; that human activity is not lawlike, but understood through its relations to power and the unconscious.

pragmatism A largely American school of philosophers who emphasized the relevance of the practical application of things, their connections to our lives, our activities and values, demanding instrumental definitions of philosophically relevant terms, and urged that we judge beliefs on the basis of their benefit to the believer.

pre-Socratics The ancient Greek philosophers before Socrates, that is, of the sixth and fifth centuries BCE. Their thought is the earliest recorded Western philosophy.

presupposition A necessary condition for the truth of a statement, assumed beforehand by the speaker, but not itself stated. The speaker of 'The present king of France is bald' assumes that there is a present king of France. Because there isn't, the statement is not true, but is it false, or rather inappropriate and lacking a truth value?

prima facie (Latin: "at first appearance") Based on the first impression: what would be true, or seem to be true in general, before we have additional information about a particular case. Prima facie duties are what we're in general obliged to do, but that might not turn out to be obligatory in particular cases. Prima facie evidence can be overridden by contrary considerations.

primary / secondary qualities Locke (and others) argued that some characteristics we perceive are really as perceived in external objects (the primary qualities), whereas others (the secondary qualities) don't exist as perceived in the real world, but are just powers of external objects to produce ideas in us which don't resemble what's out there. Something's dimensions are supposed to be primary, but its color secondary.

privileged access Supposedly a special way you alone can find out about the contents of your mind. Other people need to infer what's in your mind from your external behavior, but you can discover your mental states directly.

problem of evil A problem for religious believers: God is supposed to be all-powerful, benevolent, and all-knowing. Evil is what is bad for us, so God must eliminate all evil. But there clearly is evil. So a God with all of these features does not exist.

problem of induction Everyone believes that the basic regularities we have observed in the past will continue into the future; this principle is called the principle of induction or the principle of the uniformity of nature. Note however that it would be circular to justify this principle by our past experience. How then to justify it?

problem of other minds If only your mind and its contents can be "perceived" directly only by you, this raises the problem of what ground (if any) you have for thinking that anyone else has a mind, and is not, for example, just a body with external appearance and behavior much like yours.

proposition This term has been used in a confusing variety of ways. Sometimes it means merely a sentence or a statement. Perhaps the most common modern use is the one in which a proposition is what is expressed by a (declarative) sentence: an English sentence and its French translation express the same proposition, and so do Seymour is Marvin's father and Marvin's male parent is Seymour.

propositional attitudes These are our mental states which are, so to speak, directed at propositions. For example, toward the proposition It will snow on Christmas, one can have the propositional attitude of wishing (I wish that it would snow on Christmas), believing, fearing, and so on. Compare these with mental states which are not directed at propositions: feeling happy, enjoying an ice cream, remembering Mama.

punishment Must punishment be unpleasant? Then a judicial sentence of not-unpleasant corrective therapy wouldn't be punishment. Must punishment be given in response to a previous bad act? Then a jail sentence given to an innocent person, either by mistake or to set an example for future wrongdoers, wouldn't count as punishment.

A continuing philosophical problem is the attempt to justify the existence of punishment. The deterrence and rehabilitation theories claim punishments are justified when they have good effects: for example, the prevention of future bad acts through the deterrent threat of punishment to others, or the reform of the wrongdoer. Retributivists claim that such uses of punishment are immoral, and that punishment is justified for wrongdoers merely because wrongdoing demands it—because it's justice—or a restoration of the moral order—to inflict punishment on wrongdoers.

pure reason 1. Pure reason is often taken to be reason working on its own, as contrasted with practical reason which connects facts with desires and yields conclusions about what we ought to do. 2. Pure reason is sometimes spoken of in contrast to empirical reason; thus it's a priori reasoning, supposedly independent of what we get from the senses.

qua (Latin: as) Means considered as (such and such). Usage example: "He is investigating hip hop qua social phenomenon, not qua music."

qualia 1. = characteristics (old-fashioned use). 2. = sense-data. 3. The characteristics of sensations (of sense-data), distinguished from characteristics of things sensed; for example, the flavor of an apple, as tasted, or the feel of a headache. The existence of qualia is sometimes supposed to be a problem for functionalism.

quality / attribute / property These words are synonyms. They each mean a characteristic of something. Some philosophers argue that a thing cannot be composed entirely of qualities; there must be something else, the thing itself, which these are qualities of, in which these qualities are said to "inhere".

rationalism Broadly, any philosophical position which makes reasoning or rationality extra-important. More particularly the view, contrasted with empiricism, that reason alone, unaided by sense experience, is capable of reliable and substantive knowledge; rationalists also tend to believe in innate ideas. Sometimes by "the rationalists" one means the modern continental rationalists, notably Descartes, Leibniz, and Spinoza.

rational self-interest Acting from self-interest is seeking one's own benefit. Some philosophers have sometimes argued that sometimes one can achieve this only by fulfilling some interests of others too; so they argue that rational self-interest often involves more than narrow selfishness.

realism / antirealism Realists hold views (in a variety of philosophical areas) that some sort of entity has external existence, independent of the mind; anti-realists think that that sort of entity is only a product of our thought.

reasons / causes You sometimes have reasons for doing something, but is this to be understood causally? That is, does that mean that there is a special sort of cause for your action? One reason to think that reasons are not causes is that talk about reasons often mentions the future, but a cause of x must occur before x does.

recursive Something (for example, a definition or a function) is recursive when it is to be applied over and over again to its own previous product. For example, one can define 'integer' by saying that 0 is an integer, and if x is an integer, then x + 1 is an integer. Thus, applying the second part of this definition to the first, 1 is an integer, applying the second part to this result, 2 is an integer, and so on.

reduction To reduce some notion is to define (or analyze) it in terms of others, and thus to eliminate it from the list of basic entities in the field under discussion. Reductionism about some notion is the idea that that notion can be reduced—can be given a reductive analysis.

reflective equilibrium A goal sometimes thought to guide the construction of theories. A theory is in reflective equilibrium when the basic general principles of the theory square with the particular facts the theory is supposed to explain. We start with beliefs about particulars, and construct some general principles to explain these. Alterations might then be made in other beliefs about particulars when they conflict with the principles, or in the principles when they conflict with beliefs about particulars.

reification The mistaken way of thinking about some abstract notion as if it were a real thing.

relational / intrinsic properties A property is intrinsic if things have that property in themselves, rather than in relation to other things. Thus being 100 meters tall is an intrinsic property, but being the tallest building in town is a relational property, because this is relative to the heights of other buildings in town.

relativism / absolutism Relativists argue that when certain views vary among individual people and among cultures (cultural relativism) there is no universal truth: there is instead, only "true for me (or us); false for you (or them)." This contrasts with absolutism (sometimes called objectivism): the position that there is an objectively right view. The most common relativist views concern morality (ethical relativism).

Renaissance The period (fourteenth through sixteenth century) characterized by the diminution of the authority of the Church in favor of a new humanism, and the rapid growth of science.

representationalism Theories that hold that mental contents—thoughts, perceptions, etc.—represent reality. If these representations are the only thing directly available to the mind, how do we know that the external world is actually being represented—and what it is really like?

retrocausation "Backward" causation, in which the effect occurs before the cause. The possibility of retrocausation is debatable.

retrodiction Means 'prediction backwards'—"prediction" of the past. A historian might retrodict, for example, on the basis of certain historical documents, that a battle took place centuries ago at a certain location. This retrodiction can be confirmed by present evidence, for example, by artifacts of war dug up at that site.

rights You are said to have a right to do or have something when it is thought that nobody should be allowed to keep you from it. Thus, we can speak of a right to property, or to vote, or to life. Having a right to do something doesn't mean you must or even ought to do it, but merely that you're allowed to do it if you want. Utilitarians might be able to justify according certain rights, but usually rights-theorists insist that a right is independent of utility:

that someone morally can exercise a genuine right even if it is contrary to the general welfare. An inalienable right is a right that one cannot give up or get rid of. A civil right is a right that is (or ought to be) guaranteed and enforced by government. Conventional rights are rights produced or guaranteed by society (by government or agreement, or just by custom). Natural rights, on the other hand, are rights we are supposed to have just because we are human (perhaps because they are God-given).

rigid designator A rigid designator is a term that refers to the same thing in every other possible world in which it exists. It's often thought that proper names are rigid designators, but definite descriptions aren't—they're non-rigid.

self-consciousness In philosophical use, this may mean the sort of knowledge one has of one's self that one gets by adopting the perspective that others might have of one; or else the sort of self-awareness one gets by introspection.

self-contradiction A statement is self-contradictory when it asserts and denies the same thing (It's raining and it's not raining), or when it's logically false. An inconsistent set is self-contradictory. Sometimes (more loosely) a statement that is analytically false is called a self-contradiction.

semantics / syntax / pragmatics These terms name aspects of language and the study of these aspects. Semantics is that part of language which has to do with meaning and reference. Syntax has to do with grammar or logical form. Syntax, then, can tell you whether a sentence is formed correctly (for example, 'Is the on but but' is not formed correctly), but cannot tell you what a correctly formed sentence means, or what conditions would make it true. Pragmatics concerns the relations between bits of language and their uses by language-users.

sense-data The data of the senses—what they give us: the internal event or picture or representation we get when perceiving external objects—or sometimes, as when we dream or hallucinate, even in their absence. A straight stick half under water looks bent; we then have a bent sense-datum, the same sort of internal picture we would have if we saw a bent stick out of water. The argument from illusion is supposed to show that all we really directly (immediately) perceive are sense-data, and that we only infer external objects from these.

simple / complex ideas A complex idea is one that can be analyzed into simpler ideas. Brother, for example, names a complex idea that is "composed" of the ideas of male and sibling; but green perhaps names a simple idea.

skepticism The view that knowledge in some area is not possible. The Skeptics were a group of (skeptical!) Greek philosophers. Skeptics often don't really doubt the truth of the belief about which they are skeptical: their central claim is that we don't have justification for that belief.

slippery slope A form of moral reasoning in which it is argued that some act or practice is undesirable not because it's bad in itself, but because its acceptance will or might lead to a series of other acts that differ from each other in small ways, and eventuate in something clearly bad. It might be argued, for example, that a city's allowing street vendors on one corner isn't in itself bad, but this might gradually lead to more and more permissiveness, resulting eventually in the clogging of city sidewalks by all sorts of undesirables.

social contract A way of justifying the legitimacy of a ruler or government, or the restrictions imposed by government or by moral rules, on the basis of an agreement (whether explicit or tacit or merely hypothetical) of the people involved. It is supposed that people agree (or would agree) to these restrictions because of the resulting long-range benefits to everyone. This agreement is called a 'social contract'. Thinking about this social contract is usually intended (by contractarians) to provide not an actual history of the origin of these rules, but rather a justification of their existence and of their binding force.

solipsism The position that the self is the only thing that can be known, or, more extremely, that one's own mind is the only thing that exists in the universe. Nobody sane ever believed this latter view, but it is philosophically interesting to try to refute it.

state of nature The condition of human societies—typically but not invariably thought to be unpleasant—before the invention of governmental or conventional rules regulating conduct, typically held to justify such invention.

Stoicism The views of the Stoics, an ancient Greek and Roman school. They held that virtue is the highest good, and stressed control of the passions and indifference to pleasure and pain (thus the ordinary use of 'stoic').

straw man Straw man argument or reasoning (or "setting up a straw man") is a bad form of reasoning in which one argues against some position by producing and refuting a false and stupid version of that position.

structuralism Wide-ranging and controversial largely French twentieth-century philosophical school of thought. Its central idea is that cultural phenomena should be understood as manifesting unchanging and universal abstract structures or forms; their meaning can be understood only when these forms are revealed.

subjective / objective Whether something is objective—a feature of the real external mind-independent world, or subjective—in our minds only—is a perennial and pervasive topic in all areas of philosophy. Examples: ethical subjectivism, for example, holds that our ethical "judgments" reflect our own feelings only, not facts about externals. Aesthetic subjectivism puts beauty (and other aesthetic properties) in the eye of the beholder.

substance Any basic, independently existing entity or subject; the stuff of which things are made. Thought sometimes to be unavailable to our senses, but conceptually necessary as that which "underlies" or "supports" characteristics we can sense, and as that which is responsible for things existing through time despite changes in characteristics. Dualists believe there are two substances: (1) physical (material, corporeal, or extended substance), making up physical things, that to which material qualities (size and shape, weight or mass, etc.) apply; (2) mental (immaterial or incorporeal), what mental or spiritual things are made of, and to which characteristics such as thinking, feeling, desiring apply.

supervenience Things of kind A supervene on things of kind B (the 'supervenience base') when the presence or absence of things of kind A is completely determined by the presence or absence of things of kind B; there can be no difference of sort A without a difference in sort B (though there may be differences in B without differences in A). A clear example is the supervenience of the biological on the microphysical: things have biological properties in virtue of their microphysical properties, and there can be no biological difference without a microphysical difference. It is sometimes thought that ethical properties, and mental properties, supervene on the physical.

tabula rasa (Latin: "blank slate") The term is associated with Locke; he and others opposed to innateness think that at birth our minds have no concepts or beliefs in them—they are "blank slates" that will get things "written" on them only after, and by, sense experience.

teleological argument for God's existence Arguments based on the apparent goal-directedness of things in nature. A common version: Living things are adapted to their environment—they are built in complex and clever ways to function well in their surroundings. This could not have happened merely by the random and mechanical processes of nature. They must have been constructed this way, with their functions in mind, by a creator much more clever and powerful than humans; thus they are evidence for God's existence. The usual reply to this argument is that Darwinian evolutionary theory provides a scientific account of how these things arose merely by the mechanical processes of nature, so one need not posit something unseen and supernatural to account for them.

teleology The study of aims, purposes, or functions. Much ancient philosophical and scientific thought saw teleology as a central principle of things, and a very important basis for explanation. Teleology is much less important in contemporary thought, but philosophers are still interested in what teleology remains (for example, scientific talk about what the pancreas is for, or about the function of individual species in the ecosystem). Teleological ethics sees the aim of actions—good results—as the basic concept, from which the notions of right action and good person can be derived.

theism Belief in the existence of at least one god; often, however, more narrowly monotheism—the belief in just one God. The contrast here is with atheism.

theory Scientists and philosophers do not mean "just a guess" by the word theory. A theory here is a system of interrelated statements designed to explain a variety of phenomena. Sometimes a theory is distinguished from a law or set of laws insofar as a theory postulates the existence of unseen theoretical entities.

thought experiment A state of affairs or story we are asked to imagine to raise a philosophical question, or to illustrate or test some philosophical point. For example, imagine that the brains of two people were interchanged; what you would then say about the location of the two might have implications for the principles of personal identity. (Sometimes encountered in its German translation, *Gedankenexperiment*.)

transcendental The most general philosophical usage of this term applies to any idea or system that goes beyond some supposed limit. The word is most often encountered, however, in connection with transcendental idealism, the name of Kant's system; he produced transcendental arguments that were supposed to show truths beyond the evidence of our senses, as necessary presuppositions of any rational experience or thought.

twin-earth An imaginary planet almost exactly like our Earth, commonly referred to in philosophical thought-experiments. Suppose, for example, that rivers and oceans on twin-earth are filled with XYZ, not H_2O, though the two are (except by chemists) indistinguishable. Then when on twin-earth Twin-John asks for "water" in his scotch, does this mean the same as in English?

type / token Two different things that are both of a certain sort are said to be two tokens of one type. Thus, in the sentence 'The cat is on the mat' there are six word tokens, but only five word types. Token physicalism is the view that each particular mental event is identical with (the same thing as) a particular physical event (e.g., a brain event). Type physicalism (sometimes known as the type-type identity theory) adds that each kind of mental event is also a kind of physical event. Functionalists tend to be token physicalists but not type physicalists. Identity theorists tend to be type physicalists. Anomalous monism admits token identity, but denies type identity.

underdetermination Something is underdetermined by a set of conditions if these conditions don't determine how (or that) it will exist. Thus, the striking of a match underdetermines its lighting because it's not sufficient. Language behavior underdetermines a translation manual when different equally adequate translation manuals can be constructed for that behavior. Scientific theory is underdetermined by empirical evidence when two rival hypotheses are both consistent with all the evidence.

universalizability True of a particular action when it can be universalized—that is, when the rule behind it can consistently or reasonably be conceived of as a universal law (one that could apply to everyone). The test of consistent rational universalizability is roughly what Kant thought to be the test of ethically right action. The test of practical universalizability (not Kant's test) is perhaps what we apply when we think morally about some action by evaluating the consequences if everyone were to do that sort of thing.

universals These are "abstract" things—beauty, courage, redness, etc. The problem of universals is whether these exist in the external world. Thus, one may be a realist or anti-realist about universals. Plato's theory of forms is an early and well-known realism about universals; the empiricists are associated with anti-realism. Nominalism is a variety of anti-realism that claims that only particulars exist, and that such abstractions are merely the result of the way we talk.

utilitarianism Utilitarians think that the moral worth of any action can be measured by the extent to which it provides valued results—usually pleasure or happiness—to the greatest number of people. Thus, their general moral principle is the principle of utility, also known as the 'greatest happiness principle': "Act so as to produce the greatest happiness for the greatest number of people." Act utilitarians hold that moral thinking evaluates each act, in context, separately; rule utilitarians argue that morality is concerned with general rules for action, and that a particular action is right if it is permitted or recommended by a moral code whose acceptance in the agent's society would maximize utility, even if that act in particular does not.

utility In utilitarianism, this means the quantity of value or desirability something has. Often it is thought that the utility of something can be given a number (the quantity of "utiles" it possesses), and utilities can be compared or added.

vacuous Means 'empty'. In logic, the statement All A's are B's is understood to be equivalent to For all x, if x is an A then x is a B. Suppose there aren't any A's at all. Then it's always false that any x is an A: but this makes the conditional, if x is an A then x is a B true. It follows, then, that if there aren't any A's, all statements of the form All A's are B's are true. So, for example, because there aren't any unicorns, the statement All unicorns are mammals is true, and so is All unicorns are non-mammals. This strange kind of truth is called vacuous truth.

vagueness In a technical logician's sense, a term is vague whose application involves borderline cases: thus, 'tall' is vague, because there are some people who are clearly tall, some clearly not tall, and some who are in a borderline area, and are not clearly tall or not tall.

verifiability A statement is verifiable when there exist (at least in principle) procedures that would show that it is true or false. 'In principle' is added here because there do not need to be procedures actually available now or ever, as long as we can imagine what they are. So, for example, the statement There is a planet on a star seven million light years from here is unverifiable given our current (and perhaps future) technology, but because we can imagine what would be evidence for its truth or falsity, it is verifiable in principle.

virtue Moral excellence or uprightness; the state of character of a morally worthwhile person. The virtues are those character traits that make for a good person. Some philosophers think that virtue, not good states of affairs or right action, is the central notion in ethics: thus virtue ethics.

zombies These are, of course, the walking dead of horror movies, starring also in the problem of absent qualia which haunts functionalism. In this thought experiment, we are to imagine that zombies show normal stimulus-response connections, but no qualia—no consciousness. The functionalist would have to grant them mentality; this is supposed to show what's wrong with functionalism.

IMAGE CREDITS

Line drawing portrait by Rose McNeil:

Mary Midgley

Author image contributed by:

Virginia Held

ACKNOWLEDGMENTS

The publisher has made every attempt to locate the authors of the copyrighted material or their heirs and assigns, and would be grateful for information that would allow correction of any errors or omissions in subsequent editions of the work.

Aristotle. *Aristotle: The Nicomachean Ethics*, translated with an Introduction by David Ross [aka W.D. Ross], revised by J.O. Urmson and J.L. Ackrill. Oxford World's Classics, 1998; pp. 1–3; 11–15; 35–47; 106–122; 261–269. By permission of Oxford University Press.

de Beauvoir, Simone. "Introduction" translated by H.M. Parshley, from *The Second Sex* by Simone de Beauvoir, pp. xix–xxxv, copyright © 1952 and renewed 1980 by Alfred A. Knopf, a division of Random House, Inc. Used by permission of Alfred A. Knopf, a division of Random House, Inc.

Held, Virginia. "Feminist Transformations of Moral Theory." *Philosophy and Phenomenological Research*, Volume 50, Supplement, Autumn 1990; pp. 321–344. Reproduced with permission of Wiley-Blackwell Inc.

Hobbes, Thomas. *Leviathan*. London, 1651.

Kant, Immanuel. "Groundwork for the Metaphysics of Morals." Translated by Thomas K. Abbott with revisions by Lara Denis. Broadview Press, 2005, pp. 55–95.

Marx, Karl and Engels, Friedrich. *The Communist Manifesto*. Translated by Samuel Moore and edited by Friedrich Engels, 1888.

Midgley, Mary. "Is a Dolphin a Person?" From *In Defence of Animals*. Edited by Peter Singer. Oxford: Basil Blackwell, copyright © 1985; pp. 52–62. Reproduced with permission of Wiley-Blackwell Inc.

Mill, John Stuart. *On Liberty*. London: John W. Parker & Son, 1859.

Mill, John Stuart. *Utilitarianism*, 4th edition. Longmans, Green, Reader, and Dyer, 1871.

Nietzsche, Friedrich. From *Beyond Good and Evil*. Translated by Marion Faber. Oxford World's Classics, 1998, pp. 152–158. By permission of Oxford University Press.

Nozick, Robert. Excerpt from Chapter 7, "Distributive Justice," of *Anarchy, State and Utopia* (New York: Basic Books, 1974), pp. 149–164, 174–182. Copyright © 1974 by Basic Books, Inc. Reprinted by permission of Basic Books, a member of the Perseus Books Group.

Okin, Susan Moller. "Justice and Gender." *Philosophy and Public Affairs* 16, 1987; pp. 42–72. Reproduced with permission of Wiley-Blackwell Inc.

Plato. Book II (357a-367e), of the *Republic*. Translated by G.M.A. Grube and revised by C.D.C. Reeve. Hackett Publishing Company, 1992; pp. 33–42. Reprinted by permission of Hackett Publishing Company, Inc. All rights reserved.

Rawls, John. "Three Basic Points" and "Two Principles of Justice" reprinted by permission of the publisher from *Justice as Fairness: A Restatement* by John Rawls, edited by Erin Kelly, pp. 39–50, Cambridge, MA: The Belknap Press of Harvard University Press, copyright © 2001 by the President and Fellows of Harvard College.

SOURCES FOR QUOTATIONS

CHAPTER 1

Plato, *Apology*. In Plato *Complete Works*, ed. John M. Cooper (Indianapolis: Hackett, 1997) this quote appears on page 33.

Immanuel Kant, "An Answer to the Question: What is Enlightenment?" In Kant, *Practical Philosophy*, ed. Mary J. Gregor (Cambridge: Cambridge University Press, 1996) this quote appears on page 17.

Bertrand Russell, *The Problems of Philosophy* (Oxford: Oxford University Press, 1912), 93–94.

CHAPTER 2

Plato

Plato, *Seventh Letter*, translated by C.D.C. Reeves in his "Introduction" to Plato's *Republic*, trans. G.M.A. Grube, revised by C.D.C. Reeve (Indianapolis: Hackett, 1992), ix–x. A later fragmentary quote is from the translation of the *Seventh Letter* by Glen R. Morrow, in *Plato: Complete Works*, ed. John M. Cooper and D.S. Hutchinson (Indianapolis: Hackett, 1997), 1648.

Alfred North Whitehead, *Process and Reality*, corrected edition, ed. D.R. Griffin and D.W. Sherburne (New York: Free Press, 1978), 39.

Aristotle

Jonathan Barnes, "Introduction" to *Aristotle: Ethics*, trans. J.A.K. Thomson, revised by Hugh Tredennick (London: Penguin, 1976), 24.

J.L. Ackrill, *Aristotle the Philosopher* (Oxford: Oxford University Press, 1981), 8.

Kant

Immanuel Kant, *Critique of Practical Reason*, Preface, note 5. This translation is by Mary Gregor.

H.J. Paton, "Preface" to his translation of *The Moral Law, or Kant's Groundwork of the Metaphysics of Morals* (London: Hutchinson University Library, 1949), 7.

G.W.F. Hegel, *Philosophy of Right*, trans. T.M. Knox (Oxford: Oxford University Press, 1967), 90.

Mill

J.S. Mill, *Autobiography* (London: Penguin Books, 1989), 27, 112, 117, 68. The passage from an early draft of his autobiography, deleted before publication, can be found in *The Early Draft of John Stuart Mill's "Autobiography,"* edited by Jack Stillinger (Urbana: University of Illinois Press, 1961), 184. The quote from *Auguste Comte and Positivism* is from page 337 of Vol. 10 of the *Collected Works of J.S. Mill* (Toronto: The University of Toronto Press, 1979).

Henry Sidgwick, in a May 1873 letter to C.H. Pearson; he is quoted in Stefan Collini, *Public Moralists, Political Thought and Intellectual Life in Great Britain 1850–1930* (Oxford: Oxford University Press, 1991), 178.

Arthur James Balfour, *Theism and Humanism* (London: Hodder and Stoughton, 1915), 138.

John Skorupski, "Introduction: The Fortunes of Liberal Naturalism," in John Skorupski, ed., *The Cambridge Companion to Mill* (Cambridge: Cambridge University Press, 1998), 1–34.

John Stuart Mill, *On Liberty*, ed. Edward Alexander (Peterborough, ON: Broadview Press, 1999), 51–52.

Roger Crisp, "Editor's Introduction" to *J.S. Mill: Utilitarianism* (Oxford: Oxford University Press, 1998), 23.

G.E. Moore, *Principia Ethica* (Cambridge: Cambridge University Press, 1903), 67.

Nietzsche

Friedrich Nietzsche, *Nachlass* [Nietzsche's previously unpublished notebooks], Division VIII, Volume 3, Nietzsche's *Werke Kritische Gesamtausgabe*, ed. Colli and Montinari (Berlin: de Gruyter, 1967), 412. This translation is by Tracy Strong.

Friedrich Nietzsche, *Beyond Good and Evil*, section 5. The next quotation is from section 26, and a third from section 46. (These translations are by Marion Faber.)

Friedrich Nietzsche, quoted from a letter to Peter Gast dated June 8, 1887. (Printed in *Friedrich Nietzsche's Briefe an Peter Gast*, published in Leipzig in 1908, and cited by, for example, Walter Kaufmann in the preface to his translation of *Beyond Good and Evil* (New York: Random House, 1996), xi.)

Friedrich Nietzsche, *The Antichrist*, section 57. (This translation is by Walter Kaufmann.)

Friedrich Nietzsche, *Daybreak*, section 101. (This translation is by Maudemarie Clark.)

Walter Kaufmann, "Translator's Preface" to *Beyond Good and Evil* (New York: Random House, 1996), xvii.

Midgley

Andrew Brown, "Mary, Mary, quite contrary," *The Guardian*, Saturday, January 13, 2001.

CHAPTER 3
Hobbes

Thomas Hobbes, *Verse Autobiography* (1670), lines 27–28. This poem is reprinted in the Curley edition of *Leviathan* (Indianapolis: Hackett, 1994), liv–lxiv.

John Aubrey, *Brief Lives, Chiefly of Contemporaries, Set Down by John Aubrey, Between the Years 1669 & 1696*, ed. A. Clark (Oxford: Oxford University Press, 1898), Volume 1, 387.

Thomas Hobbes, Letter 21 in Volume 4 of *The Clarendon Edition of the Works of Thomas Hobbes*, ed. H. Warender, et al. (Oxford: Oxford University Press, 1983).

Thomas Hobbes, "Tractatus opticus: prima edizione integrale," ed. F. Alessio, *Revista Critica di Storia dela Filosofia* 18 (1963), 147–188.

Thomas Hobbes, *Behemoth*, ed. Stephen Holmes (University of Chicago Press, 1990), 16, 59.

Marx

Karl Marx, *Theses on Feuerbach*, Thesis 11.

Karl Marx, *Early Writings*, trans. Livingstone and Benton (Harmondsworth: Penguin Books and New Left Review, 1975), 425.

A.J.P. Taylor, "Introduction" to Marx and Engels, *The Communist Manifesto* (Harmondsworth: Penguin Books, 1967), 22.

Friedrich Engels, from Marx and Engels, *Collected Works*, Volume 24 (New York: International Publishers, 1989), 468–9.

David McLellan in Miller, et al. (eds.), *The Blackwell Encyclopedia of Political Thought* (Oxford: Blackwell, 1987), 322.

de Beauvoir

The quote from a friend of de Beauvoir is from a letter by Claudine Chonez and is mentioned by de Beauvoir in her autobiography *Force of Circumstances* (1963, translated by Richard Howard and published by Penguin in 1968), from which the quote about the scene at the restaurant also comes. The quote about de Beauvoir realizing she was 'only a woman' compared to Sartre is cited by Deirdre Bair in her introduction to the 1989 Vintage edition of *The Second Sex*, and comes from interviews Bair conducted with de Beauvoir in the 1980s. The subsequent quote is from an interview with de Beauvoir published in *Society*, February 1976. Praise of the book as one of the most important on women ever published comes from Terry Keefe, *Simone de Beauvoir: A Study of Her Writings*, Barnes & Noble Books, 1983 (p. 111), and Maureen Freely, *The Guardian*, June 6, 1999. The quote from Smith is from her review of the book published in *The Spectator*, November 20, 1953, and the quote from *The New Yorker* is from a review by Brendan Gill, February 28, 1953. The *Times Literary Supplement* quote is by Alison Fell, December 9, 2005. The quotation in Suggestions for Critical Reflection 7 is from Jane O'Grady, writing in the *Oxford Companion to Philosophy* (first edition, 1995, p. 179).

Rawls

John Rawls, *Justice as Fairness: A Restatement* (Cambridge, MA: Harvard University Press, 2001), 3, 10, 15.